MW00633206

Pat Neff Hall, first occupied by Baylor President Pat Neff in 1939, remains in place into the twenty-first century at the heart and center of the Baylor campus and continues to be the home of the university's president and other administrative officials. (Copyright 2006, Baylor University. All rights reserved.)

*To Sweet Biff —
I'm grateful I have been able to
finish Dorothy Jean's book. I hope
she is pleased with it.*
Terrell
3-26-07

THE LAND, THE LAW, AND THE LORD

The Life of Pat Neff

GOVERNOR OF TEXAS 1921-1925
PRESIDENT OF BAYLOR UNIVERSITY 1932-1947

DOROTHY BLODGETT, TERRELL BLODGETT, DAVID L. SCOTT

Foreword by Governor Ann Richards

HOME PLACE PUBLISHERS, AUSTIN, TEXAS

Inquiries should be addressed to:
Home Place Publishers
P.O. Box 13062
Austin, Texas 78711– 3062
www.homeplacepublishers.com

First edition
First printing: July 2007

Library of Congress Cataloging-in-Publication Data

Blodgett, Dorothy (deceased), Blodgett, Terrell, Scott, David L.

The Land, the Law, and the Lord: The Life of Pat Neff
Includes bibliographical references and index.

ISBN 978-0-9761152-2- 9

1. Neff, Pat M., 1871-1952. 2. Governors—Texas—Biography.
3. Legislators—Texas—Biography. 4. University Presidents—Biography.
5. Religious Leaders—Biography.

F 386 B78 2007   976.4 BL

Cover photo: Pat Neff—Original gubernatorial portrait hanging in Texas State Capitol rotunda.
Courtesy of the State Preservation Board, Austin, Texas. CHA 1989.1. Photographer Eric Beggs,
2/24/2000, pre conservation.

Photo of Texas Cowboy statue: CHA 1989.680; bronze sculpture by Warren; Constance Whitney
©1924; photographer: Eric Beggs 6/4/97 post conservation; © State Preservation Board (2007),
Austin, Texas. All rights reserved, including further reproduction, commercial display,
incorporation into other works, or conversion to digital media.

Lyrics: "Texas, Our Texas," copyright 1925 by William J. Marsh; copyright renewed 1953 by
William J. Marsh; Southern Music Company, copyright administrator; Owen E. Thomas and
Mary C. Hearne, copyright owners. Reprinted with permission of Southern Music Company.

Printed in the United States of America at Morgan Printing in Austin, Texas.

For Dorothy
and
For Laura

Contents

Foreword

Governor Richards went to Baylor after Pat Neff left; her connection to Neff rests in the fact that she and Pat Neff are two of only three Texas governors (Sul Ross being the third) who, to this date, were from Waco, attended Baylor, and then became governor of their state.

I never knew Pat Neff personally but over the years I have learned a lot about him. He had retired as president of Baylor University when I enrolled on a debate scholarship in 1950, but his legacy and his name permeated the campus.

That he had kept Baylor open during the Great Depression and had insisted that students from families with limited income not be turned away was well-known throughout the state. I understood at first hand what the Great Depression was. Born "out in the country" near Waco in the middle year of that economically disastrous decade, I'm not too proud to say that I wore "feed sack" dresses that my Mama sewed for me. Our food came from the garden tended by my parents. Times were hard.

When I became governor in 1991, I discovered that my fellow Wacoan, Governor Neff, had accomplished much we can all be proud of. In 1923, he persuaded the legislature to pass the first state gasoline tax, which enabled Texas to have the finest state highway system in the country. Anyone driving between Waco and Austin cannot help but notice the highway sign for Mother Neff Park. Although not the first state park, its acreage was given to Texas by the governor's mother. At its dedication, Neff spoke of his dreams for the statewide park system we now have.

I am particularly grateful to Neff for appointing many outstanding women to state boards, including the first women to the University of Texas and Texas A&M University boards of regents. I consider my selection of women to high positions when I was governor to have been one of my major accomplishments and am pleased that he, too, believed that women are capable of virtually any task.

Finally, writing this foreword to a biography envisioned, researched, and co-written by Dorothy Blodgett is a special privilege because she is considered THE authority on the Governor's Mansion and she made me understand and enjoy living there.

I hope you, too, enjoy this story of a complicated man, a hard-driving governor, and a dedicated university president.

Ann Willis Richards, Baylor '54
Governor of Texas, 1991-95

Preface

Pat Morris Neff, born on Central Texas land between Mcgregor and Moody in 1871, was destined to become the thirtieth Governor of the State of Texas and later the ninth president of Baylor University. With silver-tongued oratory reminiscent of ancient Greece and an attention to detail worthy of twenty-first century political handlers, Pat Neff introduced the art of modern campaigning to Texas. He was the first to board an airplane to fulfill a speaking commitment, the first to campaign in every section of the state no matter how sparsely settled, and the winner of more local and state elections (twenty) without a defeat than any other governor in the state's history. Even outstanding political figures like James Stephen Hogg, both Jim and "Ma" Ferguson, Dan Moody, James V. Allred, and Price Daniel tasted bitter losses at the polls.

After his governorship, Neff took on a new challenge. The Great Depression of the 1930s was decimating the country and Baylor University was about to be its next victim. With his statewide stature as a political and church leader and his unbounded faith in God and in his own leadership ability, he kept Baylor's doors open as he led it out of the economic wilderness to solid financial—and academic—ground.

Strange it is that no full-scale biography had been written of this colorful and important figure in Texas history until my wife, Dorothy Jean Chapin Blodgett, assumed the task in 1985. She had just finished writing, with former Governor and Mrs. Price (Jean) Daniel, *The Texas Governor's Mansion*, the definitive history of the residence, since 1856, of the state's chief executives. Dorothy was a journalism and history graduate of Baylor University, with an abiding love of Texas history. She had two reasons for choosing to write Pat Neff's life: her Chapin forebears owned land adjacent to that of the Neffs, and while she was a student at Baylor she worked for President Neff and was fascinated by his personality, his oratory, and his administrative style.

From the beginning of the project, Dorothy's intention was to produce the most complete, historically accurate document possible. In 1990, she enlisted David Scott, an experienced researcher and genealogist, to work with her; in 1998, I began to help her to complete the research and writing. Before her death in early 2005, she had completed writing much of Neff's Baylor presidency while I concentrated on his public service and David on his family background and boyhood.

Our work is the result of more than ten years of research by all three authors in the Texas Collection of Baylor University, which houses the Neff Papers. Those papers are contained in 348 file boxes and 60 scrapbooks. Although much of the material consists of printed documents including typewritten letters, all of the early correspondence and most of the letters of the Neff family are handwritten, and I express my personal appreciation to David Scott for his laborious transcribing of those letters so that they might be read more quickly and accurately.

The book is also the product of dozens of interviews conducted by Dorothy over a twenty-year period. In addition, David traveled extensively—to Washington, D.C., and several states, as well as within Texas—to interview relatives of Pat Neff and to collect letters and memorabilia from those family members. There is no doubt in my mind that today, David knows more about the history and genealogy of the Neff family than any descendent of Pat Neff.

Finally, my research of his public life involved hundreds of hours of research at the Texas State Archives, State Legislative Reference Library, University of Texas Center for American History, and Austin History Center, as well as numerous other resources.

David and I together acknowledge our debt to my wife, Dorothy, without whose vision and years of research and writing, this book would not exist. We hope she is pleased with the result. David and I dedicate this book to her and to David's wife, Laura.

Finally, I want to thank my daughter, Kathy, for her unwavering love and support these past two years. She has made an unbearable loss bearable by her presence.

This treatment of Neff's life is designed to be a worthy companion to the important and readable biography of Governor James Stephen Hogg, one of Neff's heroes, by Robert C. Cotner, published in 1959 by the University of Texas Press. Like Hogg, Neff was a man of prodigious talent and energy who had an enormous impact on the State of Texas. We hope this volume will foster a greater understanding of Neff's contributions and the times in which he lived and worked.

Terrell Blodgett

Other Acknowledgments

I t is easy to know where to begin when acknowledging the dozens of individuals who have helped the authors along the way. That recognition starts with Ellen Brown, archivist of the Texas Collection at Baylor University, who oversees the Neff Papers. This book could not have been completed without her guidance, patience, and professional skills, and to her, we express our deep gratitude.

It has been Terrell's pleasure, as he coordinated the writing and final production of the book, to have the talents of four other professionals whose constant and abiding skills have made what could have been an unpleasant task become a pleasure. Anita Brewer Howard was my wife's closest professional friend. Her recognized ability to "turn a phrase," honed through years of feature writing for newspapers, has enlivened several passages; her ready availability to give me sound opinions on the research and writing challenges I faced cannot be overstated. I greatly appreciate her professional assistance and her personal support. Kathleen Niendorff, an Austin book agent, has been a source of sound advice and excellent ideas and I am grateful for her expert knowledge of the publishing field as well as her friendship. I also appreciate Alison Tartt, whose editing helped shape the manuscript. I was most fortunate to have Marilyn Duncan assume responsibility for the final copy editing and manuscript production. Her professional experience, keen editorial judgment, and attention to detail sharpened the volume immeasurably.

This biography also could not have been possible without the support and guidance of the Neff family. We discovered that the offspring of Pat Neff's siblings were the greatest source of primary information. The late Charlotte Calvert, Neff's grandniece, had the largest private collection of Neff family material known outside the Texas Collection at Baylor. She could easily qualify as the Neff family historian due to her wealth of correspondence and large number of photographs. She allowed us to copy all of her collection. Three other Neff family members, each a descendant of Pat Neff's older brother Edward, held a great deal of family memorabilia and historic papers and were very helpful: Marie Taylor Neff, Patsy Crowell Britton, and Isabell Crowell Napier. Other Neff family members who contributed to the book were Barbara Christian, Sara Neff Price, Martha Frances Neff, Pauline Herberg, and Cecil Calvert. Finally, Ella Frances Dodd, niece of Pat Neff's wife, Myrtle Mainer Neff, is the family historian of the Mainer family and provided helpful information about Myrtle (Myrtie) and her family.

We owe a great debt of gratitude to many state and local libraries and collections; their staffs were uniformly helpful and friendly. At the Texas Collection at Baylor, Kent Keeth, director during much of the research phase of the book, was particularly helpful with his comments and past historical work about Baylor. The current director, Dr. Tom Charlton, and his staff supplemented archivist Ellen Brown's work with competence. We also used the Moody and Jesse Jones Library at Baylor. We express our particular appreciation to Dr. Don Carleton, director of the University of Texas Center for American History, and to his staff, especially Margaret Schlankey, Brenda Gunn, Ralph Elder, Paulette Delahoussaye, Katherine Kenefick, and Steve Arceri, whom we seemed to see more than others. Archivist Sue Soy and her two immediate predecessors, Biruta Celmins Kearl and Audrey Bateman Randle, and the staff at the Austin History Center were always helpful.

Special thanks go to Nancy Fisher, reference librarian at the Texas Legislative Reference Library, for specific help with official state documents and legislative journals. The archivist at the Texas State Archives, Chris LaPlante, and his staff endured many questions from me and always had the answers. My thanks to Jean Carefoot, Bill Simmons, Sergio Velasco, John Anderson, and Donaly Brice.

At the federal level, we utilized the resources—and express our appreciation to—the Library of Congress, the Lyndon Baines Johnson Presidential Library, and the Harry S. Truman Presidential Library. Tab Lewis, archivist at the National Archives, was most helpful to David Scott as he pursued papers related to Neff's time with the United States Board of Mediation.

At the Texas Baptist Historical Collection in Dallas, Alan Lefever, director, and particularly Naomi Taplin, librarian, provided invaluable help regarding Neff's church activities. Ali James, curator of the Capitol, and Bonnie Campbell, former curator and now director of the Bayou Bend Collection and Gardens in Houston, were key to our understanding State Capitol history, and helpful in a number of other ways.

We also express our gratitude to Hank Bass and Jeff Adams of the Bill Daniel Archives at the State Bar of Texas. In the medical field, Barbara Tims and Carlyn C. Hammons of the Texas Medical Association steered us to several key books and documents. Jan Anderson, librarian at the Texas Education Agency, was helpful with source information in the educational arena. Susan B. Rhyne, manager of information services, and Jo Lynne York, information specialist at the Texas Railroad Commission, provided key documents relative to Neff's tenure on that body.

Local libraries and museums that helped along the way include municipal public libraries of Amarillo (Donna Littlejohn), Austin, Dallas, Fort Worth, Gainesville, Galveston (Rosenberg Library), Greenville (Carol Taylor), Houston, and Mart. We also owe a specific debt of gratitude to Kathy Schwartz, director of the McLennan County Archives; Ruth Ann Baker of the Hollis Museum in Hollis, Oklahoma; Billie Sue Gaylor of the Swisher County Museum in Tulia; Linda J. Evans, director of development at the Austin Presbyterian Seminary; and the staff of the Gelman Library at George Washington University.

Individuals who should be recognized for their assistance include Betty King, former secretary of the Texas Senate; Douglas Young, architect of the Capitol (Texas); newspaperman Bill Berger; Texas Supreme Court Clerk Andrew Weber; Chris Kuykendall, senior research associate at the Texas Legislative Council; the late Bill Logue of Waco; former executive assistant to the Texas Supreme Court Bill Willis; Mary Ramos, *Texas Almanac* editor emeritus; computer consultants Mike Dempsey and Craig Meserole: *Alcalde* editor Avrel Seale and his assistant editor, Tim Taliaferro; *Baylor Line* editor Todd Copeland; archivist Edie Jeter of the International Mission Board in Richmond, Virginia; and long-time personal friends George and Virginia Nokes. Dr. Jeff Kerr was also very helpful in several ways.

David Scott found useful information and received excellent service from a number of other organizations and individuals. These include the California State Library in Sacramento; County Clerk's Offices in Bell, Coryell, Lampasas, and McLennan Counties; District Clerk's Offices in Coryell, Lampasas, and McLennan Counties; Kathy E. Van Wolfe, McLennan County elections administrator; the Lampasas Public Library; the Texas Ranger Research Center at the Texas Ranger Hall of Fame in Waco; the Masonic Grand Lodge Library and Archives in Waco; Melvin and Dorothy Maxwell; Oleta Maxwell Hamilton; Barbara Hamilton Wright; the Jones family—Tullie, V. Marie, Clyde, and Monroe (all deceased); E. A. and Vena Culpepper (deceased); Irene Gipe (deceased); Hazel Potter (deceased); Harlan and Hope Huffman; Lillie Mae Pitts; Frances Scott Thornburg; Mabel Clair Scott (deceased); the descendants of Francis Marion Scott Sr.; Keith Reed; T. Archie Monroe; Clay Patterson; Brent Campbell; Rev. Sidney Roberts; Jim and Sharon Griffith; the *McGregor Mirror* (Bonnie Mullens); Edgar Perryman (deceased); Betty Seawright; Martha Daniel; Frankie Glaze (deceased); Don and Dolores Scott; Van and Mary Massirer; Dora Lee Gentry Pharis; Tom Britton; and Estelle Shelburne.

Judge Jack Hightower and Baylor historian Eugene W. Baker both read portions of the manuscript and offered numerous valuable suggestions. In addition, veteran newsman Thomas E. "Tommy" Turner supplied invaluable information along the way.

We also appreciate the numerous thesis and dissertation writers whose work provided valuable reference material for this book.

Finally, we are grateful to the staff at Morgan Printing, Terry Sherrell, Blake Mitchell, Stephen Bright, Mark Hillis and others, who were efficient, courteous, professional—all and more than we could ask to help us complete this mission of memory.

To all of the above, we express our deep appreciation.

Terrell Blodgett, David L. Scott
June 2007

CHAPTER 1

Gone to Texas

If I hadn't had all the children that I had, I would never
have had Pat.

—Mother Neff

Baylor University President Pat Neff left his office early one crisp sunny afternoon in the 1930s.[1] The day had been full—chapel that morning, lunch with a
member of the board of trustees, visitors in and out of the office, and the usual
piles of telephone messages and mail to answer. After escorting the last visitor out,
he told his secretary he would not be back that day, got into his Chevrolet coupe,
and drove away from the campus, waving to a gaggle of students. He turned the car
southwest toward his home place, by the Leon River farm where he had grown up.

Parking under one of the towering pecan trees, he went up the steps into the
house, where he pulled on canvas pants and heavy, knee-high leather boots. Adding his old black coat against the chill in the air, he drove the several hundred yards
into the open fields. There he greeted Melvin Maxwell, the caretaker who managed
his farm. Just that day, Melvin had plowed the fields, preparing them for the new
crops to be planted.

Melvin watched as this famous man, once Governor of Texas and now president of the largest Baptist college in the world, strode across the field through the
fresh-plowed soil. Neff kneeled on the ground, then moved toward the earth as
though into the arms of a woman. Soon he was asleep. This is the way Melvin
recalled the day: "I laid out about fifteen rows and doubled back and rebedded
them and that stirred up the dirt real good. I looked back and he was lying in one
of those rows over there. . . and he went to sleep. . . lying right flat on his back in
the sunshine. That dirt, you know, it had a special smell, and it never made you
sneeze. Before commercial fertilizer, it was like perfume."[2]

Neff awakened after a spell, lying in the soil that he loved and that had succored
him all his life. The importance of land as a source of inspiration and strength was
made clear in several of his letters. "There is much strength in dirt farm land," he
wrote his son Pat Jr.,[3] a statement that would appear often in his correspondence.
He often shared his memories of playing in the fields wearing a calico dress and

1

bonnet because his mother didn't want him to be burned by the sun.[4] He also recalled the fascinating stories he had been told about the rustic conditions his parents faced when they arrived in 1855 in newly created Coryell County, Texas, considered to be the edge of the frontier.

The Roots—1851-1855

Back in Virginia before the Civil War, many young men were looking westward to participate in the boom times offered by plentiful land and promises of riches and adventure. Noah Neff and his cousin, David Deyerle, both bachelors, were seeking just such glamorous lives. Early in 1851, only six years after Texas achieved statehood, Noah and David came to Texas planning to buy land, which they believed would assure them successful futures.

Noah listed his occupation as "waggoner and farmer," while the more-accomplished David was a noted brick mason and builder, and already a well-to-do land owner in Virginia. Noah and David concentrated their land search on McLennan and Bell Counties, where they purchased several large tracts of land. They returned to Virginia, but not before they had met a man, Joel Blair, in Belton. Trusting him, they signed a power of attorney authorizing him to buy, sell, and maintain their property holdings. Their trust was well placed. Blair kept the Virginians posted on their investments, writing in January 1852 that the region was flooded with newcomers and he believed their land had increased in value to one or two dollars an acre.[5]

Apparently David Deyerle's Virginia roots grew deeper than Noah's. Soon after arriving home from Texas, Deyerle married and decided to stay in Roanoke. Noah, on the other hand, was back in Bell County by December 1852, buying and selling property for both himself and Deyerle. While Neff and his cousin were not wealthy Virginians, they had cash to buy and sell land.

Two years later, in 1854, Noah Neff's father died in Virginia. The young man returned to Virginia to take care of two matters of importance—settling his father's estate and courting twenty-three-year-old Isabella Shepherd. Isabella was no southern belle waiting around for a suitor. She had been teaching school for seven years, since the age of sixteen.[6] Her father was a well-educated man, a highly respected school teacher in the Roanoke area. Noah's courtship and marriage proposal included her going back to Texas with him. She might have had more misgivings about leaving Virginia had not three of her brothers already emigrated to Texas.

Noah and Isabella exchanged vows in an evening ceremony at the home of her parents on October 26, 1854. Eighteen days later the newlyweds, carrying their possessions in a covered wagon, began their 1,300-mile, forty-nine-day trip to Texas. They traveled six days each week, stopping on Sundays to observe the Sabbath, honoring their deep Christian convictions.[7] They arrived in Belton on January 2,

1855, staying with friends Noah had made earlier. These friends hosted a delayed wedding reception for Noah and Isabella. While Isabella immediately liked her husband's friends, she was critical of her new surroundings. She wrote David Deyerle in Virginia:

> I cannot say that I am much pleased with Texas, I hope to be better pleased when we have become settled at a house of our own. I think this is a very pretty country, but like all new countries, has many inconveniences—everything is scarce and high, and nothing but bread and meat to eat, and cornbread at that.[8]

She told David she would like to have her family visit but would be sorry to hear them sighing for their luxuriant quarters (in Virginia). She closed: "Excuse this bad writing as I have a very bad pen and no quill to make another as there is no geese out here."[9]

Building a Home and a Family

Three months after arriving in Belton, Noah and Isabella found the property they had been searching for. It stretched across the Coryell-McLennan County lines near the Leon River. On April 19, 1855, Noah paid $800 for this acreage that was to become Pat Neff's beloved "home place." The previous month Noah had purchased 241 acres of wooded property, thus providing lumber to build a house.[9]

Together, Noah and Isabella cleared the land and constructed a small log cabin. It was located near a spring so that they would not have to haul water from the nearby Leon River. They moved into their new home in the spring of 1855 when the wild flowers were in bloom, and it was here that Isabella cooked her first Texas meal in her own home.[10]

Their search for a homestead was later described in a school paper by their son Pat:

> One day as they were driving along over the boundless prairies of Texas, they came to a beautiful grove, in the middle a large spring, out of which the water was flowing freely. The buffalo and deer occupied this place, but they got out their trunk and skillet, set up a plank, and concluded that they would make that their future home.[11]

The Neffs' first child, Edward Lewis Neff, was born on December 31, 1855. Isabella had nine children during the next sixteen years. Given the tremendous amount of work required to maintain a farm the size of theirs, Isabella and Noah were partners in lives of unremitting toil. As soon as they were able to work, the Neff boys joined their father in the fields, working twelve-hour days, from sunup to sundown, six days a week. Their main crop was cotton, which had to be planted, hoed, and eventually picked, a highly labor-intensive enterprise. The Neffs also raised other farmland crops—corn, oats, wheat, and maize to feed the cattle, hogs, and poultry. Noah found that horses were the most financially beneficial, so he always kept a number of them on the farm.[12]

Meanwhile, Isabella's daily tasks included making three meals a day for the ever-growing number of eaters, sewing and mending clothes, planting and nurturing vegetable gardens for daily meals, and canning huge supplies of fruit and vegetables for winter meals. She washed clothes by first boiling them in a wash pot by the house, then giving them a scrubbing on a ribbed board, rinsing them in bluing, and hanging them to dry. Then came the ironing. No wash and wear fabric then. Isabella heated the flat iron on the wood cook stove and ironed all the family clothes.

The weather was always an important factor—there were times when it rained too much and times when it rained not at all. Only a year after the Neffs moved into their cabin, a devastating drought brought failing crops and hard times. Noah wrote David Deyerle in Virginia about the falling land and cattle prices, and the lack of rain.[13] Many years later Isabella recalled the spring when it was so dry she could only get water for her first baby by going to the spring and "dipping the water with a teaspoon."[14] The family hauled water for all other purposes from many miles away.

Noah and Isabella early on attended the Onion Creek Baptist Church, later known as the Eagle Springs Baptist Church. Noah had been reared in a Methodist household and Isabella was a strict Presbyterian. Determined to instill Christian values in their children, they joined the Baptist Church, the only denomination in the area at that time.[15]

After the birth of Edward Lewis Neff in December 1855, Isabella had two more sons in quick succession—Charles Deyerle Neff in 1857 and Samuel Herbert Neff in 1858.[16] The Neffs were clearly financially well off, reaping the benefits of their hard work. In 1859, Isabella took a break from child-bearing to travel to Galveston in a covered wagon, board a steamer for Virginia, and remain there for a year. She left Noah and the three young children in Texas, with a trusted neighbor helping Noah with the chores and child rearing.[17] After Isabella returned from her sabbatical, the babies started arriving again—Benjamin Bassel in 1860, Robert Shepherd in 1862, Sallie Jane in 1864, David Leslie in 1866, Elizabeth Frances in 1868, and Pat Morris in 1871. Later in life, when Isabella was questioned about why she had so many children, she answered, "If I hadn't had all the children that I had, I would never have had Pat."[18] As the family grew, Noah added rooms and expanded their little cabin.

The Civil War Era

In the late 1850s, the nation was being torn asunder by the division between the northern states and the "slave-holding" South. The Southern states began to secede from the Union, and soon after Isabella returned to Texas from Virginia, the Neffs were faced with the decision of voting for or against secession. With their deep Southern roots, it is no surprise that they voted with the South, although Sam Houston and a few other Texas leaders were against leaving the Union.[19] Others had been less than enthusiastic about the 1845 decision to give up the Republic of Texas to join the United States and so were inclined to want no part of either the Confederates or the Yankees. The Neffs did not hold that position.

In February 1861, Isabella, writing to David Deyerle, reported that "our election comes off tomorrow [and we are] all going to vote for cecession [sic] and some for Texas setting up for herself." Isabella reported that "times are pretty good here yet as we have no banks to close up and pinch people. Our markets are good and provisions plentiful."[20] Although financially secure, the Neffs were not "plantation owners" in any sense of the word. In the 1850 census in Virginia, neither Noah nor Isabella's parents are shown to have had slaves.[21]

The secession election was successful, and two years later, Noah donated sixty bushels of corn for the Texas Cavalry horses. He also purchased two pistols in Gatesville when the war broke out. In 1864 and 1865, they paid "Confederate taxes" on their property.[22] The Neff family was not affected in a direct way by the war. Edward Neff, the oldest son, was only five when the war began and several members of the Neff family, including Pat, had not been born yet. With the war's end in 1865, Noah served on a grand jury in Gatesville and noted in a scrapbook that "there were garrisons of Union troops at nearly every town of any size."[23] In 1867, Noah signed an oath of allegiance to the United States.[24]

Noah continued to prosper. For the 1870 federal census he estimated his real estate holdings at $3,000 and his personal property at another $3,000.[25] He apparently was recognized as one of the area's wealthier landowners, doing well compared to many of his neighbors. By the 1870s the Eagle Springs area had become a village with a general store, post office, blacksmith shop, church, and later a school. The Neffs always participated in community affairs, and contributed to the building of the church and school.

That Central Texas area, even as early as 1870, was becoming an enemy of alcoholic beverages, or "ardent spirits." When Noah Neff purchased ten acres of land for $600 from trustees of the Onion Creek Baptist Church, the condition of sale included this proviso: "In the case that 'ardent spirits' were sold, the property would revert back to the church."[26] This prohibition against the sale of liquor was part of the Baptist doctrine shared by the Eagle Springs community.

Pat's Arrival on the Scene

Four days before Thanksgiving, November 26, 1871, Isabella delivered her ninth child and seventh son. The Neffs had run out of names for boys. Isabella and Noah bandied names back and forth for several days. Finally, Noah decided that the baby would be named for a family friend, Captain Pat Morris.[27] As a little boy, the Neffs' youngest son was occasionally called "Patty." In later years, some writers thought his name must be "Patrick," but Pat always set them straight: "it is not Patrick any where or any place, but just plain Pat without a period—as I was named for a family friend who lived near my parents when I first discovered the world."[28] When Pat was two months old, Isabella wrote her brother, Josephus Shepherd in Houston: "my little babe don't grow much, is a might little fellow and cross enough for two."[29]

A school teacher herself, Isabella had taught all her children basic reading and writing in their home at night by the light of the coal-oil lamps. She refused to wait for a regular school to be established for her children to begin learning. In 1876, when Pat was five years old, the first school was built in the Eagle Springs community. This was a one-room building, with two doors at the front, a high pitched roof, and four windows on each side of the building. A wood-burning stove in the middle of the room furnished heat during the winter months. Two blackboards hung from the walls. Desks and benches were the only furnishings. Privies—one for boys and one for girls—were located on the grounds. A community well a few hundred yards from the school building supplied water for the children. The school furnished some books and educational material, and the parents provided the rest.[30]

In this school house two miles from his home young Pat Neff received his primary education. Sometimes he walked to school, but other times he rode his little pony, tying him up and watering him at noon after eating his own lunch. From the beginning, Isabella believed Pat was born for success. She saw to it that her youngest son had a Webster's dictionary, which he took to the fields with him, looking up words during the breaks to give the plow horses a rest.[31] Pat was also a fan of the *Blue Back Speller*, *Aesop's Fables*, and *Hosteller's Almanac*, along with the Bible.[32] The adult Neff remembered *Aesop's Fables* as the first book he ever read.[33] Often during recess at school, instead of playing Ante-over, Red Rover, or London Bridge with the other children, he sat in the shade under the eaves of the school building and read.[34]

As a child, Pat had a problem pronouncing the letter *R*. His mother, seeking to help him overcome this, once sent him to the Eagle Springs general store to buy a "quarters worth of squirrel shot," to practice his *R*s. To avoid embarrassment, Pat translated this to "twenty-five cents worth of small shot."[35]

Pat's first public speaking experience was at this school, debating the topic "Is Fire More Destructive Than Water?"[36] Also, at about this time the lad began showing an interest in lawyers. One day the word was passed that a lawyer was scheduled to visit the general store at Springs for a session of the Coryell County Justice Court. Pat played hooky from school to take in this event. When he returned to school, the teacher did not punish him.[37]

One of the legendary Neff stories is that he wore bonnets—like a girl's—and sometimes was taken to be a girl. All seven of the boys began working in the fields at an early age. Isabella, wanting her sons' skins to remain "white as God had made them," insisted they wear bonnets, often to their embarrassment. Neff later recalled one of these times:

> My early childhood was different from that of some boys; I wore a big sun bonnet and a dress until I was nine or ten years old, as I was very large for my age I was often taken for some of the young ladies of that country. One day I attended a horse race in which I was politely informed that they did not allow young ladies on the ground, but that was soon explained and I saw the races.[38]

Along with the required work in the cotton fields, Pat's primary chore as a child was to care for the hogs. He later gave credit to his work with the hogs for helping him gain patience: "I suppose that is where I learned to control my temper so well, for if there is anything under the canopy of heaven that will make a fellow mad and say ugly words and afterward find out that it did not do any good, it is herding hogs, especially if there is a corn field in three miles of you."[39]

While reading matter was scarce in the Neff household, Pat's uncle, Isaac Neff, who lived in Liberty, Missouri, sent his Texas kin the *Liberty Tribune* on a regular basis. Young Neff was intrigued by the Liberty news, especially accounts of what was going on at William Jewell College, a Baptist college founded in 1849, and he had day dreams about attending college there someday. He knew that higher education was possible because Noah and Isabella had sent his sister Sallie to Virginia to stay with friends and relatives while she attended high school there.

One of the articles published in the *Liberty Tribune* was a commencement address at William Jewell College by Bill Arp of Georgia, a popular Southern writer in the late nineteenth century. Arp wrote about economic, social, and political issues during the Civil War and the Reconstruction era.[40] Neff cut the commencement address from the paper and read it many times, being especially impressed by the words: "At the girdle of the educated man hangs the key that opens every door of education. The educated man turns the wheels in the affairs of church and state, and ignorance is a curse everywhere."[41]

Hardships and Rites of Passage

When Pat was seven years old, his sister and closest playmate, Elizabeth (Lizzie), contracted typhoid pneumonia, which left her an invalid until her death three years later, June 10, 1882. Only a year and a half later, Noah, then sixty-seven, died of the same disease. Typhoid still wasn't through with the Neffs. Pat's second oldest brother, Charles Deyerle Neff, died from the disease on March 29, 1885.[42] Typhoid was carried in water supplies throughout the Central Texas area in the late 1800s and into the twentieth century. Old cemeteries bear inscriptions reflecting the pain left by this disease that seemed to favor taking the young.

Pat's father did not live long enough to be a part of several important events in his youngest son's life. The first event that came after his father's death was the conversion and baptism of young Pat. The youngster joined the Eagle Springs Baptist Church of his parents and was baptized in a deep hole in Onion Creek near the church.[43] Then, early in his teens, Pat was able to take his first train ride, eat his first meal in a hotel, encounter his first beggar, and visit the "big city of Brenham, Texas," population then of 4,000.[44] In 1885, when he was fourteen, his mother took him on a five-month trip to visit relatives and friends in Missouri, Tennessee, and Virginia. To a farm boy who had spent his life in rural Texas, this was an important experience. Throughout his adult life, he was an avid traveler, believing that travel not only broadened but educated.

In a theme written in 1890, Neff told of a later trip which wasn't so pleasant:

> I was in my teens and I thought I was big enough to go anywhere; my brother was going to Lampasas County after a bunch of horses (as we had a ranch in that county). I begged my Ma to let me go along, she finally consented, so after the first day's ride or about forty miles, as the dismal luminary was setting beneath the western horizon, and as our ponies were beginning to hang their heads, we concluded that we would stop for the night. When I found out that I had nothing to sleep on but just my saddle and the shaggy rock of western Coryell County, I concluded that I had just as soon my Ma had kept me at home.[45]

Pat had had another bad experience with horses in the winter of 1887 and 1888. He wrote that the cold weather forced him and his brothers to kill several of their horses and "drag them to the bone yard." Also, one time during that winter he was riding fast on his horse, and somehow the horse fell on top of him and "knocked my knee out which laid me up for several weeks."[46]

The Neff family during Pat's teenage years had a large measure of hardships. Isabella and her large brood had hardly recovered from the terrible toll of the death of the family patriarch and two children when yet other tragedies befell them— two of the Neff sons became entangled with the law and accused of terrible crimes. The eldest son, Edward Neff, was indicted for murder, and Samuel Neff was arrested and imprisoned for attempted train robbery. To the Neffs, so proud of their good name and so determined to lead impeccable lives, the accusations were a double embarrassment.

Edward Neff in 1885 was indicted for the murder of John Adolph Witte, a local farmer and rancher. Edward and Witte, after a heated dispute over land, were involved in a violent gun battle that resulted in Witte's death. Edward was arrested and charged with murder, and he pleaded self-defense. Five years passed with several trials, all resulting in hung juries. Finally, in December 1890, a jury found Edward not guilty. If Edward had been found guilty of second-degree murder, he would have had to serve five years in the state penitentiary; if found guilty of manslaughter by sudden passion, he would have had to serve two years. The "not guilty" verdict meant that neither Edward nor his family had to bear the humiliation of a prison term.[47]

Unfortunately, the family's woes were not over. In 1888, two years before Edward was freed, his brother Samuel was indicted for attempted robbery of a Southern Pacific passenger train. While living in Lampasas County, Samuel was associated with a group of desperados, known collectively as the Harrell-Whitley Gang. The gang, suspected of several daring bank and train robberies, attempted to rob a Southern Pacific train near Harwood in Gonzales County, Texas, on September 22, 1888. Samuel Neff, accused of playing an active role in this robbery attempt, was captured by authorities and became the only gang member arrested to stand trial. William Whitley, one of the primary instigators, was shot and killed a few days after the robbery. On November 9, 1889, Samuel Neff was convicted by a jury for attempting to rob the United States mail and for assaulting the person having custody of the mail and for threatening and shooting this person with a dangerous weapon. Samuel was sentenced to the federal penitentiary in Columbus, Ohio, for five years of hard labor.[48]

Isabella Neff, widowed and still mourning the death of two of her children, sat day after day in various courtrooms listening to charges against two of her sons and waiting seemingly interminably for juries to return with verdicts. "Our good name has been injured," wrote Isabella's daughter, Sallie Calvert, to her brother Pat in January 1889.[49]

In the latter part of 1889, Isabella wrote to Pat, sharing her concerns: "I cannot think of a thing but him [Sam] and now he is where I can't do anything but grieve over his sad fate. The only comfort I can feel is that I have done the best I could for him, and will so long as I live."[50] In a letter written in 1890, while Sam was serving prison time, she asked Pat to write to Sam: "Sammy . . . can receive letters but cannot write but once per month. If you write, don't write about anything but your studies, and Sabbath School or debates—poor boy, don't tell him if you have a good time."[51]

By 1892 the proud Isabella's hopes and dreams for an educated family seemed shattered. While she continued to love and support all of her living children, her dream for success became centered on Pat. It was Pat who she felt would be her legacy, and she set her sights on pushing him forward in every way. Pat, through the years, seemed to realize his obligation to his adoring mother and tried to fulfill her wishes for him.

CHAPTER 2

Riding to Baylor on a Dream
and a Bale of Cotton

I have a chance to get on my long-tailed coat and
get before big crowds every once in a while lately. I like it!
—Pat Neff

After elementary school at home and at Eagle Springs, Pat Neff briefly attended high school in nearby McGregor, but he was convinced he was ready for Baylor and its intellectual challenges.

Baylor Days—1889-1894

Neff described his triumphant arrival at college as "riding on a bale of cotton from the family farm in Coryell County to the entrance of Baylor."[1] His grandnephew, Ed, told the story slightly differently: "Pat picked a bale of cotton by himself and sold it, and without any encouragement from anyone, he made his way to Baylor."[2] Pat arrived at the Waco campus on December 31, 1888, in time for the spring 1889 term. His family and his cotton money didn't provide enough cash for him to spend money freely. In his ledger, he listed the cost of two months' room rent at $1.75. Additional money was spent for medicine, paper and tablets, stamps, and a train ticket home on the Cotton Belt Railroad.[3] At the end of the spring term, he headed home to work on the farm over the summer, and then returned to Baylor for the fall 1889 term. When he went home for Christmas, he arrived on a Sunday and found the house empty, as his mother was away for a day or two. He seemed to enjoy the experience. Later, in a school theme, Neff described going to church and seeing old friends, finding that "everything looked natural, even the same old brindle dog came into the church and took his regular position, which was not very far from me." He also told about cooking his own meal: "[A]bout the middle of the evening I got hungry, so I killed me a chicken and made me a pie, and with what other things I could find that was good to eat, put them all together and I had a snack."[4]

Weighing 160 pounds, the five-foot-eleven-inch-tall Neff was a fine looking young man who had no trouble flirting with the Baylor coeds. In the spring of

1890, he began mentioning "pretty girls" in his letters and themes and recounting incidents at "socials" and "soirees" on the campus. University rules limited a young man's conversation with a girl to three minutes each. Of course, he could return for other three-minute sessions from time to time. It was at one of these socials at the women's dormitory, Maggie Houston Hall, that Neff met someone special, Myrtle Mainer. Usually called "Myrtie," she was an attractive music major from Lovelady, Texas. After his first three minutes with her, Neff returned again and again to fill more three-minute time spans. While in a history class together, they passed notes to each other, leading Baylor President Rufus Burleson to label Neff "mischievous."[5]

While Neff had planned to attend the 1891 summer session, his mother needed him at home. Isabella wrote, saying she was "paying a hand eighteen dollars per month," and she needed Pat to come home and "give me a little vacation of expenses and strengthen up your physical system also."[6] Both Neff and Myrtie returned to Baylor for the 1891-92 school year, and they continued their courtship. However, after Myrtie went home to Lovelady in May 1892, she never returned to Baylor as a student. Neff expressed his disappointment in a July 1892 letter, saying, "it will be a great honor to have a diploma from Baylor, and you must not think about not coming back . . . you cannot imagine how I would miss you."[7]

Despite the loss of Myrtie's presence at the end of the 1891-92 school year, that year had provided Neff with some enduring advantages and achievements. First, future Baylor President Samuel Palmer Brooks was his roommate, and the two forged a life-long friendship. Also, Neff's elocution class revealed a talent for public speaking. In February 1892 he wrote his mother:

> Last week I had a chance to recite a piece before a large crowd, being on the programme[sic] for an intertainment [sic] given by the Elocution and Music Department. I have quit taking elocution though now, I do not think it very good except for giving a boy more 'Brass, cheek, and other such necessities of life.' I think I have enough of such. I have a chance to get on my long-tailed coat and get before big crowds every once in a while lately. I like it.[8]

The summer of 1892 found Myrtie in Lovelady with no plans to return to Baylor, and it found Neff back home on the farm writing Myrtie love letters praising her and exulting that they were engaged to be married:

> I shall try to live so that you shall never regret the action in agreeing to be my companion through life. . . . I have first woed [sic] and now won the hand and heart of Texas's *fairest daughter*. One whom I consider to be the exponent of all the noble traits—a wife, a woman! I certainly do, and can but congratulate myself that I have gained the entire love and confidence of one who is so pure, noble and true.[9]

In that same letter he also admitted to her that he had read a "cheap love novel" and felt guilty about it, saying that he "generally read more substantial literature than that." In the fall of 1892 Neff returned to Baylor, but he was soon called home when his brother, David Leslie, died. Deeply grieved, he wrote Myrtie about his sorrow. She responded with a sixteen-page letter of concern and sympathy, much of it about David Leslie's widow and how she herself might react if she lost her husband. At the end of the letter, Myrtie chastised Pat for not having introduced her to his family and for failing to tell her much about them.[10] Always a proud person, Neff may have been ashamed to tell her about his brother, Sam, then imprisoned in Ohio on the train robbery charge.

In February of 1893 Neff did write to Myrtie about Sam, calling him a villain and outlaw. He described his brother as a "wild and desperate man—fears nothing—give him a pistol, Winchester and a good horse and he would meet the Devil and all his followers in combat. And would delight it seems in such, he has been the dread of a great part of Western Texas for several years." Neff also wrote that he believed Sam, when released, might not last long but would "die with boots on with his face toward the enemy."[11] Fortunately, this prediction did not come to pass. Sam eventually straightened himself out, and he and Pat became friendly and loyal to each other. After all their other brothers were gone, Sam and Pat supported each other emotionally and Pat provided substantial financial help to Sam in later years.

After David Leslie's funeral in September 1892, Pat returned to Baylor and four classes, three he considered "real hard ones."[12] He and Myrtie continued their correspondence. He still encouraged her to return to Baylor, and she told him her father also wanted her to continue her education. "I don't believe I could study to save my life now," she wrote. "I am not near rested and I do love to stay at home."[13] Pat missed her and wanted her back at Baylor, but he also was thinking ahead as he lectured her on the importance of his career and saying he didn't want his future wife to be intellectually lacking. She responded testily, not giving an inch about returning to Baylor: "I know I am not smart, never was considered so, and I am very positive graduating would not make me so."[14]

Apparently Neff's heart still belonged to Myrtie, but he continued to keep the intensity of the relationship a secret from his mother, perhaps somehow fathoming that she would not approve. He explained to Myrtie: "I never did tell my mother any thing special about us, she knows though that we are very intimate, so many persons have told her about us, she has asked me a good many leading questions concerning you at different times."[15]

At Baylor, Neff continued to take part in the socials that included women students. About one such soiree, he wrote that he "talked to the young ladies very vigerously [sic], talking to the old girls about the things that had been and to the new over the things that might be. As I had not talked to any fair damsels for some time, I started . . . very awkward, but at the end of the two hours come out with a borrowed dignity."[16]

He received excellent grades in all his fall term classes—English literature, English classics, philosophy, political economy, Tacitus, American history, and elocution.[17] He especially enjoyed debating and participating in lively competition with members of the various debate societies. He did note that this competitive spirit sometimes caused friction, writing to Myrtie: "This is the first time I ever had school mates or any one else to make unkind remarks about me."[18]

Throughout his Baylor days, Neff attended church regularly, but when he was at home during the summer of 1893, he began taking a more active part in church services at Eagle Springs. For the first time he was asked to pray and speak before the congregation. He wrote Myrtie that he and his roommate always prayed in their room before going to bed, but that this was a new experience for him. Pat told her that the preacher and several of the members had congratulated him and he had felt exhilarated:

> O, I do want to live a grand, true and noble Christian, for I know of no higher or sublimer type of true man-hood than to be a devoted servant of God.[19]

It was that summer of 1893 when Chicago hosted the fabled World's Fair— "the World's Columbian Exposition," and the inaugural scene of the Ferris wheel. In early August Pat and a friend took the train to Chicago to attend the fair they had been reading about. President Grover Cleveland called it "A Stupendous Thing," and novelist Hamlin Garland wrote: "Sell the cook stove if necessary and come. You must see the fair."[20]

The two young men took a hotel room and Pat sent his mother a postcard reassuring her: "Dear Ma, Do thyself no harm, we are here."[21] A week later he wrote her again about the marvels he was seeing. He told her that they were mingling with people from all over the world and that over 150,000 individuals attended the fair every day. He thought the entertainment and exhibits were "great, grand, sublime," and could not imagine anything surpassing it in the future.[22]

Neff was overwhelmed by the 65,000 exhibits housed in 150 buildings covering more than 600 acres, and by the 250-foot Ferris wheel, invented by the American engineer G. W. Ferris, with the specific directions to outdo France's Eiffel Tower. He was impressed by the "Midway Plaisance," the "Streets of Cairo," and an early day twenty-two-story skyscraper.[23] In a letter to his sister, Sallie Calvert, Neff described standing on top of that building and being able to see not just Illinois but also the countryside of Indiana and Wisconsin. He told her he was profoundly grateful to be living in an age of such great accomplishments and that he was having difficulty comprehending the enormity of the achievements he was lucky enough to see there in Chicago.[24]

Neff was also amazed about what he saw on the streets of Chicago, especially noting differences between northern women and the women he knew in Texas. He wrote to Myrtie:

> The people seem so different from the people of the South, especially the young la-
> dies, so bold, almost as common to see girls out at night by themselves as to see the
> men. They are not the least bashful, and one young lady from Iowa has been staying
> where I do that is real nice, good company.[25]

After this heady summer adventure, Neff returned to Waco and his last academic year at Baylor before graduation. In the fall term of 1893-94 his courses
were Latin, English literature, American classics, moral science, logic, and elocution. Again he made high marks in all his work.[26]

One of Neff's favorite professors at Baylor was Benajah H. Carroll, who
was then teaching in the Bible Department. Admiration for this professor probably deepened the student's interest in religion. "The more I see of Dr. Carroll,"
Neff wrote in a letter to his mother, "the more I admire him. I believe he has
as broad, as deep, as lofty, as sound and as sagacious a brain as any man in
these United States."[27]

In another letter to his sister, he wrote, somewhat wistfully, about his four
years at Baylor which were drawing to a close and about his future. He told
her that he had originally thought he could learn everything he needed in
about ten months and would then "have the world by the tail and a downhill
pull on it." He said he was now more mature and was beginning to realize how
little he really knew:

> Though I have walked studiously and industriously along the school boy's classic walks
> of life for some time, I am just now standing upon the shore that borders the great
> ocean of the unknown across the heaving waves of which my eyes cannot see, but by
> faith I shall push on trusting that some Moses shall with uplifted wand part the Red
> Sea of Life's unknown.[28]

Neff's early fascination with lawyers and his interest in debate and public speaking
foreshadowed his choosing law as a career. In his senior year, he wrote about an
event he was participating in:

> The [Philomathesian Literary] Society is going to give an entertainment the last of
> this month, in the form of a "Moot Court," and I am one of the lawyers for that
> occasion, and as it is to be public, it takes no little amount of work to get it up to good
> shape, we are going to try a case of "breach of promise." It will be funny too. The
> criminal will be Lyman Bryan, the one who writes for the [Baptist] Standard.[29]

Another speaking-related event during Neff's senior year was a trip to Fort Worth in January 1894, in which he represented the Philomathesian Society in meeting with other Texas university society delegates to organize a state oratorical association. While there, Neff's name appeared in print in the *Fort Worth Daily News* and in the *Gazette*. The stories merely said that Neff and others were in town for the meeting, but he noted that "'tis beautiful to see one's name in print."[30]

Neff graduated from Baylor on June 6, 1894, after a week-long series of related events that included a graduate recital, entertainment, missionary sermon, commencement sermon, graduating exercises, orations, literary society activities, and an annual concert. After graduation Neff made his life work decision: he would become a lawyer. First, however, he would have to spend two years teaching school to save money for law school, so he stayed in Waco for the next few weeks studying for his teacher's examination. By the first week in September, he had received a "first class certificate" from the state Educational Department in Austin, having passed the examination and been licensed to teach. He wrote Myrtie that the certificate was good for four years and that more than 60 percent of those taking the examination the year before had failed.[31]

After considering teaching possibilities in Brownwood and Sherman, Neff decided to take a job paying $50 a month at a new school in Magnolia, Arkansas—the Southwestern Academy. James W. Cantwell, president of the school, had just received his degree from Yale University. Neff would be "first assistant," and he would be assigned to the higher grades, which he thought would be "more pleasant and satisfactory." He wrote Myrtie about the new job, telling her the school was in a $10,000 building.[32]

In this letter, Neff also asked Myrtie: "How would you like to go?" She jumped at the idea and sent a positive reply. Neff, not really ready for marriage, hurriedly backpedaled. Reversing course, he told her that he needed to make money at Southwestern Academy to go to law school, finish his law degree, and get settled a little bit. He added: "I know I would be supremely happy and could live a better life in many ways. But we must patiently wait—perhaps it will be made sweeter by our having waited."[33]

Pat's and Myrtie's long courtship had many rocky spots, and this was one of them. Just a few weeks before, he had written to her about what he expected from a wife, scolding her for mentioning her many boyfriends. Although he bragged about his own social activities at Baylor, he did not approve of Myrtie's dating others. He had definite ideas about how his prospective wife should behave, and he wrote her that he read a little book about marriage and it advised men not to marry a girl who had too many "beaus." He assured her that he had no reason to believe that she had done anything inappropriate but still warned her that "it is no honor to have a half a dozen swear their love to you in one night."[34]

Saving Money and Saving a Life

In November 1894, as Pat Neff left his Central Texas home for Arkansas, he took a longer route than necessary, going by Lovelady to spend an entire day with Myrtie, knowing he would not see her again for a whole year. From Lovelady, he took the train to Magnolia. Winding through East Texas, he was saddened by the poverty he saw from the train. In a letter to his mother, he wrote that he saw lots of small towns filled with Negroes and poor white people and that the area did not have "the paint, push and polish that central and western Texas has."[35]

The Southwestern Academy, a preparatory school, opened December 3. Neff and Professor Cantwell spent November drumming up students for the school. On November 9, the two men spoke to an estimated 500 interested citizens at the local Opera House. Neff wrote his mother that he did "most of the gassing and one little girl went home and told her papa if he didn't send her to school, she would die."[36]

A wealthy local man, Captain William Pulliam Longino, had loaned the school board the money to build a facility for a college. However, the community decided Magnolia needed a preparatory school more than a college, so Southwestern Academy was born. The building, a two-and-one-half-story brick structure, was impressive, with a large brick bell tower above the front door. It had four classrooms on the first floor and another four on the second floor.

Neff found lodging in a local hotel. He wrote Myrtie that he had everything he needed (bureau, nice bed, washstand, nice little stove) except her, saying "it makes me long for you."[37] However, his signals continued to be mixed, as he didn't ask her to join him.

Neff's school schedule was demanding—he was teaching more than fifty students, many of them men and women older than he. He was on his feet from eight-thirty in the morning until four-thirty in the afternoon, except for a brief lunch break. He wrote his mother that he had not had to whip anybody yet as "most of my folks are large."[38] He taught physiology, oratory, mathematics, and Latin, and in later years he said he taught everything, and had to spend many evenings and weekends in preparation to stay ahead of the students.

His letters reveal that his teaching schedule did not interfere with church and social activities. He wrote Myrtie that "fifteen young ladies" at the Baptist Church had elected him to be their teacher.[39] By the spring of 1895 Neff's academy colleague, Francis G. Guittard, who later would teach at Baylor, was encouraging Neff to get out more. Neff wrote his mother that he was escorting a nice Arkansas girl from her home to church and that Guittard, a twenty-eight-year-old bachelor, was coaching him in social activities. He said he even attended a sewing club of about ten or twelve of "Magnolia's finest daughters," reporting to his mother that the girls thought he could "handle a needle real well."[40] He spent the summer of 1895 on the farm with his mother, working some in the fields but continuing to study law in preparation for law school. In September he headed back to Magnolia, again stopping in Lovelady for a brief visit with Myrtie.

More comfortable in the classroom the second year, Neff had time to keep up with the news of the world. He wrote his mother that he was reading the *Gazette* (full of prize fight news), the *New York World*, the *McGregor News*, and the *Forum* from Gatesville. He added that the hotel where he was staying got other papers. He also told her that one of his fellow professors subscribed to the *Baptist Standard*, "so every time a Sunday School is organized or a preacher runs away with another man's wife, we know about it. Thus, you can see, we are strictly in the swim."[41]

One of Neff's students in Arkansas became a multimillionaire and throughout his life gave Neff credit for his success. While many of the students were young, twelve or thirteen years of age, Harvey Couch was seventeen and felt uncomfortable in the classroom and thought about dropping out of school. Neff, recognizing this, took time to tutor and encourage the young man. He inspired him with such phrases as "a winner never quits" and "men like you have built empires."[42] Neff's words became a positive force in Couch's life and the two forged a lifelong friendship. Couch's phenomenal success included owning several railroad lines and a telephone company. He created three interconnected utility companies from scratch—Arkansas Power & Light, Mississippi Power & Light, and Louisiana Power & Light. He became a confidant and advisor to President Franklin D. Roosevelt and later to President Herbert Hoover. He often credited Professor Pat Neff as the greatest inspiration in his life next to his mother. Neff later would honor him with an honorary degree from Baylor. Couch died before Neff, and at Couch's request, Neff delivered the final oration at his funeral service.[43]

When school was over in the spring of 1896, Neff at last was ready—both financially and emotionally—to return to Texas and apply to the University of Texas Law School, as Baylor had terminated its law program several years earlier.[44] He moved to Texas, putting Magnolia behind him. His friend Francis Guittard, remaining at the academy, wrote him that there were rumors in Magnolia about the young lady that Neff had "sparked" and left behind. Guittard encouraged Neff to resolve the situation: "The fact of the matter is that no one suspected you of going to see Miss Ruth for pastime but that you were in dead earnest. This was the general opinion when you left and still prevails."[45] No record of Neff's response exists.

About this same time, before Neff went to Austin and law school, he received a letter from Myrtie, informing him that she had at least three offers of marriage. To this, Neff replied that he did not want to be a "stumbling block" if she wanted to pursue the other offers.[46]

The Rebel at the University of Texas Law School

Neff had hoped his continuing study of the law would prepare him to pass an exam to be admitted into the senior class at law school. However, he failed the exam and was admitted to the first-year class in fall 1896. At that time, the University of Texas Law School was located in Old Main, a Victorian-Gothic structure on a small hill in the center of the forty-acre campus. Besides Old Main, only two other buildings comprised the University of Texas—the Chemistry Lab Building and B Hall, a men's dormitory. The campus was surrounded by a white-washed wooden fence to prevent cattle from wandering onto the grounds. The Law School had approximately 160 students. [47]

Neff had little free time away from his studies. Movie matinees, plays, and operas furnished some entertainment. The most unusual diversion was watching the dances at the lunatic asylum. He wrote his brother Ben that the "crazy women make my hair stand up." He reported that when he asked someone what "made them crazy," the reply was, "Either religion or love." [48] One place frequented by many of the law students was a saloon located between the university and the Capitol. Scholz's continues into the twenty-first century as a popular gathering place for not only students, but legislators, lobbyists, and many others. Neff's strict upbringing prevented him from joining his classmates there, but that did not affect his ability to make friends, either then or later.

Neff's class load was so heavy that he stayed in Austin during the Christmas break. He wrote Myrtie that January 1897 would be the hardest month yet, but he was getting along well in his studies and liked his law classes. [49] About the same time, Neff wrote his brother Ben and told him his church attendance was suffering because he simply had to study every minute. He also wrote that on a recent exam, he had started at nine o'clock in the morning and did not finish until one-thirty in the afternoon. He added that he was the second person to finish the examination; the first was Will Hogg, son of Governor James Stephen Hogg. Neff added about Hogg: "He is a real sharp boy about 21 years old, but he is a real scrubby hog—different looking stock from his father." [50]

Neff's study of law often took him to the Capitol to observe the legislature and to the library in the Capitol to do some reading. He told his brother:

> The legislature is in session now and so I spend some of my spare time watching them attempt to make laws for Texas. I saw the Governor [Charles A. Culberson] inaugurated the other day. Quite an impressive scene to see him take the oath of office surrounded by such men as Hogg, John H. Reagan, Crane, Jester, and a host of other Texas heroes. I read a greater part of every evening in the Library room of the Capitol and it makes me feel very important. For a while, some of us boys would run to the top of the building for exercise after we were through

with our study, but that did not last long. By the time you trot up its stairs to the top, you are just able to grunt.[51]

Two of Neff's best friends in Law School were future U.S. Senators from Texas: Tom Connally and Morris Sheppard. Along with George Scarborough (later a successful Los Angeles playwright), the foursome were often together—studying, practicing oratorical and debating skills, and on one memorable occasion, March 2, 1897, risking the wrath of university officials.

In Texas, March 2 is almost a sacred day, commemorating the date Texans declared their independence from Mexico. For many years, March 2 was a state holiday, but not a University of Texas holiday. Several versions of the Connally-Neff-Scarborough-Sheppard prank emerged through the years, including one in Connally's autobiography, one in the University of Texas student yearbook *The Cactus*, another in the university's *Alcalde* publication, and finally, one by Neff himself in a letter to his mother a few days after the event.[52]

The "rebellion" itself began on March 1 when the students "borrowed" a cannon from the State Capitol grounds, bought forty-five pounds of gunpowder, and obtained an oversize Texas flag. Early the next day, they pulled the cannon up in front of Old Main and prepared to launch the rebellion.

George T. Winston, a native of North Carolina and the newly installed president of the university, emerged from his office in Old Main and, according to Neff, "made us a short talk." Winston told the group: "I was born in the land of liberty, rocked in the cradle of liberty, nursed on the bottle of liberty, and I've had liberty preached to me all my life. But Texas University students take more liberty than anyone I've ever come in contact with."[53]

Winston meted no punishment to the rebels but requested they move the cannon to the athletic field and fire it there. He also invited students to make short talks. Neff told his mother: "I was one of those students and of course I told them I was proud to be classed with the rebels who did not attend school on such a day."[54]

Neff also wrote his mother that most of the boys went out to the lake that night and "indulged much too freely in the drink for which the Germans have become so noted." He assured her that he was not among them, closing his letter: "So, as you see, the students down here do just as they pleased with no strings attached."[55]

While Neff and his friends exulted in their daring escapade, Winston's handling of it stands in sharp contrast with the way Neff as president of Baylor forty years later would handle infractions of Baylor rules.[56]

The rest of the school year passed without incident except for Myrtie's notifying Neff that her father had died. Neff responded with sympathy and also told Myrtie that he had just finished his last examination. He wrote his mother that he was nervously awaiting the results of his exam. If he failed, he would have to come back to school for another year.[57]

Neff rose to the occasion and in June 1897, at age twenty-five, he graduated, earning his Bachelor of Laws degree. He completed his law degree in one year instead of the normal two years by taking large caseloads and studying conscientiously. His continuous study of the law while in Magnolia was also a factor.

Practicing Law

On August 28, Neff wrote Myrtie that he was "hanging out his shingle" in Waco to practice law. He began his law practice with William W. Evans, who had previously served as county judge. Neff wrote his sister, Sallie Calvert, about preparing himself for law and his new practice:

> For *nine* long years, I have been preparing myself for the profession which I have recently entered. What, when, where, and how the goal shall be reached no one knows. With blind faith, without seeing scarcely a step in front of me, I travel into the untried and untraveled future. I am very pleasantly situated at the present and think I will like my work more and more as the weeks, months, and years roll on. I have indulged in no lofty air-castle building, but have realized in this as in all other callings, the truth of the proverb that "Every path hath its puddles."[58]

The novice lawyer found no hordes of clients overrunning his office, so he decided that fall to pursue a master's degree at Baylor while also taking law cases.[59] In January 1898, he continued his graduate work and made a decision to run for the Texas House of Representatives. He later said that he figured a campaign for the legislature would be a good way to meet people and perhaps gain some clients.

CHAPTER 3

Mr. Speaker

I never did like "politics"; it is, I think . . . corrupting.
—Myrtie Mainer

Pat Neff sought to become a member of the House of Representatives in the midst of a turbulent time in the country and in Waco. A new political party—the People's Party (usually called the Populist Party)—burst on the national scene in 1891 and quickly gained stature not only in Texas but also at the national level. However, when the Democratic Party and William Jennings Bryan, its presidential nominee, adopted many of the planks of the Populist Party, the Populists joined the Democrats in 1896, only to lose the election to William McKinley, the candidate of the Republican Party.

In other developments, the United States Supreme Court in 1896 approved racial segregation in setting forth the "separate but equal" doctrine, a ruling that would remain in effect for more than half a century. The continuing battle over Prohibition raged and, in 1900, Carrie (also spelled Carry) Nation, one of the country's best-known Prohibitionists, began praying outside saloons in her native Kansas and soon was attacking them with her trademark hatchet in some of Kansas' major cities.[1]

The morality of America's foreign relations was tested in the closing years of the nineteenth century when on February 15, 1898, the battleship *Maine* was blown up in the Havana, Cuba, harbor. The ensuing Spanish-American War lasted just four months as the United States overwhelmed Spanish forces and gained Cuba its independence. That war was also a key factor in breaking the logjam to building the long-dreamed-of Panama Canal.[2] Among the volunteers for the war was Neff's law school classmate, Tom Connally, who got only as far as Florida before the war was over.[3]

The Populist Party fell as quickly as it had risen, primarily because of the new progressivism in the Democratic Party. In Texas, that reform was led by James Stephen Hogg, who would become another Neff mentor. Twentieth century historian Joe B. Frantz called the 1890s the Hogg decade for good reason.[4] Hogg served as Texas Attorney General from 1887 to 1891 and as Texas Governor from 1891 to 1895. As the state's chief legal officer, he began enforcing laws to regulate the railroads and insurance companies and, when he believed the former were still too powerful, he advocated establishing the Texas Railroad Commission and was elected governor on this platform in 1890. During his gubernatorial years, Hogg was a major influence in Texas for stronger law enforcement as well as better higher education. Although he gave up public office in 1895, he remained interested in good government and became a significant supporter of young Neff in his fledgling career. Hogg is generally regarded as one of the strongest governors in Texas history.[5]

In Waco, Neff was set to launch his political life in a city that was never known for progressive reform. Incorporated in 1856, Waco was the center of a thriving plantation economy, with bountiful cotton grown all up and down the rich black land of the Brazos River valley. The town was a strong supporter of the Confederacy; Waco and the surrounding area supplied seventeen companies of soldiers and six Confederate generals. After the war, Waco diversified, becoming a stopping place for cattlemen taking steers to market in North Texas and other parts of the country. With the advent of three railroads between 1870 and 1885, the city became an ideal link between the cotton farmers and factories and consumers across the state and beyond. The concentration of railroads combined with the thriving cotton industry in Central Texas made Waco the seventh largest city in Texas in 1900. It was one of the most important cotton markets in the South, and at that time it had 163 factories and six banks and was continuing to expand. [6]

Also by the turn of the century, the city was really a community of three faces. The first was the very proper business and religious community. The same families who benefited from the city's business boom were actively involved in the church. In the 1890s, Waco had become the stronghold of the Baptist denomination in Texas. The city attracted a number of educational institutions in addition to Baylor and was known in some circles as the "Athens of Texas."[7] Add-Ran Christian University of Waco (later to become Texas Christian University in Fort Worth) and Paul Quinn College for students of color were the other two universities. The 1900-1901 city directory listed thirty-one churches for whites and twelve for colored people.[8]

But there was also a darker side to Waco. The presence of prostitution, gambling, and liquor continued to haunt the community. The Reservation District, with its legal prostitutes, seemingly lost none of its attraction over the years for otherwise religious men, and the saloons with gambling and whiskey and beer operated with virtually a free hand. The second face of Waco and the respectable face of business and religion were not always worn by different characters. Historians record that business and professional men patronized the district, and drinking and gambling establishments did not lack well-paying customers.[9] Periodically, preachers felt it necessary to speak on the evils of the flesh.

The African-American community represented the third face of Waco, a part of the city that many whites tried to ignore except when they needed maid or laborer services.

Because of its cotton heritage, Waco was more "Old South" than "New West." Blacks walked softly and gingerly in the community, fearfully hoping that they would not be in the wrong place at the wrong time and be swept up by a frenzied mob.

Some historians believe the Waco of the early 1900s was described fifty years later in a blockbuster novel that would blow the lid off fiction of that era. The novelist, Waco's own Madison Cooper, consistently denied before his death that the setting of *Sironia, Texas* was his own city, but historians refused to believe him.[10] Reviled by many Wacoans, the 893,000-word chronicle—twice as long as *Gone with the Wind*—was a *New York Times* bestseller for eleven weeks and received several literary awards. The *Saturday Review*, in a November 1, 1952, release written by its president, described the novel as having at least six plots which combined "sex, violence, murder, sadism, miscegenation, catastrophes of fire and blood, and class and racial hatreds." The entry on Cooper in the *Handbook of Texas* makes the statement that "Cooper based his character Calvin Thaxton on Pat Morris Neff."[11] Thaxton was one of the author's less notable characters. Cooper's handwritten notes left in his collection of papers include Neff's name as well as those of several other Wacoans living at the time.[12]

Neff's First Political Campaign—1898

However Waco and McLennan County might be characterized at the turn of the century, twenty-six-year-old lawyer Pat Neff was ready to carry the area's colors into the Texas Legislature. The county elected two individuals in an at-large election to represent its interests. After the two incumbents decided against running, seven men including Neff made the race. In this era, the top two vote-getters in the Democratic primary election were, for all intents and purposes, elected as McLennan County's representatives. There was no runoff election for Democrats and very rarely did any Republican or other opposition appear on the November ballot.

Although seven names were on the ballot, the race quickly came down to Neff, fellow attorney O. H. Cross, who would later go to Congress for several terms, and journalist James Hays Quarles. Neff and his friend O. H. Cross decided to plan their campaign appearances jointly.

On March 31, 1898, a Thursday evening, Neff launched his political career in his hometown of McGregor. Neff told the crowd assembled that he was running as a Democrat and that he believed in the policies, the purposes, the platform, and the principles advocated and maintained by that party. His principal subjects were the need for equality in taxation, more funds for education, and ballot box reform. He deplored the fact that millions of dollars left the state every year to purchase manufactured articles made from the raw material being produced by Texas labor in Texas fields and forests. He declared himself the staunch and unswerving friend of education from kindergarten to the state university and, finally, spoke strongly for "purity" of the ballot box, stating that several Southern states had adopted the payment of a "poll tax" as a prerequisite of voting. He closed with a flourish of the oratory that was to be his signature:

> The eyes of the world are turning toward Texas. She has been baptized in the blood of martyrs and consecrated to a glorious destiny by the heroic deeds of her noble sons. Through the half drawn folds of coming years, I see Texas rising to prominence and to power, not only as the Lone Star State but the biggest, best and brightest state and star that glitters in the constellation of the American Union.[13]

Neff wasted no time following his announcement in McGregor, covering seven other small towns in the next week. Except for Cross and occasionally Quarles, Neff would have the campaign trail to himself the entire spring. His letter of April 8 to Myrtie is a poignant reminder of the rigors of political campaigning. Addressed to her in Lovelady, he wrote:

> One week ago today, I left town . . . on my speaking trip. I came in from Hewitt last night at the lonesome hour of twelve. I am going to leave town again after dinner—will come back again late Saturday night. I am taking the county in a buggy. Well, Myrtie, I have been out a week and feel somewhat used up. I have been losing so much sleep I never get to bed before twelve o'clock. Every time either a good or bad report comes to me, I think of you in connection with it. In every joy and pain, I think of you as to how it will affect *us*.[14]

One is immediately struck with the difference in his campaign oratory—flowery and somewhat stilted—and his letters to Myrtie and to his family. The latter use simple, straightforward words and sentences in a more conversational tone.

From Lovelady, Myrtie was not helpful. In the middle of April, the mid-point of the campaign, she wrote Pat complaining about his not writing her often or lengthily enough and about his failing to answer questions she posed to him in her letters to him. Moreover, she wrote disparagingly of his desire to enter "politics":

> I am rejoiced to know you are getting along so nicely with your canvassing. I would be proud if you do receive the nomination yet I don't know whether I want you to be elected. . . . Of course I want *whatever* is best for you, but somehow, I *never* did like "*politics*"—it is I think to some extent corrupting—it seems that it would be so much nicer to work at your law for the next ten years to come at least—*always* for that matter.[15]

In its issue of Monday, May 9, the *Waco Times-Herald* reported that the "election was one of great interest" and proclaimed Neff and Cross the winners over the five other candidates.

After the May 7 election, Neff waited in vain for a word of congratulations from Myrtie. Finally, on May 24. two and one-half weeks after the election, he could contain himself no longer and wrote her that it had been five weeks since she had written him, despite two letters from him in the meantime. He typed a two-page letter to her, then could not resist an additional handwritten comment: "I will send you a few of my very highly appreciated letters, so you will know I received them—please return."[16]

Three months later, Neff was still piqued, this time at a letter from Myrtie in which she had lectured him and accused him of being very selfish.[17] Despite these interruptions, the long courtship stayed on an otherwise even keel, and the two exchanged loving letters over the next several months.[18]

The general election was held November 8, 1898, and Neff and Cross were elected without opposition.[19] Shortly after the election, Neff wrote his mother that he had "commenced to get my old clothes fixed up for my Austin trip."[20]

The Twenty-sixth Legislature: Neff's First Term—1899-1901

Neff returned to Austin only nineteen months after having graduated from the University of Texas Law School in June 1897. The capital city had not changed all that much. Its population continued to be similar to Waco's; in 1890, Austin had counted just 130 persons more than Waco, the latter recording 14,445. In 1900, Austin would register 22,258 persons, about 1,500 more than Waco.

For their service to their state, Neff and his colleagues received the same amount of pay and mileage as first adopted in the state's new constitution thirteen years before—the princely sum of $5 per day for the first 60 days of a legislative session and $2 per day thereafter. The maximum mileage reimbursement was $5 per 25 miles. The previous legislative session had proposed a constitutional amendment raising those figures to $5 per day for the first 100 days and the subsequent per diem to $3. It had been overwhelmingly defeated (by a seven-to-one margin) at the same election—November 8, 1898—at which Neff and the others had been elected to the Twenty-sixth Legislature.[21]

Neff would soon realize that powerful forces were at work in the state to control political elections from the governor down and to influence legislation that came before the Texas Legislature. At the corporate level, these forces included the numerous railroad companies that blanketed the eastern part of the state and several industrial concerns, including an oil company, Waters-Pierce, which would be in the limelight for several years. It would be difficult to overestimate the political power of the railroads at the turn of the century.

Three individuals stood out as the dominant political personalities in the state at that time: Joseph Weldon Bailey, James Stephen Hogg, and "Colonel" Edward M. House. The first two held a variety of official positions in state and national government; the third never held an elective position but directed (or had a key role in) the campaigns of four successive governors from 1891 to 1907 before moving on to the national stage. The House story is not well known, but he orchestrated the elections of Governors Hogg, Culberson, Sayers, and Lanham during that time, as well as U.S. Senators Culberson and Bailey. He then sat out the political scene for several years before playing a prominent role in the nomination of Woodrow Wilson for president and later serving him in a variety of advisory positions.[22]

Bailey, as a U.S. Congressman and then U.S. Senator (1901-1911), was a player in all three of Neff's legislative terms. Hogg, who left the governorship in 1895, would continue to exert influence on both state and national politics and would be pleased with Pat Neff's progressive ideas. There is nothing in the records to indicate that Edward M. House was ever cognizant of the young representative from McGregor, but Neff's relationship with Bailey would be part of the Neff story for years to come.

At high noon on Tuesday, January 10, 1899, Neff was sworn in as a member of the House of Representatives of the Twenty-sixth Texas Legislature.[23] The 128-member body was composed about equally of lawyers and farmers, with a few merchants joining them. The "freshman" legislator who was destined to become the most notable in future years was lawyer John Nance Garner of Uvalde. Garner would serve two terms as a Texas State Representative, then thirty years in the U.S. House of Representatives before becoming Franklin Delano Roosevelt's vice-president in 1933.

On the first day of the session, J. S. Sherrill of Hunt County was elected speaker of the House; six days later, the House canvassed the votes and declared Joseph D. Sayers governor and J. N. Browning lieutenant governor. One day later, on January 17, the two were sworn into office, and a week later, Sayers delivered his major address to the legislature.

The first two weeks of the session also included the legislature's election of a U.S. Senator—outgoing governor Charles A. Culberson. He had completed the traditional four years in the governor's chair and, with the influence of Colonel House, had secured the Democratic primary votes without any difficulty. The system of legislative bodies electing U.S. Senators for their states would continue until a federal constitutional amendment gave this responsibility to the voters of each state in 1916.

As a newcomer to the legislature, Neff went about learning the rules and customs of the body in a quiet way, and his name appeared in the *House Journal* only a few times. He told his mother: "Some fellows make motions, introduce resolutions and wind themselves so as to get their names in the *Journal* often. It would not do at all for us all to be just alike."[24] (The term "wind themselves" is probably a metaphor for "blow hot air.") His serious manner was reflected in other ways. He had written Myrtie the summer before, after his election, that his mother had said that "I was good for everything except one. . . . I wasn't any account to play with."[25] He seemed to conform to her description. Neff wrote to Myrtie: "I have been at my desk busy all night, not paying any attention to the jolly crowd around me."[26] He also confided to his mother in a letter midway in the session: "I do not want to be embarrassed in coming years when some one draws my legislative record on me."[27] Neff may also have been warmer at his Capitol desk; February brought the coldest temperature ever recorded in Texas when the mercury fell to minus twenty-three degrees at Tulia in the Texas Panhandle.[28] That month, some of Neff's friends in Waco enjoyed ice skating on Baylor's football turf, Carroll Field, a highly unusual phenomenon.[29]

Neff's attention to duty was also demonstrated during the week of February 14 when he refused to go with other House members to Galveston on the occasion of a visit by the battleship *Texas* to Galveston Harbor. The year 1899 appears to be the first of a series of periodic invitations to the legislature by the citizens of Galveston to take a mid-session break to visit the coastal city. This invitation was occasioned by the visit of the battleship *Texas*, but in succeeding years, whether the *Texas* or other ships were coming in or not, the legislators enjoyed the beaches and, for many years, the wide-open gambling and other worldly pleasures offered by Galveston. The Galveston trips became a tradition and continued session after session until Texas Attorney General Will Wilson and the Texas Rangers began their relentless raids on the gambling houses in 1957.[30]

Neff made only three speeches of note during the session, the most significant being an attempt to restore funding for the University of Texas. Neff made no apology for his support for and love of the University of Texas. He was distraught that the House Finance Committee recommended that the university appropriation be zeroed, a major turnaround from previous years. He knew that many of his House colleagues had minimal schooling, one remarking in the debates, "I am opposed to voting away the taxpayer's money to make lawyers and doctors."[31] In a night session on April 26, Neff summoned his best oratory and logic to sway the members whose minds were still open to the appropriation question.

> I deeply regret that the University of Texas is tonight seemingly an supplicant at the hands of this House. I speak at this hour . . . because I am a friend of the poor boys of Texas who are tonight perchance, after a hard day's work, peacefully sleeping and dreaming as I once slept and dreamed of the happy day when I would be counted as a student of this institution. . . . I remember that we read in this hall on the second of March the Declaration of Texas Independence, in which they declared that they would not live under the Mexican government because it made no provision for the education of their boys and girls.[32]

He took particular exception to the members who had said that the University of Texas was for "rich kids" and cited several examples of students working their way through school. He was upset that "in 1896, more than one thousand boys . . . had to go north for an education because we had not prepared a place for them."[33]

Neff and the other supporters of the university were successful. They did not get the $75,000 originally sought, but they did get a 23 percent increase over the previous biennium—from $32,500 per year to $40,000. This was especially note-worthy because other state agencies and institutions were given only small increases over the previous two years.[34]

The legislature adjourned May 27. The session was not considered particularly productive by most observers; it did establish, as requested in Governor Sayers' initial message, a Tax Commission "to frame and report a complete system of laws for the assessment, collection, and accounting of taxes and public revenues in the state." In addition, the legislators established "normal colleges" at Denton and San Marcos, although they did not provide any appropriation for them at this session.[35]

Neff corresponded with both Myrtie and his mother during the session, but the letters to Myrtie were fairly brief, whereas the letters to his mother—twice as many— were replete with descriptions of the legislators sitting near him, the inaugural ball and other social events, and a trip to Marble Falls.[36]

"Crossing the Muddy Waters"—The Wedding

Four days after the legislature adjourned, on May 31, 1899, Pat and Myrtie finally tied the knot that had been dangling for nine years.

Neff's opinion of marriage in the early years of courtship with Myrtie had been negative. Over several years, he had written of his friends making "mistakes" and that he would rather be single than have his wife or himself unhappy. In 1895, he had told his brother that some of his friends were going to "cross the muddy wa-ters" before the next winter had passed. A year later, he wrote Myrtie that the urge to marry had never "coursed in his veins yet, but I am looking for it to strike any time now."[37] Nevertheless, he held her off; his reason seemed to be that he wanted to finish law school and be gainfully employed. Myrtie often described herself as being lonely and unhappy during the last few years of their courtship, but Neff was unfaltering in his decision to wait. In a letter to him in early 1899, Myrtie told him that her mother believed that "Mr. Neff feels obligated to marry you."[38]

The "waiting" issue continued to weigh heavily on her mind, along with her doubts about his feelings toward her, and she pressed for a wedding date. Neff felt that marriage was inevitable and told her that he was finally ready to get married. By May 2, the date was set for May 31 and Myrtie was ordering the wedding invitations.

All finally seemed to be smooth between the two of them, but Mother Neff was not all that happy about giving up her baby boy. On May 4, Neff penned a letter to her urging her to come to Lovelady for the wedding. By May 14, he had received a negative reply from her saying her traveling days were over. Despite these protests, she would continue to make trips around the state for the next twenty years of her life. But Myrtie would not give up on her future mother-in-law and wrote her on May 20 with a final and desperate plea. Neff also wrote his only remaining sister, Sallie Neff Calvert, of Brownwood, begging her to attend, but on the day of the wedding none of his family were present.

Myrtie deferred to her mother's wish to have a small wedding at their Lovelady home in the company of a few friends and relatives. At eight-thirty on the evening of May 31, the ceremony took place in the parlor of her family's two-story Victorian home. Myrtie wore a dress of white organdy, a customary bridal veil, and a wreath of orange blossoms on her head. Neff donned a dark suit, the dress coat reaching to his knees, a white tie, and black leather gloves. A wedding supper followed in the dining room. Scattered about were "numerous and handsome presents."[39]

It is not known exactly how long the couple honeymooned in Galveston, but by June 8, Neff was back in Waco to receive his master's degree from Baylor with Mother Neff and Myrtie among others in attendance at the ceremonies. On June 16, he wrote his mother that he and Myrtie were going to "commence housekeeping tomorrow" and had rented a "nice cottage in North Waco and have bought about enough furniture."[40] In August Myrtie returned to Lovelady, which would be a regular occurrence through the years.

Just three months after renting, Neff bought their first home. Located at 1815 Fort Avenue, the house cost $1,800. Neff's papers do not reveal whether his law practice was doing that well or whether the home had been a wedding present from Myrtie's mother or her father's estate. In a November letter to his mother, he reflected on the past year, his marriage, life in the legislature, and their new home. He wrote: "I daily congratulate myself on having such a congenial and worthy companion."[41]

Early in 1900, Governor Sayers called the legislature into special session to consider his Tax Commission report. The work of the commission was presented but went for naught as legislators found themselves unable to shake free of the influence of numerous business lobbyists. The railroad and other corporate lobbyists exerted pressure from the back of the House chamber, a situation which Neff was never happy about. Among the "goodies" given to legislators were free passes on the railroads. Because the railroads were the major source of transportation in the state and virtually blanketed the central and eastern part of the state, the free passes to poorly paid legislators were a valuable perquisite. Repeated attempts to enact an "anti-free pass" law consistently failed to garner support in the legislature. Three different bills were introduced in the regular session in 1899, but none passed despite strong newspaper editorials denouncing the practice.[42] Neff himself, while railing against the lobbyists, nevertheless enjoyed the benefits of the passes and obtained them for members of his family, including his mother and sister on numerous occasions. Although an "anti-free pass" bill was finally enacted in 1907, the issue remained on the agenda for more than two decades and would even haunt Neff in his gubernatorial race in 1920.[43]

Neff was happy to have Myrtie living with him in Austin for the first time during the legislature's special session in early 1900. He wrote his mother that "Myrtie and I are thinking of going out to the lunatic asylum tonight and see the 'loonies' dance" as he had done when he was a law student at the university.[44] The recreational outing Neff described was a common diversion for Austin residents in those days.

One of the minor mysteries of Neff's life relates to his forgetting that he served in the 1899-1900 sessions of the legislature. In his press releases and other biographical information, he always stated that he began his public career with the 1901 legislative session. The first major occasion on which Neff wrote down his background was the 1920-1921 edition of *Who's Who in America*, the first year in which Neff is listed. His entry contains the line: "mem. Tex. Ho. of Rep. 1901-05, speaker of House, 1903-05."[45] The identical entry occurred in every issue of the publication through the 1950-51 edition, the last in which he is listed. The original entry must have been submitted by Neff himself or someone close to him and presumably approved by him. During his term as governor, his office issued several biographical data sheets, all with the same entry. As a result, numerous theses, dissertations, and other papers about his life carry the erroneous date. A few authors have used the correct date, but the great majority give 1901 as the beginning date of his public service career.

How or why Neff made the original error is not known. He certainly had nothing to be ashamed of in his initial legislative session. He acquitted himself sufficiently to win plaudits from his hometown newspapers and even garner two votes for speaker pro tem.[46] One would also think he would remember his service in 1899 because his wedding date was just four days after adjournment of the regular session. The unfortunate outcome is that he is frequently credited for only two terms in the legislature whereas he served three, overcoming stiff opposition to win the first two terms.

The Campaign for a Second Term—1900

Neff's decision to run for a second term was somewhat unusual. Most legislators served only one term because the position paid so little that it was really a sacrifice for most individuals to go to Austin. Serving in the Texas House was considered by many as a way for an aspiring attorney or merchant to get name recognition to further his private career or gain other better-paying public offices. In this vein, O. H. Cross decided to forego a second legislative term.

Neff drew two opponents this time: popular County Judge J. N. Gallagher and H. B. Terrell, a country newspaperman. One day before the election, Neff received help from an unlikely source. The *Houston Post* commented on Neff: "Without disparagement to other candidates, the Post desires to remark that McLennan County will do well to return Mr. Neff to the Legislature. No man stood better in the last House of Representatives, and with the experience of the former session, he will be capable of doing much good for his constituents in the coming session."[47] The endorsement of a rural representative by a leading newspaper in the state's third largest city was highly unusual. However, Neff's incumbency did not gain him the overwhelming victory he had enjoyed when he first ran in 1898. Although he led both his opponents, the race was extremely close and only 275 votes separated Neff from Gallagher, the third-place finisher. Neff received a total of 4,573 votes; Terrell 4,412, and Gallagher 4,298. Neff and Terrell were unopposed in the general election of November 6, and both began final preparations for the 1901 session to open shortly after the first of the year.[48]

Overshadowing the convening of the legislature in early January were two major events in Texas history. Remarkably, they occurred less than 100 miles from each other. The first was the devastating Galveston hurricane, which took place in September 1900, exactly four months before the session's first day. The nation's worst recorded natural disaster killed between 6,000 and 8,000 people in the city of Galveston. Estimated casualties for the entire island ranged from 10,000 to 12,000. High water and winds destroyed a third of the city, including 2,636 houses and 1,500 acres of shoreline.[49]

The second historic event was the discovery of oil at Spindletop, south of Beaumont, marking the birth of the modern petroleum industry. Various individuals had spent most of the 1890s drilling in the tricky sands of the salt dome formation in that area. Suddenly, on January 10, 1901, a terrific column of gas and then oil spewed from the rig. The geyser blew 100 feet in the air for nine days before it could be capped; it put out an estimated 100,000 barrels of oil a day, purportedly "more oil in one day than the rest of the fields of the world combined."[50]

Neff's Second Term—1901-1903

The regular session of the Twenty-seventh Legislature got under way at noon on Tuesday, January 8. One of the new members would be in the political spotlight for a long and distinguished career—Tom Connally of Marlin. He and Neff were often mistaken for each other, as they dressed and conducted themselves in similar fashion. Connally served two terms in the House and was elected district attorney in Falls County for four years (1906-1910) before going to U.S. House of Representatives in 1917 for twelve years and then to the U.S. Senate. He quickly became one of the Senate's most powerful members, extremely active in the international scene, including serving as chair of the Senate Foreign Relations Committee and as one of the authors of the United Nations Charter.[51]

With one session under his belt, Neff was now ready to step forward more aggressively and exercise his influence. Rather than dealing with substantive matters, he primarily chose to be seen as one who knew the intricacies of the legislative process and who could be trusted to be a fair and impartial arbiter of conflicting views. As a measure of Speaker R. E. Prince's confidence in Neff's knowledge of House rules and his fairness as a presiding officer, he called on Neff a total of twenty-six times during the session to preside "in the chair." The honors culminated in Neff's being one of three members to be elected speaker pro tem over the course of the session.[52]

This legislature also had the duty of electing another U.S. Senator from Texas. Senator Horace Chilton had been urged to run for reelection by former Governor Hogg and other more liberal Democrats, but he bowed out in the spring of 1900 because of illness. This left the way clear for Congressman Joseph W. Bailey, who quickly moved into the void to the dismay of Hogg, Chilton, and others. The latter group sought to persuade Hogg to run for the Senate. He declined and Bailey was elected by the legislature in January 1901, receiving 137 votes with six votes cast for a total of four other candidates.[53] Neff voted for Bailey without any comment.

Meanwhile, Neff's general demeanor was getting favorable notices from time to time in several of the state's newspapers. The *Waco Times-Herald* ran complimentary stories and also quoted Jeff McLemore, who covered the Texas House for the *San Antonio Express*:

> He [Neff] is a forcible talker and a good parliamentarian. . . and because of his able and conservative views, his people will no doubt send him here as their representative as long as he desires to come. . . . Mr. Neff is bound to go to the front on his merits. He is a close student, a conscientious worker, a steadfast friend, and these qualities, combined with a moral sense, have given him a strong hold in public favor. It is freely predicted that he will be the speaker of the next House, and the honor could not be more worthily bestowed.[54]

Myrtie (now Mrs. Neff) came to Austin with Neff for the first part of the legislative session. The couple celebrated a long legislative weekend in late February by boarding a train to Laredo and continuing on down to Monterrey. Neff wrote his mother that the entire trip cost them $25. He used rail passes for the trip and mentioned his plans to send Isabella passes so that she could visit Sallie (Neff's sister) in Brownwood and then come to see them in Austin.[55] Myrtie went home to Lovelady shortly after that to await the arrival of their first child.

The legislature adjourned April 9 with a handful of accomplishments. Its most notable failure was refusing to face up to the need for overhaul of the state's tax laws, which the governor had urgently requested in both 1899 and 1901.

Four days after adjournment of the regular session, on Saturday morning, April 13, 1901, Myrtie gave birth to a girl whom they named Hallie Maude.[56] Neff had gone to Waco to check on their house and did not make it to Lovelady until Sunday morning. He wrote his mother on Monday:

> It will be news enough for this letter to state that we have a very fine daughter at our home. She just opened her eyes upon the beauties of this world last Saturday morning. Myrtie is getting along the nicest kind, says she feels real well. I did not get here until Sunday morning. . . . Our girl has big hands, big mouth and nose, blue eyes and black hair. I will stay here I suppose until first of next week. Myrtie will remain for a month or more.[57]

After adjournment and the birth of Hallie Maude, Neff spent the next four months shuttling between Waco, Lovelady, and Austin. He had to be in Waco to get clients to support his new family, but he wanted to be with his family, and also in Austin to lay the groundwork for his bid for the speakership the following January.

When the baby was less than a month old, Myrtie wrote Pat that she was not feeling too well. In reply, he wrote her from Waco on May 12. He was obviously torn between going to Lovelady to help take care of her and the baby and, on the other hand, trying to get some cases to sustain his little family. He wrote: "I made $12 Friday—the only money I have made since I came home. The same day I got a case that has a fifty dollar fee (for the firm) in it provided I am successful."

Myrtie did not join him in Austin for the special called session that fall because of continuing health problems and inability to cope with the new baby. She spent most of her time in Lovelady, but wrote him on October 3 from a health resort. This letter was the first of many that would be written from Mineral Wells or Marlin, principally the former. These two cities were the best-known places in Texas around the turn of the century for individuals to go to benefit from both drinking and bathing in the hot mineral waters of the resort areas.

Neff introduced several pieces of legislation during the Twenty-seventh Legislature. His priority again was a constitutional amendment to require the payment of a poll tax as a requirement for voting, which had gotten nowhere in 1899. In this session, the Senate version of the amendment passed and was put on the ballot for the general election in 1902, where it was approved by the voters by a two-to-one margin. Although the officials, including Neff, would never mention it, many historians argue that the issue of white supremacy lay behind much of their reasoning for a poll tax requirement. Officials and others influential in the Democratic Party felt it should be a "white man's party" only. Frederic Ogden, in his book, *The Poll Tax in the South,* wrote: "The division of the whites caused by the Populist revolt led to bidding by Democrats and Populists for Negro support. Since the Negro vote was often controlled by intimidation and fraudulent methods, nothing prevented overtures from being made for this vote when it was needed to win elections."[58] Shortly before the 1902 election, the *San Antonio Express* captured the feelings of many in its editorial: "By requiring a poll tax receipt, secured six months previous to an election, fraudulent elections can be prevented almost entirely."[59]

Alwyn Barr, in his 1973 study, states that "the poll tax did reduce the number of voters in Texas elections, but it fell on the innocent as well as those guilty of selling votes, and had no effect on potential vote purchasers, for some local politicians bought poll taxes for their constituents. . . . But the decline in Negro voter participation from about 100,000 in the 1890s to approximately 5,000 in 1906 suggests the effectiveness of the poll tax."[60] The decline in Negro voting was also the result of the State Democratic Executive Committee's adopting a rule that county committees could exclude Negroes from the Democratic primaries. Most, but not all, counties adopted such a policy, and thus, beginning about 1904, voting in the primary elections was by white males only.

A different slant to the issue is presented in an oral memoir of Abner McCall, who was on the Baylor Law School faculty, later dean of the school, and still later president of Baylor from 1961 to 1981. McCall, appointed chairman of a commission to rewrite Texas' election laws, interviewed Neff as part of his work. Neff claimed that the poll tax amendment was not directed toward Negroes but rather at keeping the "wets" (anti-Prohibitionist factions) from stealing elections. He also claimed that the requirement that a voting official could not help a person except in the English language was not directed to "Mexicans" but rather at the "Germans" in South Central Texas, since many of them could not speak English.[61]

Neff's explanation is given credence by Walter Buenger's book on Northeast Texas politics. In writing about the poll tax amendment, Buenger had this to say:

> The expense and difficulty of paying the poll tax hit hardest at groups most likely to oppose Prohibition, and not surprisingly, leading Prohibitionists like Pat M. Neff led the charge for the poll tax in the state legislature. Pragmatism as well as ideology probably motivated men like Neff who realized that Prohibition united the state's reformers far more than the desire to restrict the black vote.[62]

Nevertheless, later in his career, Neff's actions did not always bear out McCall's or Buenger's stories. In his second term as governor in 1923, he allowed a "white primary" bill to become law without his signature. The statute—effective statewide—formally denied Negroes the right to participate in the state's Democratic primaries.[63]

The Campaign for the Speakership—1901-1903

If he were to be elected speaker, Neff first had to be reelected to the Texas House for a third term. He had carefully cultivated his home district constituents and thus was able to avoid an opponent in the Democratic primary. In fact, neither he nor Terrell had an opponent in the primary held May 3, 1902. Neff polled 8,815 votes and Terrell 8,475.[64] As usual, the general election did not produce an opponent, and on November 4, 1902, Neff and Terrell were officially reelected to the House.[65]

The contest for speaker of the Twenty-eighth Legislature in 1903 had begun fifteen months earlier, near the adjournment of the special session of the legislature on October 1, 1901. Neff had begun writing members immediately. Initially, six individuals indicated interest in being the next presiding officer. Eventually, the race came down to a contest between Representative L. S. Schluter and Neff.

For his part, Neff kept up the steady drumbeat of letters to members and to many of his friends over the state that had begun in October 1901. One of the return letters would be of particular pride to Neff in the years to come. Postmarked Uvalde, Texas, November 4, 1901, it read:

> Friend Pat—I see no reason at this time why I should not give you my support for Speaker of the next House. Any way, I wish you success. I will not go back to Legislature but will try my hand for Congress. I feel confident of winning. Expect I will have my hands full with my congressional race but may be able to secure some three or four votes for you. Your friend, Garner.[66]

Another friend Neff was delighted to have on his side was former Governor James Stephen Hogg.[67] Neff had more difficulty with attorney Joseph W. Baines of Blanco. Baines, the grandfather of future U.S. President Lyndon B. Johnson, held Neff off until near the end of the contest.[68] Nevertheless Neff had a host of persons he could call on for help with legislators—University of Texas and Baylor friends, Knights of Pythias and YMCA friends, and last, but by no means least, Baptist friends all over the state.

Speaker Neff: Twenty-eighth Legislature—1903-1905

At noon on Tuesday, January 13, 1903, Secretary of State John G. Tod gaveled the regular session of the Twenty-eighth Legislature to order. Although John Nance Garner had left, Neff was joined by his good friend Tom Connally, for what would be Connally's second and last term.

The secretary of state then announced that the first order of business was to elect a speaker. Representative Schluter was nominated by Representative H. P. Brelsford of Eastland County, who in a lengthy recitation of Schluter's qualifications stressed the "dignity and poise of his mature years," perhaps in reference to Neff's comparatively young thirty-one years. Representative Tom Connally followed Brelsford with a shorter but persuasive nomination of Neff.[69] Connally praised Neff effusively in the oratorical language of the day. Several seconding speeches followed for each man and then the vote was called for. Neff received 73 votes to Schluter's 57.[70] Neff's sixteen-vote margin would later be reduced, in the memory of U.S. Senator Tom Connally, to a hair-raising two votes. Connally, in his autobiography, claimed that the only things he remembered about his four years as a state legislator was his passage of an anti-trust bill and his work to make Pat Neff speaker. He can perhaps be excused if, in his memory, he states that only his "arm twisting" on a couple of House members turned the tables for Neff —"the vote was so close that if Miller and one other had voted for Schluter, Pat Neff would have lost."[71]

And so, after fifteen months of campaigning, the long wait was over; Neff was escorted to the speaker's stand and began his tenure as the Thirty-sixth Speaker of the Texas House of Representatives. Thanking his friends and supporters, he briefly turned on his oratorical talents, proclaiming: "In the pleasant forest fields of memory, the triumph and ovation of this hour will be to me an evergreen whose foliage the frost of the future cannot blight and whose boughs the blast of time can never break."[72]

Neff, at age thirty-one, began claiming in his biographical data sheets that he was the youngest speaker elected up to that time. Unfortunately, that claim was then repeated numerous times in subsequent publications. In a book prepared in recent years by the Texas Legislative Council (the legislature's official research body) giving brief biographical information about House speakers since statehood, that honor goes to Ira H. Evans, who was twenty-five years of age at the time he was elected in 1870 as the Nineteenth Speaker. Neff was actually fourth youngest in age.[73] Although not the youngest, Neff could rightfully have claimed to be the first speaker elected from McLennan County.

Three days after Neff's election, the legislature met in joint session and certified that S. W. T. Lanham had been elected governor and George D. Neal lieutenant governor in the November general election, both by overwhelming majorities over the Republican, People's, and Prohibition parties' candidates.[74]

Lanham was no more successful than Sayers in getting the legislature to face up to the tax problems of the state. Even though both governors pointed out that overall taxes could be reduced if the state were to collect a reasonable and just amount of taxes from the railroads and other corporations, the legislature could not bring itself to tighten the loopholes and force the companies to pay their fair share. Neff appears not to have taken an active role in trying to pass or defeat any particular legislation.

As presiding officer, Neff had a markedly successful session. His fairness and statesmanlike approach to presiding made him many friends; appeals from his parliamentary rulings to the membership as speaker were very rare. He claimed later that he was the only speaker from which an appeal of his ruling had never been taken.[75] This was somewhat exaggerated since there were three occasions when appeals were made, but one of those was withdrawn, and Neff's parliamentary rulings were sustained on the other two rulings.[76] He also claimed several times that he never missed a roll call in his tenure in the legislature; this claim was stretching the facts considerably, as he had several absences in each of the first two sessions. He did brag about one accomplishment later that was confirmed by the records: it had not been necessary to elect a speaker pro tem in 1903 because he was always in his place at the speaker's rostrum.[77]

Among Neff's perquisites as a speaker was the use of space behind the House chamber. The original drawings of the Capitol show several rooms behind the speaker's rostrum, including one labeled "Speaker's Private Room" and one labeled "Speaker's Room," but there is no specific indication that they were to be used for living quarters.[78] Historically, the Capitol was never intended to be used for overnight stay except for the judiciary department.[79] However, as early as 1884, members of the legislature were trying to save money by sleeping in the temporary Capitol. This practice continued in the magnificent new Capitol building dedicated in 1888. The *Austin Daily Statesman*, in an 1891 article, lamented the Capitol building being turned into a "cheap lodging house," and again in 1895, the *Statesman* decried the fact that visitors coming to view the Capitol were seeing "red blankets and soiled sheets aired in the windows."[80] Finally, in 1897, the *Daily Statesman* noted with pleasure that whereas there were some "eighty odd beds occupied in the capitol when Superintendent Mobley took charge of the building two years ago," Mobley had decided to enforce the 1884 law and, as members began arriving at the capital city for the 1897 session of the legislature, he turned away their "trunks and other equipment . . . and politely but positively refused to receive their luggage."[81]

Despite this history, the two houses of the legislature decided to honor their leaders—the lieutenant governor and the speaker—with private living quarters in the Capitol. There are no state records indicating the year in which the space behind the House chamber was converted to living quarters, but several papers written while Speaker and Mrs. Neff were alive give strong indication that the Neffs were the first ones to occupy the apartment.

In 1938, in response to an inquiry, Neff stated that he and Myrtie occupied the "Speaker's apartment in 1903 when he was speaker." He went on to say that he did not know whether or not anyone had occupied the quarters before him.[82] In 1945, Theodosia Bell, long-time Texas Senate librarian who was knowledgeable about Texas legislative administration, wrote about the apartment in *Today in Texas*, a newsletter/magazine published in the mid 1900s. "According to my information," she said, "it was Pat Neff who first occupied the speaker's rooms."[83] A Baylor history class paper written in 1947 and a Baylor thesis written in 1951 both state that the Neffs were the first to occupy the apartment.[84]

In 2006, professional staff at the National Conference of State Legislatures said they were not aware of any other state that provided living quarters for the presiding officer of the lower house.[85] The area continued in use as living quarters for the speaker in Texas in 2007. Texas discontinued living quarters for its lieutenant governor when that apartment was the scene of a disastrous fire in 1983. The space was converted to offices and a reception area for special occasions.

Myrtie was again sick during much of the two sessions in 1903 and stayed either in Lovelady or Mineral Wells. However, the Neffs were together in Austin, Waco, or Lovelady for a period in early spring, for Pat Neff Jr. was born December 19, 1903, in Waco.[86]

Adjournment of the regular session was set for noon on April 1. Its weighty battles fought, the House found itself with a little less than an hour to be used up, and that led to bedlam, as reported the next day by the *Austin Statesman* scribe:

> Just one word from Speaker Neff would have converted twenty more bills into laws. This the members knew and the scramble for recognition commenced. Parliamentary tones of voice soon gave place to shouts, shouts to yells, yells to screams, and screams to deafening whoops. The fragrance of the atmosphere that filled the hall two hours before was dispelled and every man in the house was perfumed to "high life." They shouted until their throats were split, gesticulated until their arms were tired, first stood on their tiptoes, then clambered into chairs, mounted their elegant oak desks, never forgetting to shout, scream and yell for recognition. While pandemonium was thus reigning, the old clock was unconscious of the value of the moments it was steadily measuring out, ticked away and finally both hands rested on the hour of 12, and actually seemed to stop and regret the ruin it had wrought.
>
> Speaker Neff kept his eye fixed upon it, and at exactly 12, he declared the regular session of the Twenty-eighth Legislature adjourned without a day. Bills were thus left to die on the calendar, resolutions squirmed in the throes of dissolution, words were half spoken, motions half made, speeches left suspended between ceiling and floor, the pencil of the *Statesman* reporter broken, and the regular session of the Twenty-eighth was no more.[87]

Neff returned to Waco immediately after the session to be reunited with his wife and daughter, who had spent most of the spring of 1903 in Waco and Lovelady.

Myrtie's Health and Pat's Future Career

Neff's trip back to Waco—four to six hours by train in those days—gave him some time to contemplate two major issues in his young life: Myrtie's continuing illness and his future career. It is not known when Myrtie first complained of illness, but as early as the fall of 1892, she had written Neff from Lovelady that she didn't want to return to Baylor because she was not rested enough to study.

In 1901, their new addition, Hallie Maude, was evidently proving too much for her, even with "Mama's help," and in October, with the baby less than six months old, a letter from Neff to Myrtie reveals for the first time that Myrtie was at a resort taking mineral baths. The location, from the letter, appears to be Mineral Wells.[88] She also visited Marlin regularly to take the "hot baths" there. She spent much of 1902 and 1903 in Lovelady or Mineral Wells. After the birth of Pat Jr. in late 1903, she continued her frequent lengthy visits to her old home and to Mineral Wells. It was in August 1904 that she first wrote from Lovelady at length about her illness. At this time, Hallie Maude was a little over three and Pat Jr. was eight months old. In a fourteen-page handwritten letter to Mother Neff, Myrtie wrote that she had had been diagnosed with "neurasthenia and nervous prostration." She wrote that, with all she had to do, she was utterly exhausted.[89] She was nursing Pat Jr. and, to aid lactation, drinking beer, which was frequently prescribed at that time to help mothers develop milk for their babies. She also indicated that the beer was helping her sleep.[90] (Companies such as Anheuser-Busch were allowed to advertise about the beneficial effects of beer for nursing mothers in the official publication of the Texas Medical Association as late as 1911.)[91]

Some medical historians believe that "neurasthenia" may be the same as the modern-day disorder known as "chronic fatigue syndrome."[92] Leland Hinsie and Robert Campbell have characterized neurasthenic patients as "typically narcissistic, self-centered, and manifest[ing] strong dependency needs."[93] Some elements of these descriptions might be said to fit Myrtie's condition. It appears that she didn't realize or later accept that she was marrying a man who would be intensely interested in a public career. She had hoped that he would be a lawyer in private practice who would be home most nights to help her with the chores and the children. His relish for the position he held as House Speaker and her realization that he might be interested in a further political career might indeed have been a mental strain that affected her health and vitality. Her frequent visits back home to Lovelady could be said to manifest strong dependency needs toward her mother.

The second matter that Neff needed to think about as he traveled home from Austin in 1903 was his future career. He had a young daughter, a second child on the way, and a wife who continued to spend time in Mineral Wells or Marlin—neither of them inexpensive places, particularly when Myrtie's stays there were measured in weeks or even months instead of a few days. Thus, Neff knew that in the short term he needed to make some money to provide for his family. In the long term, he knew he needed to begin to consider whether he wanted to engage in the private practice of law exclusively or use that profession simply as a base from which to engage in politics—the profession he had come to love in recent years.

He had thoroughly enjoyed his three terms in the House, particularly his last term as speaker. And his interest in politics must have been further whetted by some exhilarating publicity in the spring of 1903 for handling the speakership in a professional manner. The *Austin Statesman* was the first paper to laud him, writing in a March 1903 story: "[T]here is a strong and growing sentiment among the people to elect a vigorous, aggressive and uncompromising man to the position of Attorney General at the next election."[94] A month and a half later, the *Statesman* reported that Neff's friends wanted him to run for governor but, realizing that governors were virtually always given two terms unless they really performed poorly, and that the governorship was therefore not up for grabs, they were now urging him to run for the Railroad Commission.[95]

And so, as Neff left the heady atmosphere of the Capitol and returned to his law practice, he faced a critical decision. While he was heartened by the favorable stories, his survey of the political landscape disclosed that he really had few viable options in his immediate future. He had no desire to return to the House or to run for the Senate. For one good reason or another, other statewide offices were not viable options for him. He reluctantly turned to local offices as his only possibility. The only two positions in the county that merited attention were those of county judge and county attorney. A very popular John W. Baker had just finished one term as county judge and in 1904 was set to run again, so this left the county attorney's job as the last potential option. The current county attorney was his good friend, O. H. Cross, who had served with him in the legislature from 1899 to 1901. He was finishing his initial two years as county attorney and was set to run for another term in keeping with the tradition that the incumbent generally deserved a second two years. Thus, Neff realized that even the local political offices were, for all intents and purposes, closed to him in the immediate future.

CHAPTER 4

Prosecuting and Defending: Prelude to Higher Office

An Old Testament man without mercy.
—Abner McCall, describing Neff

With elective offices closed to him for the time being, Neff knew he would have to work his way up the ladder, so when O. H. Cross, the county attorney, offered him a position as an assistant county attorney in the fall of 1903, he quickly accepted. That salary, plus earnings from his private law practice, which he would be allowed to continue, would care for his growing family. At that time, the county attorney in McLennan County prosecuted both felonies and misdemeanors.

Neff took the assistant county attorney's job believing that Cross might well move back to full-time law practice when his second term expired in late 1906. Neff knew he had a lot to learn in his new position. He had run for the legislature shortly after graduating from law school in 1897, and with intensive campaigns in 1898 and 1900 plus spending a considerable amount of time in Austin participating in regular and special sessions of the legislature, his experience in the practice of law was minimal. Thus, he kept a low profile for more than a year, learning the ropes of prosecuting cases in county court and following Cross around to absorb all he could. Neff's primary duties were in county court handling misdemeanors, but he had the opportunity to try several liquor and gambling cases in 1904 and early in 1905 and to work with Cross on some of the less serious felony assault and burglary cases.

Except for Myrtie's illness, the years 1903 to 1905 were rewarding for Neff. He received accolades for his court work and, in addition, because of his former state-wide position and his oratorical ability, he received invitations to speak all over the state. In 1903, he delivered commencement speeches at Sam Houston Normal Institute in Huntsville and at high schools in Marfa and Alpine in far West Texas. On June 6, he spoke to the Texas A&M University Alumni Association in College Station. His appearances included church, YMCA, Woodmen of the World, teachers' groups, and the usual country picnics. After Neff drew some 4,000 persons to the West, Texas, annual picnic in 1905, the local newspaper reported: "Hon. Pat

41

M. Neff, in his matchless way, soared among the clouds, mixed and mingled among the stars, carrying his audience thru elysian fields of art and poetry, landing them back in West just in time for dinner."[1] Highly flattering stories were not confined to the Central Texas area. The *Houston Post*, which had lauded him several times while he was speaker, wrote of him again in late 1905: "Mr. Neff is recognized as one of the most distinguished citizens of the state. His brilliant record as Speaker of the Texas House of Representatives is remembered by all, and he is known as one of the legal lights of North and Central Texas."[2]

In addition to receiving rave notices for his speaking appearances, he was elected to two important posts by the Baptist General Convention of Texas. His honors from the Baptists were particularly pleasing to him and undoubtedly helpful politically. He had already returned to Waco as the third-ranking state official when in November 1904 he was elected to the Baylor Board of Trustees at the annual meeting of the Baptist General Convention of Texas.[3] In assuming his board position, Neff became the youngest member of that governing body. At a board meeting on June 5, 1905, he received more honors when he was elected vice-president of the Baylor Board after less than six months' service.[4] Still more accolades came at the annual session of the Baptist group in 1905 when he was elected a vice-president of the convention.[5] At that time, this position was a rotating honor and the vice-presidents changed each year, but his election couldn't have come at a more fortunate time.

County Attorney—1906-1912

When Cross indicated that he would be favorably disposed to having Neff succeed him as county attorney in 1906, Neff quietly began laying his plans, which by the summer of 1905 became an open secret. Neff was not alone in this ambition. Justice of the Peace Minor Lee Moore was also interested in a promotion and started making his own plans for the July 1906 election. Neff received the endorsement of the *Waco Semi-Weekly Tribune* in an editorial on April 4, 1906, which stated that the county attorney "cannot be an untried and incapable lawyer. If he is, the interests of the state and county will surely suffer. . . . Mr. Neff will be capable . . . of meeting the very responsible duties that will confront him."

By early June, six weeks before the election, Moore decided the race was getting away from him and paid to print a fifty-six-page booklet filled with figures, tables, charts, text, and affidavits—all designed to defend his record and destroy Neff's reputation as an aggressive prosecutor. A statement on the front cover provided the essence of Moore's campaign: "I charge that the Honorable Pat M. Neff has a tender foot, a lame hand, a suave mien, an eloquent tongue and a timid heart."[6] Neff did not let the charges go unchallenged. A few days later, he published an extensive rebuttal to Moore's charges, complete with his own set of affidavits and letters supporting his record and outlining his complaints against Moore.[7] The net result of the campaign could well have been confusion on the part of the voters as to whose claims were correct and who was quoting the right statistics. Moore had been a popular and honored graduate of Baylor but could not begin to compete with the high profile Neff enjoyed in the community. At the primary election on July 28, Neff won 59 percent of the vote. In the general election November 6, Neff was unopposed.[8]

Neff's income as county attorney continued to be augmented by his private law practice. The family's financial status was constantly in flux, resulting in mixed signals—one month, Neff would claim to be making money "on the side" so the family could "get by"; the next he would tell his mother to buy whatever she needed, that he had money he had not touched. In October 1906, Neff bought a home at 2110 Austin Avenue in Waco for $3,200. This remained home base the rest of his life. The property included two lots facing on Austin Avenue and two on Franklin and thus was a full block deep. He agreed to make two payments, $1,600 on June l, 1907, and the remainder on November l of that year. The notes were paid off a week early in October 1907.[9] However, only three months after the house purchase, in January 1907, Myrtie complained to her mother-in-law that they were overdrawn at the bank $700 and that "I am going to do without; I haven't bought a garment for myself, or the children and now will go without rugs in the halls."[10] Court was not held in the summer, so Neff was free to pursue his private law practice full-time. He wrote his mother in June that he would not be at home for several weeks and later that summer wrote her from Wichita Falls, where he was conducting some of his work. The family did take time out in July to go to the summer Baptist encampment in Palacios for a week.[11]

In his first two years in office, Neff kept up his contacts by active membership in both the Knights of Pythias and the Modern Woodmen of America. He was a popular speaker with the Knights and became a frequent lecturer for the Woodmen, being invited to different parts of the state to deliver his orations. By 1906, the Woodmen group was printing up posters with blank locations and dates, inviting people to hear "one of Texas' most brilliant young men." The local Woodmen camps (lodges) had only to get Neff's commitment, fill in the name of the locality and the date, and post the flyer.[12]

The highlight of 1907 was Neff's election as president of the Baylor University Board of Trustees in November. Dr. B. H. Carroll, president of the board for more than twenty years, had requested that the Baptist General Convention relieve him of membership on the board. Not in the best health, he wanted to devote his time to the work of a new Baptist seminary that was in the process of being separated from Baylor. Neff was elected president without opposition at a special called session of the board on November 19, 1907.[13] Now, he and his former roommate, Samuel Palmer Brooks, president of Baylor since 1902, would have a new relationship—one that would endure for twenty-four more years until Brooks' death in 1931.

Neff's election as presiding officer was a remarkable testimony to his leadership abilities and the respect with which he was held by his elders. At the time Neff was elected president of the board, he had been on the board only three years and was the second youngest member of the thirteen-member board. Neff at thirty-five was half the age of member M. H. Standifer, and indeed most of the members were in their fifties and sixties.[14] He felt compelled to defer to the other board members and to President Brooks in many ways, and although he made himself available to Brooks for advice and consultation, Neff was careful to avoid the limelight at Baylor. After all, Brooks was older than he—by some eight years—and Neff had great respect for his friend from college days.

The year 1908, the second year of Neff's first term as county attorney, was marked more by a national speech he made than by any cases he prosecuted. In that year, Neff again made talks all over the state for the Modern Woodmen of America and was invited to go to Peoria, Illinois, with the state delegation to try to bring the national meeting to Dallas in 1911. Although the Woodmen was primarily an East and West Coast fraternal lodge, Texas had recruited 17,000 new members in the previous four years, leading all other states in membership. The total membership of the order nationally was 1.2 million.[15] The 1908 conference in Peoria attracted several thousand delegates, but few outside the Texas group were prepared for the Texas orator. The local newspaper headlines read, "Buffalo Defeats Dallas—Delegate Neff Nearly Stampedes Convention in Favor of His State." The story reported that "the politicians [in the lodge] who had framed up the deal to take the conclave to Buffalo had an uncomfortable half hour" before they were able to quiet the group down and obtain their vote for Buffalo. Of Neff's speech, the paper reported:

> For ten minutes the convention ran riot, heedless of the appeals of the leaders and the sound of the gavel wielded by the head consul. The adherents of Buffalo became alarmed and a good deal of quiet work was done in the different delegations. . . . Notwithstanding his eloquent description of Texas, if his town had been anywhere else but in Texas, it is likely that the delegates would have bolted and given him everything he asked for.[16]

Despite not getting the vote for Dallas, Neff made a deep impression on several thousand delegates from all over the country. And he broadened his political experience by attending one day of the Republican National Convention then in session in Chicago before returning home.[17]

While he was succeeding in public life, he was worried about Myrtie's health. Hallie Maude was now nine and in school, and Pat Jr. was almost five. Myrtie's nervous condition continued to plague her, and in October 1908, a neighbor wrote Pat's mother that Myrtie "can't turn herself in bed, and the neighbors think she is in critical condition, and wonder why her mother is not with her. I think she has been in bed most of the time, for 6 or 7 weeks."[18]

Neff's intensive, high-profile campaign in 1906, his attention to duty his first year and a half in office, and his Baptist and Baylor honors paid off—no opponent for county attorney came forward in the Democratic primary on Saturday, July 25, 1908, and Neff was reelected. [19] Thus, Neff was saved several thousand dollars and lots of shoe leather; he could and did use the summer to accept several cases in his private law practice and also make a number of speeches over the state. As usual, most Democratic Party candidates, including Neff, were unopposed in the general election on Tuesday, November 3, 1908.[20]

His most noteworthy case during this second term was, without doubt, the trial of W. I. Fitch of McGregor for operating what was known as the K Club in violation of the state liquor law. Fitch had opened what he called a private club, but which, according to several of Neff's witnesses, was actually an open bar. In his final argument, Neff combined solid evidence, reliable witnesses, and a sound knowledge of the law to overwhelm the jury. Widely known for his oratory, Neff put on a virtuoso performance for the jury. He used more than a dozen quotations or paraphrases of poetry by John Greenleaf Whittier, Sir Walter Scott, Edgar Allen Poe, Alfred Lord Tennyson, Henry Wadsworth Longfellow, and William Shakespeare. He paraphrased Whittier's "Maude Miller," saying that when he shut the K Club down, the devotees of the beer keg were crying: "Of all sad prayers of tongue or pen, The saddest of these, no beer, Amen." When he backed Fitch into a corner while Fitch was figuring the number of club members, Neff reminded the jury of Scott's line: "Oh, what a tangled web we weave, When first we practice to deceive." About midway through his presentation, he accused the K Club of having its own national anthem patterned after "The Star-Spangled Banner":

> My K Club 'tis of thee, Sweet distributor of beer, Of thee I sing, Beer that was Anheuser-Busch's pride, Beer that Winn said marked Temple's high tide, From the K Club's every side, let beer bottles fly.[21]

Finally, near the end of his address, he could not resist chastising Brother Ament, one of Fitch's witnesses. Neff stated that he had known Ament since "I wore nothing but a freckled face, a calico apron, and a stone bruise." And he remembered that Ament as an elder in the church who read the scriptures and broke bread with the Christian flock there. But now, Neff said:

> Judging from the testimony in this case, I would think of late years, perhaps, he has worshipped with Fitch's flock more than the brethren of other days. I think I can hear him now reading the 23rd Psalm as follows: "Fitch is my shepherd, I shall not want. He maketh me to lie down in a cool place till the train from Temple comes in, and

then he leadeth me to the beer keg. Though I walk through the valley of the shadow of a prohibition precinct, I fear no thirst and I fear no evil, for Fitch's club and Fitch's beer, they comfort me. He prepareth for me a lunch; my cup runneth over for 25 cents with beer. Surely goodness and mercy shall follow me and I would be willing to dwell in the Fitch Club forever."[22]

Neff had won them over—with his logic and his humor. Seven of the twelve jurors came back first for the maximum five-year sentence; the other five, however, wanted to assess a shorter term, and thus the jury compromised at a three-year sentence. This was enough for the local newspaper to headline: HARD PENALTY PUT ON FITCH.[23] The paper noted that this was the first conviction under the law passed by the previous legislature making it a felony to sell intoxicating drinks in local option territory. It also reported that since the September raid all other questionable establishments in McLennan County had closed their doors. McGregor had another local option election during the trial, and the Prohibitionists continued to be victorious. Neff's closing argument was so widely read, reread, and praised that a few years later when the Baylor Philomathesian Literary Society honored Neff by publishing a select list of his literary addresses, he chose it as one of twenty-three to be printed and distributed by the society.[24]

The grand juries in 1909 and 1910 praised Neff for his outstanding work, and the newspapers joined in the laudatory comments. In the spring of 1910, at the conclusion of the Fifty-fourth District Court for that term, the *Waco Semi-Weekly Tribune* reported thirty-four cases disposed of, many with unusually heavy penalties, "evidence that our county attorney has prosecuted with his accustomed vigilance and vigor, and that more and more, he is becoming a terror to the violators of the law."[25] Neff's salary compared favorably with salaries of other city and county officials at that time and did not include his earnings from his private law practice. He was able to purchase property in 1909 in both far West Texas near Rotan and in the Rio Grande Valley.[26]

The county attorney's job and his private law practice took most of Neff's time, but he determinedly found time for his other passions—Baylor University and making speeches around the state. Perhaps even then he was anticipating a statewide political race. Neff, by 1909, was beginning to feel more comfortable chairing a board comprising older individuals. Nonetheless, he still felt compelled to defer to them and to President Brooks in many ways. He continued his stewardship in November 1909, when he bought a $500 endowment bond to endow the general university and paid this off in five years, with the bond marked paid on May 5, 1915.[27]

Early in 1909, Neff went to Austin and visited with old friends in the legislature, which was in session. He seemed to have a knack for being mentioned in newspapers, and during that visit, the *Austin Tribune* commented that he was "prominently mentioned as a candidate for Governor in 1910."[28]

As in the past, his speechmaking increasingly took him outside his native Central Texas area. As state lecturer for the Modern Woodmen of America, he was delighted to accept invitations from local organizations of the Woodmen in West Texas, including Weatherford, Stamford, Haskell, and San Angelo. One of the beauties of Neff's oratory was that he could dwell on the most serious and critical ethical and political issues of the day or he could address mundane subjects. Even in the latter cases of what appeared on the surface to be humorous talks, a message would emerge. His lecture on "A Glass of Pure Water" was an example. The occasion was the annual opening of the Texas Cotton Palace. If Baylor was Waco's educational pride in the early 1900s, the Cotton Palace was its entertainment glory. The facility was originally built in 1894 to celebrate the rich cotton culture of Waco and the surrounding fertile black lands of the Brazos and Bosque river valleys. A spectacular opening of the fair and exposition was held in November 1894, to be tragically followed only two months later by an even more spectacular fire that destroyed the building. The Cotton Palace finally reopened in 1910 to usher in a twenty-one-year period of glamour and excitement that made it the superlative showplace of Texas. The fairgrounds, located about a mile south of downtown Waco, eventually consisted of half a dozen buildings, including a 10,000-seat coliseum. According to the *Waco Tribune-Herald,* the Cotton Palace offered everything from "grand opera to carnival acts, races, vaudeville, glittering society balls and exhibits" of all kinds.[29] Governors frequently opened the annual exposition. Attendance, which hit 200,000 in 1911 and 300,000 in 1912, would peak later in 1917 with a turnout of more than half a million. On several occasions through the years, Neff opened the fair, and one of his favorite short introductions at the opening dinner was his toast to "A Glass of Pure Water." Comparing it to the evils of whiskey, he would end his remarks with these words:

> Water is the drink of the winning pugilist, of the conquering athlete, of the fearless ocean flyer. . . . In it, no fungus ferments to steal away the brain, no demon lurks to destroy a good name; no poison pollutes it; no blood stains it, and around it there are no tears. The most popular liquid, the beverage best beloved, the elixir of life, the drink of all drinks—is a glass of pure water.[30]

Neff's popularity as a speaker served him well as county attorney. Most prosecuting attorneys before him had served a maximum of two terms, but at some point, Neff decided to run for a third and final two years. He was challenged by one of his former assistants, W. H. Forrester, who announced that he would seek the position in the 1910 election. Forrester was five years older than Neff and had served as assistant county attorney under O. H. Cross from 1902 to 1906 and then under Neff for one year. He had resigned (Neff said he was fired) in 1907 to enter private practice full-time. Neff was embarrassed two days before the 1910 election when Forrester cited a *Waco Times-Herald* article of December 19, 1907, which quoted Neff as saying that he regretted Forrester's resignation and considered him his right-hand man.

During the campaign, Neff received one of many timely assists from Baylor; this time, the senior class editors of the school yearbook, *The Round-up*, dedicated the 1910 edition to Neff. He was also able to use his solid record to advantage in the campaign. One of his most effective arguments was that during his three years as county attorney, he had not cost the taxpayers of the county a single dollar, but had made $10,000 over and above his salary for the citizenry. Whether he could prove these claims or not, his new methods of operation had certainly been effective and had accrued money to the county treasury. He had every reason to be proud of his accomplishments. The *West News* editorialized that "the state has no better official than Pat M. Neff. He is honest, upright, capable and industrious."[31]

The day of the election, the *Waco Times-Herald*, an afternoon paper, reported a heavy vote over the state, exceeding the 325,000 recorded in July 1908 in the Democratic primary. McLennan County turned out approximately 70 percent of its voters. Neff polled 4,580 votes, or 60 percent of the total in his race. Forrester's total was 2,980.[32] As usual, Neff had no opposition in the general election of November 8, 1910.[33]

Although he was a tough prosecutor, Neff valued high ethical standards and demonstrated on several occasions his capacity for fairness and compassion. One illustration occurred in October 1911, when he moved for dismissal of a murder case against A. V. Cantrell and Alfred Mitchell. Both had been indicted for the murder of Ira Wall. The case had been called for trial, and Neff's move caused a sensation at the courthouse with news headlines shouting IN THE INTEREST OF IDEAL JUSTICE—"County Attorney Neff Makes a Move That Causes Sensation—Urges Dismissal of Suits—States His Reasons with Eloquence and Force."[34] Neff's motion to dismiss was based on his extensive cross-examination of Mitchell, who confessed to the crime but told three different stories at three different times. Neff's address to the court covered some eighty column inches of newspaper space as he laboriously and in extensive detail went into Mitchell's three confessions, implicating first one, then another of some five other persons. Neff said he was asking for dismissal because he could not believe anything the defendants said. The judge agreed with Neff and charges against the two men were dropped.[35]

The most publicized murder case of Neff's six years occurred just before he left office in late 1912. Neff's closing argument in the Alex Johnson case was considered a forensic masterpiece and was reprinted in a widely known eight-volume series of legal speeches published over a period of several years in the late teens and early 1920s. Alvin V. Sellers, the author, chose a handful of cases for each volume. Neff was in distinguished company, as the various volumes included addresses by such notables as Clarence Darrow and even a dissent by U.S. Supreme Court Justice Oliver Wendell

Holmes in an espionage case during World War I. The volumes also included cases from England, Ireland, and France. Neff was further honored by being one of fewer than half a dozen attorneys whose pictures were featured in the series. The release of volume five in 1919 came at a fortuitous time for Neff's political career.[36] The Philomathesian Society had previously included the closing argument in this particular case (Johnson case) in its publication *Twenty-three Addresses.*[37]

The trial in question was that of Alex Johnson, a local salesman accused of killing his employer, A. P. Duncan, in March 1912. Duncan and Johnson were purportedly arguing over Johnson's work schedule. Johnson, claiming that Duncan threatened him, pulled out a gun and shot Duncan several times. Duncan died the next day and Johnson was indicted for murder. Johnson's plea was self-defense. The trial took place that fall in Waco, and Neff's closing argument to the jury, covering two full pages of the *Waco Times-Herald,* was reprinted as an advertisement in the October 20 issue of the paper (paid for by the son of the murdered man).[38] Neff used no notes during his speech and did not know it was going to be recorded by a courthouse stenographer in shorthand until shortly before he began. Despite the strong argument for self-defense advanced by Johnson's attorneys, the jury came back with a verdict of murder in the second degree and sentenced Johnson to five years in the state penitentiary.[39] One day after this conviction, Neff wrote his mother and, among other subjects, commented on the trial: "The jury gave him [Johnson] five years in the 'pen.' I feel sorry for him but troubles come easy and are hard to get away from."[40] The Texas Court of Criminal Appeals later affirmed the decision of the lower court.[41]

Several years later, Neff received a letter asking for a copy of his "Johnson" speech. Neff sent the writer a copy and commented in part: "About two-thirds of this address went up to the High Court on a Bill of Exception on the theory that the speech was improper. The Court, however, said the speech was within the record. It is the only speech I made that had the approval of the High Court."[42]

Less than a month after the Johnson trial, Neff tried his last case as county attorney, securing a life sentence for a young Negro, Will Montgomery, accused of murdering his grandfather.[43] Neff asked and received permission of the court to make some farewell remarks before his summation of the state's case against Montgomery. The highly effective prosecuting attorney was proud enough of the final address to request that it be included in the collection published by the Philomathesian Society a few years later. Claiming to have "dealt out justice with an impartial hand," he restated his belief "in the equality of all men before the law; those who wore the rags of poverty and those who fared sumptuously." He also boasted that his duty was as much "to protect the innocent as to prosecute the guilty." He pointed out that during his administration, "352 cases were tried, and in 336 of this number, I felt the flush, but not the blush, of victory. Only 14 of the 352 escaped the penitentiary, and these 14 were guilty."[44] (Neff's statement of his cases left two cases unaccounted for.)

Neff had many admirers in his work as prosecuting attorney. District Clerk Bob McClain served hundreds of judges and attorneys in his post from 1900 to 1954. In an interview a few years before his retirement, he said of Neff: "Neff was a fearless, hard district attorney, the toughest we have had. He was always cool and collected, and never deviating. . . .When Pat Neff was in court, it was next to impossible to keep the Waco High School students or the students of Baylor in school. Everybody came. Pat Neff could do anything to a jury."[45]

Neff's own feelings about his law cases was expressed in a 1951 interview with dissertation writer Chase Winfrey: "I enjoyed trying cases; in fact, I enjoyed all my cases. I always preferred to have two or three really smart lawyers against me on the other side—whetted my appetite. It added zest to know that I was measuring my lances with real brains against me."[46]

In Neff's final report to the McLennan County Commissioners Court, he bragged that he had inherited nearly 1,100 pending cases on the docket when he took office in 1906, but that he was leaving his successor with a completely clear docket. He also took a great deal of pride in pointing out the short but efficient work he had done with the grand juries during his six-year tenure: "I find that for each person sent to the penitentiary in Dallas County, it cost the county for grand jury alone $180, while in this county for that purpose it only cost $12."[47]

There has never been a question that he was a highly effective prosecutor—and a tough one. Abner McCall, who would later serve as law school dean under Neff at Baylor, called him a "hawk-nosed prosecutor." McCall recalled that Neff told him: "I collected more fines from people under my prosecution than all the rest of the county attorneys in Texas put together. . . . I didn't care who they were, friends or foes. . . . Some of my best friends, when they violated the law, I prosecuted them to the hilt." McCall described him as an "Old Testament man without mercy" and recalled how Neff said that "my theory was that I was employed to enforce the law." McCall asked: "Did you ever hear of mercy?" Neff's reply was: "That's not my function. That's the Governor's prerogative to pardon. It's not the function of the prosecutor. Whenever anybody violates the law he prosecutes."[48]

In June 1911, leaving Hallie Maude and Pat Jr. with Grandmother Mainer in Lovelady, Pat and Myrtie left for a month's trip to the Northeast that included stops in Detroit, Niagara Falls, and Toronto, as well as Buffalo. The stay in Buffalo was for the Modern Woodmen of America head camp meeting, which Neff had unsuccessfully fought to bring to Texas three years earlier. As state lecturer and legal counsel for the organization, his expenses were presumably paid for by the Woodmen.

Although Myrtie evidently enjoyed the trip to Buffalo, the last two years had been a definite strain on her, and she appears to have been ill continually from about mid-1911 until shortly before Neff left office at the end of 1912. Her health was the principal subject of letters between her and Mother Neff, as well as letters between Mother Neff and Patsy Neff. In letters primarily to Mother Neff, Myrtie lamented her condition. In September 1911, she wrote that she was "on the verge of a collapse," having taken care of Pat for a week while he was sick, entertained a friend from out of town, and nursed Hallie Maude after she had her tonsils removed.[49] She evidently improved for several months, but between May and October 1912 she again became ill, and a neighbor, writing to Isabella in May 1912, said that she and the other neighbors thought she was critically ill.[50] That summer, Myrtie started camping in the backyard—not an unusual practice in those days—and apparently spent most of July and August, day and night, outside.

A twelve-page letter dated October 11 from Myrtie to Mother Neff reflected her depressed state:

> I am so broken in spirits and health that I seldom write to my own mother who is left alone at Mineral Wells. Mr. Neff has been away six weeks leaving me to take the same hot water treatment all the night and morning which of course has become almost a constant dread as it seems long since to have lost its effect. I am exhausted and feel as if I will go to pieces. I am living night and day outdoors except of course when the house is cleaned. Most of his [Pat's] time is spent at the courthouse; it makes me feel so lonely to be without him. I think I will take Hallie Maude and go to Mineral Wells. If I go, he [Pat Jr.] will go to his papa's after school and play on the Courthouse lawn—they will eat supper in town and come home to sleep.[51]

Near the end of October 1912, Sallie Calvert, Pat's sister, wrote her mother that she had just left after a visit with Pat and Myrtie and that the latter was "a good deal improved."[52]

Full-Time Private Law Practice—1913-1919

In December 1912, Neff left public office for the first time in fourteen years. He began a seven-year period of private life that included a thriving law practice and a host of civic and other interests. This period is scarcely touched in the two dozen theses and dissertations written about his life but provides significant insights into his ambitions and work habits.

To put bread on the table, he immediately plunged into a busy law practice. He was fortunate to establish an ongoing relationship with both the International and Great Northern Railroad and the San Antonio and Aransas Pass line. During these years, both railroads were in and out of financial difficulties and provided considerable work for Neff. During the 1913-1919 period, court records indicate that he was both a plaintiff's attorney (including sometimes assisting a prosecuting attorney in a criminal case) and a defense attorney. His practice encompassed civil as well as criminal matters. In addition to representing the Modern Woodmen of

America in its insurance practice for several years, he handled estates, debts, land disputes, and divorces. He did not hesitate to take cases in other cities; the record of appellate cases in the various Texas courts of civil appeals and in the Texas Supreme Court show that, in addition to his extensive practice in McLennan County, he represented parties in San Antonio, Fort Worth, Marlin, Corsicana, Abilene, Athens, and Post in far West Texas. His record in appellate court was commendable, but not outstanding; he won decisions for his clients in just over 50 percent of the appellate cases.[53]

The civil cases generally provided few fireworks that made newspaper headlines. The only notable exception in this period was the so-called "chicken salad" case. The lawsuit was filed by State Representative W. C. Middleton in 1915, seeking an injunction to recover payment of certain Governor's Mansion expenditures by Governor O. B. Colquitt while he was in office. Although the suit was filed against H. B. Terrell, state comptroller, it was Colquitt who was really on trial. Both men hired Neff to defend them. Middleton was particularly unhappy about monies paid to the Driskill Hotel for chicken salad and punch—hence the name by which the case came to be known. In 1915, Governor Colquitt submitted a detailed report to the House that consumed twenty-eight pages in the *House Journal* of May 22. He vigorously defended the expenditures of the past two years and enumerated in detail the expenses for the mansion, including a number of purchases for which he said he had reimbursed the state at the time of purchase. Although the chicken salad and a number of other items had been used for entertainment of official guests, Mrs. Colquitt would regret his listing of the personal expenditures, including twenty corsets and seven "brasiers" for the governor's wife in the last two years of his administration. In those Victorian times, the revelation in the official House record must have been traumatic to Mrs. Colquitt. Neff lost the case in the courts, and Colquitt was forced to repay the monies.[54]

Although the civil cases did not bring headlines, they did consume most of Neff's time in his practice. However, as a former prosecuting attorney, he was frequently seen as a highly qualified individual to serve as a criminal defense attorney as he would know the state's approach on a criminal case and hence could mount an effective defense. Neff's reputation as a fearless and articulate prosecuting attorney therefore brought him four high-profile criminal cases during this period, each of which garnered more newspaper coverage than all of his civil cases combined. In one of the four, he assisted the prosecuting attorney; in the other three, two of which were capital murder cases, he was the defense attorney.

Neff's first noteworthy case as a criminal defense attorney in private practice was defending Dr. Charles C. Lemly, a local chiropractor, who was accused of practicing medicine without a license. The medical profession claimed that chiropractors were covered by the Medical Licensing Act enacted much earlier by the Texas Legislature, and the State Board of Medical Examiners assisted local officials in prosecuting offenders. The act provided for both a fine and a jail term of six months for violators. Several chiropractors appealed convictions under the act, and the appellate courts routinely upheld the contention that chiropractors were covered and guilty as charged. At Lemly's first trial, he employed Neff but had a Kansas City lawyer take the lead. He was convicted and given a $50 fine and an hour in jail. Neff convinced Lemly not to appeal but to serve that sentence, continue his work, and let Neff be the sole attorney the next time. The State Board, backed by the Texas Medical Association, was determined to drive Lemly out of the state and persuaded Neff's successor, County Attorney John McNamara, to file numerous cases. But in subsequent cases, Neff put Lemly's patients on the witness stand, and when they told of favorable results at Lemly's hands, the juries continually acquitted Lemly. After the tenth trial, the Medical Association and the county attorney gave up; by 1920, Lemly was taking out quarter-page ads in the city's daily newspaper, and he was not prosecuted for another five years—again unsuccessfully.[55] The McLennan County Medical Society attempted to get the state's medical establishment to oppose Neff when he ran for governor because of his representation of Lemly, but the maneuver failed.[56]

Neff's second notable criminal case would also cause him some problems in his gubernatorial race. Neff's spirited defense of T. R. Watson, who shot and killed State Commissioner of Banking and Insurance John S. Patterson on August 28, 1916, brought rebuke from Patterson's widow as well as critical letters from other friends of the state official. They were disturbed that Neff had served as a pallbearer at Patterson's funeral and then defended the man who shot him. Neff was the leading counsel for the defense and argued strenuously for a verdict of manslaughter at worst. One Waco daily newspaper called the case "probably the most noted criminal case in the history of Texas."[57] The city's other daily, the *Waco Morning News*, reported that "it was estimated fully 100 more people had crowded the courtroom on this occasion than on any previous one. No standing room was left. The skylight was opened that spectators might get a place to see and hear, and yet many could not get in earshot of the speaker."[58]

Neff was able to save Watson from hanging, but the jury gave him a ninety-nine-year sentence. Neff appealed the case to the Texas Court of Criminal Appeals to no avail.[59] Because of ill health, Watson was pardoned after serving less than two years of his term. Although Patterson's widow tried to keep the issue alive even during Neff's subsequent run for the governor's office, Neff was able to successfully parry her arguments. It turned out to be a minor issue in that race.

Neff's other two newsworthy criminal cases did not command as much attention as the first two, but they are instructive nevertheless. The murder of Hal St. Clair, a young Falls County farmer, brought him the largest single legal fee during the 1917-1919 period—$l,500. In this case, he assisted Falls County Attorney Tom Bartlett in prosecuting Frank Finks in a trial that received detailed coverage in the local newspaper, the *Marlin Daily Democrat*, over a period of several months in 1917. Although the prosecution, aided by Neff, obtained a ninety-nine-year sentence for the defendant, a Texas Criminal Appeals Court overturned the verdict with a stinging rebuke to the trial judge and the team of prosecutors who had tried the case. The appellate court upheld the defense argument for a change of venue and for not allowing the defense to show that at least two witnesses were coerced by a number of whippings. Neff's argument to the jury, contained in his papers, illustrates that even the cool-headed Baptist could get carried away in the heat of a trial, arguing at one point: "I don't know whether they hit him five licks or fifteen. Don't care."[60] The new trial ordered by the appeals court became moot when Finks was killed by a former sheriff.

The second largest legal fee that Neff recorded for the 1917-1919 period—$500—was for defense of two young men who murdered Max Rubin, a merchant from the town of Mart in McLennan County. The two youths, Jewel Hale, eighteen, and Eugene Spencer, twenty, were captured shortly after the crime in 1919 and pleaded guilty to the charge. Prosecuting Attorney Frank Tirey made an impassioned plea for the death penalty for the two. With confessions from both young men, acquittal was not an option. Neff's only hope was to try to defeat the death penalty for the two boys and persuade the jury to give them prison sentences. With the two mothers in the courtroom, Neff did not make a lengthy address. He again appealed to the jury's religious outlook and, in this case, to their "fatherly" instincts by constantly referring to the two as "boys" or "lads."

The jury was out only thirty-five minutes and came back to assess punishment for each defendant at ninety-nine years in the penitentiary. Neff evidently found no reversible error in the court's proceedings or realized that the prosecution had such a strong case that even if there were a new trial, the outcome would be the same or worse. Accordingly, he promptly announced that there would be no appeal of the verdict. Neff really "won" the case by saving the two from the death penalty. Indeed, the sentence turned out to be relatively light. The two were both freed with full pardons in less than ten years.[61] On Spencer's release in 1927, Neff actually put the young man to work in Mother Neff Park, where he also furnished him housing until the Depression forced Neff to eliminate his expenses there.

The Hale-Spencer case effectively marked a sharp curtailment of Neff's law practice in the 1913-1919 period. For the three summer months of June, July, and August 1919, Neff recorded fees from only ten cases for a total income of only $402. But for the two-and-one-half years from 1917 to mid-1919, he had recorded a total income of $26,889.05. While this was probably not the most for any attorney in Waco for that period, it certainly was a substantial sum. To put these figures into perspective, February 1919 issues of the *Waco Daily Times-Herald* advertised rooms at the Raleigh Hotel for $1.50 per night, a round-trip train ticket to Kansas City for $22.95, and a box of chocolate-coated cherries for $.39 at Morrison Drug Store.

Extracurricular Activities during Those Years

Neff made a comfortable living in private practice, but he had never really worried about this aspect of his life. It is obvious his real goal in life was to meet the expectations of his beloved mother, who constantly urged him to "be his best" and to make the world a better place to live in. His six years as a public prosecutor had taken much of his time—particularly in the spring and fall each year when grand jury indictments launched a series of trials. Relieved of those duties, he could determine his own daily schedule better and could wear the many other "hats" he enjoyed, including education, politics, and matters involving Prohibition, fraternal activities, Baptist and Baylor commitments, and, last but not least, patriotic service.

When he left the prosecuting attorney's position in late 1912, Neff immediately began taking an active role in the Conference for Education in Texas, culminating in his being named president of that group in November 1913 at its sixth annual meeting in Dallas.[62] Substantial improvement in the status of education had been one of his political passions when he opened his legislative campaign in 1898. His first major speech to the legislature in 1899 had been to urge a higher appropriation for the University of Texas. As he was completing his term as county attorney in 1912, he saw the Conference for Education as an opportunity to work with other statewide leaders to improve Texas' poor standing in education. The conference had been organized in 1907 by a group of Texas educators to "provide a campaign agency for needed constitutional amendments and better school legislation."[63] After some five years, the organization floundered in some people's minds; indeed, renowned University of Texas Education Professor Frederick Eby wrote later that "the Conference ceased to function effectively about 1912."[64] This statement is contradicted not only by Neff's files but by other books and documents. Neff persuaded sixteen college presidents, other educators, and lay persons to join him on the board in continuing the organization's agenda. He also convinced Dr. Thornton Rogers Sampson, then serving as the first president of the Austin Presbyterian Theological Seminary, to become the group's chief administrative official. Neff and Sampson successfully lobbied the 1915 legislature to enact the long-sought compulsory attendance law and a million-dollar appropriation for rural schools. An exhausted Sampson left for a short Colorado vacation in August 1915 and, although an experienced hiker, fell to his death in the mountains there.[65] His death seemed to drain all the energy from the group, and no further activity of the Conference for Education is found in Neff's files or in several books on the history of educational efforts in Texas.

During the period following his county attorney tenure Neff also flirted with the idea of running for the U.S. Congress, but he finally decided against it. The most probable reason for declining was that Baylor President Samuel Palmer Brooks had decided to run for the Senate, and Neff wanted to help his close friend. No doubt he also felt it would not be good for Baylor if Brooks and he were both to be elected to national offices that would take them away from the campus. Neff made numerous speeches for Brooks and endorsed a note for Brooks for $1,500 in the middle of the campaign. Despite the work of the candidate himself, campaign manager John K. Strecker, Neff, and thousands of supporters, Brooks finished in third place.[66] In November, in the first Senate race not decided by vote of the Texas Legislature, incumbent Senator Charles A. Culberson was reelected.

In the congressional race, Neff's law school colleague and good friend Tom Connally had announced early and was very concerned that Neff would get in the race. In his autobiography, Connally gave another reason for Neff's decision not to run. One can almost see the wide smile on Connally's face as he wrote it. Connally admitted that he first got "Washington fever" when he attended President Wilson's inauguration in 1913. But two years later, he realized that he had formidable opposition to overcome to get to Congress. Neff was a real possibility, and in a chance meeting at the federal courthouse in Waco one day, Connally tried to draw him out:

> "You know something, Pat," I finally said. "You're too good to run for
> the House. Congress is too small for you." At this, his eyes lit up. "You ought
> to be Governor, Pat," I added.
>   "Yes," he said dreamily, "maybe I should."[67]

Neff decided not to run for the House, but to prepare himself for the Governor's Mansion.

While Brooks, Connally, and others were campaigning across the state in the spring and summer of 1916, Waco became the scene of one of the most horrific lynchings in the history of the nation. Waco was no stranger to the butchery of Negroes, and in 1916 most Wacoans could still remember the savage lynching and burning of Sank Majors in 1905. However, the lynching of the young, illiterate black man named Jesse Washington set a new low for the city that prided itself on its churches, Baylor University, and its middle-class respectability. On May 15, 1916, the city set the unenviable record for what is believed to be the largest lynch mob in the country's history—15,000 men, women, and children by the estimate of a reporter present.[68]

Jesse Washington worked on the George Fryer farm in Robinson, just south of Waco. In the early evening of Monday, May 8, Mrs. Fryer, fifty-three, was found dead in the family seed shed by her son and daughter. Washington was soon fingered as the murderer and arrested. Anticipating an enraged community, McLennan

County Sheriff Samuel S. Fleming first moved him to Hillsboro, thirty miles north, and then later to Dallas, another sixty miles northward. In Dallas, Washington gave a signed confession to Dallas County Attorney Mike T. Lively in which he admitted raping and murdering Mrs. Fryer. A report of a special agent of the National Association for the Advancement of Colored People later concluded: "There was some, but not much, doubt of his guilt. The confessions were obtained, of course, under duress, and were, perhaps, suspiciously clear, and not entirely in the boy's own words. It seems, however, probable that the boy was guilty of murder, and possibly of premeditated rape."[69]

The trial was held in a packed courtroom in Waco with thousands of curious spectators from all over Central Texas congregated around the courthouse on all sides. The jury took only four minutes to convict Washington, but the drama started when the judge started to write the verdict. The next few minutes were captured by the chillingly succinct account in the Tuesday, May 16, story that appeared in the *Waco Daily Times-Herald.* Under the headline COURT'S ENTRY NOT FINISHED WHEN MOB SECURED NEGRO, the paper reported that the mob dragged him from the courtroom and down the backstairs of the courthouse, tearing off his clothes as they went. The crowd grew, coming in buggies, afoot, and in automobiles. Washington was hanged from a tree in the City Hall yard, and then, with boxes and litters piled around him, his body was torched. Not satisfied, one person tied a rope to what was left of the body and, as he rode horseback, dragged the body through downtown streets. The body was finally taken to Robinson, near where the crime occurred, and hoisted high on a pole.[70]

City and county officials had stood by with no effort to stop the action. In the next week, a special committee of Baylor faculty issued a resolution condemning the mob's actions, and sermons denouncing the lynching were delivered by at least four Protestant ministers the following Sunday.[71] These included Dr. Joseph Martin Dawson, Neff's pastor. Neff's office was only two blocks from the scene; there is no indication in the Neff Papers or the newspapers as to Neff's whereabouts that day. He was out of town frequently during that spring, making speeches for Dr. Brooks, the Knights of Pythias, and the Modern Woodmen of America, or trying a law case. The event has remained a blot on Waco's history for almost a century.[72]

The year 1916 was a tumultuous one for Waco and Neff for other reasons. In the midst of politics and racial problems, Neff and other leaders in the Prohibition movement decided it was time to force the Prohibition issue again. The most recent statewide loss of the "drys" had been in 1913. Seeking to avenge that loss, they had hoped to elect a Prohibitionist governor in 1914, only to be thwarted by Jim Ferguson, who was elected governor and declared opposition to Prohibition. As they licked their wounds, the Prohibitionists resolved to come back for a statewide effort in 1916. The question was put on the primary ballot and carried, but Ferguson, and later the legislature, ignored the vote. Neff and his Prohibitionist colleagues decided that if they couldn't win at the state level, they would wage local fights to "dry up" the state county by county. The group had failed to convince McLennan County voters in 1895, 1907, and 1912, the last two times by fewer than 1,000 votes, but they were convinced that this time they would succeed. They began a campaign that would culminate in the fall of 1917. Prohibition advocates held a rally on October 1 at the First Baptist Church, and a large crowd heard Neff point out that the authorities, both of the U.S. Army at Camp MacArthur and of the City of Waco, were making every effort to keep liquor from 35,000 soldiers stationed locally. Neff was in his best form as he orated for more than an hour, closing with the statement:

> The world is constantly moving onward and upward, and during the next generation, students of thought will walk the halls of learnings, and inquire why and how their forefathers endured so long a traffic that dethroned manhood, debauched womanhood, destroyed childhood, corrupted the ballot box, commercialized virtue, brutalized civilization and squandered the world's wealth.[73]

Neff was proud enough of the speech to include it in his second book of addresses, *The Battles of Peace*, published in 1925.

Meanwhile, the opposition was not quiet. Striking back at the Prohibition faction's appeal to patriotism, the "anti" faction had its own interpretation of patriotism. An advertisement in a local paper stated that President Wilson's policy was to prohibit the manufacture of strong drink while permitting the manufacture and use of light wines and beer.[74] But the work of Neff and his adherents paid off. For the first time in four elections, McLennan County voted 5,208 to 3,935 to dry up the county—all of it, even those precincts that had previously voted "wet."[75] In that same year, Dallas also voted "dry," whereas Houston chose to keep liquor legal.[76]

Neff and His Organizations

Like others in those years, Pat Neff was a "joiner." To borrow a familiar phrase, it seemed he never met a club or organization he didn't like. He was active in civic and fraternal functions and organizations from his college days. As noted earlier, he joined the Knights of Pythias and the Modern Woodmen of America and climbed to positions of great responsibility in both organizations. In 1905 he joined the Masons, oldest and largest of the fraternal organizations; however, he did not take a leading part in that organization until after his gubernatorial days. All three organizations, very popular in the early 1900s, were male social organizations, offering a variety of activities, sometimes including the provision of insurance for members and their families. Although struggling for membership, all three remain active into the twenty-first century. Neff's motivation for taking part in fraternal activities is not revealed in his writings, but it doubtless stemmed from an inherent gregariousness that saw him delight in the public speaking and rough and tumble of a political encounter from his earliest days of running for the Texas Legislature in 1898. His ultimate political ambitions were never expressed in his early letters to his mother, but he probably knew that his political career would benefit from his affiliations with these organizations. His club activity may also have provided respite from dealing with Myrtie's illnesses and depression.

Neff began making speeches statewide for the Pythians as early as 1898. He steadily worked his way up the ladder, and on May 14, 1918, at the annual meeting in Fort Worth, he was elected to the organization's highest state position—the grand chancellorship.[77] The organization had been losing membership for the past seven years, but Neff was undaunted. Writing both "Official Communiques" from his office and articles in the Pythian's two organs, his enthusiasm captured the members' imagination. By the spring of 1919, in spite of more than 1,200 of their number being called to war service, a crippling influenza epidemic, and a severe drought in West Texas and the Panhandle, Neff reported that Pythian membership was up by eighty-three members.[78] Little wonder then that the *Grand Lodge Newsletter* called for Neff's reelection, a virtually unheard-of move. Neff had put the Pythians back on stage as the third largest fraternal organization in Texas and started them on the road to the largest membership in their history—30,507 in 1922.[79] Despite calls that he serve an unprecedented second term, he stepped down in May 1919. He left having made a significant impact, and he was pleased with his contributions. One source of particular pride was the Pythian Children's Home in Weatherford, where more than 100 children of deceased Pythians lived.[80]

Neff continued to be an active member of the Modern Woodmen of America, making frequent speeches for the group. Representing the Woodmen's insurance plans gave him the opportunity to attend national meetings of the organization in Chicago, New York, Boston, and Minneapolis, among other cities. During this period, he also delivered several keynote addresses in Chicago for the Woodmen's Lincoln Birthday banquets. These trips broadened his experiences and outlook and partially set the stage for his being considered later for national political offices.

Perhaps the highlight of Neff's extracurricular activities in these years was his being asked to join in a barnstorming tour of South Texas aboard a Liberty Loan train in 1918. Most of the cost of World War I was to be paid by a new federal income tax, approved by the nation's voters in a constitutional amendment in 1913. However, President Woodrow Wilson called on the populace to buy war bonds, and the government used a variety of methods to stimulate participation, ranging from parades to community celebrations honoring men who had been killed in the war. The fourth drive featured special trains traveling from place to place to drum up sales of bonds. Neff was asked to be one of five speakers on a train in Texas. His unit left Dallas on September 28, 1918, and covered primarily East and South

Texas. Although the state's daily newspapers covered the tour thoroughly, none of these accounts could rival Neff's own colorful description of his ten days on the train, contained in a letter to his mother the day after he returned to Waco. He wrote that the train's engine was decorated with the American colors, and following it were two flatcars loaded with several U.S. guns as well as French and captured German cannons. The train also featured two wounded French and American soldiers just back from the war front. At each stop, a band revved up the crowds, varying from 2,000 to 10,000. The audience was required to listen to a spiel for war bonds before being allowed to tour the train.[81] The *Dallas Morning News* of October 20, 1918, reported that the Dallas Federal Reserve District had exceeded its goal by several thousand dollars, with money still coming in. Neff must have been pleased at his part in exceeding the target. His participation also brought him more new friends and favorable publicity, both of which would be welcome just two years later when his patriotism would be questioned.[82]

Although he thrived on the stimulation of all of his various extracurricular activities, he never forgot that his first priority for these activities was his church and Baylor. Neff had transferred his membership from the Eagle Springs Church to the First Baptist Church in Waco in 1898 and was elected church clerk in 1909, serving in that position until 1918, when he resigned because of the burdens of his law practice.[83] At the church, Neff was instrumental in bringing Dr. Joseph M. Dawson in 1915 to begin a thirty-two-year pastorate at what many considered the flagship church of Texas Baptists. Dawson took the church from a membership of some 1,200 to more than 2,000, all the while preaching strong sermons, many of them oriented to challenging its members to tackle social issues. Neff and Dawson, already friends, became even closer as the Neffs continued their membership there and Dawson joined the Baylor Board of Trustees just one year later in 1916. Myrtie was also quite active in the church, "teaching a Sunday School class, doing more than her share of visiting the sick, and taking flowers that she had grown in her garden to the hospitals," according to one of her friends.[84] Although Dawson and Neff did not always agree on social issues, their friendship was never sorely tested. Dawson, in his autobiography, speaks endearingly of Neff and his family.[85]

Neff's most important work for his denomination in these years was as president of the Baylor University Board of Trustees. The university always seemed to be in financial trouble and, as a part of the Baptist General Convention of Texas, continually looked to the organization for financial leadership. Neff also found time to serve as moderator of the Waco Baptist Association, composed of the Baptist churches in McLennan County.

One of Neff's more challenging times came in 1917 when Camp MacArthur brought 35,000 soldiers to Waco from all over the country. The streets of Waco were jammed with service personnel. The Baptists saw the soldiers' presence as a formidable challenge and began an intensive campaign to minister to the men's spiritual as well as personal needs. The *Baptist Standard* of October 18, 1917, reported that "services are held every night and many conversions are being had."

During these years, Neff served as chair of several committees of both the Baptist General Convention of Texas and the Southern Baptist Convention. One of his major jobs in 1919 was to play a key role in the Southern Baptist Convention's $75 million fundraising campaign. Texas' share of that overall goal was $16 million, and Baylor was slated to get $3 million of that amount—$2 million for Waco and $1 million for Baylor-Dallas. Having taken his place on the Baylor Board in 1904 and being elected its president in 1907, Neff, by this time, was an experienced chair and had a good relationship both with the rest of the board and with President Brooks. The board minutes do not reflect a single split vote among members between 1913 and 1920. The board was, throughout these years, a very homogenous group of white males, who might be expected to think alike. The most notable membership change in those years was the addition to the board of Dr. Dawson in 1916; he would serve on the body for thirty years, rarely disagreeing with Neff.

Although the Baptist Convention elected new blood to the board from time to time, the three stalwarts of the board for the first half of the twentieth century were Dr. George W. Truett, Judge W. H. Jenkins, and Dr. J. T. Harrington. Those three were the dominant members of the board during the decade preceding the 1920s, but it can be safely said that President Brooks, while not a member, was the real driving force behind the board. His devoted and energetic leadership of Baylor brought him nothing but praise from the board as the university grew to meet the increasing demands of a burgeoning enrollment and a changing society. The board's agendas were generally confined to four subjects: financial matters; property acquisition and disposal; approval of the president's recommendations for faculty appointments, leaves, and salaries; and the perfunctory approval of the university's graduates each semester. Real estate acquisition frequently involved buying properties on South Fifth Street or Speight Street, both adjacent to the campus and thus logical locations for dormitories and other facilities. The financial affairs most often involved requests from Dr. Brooks or the finance vice-president to borrow money to meet current operating expenses. The university was literally surviving from month to month. At many meetings, the only major topic on the agenda would be to authorize the president to borrow anywhere from $500 to $35,000.[86]

Family Life

Neff's income allowed his family to live comfortably, if not extravagantly. Neff had paid off his home on Austin Avenue in 1907. He was clearly gone from home a substantial amount of time during those years: his law practice was statewide and sometimes took him outside the state; his fraternal and other activities also took him away from Waco on many occasions; and on his business and fraternal trips, he went by himself virtually all the time. He also did not accompany the family on many of the vacation trips which they took, but a 1915 trip to California was a full family affair—Neff was with them five of the seven weeks. The family's summer trip to the West Coast in 1915 was a combination vacation, educational experience, and, most likely, a few days of therapeutic treatment for Myrtie. The trip was the subject of a double-spaced, eleven-page typewritten letter from Neff to his mother in which he described in some detail the family's visits to the Grand Canyon, Los Angeles, Pasadena, San Francisco, Yellowstone Park, Salt Lake City, and finally Manitou, a resort near Colorado Springs. Neff's summation of the trip is insightful: "The West and Northwest is the place to go to see the wondrous works of nature; the East to see the handiwork of man."[87]

Only two letters from Hallie Maude to her father survived the return trip to Long Beach in 1917, but she was now sixteen and Neff was in for a shock. On a Sunday in August, after telling him that the water was even better than last year, she informed him: "I am learning to dance. I know you don't like this quite so well, but I knew if I ever intend to have a good time, I would have to learn here because I would not do it at home."[88] Hallie Maude was properly hesitant. Two years later, in 1919, the *Baptist Standard*—revered next to the Bible in the Neff household—would have an editorial stating that "A good dancer cannot make a good Sunday School teacher or good B.Y.P.U. [Baptist Young People's Union] worker."[89] Despite these lapses from proper Baptist behavior, there is no evidence that Hallie Maude and Neff ever had a serious breach in their relationship.

Other than the three long journeys to the West, Myrtie's trips were confined to Texas, principally to Mineral Wells to take the hot water treatment offered there. She had begun her visits to Mineral Wells and Marlin in 1901, utilizing the baths at Marlin for the most part while Neff was county attorney since it was closer and cheaper. But she frequented Mineral Wells more and more beginning in 1913, and from 1917 to 1927 she missed her annual trip to the wells only twice. On many of these occasions, Hallie Maude was with her, and on a few, Pat Jr., but there is no record of her husband's ever being in that city at the same time that she was. Myrtie's illnesses, which had proven difficult if not impossible for doctors to diagnose and treat, seemed very well suited for the cures promised by Mineral Wells. At that time, when doctors could not diagnose an illness, they often thought that the cure was to clean out the poisons or impurities in the body and that the best way to do this was to have the patient drink gallons of very hot water and take extremely hot baths. The favorite place in Texas to take this cure was at Mineral Wells.[90]

The period from 1913 to 1919 had been an eventful time for the Neff family. And the final year, 1919, was especially momentous. Neff saw Prohibition, a lifelong passion of his, adopted at both the national and state levels; he finished a highly successful year as grand chancellor of the Knights of Pythias in Texas; and he had played an integral role in the $75 million Southern Baptist Convention fund-raising campaign. In the midst of all this, he still had a law practice that made him a respectable living and took him to many interesting places during the year.

In July 1919, in the midst of all this almost frenetic activity, Neff, without any prior warning, casually notified his mother that he had decided to run for governor of the state. The news was met quietly, both in the family and by the general public, but this decision became the prelude for an exhaustive campaign by Neff and three opponents in late 1919 and the first half of 1920.

CHAPTER 5

From a Mule to an Airplane: Campaigning for Governor

*I did not confer with any politicians in regard
to my candidacy.*

—Pat Neff

P at Neff was restless in 1919. It was not that he needed to do better financially. His last two and one-half years in private practice had been lucrative. He had earned $26,889.05 in law fees, rents, interest and dividends, and fees for speaking.[1] Not bad, considering that the Governor of Texas made only $4,000 in 1917, and the president of the University of Texas was in the appropriation bill for an annual salary of $6,000.[2]

But something was missing in Neff's life. He relished public service and felt that when he was away from it he was not fulfilling his mother's hopes and dreams for him. She had always insisted that he was destined to serve God and his fellow man, and she kept urging him to "be his very best." It is true that he was partially living up to her dreams by serving as president of the Baylor University Board of Trustees, by being active in the Baptist brotherhood, by working in such organizations as the Knights of Pythias, and by doing his share of pro bono work as an attorney. But there had to be more than this in his life.

His six years in the Texas House of Representatives and his six as McLennan County prosecuting attorney had been the most satisfying times he could imagine, but they seemed to be only a prelude. In 1903, at the zenith of his popularity as speaker of the House, several of the state's newspapers and numerous friends had suggested that he run for attorney general or the Railroad Commission. As he had studied the situation, neither of these was a reasonable possibility at the time, particularly at his relatively young age of thirty-two. Now he was beginning to receive letters again, this time suggesting that he should set his sights on the governor's office.[3] Newspaper speculation renewed when the *Houston Post* of October 7, 1917, reported that it was "practically certain that Neff would run for governor."

Neff, as an avid reader of the newspapers and an astute political observer, would have known that he should at least consider a run for the governorship. It is reasonable to assume that in the early months of 1919, he began to approach his decision as he would one of his law cases—through a painstaking examination of all aspects of the various factors that should go into his decision.

Formidable Opposition

Neff's prospects for the governorship were backed by several strengths: outstanding speaking ability and persuasiveness as an orator, twelve years of public sector experience, and many friends in various fields. Equally important, he now had the financial resources to conduct a campaign. He had saved some money, and he could continue to take a limited number of clients during the campaign. If worse came to worst, he had several pieces of property around the state that he could sell to provide some money for travel and printing costs. If unsuccessful, he could resume private law practice without too much difficulty.

His weaknesses were not insignificant. First, despite the fact that he had held two public offices for a total of twelve years, neither was a statewide office. Although the speaker of the House was generally regarded as the third-ranking office in the state hierarchy, he was elected by his peers in the House, not by the voters of the state—and the Texas Legislature was not generally held in the highest esteem by the citizenry. Sixteen years had passed since his name had appeared in the statewide press conducting the business of the House of Representatives.

A second weakness was that his most recent experience was in Waco, a city of fewer than 40,000 that was losing ground each census period. Although most previous governors had come from small towns, the demographics of the state were rapidly changing. One-third of the state's 4.5 million people lived in urban areas. Neff identified himself, and was probably identified by others, with rural Texas. Furthermore, Neff would surely have reasoned that the voters would regard him primarily as a Baptist and Baylor candidate and not as a representative of the state as a whole. An analysis of his strengths and shortcomings would lead him to conclude that he might have a reasonable chance to be successful, but it would be no cakewalk.

Another factor in his decision would have been his potential competition. As many as two dozen opponents were possibilities at that time. The first two names on that list had to be incumbent Governor William P. Hobby and Baylor President Samuel Palmer Brooks. In early 1919, Governor Hobby enjoyed considerable success with the legislature and was highly regarded by a number of citizens across the state. However, the "accidental governor," as some called Hobby (since he had succeeded to the position when Jim Ferguson was impeached), did not really have his heart set on being governor.[4] Hobby had been happy in 1914 in his position as editor-publisher of the *Beaumont Enterprise* when he was drafted to run for lieutenant governor. The newspaper business was his life; he had quit high school to begin work for the *Houston Post* and worked his way up to managing editor of that newspaper. In 1907, at the age of twenty-nine, he had gone to Beaumont as editor and half-owner of the *Enterprise*, Beaumont's morning newspaper. Hobby had been taken aback when friends approached him in 1914 to run for lieutenant governor. The post was about to go by default to State Senator B. B. Sturgeon, an ardent Prohibitionist. Hobby was not a strong anti-Prohibitionist, but he felt strongly enough for their cause that he certainly did not want to see a Prohibition candidate elected.[5] Hobby ran and defeated Sturgeon by fewer than 7,000 votes out of more than 400,000 cast in the Democratic primary.[6] Ferguson was (effectively) elected governor in the same election, and two years later the two were reelected.[7] By the time the 1916 campaign was over, Ferguson was in a full-fledged fight with the University of Texas. In 1917, the governor was indicted for misapplication of public funds, and the whole mess ended with his impeachment by the House of Representatives and conviction on ten different charges by the Senate. On September 26, 1917, Hobby was administered the oath of office as governor.[8]

Newly invested Governor Hobby now moved forward aggressively on several fronts and ran for reelection in 1918, only to be faced by Ferguson. Despite being barred from public office by his impeachment, Ferguson was determined to run and Hobby, rather than try to force him out of the campaign by court action, decided to let him stay in the race. In a bitter campaign, Hobby ran away with the primary election, polling 461,749 to 217,012 for Ferguson.[9] In 1919, as Neff was contemplating his future, Governor Hobby generally had been successful in regular and special sessions with the legislature and might well win reelection if he chose to run. He had drawn particular praise for the fourth called session of the body which met from February 26 to March 27, 1918. Under Hobby's prodding, that session produced a statewide prohibition law (in advance of the U.S. constitutional amendment on liquor), a law granting women the right to vote in all primary elections and nominating conventions, a new statute requiring a majority vote for all state and district offices, and finally, a tough prostitution law to protect the thousands of military men in Texas.[10]

The long-time tradition of Texas governors was to serve two two-year terms. At the end of his term in 1921 Hobby would have served three years and five months, short of the four-year tradition but still reasonably close to the traditional maximum. It cannot be determined when Governor Hobby officially took himself out of the 1920 campaign. The *Waco News-Tribune* reported on December 3, 1919, that the governor was home in bed with tonsillitis and had definitely decided not to ask for a second full term. However, Hobby did not openly declare his non-candidacy until February 1920, after the field already had four prospects.[11]

What Neff knew and when can only be speculated. Likewise, whether Neff would have proceeded with his plans early in 1919 if he had thought Hobby was going to run for reelection remains a mystery. But it is known that Neff did proceed with his plans—one of the best indications is that he resigned his monthly retainer fees with International and Great Northern Railroad and the San Antonio and Aransas Pass line, effective at the end of May 1919. This took some courage, for together, they represented almost $4,000 per year in retainers.[12]

The second person Neff had to think about in considering his potential candidacy was his long-time friend, Baylor President Samuel Palmer Brooks. Brooks had a lifelong interest in civic affairs and, like Neff, had been receiving letters from admirers as early as 1911, telling him that he should run for U.S. Senator or governor. The only document actually pointing toward the governorship, however, is an interview given by Brooks' two children, Sims Palmer Brooks and Aurelia Brooks Harlan, in the 1980s. In the interview, Harlan was adamant that her father had planned to run for governor in 1920: "He was ready to make his announcement. . . . Then, one day the door to his office opened and Pat Neff walked in and said, 'Well, Palmer, I've decided to run for the governorship.' And that was that! So he [Brooks] never announced."[13] Harlan stated in the interview that her information came from her mother. Mrs. Brooks may have made the statement, but if true, it would be contrary to the letters on the subject retrieved from the Brooks Papers at Baylor. From the beginning, it appears that Brooks was interested only in the U.S. Senate, not the governor's chair. Two letters in 1913 both point to the national office. In one letter, he stated that if he ran at all, it would be for the U.S. Senate. In another, he lamented that he did not have the financial resources to run for governor and discouraged the letter writer from considering him for a gubernatorial campaign.[14] After his defeat for the Senate in 1916, Brooks continued to talk about running for the same seat again in 1922. As late as 1921, he admitted that "the senatorial bee has clung to my bonnet."[15]

Neff, having considered the background and interests of the two men, must have determined that neither Hobby nor Brooks would be interested in making the governor's race in 1920. This still left a long list of potential candidates. However, the list could be shortened considerably by ruling out current federal officeholders (such as Tom Connally) who had indicated a preference for service in Washington. Likewise, the list of current and former state officials was quickly narrowed by eliminating those whose age (like Railroad Commissioner Allison Mayfield) or lack of statewide exposure (for example, Land Commissioner J. T. Robison) made them unlikely candidates.

It was actually fairly easy to reduce the potential competition to the three men who ultimately decided to run—Joseph Weldon Bailey, Benjamin F. Looney, and Robert Ewing Thomason.

Joe W. Bailey was arguably one of the two most influential politicians in Texas at the time even though he had been out of the state for the last seven years. Born in 1863 in Mississippi, Bailey moved to Gainesville, Texas, where, in 1885, he began practicing law and promptly took an active part in politics in the area. Only five years after becoming a Texan, he was elected to Congress and served in the U.S. House of Representatives until 1901, when he was elected by the Texas

Legislature to the U.S. Senate. A flaming orator, he held crowds spellbound and was compared to William Jennings Bryan. From the beginning, he was known for his very conservative views. While in the Senate, he was charged with illegally representing the Waters-Pierce Oil Company, which had been banished from Texas for violating the antitrust laws because of its connections with the Standard Oil trust. The revelation that Bailey had received large fees as a corporate attorney and that Waters-Pierce had never broken its ties to Standard Oil ended Bailey's career as a senator, and he resigned in 1913 to enter private law practice in Washington. Bailey never accepted Woodrow Wilson as the leader of "his" Democratic Party and for the next years after he resigned from the Senate, he fought both the domestic and the foreign policy initiatives of the Wilson administration. Bailey also fought woman suffrage, Prohibition, and other major Democratic Party policies and was bitter about Wilson's foreign policies. Nevertheless, the former senator had his share of supporters in Texas.

State Attorney General Looney of Greenville was a definite possibility to run. In January 1919, he had completed six years in the state's top legal post with an outstanding record and had previously served short stints in both the Texas Senate and the Texas House. Bailey had tried desperately to get Looney to run for governor in 1918 against Hobby but Looney demurred.[16] In the legislature, Looney had authored many progressive measures and was an arch Prohibitionist.[17]

Speaker of the Texas House Thomason of El Paso was another story. Eight years younger than Neff, he had been elected presiding officer of the House in only his second term in the legislature.[18] Obviously bright and ambitious, he would make a capable opponent.

One political figure that Neff would not have to worry about running was former Governor Jim Ferguson. After Ferguson's defeat in 1918, the Texas Legislature enacted a law preventing a person who had been convicted after impeachment from having his name printed on the ballot. Historian Norman Brown calls Ferguson "the most important figure in Texas politics from 1914 to 1934."[19] This statement is well taken but it is also true that Ferguson would not play a pivotal role in the 1920 election and would be content to operate through surrogates in that contest. Neff's listing of the two dozen possible opponents would have been sobering to him but not overwhelming. Neff had a great deal of confidence in himself and was not afraid to take on the field, whoever might be in it.

One other analysis Neff would have undoubtedly undertaken would be the total political and governmental climate within which the race would be conducted and the climate that a new governor would face. In this review, national issues would be more important in the 1920 election than state issues. The end of World War I only months before had brought problems to the state. Jobs for veterans became a high priority, and the end of the war saw prices on virtually all commodities rise sharply. The end of the war had set both capital and labor free to push their respective demands for higher profits and higher wages. Labor strikes proliferated throughout the Northeast as individuals and families found the cost of living soaring. Two national issues—Prohibition and woman suffrage—had been taken off the table as campaign issues in Texas because of Governor Hobby's leadership. A stiff Prohibition law passed in 1918 had been followed by ratification in Texas, and then in January 1919, by the necessary three-fourths of the states, as the Eighteenth Amendment to the U.S. Constitution. Neff would have known, however, that with the division in Texas between Prohibitionists and those opposed to it, enforcement of the laws would be a contentious issue for the next governor.

Woman suffrage had also been given a big boost in 1918 by the passage of the state law; however, Texas voters turned down a state constitutional amendment, with the same objective in mind, on May 24, 1919, by a 54 percent vote.[20] It would be up to a federal constitutional amendment to accomplish this goal; just five weeks after the failed state constitutional amendment, the legislature ratified the Nineteenth Amendment to the U.S. Constitution giving women the right to vote. The federal amendment became effective August 18, 1920, when the thirty-sixth state ratified it.

Other state issues facing the next governor included the continuing penitentiary and pardons/paroles problems, the challenges of adequately funding public and higher education, the pink boll worm infestation, and the question of the continuing growth of state government.

Neff obviously concluded that the issues, personalities, and challenges facing him were manageable and that he wanted to move forward. There is no evidence in his papers that he counseled with anyone on his decision to run for governor. Similarly, there is no correspondence with his mother or other members of his family indicating they had any concrete knowledge of his plans. It was one of the few times he would make a decision without consulting with his mother.

"I Want to Be Your Governor"

In the summer of 1919, the race to be the governor who would take office in January 1921 was far from most politicians' minds. So Neff decided this would be a perfect time to get a jump on any and all aspirants. Thus, with no warning, on Friday, July 25, Neff wrote his mother, addressing it to Brownwood where she was visiting her daughter, Sallie Calvert. Addressed "Dear Ma," it laid out his decision to run for governor of the state:

> In the papers of Sunday will appear a notice of my intentions to run for governor next year. I desire to convey this information to you ahead of the notice, because I would not be willing for you to get this from anyone, originally, except myself. You may not approve of this, but I trust you will. To be governor of Texas to my mind is next in

dignity and importance to the presidency of the United States. It is an honor worthy of any one's ambition. It places a person in position to render valuable service to the country. If elected I hope to be of service. . . . I can make more money at the practice of law, but whether I make much or little money, I only get "a suit of clothes and three meals a day" out of it. I would rather leave to those who come after me my work as governor of my native state than to leave them much wealth. Then you see, I think it will be an additional honor to you, that the people thought that much of your son. If I am defeated, it will leave no sore spots with me, but I will begin my practice anew with a hopeful spirit and a cheerful disposition. So if I am elected, I shall try and fill the office with credit; if I am defeated, I shall console myself that it is better "to have run and lost than never to have run at all." Trusting you will get much pleasure out of the thoughts of my candidacy, and with much love to you, I am, your baby

Pat M. Neff[21]

The always supportive mother replied, wishing for him "the greatest success."[22] Neff's papers do not reveal reaction from any others of his family.

As one might expect, his announcement received considerable front page coverage in the Waco newspapers. It caused little stir in the rest of the state. The major dailies—the *Dallas Morning News*, the *Houston Post*, the *San Antonio Express*, and the *Austin Statesman*—all buried the story on inside pages.

Getting an Early Start

Neff's announcement a full year ahead of the primary gave him a head start in the race and enabled him to make maximum use of the countless invitations he received each year to speak at all manner of events. It also meant that he would get newspaper coverage for his addresses. Less than a week after his original announcement, he spoke to an estimated crowd of 5,000 at a barbecue on the ranch of a good friend in Brownfield in Terry County. The Waco paper reported on November 19 that the McLennan County Medical Society had unanimously adopted a resolution opposing his candidacy because "he has been counselor and defender of unlicensed and unlawful practitioners of medicine in this community."[23]

When not making speeches in the fall of 1919, Neff spent time writing letters. He had a prodigious storehouse of names in his file cabinets. It is almost certain that, at least up to that time, no gubernatorial candidate had ever had as wide a range of friends across the entire state as Neff. In the early fall of 1919, he also began spending substantial sums of money for campaign letterhead and envelopes, posters with his picture, and campaign cards. He began writing numerous people across the breadth and width of the state; where he felt he knew persons well enough, he did not wait for them to ask in a return letter for campaign literature—he sent it out with his first letter. Many of the letters were personal. To John B. Nichols of

Crawford in McLennan County, he wrote on August 6: "You furnished the calico to make my dresses when I was a youngster, you have known me from that day to this, and if my conduct has been such as to meet your approval, I am most grateful."[24] To Walter Stewart in Simonton (Fort Bend County) on August 23, 1919, he wrote: "When we picked cotton together, we little dreamed that the time would come when you would write me offering your support to me as a candidate for governor."[25] The month of August also saw the first Neff for Governor Club organized, this on the Baylor campus. Such organizations would continue in the new year until almost 200 clubs were formed across the state.[26]

In September, he wrote to current members of the Texas Legislature, to preachers, and to individuals who went to Baylor with him. Asking for support in his race, his communiqués to current legislators included a letter to Honorable Sam E. Johnson, Johnson City, Texas, father of the future U.S. President. To Baptist preachers he knew over the state, he wrote identical letters, stating that "the Gospel and the Law have always gone together, and I see no reason why the preacher could not now join hands with the lawyer in fighting a common battle for the uplift and ongoing of our State."[27] To former fellow students he knew even better, he wrote that he expected their help and gave one of them instructions that he wanted a unanimous vote in that county.[28] One of the letters to former House colleagues was to E. B. Pickett Jr. of Liberty, member of a Southeast Texas family of distinguished attorneys. Although another "form" letter, it was nevertheless a poignant tribute to their time together. Neff recalled their days in the House of Representatives when they "saved the country" and wrote that he was now asking for his vote and influence.[29]

The letter to an E. J. Neff of Grandview, someone whose only connection was his surname, was an indication that Pat Neff was not going to leave any stone unturned in his campaign. The only other known instance of a candidate's writing individuals with the same surname would occur nearly a half century later by then Lieutenant Governor Preston Smith. Journalist and author Jimmy Banks has written that when Smith was running for governor, he realized that there had never been a governor named Smith. He sent out letters to 47,000 "Smiths" in Texas, asking, "Don't you think it is about time one of us was governor?"[30]

It was also in October that Neff sought to call in a "chit" from earlier days. To Vernon McIntyre of Marathon—a small town in Brewster County in far West Texas, much closer to Mexico and New Mexico than to either Waco or Austin—he wrote: "I recall writing for you some years ago a recommendation in behalf of your application for the position of Postmaster at Marathon. . . . I am running for Governor and I need your help."[31]

November saw letters to fellow Pythians and to several members of the Texas Federation of Women's Clubs. In letters to good friends in the Pythians and other organizations, he enclosed posters and campaign cards with the letter, asking the recipients to post them in public places such as hotel lobbies, restaurants, shop windows, and garages.[32]

If there were any hard feelings between Brooks and Neff about who should run for governor, they were not apparent in the fall of 1919. On November 5, Brooks wrote W. S. Davis, publisher of the *Redland Herald* newspaper in Nacogdoches, about Neff's race. In recommending Neff, he stated: "Mr. Neff and I were roommates in college. I know him like a book. He is one of the most trustworthy men I ever knew. . . . We have not had his like for Governor in a long time. Should we get him, we will be proud of him and the work he will do. This is my candid judgment."[33]

Joining the Battle

Neff did not anticipate that he would have a "free" run at the governor's office, so he was not surprised when November brought three other candidates into the race. One aspirant, State Comptroller Henry B. Terrell, announced but then withdrew because of ill health and died within eighteen months. The other two, R. Ewing Thomason and Ben F. Looney, both announced for governor in November and stayed in the race to the end.

Thomason, born in Tennessee in 1879, became a Texan at one year of age when his parents migrated to Texas in 1880 and settled near Gainesville in North Texas, the same city where a young lawyer named Joseph Weldon Bailey settled five years later. Thus, the little Cooke County farming town less than a hundred miles north of Fort Worth in the early 1900s became the home of two political figures who were as dissimilar as night and day. Graduating from the University of Texas Law School in 1900, Thomason returned to Gainesville to open his law practice. In his autobiography, he related how his thirty years in Gainesville had ended: "In the late summer of 1911, I was stricken with a prolonged attack of malarial fever. The doctor told me that I would have to seek a higher and drier climate."[34] After agonizing over a move, the Thomasons became permanent citizens of El Paso in 1912. He became a part of a prominent law firm there and in 1916 was elected to the Texas Legislature. Thomason wrote in his autobiography that he volunteered to serve in the armed forces in the World War but was deferred because of his family status—a wife and two small children. In the book, Thomason also boasted of his key role in the impeachment of Governor Ferguson and support of bills establishing the State Highway Commission, providing compensation for workers injured in industrial accidents, and providing for woman suffrage. He was reelected to the Thirty-sixth Legislature in 1918 without opposition and became one of the few House members to be elected speaker of that body in their second term and without opposition. Newspapers in the spring of 1919 gave Thomason the same high marks for fairness and a businesslike attitude in the speaker's chair that they had given Neff sixteen years before. The press and friends began talking of him as the next governor, but Thomason later wrote: "I can truthfully say that I did not initiate or encourage it. As I look back on it now, I feel sure my heart was never in it. I know I was not enthusiastic about it."[35] Thomason felt that Bailey would get in the race and that he could not defeat the veteran senator and campaigner. His friends back in Gainesville convinced him that Bailey would not run, and so on November 8, 1919, he announced for governor.

Twelve days after Thomason's announcement, Ben F. Looney of Greenville tossed his hat in the ring. Looney, born in Louisiana in 1859, came to Texas with his widowed mother at an early age and was educated in Marion County. He spent two years at the University of Mississippi and then enrolled in the law department of Cumberland University in Lebanon, Tennessee, where he received his Bachelor of Laws in 1882. Returning to Texas, he opened a law practice in Greenville, served in the Texas Senate from 1905 to 1909, and filled an unexpired term in the Texas House of Representatives in 1910.[36] While in the legislature, he compiled an impressive record as a progressive, and went on to be elected Texas Attorney General in 1912 over two strong opponents and to build an outstanding record in that post for six years. According to historian T. C. Richardson, Looney's administration as attorney general was "distinguished for the rigid, uniform and impartial enforcement of the anti-trust laws, and the prosecution of corporations for acts in excess of granted powers."[37] Retiring from the attorney general's post on January 1, 1919, he had returned to Greenville and was engaged in the practice of law there when he decided to run for governor. The platform he laid out on November 22 included favoring full suffrage for women, rigidly enforcing the Prohibition laws, improving the public school education system, lowering the state tax rate, and establishing a state budget system.

My Platform is . . .

Neff had planned to wait until after the first of the year to open his campaign, but he could not wait. Thomason and Looney were now in the race and Bailey and Henry had been making speeches throughout the fall. Neff decided it was time to make his formal opening and begin campaigning in earnest on the platform of things he wanted to accomplish in the governor's chair. He chose to make his opening address in Waxahachie on December 6, 1919. The county courthouse was filled to overflowing with a crowd estimated at anywhere from "a few hundred who braved the rain" to estimates as high as 1,200.[38] Crowd estimates for the entire campaign would vary wildly. One newspaper, somewhat disapproving, reported that Neff "treated them to a 10,000 word speech that covered every known subject in the calendar of political, social and economic life."[39] Another newspaper was kinder: "Neff's hour and a half address was received with enthusiasm as he spoke in a deliberate yet forceful manner and his speech was interspersed with frequent flights of oratory and outbreaks of original witticism."[40]

The first newspaper was not exaggerating that much in describing Neff's wide-ranging discourse. Nineteen different subjects were covered with particular emphasis on education, agricultural policy, and public health. Neff stated that Prohibition and woman suffrage were the law of the land, and that he would vigorously enforce the constitution and laws relating to each.[41]

He spent much time on education. Deploring the fact that 25 percent of Texas boys in the recent war could neither read nor write and that only a small percentage had advanced beyond the fourth grade, he also pointed out that roughly half of the state's 1.25 million school children—those in rural areas—did not have access to high schools. He went on to lament the low salary of teachers—an average of $436 per year in the country and $544 in the city—and pointed out that they received an average of 16 cents an hour while a manual laborer received 60 cents. Neff also addressed agriculture, water conservation, hydroelectric power, irrigation, conservation of overflow lands, highway construction and beautification, home ownership, equalization and reduction of taxes, law enforcement, labor and capital, state forestry, the purity of the ballot box, public health, and ownership of large parcels of land. Speaking on public health, Neff first paid tribute to the state's doctors, a paragraph undoubtedly inserted to try to calm the seething medical profession for his defense of the chiropractor Lemly. But his litany of statistics on the matter of the state's health was similar to the figures quoted on education. He noted that 34 percent of Texas boys were unfit for recent military service because of physical defects, that more than 100,000 infants had died the previous year for want of proper attention, that 315,000 children had died under five years of age from preventable diseases, and that more than 5,000 Texans had died the year before from tuberculosis.

Midway through his speech he touched on what would become the only controversial subject in his platform. He opened a firestorm of debate in the campaign when he stated:

> Texas has one hundred and thirty million acres of uncultivated land. Most of this is owned by a small number of individuals. . . .Texas should not permit a few people to hold for speculative purposes, her agricultural lands unused, while thousands of our people are clamoring for homes, and while humanity is starving for the products of the soil.[42]

There is no indication in Neff's papers how or why he decided that this should be a part of his campaign, but with some explaining and variation, he stuck with it the entire nine months of the race.

Neff received extensive coverage of his speech in newspapers all over the state. Letters of congratulation and support poured into his office. Again, he did not take anything for granted. Before he spoke, he had written numerous newspapers over the state offering to pay them to run his opening speech as a supplement to one of their issues. He enclosed a postcard for them to reply—all they had to do was fill in a few blank spaces.[43]

Neff then spoke in Lubbock and Plainview, and just before the new year, traveled to Southwest Texas to speak in Del Rio, Marfa, Alpine, and Fort Davis. As the year ended, he had already visited more than two dozen counties in the state and had received much encouragement in his race.

Bailey and Henry Strike Back

It was well that Neff made an early start, for not only did Thomason and Looney get in the race in November, but the dissident forces in the Democratic Party were far from idle that fall. The leader of the anti-Wilson group in Texas was Joseph W. Bailey. Neff, President Brooks, and the "Progressive" Democrats in Texas had continued to support Wilson through all his travail in obtaining U.S. Senate approval of the peace treaty ending World War I and of establishing the League of Nations.[44] But others, including Jim Ferguson, former Congressman Robert L. Henry, and Bailey, had fought Wilson from the time of his inauguration in 1913. They opposed Prohibition, woman suffrage, foreign entanglements of any kind, and what they saw as increasing centralization of government. Bailey insisted in early 1918 that he was through with public life, but he couldn't resist. On July 29, 1919, only two days after Neff announced for the governorship, the Bailey-friendly *Waco News-Tribune* trumpeted that Bailey was "headed for the hill country" to consider the state of the Democratic Party. The newspaper later reported that at a picnic held on July 31 in Covington, some forty miles north of Waco, Bailey blasted the party before thousands of his supporters and stated that he could no longer be a part of the organization that had deserted the Jeffersonian principles of democracy. He went on to say that he would be in Fort Worth on August 14 to consider organizing a new political party. When Bailey, joined by Henry, arrived in Fort Worth, they found that Jim Ferguson had his own ideas. Although the three men agreed on opposition to Prohibition, woman suffrage, and the League of Nations, the conservative Bailey people did not like, in historian Lewis Gould's words, "Ferguson's sympathy for labor, his call for federal loans to small farmers, and his criticism of profiteering."[45] Although all three denounced Wilson and the League of Nations, they could not reconcile their other differences, and the Ferguson forces walked out of the conference (to form the American Party) while the Bailey-Henry forces decided to try to "reform" the Democratic Party in the coming election. Bailey and Henry were much more interested in trying to change the direction of the party at the national level than they were in state issues. Nevertheless, they felt they needed to work at the state level also, hence Henry announced his candidacy for governor on August 29 on the "Bailey platform." Both Henry and Bailey started speaking across the state.

Bailey was receiving increasing pressure to announce for governor, as many supporters believed he would make a much stronger candidate than either Henry or Houstonian John Henry Kirby, who had thought about making the race. The 1920 gubernatorial campaign would be a referendum, no less, on the Wilson administration and whether Joe Bailey was going to come back in power—regardless of whether or not he sat in the governor's chair. Many groups and individuals, including the state's major newspapers, would not particularly be for any *one candidate* for governor, they would just be *against* Bailey.

The 1920 Campaign: Driving, Riding the Rails, Flying, and Walking

Neff began his intensive campaign shortly after the first of the year.[46] He initiated the new year with a mid-January trip to the Lower Rio Grande Valley, where he spoke eleven times in one week.[47] Just days later, Neff registered another first to add to his resume. He had agreed to make a talk in Canyon on January 21 and decided to go a day early and add Amarillo to his schedule. Arriving in Amarillo, he found snow on the ground and highway travel next to impossible. His host told him of an airplane pilot who was operating in the area, and he decided to make the seventeen-mile trip by air. He is believed to be the first political candidate in Texas to use this means of transportation. Writing to editor Sumner N. Ramsey of the *Amarillo Globe* on his return to Waco, Neff thanked him for his courtesies in that city and then added:

> Of course, when I last saw you I was climbing directly toward the North Star, and I thought the pilot would never quit going up. However, after he made a circle in the sky and we struck a bee-line towards the sun I enjoyed the ride very much. We made a safe landing in Canyon and in a few moments I was talking to the Swine Breeders of the Panhandle, notwithstanding I still felt that I was going through the air.[48]

The initial story is enhanced by two related incidents—one near tragic. Shortly after Neff's flight, the West Texas newspapers carried a short item that F. W. Hinds, an aviator from Amarillo, and C. D. Boyd, a traveling salesman of Plainview, were thought to have been killed when the airplane in which they were flying plunged 800 feet to earth. Neff's letter to Ramsey indicated that he had seen the story and "was grieved to read several days ago that my pilot had an accident, probably fatal."[49] Although the local newspaper had reported that the pilot and passenger were probably mortally injured, the two actually escaped serious injuries.[50] Neff had taken a courageous step to get into the airplane—that mode of travel was very much still in its experimental stage. Neff's airplane ride was another illustration of the resoluteness with which he pursued his campaign—he was single-minded in his determination to sit in the governor's chair in 1921.

The second part of the story took place several years later and is memorable because it involved Pat Neff Jr. In 1924, Governor Neff wrote his son a letter of congratulations on his twenty-first birthday and presented him with a "grip" (suitcase) that the Waco Lodge of the Modern Woodmen of America had given him as a Christmas gift in 1904. Neff told his son that he had carried the suitcase with him on all his trips and "tied it to the wing of the flying machine in which I rode from Amarillo to Canyon during my first campaign for governor."[51]

Neff referred to his historic airplane flight many times during the remainder of the campaign, and in his remembrance of the race in his book, *The Battles of Peace*, he fondly recalled that "I used every means of transportation from a mule to a flying machine."[52] The half-mile mule ride occurred in East Texas when roads had overflowed after a downpour.

Neff's last trip in January was to Southeast Texas. On that trip, he spoke in Silsbee, San Augustine, Center, Liberty, Orange, Groves, Sour Lake, Newton, and Brookland.[53] In Orange, Neff said it was not right for Texas

> to sell a bale of cotton to New England for $150 and then buy it back in the form of cloth for $1,000. He decried Texas' system of selling steers to northern packers for $100 and then buying them back in tin cans for eight times that much. In further defending his argument for more and better industries for Texas, Pat Neff stated that the average man in Texas arose each morning from his Pennsylvania bed to the sound of an alarm clock made in New England, and put on his pants which were made in New York. He then washed his face with Massachusetts soap in a pan from Indiana, and at breakfast, the typical man sat down to eat a Michigan cereal, Chicago bacon, and flour manufactured in Kansas.[54]

Returning to Waco, Neff was greeted by the news that two other candidates had announced for governor. Dwight L. Lewelling, age forty, former district attorney in Dallas County and a two-term member of the Texas House of Representatives, threw his hat into the ring on February 2 as a supporter of President Wilson and a Prohibitionist. And Bailey, who had been rumored for weeks as a candidate on an anti-Wilson platform, made it official on February 18; Robert L. Henry thereupon withdrew in Bailey's favor and began to make speeches for him over the state.[55] Neff must have been somewhat concerned about Lewelling's announcement, since his similar stance on issues might pull some votes from Neff in the Dallas area. It was clear, however, that Bailey would become Neff's most formidable opponent, so Neff decided to challenge him early. On Saturday afternoon, February 21, Neff traveled the thirty miles to Hillsboro to make one of the major speeches of his campaign. The address became a front-page story in hundreds of Texas newspapers over the next week. As an estimated 500 supporters applauded and cheered frequently, Neff "handled . . . Bailey . . . without gloves." He began by claiming that

Bailey was "legally disqualified . . . to become governor of Texas" because he had lived in Washington, D.C., the past ten years and owned his home there. He went on to say that Bailey was "out of touch and sympathy with Texas institutions and enterprises." Warming up, Neff stated:

> Mr. Bailey does not stand affirmatively for any kind of constructive legislation. He is opposed to everything. . . . Mr. Bailey approves of the conduct of no living statesman, except himself. He works with his face to the past and his back to the future.
>
> Politically speaking, Mr. Bailey is satisfied with everything except the League of Nations, the national administration, the state administration, the Democratic Party, the president of the United States, Congress, the two senators, the eighteen congress-men, the state legislature, prohibition, woman's suffrage, and the enforcement of the prohibition law. Joe is highly pleased with himself.[56]

Neff proclaimed that Bailey had never sponsored any worthwhile legislation, but on the other hand, had been against the Panama Canal, the Federal Reserve Bank, the parcel post law, and the federal savings banks. Neff challenged him to discuss state issues.

Clearly, Bailey was also the one that supporters of President Wilson were worried about. The Prohibitionists were concerned that Bailey and his supporters would take over the State Democratic Convention in Dallas in late May and elect a slate of anti-Wilson men to the National Democratic Convention in San Francisco. Neff, Looney, and Thomason agreed to minimize their own campaigns until after the May conven-tions and concentrate on speeches supporting the national administration.[57]

There was one break in the "be nice" campaigning. Early in March, speaking from the chamber of the Texas House of Representatives in Austin, Thomason tore into Neff, stating, among other charges, that Neff had once represented Governor Colquitt in the so-called "chicken salad" case, that he was traveling on his cam-paign trips on free passes issued by the railroads, and that he was misrepresenting Thomason's votes on woman suffrage and Prohibition. Neff would respond later.

In April, Neff made a week-long swing of East and North Texas speaking in behalf of the present national administration. Driving himself, he spoke in eleven counties in one week.[58] He followed that trip with one to the north Central Texas area. His busiest day was April 21 in the Fort Worth area, where he spoke to an estimated total crowd of 6,000 people. He began at the packing houses at twelve noon, continued at the First Baptist Church, addressing a crowd of 3,500, then spoke at Arlington and finally at Mansfield that night.[59]

In May, Speaker R. Ewing Thomason's campaign swung into high gear. In the Lower Valley, he visited ten towns in a single day, most of them the same commu-nities that Neff had campaigned in earlier in the year. He spoke to an estimated crowd of 5,000 at the American Legion celebration at Donna.[60] Thomason was obviously gratified in mid-May to receive the warm endorsement of the *Houston Post.*[61] The editorial included many laudatory comments, and closed with an opinion shared by many other newspapers—anyone but Bailey. On May 30, the *Houston Chronicle* editorialized that either Neff or Thomason would be satisfactory—again, anyone but Bailey: "In the *Chronicle*'s opinion, one of the two [Neff or Thomason] will win, and no matter which, Texas will not lose."[62]

On May 22, Ben Looney formally opened his campaign in his home city of Greenville. The local paper indicated that he had been devoting the time before the State Democratic Convention to supporting the pro-administration faction of the party. That State Convention on May 25 proved to be a runaway for the Wilson forces.[63] The Texas delegation to the National Democratic Convention in San Francisco was committed to pushing William G. McAdoo for the presidency, but McAdoo faltered, withdrew from the race, was placed back in the race by his friends, and then lost the nomination to James M. Cox, who lost the November presidential election to Republican Warren G. Harding.

Neff was certainly pleased that the threat to the administration had been beaten down, but he was even more pleased that Dwight Lewelling of Dallas announced at the convention that he was withdrawing from the governor's race because of lack of financing and that he would be endorsing Neff.

During the campaign, Neff wrote to his mother at least once a week, keeping her informed of his progress and inquiring as to her health. On May 20, he wrote from a hotel in Eagle Lake: "Every now and then I run into some old time citizen who knew you in your early days. . . . I have never met one who knew you in your early days and enjoyed the hospitality of your home, but know many nice things to say about you. So thus you see that even then you were aiding me in my race for Governor."[64]

In June, with the Democratic Party machinery firmly in the hands of people friendly to the national administration, the governor's campaign concentrated more on state issues and the three "progressive" candidates intensified their campaigns. In early June, Bailey was confined to Washington, D.C., by business obligations and family troubles, but then, despite his defeat at the convention, he returned with new vigor to begin an anti-union campaign. Neff mapped out a back-breaking schedule for June and plunged into it with enthusiasm and vigor. To do so, he needed campaign contributions to supplement the personal funds he was putting into the race. On June 9, his campaign sent out hundreds of letters to prominent citizens throughout the state asking for extra contributions to help replenish Neff's fast-depleting financial resources. The solicitation was effective, resulting in a number of checks of varying amounts.[65] Neff first traveled to almost a dozen towns around and west of Abilene, then spent a week in a wide-ranging area of west Central Texas. At the end of fourteen days, Neff wrote a friend in Seymour that he had driven by car 1,700 miles, campaigning in twenty-six counties and making a total of fifty-two speeches.[66] Clyde Essex, reporter for the *Farm and Labor Journal,* accompanied Neff and did not enjoy the second week nearly as much. Under dateline of San Saba June 12, Essex reported:

> The Pat M. Neff Special rolled into this, the county seat of Mills County at about 10 o'clock after a cross-country run of some 55 miles from Hamilton. Some run, brother, believe me. The roads between Hamilton and Goldthwaite contain more curves than a corkscrew; pass over more little and big rocks and up and down more hills than any other road in any county in the state.[67]

The Abilene address on Friday, June 4, and the speech at Italy (Ellis County) on Tuesday, June 29, received major coverage. Neff bragged:

> Last July I announced myself for the office of Governor. I did not confer with anyone about it. I did not confer with any politicians in regard to my candidacy. I announced on my own responsibility and commenced taking my candidacy to the voters of Texas as never before by any candidate for Governor. . . .When I become your Governor next January, I will go in the office with no fetters on my feet and no muzzle on my mouth.

He closed, paraphrasing the words of the old gospel hymn "I Would Be True." This comparison undoubtedly resonated with the many Baptists in the audience:

> I promise to be honest for there are those in Texas who think me honest; I promise to be true for there are those who think me true; I promise to be strong, I promise to be brave. I shall serve and forget the serving. . . . I shall be humble; I will look forward and not backward, up and not down, out and not in. I will laugh and love and live as your Governor.[68]

Neff continued to stand with his land plank even though he was receiving more letters of criticism on this and on his riding on railroad passes than on any other issues. Many of the letters from West Texas begged him to scrap his land plank, and newspapers all over the state were also stating their opposition. In a major speech delivered in the chamber of the Texas House of Representatives in Austin on July 7, Neff made a long and impassioned plea, refuting several charges made against him by Thomason in the same chamber earlier in the campaign. Regarding the land plank, Neff amended his original statement by saying that the state should require "non-resident" owners of the large tracts to "either improve and cultivate their lands or make it unprofitable for them to hold it off the market for any length of time."[69] He went on to claim that his proposition was based on Governor James Stephen Hogg's stand when he ran for governor in 1892.

The problem about free passes on railroads for public officials began almost as early as railroads assumed their key role in the country's transportation. A noted railroad historian wrote that "such [free] transportation was beyond question given for the purpose of influencing legislation or the courts of justice."[70] Now, in 1920, one state representative wrote Dr. Brooks a three-page single-spaced typewritten letter, bitterly attacking Neff for his use of the passes during the campaign.[71] Several of Neff's friends wrote him that the issue was affecting his campaign negatively.[72] The subject remained one of controversy, but it did not stop Neff from utilizing the transportation for all of his family on several occasions.

As the race grew hotter with the weather, Neff realized that the land plank was the only part of his campaign platform that was getting much attention. The campaign was turning more and more negative. He also realized, with less than four weeks to election time, that it would be difficult to keep Bailey out of a runoff and that he needed to concentrate on getting one of the two runoff spots. Thomason was making a stronger race than Looney, so Neff began concentrating most of his fire on the El Paso legislator.

The Push for a Runoff Spot

President Brooks broke Baylor precedent one day in the spring to endorse Neff at the daily university chapel, which mandated student attendance. He said that Neff had been of great service to the school and urged the students to wear Neff buttons and to join the Baylor Neff Club.[73] It also became known that some Baptist churches were forgetting their neutrality—one church in Mineola had a prominent picture of Neff in its church bulletin, and it was charged that some Baptist ministers had pinned Neff buttons on their members' coats after services.[74]

The high point of the month came on June 25 and 26 when the *Brownsville Herald*, the *Houston Chronicle*, and numerous other papers reported that the Neff campaign had launched a bombast of oratory. Over a period of two days, 50,000 people had heard 300 speakers for Neff.[75] The idea was not new, of course. Statewide campaigns in earlier years had undertaken similar projects to reach out. The effort took an enormous amount of planning. The Neff headquarters began writing letters early in June. Target communities had to be selected, speakers secured, and the events publicized. The action required so many communications that the office resorted to form letters with all the wording pre-printed except the name of the speaker, his town, and the date of the speech.[76]

The all-out effort should have removed all doubt from anyone keeping up with the gubernatorial race that Neff was operating a full-time, professional campaign. Neff bragged throughout the campaign, including in his speeches in June at Abilene and Italy, that he had no campaign manager and still answered his own mail. He went on to say that two of the candidates had extensive space in Dallas hotels for their state headquarters.[77] He also often said that his headquarters was in his car. One time he even told an audience that his headquarters had two blowouts the day before on the road.

His headquarters was not in Dallas and not in a big hotel room, but there was indeed a headquarters in Waco located in his law office. Neff had said that he wrote all his own letters, and this was the case in 1919 and perhaps early into 1920, but by mid-spring with his traveling two to three weeks out of each month, he could not possibly reply to every piece of the mountain of correspondence coming in, asking for posters, speech commitments, campaign cards, buttons, and his stance on various issues. It would be physically impossible for one person to both travel the state extensively as Neff did and provide responses to those thousands of letters. As Neff traveled more and more in the last four months of the campaign, the letters increasingly came to be signed or written by George W. Barcus or Joseph W. Hale.[78]

Barcus, forty-six, was two years younger than Neff. A long-time trusted friend, Barcus had been admitted to the bar in 1898, served in the legislature two terms, worked as an early law partner of Neff's, left Waco, and then returned to open his own practice.[79] In 1919, Barcus agreed to help Neff in his campaign and he virtually gave up his own law work for the first eight months of 1920. Hale was only twenty-nine at the time, had received an undergraduate degree from Baylor, and then had read law in the offices of Neff and Walton Taylor. He was admitted to the bar in 1917 and was brought into the Neff law firm. Although Neff probably made most of the major decisions in the campaign, Barcus and Hale both qualify as Neff's campaign managers without doubt.

None of this is to take away from the unprecedented pace and coverage of the candidate's labors. In his essay on his campaign in *The Battles of Peace*, Neff boasted of visiting thirty-seven counties that no governor or candidate had ever seen.[80] His travels and speeches in June alone ranged from Seymour in the west to Tyler in the east, a distance of more than 250 miles, and to Beeville in South Texas, more than 300 miles from Tyler—all this in a Buick Roadster that was not immune to engine breakdowns and tire blowouts.

> I drove my car some six thousand miles, patched my own blowouts, pumped up my own tubes, and never but once went in on the rim. . . . Often during the campaign, I would drive my car a hundred miles in one day, and fill four or five speaking dates. . . . Undoubtedly I traveled more miles, visited more counties, made more speeches, shook hands with more people, and had more fun than any other person who had ever sought public office in Texas.[81]

The month of July was a rough one for all four candidates. Trouble started for Neff on the first day when an editorial in a small West Texas newspaper joined several other Bailey-leaning papers in impugning Neff's manhood. Bailey supporters had been running several cartoons picturing Neff in short pants. The *Quanah Observer* quoted Dr. Brooks as saying that Neff "has never shot a gun. He has never baited a fishhook. He has never touched tobacco in any form. He does not know one card from another and he cannot play any kind of social game."[82]

The newspaper went on to speculate that "Pattie wore lace on his nighties and was never known to be away from home after sundown." The editorial concluded that Neff would be better suited as a principal of an old maid's college.[83] To offset such editorials and cartoons, Neff's friends began to invite him to spend weekends with them in their lakeside cabins. There they purposely photographed him with a gun in his hands and a hunting dog at his feet. Frequently, they posed him baiting a hook beside a river or casting a line into a lake.[84]

Neff made a mass mailing on July 14 to supporters all over the state that must have cost several thousand dollars in printing and postage. The letter enclosed a complete round of Neff's latest campaign literature. The enclosures are not attached to the letter filed in the Neff Papers, but they must have weighed at least several ounces.[85]

Neff's decision to focus his attention on beating Thomason for the runoff spot with Bailey reflected good judgment. Thomason was competing intensely for the women's vote, and he had formidable help. Two of the leading suffragists in the state supported Thomason: Jessie Daniel Ames and Minnie Fisher Cunningham. Ames began writing a column on woman suffrage activities for the *Williamson County Sun* in 1916 and joined Cunningham in fighting for ratification of the Nineteenth Amendment giving women the right to vote. Cunningham, an East Texas teacher and pharmacist, had quit the latter job because of the inequity in her pay and had became a full-time activist for woman suffrage. She served as president of the Texas Woman Suffrage Association from 1915 to 1919 and lobbied Congress for adoption of the Nineteenth Amendment. When she saw that Joe Bailey was going to run for governor, she determined to take an active part in the 1920 campaign because Bailey had testified in Congress against the amendment. Cunningham found Neff to be more show than substance, a politician without a vision running on a platform of "glittering generalities." When Neff's opening campaign speech appeared in the newspapers, she went through it paragraph by paragraph, scribbling indignant comments in the margins: "bombast," "rhetoric," "old stuff."[86]

Ames fired another shot against Neff in a circular sent to a wide range of friends and other activists in June. In the circular, Ames cited Thomason's record on woman suffrage and Prohibition and criticized Neff's record on these two issues.[87] Although Cunningham and Thomason had many friends who followed their lead, these numbers paled beside the devoted believers in Neff and his record—and his advance work very early in the campaign. The Waco native had cultivated not only women in the Baptist Church and alumnae of Baylor but also wives of fraternal brothers as well as leaders in the Texas Federation of Women's Clubs, an influential group at that time. Neff began writing women active in the latter group in the fall of 1919.[88]

Neff brought his campaign to a close on the night before the primary election in his hometown of Waco. He claimed that he had spoken in 152 counties, making approximately 375 speeches.[89] The election on Saturday, July 24, failed to draw a heavy turnout. A total of 449,800 voters went to the polls, thousands fewer than Hobby had drawn in his race with Ferguson two years before. That race had brought out a total of 678,761 voters, 50 percent more than the 1920 race.[90] As the results came in, it was soon apparent that Bailey and Neff would be in a runoff, with Thomason trailing significantly and Looney polling poorly. The final results, however, were not compiled and published until more than two weeks after the election. The *Dallas Morning News* of Monday, August 9, carried the returns that were used subsequently in books and publications as the official returns. That final canvass showed Bailey with 152,340 or 33.9 percent of the vote, and a 2,522 plurality over Neff, who polled 149,818 or 33.3 percent. Thomason received 99,002 votes or 22 percent of the total, and Looney 48,640 or 10.8 percent. Bailey led in 81 counties, Neff in 111, Thomason in 48, and Looney in only 4.

Thomason was disappointed with the results. In his autobiography, he wrote that if Bailey had stayed out of the race he could have defeated Neff.[91] Although he was a highly regarded state official, he was undoubtedly hurt by being from El Paso. A Bailey supporter dismissed him one time by saying, "He's almost from Mexico." In spite of his geography and youthfulness, Thomason might have made the runoff except that during a crucial portion of the campaign, he was confined in Austin in a legislative session. Raymond Brooks, veteran Austin political writer, in a column penned in 1954, referred back to the 1920 election in discussing the 1954 gubernatorial race of the then speaker of the House, Reuben Senterfitt. Senterfitt bowed out of a race at that time because of a special session in March-April 1954. In making comparisons, Brooks wrote:

> Ewing Thomason, who was a candidate, would have been elected governor in 1920, according to those who recall that year's campaign, had not a May special election been called. The El Pasoan was considered well out in front on his way to nomination, when suddenly he was frozen in the Speaker's chair for a full 30 days, just in the crucial stages of the state race. Issues built up during the month that bypassed him. His campaign sagged, and never got up steam again. Pat Neff, the white-maned ex-speaker from Waco. . . came on to take the nomination and the office.[92]

The special session had been called by Governor Hobby to deal with a pink boll worm crisis and to a lesser extent a school funding problem. Thomason could ill afford to abandon his presiding role to campaign for governor and undoubtedly lost much of his momentum because of the session.

Looney's defeat was as devastating as Thomason's. Despite a successful six-year career as Texas Attorney General, his campaign never caught on with the voters. It would appear that he ran against three formidable opponents who simply left no room for a fourth candidate. Looney no doubt would have run well in a governor's race in other years, for he was an attractive candidate, but 1920 was not his year.

Runoff: Bailey Turns up the Heat

Overall, Neff was pleased with the primary results. He had finished fewer than 3,000 votes behind Bailey and he felt he could draw a substantial portion of the Thomason/Looney voters in the runoff on August 28. Endorsements by the latter two were not long in coming. As in the case of some of the leading newspapers like the *Houston Chronicle*, the *Houston Post*, and the *Dallas Morning News*, the endorsements by Thomason and Looney were as much or more a condemnation of Bailey as they were a recommendation of Neff. The *Fort Worth Star-Telegram* continued to back Bailey with strong editorials during the month of August. Among the unhappiest of voters were State of Texas employees. They noted that both Bailey and Neff called for slashing government payrolls and that meant hundreds of state employees would have to go job hunting shortly.[93]

Neff officially kicked off the runoff campaign at an August 2 meeting in Dallas, denouncing Bailey's Prohibition views and saying that no one who was not in favor of the total enforcement of the Prohibition law should be governor of the state. Bailey launched his runoff bid the following day in San Angelo, attacking Neff's labor stand and particularly his land plank. Although Bailey had earlier turned down Neff's challenge to debate, he agreed to a joint appearance in Coleman on August 4. Bailey spoke first, continued his assault on Neff's labor and land planks, and pleaded for the "return of old fashioned things."[94] Neff came on stage to a somewhat hostile crowd but managed to defuse several hecklers. In his speech, he accused Bailey of carrying a "water keg on his shoulder in North Texas and a beer keg in South Texas."[95]

Neff's family added its weight to the cause. Patsy Neff, Pat's sister-in-law, visiting her son Morris in Justiceburg (Garza County), wrote Isabella about the campaign sign Morris had ready for the front of his house: "If you are going to vote for Neff, to the water help yourself. If you are a Bailey man, just move on as fast as you can."[96] Morris had delivered the votes in the primary: Garza County gave Neff half again more votes than the other three candidates together. In the runoff, Neff swamped Bailey 405 to 171.

Looney made a logical argument to Neff that he could best help him where Looney himself had been strongest. Looney had carried four counties in the primary—his home county of Hunt, neighboring small counties of Raines and Rockwall, and sparsely settled Martin County in far West Texas.

But Neff had to face an assault on his personal life before he could rest. Only eight days before the runoff election August 28, Bailey launched a broadside which quickly became the biggest issue of the campaign—an attack centered on whether Neff had falsified his age and thus avoided registering for the draft in World War I. In an August 20 speech in Temple, Bailey produced a book printed during Neff's last term in the legislature that stated that Neff was born November 26, 1872. Bailey pointed out that if this were true, Neff, not having passed his forty-sixth birthday, had been within the age limit of those required to register. The crowd finally understood that, if true, this meant that Neff had avoided the draft and could be called a "slacker." Neff, speaking in Sherman that afternoon, received a message telling him of Bailey's charge and quickly branded it as a malicious falsehood. Emboldened by the possibilities of putting Neff on the defensive just a week before the election, the Bailey forces quickly sought out other directories, records, and books and just as quickly found numerous sources listing Neff's birth year as 1872.[97] Newspapers fanned the flames of a white-hot battle, and the Bailey headquarters immediately flooded the state with advertisements, some occupying an entire page, detailing the charges and citing their sources. Extremely concerned, Neff headquarters got in touch with his mother, asked her to check the family Bible, and then issued a notarized statement from her that the family Bible showed "Patty Morris Neff was born November 26, 1871." The family Bible was even placed on display for a short time in Dallas so that everyone could satisfy their questions.[98] The Bible was later placed in a bank vault to prevent its theft. Nevertheless, Neff did not help matters by remarking on more than one occasion that he was not sure when he was born.

As the runoff race reached a climax, Neff continued his whirlwind campaign across the state. Thinking back on the 1920 race thirty years later in a rare interview with a doctoral student at the University of Denver, he told the student:

> My tongue elected me Governor of Texas. Why, in that first campaign for Governor, I spoke over 800 times. I spoke in seven county seats in one day. I just went out and sold myself. . . . I got into my old Buick, and ran for office. . . . I was introduced in Leon County by some bewhiskered old gentleman who said I'd be the first candidate for governor to speak there since he heard Sam Houston speak there 65 years before.[99]

In writing his dissertation, the student also received a response to a query to James V. Allred, who served as governor from 1935 to 1939 and who in 1951 was serving as a federal district judge. In 1920, Allred was a twenty-one-year-old war veteran studying law in a Wichita Falls law office. Allred heard Neff one night and was so captivated that he resolved not only to vote for him but to actively work in his campaign. Allred said Neff's face depicted dignity and character. "His voice was vibrant—there was nothing stereotyped about it. . . . Somehow, it seemed that he was soliciting my support alone."[100]

Reminiscing about his style of campaigning in his *Battles of Peace* book after his governorship, Neff validated Allred's feeling of receiving individual attention:

> I stopped at all blacksmith shops and cross-roads stores to exchange greetings with those thereabout. At these places one meets real folks: people who think straight and vote right. When I campaigned in a small town without a speaking date as I frequently did, I made it a practice to shake hands with every person I could find, never skipping the man handling bacon in the back of the store, or the carpenter building a shack in the alley.[101]

As the runoff campaign wound down, Thomason delivered his support as he had promised.[102] The last days also brought word that Governor Hobby had issued a press release stating that he would vote for Neff on Saturday, and United States Senator Morris Sheppard was coming home on the weekend to cast his ballot for the Waco native. Congressman Tom Connally had already announced his support early in the campaign.

The election on Saturday brought Neff a clear victory with 264,075 votes to Bailey's 184,702. Neff's majority of 79,373 reflected his securing almost 59 percent of the total vote to a little over 41 percent for Bailey. The total vote of 448,777 was about 1,000 fewer than the total vote in the primary. In the runoff, Neff carried 192 counties and Bailey 49, for a total of 241 counties reporting results.[103]

The victory in the runoff was a source of delight and relief to the Democratic Party faithful, from President Wilson, to the great majority of the Texas Congressional Delegation, to the thousands of progressive Democrats in the state. Bailey was doubly chagrined that his own city of Gainesville and Cooke County had gone against him (2,189 to 1,744) whereas McLennan County had given Neff a big margin (5,805 to 3,822). Bailey's biographer, newsman Sam Hanna Acheson, wrote: "The blow fell heavily on Bailey. . . . At fifty-seven years of age, still a comparatively young man, this first and complete repudiation at the hands of his own people aged him twenty years at one stroke."[104] Bailey's defeat was in fact a repudiation of the Old South he had represented. Walter L. Buenger wrote that women had done much to kill the Confederate myth, "especially when it was used to attack an active government and woman suffrage."[105] Opposing a strong federal government was no longer the popular stand as Texans came to feel more a part of a progressive Southwest and increasingly welcomed a partnership with Washington in overcoming the challenges of a new decade.

Neff's tremendous base of friends and supporters statewide paid off. Apparently he knew men—and women—in every nook and cranny of the state. Friends and acquaintances from all walks of life supported him. He had initially built up a reservoir of good will as Speaker of the Texas House of Representatives, strengthened it in his six years as a highly effective prosecutor, and matured it during his seven years in private practice as he went from one end of the state to the other representing clients. Through all those twenty years, his activities in the Knights of Pythias, in the Modern Woodmen of America, and especially at Baylor and in the Baptist Church, earned for him such a solid reputation that none of the stories told by Bailey and his lieutenants about his age discrepancy or any other failing really caught on with the voters. By 1920, Neff had accumulated what would later be called in politics a Teflon image, that is, an image to which a story of malfeasance or deceit would simply not "stick." Neff was fortunate that this was the case; a lesser man might well have been brought down by the tale of his age discrepancy, by his legal representation of several persons in what some saw as questionable circumstances, and by his use of free railroad passes.

No question it was a dirty campaign. The 1918 Hobby-Ferguson contest had been a very bitter one, but the 1920 race reached new lows. Although Neff, Thomason, and Looney started their campaigns on a positive note, Bailey was castigating President Wilson and the Democratic Party from the very beginning. As the race developed, even Neff and Thomason swapped charges and counter-charges, and in the runoff Neff and Bailey spared no invective. Neff called Bailey a "coward" and an "unmitigated liar."[106] Bailey accused Neff of being a "war slacker" and more.[107] The battle did nothing to enhance the reputation of either, and the negative tone of the race may have contributed to the smaller turnout of voters in both the primary and the runoff elections.

Although campaign expenditure reports did not reflect it, the race and the two elections were also very expensive. The first Texas law limiting campaign expenditures in a state election went into effect June 18, 1919, and thus the 1920 state and district races were the first to be affected by its terms.[108] The first attempt in Texas at what would become a recurring challenge into the twenty-first century was, as might be expected, convoluted and poorly drawn. The law did not take into account runoff elections, and it did not even speak to the general election in the fall. Furthermore, the law mandated separate reports by a candidate and his campaign manager. Each candidate filed a sworn statement that they had spent less than $10,000, the legal limit.[109] But because the confusing law had required no standard reporting format, expense reports defied accurate, simple arithmetic. An analysis of the expenditure reports reveals wide discrepancies. More than correct addition, however, it strains credibility to believe that any of the reports were comprehensive renditions of the money actually spent on the campaign. The tremendous amount of newspaper advertising compounds doubts of accuracy. By comparison, Governor Hobby—just one candidate—in 1918 reported contributions of more than $80,000, all of which was spent. His statement, after he defeated Ferguson, said in part: "The cost of the campaign, in my judgment, is less than any other successful campaign in very recent years in the state."[110]

Neff himself paid dozens of newspapers to reproduce his opening speech of December 6 and include it as a supplement in their publications.[111] Immediately following his speech attacking Thomason in the chamber of the House of Representatives in Austin, he wrote one of his key San Antonio supporters: "Our supply of buttons is exhausted [but] we have already sent you a liberal supply of large posters, and approximately four thousand small cards. We also sent you yesterday, fifteen hundred copies of the Austin speech. . . .We are also sending you an additional six thousand small cards."[112] From Neff headquarters, George Barcus told one East Texas supporter that he could raise and spend any amount he wanted to because he had not been designated as an assistant county manager who was required to report.[113] It is highly unlikely that the reports submitted were anything close to accurate or complete.

Readying to Take Over

Three weeks later, Neff went to Fort Worth to the State Democratic Convention, arriving there Monday morning, September 6. His family—Myrtie, Hallie Maude, and Pat Jr.—joined him Tuesday. The family members were basking in the afterglow of Neff's tremendous victory, and they were expansive and talkative to a reporter covering the convention.

The reporter spent some time describing Myrtie: "Mrs. Neff is woman of medium height with blue-gray eyes and light brown hair. She is modest and retiring with a charming, gracious personality. . . . Very quietly and thoroughly she campaigned for her husband in her home county [Houston] and carried it by a surprising majority [1,376 to 638]." Hallie Maude told the reporter: "She [Myrtie] hasn't been feeling well lately and just stays around home, always fixing things and working in the garden. We have a big garden and Mother's flowers are just beautiful. She belongs to a couple of literary clubs in Waco and is interested in church work. . . . Mother believes in suffrage good and strong, but she never was militant."[114]

The business of the convention proceeded relatively smoothly. Thomason had let it be known ahead of time that although he supported Neff strongly, he was dead set against Neff's land plank and notified all concerned that he would fight its inclusion in the party platform. Neff did not want to start his duties with a squabble and in a public statement at the beginning of the convention stated that the entire platform would be left up to the delegates and that he would not dictate any part of it. In his acceptance speech, Neff pledged: "I do not expect to be a meteor across the political sky of Texas, but I do intend, by hard faithful work, to try to render you some real service. I intend to be a steady-working plow horse; maybe not so much show and speed, but in the end, I believe by long, hard, faithful work, I can show you something done."[115]

And now the Democratic nominee for governor was ready for some rest and relaxation. Traveling on passes from the International and Great Northern Railroad, which he had represented for many years, he and the two children boarded a train the following Sunday for a ten-day trip to New York, but not before penning his mother his devotion: "The Convention directed that you be sent a telegram of good cheer. Your name was frequently mentioned. I am proud of my nomination for your sake. The people properly so give you much credit for raising me."[116] In his letter, he added that "Myrtie will stay at Mineral Wells while we are gone." This time, she stayed almost a month.[117] In October, Mother Neff had begun to worry about a new wheelchair. It is unclear in her letter of October 1 to Neff as to whether she was talking about one that would be suitable for her current home or was hinting at one suitable for use in the Governor's Mansion. Neff committed the next day to having her at the mansion, and the question became moot.[118] There are no files to indicate whether or not Neff talked with Myrtie about his mother's new abode.

In a thoroughly Democratic state, the Democratic primaries were tantamount to election; thus Neff and the electorate paid scant attention to the November 2 general election. In that election, Neff had four opponents, with the major opposition split between the Republican nominee, John G. Culbertson, and that of the American Party, T. H. McGregor. A Black and Tan Party candidate (H. Capers, nominee) and a Socialist Party candidate (L. L. Rhodes) completed the lineup. The election turned out as expected. Neff received 289,188 votes, or 60 percent. Culbertson was second with 90,217 votes (18.7 percent), McGregor was third with 69,380 (14.4 percent), and Capers and Rhodes drew a total of 6.9 percent. Neff led in 228 counties, Culbertson in 5, and McGregor in 13.[119] Neff thus officially joined Richard Coke and Sul Ross and became the third chief executive of the state from Waco.

On November 26, Neff and Governor Hobby left for Mexico to attend the inauguration of President-Elect Alvaro Obregon. Neff wrote his mother that he was taking the ten-day trip as the guest of the Laredo Chamber of Commerce with all his expenses paid.[120]

Meanwhile, other preparations for assuming the governor's office were moving along—but not without some hitches. The question of the inaugural ball for 1921 began on November 15, 1920, when J. L. Peeler, an attorney in Austin, wrote Neff: "Since the days of Sam Houston, the citizens of Austin have given an Inaugural Ball and Reception to each new governor and we do not intend to now abandon this honored custom. . . . If you or Mrs. Neff have any suggestions do not hesitate to make them. . . . Please send us a list of the names and addresses of the persons to whom you desire invitations mailed."[121] Neff immediately replied to Peeler that he was neither a participant nor defender of "the dance" and suggested an informal reception instead. It took another exchange of letters, but Peeler finally got the message and the planners proceeded with only a reception—no ball at either the Capitol or the Driskill Hotel. Neff's stand, which had been made public, brought hearty approval from more than thirty letter-writers, along with resolutions of support from church groups and a laudatory editorial from the *Baptist Standard*.[122]

Finally, Neff's family was getting ready for the big event in January. Neff wrote that he was expecting his sister Sallie to attend his inauguration: "Tell her to get a dress and stick a new feather in her hat and be ready."[123] His mother was all a dither. As she grew older, she was not above manipulating her youngest son a bit. Writing from Brownwood in late December, where she was visiting Sallie, she told him:

> I cannot even imagine how I am to get to your inauguration. . . . How can I fix to go? Away out here, in the middle of the ocean (as it seems) without chart or compass. Do hope I will hear from you today. If I only get an envelope addressed in your own hand and only the one sweet little word 'Pat' in it, I kiss my Baby's name and rock on in silence.[124]

In early January, she wrote him again about coming to the inauguration, concluding with the question: "Do you expect me to stay with you or do I have to come back with Sallie?"[125] The mother must have forgotten Neff's commitment to her just three months earlier, but Neff had not. Myrtie may have been the First Lady-Elect, but for the next few months at least, the First Mother-Elect would outrank her.

CHAPTER 6

Fussin' and Feudin':
First Gubernatorial Term, 1921-1923

I work about eighteen hours each day, but do as
I please the rest of the time.

—Governor Pat Neff

When Neff assumed the governor's office on January 18, 1921, Texans had every reason to believe the coming legislative session would be harmonious and productive. The *Dallas Morning News*, generally recognized for its astute political reporting, headlined its January 16 story about the new administration in Austin, HARMONY IN NEFF REGIME EXPECTED.

Even the most knowledgeable political observers failed to note the inherent differences between the handsome, erudite new governor and the mostly unschooled legislators. Neff was a strong Prohibitionist, and many of the legislators believed hard drink their due reward after a hard day's work and professed little interest in enforcing Prohibition. Moreover, many of the Senate and House members had supported Joe Bailey or Ewing Thomason and were still smarting over the vicious campaigning before the summer primary and runoff election.

As a prosecutor, Neff had been successful with juries composed of these types of individuals by playing to their prejudices, but Neff the governor seemed to have lost this knack, and the feuding between Neff and the legislature began almost at once.

Inauguration

Neff, sitting at home in Waco the day before the inauguration, could not foresee the difficult times he would have. Boarding a train that afternoon with Myrtie and Pat Jr., they arrived in Austin in the evening, joining Hallie Maude, who was already there, and went to the Driskill Hotel for the night. Inauguration Day began for the Texas Governor-Elect with breakfast in the company of the Mexican delegation and the Laredo Chamber of Commerce. Then it was time for the traditional parade up Congress Avenue to the Capitol, where Neff saluted "his band," the 142nd Infantry Regiment Band from Brownwood, lovingly called the "Old Gray Mare Band." General Perez Treviño, Mexico President Alvaro Obregon's official representative, joined Neff in the parade up Congress Avenue and took a seat of honor with him on the platform in the House of Representatives, where the inauguration ceremonies were held. Mother Neff, in her ninety-first year, sat in an honored seat at the front of the hall. Neff "kissed her tenderly as he walked past her on his way to the platform."[1] After Neff took the oath of office, Governor Hobby praised Neff as "one whose eyes turn to progress, and whose every pulse beat as a native son throbs for the unselfish glory of the Lone Star State."[2]

Then Neff, summoning his most eloquent oratory, articulated his vision:

> While the solemn oath of office is fresh on my lips, I wish to plight anew my love and loyalty to my native state and pledge to her my unselfish service. Born and reared on Texas soil, educated and trained in her institutions, honored beyond measure by her people, proud that her sacred soil shall at last entomb my ashes, I am ready to give my very best to her upbuilding.[3]

And so with Neff's solemn oath of office, Tom Connally's 1916 wishes were fulfilled—he was in Washington and Neff was in the governor's chair, and never would they compete in a political election.

That night, 12,000 surging, pushing people challenged the Capitol spaces and halls to the limit. Neff's call for a reception open to all instead of the traditional inaugural ball, along with the presence of the Mexican delegation with its "uniforms of brilliant color and the famed Mexican orchestra,"[4] drew an unusually large crowd. The Mexican orchestra played from an improvised platform in the House of Representatives, the University of Texas band played in the rotunda, and the Austin Majestic Theater orchestra was stationed on the rostrum of the Senate.

Neff became the fourteenth Governor of Texas since Reconstruction. He was the fourth Baptist versus eight who claimed Methodist affiliation; one Presbyterian and one Episcopalian completed the group. He was the twelfth lawyer of the fourteen and the first graduate of the University of Texas to claim the office. Three of his predecessors, including William P. Hobby, were thirty-nine years old when they were elected. Oran M. Roberts was sixty-three. Several had been in their late fifties. Neff's age of barely forty-nine placed him in the middle of the group agewise. The majority of the earlier governors were in elective office at the time of their election—two each as attorneys general, lieutenant governors, and members of the U.S. House of Representatives.[5] Although less experienced, Neff's six years in the Texas House and six years as prosecuting attorney gave him both state and local as well as legislative and judicial training. He was rated by most observers as being fit in every way for the responsibilities of the post-World War I era.

The morning after the inauguration, Neff, sitting behind the massive walnut desk first used by one of his heroes, James Stephen Hogg, would surely have contemplated the months ahead and those just past. In his opening campaign speech in December 1919, he had barely mentioned law enforcement and had even stated that Prohibition was an "issue of the past." Now, he was faced with the fact this was not true. Most of his Baptist brethren still believed in Prohibition, but were they as intent as he in enforcing the laws against the Demon Rum? Neff could count, and he knew that the state constitutional amendment outlawing liquor in Texas in 1919 had been favored by a mere 53 percent. Forty-four counties, almost 20 percent, had voted against the amendment.[6] But Neff knew where his mother stood on Prohibition and he himself would not waver in vigorous enforcement of the ban against liquor.

Another of Neff's post-election concerns would be the bulging file boxes of letters he had received immediately after the runoff election from people begging for jobs in the new administration. Where was he to find jobs for these people? He had also made campaign promises to equalize and reduce taxes, but what would that do to state services? Texas was growing in population: a 20 percent increase between 1910 and 1920 when 4.5 million Texans kept the state as the fifth most populous in the country. Also confronting the new governor were such challenges as finding better pay for school teachers and cleaning up the disreputable practices of mismanagement and abuse in the state penitentiaries. Yes, the campaign was over and Neff had much to do.

Neff was returning to a capital city, described much later by Lyndon Johnson biographer Robert Caro and others as the city of the "Three B's" (beefsteak, bourbon, and blondes). Caro wrote that as late as 1929, "Congress Avenue was still lined with bars and whorehouses at which lobbyists maintained charge accounts for cooperative legislators."[7] Austin's population in the 1920 census had actually fallen behind that of several other Texas cities. Although the city increased from 29,860 in 1910, seventh largest in the state, to 34,876 in 1920, three other cities leapfrogged it and pushed Austin to tenth place. Waco, Beaumont, and Wichita Falls all surpassed Austin, whose economy consisted of government and the university and little else.[8]

Assuming command of the state government, Neff found that as of December 1920, the state had 4,433 persons on the state payroll, including colleges and universities, but not including the prison system and the Texas National Guard.[9] About the same time, the University of Texas had a total income from all sources of $1,476,000. Of that amount, $839,000, or some 57 percent, came from legislative appropriations.

The great majority of state officials originally housed in the Capitol were still in their assigned Capitol offices when Neff took the oath of office. What would become known as the "Capitol Complex" consisted, in 1921, of only the Capitol and two state buildings—the General Land Office Building, just southeast of the Capitol, and a state office building at the southeast corner of Brazos and East Eleventh Streets. The second state office building was authorized by the legislature in 1917 in response to the need for a new Land Office and to alleviate the crowded conditions in the Capitol. The old Land Office Building was turned over to the Daughters of the Republic of Texas and the United Daughters of Texas for their archival collections.[10] Only five state agencies and the eleemosynary institutions were housed away from the Capitol when Neff took office.

The governor and his staff occupied the same space originally assigned to the chief executive by the Capitol architect, Elijah E. Myers of Detroit. The original design emphasized the importance of the chief executive's office. The governor's public reception room on the second floor had a sweeping view down Congress Avenue stretching southward toward San Antonio. From the beginning, the Governor's Office, as a totality, occupied space on both the first and second floors, as it continues to do into the twenty-first century. The two small rooms on the second floor were used for conferences. Until Governor James V. Allred moved upstairs in 1935, governors, including Neff, used the first floor rooms as their personal office. The governor's stenographic pool and his file clerk worked in the "Governor's Business Office" on the first floor just to the north of the governor's rooms.[11]

Thirty-seventh Legislature Tackles the Challenges

The legislature had been in session for a week when Neff was sworn in. Both houses had many new members, 14 of 31 in the Senate and 80 of 142 in the House. Denton County businessman Charles G. Thomas was elected speaker. The lieutenant governor after January 18 was wealthy Houston lumberman Lynch Davidson. In the Senate, lawyers dominated. The roster included several individuals who would be heard from in other venues in the future. Another Davidson, Senator T. W. Davidson, would become lieutenant governor in Neff's second term and would later be appointed a U.S. district judge and serve on the federal bench for more than thirty years. Senator R. M. Dudley, an El Paso banker, was elected mayor of El Paso in 1923 in a bitter campaign in which he campaigned against the Ku Klux Klan. He was reelected without opposition and sworn in April 16, 1925, only to die two weeks later after a surgical procedure.[12] Senator Edgar E. Witt of Waco served in the Senate until 1930, at which time he was elected lieutenant governor for two terms, then ran for governor and was defeated by James V. Allred in 1934.[13]

One of Neff's chief nemeses in the Senate should be noted—Archer (Archie) Parr, the longtime political boss of Duval County. Parr utilized a variety of circumstances in the South Texas county to control the Hispanic vote over an extended period through a combination of paternalism, corruption, and coercion. Elected to the Senate in 1914, Parr served until 1934; in 1919, he was almost forced out, but the Senate voted 16 to 14 to uphold his election despite continued charges of election fraud and manipulation.[14]

Few young people served in the House in 1921. The group did include men who would be a part of Neff's life for more than just the four years of his governorship. Two of them were Wright Patman and Sam Ealy Johnson. Neff later appointed Patman to a district attorney position in East Texas, after which he went on to a forty-seven-year career in the U.S. Congress. Johnson, father of President Lyndon B. Johnson, was a veteran state legislator, having already served four terms, including the two immediately preceding Neff's election.

One of the few privileges of the Texas Governor was the appointment of numerous state officials, the great majority being nonpaid positions. One of Neff's early nominations to the Senate for a paid position was Dr. M. M. Carrick of Dallas as state health officer. Dr. Carrick, a medical doctor, wasted no time making his mark in a nonmedical field by ordering that "paint, powder, and lipstick were taboo" in his offices and that bobbed hair for his female employees was looked upon with disfavor. According to the *Austin American* of February 16, other agency heads followed Dr. Carrick's edicts.

Neff's final round of appointments during the early part of the legislative session came February 16 with the appointment of three state highway commissioners and three new livestock sanitary commissioners. His most notable appointment of the six was D. K. "Dock" Martin of Itasca to the Highway Commission. Martin became a lifelong friend of Neff's and one of his strongest supporters on the Baylor University Board of Trustees when Neff was president of that institution. All of Neff's 1921 appointments were confirmed.[15]

Neff was accustomed to operating by himself and in his political races liked to boast that he had no campaign manager. He was not comfortable delegating tasks, a problem for him in all his dealings. The ranking staff individual in his governor's office was the governor's private secretary or officially titled the "Secretary to the Governor," a position paying a low salary and having none of the influence the governor's chief of staff would have later. Neff had no representative "working the floor" of the Senate and House. This was a problem for him during the legislative session.

For secretary to the governor, Neff turned to Nacogdoches County District Clerk R. B. Walthall, a friend, but not one to play a major role in substantive decisions. Walthall's salary was set in the appropriation bill at $229.16 per month. To serve as assistant secretary to the governor, actually the governor's top secretarial position, Neff brought Espa Stanford with him from Waco and paid her $150 monthly. A corps of four stenographers were paid $125 each per month.[16] Even in those times these were bare-bones wages.

Governor's appointments in Texas were few in number compared to those in many other states. During Reconstruction days, there had been such strong governorships that a backlash led the makers of the 1876 Constitution to severely restrict the governor's powers, including appointments. Also, low state salaries forced several persons whom Neff wanted to appoint to turn down his offers.[17]

Neff's first substantive act as governor was to ask for the resignations of the members of the State Board of Pardon Advisors as well as all that board's employees. He personally took over the processing of applications for pardons and paroles and announced none would be considered without a recommendation from the district judge who had presided at the inmate's trial.[18] This was his way of dealing with what he believed was a mockery of the law by Governor Jim Ferguson, and to some extent Governor Hobby, in granting too many pardons. He often said he had been told the Fergusons pardoned three convicts each day. Several newspapers criticized Neff for his tough stand, but he was unrelenting throughout his four years as governor.

The next most frequent theme in his administration was law enforcement, translated into "local officers enforce the Prohibition laws or be fired." He also wanted repeal of the suspended sentence law and a tighter law on concurrent sentences.

Both in his campaigning and in office, Neff stated his other priorities to be eliminating "waste and duplication in state government" and cleaning up the penitentiaries. His first of four messages in an eleven-day period (January 28 to February 7) to the legislature targeted government economy, efficiency, and reorganization. He named half a dozen state agencies that should be either abolished or combined with others, and declared that at least $100,000 could be saved by operating efficiently.[19] His first message called for merging the Warehouse and Marketing Department into the Department of Agriculture, the Dairy and Food Department into the State Health Department, the Tax Commissioner and the State Tax Board into the Comptroller's Office, and the Mining Board and Mine Inspector into the Labor Department. In addition, he wanted to abolish the Industrial Welfare Commission.[20]

The general thrust of Neff's economy messages was highly popular with the people. His files contain numerous letters from businessmen and ordinary citizens lauding him for his stance. His message drew a highly complimentary editorial in the *Houston Chronicle* that offered the opinion that "Governor Neff's message will not fail to harmonize with public opinion."[21] The *Dallas Morning News* was not as kind. In an editorial three days later, the *News* called his address "somewhat divagatious" (straying from a subject), chided him for not naming names of superfluous agencies, and doubted whether "there were more than two or three which any considerable number of people would pronounce useless."[22] Despite the legislators' general agreement with Neff, the only reorganization approved in the regular session was for the Dairy and Food Department to be absorbed by the State Health Department, signed into law by Neff on February 18, and the abolition of the Industrial Welfare Commission, signed after the session adjourned.[23]

On February 1 and 3, Neff delivered, by messenger, recommendations on law enforcement. He had received numerous letters charging lax law enforcement in many communities. One of the most alarming, four typewritten pages, came from a Del Rio lawyer who wrote that more saloons were being opened and "booze" was being smuggled across the Rio Grande. The letter writer went on to say that in the recent campaign his group had offered a candidate for sheriff who pledged to enforce all the laws, but that the person elected, if not corrupt, was "fat and lazy." The letter writer said one of the Rangers assigned to Del Rio was discharged for bootlegging and that the Ranger captain had done nothing to "interfere in the least with this traffic."[24] This letter was typical.

Incensed, Neff wrote his first law enforcement message to the legislature on February 1, stating that "a wave of crime . . . [is] sweeping over Texas." Offering four recommendations, he first sought the outright repeal of the suspended sentence law. He lamented that an average of 1,000 sentences each year were suspended without the culprit's being incarcerated. Second, the governor expressed concern that certain local officials were "corruptly" standing in the way of enforcement and recommended that "such officers should be speedily removed from office." Next he asked that the Dean Law (the state Prohibition law) be amended to provide a more effective trial of violators by allowing the liquor buyer to testify in court against the seller. Finally, he told the legislators that prosecuting attorneys should not be permitted to let a defendant charged with a number of violations to plead guilty and serve all sentences concurrently.[25]

The officer removal bill was introduced in the House on February 4 and a week later had an unfavorable report. Local law enforcement officials (police and prosecuting attorneys) had begun worrying about the possibility of such a bill's being enacted and contacted friends to oppose Neff's initiative.

The change in the Dean Law to allow the uncorroborated testimony of an accomplice or purchaser of liquor to be sufficient to obtain conviction had been introduced early in the session, and the *Houston Post* had been among those calling for the Prohibition law to be more rigidly enforced. But on February 22, the House had narrowly (61-59) killed the bill, setting off a tirade by Governor Neff. He wrote an impassioned rebuttal in a press release on February 24. The *Dallas Morning News* on its front page the next day headlined: NEFF SAYS VICTORY WON BY BOOTLEGGER. The following day, February 26, another *Dallas Morning News* front-page story headlined: NEFF'S BREAK WITH HOUSE THREATENED. The story's lead read: "What is regarded as an open break between Governor Neff and the House of Representatives came to pass this afternoon when the House voted to print in the Journal the personal privilege speech of Representative Sid Crumpton." The House also voted to print Neff's comments, this by a vote of 110 to 8. The newspapers stayed with the governor on this issue. The *San Antonio Express* on March 2 editorialized that "the survival of the Republic rests on those who stand for law and order."

Neff's break with the legislature had begun February 18, only a month after his inauguration, when he vetoed a bill repealing the 50 percent tax on pistol sales, stating that the bill would increase crime. The Senate overrode his veto, but the House, with many members sympathetic to an override, nevertheless finally sustained the governor's veto by a 71-43 margin. The next embroilment came a few days later over the Dean Law amendment. On February 26, the *Austin American* began a story with this headline: WAR AGAINST GOV. NEFF PLANNED BY LEGISLATORS IS REPORT AT CAPITOL. Just before the end of the regular session in March, an *American* editorial stated: "We have faith in Governor Neff. . . . [W]e are willing to admit that Governor Neff has made mistakes . . . [and] Governor Neff has been unwise in scolding the Legislature. . . . But, on the whole, Governor Neff is *proving* himself to be a capable and efficient administrator."[26]

Neff was also caught in a firestorm early in his tenure about the location of the University of Texas campus. George Washington Brackenridge of San Antonio had deeded an expansive tract of land on the banks of the Colorado stretching eastward from what would be the Tom Miller Dam. The University of Texas Board of Regents had petitioned Governor Hobby, just before he left office, to move the university from what were already cramped quarters north of the Capitol to the new site. The plan went awry in February. Twenty-eight House members signed a resolution calling for a statewide election to determine the permanent location of the University of Texas. Senator J. C. McNealus of Dallas stepped in, proposing that the university be moved to a location between Dallas and Fort Worth. Representative Lee Satterwhite, who had favored the Brackenridge tract, felt he had to keep the university in Austin, so he asked University of Texas President Robert E. Vinson to provide information about how much additional land would be needed at the present site for an adequate campus. This was delivered and the legislature passed an appropriation bill of $1.5 million to allow expansion of the existing campus. Neff signed the bill to the cheers of Austin business and civic leaders.[27]

Along with other issues during his first term, Neff could not avoid addressing the continuing penitentiary crisis that had plagued every chief executive since statehood and even before. On February 3, responding to allegations of mismanagement and mistreatment of prisoners in the system, the governor delivered a message to the legislature asking for a penitentiary investigating committee composed of three to five "intelligent, honest citizens, not holding public office."[28] The legislature ignored his recommendation and set up a committee composed entirely of legislators. After a series of hearings and visits to Huntsville and prison farms, the committee issued a brief report on the last day of the regular session, March 12, concluding, "We find nothing in the entire system in any department to commend the penitentiary system."[29] The committee promised a detailed report ready for the special session of the legislature whenever it was called.

The regular session was called a "murderous Legislature" by one of its members.[30] While 742 bills had been introduced by mid-February, fewer than 30 passed, and none was of statewide importance.[31] On the last day of the session, Lieutenant

Governor Davidson said the state was "law-ridden" and that "no great piece of constructive legislation was passed."[32]

Both major and minor bills failed to survive a negatively oriented legislature whose members agreed with the lieutenant governor. The legislature also nixed the calling of a constitutional convention to simplify the state constitution. Neff called on opinion leaders, such as representatives of the state's four leading newspapers, and political leaders, including former Governor Campbell, for their opinions about a constitutional convention. The *Houston Chronicle* editorialized for such a convention, but others suggested such an effort should wait for calmer times.[33] A concurrent resolution for revising the constitution was introduced, but went nowhere, dying in the do-nothing epidemic that also killed congressional and legislative redistricting, tax reform, an amendment on home ownership that had been favored by a former governor, a revision of the Medical Practice Act, and a proposal to construct apartment buildings on the Capitol grounds for legislators.[34] Most of the bills passed were local in nature, or of limited scope. One successful bill provided for the organization of cooperative marketing associations, permitting such associations to make contracts for marketing agricultural products.[35] Two new counties were added: Kenedy County was created by legislative action, and Hockley County, previously attached to Lubbock County, was formally organized without legislative action. The two new counties put the statewide total at 251.[36]

During the regular session, Neff vetoed twenty-one bills plus some line items in an emergency appropriation bill for the state agencies. In addition to the pistol bill, he vetoed a $300,000 appropriation for establishing and maintaining a state tuberculosis sanatorium for Negroes.[37] He argued that the state already operated one such sanatorium and that, if a hospital were to be built for Negroes, it should be located adjacent to the existing facility so as to utilize the central plant and equipment of the existing installation. He also vetoed a bill appropriating $400,000 for wolf scalps.[38] Neff vetoed sixteen other bills, most of them relatively unimportant.[39] Three vetoes, however, caused shockwaves. The most controversial was his veto of $50,000 to launch West Texas Agricultural and Mechanical College at a site to be determined. In his veto message, Neff first cited the rejection by the State Democratic Convention in its meeting the previous September of a resolution recommending the establishment of the college. He stated that he had pledged to abide by the dictates of the Democratic Party and felt that any contrary action on his part "would be fundamentally wrong."[40] The veto produced a firestorm in West Texas. A mass meeting of some 5,000 citizens April 2 in Sweetwater angrily denounced Neff and the legislature and threatened to secede from the rest of the state. The *San Antonio Express* the next day ran the headline: NEFF VETO REVIVES OLD MOVE TO DIVIDE TEXAS. After a few days, cooler heads prevailed as the West Texas Chamber of Commerce officials moved to quiet the storm.[41]

A second veto cut off $4 million appropriated by the legislature for rural school aid. At the same time, Neff approved $3 million to supplement the Available School Fund for the fiscal year ending August 31, 1922. Neff's reasoning revolved around the money that he estimated might reasonably be available for all purposes during the coming year. Several of the state's dailies, including the *Houston Post*, decried the veto of the rural school appropriation, the *Post* even supporting a possible temporary tax increase of six cents per year.[42]

Neff's third veto of note left the state without any minimum wage legislation of any kind. In his veto proclamation, he cited several reasons for vetoing the bill, one of which was that he considered it to be "class legislation," penalizing certain classes of workers, and therefore unconstitutional.[43]

Because the regular session failed to pass the necessary appropriation bills to operate state government and institutions during the forthcoming biennium, a special session would have to be called later for this purpose. This was not uncommon, particularly in light of the fact that the regular session lasted only sixty days at that time.

As governor, Neff continued to be a slave to detail and hard work. His work days were long and arduous, made so by his apparent determination against delegating any authority. In a letter to a friend in Dallas in March, he claimed to have 1,000 unanswered letters on his desk.[44] In a letter to a cousin in Houston, he reported: "We are well at this end of the line. Nothing out of the ordinary is happening. I work about eighteen hours each day, but do as I please the rest of the time."[45] He bragged in speeches about signing his name 200 times a day, and another time reported that he had personally signed 1,500 souvenir postcards to boys and girls attending the Interscholastic League meet in Austin.[46] His family suffered from his long workdays and weeks. Pat Jr. graduated from Waco High School on February 11. Although Waco is only 100 miles from Austin, Neff sent a telegram of congratulations and did not attend.[47]

Meanwhile, Back at the Governor's Mansion

The Texas Governor's Mansion, into which the Neffs moved in January 1921, predated the Texas Capitol building by some thirty years. The mansion was and continues to be regarded as one of the finest examples of nineteenth-century Greek Revival architecture. Begun by master builder Abner Cook in 1854 and finished in 1856, it is the oldest executive mansion in continuous use west of the Mississippi and the fourth oldest in the country.[48]

The mansion had never been a model of comfort or convenience. A major contribution to the building occurred during the Hobby period: the addition of steam heat throughout the structure. When told that spending money for that purpose might hurt her husband politically, Mrs. Hobby replied that she had rather be "warm for two years than to freeze for four."[49] The Neffs' major addition was the creation of a screened porch and glazed sun parlor on the rear upstairs gallery; they continued to use the screened front porch for sleeping.[50] The mansion's furnishings consisted of a mixture of heirlooms, fine period furniture, and hand-me-downs from previous governors. The Hobbys had added some furniture pieces to the collection; the Neffs contributed a player piano. Neff used the small northwest bedroom upstairs as his den. The mansion was continually in need of some renovation, and the legislature tried to help the situation when the Neffs came in by appropriating an additional $5,000 for repairs and refurbishing, but Neff vetoed the effort.[51]

In moving into the mansion, Myrtie gave up what she described as "the fireside of our home around which I had sat all those evenings with my children from infancy and sometimes my husband, so sacred and dear only because of its association."[52] She would later be quoted as saying: "I came to the mansion reluctantly, because I have never been in any sense of the word a society woman, having felt that my time and the strength which has been given me rather sparingly belonged to my home and my family."[53]

Myrtie's letters to her children reflected her loneliness. She was left by herself many evenings while Neff attended meetings or worked in his den upstairs. She also had not counted on her mother-in-law's being in the mansion with them. Neff's attention to his mother's every wish had been a source of irritation to Myrtie. Now she had the partial burden of caring for her, although Isabella's nurse, Sallie Lasater, also moved to the mansion.

Despite her ninety-one years, Mother Neff was able to take part in at least two social events before falling ill in April. Only three weeks after the inauguration, Isabella wrote her daughter-in-law, Patsy Neff, in Waco, about her first mansion reception the day before. She wrote that more than 400 callers came, and she took particular pride in the fact that Neff seemed proud of her.[54]

Mother Neff fell ill in mid-April and died May 18, exactly four months to the day after her son's inauguration. Neff cancelled all speaking and most other engagements the last ten days of her illness and did not leave her bedside. The funeral service was held in the mansion with burial at Post Oak Cemetery in Coryell County, next to her husband Noah, in the Neff lot.[55] It is difficult, if not impossible, to overestimate the impact of Mother Neff on her youngest son. Left a widow at age fifty-two and disappointed in some of her older sons, she spent her life lavishing attention on Pat. She constantly pushed and encouraged him to "be his best." He, in turn, responded to meet her every expectation. Just two years earlier, in 1919, he had written her, using one of his typical phrases: "The thoughts of your sacrifices for me has always been and still is a stimulant for me to do my best. For your sake, I have tried to make the most of life and render service to others as best I could."[56] Neff received many letters of condolence on her death. His replies to most of them were sincere, but brief. To two of his closest friends, he was more personal and revealing. He told one, "Her Christian example has been and is the greatest thing in my life."[57]

The Neff Papers contain hundreds of letters between mother and son, dating back to his college days. He wrote her virtually every week when he was away from the home place and shared his innermost thoughts with her. On a trip, it was not unusual for him to pen a letter or postcard to her every day. In contrast, the collection has very few letters between Neff and his wife. It could well be that Myrtie destroyed his letters to her.

Despite Myrtie's aversion to social activities, the Austin newspapers referred to her as a gracious first lady. Mary Farrell and Elizabeth Silverthorne, in their book *First Ladies of Texas*, wrote: "She set aside every Tuesday to be at home at the mansion to the public and she also planned and carried out with great care and attention all the traditional formal entertainment that went with her role."[58] She kept the mansion filled with floral arrangements from the greenhouse and assumed the responsibility of arranging flowers for Sunday service at the First Baptist Church across the street from the mansion, which she and Governor Neff attended regularly.

Myrtie's assistants were her daughter, Hallie Maude, and a woman named Martha Johnson. In a 1992 interview, Hallie Maude's role at the mansion was described by a friend, Mrs. Maurice (Bobbie) Barnes of Waco: "I do know that . . . Hallie Maude was really the hostess at the mansion. . . . She presided at things held there. She planned all the meals. She would tell me often, 'When Dad was governor, I bought thus and so by the case.'"[59] Two paroled convicts—Jody, who cooked, and a young man named Thomas—also worked in the mansion. Myrtie continued her periodic trips to Mineral Wells, but now the bashful first lady would occasionally go in disguise, and would frequently change hotels when she saw someone in the lobby she recognized.[60]

After his high school graduation in February 1921, Pat Jr. came to live in the mansion for a short time. The family decision was that it would be better if he did not try to enter college for the spring and summer semesters but take some time off. Neff wrote his brother Sam, asking whether Pat Jr. could spend the spring with him and his family in the community of Tennyson in West Texas. Neff offered to send $15 per month to Sam to pay Pat Jr. for his work. The son wrote several letters home during the spring months, all expressing positive feelings about his experiences.[61]

Because of his financial situation (his salary as governor was not generous), Neff appreciated the little gifts that came his way. Shortly after he came into office, the National Association of Straw Hat Manufacturers of America wrote him, offering a hat for the "coming season." Neff accepted, advising them that his height was six feet, his weight 190 pounds, and his hat size 7 1/4. He wrote that he usually wore what was known as a standard Stetson with a "rather large brim."[62] At age forty-nine, Neff was still a fine-looking gentleman who took pride in his appearance.

The Appointments Conundrum

One of the governor's chief tasks during the spring and early summer was to make appointments to numerous boards and other positions. Neff appointed an unprecedented number of women—twelve in all—to various posts, including the first female members of the University of Texas and the Texas A&M Boards of Regents.[63] In the 1900s, the UT and A&M boards, along with the State Highway Commission, were considered by most political observers to be the most prestigious appointments a governor could make. Until Neff appointed Mrs. H. J. (Mary McClellan) O'Hair of Coleman to the UT Board and Mrs. J. C. (Willie) George of Brownsville to the A&M Board, those governing bodies had been strictly men's clubs. O'Hair, journalist and civic activist, was an early supporter of woman suffrage, served as president of the Texas Women's Press Association in 1910, and remained active in that organization the rest of her life. Married to wealthy rancher H. J. O'Hair, she served not only the full six-year term as Neff's appointee, but another two-year unexpired term by appointment of Governor Dan Moody. She was the only woman to serve on the University of Texas Board of Regents until 1935. Willie George of Brownsville, newly elected president of the Fourth District Women's Federated Clubs, was appointed to the Texas A&M Board May 11.

Margie Neal, whom Neff appointed to the Board of Regents of the State Normal Schools on April 20, 1921, would become one of the most widely known of all of Neff's appointees. Born and reared in Panola County in East Texas, she was editor and publisher of the *Texas Mule*, a newspaper her father bought for her. She renamed it the *East Texas Register* and covered the Panola County area from 1902 until 1911, when she sold it. She used part of the proceeds to lobby for woman suffrage, and then, using her teaching background, she made her first speech "selling Liberty Bonds [during World War I] from the back of a pickup truck in her hometown."[64] Neal was active in the Democratic Party and was one of Neff's stalwart supporters in 1920. In 1927 she became the second woman legislator in the state and the first woman state senator. In 1952, she was honored at an appreciation party in Carthage. Among the speakers were U.S. Senator Lyndon B. Johnson and Governor Allan Shivers.[65]

The power of appointments is one of the few powers left to Texas governors by the Constitution of 1876. This included in the early 1900s several hundred board appointments, virtually none of them carrying any compensation. These were nearly all one- or two-year appointments. The privilege also extended to replacing state judges and district attorneys who died or resigned their offices. Those appointments were subject to the electoral process at the next election, but they were prized by attorneys since their campaign posters and signs could say "Keep Judge Jones on the Bench," if not "Reelect Judge Jones." The competition for district judge and district attorney positions may best be gauged by the fact that the Neff Papers contain three bulging file boxes of letters and recommendations concerning these positions. Neff did not hesitate to let his district attorney nominees know his expectations. In a typical letter, Neff wrote one appointee that he expected him to vigorously enforce the Prohibition law and that if he could not assume that responsibility he would be expected to decline the appointment.[66]

If the power of appointments was a perquisite of the office, it was also an awesome chore. Neff learned early what governors before him had learned and governors after him would swear to: when you appointed an individual, you made that person and a few of his or her supporters happy, but you made many other of your supporters unhappy. Neff's carefully crafted replies, with variations, had to be used several times in the four years as he filled the vacancies at his disposal. Neff generally wrote a full-page, typed letter to try to soothe an unsuccessful individual's feelings and retain his or her friendship. He often concluded by praising the unsuccessful candidate: "You should indeed be proud of the many splendid testimonials your neighbors and friends have given in your behalf—a rich heritage to you and yours."[67]

The most important matter Neff had to deal with in the four months between the regular and special sessions was the issue of penitentiaries and pardons and paroles. Allegations of financial mismanagement, mistreatment of prisoners, graft, and other irregularities harassed governors throughout Texas' history, and in 1921 it became Neff's turn to correct the problems. Neff was well aware that countless governors before him had struggled with this challenge but not succeeded. He was determined to make his mark in this area. Neff had a golden opportunity to do what no governor before him had done—to develop a rehabilitative prison system that treated inmates in a humane manner and gave them an opportunity to rebuild their lives.

With one appointment on the Board of Prison Commissioners available when he took office, Neff promptly named Captain J. A. Herring to that body and made him chairman. The *Austin Statesman* responded with the comment that Herring was probably better informed about penitentiary matters than any other man in the state.[68] Herring had been a manager of one of the prison farms and, in 1907, Governor Thomas Campbell had appointed him as superintendent of the prison system. In his new position with Neff, Herring quickly assumed responsibility and began writing the governor frequently in the spring of 1921 about conditions at Huntsville. He had to deal with several escapes; a few commentators blamed Neff's tough policy on pardons and paroles as the reason. The *San Antonio Express* reported on May 13 that the largest prison escape ever had taken place the day before, with forty prisoners making their way out after wounding two guards.[69] Just a month later, Herring had to report that thirty-four Mexican prisoners had escaped. An extensive story in the July 21 issue of the *Dallas Morning News* by reporter Robert R. Penn catalogued prison escapes in the first six months of 1921.

Penn reported that the number exceeded the figures for the entire year of 1920. When asked the reason for so many escapes, Herring defended Neff's policy of tighter rules for pardons and stated that he did not think that policy had "much to do with the number of escapes."

The Two Special Sessions and a Perspective

Neff's failure to have any of his law enforcement bills passed during the regular session did not lessen his resolve. He was spurred on to call a special session by letters specifying abuses as well as editorials supporting his position. A letter from the Rio Grande Valley pleaded with him to send in a "good man" to enforce the law.[70] Another from Johnson City told Neff that the writer and his friends had put a "dirty little saloon" out of business in the town but that he had paid the price: "I had my place of business burned out three times within twelve months."[71] The *Amarillo Daily News* of July 16, 1921, reinforced Neff's beliefs that Prohibition laws were being flouted even by law enforcement officials. The lead editorial that day recounted the recent meeting of the Texas Sheriffs' Association and lamented the fact that "a number of the men became thoroughly intoxicated," resulting in "loud and unquestionably offensive language."[72] Much of Neff's backing came from rural newspapers. The *Hearne Democrat*, for example, on July 15 called on its readers to "rally to the assistance of the Governor." But not everyone was supportive. Former Governor Hobby's *Beaumont Enterprise* editorialized opposition to several of Neff's proposals on July 9.

On the eve of the special session, it was apparent that Neff had real problems with the legislative leadership. Arriving in Austin on July 17, the day before the convocation of the legislature, Lieutenant Governor Davidson was quoted in the *San Antonio Express* as saying that the legislature should pass the appropriation bills and go home. In the same story, influential Senator R. M. Dudley, chair of the Senate Finance Committee, expressed the same sentiments. Other senators were known to favor Governor Neff's program, some with modifications. The same newspaper the next day, the first day of the session, reported that "it would take but very little to cause outward antagonism to develop between the Governor and the Legislature."[73]

For his part, Neff was undeterred. Rather than working with the leaders for some kind of compromise, he continued to think he could go over their heads to the people of the state and force action by the legislative body. For the special session, he ignored tradition and called the legislators back to duty at nine o'clock instead of the usual noon opening time. He listed the unfinished items of business that he expected the body to enact: appropriations for the support of the state agencies and institutions; additional money for the public schools; his three law enforcement programs, including repeal of the suspended sentence law, strengthening of the state Prohibition law, and removal of officers who fail to enforce the law (he had long since dropped his request to tighten the law concerning concurrent sentences); consolidation of overlapping departments and abolition of useless offices; and redistricting of senatorial and representative districts. At the same time, he delivered a ten-page message detailing reasons for his recommendations.[74] This message called particular attention to the business depression prevailing in the country, noting that Texas itself was "passing through a financial crisis" and that this was "a time to conserve rather than consume, a time to retrench rather than enlarge." He itemized his vetoes, a total of $5,245,420 in the regular session, and stated that either revenues had to be increased or appropriations slashed.[75]

Neff's law enforcement program underwent several days of committee hearings and debate, and on July 25 the House reported out a modified suspended sentence law that would add rape, automobile theft, and violation of liquor laws as crimes in which the law could not be invoked. On that same day, the House also adopted a bill amending the Dean Act, which substantially followed Neff's wishes. The next day, July 27, the House Judiciary Committee supported the officer removal bill in felony cases only. Despite these favorable signs, the votes were simply not there in the end, and none of them reached the governor's desk for his signature.

Sparring between the governor and the legislature occurred about virtually every issue. Neff's six years as a prosecutor seemed to have hardened his resolve to win every argument. When he was speaker of the House in 1903, he had been known as a friendly and open presiding officer, but by 1921, he appeared to be rigid and stand-offish, loath to compromise. His determination to do everything himself without help from lieutenants who might have smoothed the way to some compromises hobbled his effectiveness.

So contentious was lawmaking in Texas in 1921 that many voters were turned off, placing a pox on state government in general. For example, in the regular session, the legislature authorized five constitutional amendments, with the vote set for July 23. Only one passed: the amendment limiting voting rights to native or naturalized citizens and incorporating woman suffrage to conform with the Nineteenth Amendment of the U.S. Constitution.[76]

While the governor and the lawmakers agreed that prison conditions in the state were abysmal, they disagreed on how to correct the situation. Neff disagreed with the recommendation to sell all the prison farms, close the main prison at Huntsville, and relocate it to within fifty miles of Austin. His skepticism here had two parts: first, no money had been allocated to buy new land and build new buildings; and second, the proposal ordered the sale of all twelve farms in the system, even though the cotton revenue from the farms provided the bulk of operating revenue for the system. It was true that unpredictable weather caused unpredictable revenue, making budgeting a nightmare, but Captain Herring had a suggestion to counter some of that uncertain revenue. He proposed that farming be confined to men unfit for factory work (primarily Negroes) and that he be allowed to develop factories to employ many of the prisoners suitable for industrial training.[77] When it was revealed that Herring had in mind a convict labor factory to manufacture shirts and overalls, it set off a storm of protest from labor groups and the outcry forced Neff to table the whole idea.[78]

The legislature spent much of its time in the thirty-day session considering the four major appropriation bills required to run the state government and its institutions for the next two years. These included money for the judiciary, state departments and agencies, the eleemosynary institutions, and the state colleges and universities. The money for the judiciary, with little opposition, was the only bill approved by Neff during the session.[79] It had the distinction of being the only one of the four bills in which the governor did not line-item veto several items. After extended debate, funds for the various state agencies and the eleemosynary institutions were passed, but Neff did not have to make his decision on them until after the legislature departed. The higher education bill drew opposition in both houses, and the session ended with the matter still unresolved. Neff had indicated a week before the end of the first called session that he had no intention of calling a second session, but the legislature could agree only on a senatorial redistricting bill with no revamping of the House districts and failed to pass an education appropriation bill. Neff thus was forced into calling the second session, which he did immediately. The second session began on August 17, the day after the first session ended.[80]

Although the legislature had passed a bill for support of the various state agencies in the first special session, Neff returned it with the message that the amount in the bill plus an estimated $5 million for higher education would total $22 million. Estimated revenues at the current tax rate would total only $19 million, thus leaving a shortage of some $3 million. He urged legislators to "cut the garment to the cloth" and challenged them to give him a revised departmental bill and a college and university bill totaling no more than $19 million.[81] The eight-day second special session was marked by bitter debate on the higher education appropriation bill. The bill was finally passed on August 24. The legislature adjourned the next day, leaving Neff to sort out the mess.

Neff's twenty-day period to take action on the three major appropriation bills and a small number of other bills did not expire until early September, so during the last week of August, he studied the various bills and made his decisions. On August 31, he signed four bills, including the one covering all the eleemosynary institutions. Although he eliminated $624,480 from the bill through line-item vetoes, the overall total still reflected an increase of 11 percent over the previous biennium. The increase included two new institutions, a Northwest Texas Insane Asylum and a Home for Dependent and Neglected Children. Also on August 31, he signed bills providing $60,000 for a school building at the State Orphan's Home in Corsicana and a two-year $321,660 appropriation for a new American Legion Memorial Sanatorium in Kerrville. Finally, that same day, he approved $2.5 million in rural school aid, a figure $1.5 million less than he had vetoed in the spring.[82]

Three days later, Neff had finished his journey through the lengthy bill for support of the state departments and agencies. The legislature had ignored him on the departmental appropriation bill, but on September 2, he signed the $4,941,842 bill after cutting a miniscule $68,945, less than 2 percent of the total. The total allotted state employee complement of 772 positions thus, by and large, escaped the hatchet that so many had feared.[83] As the *Austin American* headlined the next day: EMPLOYEES AT TEXAS CAPITOL RELIEVED BY CHIEF EXECUTIVE'S ACTION. The appropriation bill also reflected Texans' early love for the open road. The State Highway Department was included in the general appropriation bill for the first time and, just as quickly, became the highest dollar agency of the twenty-five for which funds were provided.[84]

Neff was left with only one appropriation bill to consider, that of the state-supported institutions of higher education. The battle centered almost entirely on the proposed money for the University of Texas. The Senate's version of the bill did not treat UT as badly as the House's did, so the issue had gone to a conference committee. On the third day of the second session, August 20, the conference committee reported out a bill cutting by 20 percent those faculty salaries that were above $2,000.

Will Hogg, Governor Hogg's son, who was a graduate of the UT Law School, a former UT regent, and a strong backer of the university, was dispirited by the salary cuts and what he perceived as Neff's inaction to prevent such cuts. He was outraged that President Vinson's and most of the professors' salaries had been cut and tighter restrictions put on the university than ever before. In a letter to Alvin Ousley on October 24, 1921, Hogg wrote that as the first graduate of UT to become governor, Neff, he hoped, would have the "guts" to rectify the mistakes.[85] Hogg had written Neff early in the year recommending a tax of "at least twenty five cents a barrel on every barrel of marketable crude petroleum produced in the State of Texas, the tax to be paid by the producing company, but a proportionate part to be passed on to the royalty owner."[86] Thus Hogg was offering to increase his own considerable taxes to bring in what he estimated as a total of more than $25 million to the state.

Neff vetoed twenty-nine bills in his first term, not including two bills in which he line-item vetoed specific items. The vetoes totaled twenty-one (plus one line-item veto) in the regular session and eight in the first called session of the legislature. The only veto in the second called session was a line-item veto of certain items in the education appropriation. His total of twenty-nine exceeded the number of first-term vetoes of any governor before him except Governor Edmund J. Davis in 1871.[87]

Neff's demeanor toward the legislature is puzzling. Instead of co-equals, he seemed to treat the legislature as a trial jury, virtually ordering it to deliver punishment of wrongdoers, particularly violators of the gun or Prohibition laws, and to follow his other entreaties without compromise. It is curious that he misread the legislature (jury) so many times. As a prosecutor, one of his strengths was "knowing" the jury that would be trying his case. He was lauded for his ability to ferret out the birthplace and date, family background, business or profession, religion, hobbies, and other attributes of the jury pool from which the final twelve were selected. He did not seem to undertake this critical analysis of the legislators with whom he would deal, or if he did, he ignored the picture it presented.

Neff did have some victories, although few could be considered major pieces of legislation. As described earlier, the most significant bill authorized money for additional land for the University of Texas, thus fixing its location once and for all. He also persuaded the legislature to allow the State Textbook Commission to extend its current book contracts, thereby saving the state more than $1 million. In addition, he was able to keep his promises to rural school advocates by approving $2.5 million of aid to those districts. Finally, he was successful in obtaining appropriation bills that held the line on the state tax rate, an objective that he considered quite important.[88]

The Ku Klux Klan and Other Ongoing Challenges

Neff's predecessors as governor had traditionally breathed a sigh of relief when the legislature adjourned and left Austin—"now, we can get something done." But Neff was not to have any relief in early September 1921, when he finished the last of his bill signings and vetoes. The Ku Klux Klan had been resurrected in Texas after a fifty-year absence, and Neff would have to deal with it.

Originally founded in Tennessee in 1866 for social purposes, the Klan spread through the South during Reconstruction and began to oppose the post-war Republican rule and espouse white supremacy, opposing mixing of the races and the pervasive encroachment of the carpetbaggers. After several years, federal authorities and the white leadership of the state began to exert positive influence against violence and the Klan effectively disappeared.[89]

It was almost half a century before the group would resurface, first in Georgia in 1915, followed by Texas in 1920. Norman Brown, in his extensive chapter on the Klan in *Hood, Bonnet, and Little Brown Jug: Texas Politics, 1921-1928*, records the resurrection of the organization in Houston in some detail.[90] Playing to many of Houston's leading citizens in the race riot in that city in 1917, in which sixteen whites, including five police officers, were killed, a Houston chapter of the Klan was established October 8, 1920, complete with an initiation ceremony featuring flaming crosses.[91]

In reality, the twentieth-century Klan was much different from the organization of the previous century. While still citing fear of the Negro, the 1920 reemergence was based on other factors. Klan authority Charles C. Alexander described the culture of that era within which the Klan was revived:

> The white Protestant citizen of the Southwest had many anxieties. His fears for the safety of his property, the chastity of his daughter, the honor of his wife, and the peace of his community were supplemented by concern over foreign immigration, the Catholic hierarchy, insolent Negroes, greedy Jews, and Bolsheviks.[92]

Neff's message of February 1, 1921, to the legislature sounded much the same alarm:

> There is sweeping over Texas, as never before in her history, a wave of crime. Murder, theft, robbery, and hold-ups are hourly occurrences that fill the daily press. Criminals fill the land with terror and make unsafe both life and property.[93]

Alexander, in his 1959 master's thesis, responded to Neff's statement, writing that Neff's sentiment was an open invitation for the operation of an extralegal law enforcement body like the Klan.[94]

The Klan attracted members from the entire spectrum of communities. Although some portrayed it as an organization of "ignorant farmers and laborers," in truth, it sought and obtained members from every stratum of society—working class men as well as doctors, lawyers, businessmen, and even preachers. It was particularly successful in the burgeoning cities. Joining the Klan, members found a variety of activities to fulfill their needs. In her comprehensive master's thesis on the Klan in Texas, Linda Elaine Kilgore wrote that the organization actually sponsored four different types of activities—social, benevolent, political, and finally extralegal violence.[95] Of course, the activity most commonly associated with the Klan was the enforcement of moral and legal codes through extralegal violence. The political activities of the Klan came to the forefront in 1922 and 1923 as it maneuvered to control state and local political offices.[96]

Neff's first public acknowledgment of the Klan occurred on June 17, 1921, when he addressed National Guard troops at Camp Mabry in Austin: "The National Guard stands for law and order and is against lawlessness, whether lawlessness wears a mask and marches through the streets of our cities at midnight or whether lawlessness unshields its sword of anarchy in broad, open daylight."[97] Clearly, this statement was directed to the Klan without using its name. But it was not enough for the *Dallas Morning News*. The first major newspaper to challenge the Klan, the *News* hammered Neff for the next year because he would not condemn the Klan by name. State Representative Wright Patman from Cass County was the first state official to oppose the Klan openly. A law graduate of Cumberland University in Lebanon, Tennessee, as were many other early Texas lawyers, he returned to Texas to practice, enlisted in the Army in July 1917, and volunteered for overseas duty, only to be rejected because of a minor heart problem. He later went to Congress and supported virtually all of President Roosevelt's New Deal economic and social reforms.[98] Elected to the Texas Legislature in 1920, Patman came to Austin to be a deskmate of Sam Ealy Johnson, father of the future U.S. President. Patman had not been particularly vocal during the regular session, but on July 25, 1921, he spoke up, introducing a resolution condemning the masked organization and demanding that national Klan officer William J. Simmons stay out of Texas. Patman said that the state and local officials in Texas could and would enforce the law and did not need the Klan to be self-constituted law officers. Patman then persuaded forty-eight other representatives to call on Neff to submit legislation curbing the Klan. The resulting defeat of his resolution, 69-54, revealed the deep inroads that the Klan had already made in the state in less than one year.[99] Patman prepared three bills designed to cripple the Klan, but all three died in the House when the first called session adjourned August 16.

Meanwhile, Klan activities continued in every part of the state. On September 2, approximately 500 Austin and San Antonio white-robed Klansmen paraded through the Austin business district behind fiery crosses.[100] In El Paso in early October, County Attorney Will H. Pelphrey announced that he had received a threatening note signed "KKK" that demanded he resign his office because of a perceived lack of strong law enforcement.[101] Not all state and local officials were cowed by the hooded organization. District judges in Dallas, Georgetown, El Paso, and Beaumont were among several who challenged the Klan.[102]

Neff's general statements had not proved strong enough for many throughout the state, including one of the state's leading newspapers, the *Houston Chronicle,* which took strong issue with the governor in the fall of 1921. Marcellus E. Foster, president of the Houston Chronicle Publishing Company, writing on company letterhead on November 10, added his own personal views, gently chiding Neff for not coming out early in the year against the Klan:

> I do think that your statements in regard to law and order have been very helpful recently. I am inclined to believe, however, that the exposure of the Ku Klux Klan by two or three of the leading newspapers of Texas has done more to suppress the lawlessness of the mask organization than all else that has happened.[103]

In a reply, Neff stubbornly refused to give any ground or admit any weakness.[104]

Neff was more open about what he saw as a major scandal—the liberal granting of pardons and paroles by Governors Ferguson and Hobby—and he vowed to personally review all cases brought before him. This was a popular decision with district judges, who had watched helplessly when court decisions were overturned by governors.[105]

Neff's goal of clamping down on paroles, however, often brought him personal pain. Recalling difficult decisions he had had to make, Neff later told Baylor Professor Robert Denny:

> "Once when I was governor, a mother got through the door of the outer offices and came into my office, fell on the floor, held my feet, and begged for the life of her son who had been condemned to die."
>
> "What did you do?" Denny asked.
>
> "I couldn't do anything except say, 'Lady, I'm sorry. I have reviewed the case. I think justice has been done as far as justice can be humanly done, and so the decision of the court must stand. I am sorry.'"[106]

Neff was so jealous of this pardon and parole responsibility that he refused to leave the state in the fall of 1921, fearful that Lieutenant Governor Lynch Davidson might grant prison releases in his absence.

Although penitentiary and clemency matters took much of his time in the fall of 1921, other state business had to be cared for. Chief among these were the continual rounds of appointments to state executive positions and boards and commissions. Neff was beginning to build a reputation for outstanding appointments that would stand in stark contrast to the "good ole' boy" system prevalent under Governor Jim Ferguson and revived later by Miriam "Ma" Ferguson when she succeeded Neff. Neff's breadth of experience in government, Baylor and Baptist affairs, and fraternal and legal groups brought him in touch with the state's leaders and the movers and shakers in a wide range of organizations. His integrity and high standards of conduct drew many to his service, even though the salaries were generally much lower than these people could have drawn in the private sector. He had an uncanny knack for picking future leaders of the state—and even the nation—individuals who would go on to noteworthy careers in government as well as business.

An example of his good judgment and foresight was his appointment on October 3, 1921, of twenty-seven-year-old Robert Gerald Storey of Tyler to be the assistant attorney general assisting the Texas Court of Criminal Appeals. Storey, who had passed the bar exam in 1914 without the benefit of a bachelor's or law degree, served as assistant attorney general two years, and then left for Dallas to open a law practice. Neff appointed him shortly thereafter (1924) to serve on the University of Texas Board of Regents, and from there it was one honor after another. Over a period of years, Storey became president of the Dallas Bar Association, the Texas Bar, the American Bar, and later the American Bar Foundation, and still later, the

International Bar Association. In 1945-1946, he acted as executive trial counsel to Justice Robert H. Jackson of the U.S. Supreme Court in the prosecution of Herman Goering, Rudolf Hess, and other high-ranking Nazi officials in the Nuremberg war crimes trials. After the war, he was urged to run for governor, but he chose instead to become dean of the Southern Methodist University Law School and president of the Southwestern Legal Foundation.[107]

Second Year in Office—1922

Governor Neff's second year began with an Old West drama worthy of cinema and the vehicle for showcasing his devotion to law and order. This occurred in Mexia, forty miles east of Waco, when an oil promoter struck it big, predicting Mexia would become the greatest oil town in Texas. Colonel A. E. Humphreys, called "a veritable P. T. Barnum," by the authors of *Oil in Texas*, spread the word and caused a frantic rush to the town, swamping local facilities.[108] One enterprising citizen "erected a large circus tent, renting cots to sixty workers for a dollar a night."[109] Along with the get-rich-quick crowd came the criminal element, which the law enforcement officials either couldn't or wouldn't suppress. Neff, at the invitation of local citizens, made an incognito visit to Mexia, by then swelled to 30,000, and was appalled at what he saw. Narcotics and whiskey were plentiful, along with numerous gambling halls. Immediately, the governor ordered Adjutant General Thomas D. Barton to raid the area on the night of January 7. Barton and his men found whiskey and gambling at the two most disreputable places, the "Chicken Farm" and the "Winter Garden."[110] The next day, Barton called a meeting of the district judges, district attorneys, county judges, and sheriffs and county attorneys of both Freestone and Limestone Counties. Barton and Assistant Attorney General Clifford Stone met resistance from these local officials and concluded that martial law was the only solution. Three days later, January 11, 1922, Neff proclaimed martial law, sending in Brigadier General Jacob F. Wolters of the Texas National Guard with two companies of Texas Rangers and a contingent of guardsmen. "More than three thousand persons left Mexia the first day after martial law was declared," Neff later wrote. "These three thousand were part of the outlaws who were operating there, and they wanted to get away while getting away was good."[111] Martial law remained in effect for forty-seven days, during which time the militia hauled in an astounding amount of illegal liquor and gambling paraphernalia and arrested 602 individuals.[112]

Back in Austin, Neff resumed his normal executive duties with another round of appointments during the spring months. One of his district attorney appointees was Daniel J. Moody of Georgetown. In 1923, in the midst of Klan strength in Williamson County, Moody would successfully prosecute a group of Klansmen and parlay that into an acclaimed political career in Texas state government as attorney general and then governor.[113] Although not a direct appointment of the governor, J. D. Fauntleroy, state highway engineer, was another example of the type of professional men brought into state government during the Neff administration. When appointed in Texas, Fauntleroy was district engineer for the U.S. Bureau of Public Roads in charge of federal aid work for highways in four states, including Texas. His appointment was significant, as it was another step in positioning Texas to take full advantage of the federal aid to highways that Congress was increasing every year.[114]

Neff, early in 1922, took stock of his first year as the state's chief executive and began to plot his course for a second term. In the latter 1800s and early 1900s, two two-year terms as governor were a virtual given. Since Oran Roberts had begun his governorship in 1879, all eight successive governors up to Jim Ferguson had served their four years and then bowed out. Ferguson's second term was cut short. Hobby, following him, voluntarily stepped down after three and one-half years. Neff apparently had no thought other than to continue the four-year tradition. Few of the nine governors beginning with Roberts had faced any strong foes in their bids for reelection, and Neff must certainly have felt that he wouldn't either. Nevertheless, knowing that his first year had not been spectacular, it is reasonable to assume that Neff believed he had not lived up to the expectations of his legion of supporters. To recapture the initiative as the state's political leader, he needed to broaden his appeal and his legislative goals. In his first legislative sessions, he had concentrated heavily on law enforcement matters. The legislature had rebuffed him on all of these proposals, and Neff now must have realized that he needed to mix those requests with a wider assortment of bills that would receive a more favorable response. Three of the major problems facing the state were challenges in which Neff had a deep interest: education, highways, and flood control and water conservation.

Although aspirants for his job began to announce in March 1922, Neff held his fire and planned a series of "educational" talks across the state to inform citizens about their government and its operations. He decided to begin the educational tour by spending the last week of April in West Texas. For his theme, Neff chose "Texas: Its Perils and Possibilities." The itinerary, announced in early April, would cover eighteen cities and towns in seven days, beginning in Wichita Falls on Sunday afternoon, April 23, and concluding Saturday night, April 29, in Hereford.[115] He used these occasions to emphasize his new goals for education, highways, and flood control. He also was giving his audiences detailed figures on the cost to the state—and to them as taxpayers—of the many educational, penal, and eleemosynary institutions supported by state government. His speech in Pampa on April 28 elicited *Dallas Morning News* headlines the next day and, in modern times, might have plunged him into deep political trouble, but the headlines and his remarks caused hardly a ripple in West Texas. The headline, NEFF SAYS TEXAS BREEDING LUNATICS, referred to his statement that "we have over 6,000 lunatics in the institutions of Texas; . . . we are just breeding lunatics and it must be stopped." Both the *Dallas Morning News* and the *Fort Worth Star-Telegram* speculated that Neff favored some sort of birth control or a modified form of eugenics to correct the problem.[116] After Neff's return to Austin, his office summarized in a news release the scope of his prodigious two-week trip "visiting twenty-one counties, speaking thirty-two times to approximately thirty thousand people, and traveling a total of sixteen hundred miles by automobile and train."

These bare facts, however, were pale compared to the vivid coverage given the trip by E. M. Dealey, a reporter for the *Dallas Morning News*, the state's leading newspaper. "Ted" Dealey, as he came to be known, represented the fifth generation of his mother's family in the newspaper business, and would become president of the *News* in 1940. Dealey reported daily on Neff's trip, capping it off on May 7, 1922, with a *News* column entitled "Sidelights on Neff's Trip through the Panhandle." Recounting half a dozen amusing incidents during the trip, Dealey remembered that at Quanah, Governor Neff borrowed a needle and thread to restore, by himself, an errant button on his pants. Dealey wrote that at every stopping place, one could hear several individuals remark, "Sure is a fine looking fellow, ain't he?" Dealey also wrote that Neff proved that, although some persons thought his speeches "sounded like a sermon," he could also lighten his delivery with the best of politicians. Undertaking to define the difference between "life" and "love," Neff told the audience at one stop: "Life is just one fool thing after another, while love is two fool things after each other."[117]

Neff's emphasis on education, highways, and water conservation found enthusiastic interest not only in West Texas but throughout the state. Organized support for education legislation already existed—Neff's Conference on Education in Texas no longer existed, but a strong Texas Parent Teacher Association, an active Texas State Teachers' Association, and the Texas Federation of Women's Clubs all would help him in pushing for more money for public and higher education in 1923. Despite criticism for not fighting harder against the cuts in education, he had the backing of the vast majority of education proponents, including the continued support of H. T. Musselman and his influential *Texas School Journal*, which was highly regarded by school superintendents and teachers.

A state highway system was another of Neff's high priorities for his second term. In a speech to the Texas Bankers Association in May 1922, Neff noted that one of the accomplishments of his first year in office was the continuation of a fledgling effort to build a coordinated system of highways in Texas.[118] Although the legislature had established the State Highway Department in 1917, its funding was still limited to miniscule vehicle registration fees. Federal aid was available, but for now, the state had to depend heavily on county road bond issues for the greatest portion of matching funds for the federal money. From his 6,000-mile often-muddy odyssey by way of his Buick Roadster in his 1920 campaign, Neff knew firsthand the critical importance of good roads. His travels across the state that year revealed the unevenness of Texas highways—he had traveled on concrete in one county only to wallow in mud in the next. Automobile travel was increasing exponentially.

The first formal steps toward a citizen support organization for better roads came in a call reported in the *Dallas Morning News* of April 9 stating that the organizational meeting would be held in Austin on April 17. The purpose was "to promote the advancement of good road building and to provide an adequate fund for road maintenance." Speaking in the capital city before some 200 good roads advocates from every corner of the state, Neff challenged the group to develop a "big road building program, not a little, sickly puny one" and told them if they did that, he would carry their program to the people of Texas.[119]

Meanwhile, the State Highway Department became one of the first state agencies to trumpet its own work and needs. The department began publishing a monthly *Bulletin* containing "news and accomplishments" of the young agency. At first, the publication consisted of only a few mimeographed pages bound in magazine form; within a year, however, it had developed into a printed news magazine with a circulation of more than 4,000 public officials and interested citizens. The state's dailies and weeklies made full use of the articles in the *Bulletin*, thus preparing the electorate for highway legislation in 1923.[120] The Highway Department emphasized the need for a state tax on gasoline to rectify the muddy, pot-holed highways and allow Texas to take full advantage of the federal monies.

Neff's third priority for his second term was flood control and conservation. Here again, nature delivered him strong support. Spring rains fell heavily all over the state—the international bridge over the Rio Grande at Eagle Pass was swept away in a torrential flood and the Laredo bridge that Neff had dedicated only months before was threatened. In cities and towns all over Texas, individuals were forced from their homes. Thus, the predicate was laid for the governor to voice his concerns and plans to respond to these critical problems.

Neff proposed these initiatives in the face of disastrous cotton prices from late 1920 to 1922. Despite low prices, farmers continued to expand their acreage. Neff developed one counterattack on their behalf. In the spring of 1922, he asked Bebe Daniels, a highly popular actress at the time, to aid growers by wearing dresses made of cotton.[121]

The Klan Continues to Grow

Even with many other pressing problems, Neff was faced with growing Klan problems that would affect his bid for a second term. By January 1922, the Texas Klan membership was estimated at 75,000 to 90,000 by Edward Young Clarke of Atlanta, imperial kleagle of the Knights of the Ku Klux Klan.[122] Clarke estimated total U.S. membership at about 225,000, located in every state but Montana and

Maine. The organization was growing daily and savoring its strength among all classes of persons, with strongest growth in Chicago and Texas where "real men" resided.[123]

Clarke visited Dallas the weekend of January 21-22, and his bold and chilling interview with a *Dallas Morning News* reporter plus a description of the Klan parade Saturday evening occupied some forty column inches in the Sunday edition of the *News*. Clarke forthrightly told the reporter that the Klan membership in Dallas already numbered 7,000 and that the group was preparing for 2,000 more. He stated that the Klan stood for five things: "A revival of patriotism, white supremacy, separation of church and state, a greater sentiment in favor of the home, and a recognition of woman's place in the home." He went on to proclaim: "This country was created for the Caucasian race. It was not created for the Greek, the Italian or the Jew. [In addition,] women are entering business and politics, and this is a real danger unless there is some strong organization constantly preaching that woman's place is in the home."[124] In Dallas, the parade, estimated at 1,300 robed and masked men, included some Klansmen from Fort Worth and Waco.[125]

In February, the *Dallas Morning News* continued its criticism of the governor for not singling out the Klan in his speeches. Alonzo Wasson, chief editorial writer for the *News*, wrote Neff that he had gone after other forms of lawlessness but had ignored the Klan.[126] In March alone, the *News* ran three critical editorials, the one on March 25 comparing Neff unfavorably to Governor John M. Parker of Louisiana, who the day before had called on all peace officers in that state to "suppress with an iron hand the evil of Ku Kluxism wherever it raises its head."

The state's newspapers represented a wide range of opinion. In her examination of several of the big city dailies of that period, Linda Elaine Kilgore found that the *Dallas Morning News* took the strongest stand against the Klan, followed closely by the *Houston Chronicle*.[127] Kilgore wrote that the *Houston Post* "seemed to advocate objective reporting of every aspect of the incidents, with a minimum of editorial comment."[128] Other papers with neutral stands similar to the *Post* included the *Austin American* and the *Fort Worth Star-Telegram*.[129] Kilgore was astounded by the fact that the *Star-Telegram* could print several column inches of news stories about activities of the Klan without once taking an editorial stand.[130] Her reading of the *Waco Times-Herald* placed that newspaper "well on the side of the Klan."[131] Her study also included a chapter on the *Denison Herald*, where she found a courageous editor, J. L. Greer, who repeatedly editorialized against the Klan over a five-year period, beginning in 1921. Despite being located in the North Texas area where public opinion strongly supported the Klan, Greer wrote tough columns attacking the secrecy of the group and its racial and religious intolerance.[132]

Although the Klan's small benevolences to churches and its stand against liquor and immoral living brought support from some clergy, others took strong issue. Among them was Neff's own pastor, Dr. Joseph Martin Dawson, minister of the First Baptist Church in Waco. Dawson began his outspoken interest in social issues in 1915 when he arrived in Waco and preached often on such subjects as child labor, the exploitation of immigrants, and women's rights. He condemned the lynchings in Waco, and when the Klan came to Waco in 1921, he used the pulpit to decry their methods and activities, even though many of his congregation were members.[133]

There is little question that mob violence was peaking in the state. The violence certainly included beatings and tarring and feathering. Beyond that, the spring of 1922 saw a frightening increase in lynchings, primarily of Negroes, but also a few white persons. The most horrendous of the killings occurred in the small Central Texas town of Kirvin, some fifty miles northeast of Waco, on May 4, 1922. Monte Akers' *Flames after Midnight: Murder, Vengeance, and the Desolation of a Texas Community* paints a graphic and detailed account of the burning alive of three black men who were almost certainly innocent of a brutal murder of a young white woman in Kirvin. The story is all the more tragic because local authorities concealed the identities of the white probable murderers and allowed them to go free, and because within the next month, outraged white men killed, by at least one person's estimate, an additional twenty-seven black persons.[134] Neff did not challenge the Klan in this incident, just as he had not taken note of an earlier KKK parade and violent episode just outside Waco in 1921.[135]

By the summer of 1922, the Klan was into politics in a big way. Nevertheless, the organization did face scrutiny from some of the media and ministers, and all of the major cities and several of the second-tier cities organized citizens' leagues to combat their activities. Neff had steadfastly refused to tackle the Klan head on, so if he wanted a second term, he was almost sure to have more than token opposition. For all intents and purposes, Neff's first term ended eight months shy of its official termination on January 1923. Those months would be devoted to his campaign for reelection, which was to be more challenging than he had originally thought.

CHAPTER 7

Reelection and Second Term

I feel I have been a missionary in a strange land.

—Pat Neff

Talk of denying Neff a second term began almost before he could settle into his chair in the governor's office. In October 1921, the *San Antonio Express* ran a lengthy story relating the search by several individuals for a suitable opponent for Neff in 1922. The reporter wrote that there had been "probably a hundred conferences aimed at unhorsing" Neff, but the ringleaders had been unable to find a man who they thought could defeat Neff. The group felt that Neff was not anti-Klan enough. They wanted to field a person with strong feelings about the Klan. The reporter noted other opposition to Neff but quoted an unnamed anti-Neff "man of consequence" as cautioning the others:

> Of course it is possible to run somebody against Neff. Of course Neff has enemies inside the party. Every executive has. But I have heard this second term stuff before. If Tom Campbell and Jim Ferguson and Oscar B. Colquitt could not be beaten for their second terms, what on earth is the use of trailing Neff?[1]

As finally constituted, the Democratic Party primary ballot included three men in addition to Neff: Fred S. Rogers of Bonham, Harry T. Warner, editor of the *Paris News*, and W. W. King of Sabine County.

Rogers presented himself as a former army major and combat veteran of the World War, a founder of the Farm Labor Union, and a person who "knew his age."(Rogers was undoubtedly referring to Neff's having trouble remembering his birth date.) Although he said he was not a member of the Klan and did not intend to become one, he upheld the right of the Klan or any other organization of a social, political, or fraternal nature to organize and operate.[2] Rogers was former Senator Joe Weldon Bailey's choice to oppose Neff, but Bailey did not take an active part in the 1922 campaign.

Neff ignored Rogers throughout May and finally announced for reelection on June 3, only seven weeks before the primary election.[3] Neff decided to wait until

June 24, only twenty-eight days before the primary, to make his "opening speech" and thus made a conscious decision to let Rogers have the stage to himself for the first three weeks of June.

Warner announced for governor the day after Neff, severely chastising Neff for his lack of leadership in funding the public schools.[4] Warner was well known in the newspaper fraternity, since he had been the Capitol correspondent and later managing editor of the *Houston Post* before moving to Paris, Texas. Warner formally opened his campaign in Brownwood at a Fourth of July picnic, blaming Neff for the rural school crisis, the prison system quandary, and particularly the assaults being perpetrated by the Klan.[5] Neither Rogers nor Warner had the time or resources to conduct an extensive or expensive campaign. The October 1921 warning of the prominent but unnamed anti-Neff man regarding the futility of challenging a popular incumbent was proving to be well founded. Another Joe Bailey or other dominant figure failed to materialize, and the power of incumbency was still overwhelming, particularly because Neff's strong stand on law enforcement and his pleas for economy in government had found a receptive audience. Rogers was reduced to hoping that the Bailey influence would rise again. Warner had to be content to appeal to those who wanted a stronger anti-Klan candidate. W. W. King was never a factor in the campaign.[6]

Neff Opens His Campaign

For his part, Neff made the most of the four weeks he had allotted for the campaign. He decided to open his campaign in Plainview and spoke to some 2,000 supporters the afternoon of June 24. For the occasion, he prepared a text that ran seventeen legal-size pages. Speaking to farmers, stockmen, and small businessmen who were suffering from the depressed economy, he emphasized his drive for an "economically administered government." The major part of his address was directed to public schools and law enforcement issues. Neff reiterated his long-standing commitment to proper support for education, from "the obscurest rural school to the University of Texas," but stated that he wanted to find new revenue sources for education and not raise the tax on "over-taxed real property." Although he spent more time during his address on the subject of law enforcement than any other area, he still refused to address the Klan question in a clear way. His overriding focus continued to be enforcing the Prohibition law and railing against local law enforcement officers who refused to vigorously prosecute violations of that law. He also laid out, for the first time, his vision for a full-fledged system of state parks, saying the state "should establish parks, large and small, throughout her broad borders."[7]

The Denison Railroad Strike

Neff planned his July schedule to be far less frantic than the one he had endured two years earlier. But he reckoned without a railroad strike at Denison that began July 1 and engulfed his attention before the election. The month started quietly enough with a nonpolitical address in Athens on July 4. Neff stayed the night before with a family who must have been very close friends based on his advance letter to them:

> Your invitation to stay with you is accepted. I am to be "home folks" and I now give you instructions as to what I want for breakfast. You and your wife can eat whatever you desire. I am to have a bowl—a large bowl—of milk toast, the milk to be partially skimmed on one side. The toast is to be browned on each side, the milk boiled and poured over it. The toast is to be made of either light bread or biscuit, not corn-bread. In addition to this, I am to have two boiled eggs—hen eggs—boiled in the way the restaurant people call "soft" hard boiled. I mean by this, just hard enough so that the eggs will stay together while being peeled. This menu is to be supplemented by a glass of water—pure water. If you have more to drink than water, keep it on your side of the table. Your conscience should be your guide as to what you drink.[8]

His carefully planned schedule, however, was about to be disrupted.

The nationwide railroad union dispute that began July 1 soon flared into violence at Denison, in far North Texas, where 1,400 rail employees walked off their jobs. The railroad companies began hiring replacements, causing volatile reaction from the strikers. Every day the state newspapers reported violent incidents.[9] The federal government and the railroad companies (Texas and Pacific and the Missouri, Kansas, and Texas) all appealed to the governor on July 12 to send in National Guard troops.[10] On the same day, the shop craft union warned Neff that the workers would protest any use of state troops.[11] In Washington, U.S. Secretary of War John W. Weeks, after consulting with President Warren G. Harding, wired the army commander in San Antonio to be prepared to act if Governor Neff did not.[12] Neff tried to stay neutral about the labor dispute, keeping a close watch on developments but never taking any direct action.

Former Governor William P. Hobby recommended to Neff that he invoke the Open Port Law, enacted during Governor Hobby's tenure in a 1920 shutdown of the port of Galveston by a dock strike. A bitter gang-type war had broken out in Galveston after strikers demanded the shipping companies employ only union men and increase wages. Galveston authorities hesitated to interfere, so Governor Hobby sent in four Texas Rangers. When the Rangers failed to quell violence, Hobby declared a state of martial law on Galveston Island.[13] The legislature, backing up Governor Hobby, enacted the Open Port Law, which was later extended to apply to all operations of common carriers, thus its relevance to the Denison strike.[14] However, after conferring with Adjutant General T. D. Barton and Texas Ranger Captain Tom Hickman, Neff decided no action from him was warranted at that time.[15]

He did take time on July 11 to add another "first" to his record. He became the state's first chief executive to make a radio address, which was broadcast through the wireless telephone station of WCM of the University of Texas. Some seventy-five persons were in the station, and a large crowd gathered outside to hear Neff directly. The governor made a nonpolitical speech entitled "Peacetime Patriotism" while the revered melody "Silver Threads among the Gold" played in the background.[16]

But the Denison strike would not go away. On the Thursday before the election, Neff canceled all remaining political engagements and hurried to Denison, where he talked to the strikers during the day and, "in disguise," to more of them Sunday night.[17] (Neff never explained what he meant by "in disguise.") Then he returned to his home in Waco to await election day, having taken no decisive action on the Denison situation.

The Denison strike was not the only issue during the campaign on which Neff was perceived as waffling by his critics, including the *Dallas Morning News*. What his opponents saw as equivocation on vital issues, Neff and his adherents viewed as calm deliberation—and smart politics—on critical problems. Nevertheless, it must have caused his supporters some concern as they observed his lack of decisive action on the strike as well as his refusal to challenge the actions of the Ku Klux Klan in a straightforward manner.[18]

The Klan and Politics

The Klan reached its peak of influence in the period from mid-1922 to early 1923. The organization pitted brother against brother, neighbor against neighbor. It was both encouraged and denigrated by various Protestant preachers and in fraternal halls. The issues it raised—Prohibition, morality, family values—were strongly debated in cities and at the forks of the creek.[19]

In the summer of 1922, the Texas Klan was ready to enter the final phase of its organizational development: politics. Revived in 1920, the Klan concentrated in 1921 on recruiting members and imposing its moral order on Texans. By 1922, its members, particularly Hiram Wesley Evans, a Dallas dentist, hungered to extend their influence to political offices and set their sights on electing officials at all three levels of government—local, state, and national.[20] Concerned citizens in a number of cities reacted with alarm. Bolstered by opposition to the Klan by such major newspapers as the *Dallas Morning News* and the *Houston Chronicle*, they began to organize to prevent the Klan from electing members or sympathizers to public office. The first group to mobilize was the Dallas County Citizens' League, formed in April 1922. Citizens in Fort Worth, Beaumont, Austin, Waco, and a number of other cities also organized. Four days before the primary election, the Dallas League staged its final rally, drawing 3,000 "lustily cheering people" to hear candidates who opposed the Klan.[21] The KKK held its own rally for aspirants favorable to its cause, and in the Saturday election, the Klan swept all local offices except one. That night, the Klan paraded—unmasked—through the streets of Dallas.[22] In the Sunday and Monday papers after the election, the *Dallas Morning News* ran stories of Klan victories in Houston, Fort Worth, and Waco.[23] It was feared that in addition to victories in local races, the Klan would control the Texas Legislature in 1923. Klan candidates did claim a substantial majority of seats in the House of Representatives and would be a strong presence in Austin in January 1923. However, the organization's failure to win a majority in the Senate meant that its agenda could be blocked by the upper house.[24]

The biggest victory for the Klan was the vote registered by Klan-supported Earle Mayfield for the U.S. Senate. Mayfield, a forty-one-year-old attorney from East Texas, had served in the Texas Senate from 1907 to 1913 and was a member of the Texas Railroad Commission when he ran for the Senate. U.S. Senator Charles A. Culberson's term was to expire in 1922 and opposition to him was widespread. Several names were mentioned, including Baylor President Samuel Palmer Brooks, Congressman Tom Connally, and others, but all demurred for one reason or another.

The four who finally made the race in addition to Mayfield and Culberson were former Governor Jim Ferguson, Cullen Thomas, Clarence Ousley, and former Congressman Robert L. Henry. Two, Mayfield and Henry, were avowedly pro-Klan, although Mayfield tried to downplay his endorsement by the organization. Three of the candidates, Ferguson, Culberson and Ousley, were clearly anti-Klan, while Thomas tried to straddle the fence and keep both sides happy.

In his extensive chapter on the 1922 Senate race in his book, *Hood, Bonnet, and Little Brown Jug*, historian Norman Brown wrote that Ferguson was "the most colorful and controversial candidate in the race."[25] The Temple banker-farmer—ousted by impeachment in 1917, defeated by Governor Hobby in 1918 when he attempted to return to the governor's office, and defeated yet again in 1920 as a presidential candidate on the American Party ticket—was still looking for vindication for what he thought was a terrible injustice in deposing him from his office in the State Capitol. To keep his name before the people, he had started a weekly newspaper, the *Ferguson Forum*, in 1917 and used it to berate his enemies, near and far. On February 2, 1922, he used the *Forum* to announce his candidacy for the Senate. Ferguson came out against the Klan in April but also added that he was not running solely as an anti-Klan candidate but as a full-fledged Democrat.[26]

Although other candidates scored points from time to time, it was clear in mid-summer that Mayfield and Ferguson were the frontrunners—one backed by the Klan, the other openly anti-Klan. In the primary, the Klan gave Mayfield a lead of some 30,000 over Ferguson, who finished strong enough to force a runoff.

Culberson, Thomas, Ousley, and Henry finished in that order, and the stage was set for another contentious election.[27] The choice in the runoff was clear: between a Klan candidate and a former impeached governor. The ensuing contest saw law partners, women's advocates, and political friends on opposite sides of the fence. Strong Prohibitionists generally chose Mayfield, individuals who could not stomach the Klan reluctantly sided with Ferguson. Mayfield won the seat with 317,591 votes to 265,233 for Ferguson, a margin of 52,358. Ferguson put out a poster that stated that Neff was going to vote for him;[28] Neff's actual vote is unknown.

The senatorial battle completely overshadowed the governor's race. The state's newspapers consistently spread stories of the six senatorial candidates across the top of their pages while relegating Neff and his contenders to smaller and less visible space. This suited Neff fine and perhaps lessened his chagrin that he received endorsement for reelection from only two of the state's major newspapers, the *Houston Post* and the *Corpus Christi Caller.*[29] There would appear to be little question that the big-city newspapers, certainly the *Dallas Morning News*, were displeased that Neff failed to be more forthcoming on the Klan issue and more decisive on the Denison strike. They must have felt that Neff would win—and they really hoped he would—but they were not going to give him the satisfaction of an endorsement, which would congratulate him on what many of them saw as a less than sterling first term and a failure of leadership on crucial issues during the campaign.

As the governor's campaign launched into its final month, Neff received an increasing number of letters imploring him to take a firm stand denouncing the Klan. One of his supporters in Dallas wrote in part: "If you are not a member or a sympathizer, for God's sake, come out and deny it."[30] Similar letters came from half a dozen other individuals. Neff's office replied to all of them with the simple statement that Neff had said he had never been a member of the Klan or expected to be.[31] This ambiguity resulted in his name appearing on both pro-Klan and anti-Klan sample ballots.[32]

Neff was obviously conflicted regarding the Klan. He did not support violence of any kind, but he was also exceedingly unhappy with numerous sheriffs, police chiefs, and district attorneys who were turning their eyes away from open violations of the Prohibition laws. The Klan was, in some areas of the state, the only mechanism enforcing these laws. Although the governor was a man with some inconsistencies in his political stands, the enforcement of Prohibition was one principle from which he would never retreat. A second factor in not being explicit about the Klan was that "good politics" told him that to take a strong stand for or against the Klan before the primary election would probably not be to his advantage.

By Saturday night, July 22, Neff was the clear winner, with a convincing if not overwhelming victory.[33] Neff and his supporters had not really worked that hard or long, and although he would express disappointment in letters during the coming weeks, he had won another two years without a runoff election. On July 25, the *Dallas Morning News* ran three editorials commenting on the events of the previous week. Regarding the governor's race, the *News* expressed the sentiments of probably many Texans when it reported that no one expected Neff to lose but that certainly "Texas would have its Governor more frank and courageous than he has shown himself to be."

Records of the Texas Election Bureau and of the Texas Democratic Party are no longer available for that election, so the *Dallas Morning News* results have been used as the unofficial "official" results for the election. The *Dallas Morning News* of August 6, 1922, carried the tabulation as "complete unofficial returns from the Texas Election Bureau." The election produced 618,928 votes. Oddly enough, this was 20,000 more than the hotly contested Senate race. Neff polled 332,961 or 53.7 percent of the vote, Rogers 208,318 or 32.9 percent, Warner 60,636 or 9.8 percent, and King received 22,013 votes, or 3.6 percent. A color-coded map found in the Neff Papers revealed that his support was widespread over the state. Although Rogers carried a few counties in all parts of the state, Neff's strength overcame the Bonham candidate's appeal.

The Denison Strike Revisited

With the election behind him, Neff quickly got back to the problem of the Denison railroad workers' strike. In his book *The Battles of Peace*, he makes no mention of the fact that he had held off action in sending in the Rangers or declaring martial law until after the election. Whether the federal government deliberately held off making its final demands on Neff until after the election is not known.

The first action occurred the Monday after the election, July 24. In *The Battles of Peace*, Neff relates how he received a Colonel Lincoln that Monday and was informed that the officer had been sent to determine whether Neff was going to use state militia to protect life, property, and commerce in Denison. According to Neff's account, the Colonel remained in his office for three hours, Neff finally stating that he was unwilling for federal troops to march on Texas soil for the purpose of enforcing Texas laws: "I took my stand for the supremacy and sovereignty of the State."[34] Neff told Colonel Lincoln that by daylight Denison would be put under martial law; National Guard troops moved to the city the following day. The troops brought order out of chaos and respect for law out of threatened open violence. Accused lawbreakers were brought to court, but Adjutant General Thomas Barton's official report to the governor told of the failure of most charges to result in convictions by local courts. Barton reported widespread sympathy for the strikers: "I believe that these parties would have been convicted in any other county in the state."[35]

Fall 1922 Activities and Preparations for the Legislature

Having resolved the railroad strike problems, Neff was ready to start thinking about his promises to the people of Texas for his second term. He had said his priorities for the legislature in January 1923 would be proper support for education, highways, and flood control and conservation. In August, he convened approximately 200 engineers and interested citizens in the Senate Chamber in Austin to plan how to reclaim the millions of acres of fertile Texas land hit by recurring floods, and to work toward harnessing the floodwaters of Texas rivers. The governor challenged the audience to consider the possibilities of dams and reservoirs that would reclaim four million acres of the finest land "in all the world" and thereby add $200 million to the tax rolls.[36]

Also in early August, he took time out to travel to Waco to see Hallie Maude graduate from Baylor. Myrtie did not attend, having gone to Mineral Wells for her periodic visit for her health. Again, she stayed at least a month.[37] In her mother's absence, Hallie Maude also continued to play the lead role in Governor's Mansion activities, from furnishings to hosting social events. Late in August, Neff wrote her: "Make out a list of all the furniture you want to purchase for the Mansion. If you will make the list at once, stating the different articles you desire to purchase and send it to me, I can arrange it so that the selection of this furniture can be made after September 1. Do this at once."[38]

Family matters also inserted themselves on September 5 when Sam Neff and Sallie Neff Calvert deeded their title and interest in the original Neff homestead to their brother Pat. This land was in the estate of Isabella Neff and consisted of 129 1/2 acres on the dividing line between McLennan and Coryell Counties. In the early twenty-first century, this acreage was still owned by Pat Neff III.[39]

As expected, Neff won the general election overwhelmingly. After a flurry of lawsuits and counter suits, Earle B. Mayfield, Democratic Party nominee, won the U.S. senatorial race over George Peddy, the Independent Democratic and Republican Party nominee.[40]

If Texans sometimes thought they had elected a governor who was a combination Baptist preacher and prosecuting attorney, the lead story in the November 26 *Austin Statesman* would have borne that out to the delight of some and the trepidation of others. In a move decidedly unusual to political observers, Neff announced that, before the convening of the legislature in 1923, he was going to make a series of eight speeches based on Bible texts from both the Old and New Testaments. The speeches would lay out his priorities for the 1923 legislative session. Ranging from, "No man seweth a piece of new cloth unto an old garment" (Matthew 9:16), referring to his call for a new constitution, to, "Sirs, ye know by this business we have our wealth" (Acts 19:25), referring to his interest in economic development, the Bible texts would highlight his proposed agenda for the legislators. The topics were the need for a new constitution, education, taxation, law enforcement, highways, flood control, prison reform, and, finally, economic development.

On November 28, he made his maiden talk of the series at Brenham on the need for a new constitution. Arguing that the current constitution was completely out of date, he said the men who wrote it in 1876 "knew that men could not make a flying machine and they would have been turned out of church for heresy had they believed in wireless messages or contended that ice could be made in August."[41]

Neff traveled to Houston the evening of Friday, December 1, to address the State Teachers' Association in the second of his series. Making the case for a better educational system at both the public school and higher education levels, he came out against an increase in the state property tax but brought up the possibility of an oil production tax that could bring in $9 million per year.[42]

In mid-December, Neff decided to take a short break in the middle of his speech series. He left Austin on a week-long vacation trip to the Rio Grande Valley. The press was friendly, the *San Antonio Express* reporting that the governor had been working back-breaking hours, arising at six in the morning and many times working until eleven at night, and that he was due his first real vacation of the year. Although he mixed in some duties, Neff did find time to participate in his first deer hunt and shattered the statement by Baylor President Brooks that he had "never baited a hook or fired a gun." Neff confessed to the *San Antonio Express* reporter that "the big buck got away."[43] He brought the exploded rifle cartridge home as a souvenir.

Neff's third and fourth addresses in his eight-part series came on the afternoon and evening of December 22, the first at Fredericksburg and the second at Johnson City. At Fredericksburg, he gave strong backing to the centralizing and standardizing of highway construction. That evening, in Johnson City, he waded right into the middle of the controversial subject of taxes. The *San Antonio Express* the next morning gave him banner headlines: NEFF SCORES TAX EVADER: LITTLE FELLOWS PAY AND WEALTH GOES FREE.[44]

Spending a quiet Christmas week at the mansion, Neff issued his annual Christmas proclamation and prepared a new talk on his favorite subject—law enforcement—and on December 30, he traveled to Floresville, just southeast of San Antonio, and made another hard-hitting speech on the subject.[45]

One week before convening the 38th Legislature on January 9, Neff made the final two speeches in his series. In Navasota on January 2, he talked of prisons; the *San Antonio Express* the following day (January 3) reported that the governor advocated factory work for state prisoners. The next day he journeyed on to Liberty, where he made a major address on the need for industry and other economic development, reminding Texans that with the state's vast raw materials, they must find a way to benefit financially from the manufacture of finished products.[46]

A young Noah Neff, Pat's father, circa 1854. (Charlotte Calvert Papers, David L. Scott Collection)

A young Isabella Neff, Pat's mother, circa 1854. (Charlotte Calvert Papers, David L. Scott Collection)

When Pat was about ten years old, his mother took him on a train trip to Houston, where this formal portrait was made. This is the earliest photo of Pat Neff known to exist. (Isabell Crowell Napier Collection)

Pat as a Baylor student, circa 1892. (Charlotte Calvert Papers, David L. Scott Collection)

Myrtie Mainer in her freshman year at Baylor, circa 1890. (Texas Collection, Baylor University)

Myrtie Neff in the early 1900s. (Ella Frances Dodd Collection)

Southwestern Academy in Magnolia, Arkansas, where Pat taught for two years (1894-96) to save money for law school. The building was finished in the late fall of 1894, when Neff began teaching. It was destroyed many years ago. (Postcard, 1907)

Formal portrait of Neff in the Texas Legislature, 1899-1905. (Charlotte Calvert Papers, David L. Scott Collection)

Pat and Myrtie's wedding picture. The ceremony took place in her hometown of Lovelady, Texas, on May 31, 1899. (Texas Collection)

Hallie Maude (b. 1901) and Pat Jr. (b. 1903) circa 1915. (C. J. Wright Studios, Ella Frances Dodd Collection)

"A Plain Democrat," poster for Neff's first campaign for governor in 1920. (Courtesy of Jud Thomas R. Phillips, Baylor '71, former Chief Justice, Supreme Court of Texas)

Neff, the hunter. To counter opponents' claims in his first gubernatorial campaign (1920) that he was a "sissy," friends invited him to go on hunting and fishing trips, photographed him, and circulated the photos to the news media. (Texas Collection)

Neff's inaugural ceremony as governor, January 18, 1921. At his request, no inaugural ball was held that year in consideration of his Baptist beliefs. (Texas Collection)

*Myrtie in her inaugural gown,
January 18, 1921. (Ella Frances
Dodd Collection)*

*Mother Neff at the inauguration.
She moved into the Governor's
Mansion with her son and the First
Lady but died just four months into
Neff's first term. She was
undoubtedly the single greatest
influence in his life.
(Texas Collection)*

The Cowboy statue, which stands just outside the front door of the Texas State Capitol to the southwest, was dedicated by Governor Neff on his next to last day in office, January 19, 1925. (State Preservation Board, copyright 2007)

Although the inmates standing with Neff in this photo are not identified, the governor made several visits to the Sugar Land prison farm in 1924, where he enjoyed the music of a blues singer named Leadbelly. One of Neff's final acts as governor in January 1925 was to issue a pardon for the talented convict. (Texas Collection)

Mother Neff Park, a gift to the State of Texas from Pat Neff and his mother, was the first nonhistorical park in the state park system. (V. Marie Jones Papers, David L. Scott Collection)

CLUB HOUSE
MOTHER NEFF STATE PARK

WHITE AND CARTER
BELTON TEXAS

The clubhouse at Mother Neff Park was built by the Civilian Conservation Corps in the 1930s under Neff's supervision. (V. Marie Jones Papers, David L. Scott Collection)

Neff with a lamb at his "home place," the family farm in Coryell County, circa 1945. (Marie Taylor Neff Collection)

President Neff rides a donkey during "All University Day" at Baylor, circa 1940. Each year at this spring holiday festival, Neff would race Education Dean Lorena Stretch. (Texas Collection)

Neff and the Keys quadruplets (l-r, Roberta, Leota, Mary, and Mona Keys) board a train to go to Canada to visit the Dionne quintuplets in May 1936. The trip generated over 4,000 newspaper clippings and was worth an estimated $250,000 in publicity for Baylor and the Texas Centennial. (Gildersleeve photo courtesy of the Texas Collection)

The family at Hallie Maude and Frank Wilcox's wedding, December 5, 1933. (l-r) Pat Jr., Wilcox, Hallie Maude, Neff, and Myrtie. (Texas Collection)

Neff (center) awarded both Vice-President John Nance Garner (left of Neff), a friend of his from his years in the Texas Legislature, and Mrs. Garner (second from far left) honorary Doctor of Laws degrees in 1936. Pictured to the right of Neff is former Governor Miriam "Ma" Ferguson. At the far left is U.S. Senator Tom Connally. (Texas Collection)

First Baptist Church in Waco, Pat and Myrtie Neff's long-time "home" church. The church was founded in 1851. (Courtesy of First Baptist Church, Waco, Texas)

Neff invited Eleanor (Mrs. Franklin D.) Roosevelt to the Baylor campus to speak in 1939, but he did not use the occasion to award her an honorary degree in deference to several of his board members' feelings toward her husband's administration. (Texas Collection)

Despite the Texas Baptist Convention's opposition, Neff awarded an honorary Doctor of Laws degree to President Harry S. Truman in 1947. Upon hearing of the Baptists' objections, Truman wrote a friend, "It is a wonderful thing we don't have a Baptist Pope." (Marlan and Ockander photo courtesy of the Texas Collection)

Neff poses with his old friend, U.S. Senator Tom Connally, circa 1945. The two were classmates at the University of Texas Law School and peers in the Texas Legislature. Connally had a long and distinguished career in Congress, serving in the U.S. House of Representatives from 1916 to 1928 and then in the U.S. Senate from 1929 to 1953. (Texas Collection)

The traditional Speakers Day event in 1947 honored former speakers of the Texas House of Representatives. The group included three speakers who later became governors: Coke Stevenson (front row, second from left), Pat Neff, and Price Daniel (right). (Photo courtesy of the children of Claud H. Gilmer, speaker in 1945, pictured back row, top right)

Neff with Harvey Couch, the Southwestern Academy (Arkansas) student whom Neff challenged to stay in school in 1895. Couch went on to become a railroad and electric utility magnate and a confidant of U.S. presidents. He credited Neff, next to his mother, for his success in life. This picture was taken at Couchwood, Couch's summer home in Arkansas, circa 1940. (Photo courtesy of Broadman Press)

The Thirty-eighth Legislature—1923

The Klan's victories in several local elections and some state elections in the summer of 1922 represented the zenith for that organization. When the new session convened January 9, the organization controlled the House of Representatives by about a two-to-one margin, but its supporters were a minority in the Senate. Representative Lewis T. Carpenter of Dallas tried to rally the anti-Klan members of the House to oppose R. E. Seagler of Palestine, a Klan sympathizer, for speaker, but failed.[47] The Senate kept up its opposition to the Klan, adopting a resolution on January 16 to commend the efforts by Louisiana Governor J. M. Parker against "the rule of hooded mobs and masked political organizations."[48] The resolution was seen by some as a rebuke to Neff for what many perceived to be his too-mild opposition to the Klan. The House refused to follow suit on the resolution. As early as February, the *San Antonio Express* carried a story from its Austin bureau that the "Three K Issue [Is] Fast Fading in Texas Politics." The state continued to show its division on the question when the Klan lost local elections in the spring of 1923 in El Paso and several other communities.[49] Offsetting that was an incursion of seventy robed and hooded Klansmen onto the floor of the Texas House of Representatives on April 19. A program of Negro music by the chorus of St. John's Orphanage was under way at the time; when the singing stopped, the leader of the Klan stepped forward and presented the group with cash and coins totaling $64.75 and declared that the Klan was the friend of the Negro.[50] The uninvited visit was deplored the next day by the lieutenant governor, who expressed his "unqualified disapproval" of the act.[51]

Against this backdrop of the split legislative makeup, Neff received some excellent advice from George Barcus, his former Waco law partner and wise friend. Barcus, who had worked in Neff's 1920 campaign without pay for several months, was one of the few individuals in the state who could speak openly and candidly to the governor. On January 2, exactly one week before the legislature was convened, he wrote Neff one of his periodic letters, full of politically astute advice. Speaking of several key issues, Barcus first advised Neff to recommend a constitutional convention to the legislators but to suggest to them that, if in their judgment the people would not favor such a convention, the legislature should take no further time discussing the matter. Addressing the question of law enforcement, Barcus told the governor he thought frankly that Neff "was asking for more than you can ever get the legislature to give, and . . . you will make a mistake if you try to force your drastic program . . . onto the statute book."[52]

As the legislative session got under way, newspapers heralded the first woman legislator—Edith Wilmans, a Dallas lawyer, who had been elected to the House. She was active in both woman suffrage and Democratic Party activities. She got into the middle of things immediately, making a seconding speech for one of the losing speaker candidates.[53] The state's newspapers also reported that, for the first time, the House would have its constitutional limit of 150 members and that an electric voting machine had been installed to replace the tedious and time-consuming roll call system.[54] Neff could not wait for his second inaugural and sent up a message at the end of the legislature's first week that he would like to be heard before the ceremonies on January 16. The legislature acceded and on Friday, January 12, Neff made one of his few personal appearances before a joint session: "I come to this occasion not as one who would dictate. . . . I come at this hour with that fine spirit of friendship and fellowship and comradeship. . . . [I want to] become better acquainted with this splendid type of lawmakers."[55]

But then he virtually contradicted himself when he again said that he would have no one to represent him on the floor of the House or the Senate, despite the lack of success with this operating method in 1921. He also repeated that there would be no administration bills from his office. In taking this stand, he ignored Barcus' last and best plea in his letter. To get all or at least most of his program adopted, Barcus had suggested:

> Make friends with the members of the legislature and give them a little "taffy" and take them into your confidence and have certain men in both branches of the legislature that are your recognized spokesmen in legislation and be careful to have them fight for only the real constructive matters you wish. In other words, in a great many of the small things, do not try to force your word.[56]

At Neff's request, social activities for his second inauguration were minimal. His favorite band, the 142nd Infantry Band (the Old Gray Mare Band) of the Texas National Guard unit in Brownwood, played a concert Monday night before the inauguration. The only other event was a dance the night of the inauguration—not for or involving the governor but for members of the legislature and their families.[57]

Law Enforcement

Neff's first detailed message to the legislature was on his highest priority, law enforcement. The exhortation was not delivered personally by the governor but filed and read into the records in the two houses. Neff had addressed eight subjects in his presession addresses in Central and South Texas, and between his inauguration and the end of January, he sent official messages to the legislature on all but water conservation and flood control. No one familiar with state politics had any doubt, however, as to his highest priority. He made sixteen recommendations on law enforcement, one fewer than in his presession speech at Floresville.[58] He did get some of the Klan problem "off his back" by castigating mob rule, leading the

San Antonio Express on January 16 to headline the story about his message: HIT
AT HOODED BANDS SEEN IN NEFF MESSAGE ASSAILING MOB RULE.

The great majority of Neff's sixteen recommendations concerned enforcement
of the Eighteenth or Prohibition Amendment to the U.S. Constitution. Neff's
fight was but a microcosm of the nationwide battle on the amendment. Sparked
partially by the desire to protect young soldiers, the U.S. Congress had submitted
the amendment (titled informally the Volstead Act) to the states in December 1917
and in less than fourteen months (January 16, 1919), Nevada had become the
thirty-sixth state to ratify the amendment and put it into effect. Just three years
later, the amendment was already facing increasing opposition. The *Austin Statesman* of November 20, 1922, reported that the forces seeking modification of the
act were meeting in St. Louis to organize a national group to offset the influence of
the Anti-Saloon League of America, promising to make it an issue in the 1924
elections. Two weeks later, the *Statesman* reported that President Warren G. Harding
was going to call the governors together to work out a program of joint federal-
state enforcement of the amendment.[59] The week before Christmas, fifteen governors, including Neff, met with the president in Washington and assured him of
their cooperation in enforcing the act.[60]

The split in the country between Prohibition and anti-Prohibition was reflected
in Texas. Texas had joined the states ratifying the amendment, but after the war
anti-Prohibition forces regrouped as the mood of the people changed. Neff had the
unhappy experience of coming to the governorship when the majority of legislators were against any new programs and increasingly sympathetic to loose enforcement of Prohibition. Despite numerous favorable newspaper editorials and church
group endorsements, his law enforcement recommendations fared no better in
1923 than they had in the three legislative sessions of 1921. George Barcus' letter
proved prophetic: Neff asked for much more than the legislature was willing to
enact, dooming him to disappointment. Several of his points were never even introduced, several others were killed in committee, and the few that survived were
weakened considerably. The only two that passed in the regular session were a
vastly weakened officer removal law and one requiring detailed preservation of
reports and records of liquor seized by officers.[61]

The governor fared little better in the three special sessions he called. In his
message to the second called session, he reduced his sixteen demands to four, couch-
ing several in broader terms. The legislature again refused to enact his officer removal request and passed only three minor bills: a general bill restating the basic
Prohibition law, a second one strengthening the penalty for driving a car while
intoxicated, and a third providing for injunctions against hotel proprietors who
allowed alcohol violations on their premises.[62] The other message Neff sent up the
day before his inauguration was a call for a new state constitution.[63] A concurrent
resolution later passed the House, only to die in the Senate by a tie vote.

After his inauguration on January 16, Neff had private secretary R. B. Walthall hand-deliver five other substantive messages to the legislature over the following two weeks. The governor called for improvements in education, the taxation system, and the prison system and urged attention to highways and the status of manufacturing in the state.[64] There is no record of why Neff, so successful in persuading trial and civil juries for more than fifteen years, chose to have the great majority of his messages read to the legislature instead of delivering them personally. Presumably his highly effective style of speaking to juries would have been equally effective before the legislature, but we will never know. Fred Gantt, in his comprehensive study of the Texas governor's office, devotes a major portion of one chapter to the use of messages by Texas governors from 1876 to 1963. Gantt references Neff's extensive use of the "message device" but does not address the issue of Neff or any other governor's delivering such messages in person. For the most part, the legislature responded coolly to Neff's entreaties. Gantt stated that the legislature "was not impressed by this free flow of words" and that much of Neff's progressive program "fell far short of his expectations and hopes."[65]

Education

The governor's message on January 17 confirmed Neff's longtime interest in education, lamenting Texas' standing as thirty-fourth among the states in education. He was particularly critical of the state's lack of attention to rural schools. He urged the legislature to "make a thorough, scientific, impartial survey of our entire educational system" before making specific changes.[66] In response, the legislature enacted Senate Bill 256, establishing an educational survey commission composed of twelve persons, of whom at least six had to be outside the teaching profession. The members of the commission were to be chosen by a broad committee of educators, chaired by the governor. The body was given $50,000 for the survey with the requirement that neither the executive director nor any staff could be from Texas. The commission was mandated to make a study of the entire educational system, including higher education, and was to report back to the governor and legislature no later than December 1, 1924.[67]

The legislature also enacted several other education bills during the regular session. It voted $3 million of aid to supplement the available school funds for the scholastic year then in progress, exempted ex-servicemen and women from paying most fees and charges collected by the institutions of higher education, and designated the State Board of Education as the State Board of Vocational Education in order to qualify for federal funds. Of most importance to the normal colleges, the legislature scrapped that hated and puzzling name and changed the name of each of the eight colleges to "Teachers College." Thus, Sam Houston State, North Texas State, Southwest Texas State, West Texas State, South Texas State, Stephen F.

Austin State, East Texas State, and Sul Ross State simultaneously took on new, more descriptive suffixes.[68]

Two special education appropriation bills were passed in the third called session, one appropriating $2 million for each of the fiscal years ending on August 31 of 1924 and 1925 for the public schools of the state. Section 2 of the act gave the rationale that "many of the public schools require additional funds to pay the salary of teachers." The other bill gave an additional $1.5 million in each of the two years to the rural schools of the state.[69] Both bills were presented to the governor on the last day of the third session, and Neff, despite his general support for educational matters, let both bills become law without his signature in protest of the legislature's failure to provide the revenue required to implement them.[70]

Taxation

Neff's fourth substantive message to the legislature occurred on January 19 when he took up the subject of taxation.[71] The governor spent the first part of his message on the state property tax, lamenting that under the present "non-system of taxation, our taxes are neither equal nor uniform." Belying his conservative reputation, Neff then laid out several recommendations for additional methods of taxation. One of his principal suggestions was for an increased severance tax, one that taxes "our natural resources which have accumulated by the gradual operation of nature." Citing such taxes in Pennsylvania, West Virginia, and Minnesota, he declared the Texas tax to be entirely inadequate and went on to state that the severance tax was "clearly well within the class of subjects having ability to pay." He blasted the pipeline companies for refusing to pay the severance tax and said the state could bring in more than $2 million per year if this law were enforced. He also proposed a state income tax as one way of getting money to support Texas government. In addition, he called for revamping the inheritance tax and called attention to the fact that more than $6 million in taxes was currently owed and should be collected. Finally, he said if it were left up to him, he would abandon the property tax for state purposes and leave it entirely to the counties.[72]

For the next two months, numerous newspaper stories around the state reported on the machinations of legislation, as the Senate and House struggled to find the least painful way to provide for state government and the public schools. In late January, the House passed a production tax on oil; early in February, Representative Sam Johnson decried the emphasis on new taxes and lamented that the state would soon be known as the "State of Taxes instead of the State of Texas."[73] By the end of the regular session in mid-March, the legislature had managed to agree only on an occupation tax on gasoline dealers and on sulphur produced in the state and a gross receipts tax on textbook publishers.[74] The major fight on oil would carry over to the special sessions.

In the second called session, the legislature enacted a 2 percent gross production tax on oil, which was immediately challenged in court.[75] The body also passed an inheritance tax bill, and an occupation tax on amusements, and cleaned up the previously enacted bills on the sulfur tax and the occupation tax on gasoline. An income tax, which Neff had suggested, actually passed both houses, but then the two different versions could not be reconciled by the free conference committee; hence the bills died.[76]

Prisons

Neff delivered two separate messages on the penitentiary problem, the first on January 22.[77] Near the end of the regular session, the legislature was forced to appropriate another $600,000 to keep the penitentiaries operating.[78] The prison system's heavy reliance for much of its income on sales of agricultural products grown on the prison farms was a constant source of frustration and worry for Neff and the legislature and would remain a problem for many years. In his second message sent up on January 23, Neff told the legislators that the system owned more than 80,000 acres of land, with about half in cultivation. He related that there were twelve prison farms, all but one in far South Texas, with the headquarters of the system located on a ten-acre tract of land at Huntsville. The prevailing prison census was approximately 3,700, with almost a third of those added in the two years he had been governor.[79] Clearly, Neff's stringent pardon and parole policy was adding considerably to the prison population. Approximately half the inmates were white, some 90 percent were illiterate, and a quarter were too sick or otherwise limited in ability to work. Neff pushed for prison industries, not to sell goods to the public but to produce goods to be used at the penitentiaries and by other state institutions. He cited the making of automobile license plates and the canning of the prison-produced vegetables as two examples of work that would profit both the system and the individual. He also proposed that a number of the convicts work on public roads and that one of the farms be designated an "Honor Farm," with inmates working under the direction of a superintendent but without guards.[80]

Highways

On January 25, the governor sent up his sixth substantive message to the legislature. If there was any Neff legislative matter about which he could claim intimate knowledge, it was this one—Texas highways. Neff boasted more than 6,000 miles of experience with this topic. In the four years since he had begun campaigning for the chief executive's office, he had literally traveled the length and breadth of the state, from Texarkana to El Paso and from Texline to Orange. Although a considerable part of his travel had been by train, the majority was in his trusty Buick. Neff felt he knew every mud hole in the state, and there were a lot of them. He knew firsthand what it was to travel on a nice concrete ribbon for a while only to come to a county line and be tumbled into a muddy, barely navigable swamp. In fact, even as his highway message was being considered, the *San Antonio Express* was reporting that the main highway between San Antonio and Houston was impassable because of heavy rains in the area.[81] Neff had pledged to the Texas Highway Association in 1922 that he would stump for better highways, and he had done so. His message to the legislature on January 25 carefully and painstakingly built the case for state control and financing of a coordinated system of roads.[82] Of course, Neff's contention was made considerably easier by his citing the Federal Highway Act of 1921, which mandated that federal funds were available only where construction and maintenance were vested in the state. The governor's and the legislature's task in meeting the highway challenge was also greatly aided by the lobbying of the Texas Highway Association. In 1911, a Texas Good Roads Association had been formed to "carry out educational programs in the interest of road development."[83] Six years later, in 1917, the Highway Department was established, but county control of roads and funds continued. After the department was established, the Texas Good Roads Association disbanded to reemerge in 1922 as the Texas Highway Association.[84]

By 1923, cars were considered indispensable by Texans traversing the wide open spaces of their boundless state. Newspaper advertising by automobile dealers was supplying much of the revenue of the state's dailies, and four-to eight-page special "Automobile" sections appeared in many Sunday newspapers.[85] Add to that the strong support of contractors, suppliers, and the motoring public, and the legislature had few hard decisions to make in this area. On March 14, Neff approved House Bill 51, passed during the regular session, increasing the registration fees of cars and trucks and directing county tax collectors to transmit a portion of those fees to the Highway Department. A little-noticed section became more important later; it provided that effective January 1, 1924, the Highway Department was authorized to take over and maintain the various highways designated as "State Highways" in the several counties. Significant progress in highway matters was Neff's most notable accomplishment in 1923. He succeeded in getting a one-cent gasoline tax to finance highways, signed a bill for state control of the system, and obtained six-year terms and a pay raise for his three-member Highway Commission.[86]

Flood Control

Although flood control and conservation had been the subject of one of his presession addresses, Neff did not make a separate message on this subject to the legislature. Nevertheless, one of the first bills he signed in 1923 was on January 31 for an appropriation of $300,000 per year for two years to conduct topographic and hydrographic surveys in the state. The signing brought kudos from engineers and conservationists around the state and prompted a favorable editorial from the *Austin American* on March 30, 1923. During the third called session, the legislature sought to reduce the amount by half, but Neff stood with those concerned about flood control and vetoed House Bill 35.[87]

Higher Education: Texas Tech

Another of Neff's important accomplishments in the Thirty-eighth Legislature was the establishment of Texas Technological College. In 1919, a West Texas Chamber of Commerce had been formed, and it became the driving force for the new college in the Lubbock/Panhandle area.[88] In Neff's first term in 1921, he had vetoed a bill appropriating $50,000 to establish West Texas Agricultural and Mechanical College at a location to be picked. The veto had set off a storm of protest in West Texas, but Neff had calmly pointed out that the State Democratic Party platform had rejected a resolution recommending the creation of such a college and, besides, Texas was in desperate financial condition and could not afford another college then.[89] Neff had been besieged by West Texans and roundly cussed for his action, but he had given no hint of backing down. Proponents of an institution bided their time and determined that they would come back to the legislature in 1923 with "all their ducks in a row."[90]

In September 1922, a delegation from West Texas descended on San Antonio, the site of the State Democratic Convention, and succeeded in getting a favorable recommendation.[91] Over the fall, arguments went back and forth over the name of the proposed college and whether it would be independent or a part of Texas A&M. In January 1923, it was time for Governor Neff and the 38th Legislature to consider the matter. Searching for a college name which would be acceptable to all, Representative Lewis T. Carpenter suggested "Texas Technological College" and the legislators quickly agreed. The next move was up to Neff, and the West Texans left nothing to chance. They flooded him with calls, telegrams, and letters; one estimate was that a total of between 5,000 and 6,000 such communications came into his office in the next few days.[92] After keeping the supporters on pins and needles for several days, the governor, on February 10, signed the bill in appropriate ceremonies and the celebrations began. Nine days later, Neff sent his nine nominees for the college governing board to the Senate and they were quickly confirmed. He named five West Texans and four other outstanding individuals, including former Governor William P. Hobby, to serve. A tumultuous celebration was held in Sweetwater on March 2 at which Neff, who was accompanied by Hallie Maude, was lauded by all present.[93] The *Fort Worth Star Telegram* gave strong support to the college over a period of years, and Neff named publisher Amon Carter to the board. He was elected the first chairman by the remainder of the board members.[94]

State Parks

The work for which Neff is best remembered as governor is the beginnings of a formal state park system. The concept started simply: dedication to the public by Mother Neff of a small portion of land on the Leon River (part of the Neff property), described simply in her 1916 will as the "Neff Picnic Grounds."[95] In her will she prescribed that these grounds be permanently enclosed, that a pavilion be built for public gatherings, and that a gate and archway be erected with the name "The Neff Park" inscribed. Finally, her will provided that the park would be under the "management and control of my son, Pat M. Neff," and after he died, his descendants.[96] The six or so acres had indeed been a popular meeting place for church, family, lodge, and political reunions and events since Pat was a boy. He had made one of his campaign speeches for the legislature at the park in 1898. The value of his mother's gift to the people of Texas cannot be overestimated. As one writer put it: "Neff revered his mother and there is every indication that he believed there to be no more fitting legacy for her than a first class system of state parks with her own land donation as the crowning jewel."[97] In his campaign kick-off at Plainview on June 24, 1922, Neff had come out strong for parks:

> The State should establish parks, both large and small, throughout her broad borders. The people should have these breathing spots, where they can enjoy nature in stream and tree, in rock and rill. These are valuable things in this world that do not bear the dollar mark.[98]

Neff did not include a park system in his nine substantive messages to the legislature in January but, at the second called session on May 1, he had read into the record his brief but specific parks message. Citing the need for places where people might go for "rest, recreation, and relaxation," he called on the legislature to set up an unpaid six-member State Parks Committee to solicit "donations of land in tracts large and small" for conversion into public parks. He anticipated that if not then, perhaps later, the state might make money available to purchase such land so as to establish a "system of State parks."[99] A bill to carry out the governor's recommendation was introduced in the Senate two days later, wound its way through the legislative channels, and was approved by the governor on May 31. The final bill called for a five-member board to be appointed by the governor for six-year terms. The only appropriation was $1,500 for board members' travel expenses. The board was directed to solicit donations of land and to investigate the possibility of purchasing land, both subject to approval of the legislature.[100] The act did not go into effect for ninety days, but in the fall of 1923 furious activity toward a park system got under way.[101]

"White Primary" Bill

One major bill was enacted that does not reflect favorably on Pat Neff: the so-called "white primary" bill. Although Negroes had been effectively excluded from participating in the Democratic primary elections for many years, they were increasingly challenging their status. In early 1923, Representative Douglas Davenport of Bexar County introduced a bill to legally prevent blacks from voting in those elections. Senator R. M. Dudley of El Paso successfully derailed it in the Senate in the regular session, and it could have died there. However, Neff revived it in a message to the second called session of the legislature in 1923, saying, "It's a demand of the Democratic platform, isn't it?" Dudley was unable to defeat it this time, and the House passed the bill by a vote of 93 to 11. It was presented to the governor on May 10, and he allowed it to become law without his signature.[102] Apparently, he was not proud enough of the bill to put his signature of approval on it.

As usual, the regular session of sixty days did not produce the required biennial appropriations bills and failed to act on most of Neff's agenda. He was determined to keep the two houses in continuous session until they produced results. His message of March 10, four days before adjournment of the regular session, had a sarcastic tone, saying the Senate had "smothered to death" one of his law enforcement recommendations. That message told the legislature that he was calling it back into an immediate thirty-day session.[103] The legislature responded on March 15 by convening and then adjourning in thirty minutes for the shortest special session and the only one-day session in the history of the state. Neff had no choice but give the lawmakers a thirty-day breathing period, calling them back April 16 for a second called session. The second and third special sessions worked straight through from April 16 to June 14 to complete their work.

Neff's testy relations with the two legislative bodies was also vividly illustrated by the number of vetoes he issued during his second term. Neff vetoed sixty-two bills in the four legislative sessions in 1923.[104] Added to his vetoes in 1921, he gained the unenviable distinction of vetoing more bills than any governor before him except Edmund J. Davis, a Reconstruction governor.[105] His most controversial vetoes were those decrying the establishment of additional courts in the state. Legislators had long considered the creation of new courts in their district to be a "perk" of their jobs. Pointedly ignoring his wishes, the legislature in early March 1923 overrode eight Neff vetoes to establish seven trial (district and extra-jurisdiction county) courts and one new civil appeals court at Waco.[106] Most of the votes were overwhelming, with as many as 80 percent of the legislators voting to overrule the governor. The legislature did sustain Neff on one veto of a court bill and two vetoes of other bills in the regular session. No explanation is apparent for the governor's allowing two other courts to be established by letting the legislation become law without his signature.

One of the few moments of levity of the summer—although macabre—occurred during the second called session when the legislature was again considering abolishing hanging for capital offenses, which always took place in the county where the offender was convicted. The events usually attracted a gawking crowd of spectators. One of the last legal hangings in Texas was in Waco and was reported in the July 31, 1923, edition of the *Waco Times-Herald*. The newspaper reported that 4,000 to 5,000 persons attended, including at least 500 women.[107] The last legal execution by hanging occurred on August 31, 1923, at Angleton.[108] The bill to provide for electrocution at Huntsville for all capital crimes moved along smoothly in both houses of the legislature until a member of the House from South Texas rose to oppose the bill. With sincerity and eloquence, he argued against electrocution, closing with words that set off a loud uproar:

> Why, Mr. Speaker, one of the few attractions now left in the country is for the people to gather together at their own county seat and witness an occasional hanging, and now you want to take even that away from them. Mr. Speaker, I don't know what you think about it, but as for me, hanging was good enough for my father and it's good enough for me.[109]

Three notable appointments highlighted the spring of 1923. The Texas Railroad Commission suddenly had two vacancies—one following the death of Commissioner Allison Mayfield and the other resulting from the resignation of Commissioner Earle B. Mayfield (a distant relative), who survived hearings in the U.S. Senate to claim his seat there after a disputed election. Neff was besieged with individuals clamoring for those prized state jobs. On February 26, the governor surprised virtually everyone by naming University of Texas Professor Walter M. W. Splawn and attorney W. A. Nabors to those positions. The Texas Senate quickly confirmed them, the ambitious senators passing a resolution praising Neff and the two appointees for agreeing that, while on the commission, they would seek no other elective office. Nabors, from Winnsboro in northeast Texas, was a fellow Baylor graduate, an attorney, and a prominent produce shipper, and his appointment had been rumored; but Splawn, a highly regarded professor of economics, was a complete surprise to the writers and observers who expected Neff to name another of his political supporters.[110] The governor could thus claim another distinction in his long line of outstanding appointments—he was the only governor, before or since, to appoint a future president of the University of Texas to a key state office. Splawn left the Railroad Commission to serve as the university's president from 1924 to 1927.[111]

The third notable appointment was no less groundbreaking. When Neff's initial private secretary (chief of staff), R. B. Walthall, went to a higher-paying job at the Railroad Commission on April 1, 1923, Neff appointed the second-ranking person in the office, Espa Stanford, to Walthall's position. Stanford is believed to be the first woman in the country appointed to the top staff position in a governor's office.[112]

Finishing the Course

Finally, on June 14, the legislature adjourned. On June 27, Neff vetoed his last bill and the long four-session biennial grind was over. With the necessary executive and board appointments also taken care of, the governor was finally free to have a little rest and relaxation. He joined a West Texas Chamber of Commerce ocean trip to Cuba and Panama on June 30, joyfully pocketing a collection of money given him for the trip by his colleagues at the Capitol.[113] In the summertime, the Neff family was traveling in several different directions. While the governor was off on his voyage, Myrtie was lamenting the absence of Pat Jr., who was in Dallas for the summer working for the State Fire Insurance Commission. Pat Jr. later worked for the State Health Department while attending the University of Texas in Austin, both jobs being in apparent contradiction to Neff's opposition to nepotism on the part of state officials. Writing her son in August, Myrtie urged the nineteen-year-old to follow his father's example and not sow any wild oats.[114] Shortly after her letter, she went to Mineral Wells for her periodic visit, staying this time from August 21 to September 18 and writing Hallie Maude, who stayed home at the mansion: "If I had the time and money, I would stay here months."[115]

In early August, a new level of excitement swept the mansion and Austin, as William Jennings Bryan, in an Atlanta interview, named Neff as one of three possible U.S. presidential candidates from the South.[116] Bryan's comments came after reading a stirring speech Neff made at Chautauqua, New York, on Prohibition. Bryan wrote Neff that he was going to California to visit his children and would be happy to try to see Neff in Houston or San Antonio when the train stopped briefly.[117] Ever alert, Neff arranged for the train to make a special stop in Liberty and pick him up so that he could visit unhurriedly for an hour with Bryan on the way to Houston.[118]

Neff's Chautauqua speech found other admirers. C. W. Osborne, a Pittsburgh capitalist who was visiting some of his holdings in Texas, was quoted as saying that "Governor Neff's speech in New York August 14, has caused more of a sensation there than in his own state."[119] Osborne's and Bryan's favorable remarks, however, resulted in only one county organizing a Neff for President Club in the summer of 1923.[120] Neff kept his thoughts to himself, telling people only that he was flattered to be talked of for president, as well as the U.S. Senate, but that he had not made up his mind what his next move would be.[121] In December, the State Democratic Executive Committee endorsed Neff for the presidency, but Neff and his supporters were jarred two days later by Bryan's announcement from his home in Florida that he was going to offer University of Florida President A. A. Murphree as a "favorite son" Democratic candidate. In November, all Democratic efforts were in vain, and the Republican ticket of Calvin Coolidge, who had succeeded to the presidency on Harding's mid-term death, and Charles G. Dawes coasted to an overwhelming victory. The Democratic candidate, John W. Davis, won only Oklahoma and the eleven former Confederate states.

Parallel to all of these national political fights, Neff's name was being discussed even more for another presidency, that of the University of Texas. President Robert E. Vinson's resignation in February 1923 set off wild speculation on his successor, much of it centered on Neff. One Austin newspaper had a long story on the situation, stating that Dr. H. Y. Benedict was in line to be acting president, but the story's subheadline read: "Governor to Take Charge in June, Say Rumors."[122] Neff appointee and now chairman of the University of Texas Board of Regents H. J. Lutcher Stark was reported closeted with the governor for more than an hour after a board meeting the previous night. Neff's friends pointed to his educational background, including his two degrees from Baylor and his law degree from the University of Texas. In addition, they noted his presidency of the Baylor Board of Trustees since 1907 as giving him credibility in educational circles.[123]

However, opposition to Neff was not long in rising up. Faculty members at the University of Texas saw him only as a politician with all the negatives that word could conjure. At its annual meeting in June, the Ex-Students' Association went on record as opposing any person for the presidency who had political enemies.[124] The board put off its decision for a permanent president month after month and finally in August decided to let W. J. Sutton, dean of the School of Education, continue as acting president for the 1923-24 school year.[125] Speculation arose that Neff backers on the UT Board of Regents took this action to allow time to see if a "Draft Neff for the U.S. Senate" movement was going to develop. Finally, on Thursday, May 15, 1924, the regents and the executive council of the Ex-Students' Association—which had kept up a constant drumbeat against the selection of Neff—met. Will C. Hogg, a member of the council and a former regent, was the spokesman for the ex-students. The August 1924 issue of *The Alcalde*, the publication of the Ex-Students' Association, carried a detailed, dispassionate story of the unfolding events. Hogg stated that the ex-students did not have a candidate for the position, asking only that the regents select "a trained and experienced educator, not a politician or anyone tainted by politics." The exes felt that they had a good meeting with an understanding that "the regents would elect no one except some experienced educator." Nevertheless, the regents in its formal meeting on Friday offered the presidency to Neff. The board's vote for Neff was 7 to 2. Contacted in Eastland, the governor immediately wired back his refusal. Neff expressed his appreciation to the regents but told them: "I deeply regret that the only light I have to guide my feet does not reveal at this time the path of duty with sufficient accuracy to enable me to see my way clear to accept the proffered position of trust and responsibility."[126] The effort to find a president proved difficult. After Neff declined, the board offered the presidency to Dr. Guy Stanton Ford, graduate dean at the University of Minnesota. Ford declined the next day.[127] Ten days later, the board then tried to bring historian Herbert Eugene Bolton of the University of California back to Texas.[128] He also declined. Finally, in early July, Walter Splawn, then serving as Neff's appointee on the Railroad Commission, accepted the office.[129]

There are no records to specifically indicate the depth, if any, of Neff's actual interest in the University of Texas presidency. Undoubtedly, he was giving thought to his future in both 1923 and 1924, but he must have been shaken by the furious opposition of his friend Will Hogg. His decision not to accept the position did not deter him from continuing to support the university in every possible way, however, even as his successor, Governor Miriam A. "Ma" Ferguson, continued her husband's relentless attack on that institution.

While the scenarios of the U.S. and UT presidencies were being played out, Governor Neff was still responsible for the affairs of the state. In the closing period of his administration, Neff sought to ameliorate his "anti-pardon" reputation by instituting an "Honor Farm" for convicts whose conduct in the prison system appeared to justify treating them with some freedom. When the farm opened in 1924, he told the convicts: "If I can, I shall make this Honor Farm the approach to pardon."[130] Neff had appointed prominent Texas clubwoman Mrs. J. E. King as chair of his Prison Advisory Board, and Neff shared credit with her for the Honor Farm idea. Ex-Governor Jim Ferguson, inspecting the prisons for his newly elected wife Miriam in early 1925, pledged that she would continue the Honor Farm. However, a simultaneous escape of some forty-five prisoners in the spring of 1925 caused the Fergusons to abandon the concept.

Politics took a brief backseat in the fall of 1924, when Neff made the main address to dedicate the University of Texas Memorial Stadium "to the 198,298 Texans who served in the World War and especially to the 5,280 who lost their lives."[131] Neff's Baylor Bears ruined the occasion for the Longhorns by beating them 28-10 on their way to their second Southwest Conference football championship in three years. After the game, Baylor fans marched up Congress Avenue, Austin's main street, to the Capitol, where Neff greeted them.[132]

Another nonpolitical thread in Neff's second term was tied to his deep interest in history and his particular pride in Texas history. In November 1923, a New Yorker came to Texas to suggest that the state was overlooking an economic and tourist bonanza by failing to advertise its romantic history of struggle, independence, and statehood. Theodore H. Price, publisher of the business weekly *Commerce and Finance*, was in Corsicana to address a meeting of the Advertising Clubs of America when he suggested some type of centennial exposition to celebrate

Texas' rich heritage. There had been talk before of some type of commemorative celebration—by veterans of San Jacinto and by Governor James Stephen Hogg—but nothing had come of it.[133] Before the Corsicana meeting adjourned, however, the delegates decided that Texas should hold a great celebration to honor the heroes of the past and advertise the wonders of Texas. The Advertising Clubs were joined by the Texas Press Association, cohost of the meeting. This time, a governor steeped in Texas history read the *Dallas Morning News* story reporting the talk and the action of the group and in less than a week was giving it official recognition.[134] In Fort Worth to attend the city's diamond jubilee, Neff announced that a "Texas Centennial should be held and every energy of the state placed behind it."[135]

On February 12, 1924, more than 2,000 patriotic citizens jammed the Senate Chamber to demonstrate their support for the proposed celebration, originally envisioned to take place in 1945. (Later, a decision was made to celebrate 1936 and independence rather than 1945 and statehood.) An official organization was formed—the Centennial Governing Board of One Hundred. Finances were discussed, and a second unofficial meeting was scheduled for May 21, 1924. The first official meeting of the board was held in Austin on Neff's next-to-last day in office, January 19, 1925.[136] The next month the 39th Legislature gave the group its sanction, and the organization then turned to the challenge of keeping the movement alive for the twelve years until 1936 and obtaining the funding to make the Texas Centennial a reality. Neff's involvement as governor had ended, but in the next eleven years, he would be called on numerous times to add his luster to the success of the great celebration.[137]

The Final Nineteen Whirlwind Days

In the past, most Texas governors had gone away quietly during their last days in office. However, in his last nineteen days in office in January 1925, Neff took these actions:

— Appointed an unprecedented all-woman Texas Supreme Court;

— Issued the most famous pardon of his four years—to a man known simply as Leadbelly;

— Had dozens of noteworthy appointments confirmed by the Senate, including future Governor James V. Allred and future influential Congressman Wright Patman as district attorneys. (Although Patman and Neff occasionally disagreed, Patman so respected Neff that he gave one of his four sons the name William Neff Patman. That son served in the Texas Senate and then two terms in Congress.)[138] Allred and Patman had both won elections to full terms as district attorneys in November 1924; thus confirmation by the Senate was really not in question.

— Announced the dedication of forty-five state parks aggregating 3,483 acres of land for the enjoyment and benefit of Texans throughout the state;

— Unveiled a striking statue of a Texas cowboy, which still stands in the southwest quadrant of the State Capitol grounds; and, finally,

— Capped it all by leaving a marked verse in a Bible in the governor's office for the incoming governor, a first for Texas.

The first all-woman Supreme Court in the history of the country came about through the nature of the single case it was called upon to hear—a civil case involving the Woodmen of the World (WOW) fraternal organization.[139] In those days, WOW membership numbered virtually all public officials and many, if not most, of the prominent attorneys in the state. This meant that they were proportionate owners of the assets of the association and had an impermissible interest in cases involving the organization. On March 8, 1924, Texas Supreme Court Justice Calvin M. Cureton certified to Neff that he and the court's two associate justices, Thomas B. Greenwood and William Pierson, were disqualified to hear the WOW case from El Paso County, which was on appeal from the court of civil appeals in that city.[140]

Neff did not make the three appointments to serve on the case until January 1, 1925, ten months after Chief Justice Cureton's letter was written. On January 2, newspapers around the state hailed the appointment of Nellie Robertson of Granbury, Edith E. Wilmans of Dallas, and Hortense Ward of Houston.[141] During the next week, Neff learned that neither Robertson, who had been named chief justice, nor Wilmans, a former legislator, had the required seven years of law practice to serve on the Court, and he replaced them with Hattie Henenberg and Ruth Virginia Brazzil. Neff named Ward to preside as chief justice. Whatever his reasons for appointing an all-woman Court to hear the case, Neff's action served to add a crowning note to his long record of appointing women to important posts.[142]

Neff's stinginess with pardons for Texas convicts was well known. It took only one pardon, however, signed on January 16, 1925, to soften Neff's reputation as a hard-hearted governor. On that day, he took twenty-three years off a thirty-year sentence of a convicted killer known simply as Leadbelly. In the prisoner's biography, authors Charles Wolfe and Kip Lornell maintain that Leadbelly was probably the most famous black folksinger in American history.[143] Under the name of Walter Boyd, the Louisiana native who moved to Texas at an early age had been convicted of murder. John Lightfoot, in his essay on Leadbelly, wrote that he was a "musical child prodigy" who learned to play several instruments before age six."[144] By 1924,

Leadbelly (also known as Huddie Ledbetter) had become well known in prison as an entertainer, and when he heard that Governor Neff was making one of his visits to check on the prisoners at Sugar Land prison farm he prepared. He had been saving a white suit for special occasions, and he paid another prisoner a nickel to wash it. Leadbelly's biographer notes that he wrote two different songs for the occasion. The more familiar one ended with these lines:

> If I had you, Hon. Governor Neff, where you got me,
> I'd wake up in the morning and set you free.[145]

Neff loved his singing but told him he would not set him free in early 1924, but rather wanted to hear him again and again as he visited the prison on future occasions. A year later, three days before he left office, Neff signed the full pardon for Leadbelly.[146]

After the Thirty-eighth Legislature's third called session had adjourned on June 14, 1923, Neff had continued his appointments to state offices and boards, all pending approval by the Senate. When the Thirty-ninth Legislature convened in January 1925 with a new governor (Ma Ferguson) coming into office, the Senate confirmed 195 appointments and refused approval of 18. Key confirmations included all state agency heads except Charles Baughman at the Department of Markets and Warehouses, whose appointment was held up. Neff lieutenants R. B. Walthall and Espa Stanford, appointed to the Board of Control and to the Industrial Accident Board, respectively, survived the new administration. On the first consideration, the Senate also approved all of Neff's higher education board appointments except for those to the University of Texas Board of Regents.[147] It gave the green light to only two of the five regents Neff had named between June of 1923 and early January of 1925.[148] On his last day in office, Neff valiantly tried to appoint three new University of Texas regents but to no avail.[149] Ferguson left only Mary O'Hair, Robert G. Storey, and H. J. Lutcher Stark on the board when she submitted her own list on January 29. At that time, she sent the Senate thirty-nine new names for key state official and board positions.[150] On February 9, she added another thirty-nine names, replacing several Neff appointees who been confirmed earlier but had no set term.[151] Virtually all key positions were then in her hands.

Neff's intensive interest in state parkland, formally initiated in his second gubernatorial campaign in 1922, continued unabated to the end of his second term and beyond for virtually a lifetime. His appointments to the Texas State Parks Board included good roads promoter David E. Colp of San Antonio; Hobart Key Sr., Marshall businessman; Mrs. W. C. Martin, Dallas newspaper correspondent; Phebe Kerrick Warner, Claude newspaper columnist; and Katie Owens Welder, Victoria rancher. The appointment of three women to the board was indicative that Neff was counting on the Texas Federation of Women's Clubs to enthusiastically support the work. In his initial letter to Colp, Neff did not hesitate to lay out seven conditions for Colp and the others—including a commitment to travel all around the state, not just in their own geographic areas, to obtain land.[152] It would be difficult to overstate the zeal with which Colp attacked his assignment.[153]

To secure land donations, Neff made at least three trips with the Parks Board before he left office. The initial trip began March 12, 1924, in San Antonio and headed for South Texas and the Valley. Neff was accompanied by Hallie Maude on this first one, which covered more than 1,500 miles and included visits to twenty-four proposed park sites in eighteen counties.[154] In mid-July, Neff and the board made its second trip, this time to West Texas. In Van Horn, New Mexico Governor James Hinkle met Neff and they discussed Carlsbad Caverns, the huge underground cave in New Mexico. Neff wanted to dig a tunnel from the Texas side, hoping to connect with the caverns, but it never materialized.[155] Neff was indefatigable, speaking as many as six times a day until nearly midnight.[156] The board's final trip was to North and East Texas and to the Panhandle in late November and early December 1924.[157]

It would be a fitting climax to the work put forth in 1924 to report that the legislature in 1925 accepted the parks and appropriated the $50,000 Neff requested for expenses of the board. Unfortunately, in February 1925, a parsimonious Thirty-ninth Legislature adopted a formal position: the state appreciated the offer of land, but other "urgent demands" precluded the state from accepting the land unless the donors would take care of all of the maintenance and upkeep of the parks.[158] But the legislature's rebuff would not stop the movement. Historian James Wright Steely, in his comprehensive story of the development of the state parks system, closes the prologue to his book by writing that in the decade following Pat Neff's proposal for a state park system, "widespread community interest in parks emerged even at the remote frontiers of Texas."[159] In 1927, when Neff had moved on to a new job in Washington, D.C., Parks Board member Colp secured designation of twenty-three parks. Despite this success, the parks movement subsided for several years until President Franklin Roosevelt's New Deal opened up a whole new set of opportunities. Neff was recalled by Governor Ma Ferguson in her second term in 1933 to help direct the state's response to the federal initiatives.[160]

One of Neff's lasting contributions to his beloved state still stands, now professionally conserved after seventy years, just a few yards from the front door of the Capitol. The *Texas Cowboy* statue, a lifelike figure of a Western cowboy sitting astride a bucking bronco horse, was sculpted by New York-born artist Constance Whitney Warren. She moved to Paris and was exhibiting the statue there in 1924 when Neff learned that she felt that the statue should really find its home in America. The governor got in touch with Charles Cason, vice-president of the Chemical National Bank of New York, and Cason arranged for the statue to come to Texas.[161]

Neff's final act of his four years as governor came at Miriam Ferguson's inauguration. Although Neff had drawn fire from Jim Ferguson for not endorsing "Ma" in her race for governor against the Klansman Felix Robertson, Neff was very cordial to both Fergusons when the day came for the changeover of administrations. As Neff introduced the new governor, he told her he had left her a portrait of Woodrow Wilson, a white rose, and a Bible in which he had marked, underscoring each word separately, the 105th verse of Psalm 119: "Thy word is a lamp unto my feet, and a light unto my path."[162] One of Neff's secretaries later remembered the rest of the story:

> We went back to the Governor's Office and back into the room with the open Bible. Jim [Ferguson] sat down at the table in the big chair and took the rose and smelled it and threw it in the window sill. He said: "Come on, let's get to work. Sunday School is over."[163]

This story became well known over the years but was omitted from the biography of the Fergusons by their dutiful daughter, Ouida Wallace Ferguson Nalle.[164] Nevertheless, Ferguson followed the new tradition and left a verse for her successor, Dan Moody. The tradition has continued into the twenty-first century, broken only once by the failure of Governor Ross Sterling to leave a marked passage for Ma Ferguson as she returned to the governor's office for a second term in 1933.[165]

The Neff-Ferguson relationship was an intriguing one in Texas politics. When Ma Ferguson took office in 1925, Hugh Nugent Fitzgerald, state political columnist for the *Austin American* during this era, wrote that Neff was not close to the Fergusons, and never "kowtowed" to them when they were in office, but neither did he "kick them in the teeth" when they were down. Fitzgerald wrote that Neff never criticized Ma Ferguson, regardless of the Ferguson acts with which he disagreed.[166]

Governor Pat M. Neff: A Retrospective

It is fair to say that all Texas governors have had both high and low points during their years of service. Some have had more outstanding administrations than others. James Stephen Hogg and John B. Connally are seen by many historians as governors who acted boldly and most often wisely in their tenure.[167] The low points in Texas gubernatorial history are generally thought to be represented by the two Fergusons, who took a courageous stand against the Klan but who, in a combined six and one-half years in the office, otherwise brought shame and reproach to an office held by individuals of generally good character and integrity.[168] Neff may not have been a Hogg or Connally, but he brought impeccable integrity to the office and left it having achieved greater accomplishments than he is generally given credit for.

He was the first governor with a degree from a Texas institution of higher education. Thrice degreed and well traveled before he became governor, he brought a vision of what Texas might become unlike any projected before. An unresponsive legislature and the economic situation quashed many but not all of his dreams. Neff's unwillingness to compromise on virtually any legislation and his refusal to properly utilize his staff and key legislators who could have helped him realize his goals cost him dearly. Despite those failings, he had some clear victories that mark him as a successful chief executive.

The first area of success, largely overlooked by gubernatorial historians, was in the quality and diversity of his appointments. No other Texan can claim in his or her portfolio as governor to have appointed two men who would later become governor (Dan Moody and James V. Allred); an individual who would become one of the most formidable Congressmen of his period (Wright Patman); a state official who would become president of the University of Texas (Walter Splawn); and an attorney who would become president of the American Bar Association and later the International Bar Association (Robert G. Storey). Beyond those selections, he consistently appointed to key offices and state boards men and women of good reputation in their communities. He drew fire more than once from his political supporters for appointments of persons who had not supported him initially but whom he considered good citizens.

One of his proudest breakthroughs was the appointment of numerous women to high positions. He not only appointed the first women members of the boards of regents of the University of Texas, Texas A&M, and the state teachers colleges, he also put women, for the first time, on dozens of other boards. He capped this achievement by appointing Espa Stanford as the first female private secretary to the governor (now generally called chief of staff) in the history of the state. In addition to the three women appointed to the Supreme Court, his most notable female appointments were renowned clubwomen Mrs. Percy (Anna Hardwicke) Pennybacker and Mrs. J. E. King and Margie Neal. As noted earlier, Neal was later elected to the Texas Senate for four terms and ended an eventful public service career in Washington, D.C.

There is every reason to call Neff the "father of the Texas park system." At least three historians call him the "originator of the state parks system."[169] Describing Neff's key role, the dust jacket of James Wright Steely's state parks history notes that the book "follows the fits-and-starts progress of park development through the early 1920s when Governor Neff envisioned the kind of park system that ultimately came into being between 1933 and 1942."[170] Building on his mother's dedication of the small plot of land on the Neff homeland, he began talking parks in 1922 and in succeeding years traveled the length and breadth of the state to promote the parks movement. As recounted earlier, he persuaded the legislature in 1923 to create the State Parks Board and traveled extensively in 1924 to secure park sites.

Neff had major accomplishments in two other vital areas of state government responsibility: highways and education. His success in laying the foundation for a broad and extensive road-building program must be considered as one of his major achievements. With the enthusiastic and effective support of the Texas Highway Association, Neff, who was stymied in so many initiatives, found a willing legislature in his second term, and the resulting laws propelled Texas' highway system into the front ranks of programs nationwide. The lengthening of the highway commissioners' terms from two to six years gave some political stability to the State Highway Department. Key legislation also took control of so-called "state" highways away from the counties and gave it to the Highway Department, thus launching the "Texas" highway system. The final accomplishment was the one-cent gasoline tax, three-fourths of which went to highways and the remainder to public schools. That tax became the mainstay of the department's revenue-matching federal aid, which increased virtually every year, and made Texas highways the envy of every other state in the country. D. K. "Dock" Martin, member of the State Highway Commission during three different administrations, wrote Neff staffer Emma Shirley in 1937 that in his judgment, "Governor Neff's administration laid the foundation for the highway program that is now underway in Texas."[171]

Neff's strong support of an adequate public educational system was demonstrated throughout his life. From defending appropriations for the University of Texas on the floor of the Texas House in 1899 to serving as president of the Conference on Education in Texas in 1913, he had earned his credentials in educational circles long before he became governor. He accelerated that advocacy in his first gubernatorial campaign, constantly pushing the state's citizens and lawmakers to increase their support for both public and higher education. In the field of education, Neff's two terms were marked by the establishment of Texas Technological College in West Texas and South Texas State Teachers College at Kingsville, specific appropriations for rural education in both terms, acceptance of federal aid for vocational training in the public schools, and a law permitting former armed service personnel to attend state colleges tuition free. Neff's call for an educational survey commission to review the whole field of education was also approved.[172]

The passage in 1923, on Neff's recommendation, of $600,000 for topographic and hydrographic surveys of the upper reaches of the state's major rivers must also be ranked as one of Neff's major achievements. In fact, in 1938, as he reviewed his governorship, he considered his park work and the attention to conservation of floodwaters as the most far-reaching of any of his accomplishments.[173]

Emma Shirley lists a number of Neff's miscellaneous accomplishments in her thesis:

The criminal and civil laws were codified for the first time since 1911; a blue sky law to protect investors from fraud was passed; cooperative market associations were authorized; it was made a violation of the law to drive an automobile while intoxicated; pensions to Confederate veterans were increased; a law was passed authorizing cities to establish and maintain city hospitals. . . . The American Legion Memorial Hospital, costing more than a million dollars, was built for nursing back to health ex-soldiers of the state; the Texas Historical Commission was created [actually a State Historical Board—the present-day Texas Historical Commission was not created until 1953]. The Texas Centennial celebration movement was inaugurated.[174]

Neff left a rich legacy of major accomplishments. He also left a feeling with some, however, that he had not lived up to his potential. Of the state's leading newspapers, only the *Austin American* lauded him as he left office.[175] The *Dallas Morning News* criticized him on a regular basis throughout his four years. Even as he came forward with the donations of park land in his last days in office, the *News* belittled his and Colp's exhaustive work by labeling the lands "a string of tourist camps, for commercial purposes."[176] Neff prided himself on the fact when he first ran that he was not a member of the Democratic Party machine or any other machine. This deviation from most past gubernatorial practice led Fred Gantt, in his chapter "The Governor as a Political Leader," to observe that Neff's "'hands off' attitude in party affairs" possibly "compounded his legislative difficulties."[177]

Neff had other failures—administrative reorganization and constitutional revision among them. He was basically unable to get the state's tax system modernized and broadened to reap the benefits of a growing oil industry, and he failed utterly to bring about more laws and stronger enforcement of Prohibition. In later years, it's fair to say he would not be proud of his passive approval of the "white primary" law or his failure to make any real inroads in reform of the penitentiary system. Lee Simmons, a noted prison official in the 1920s and 1930s, said in 1957 that Neff probably "knew more about the penitentiary and did less about it than any other governor I know of."[178] In Neff's defense, the prison system had vexed all of his predecessors and would continue to be a thorn in the side of subsequent governors.

In his last week in office, Neff was honored with a banquet at the Stephen F. Austin Hotel and presented with a new car. At the banquet, he repeated his public remarks that he had enjoyed "every day of his four years in office."[179] In private, according to H. T. Musselman, his longtime friend in the education field, it was a different story. Musselman wrote that he was alone with the governor in his office just before he went up the stairs to the reception room to meet the new administration. Musselman asked Neff how he felt about his four years, and the governor's reply was, "I feel I have been a missionary in a strange land."[180]

His mixed feelings were also evident in his *Battles of Peace*, a book of essays published in 1925. Lamenting that it cost him $56,000 more than his salary in four years to be governor, he also complained that the falsehoods that had been spread about him were a "loss of respect [that] is largely irreparable." He closes the essay, however, by writing that any sacrifice had been worthwhile, especially because of the friends he had made and to whom he would be eternally grateful and the opportunity to serve his state "in the highest office within their gift."[181]

In his last six months in office, Neff received several letters offering employment. Baylor desperately tried to get him to take a position raising money statewide for the institution with an opportunity to head the law school at a later date.[182] Congressman Tom Connally presented his name to President Coolidge for appointment to the Interstate Commerce Commission.[183] A Chicago firm wanted him to sell real estate for them in the Texas Panhandle. And a Los Angeles law firm tried to persuade him to come to California. It appears that Neff had determined to go back into the practice of law; his only wavering was whether he would locate in Dallas, Houston, or Waco. Neff kept people guessing to the end. The *Dallas Morning News* of January 19 announced that he would move to Houston, but immediately after the inauguration of the new governor, Neff and his family headed to Waco to settle there once again.

CHAPTER 8

Two Appointments, Two Headaches

By God, I'll make a speech for Pat Neff.
—Lyndon B. Johnson (age 21)

Four years in the governor's office took a toll on Neff—physically, financially, and psychologically. He had been through grueling primary and runoff campaigns in 1920, followed by a contentious legislature in a regular session and two special sessions. The 1922 campaign had been much easier, but his relations with the legislative branch in 1923 were still strained and often hostile. He calculated that between his lost income as an attorney and his net campaign expenditures, his public service had cost him some $56,000 more than his gubernatorial salary.[1] He had gone into the governor's office with notes payable to him of more than $30,000, only to realize at the end of four years that they were virtually uncollectible.

It is little wonder that Myrtie worried that he could not come down off his "high" after such a demanding schedule. Early in the spring of 1925, Myrtie wrote Hallie Maude: "Your Daddy, I feel, is on the verge of a breakdown. He has never relaxed even *one* day and seems so tired."[2] Neff tried to relax but plunged almost immediately into his legal work and the renovation of their house in Waco. Before he left the governor's office, he had contacted some of his old clients. To get back to his law practice, he had to borrow $5,000, only the third time in his life that he had borrowed money. He did not make the last payment on that loan until January 19, 1931, six years almost to the day after leaving Austin.[3] The Neffs' home on Austin Avenue in Waco had been rented while they were in the Governor's Mansion and, on their return, they decided it needed major refurbishing. In mid-spring, they moved to the Raleigh Hotel downtown. Living in the hotel with no household responsibilities, Myrtie blossomed. She regularly attended several church and club meetings and seemed overwhelmed by the compliments and attention bestowed upon her.[4]

Neff was not so busy with his law practice and worrying about the house remodeling that he would pass up giving advice to Hallie Maude. In May, he told his daughter he had paid Dr. A. J. Armstrong in full for her annual trip to Europe ($1,358), encouraged her to buy new clothes for the trip, and then wrote:

I want to urge again that you get yourself in good shape physically and mentally. Cut out all pink teas, picture shows, late hours. Instead of sitting up in some picture show looking at some fool story that never happened, never could happen, and never will happen, and if it did happen, it would not be of any value to anybody, put in your time "breaking" in a good pair of everyday horse sense shoes, shoes that are really made for walking and not for exhibition.[5]

"Winding Down"

Neff was also never too busy to look after Mother Neff Park. In June, he wrote Ione Neff, his sister-in-law in Dallas, telling her proudly what he had done: "[T]he park has been fenced; a pavilion built on it; a house for a custodian to live in has been constructed; a cemented well [with] pump, and fixtures, has been provided for; an archway placed above the gate; a barbeque pit of fire brick constructed; all to make the park an interesting and attractive place."[6] Neff added that he was proud that he had secured the services of ten convicts under supervision of a Texas Ranger to work more than two months in cleaning up, fencing, beautifying, and constructing the improvements—at no cost to any of the family.

He had already planned the first of what would become his own annual "Chautauquas" at the park,[7] scheduling his initial undertaking for July 5-12, 1925. The plan included three services on each of the beginning and ending Sundays, two addresses on Saturday, July 11, and one program each evening at 8 p.m. during the week. To attract a crowd, he persuaded Congressman Tom Connally, Texas Attorney General Dan Moody, University of Texas President Walter Splawn, and Texas A&M President W. B. Bizzell to speak at various times. To keep the programs from being too heavy, he mixed in some music and entertainment. Despite the Texas heat, the crowds came and loved it.[8]

On Christmas Eve 1925, he received from Pioneer Publishing Company in Fort Worth the first hardbound copy of *The Battles of Peace*, containing forty-six of his speeches, patriotic orations, and essays over a twenty-year period. He produced the book in answer to numerous requests for copies of some of his notable speeches. During the year, he had written checks totaling $2,761 for the printing, and he immediately sent copies of the book to family members.[9]

Early 1926 brought a sobering event to the Neff household. In 1922, Hallie Maude had met a young Austin lawyer named Harris Bell. Bell began to court Hallie Maude shortly after they met, and in 1923 they were dating "every other week."[10] By 1924, he was sending her more telegrams than letters as he tried law cases around the state and she traveled around the world. In early 1926, Bell bought a home for the couple in Austin, and Myrtie announced their daughter's engagement in a *Waco Times-Herald* story of March 10, with a wedding date of March 31. Wedding invitations were mailed shortly thereafter, and a mountain of gifts began to come in.[11] Unfortunately, although the Neffs were not aware of it yet, Harris Bell was in trouble. He had received a citation on December 8, 1925, to appear in district court in Austin on January 4, 1926, to respond to a civil suit brought against him by Jesus Ramirez and his wife, Refugio.[12] Ramirez had engaged Bell to represent him in fighting four felony indictments charging violation of liquor laws. According to Ramirez, Bell, to secure his legal fee, had persuaded the couple to sign a deed to their farm in Bastrop County, while representing to them that they were executing a mortgage. On March 24, with the civil suit against him pending, Bell was indicted by a Travis County grand jury of swindling in the same transaction. Neff was ignorant of all of this until late March. In a March 27 story reporting the cancellation of the wedding, the *San Antonio Express* ran a picture of Hallie Maude and quoted her as saying that the engagement had been permanently cancelled about two weeks before. No story of the broken engagement appeared in either of the Austin papers or the *Dallas Morning News*. No records were found, but it was generally believed at the time that Neff himself made the call to Bell and told him the wedding was off.[13]

Bell lost the civil suit in district court, and the court of civil appeals upheld the judgment of the lower court. Finally, in August 1928, Bell and Ramirez made an out-of-court settlement that returned the property to the Ramirez family.[14] Although Bell had been indicted by the grand jury for swindling (a felony), the case lay dormant and was finally dismissed, also in 1928.[15] With both cases settled, Bell's legal problems were behind him, and he moved to New York, where he lived for a number of years before returning to Texas to live a productive and rewarding life.[16]

Neff had other challenges to face. As president of the Baylor Board of Trustees, he had been bombarded for several years by fundamentalist preacher J. Frank Norris of Fort Worth, who attacked the alleged teaching of evolution at Baylor. Norris was particularly upset with Baylor President Samuel Palmer Brooks, claiming that he and most of the Baylor faculty were not making strong, unequivocal statements against the theory of evolution. At the annual meeting of the Baptist General Convention of Texas in 1924 in Dallas, the delegates had given Brooks a rising ovation as he read the report of the Baylor Board of Trustees, calling the attacks "false" and "diabolical."[17] Norris was not deterred. Writing to Neff several times in 1925, he kept up his attack on Brooks and threatened to "carry this issue to the people of this state."[18] Neff kept Norris at bay. Then in mid-1926, the preacher had a more pressing problem of his own—he shot and killed a man. On Saturday, July 17, Norris was confronted in his office by Fort Worth lumberman D. E. Chipps, and after some words, Norris pulled a gun and shot him dead. Norris showed little remorse. He stated that the common opinion was that the case would never come to trial but if it did, he wanted Neff to represent him.[19] Neff did not represent him and, in the trial that ensued, Norris was acquitted on grounds of self-defense. Norris continued to fight both the Texas Baptists and the Southern Baptist Convention until he died in 1952.[20]

During Neff's "sabbatical" from public life in 1925 and 1926, he spent a substantial amount of time on the road supporting causes he believed in. He was particularly popular with "dry" forces, responding every time he could to put in a few words against the Demon Rum. His Baptist affiliations continued to be an important part of his life: he was elected president of the Baptist General Convention of Texas at its meeting in San Antonio in 1926,[21] and also served on the Executive Board of the Southern Baptist Convention. But he was not too busy to stage his second annual "Chautauqua" in the summer of 1926, sharing the platform at Mother Neff Park during a week of meetings and speeches.[22]

A Lesson in Washington Politics

In early 1927, after a public service career spanning sixteen years in three elective offices, the fifty-five-year-old Neff accepted his first appointive public office, a federal appointment dealing with a subject with which he was intimately familiar—railroads.

Following a series of bitter strikes by railroad employees in the late 1800s, the federal government belatedly sought laws to bring the railroads and their employees to the table to talk about wages and benefits. After earlier acts were faulted for one reason or another, the Railway Labor Act (Public Law No. 257, Sixty-ninth Congress) was signed into law by President Calvin Coolidge on May 20, 1926. The act was to be administered by a five-member, presidentially appointed board—the United States Board of Mediation—established as an independent agency within the executive branch. The act made it the duty of the railroads and their employees to make wage and benefit contracts without outside intervention. If this process failed, the parties could apply for the Mediation Board's assistance to mediate the dispute. The board also had the authority to interpret agreements and to try to persuade arbitration if mediation failed. Under the law, however, the board could not require either the companies or the unions and their employees to mediate or to seek arbitration.[23]

On November 26, 1926, Mediation Board member Carl Williams of Oklahoma notified President Coolidge that he planned to resign from the board. The president asked then Secretary of Commerce Herbert Hoover for recommendations, indicating that he was open to appointing a Democrat. On February 7, 1927, Coolidge announced Neff's appointment, and two days later U.S. Senator Earle Mayfield of Texas wired Neff that he was a member of the committee that would consider the nomination and that he would "look after the same and expedite the confirmation."[24] The nomination sailed through the Senate Nominations Committee; four days later, on February 14, Neff was confirmed by the Senate for the remainder of Williams' term, which was to expire December 31, 1928.[25] Shortly after his appointment, in a letter to a good friend, Neff said that he had reluctantly decided to try the position, having found out that it would not take his full time and he could continue to maintain his Waco residence and a limited law practice.[26] Neff left Waco in late March to begin his official duties in Washington. Plaudits from Board Secretary John Marrinan were not long in coming, with a short "Good Work" note following just two weeks later.[27] Board Chairman Samuel E. Winslow added his own congratulations in a September telegram commending Neff for the "Burlington settlement."[28] An overconfident Neff displayed a lack of political acumen the following month when he wired the chairman, stating that his daughter was anxious to take the place made vacant by the resignation of Neff's secretary, conceding that he was not sure the idea was in good taste.[29] Two days later, Winslow wired Neff saying that he agreed that it was not a good idea.[30]

Neff continued to get commendatory letters on his mediation work in 1928. He was particularly proud of settling five dispatchers' cases in the St. Louis area at one time. This work brought a warm letter from Secretary Marrinan: "I may add that not least in this accomplishment was the effect of these settlements in stabilizing dispatcher rates at a common level on railroads in the contiguous territory covered. This latter makes for that foundation which minimizes the chances for recurring wage difficulties in any area."[31]

Although Neff held the Mediation Board job and was busy with his law practice, it was impossible for him to completely avoid politics in 1928. In the U.S. Senate race, Mayfield was vulnerable, partially because he had been elected as a Klan sympathizer and the Klan was no longer a force in Texas politics, and partially because of his lack of an outstanding record in the Senate.[32] Several of Neff's friends, including F. S. Groner, general secretary of the Baptist General Convention of Texas, had earlier urged Neff to run, and rumors of a Neff candidacy continued until he agreed to take the Mediation Board position.[33] Later, when his good friend Congressman Tom Connally decided to run, Neff was glad that he had declared early he would have to remain neutral—in the face of Mayfield leaning on him to support his reelection. Connally defeated Mayfield to win the Senate seat.

Concurrent with the Senate race, the campaign for the presidency became heated, with the Democrats struggling over the Prohibition issue. The Republican National Convention, meeting in June 1928, was much quieter, nominating on the first ballot Secretary of Commerce Herbert Hoover for president and Senator Charles Curtis of Kansas for the second spot. The Democratic National Convention, held at the end of June, produced as the Democratic nominee for president Alfred E. Smith, the New York governor who strongly opposed Prohibition and was a Catholic. Despite Smith's "wet" stand, Neff found him satisfactory, writing Hallie Maude shortly after the convention that "the country has been made safe."[34]

Shortly after the conventions, Neff began to receive requests from both parties to help in the fall campaign. John Raskob, chairman of the Democratic National Committee, wired Neff on August 10 that he hoped Neff could "come east and give us the benefit of your counsel and advice with reference to the conduct of the campaign in your state."[35] Others from the party sought his oratorical skills in behalf of Smith. Republicans and a considerable number of Texas Democrats who had formed an "Anti-Smith Democratic Organization" wrote and begged him to come out against Smith. They knew Neff was an ardent Prohibitionist and that Smith's continued attacks on the Eighteenth Amendment, even in the face of a Democratic platform that supported its enforcement, must have galled Neff. However, he refused all entreaties to get involved. As to how he voted, Neff remained enigmatic to the end. He continually parried a newspaper reporter's question as to his vote even after the reporter rephrased his question. Neff's final answer was, "This is a nice afternoon, isn't it?"[36] On November 6, Hoover overwhelmingly defeated Smith with 58 percent of the vote and 444 electoral votes to Smith's 87. Texas voted Republican, Hoover defeating Smith in the state by more than 26,000 votes out of 709,000 cast.[37]

Neff's short term on the Mediation Board would expire December 31, and on December 6, President Coolidge submitted his name for reappointment, one day before receiving a letter from now lame duck Senator Mayfield asking him to wait until he could talk to him.[38] Senator-Elect Connally wired Neff in mid-December that he had received stories that some of the labor unions would oppose Neff and that he had heard one story that Mayfield might want the job himself.[39] Neff decided to seek a direct meeting with Mayfield but was rebuffed. Mayfield, who was in Austin for the holidays, informed Neff that he had already made up his mind to oppose the confirmation and a meeting between the two "would result in no change of attitude in the matter."[40] Texas' other U.S. Senator, Morris Sheppard, was trying to help Neff, wiring and writing him advice based on objections to Neff he had received in letters from four different labor unions.[41] Thus, Neff's biggest political fight since his runoff election with Joe Bailey in the summer of 1920 was underway. The formal hearings were held on January 9, 28, 29, 30, and 31.[42] The most influential labor unions had supported Mayfield in his losing bid for reelection, and although they had posed no objection to Neff until prodded by Mayfield, they readily responded to his call. Neff found himself defending his handling of several Mediation Board cases as well as his actions in sending in National Guard troops to the railroad strike in Denison as governor. At the end, Neff claimed that eleven of the seventeen committee members favored him. In the formal vote on February 11, the committee voted 8 to 6 to confirm his appointment.[43]

Mayfield was not through. He vowed to keep the Senate from taking a vote on Neff and was successful, bottling up the nomination until its adjournment on March 4, 1929. With the expiration of Coolidge's term as president on that same day, Neff's nomination died; it would be up to President Hoover to make the appointment. Neff sought and received widespread support from his Texas friends and several out-of-state friends, including his long-time friend Harvey Couch, who had hosted Hoover for a short visit to his state several months earlier. Couch, now a big utility company executive in Arkansas, told the president that he was "greatly indebted to Neff for what he had done for me as a struggling country boy."[44] In a lengthy letter, Neff pleaded his case directly to Hoover, stating that he had the support of both current Texas senators and all eighteen congressmen from Texas.[45] All was to no avail. Neff, by remaining neutral in the 1928 presidential race, had alienated both parties—Mayfield was angry because he felt Neff should have supported him, and the Texas Republican Party was unhappy because they felt that Neff had not helped their cause. Hoover soon nominated former Texas Governor Oscar B. Colquitt, who was easily confirmed by the Senate.[46] Neff returned home to Waco, a sadder but wiser man about Washington politics.

Meanwhile, Back at the Farm

Neff had told his good friend F. S. Groner that the Mediation Board job was to his liking because he could continue many of his other activities at the same time. Indeed, he had spent about one-half of his time back in Waco or on the road making speeches for Baylor or the Baptist Church and keeping up his seemingly never-ending round of commencement addresses in May and June of each year. Particularly after his rejection by the Senate, he seemed to find solace in going to small towns and receiving adulation and royal treatment as he orated at their high school commencements.[47]

To maintain the level of income regained after his governorship, Neff also needed to spend time on his law practice. His family had never really adjusted to his reduced compensation as governor. After they left the Governor's Mansion, Myrtie treasured her time at Mineral Wells each year, Pat Jr. was in Baylor Law School until he graduated in May 1928, and Hallie Maude took her summer-long trips to Europe in 1928 and 1929.[48] Neff's law cases during these three years included both civil and criminal matters. Although he left no record of the specific income from his practice, the very nature of the cases and the lifestyle that the family enjoyed indicate that he received sizeable fees.

Neff continued to serve as president of the Baptist General Convention of Texas (BGCT) until November 1929, when the customary three one-year terms expired. But Neff's biggest involvement with his church in this period concerned Baylor University and its possible move from Waco to Dallas. In November 1927, at the annual BGCT meeting in Wichita Falls, the messengers (convention representatives) adopted a recommendation of their Budget Control Committee to appoint a commission to review the entire Baptist educational work in the state.[49] Baptist leaders in Dallas, already the site of Baylor's medical, dental, pharmacy, and nursing schools, decided that this would be an excellent opportunity to consolidate Baylor and improve the financial well-being of the total institution by moving the remainder of the university from Waco to Dallas. The Dallas Chamber of Commerce pledged $1.5 million in cash and 1,000 acres of land in Dallas for a new campus.[50] This was not the first attempt by Dallas to relocate Baylor. In the late 1890s, Dallas made its initial move to lure the university to the growing North Texas city. The offer was turned down, but not before W. C. Brann, the fiery iconoclast and the bane of Baylor and all Baptists in those days, wrote that he would personally help underwrite the move to Dallas.[51] In 1920, President Brooks and the Baylor Board of Trustees turned down a second offer from Dallas, believing this would be the end of the matter.

The 1927 action by the BGCT emboldened Dallas business leaders again, and this time the threat was taken seriously by the newly created Baptist Education Commission. In a meeting in Dallas on April 28, 1928, the commission voted 13-2 that Baylor pick up and move to Dallas. Only Neff and Judge O. S. Lattimore of Austin dissented in the decision.[52] Neff was unable to sway the commission, but he promptly filed a minority report and then began huddling with President Brooks, who again vigorously opposed the move and gathered financial information to refute the commission's findings.[53] With Neff and Brooks giving strong moral encouragement, Waco business leaders mobilized to submit a counter proposal: if Baylor would remain in Waco, the citizens of Waco would raise and contribute $1 million to the university over the next seven years.[54] The city asked only that BGCT match that amount. Faced with this offer, the commission reversed its stand and voted to recommend that Baylor remain in Waco.[55] Responding, Wacoans vowed to immediately raise more than $400,000 to build an auditorium to replace the burned-out Carroll Library and Auditorium, where chapel services had been held for decades. In the depths of the Great Depression, the citizens came through, and a new auditorium seating 2,000—appropriately named Waco Hall—was completed in less than two years after the action of the commission.[56]

Although Neff enjoyed traveling around the country, his favorite relaxation from his law practice and the demands of Baylor and his church was his beloved Chautauquas. His 1927 program featured women. As the *Waco News-Tribune* issue of July 31, 1927, put it, "Neff bows sincerely to women, recognizing the combination of beauty and brains." In 1929, he staged his fifth consecutive Chautauqua at Mother Neff Park. The opening speaker was Dan Moody, by then governor and a highly popular one. As Neff held his Chautauquas and made commencement speeches that summer, Austin was already alive with talk of the next governor's race. Governor Moody wouldn't finish his traditional two terms until January 1931, but his successor was already being discussed. Earle Mayfield as well as Neff were being mentioned. In fact, the *Dallas Morning News* of July 12 reported that Neff's entry into the race was almost certain. He received some sound advice from a respected friend—M. P. Daniel of Liberty (father of future Governor Price Daniel). Daniel wrote him in the summer of 1929 that he thought Texans would not take kindly to an individual who had already served his two terms and was trying to come back for more.[57] The elder Daniel and Neff both knew that two former governors, Tom Campbell and Oscar Colquitt, had tried political comebacks, and both had been defeated handily. Neff apparently took heed, as he didn't make any moves to reclaim the office. However, he did not lack for other job opportunities that summer. He had at least two offers to head insurance companies in Dallas, and longtime Baptist leader Dr. J. B. Cranfill urged him to "give the balance of your big life to the cause of God."[58] There is no indication Neff gave serious thought to any of these entreaties. In September, to help assuage his feelings over his Mediation Board rejection, about 100 of Neff's friends feted him at a lunch in Austin. During the lunch, Governor Moody and Neff traded effusive compliments.[59]

Learning Some New Things about Texas Politics

Less than a month later, Texas Railroad Commission Chairman Clarence Gilmore unexpectedly died of a heart attack, and Governor Moody immediately called Neff and asked him to take Gilmore's seat on the commission. The appointment would be for Gilmore's unexpired term. Neff would have to face a primary election in only nine months, but the former governor was eager to get back into the political fray. He readily accepted and was sworn in on October 16, 1929.[60] The appointment gave Neff some quiet satisfaction since Earle Mayfield was known to covet the job. It is conceivable that Neff took the position to spite Mayfield, his Washington nemesis. If so, he may have later regretted his move. In less than a year from Neff's appointment, huge amounts of oil were discovered in East Texas, embroiling Neff and the other two commissioners in heated discussions as the commission was caught in mammoth fights between major oil companies and independents, conservationists, free-enterprise businessmen, and legislators favoring one view or the other.[61] At the time of Neff's appointment, the other two commissioners were C. V. Terrell, whom Neff had appointed to the commission in 1924 to succeed Walter Splawn when Splawn left to become president of the University of Texas, and Lon A. Smith, who was elected in the fall of 1924 to succeed W. A. Nabors. Terrell was sixty-eight years old when Neff came to the commission. He had been in the Texas Senate many years before and was serving as state treasurer when Neff appointed him to the commission. Gilmore had really been the glue that held the commission together. A journalist and an attorney, he had served in the legislature for three terms before he was elected to the commission in 1918. Gilmore took hold and was the stabilizing influence in the agency during the 1920s. His death thus left a noticeable void. Perhaps Governor Moody thought Neff could be the new anchor, but it didn't work out that way.

The early years of the Texas Railroad Commission have been most recently captured in a volume written in 2005 by William R. Childs.[62] As Childs explains, the Railroad Commission was established to secure some control over the railroad industry in the state. It was Texas Attorney General James Stephen Hogg who proposed the regulatory body, and he was elected governor at the same time the constitutional amendment authorizing the commission was passed in 1891. The agency's original mandate of railway regulation expanded from year to year. By the time Neff joined the commission in the fall of 1929, the legislature had added pipelines (1917), petroleum production (1917-1919), natural gas utilities (1920), motor buses (1927), and trucks (earlier in 1929) to the commission's jurisdiction.

Neff and the other two commissioners appeared to get along well in his first few months in his new position. However, after only five months, Neff had to look beyond his everyday commission duties to plan for reelection in the primary of July 28, 1930, only four months away. It had been eight years since the former governor had geared up for a race, and he was now fifty-eight years old. Despite his apparent popularity, Neff did not get a free pass to a six-year term on the commission. His most formidable opponent was W. Gregory Hatcher from Dallas, who was finishing three terms as state treasurer and seeking to move up to a more lucrative position. Two others announced but were nonfactors in the race. In the primary, Neff campaigned mostly by letters to his friends but did make several trips around the state.[63]

During the campaign, a young man made an extemporaneous speech for Neff one summer night at Henly, a wide place in the road southwest of Austin. No one would realize the significance of the young man's name until several years later. Twenty-one-year-old Lyndon Baines Johnson had been raised in a political—and Baylor—family. His mother's grandfather was a preacher and president of Baylor from 1861 to 1863, and his mother went to Baylor College in Belton.[64] His father, Sam Ealy Johnson, served in the legislature when Neff was governor, but he was not a great fan of Neff. Sam was a "wet" and disliked the Klan; Neff was a "dry" and, in Sam's view, coddled the Klan. Sam liked Pa and Ma Ferguson and was happy to see Ma elected in 1925.[65] On the other hand, Sam's wife, Rebekah, was "keen on Neff."[66] Rebekah was a strong-willed woman and a Prohibitionist who exasperated her husband in 1920 when she voted for Neff for governor against her husband's wishes.[67]

Neff and Lyndon Johnson had their first encounter by mail. Neff wrote what would appear to be a form letter to the young man when he graduated from high school in 1924.[68] Form letter or not, in a meeting with biographer Ronnie Dugger years later, Johnson is quoted as stating that the letter "may have been the greatest single influence on my life."[69] Johnson's first cousin, Ava Johnson Cox, remembered that Lyndon was "proud as a peacock" of that letter and carried it with him everywhere he went.[70]

Lyndon's father, Sam Johnson, had left the legislature in 1925 to take better care of his family. Despite good times in many parts of the country in the late

1920s, the Hill Country was not one of those places, and in 1929 Sam was having a difficult time making ends meet. On January 1, 1930, Neff, exercising his right to appoint one-third of the Railroad Commission employees, placed Sam on the commission payroll as a bus inspector at $100 per month.[71] It was a tribute to Rebekah, not Sam, but Sam was grateful. On June 7, Neff wrote Sam asking for his support in his bid for reelection, and the next day Sam replied that he would be happy to do whatever he could.[72] Thus, Neff followed the lead of Commissioners Terrell and Smith, who had utilized Railroad Commission employees to campaign for them in 1926 and 1928, respectively.

On June 26, 1930, Neff was scheduled to go to Henly for a big political rally. Earlier in the week, Neff had written Sam that he would be unable to be there and told Sam he would send someone from Austin to represent him.[73] But when the day came, no one was at the rally to represent Neff. Two different accounts by persons present at the rally tell the story of Lyndon's speaking. Welly Hopkins was at the rally to speak for his own candidacy for the Democratic nomination for the Texas Senate. Hopkins recalled 200 to 300 persons in attendance, a speaking platform that was "a country delivery wagon with the tailgate let down," and a local master of ceremonies "calling on first one candidate, then another." When the emcee called for Neff, no one answered. Then, said Hopkins, "he was about to pass on to the next one, when I remember very well, I saw coming through the crowd, a young fellow, kind of waving his arms about calling out, 'By God,' I think that's what he said, 'By God, I'll make a speech for Pat Neff.' Whereupon he climbed up on the tailgate, and in the next ten minutes or so, he made a stem-winding, arm-swinging speech in behalf of Neff."[74] Hopkins recalled that the crowd didn't object to the youngster—he was introduced as Sam Johnson's son and everyone knew Sam Johnson—and that in fact Lyndon got some nice applause. Wilton Wood, a boyhood friend of Lyndon's, remembered that Lyndon's mother was there and Lyndon told her, "I'd better talk or someone better talk," and she gave her approval for him to speak.[75] Neff heard about Lyndon's speaking for him and thanked him in a letter asking for his continued help in the runoff election that he faced.[76]

In the July 26 primary, Neff carried 231 of 253 counties with a margin of almost 200,000 over Hatcher, but lacked just a few thousand for a majority; thus Neff was forced into a runoff on August 23. Sam Johnson was not the only commission employee Neff asked to help him in his campaign. Papers in Neff's 1930 campaign folders reveal that he corresponded with at least twelve other agency employees, stationed from Texarkana to Odessa and Amarillo to Beaumont. He asked them to put up posters and to talk to newspaper editors about the campaign. The employees replied to him on a regular basis, many of the letters written on Railroad Commission letterhead and dated on weekdays—a practice that was not illegal at that time.[77] In the runoff, Neff carried 223 counties to Hatcher's 30, with a vote margin of 122,000.[78] As usual, the general election in November was a foregone conclusion.[79]

Railroad Commission, Part Two

On January 28, 1931, less than a month after he officially took his seat for a full six-year term, Neff was jarred by a sudden move on the part of the other two commissioners. With no warning, they voted to install Terrell as chairman, on the grounds that he was senior on the commission and that this practice had prevailed before Neff joined the board.[80] The move was the final split between Neff and the other two, and from then until the end of his tenure seventeen months later, the commission's operation was characterized by the two commissioners' making decisions without consulting or informing Neff. Any semblance of civility ceased. Neff had begun to have his differences with the other two within months of his appointment. He had joined an agency trying to deal with the loss of its leader (Gilmore), who had given it cohesion and direction. In addition, Neff was in a new arena, having had no regulatory experience. And the commission was undergoing tremendous organizational and personnel challenges as it expanded from a railroad regulation agency to one dealing with half a dozen other industries. To make matters worse, Neff was not of the same political mold as Smith and Terrell. In his book on the Railroad Commission, Childs observed that "Neff epitomized the older, idealistic approach to reform and regulation. . . . He was not the outdoorsman many of the commissioners had been." Neff, the lawyer, was used to following laws and regulations almost religiously; the other two "encouraged the staff to serve their individual interests rather than the public's interest."[81]

Outside circumstances also worked against a smooth environment within the commission. Neff could not bring himself to commit his complete time and devotion to the work of the commission, including a move to Austin. He continued to chair the Baylor Board of Trustees and accepted a number of speaking invitations, both in and out of state. Although his election campaign in the spring and summer of 1930 was nothing compared to his gubernatorial races, when added to the other meetings and speeches, it meant that he did not have the time to get to know the commissioners and staff or the background of the problems facing the agency.

When 1931 began with the other two commissioners deposing him as chairman, it seemed to presage a difficult period for Neff. The entire year was undoubtedly the most stressful time that he had endured in his personal life since the death of his mother ten years earlier. It is little wonder that he could not take the time to try to smooth out the disagreements in the commission. The year began with his having to face the fact that his close friend Samuel Palmer Brooks was dying. Neff spent several days in Waco with Brooks, then found out that his last living brother, Sam, had suffered a stroke in West Texas, and he spent time with him out there.

Finally, Neff and Myrtie received word in September that Hallie Maude, returning from her annual summer trip to Europe, had taken ill in New York City. (She had moved there in 1929 to take a sales job with B. Altman and Company.)[82] As Neff was about to leave to go see her, she wrote that she was out of the hospital and recovering.[83] The nature of the illness was not revealed in her letters.

While Neff was occupied with his multiple personal crises, the world moved on. By 1931, the effects of the stock market crash of October 29, 1929, were finally being felt in Texas. Bread lines in the state's major cities were a stark contrast to the five-county East Texas area where, for a time, the countryside was awash with oil and money. When overproduction dropped prices to the floor, East Texans joined the many other Texans in looking to soup kitchens for their daily food. Banks closed, hobo jungles of unemployed and homeless people sprang up all over the state, farm foreclosures became common, and older people moved in with their children.[84]

The election of Franklin Delano Roosevelt in 1932 gave hope to millions that aid would be forthcoming. In the November election that fall, Neff's old legislative friend of the early 1900s, John Nance Garner, was on FDR's ticket as vice-president, and this gave Neff the opportunity to congratulate his former colleague:

> When you and I saved the country in the Texas Legislature too long ago to mention dates, no one thought you would ever be vice president of anything. It is impossible to tell however what a scrub yearling raised on acorns, prickly pears and chaparrals will produce. It is hard to keep a steer thus produced from being recognized as such by ranchmen in far distant pastures.[85]

The Railroad Commission, in changing its emphasis from railroad regulation to oil and gas, had initially acquitted itself quite well in the regulation of the petroleum industry. As Childs noted: "The first decade or so of petroleum-conservation regulation by the TRC, covering the years from 1917 to 1929, proved to be a relative success story in the implementation of public policy compared to the contentious decades that followed."[86] In those days, the oil fields in the news were Burkburnett, Laredo, and the Permian Basin (Yates and Winkler fields). Problems of overproduction leading to low prices and a shortage of pipelines to carry the oil from the derricks to the refineries were met by a constitutional amendment, in addition to legislative enactments and Railroad Commission rules. It was during this period that the term "proration" became common in the oil industry as the commission strove to treat all participants equitably by "distributing proportionately" the right to market oil and gas produced. By the late 1920s, the commission was beginning to be seen by the oil industry as a legitimate government agency. Nevertheless, it was still one with limited capacity, both in number of employees and in their lack of experience. That factor, combined with attorney general opinions and court cases that kept the commission staff on the defensive, meant that the commission's proration orders were still only as good as the good faith of the oil company involved.[87]

All of this was about to change—not overnight, but over a several-year period instead of decades. In October 1930, a promoter from Oklahoma struck oil in Rusk County in East Texas. In the next four months, three other wells came in and the East Texas oil boom was underway. According to one description, in Kilgore, the center of the boom, "wells were drilled in the yards of homes and derrick legs touched those of the next drilling unit. One city block in Kilgore contained forty-four wells."[88] Historian David Prindle described the scene in these words: "To an impoverished farmer in the Depression, an oil well was a lifeline, and landowners eagerly signed leasing agreements with the thousands of legitimate and crooked promoters who swarmed into the Kilgore area."[89] As drilling continued frantically and supply exceeded demand, oil prices dropped precipitously. In the spring of 1931, the Railroad Commission attempted to limit production by a series of proration orders that were largely ignored.[90]

When oil prices continued to drop, violence flared in East Texas while the three commissioners continually wrangled over conservation and the appointment of agency employees.[91] Governor Ross Sterling had little choice but to step into the picture. On July 14, 1931, Sterling called the legislature into session to address the East Texas oil problems. In the session, unsuccessful bills were introduced in both houses to establish a separate agency to deal only with oil and gas. The House did form itself into a committee of the whole to hear from industry representatives with proposed solutions and to investigate the continuing disagreements among the three railroad commissioners. The resulting testimony from major oilmen as well as independent producers and others occupies more than 500 pages in the *House Journal* of that summer.[92] In the session, Smith, Terrell, and Neff testified individually.

Neff launched a bombshell when he testified on Friday, July 24. Speaking of his two fellow commissioners and the status of proration, Neff stated: "We just prorated the people who wanted to be prorated, and nobody else, and we have not had proration in Texas or even an intelligent gesture looking to proration." Asked why the commission was indifferent to enforcement of proration, Neff blamed the laxity on "physical inactivity, mental inalertness, and the desire to work along the lines of least resistance."[93] The statement brought cheers from some of the legislators and bold headlines the next day. Neff was also highly critical of the commission for failing to eliminate the burning of waste gas in the air and for allowing referees (who monitored production at the wellhead) to be paid by the oil companies. After Neff's appearance, Terrell was granted rebuttal time and he blasted Neff's testimony, arguing that Neff had earlier approved private payment of the salaries to the referees.[94] Smith did not testify again but issued a bristling statement to the newspapers: "Mr. Neff has been spoiled by footlights, bouquets, brass bands and newspaper publicity. He has an inordinate pride which has had a fall, and he cannot adjust himself to his new environment."[95] Obviously, the week had done nothing to repair the rift between Neff and the other two.

While the legislative hearings were going on, matters were reaching the boiling point in East Texas, and a federal court was making the crisis worse. On July 28, the court held the April 4, 1931, proration order for the East Texas field invalid, stating that it was an attempt to solve production glut and to fix price.[96] Facing a similar situation, Oklahoma Governor William H. "Alfalfa Bill" Murray had declared martial law in that state and shut down all oil production.[97] On August 14, meeting in Tyler, Texas, 1,500 East Texas operators, in the words of Olien and Olien, "protested against other producers who were running more oil than TRC orders allowed. They asked for martial law to enforce the shutdown of East Texas."[98] Texas Governor Ross Sterling knew the situation was getting out of hand and on Sunday, August 16, declared "a state of insurrection against conservation laws" by a number of East Texas producers and ordered in troops the next day to shut down illegal operators and enforce Railroad Commission orders. In the fall, the commission issued new proration orders. Some individuals and companies complied, others ran "hot oil."[99] Federal courts ended martial law in Texas on February 2, 1932, and continued to rule proration orders illegal. Finally, in May 1932, the U.S. Supreme Court upheld Oklahoma's proration law,[100] and the Texas Railroad Commission staff could also breathe easier. For his part, Neff continued to oppose actions of the other two commissioners. In references to Neff in his book, Childs generally does not fault Neff for his substantive views but seems to attribute the problems that Gilmore had avoided to Neff's lack of interpersonal skills.[101]

In February 1932, the Baylor Board of Trustees offered Neff the job of presidency of Baylor. After delaying acceptance for several months, he finally resigned from the Railroad Commission on June 4, 1932, at a commission meeting. At the same time, his successor, Ernest O. Thompson of Amarillo, was sworn in.[102] Neff was glad to be freed from the four and one-half years remaining on his term. He would be trying to fill the shoes of the giant Brooks, now deceased, fully aware that educational and religious politics were tough, but he was going home to his beloved Baylor and *he* would be the sole administrator.

CHAPTER 9

The Miracle on the Brazos

We have no money. We cannot borrow a penny.
—Pat Neff, 1932

"T he saddest day of my life" was Neff's description of his first day as Baylor's president—Wednesday, June 8, 1932. In a talk to his faculty many years later, Neff said he remembered the day as if it were yesterday, when he faced three alarming facts: Baylor was in debt almost a million dollars; the faculty really didn't want him there in the first place (they had preferred Acting President William Sims Allen); and, finally, he would have to perform miracles for Baylor to open for its eighty-eighth year in the fall.[1] Baylor was feeling the full fury and might of the Great Depression.

But sitting there in his little office, "unkempt," as he described it, he also knew that financial struggles were nothing new to Baylor. History was just repeating itself.

1845—Baylor Founded and the Struggles Begin

The Congress of the Republic of Texas approved Baylor University's charter, and Anson Jones, last president of the Republic, signed it on February 1, 1845, thus making Baylor the oldest institution of higher education in continuous existence in Texas.[2] Baylor was originally located at Independence (some seventy-five miles northwest of Houston), which had outbid several nearby towns.

The most notable early president was Rufus Burleson, a minister as well as an attorney. Preaching often, Burleson held several revivals while he was president and baptized hundreds of converts. The most dramatic was the immersion in Rocky Creek, near Independence, of General Sam Houston in 1854. Houston, the famously rambunctious, drunken Indian fighter, had married a devout Baptist woman who took it upon herself to reform him. Told that the baptism had washed all his sins away, Houston replied: "I hope so, but if they were all washed away, the Lord help the fish down below."[3]

Burleson resigned in 1861 after serving ten years and went to Waco to become president of a new institution, Waco University. Over the next twenty-five years, Baylor at Independence had three presidents: George Washington Baines (1861-

1863), the grandfather of Lyndon Baines Johnson's mother; William Carey Crane (1864-1885), who holds the record for the second-longest presidential tenure next to that of Samuel Palmer Brooks; and Reddin Andrews (1885-1886). The university moved from Independence to Waco in 1886 and merged with Waco University. The name Baylor was retained and Burleson was asked to stay on as president.[4]

Baylor at Waco opened in September 1886, using the inadequate but available buildings of Waco University. Citizens of Waco contributed money to purchase twenty-three acres in South Waco, which was where the permanent Baylor campus was established. The initial building on the new campus, called Main, was completed in 1887 along with a companion women's dormitory, named Georgia Burleson Hall for the wife of the president. As at Independence, the university maintained a preparatory department with a five-grade primary school and three upper levels.[5]

In 1892 the new university in Waco faced a $92,000 debt. A twenty-three-year-old youngster named George W. Truett with no college experience came to the rescue. Truett traveled all over the state talking to Baptists, and he raised the money.[6] He entered Baylor, and on his graduation in 1897 accepted the call to the First Baptist Church in Dallas, where he served as pastor until his death forty-seven years later. Baptist historian Harry Leon McBeth later wrote that Truett was "generally regarded as the greatest pastor Baptists in America have ever produced."[7] He was one of many early graduates of Baylor who achieved national prominence, Pat Neff being among that elite group.

In 1897, Baylor trustees encouraged President Burleson to retire (he was by then seventy-three years old, having served forty-six years as president of Baylor at Independence, Waco University, and then Baylor at Waco). Over the next five years, the university would have two short-term chief executives: faculty chair John Compere Lattimore, who managed the school from 1897 to 1899, and then Oscar Henry Cooper, who served as president for two and one-half years until 1902.

Samuel Palmer Brooks and His Legacy—1902-1931

On Cooper's resignation, the Baylor trustees unanimously appointed Baylor graduate Samuel Palmer Brooks as president with an annual salary of $2,500. Beginning his tenure in 1902, Brooks found that Baylor's only financial resources were tuition and an endowment of $14,750. The university at that time had an enrollment of 783, with thirty-two faculty members and another ten part-time faculty in the academy. The campus consisted of two buildings (Main and Burleson) and two more under construction (Carroll Science Hall and Carroll Chapel and Library) on the new campus; and the two older buildings at Waco University, located several blocks from the campus, then used as men's dormitories.[8]

During Baylor's first half century, the institution had existed without endowment and with virtually no resources except the rent on some dormitories and student tuition.[9] In 1903, Brooks secured the first of several grants from the Rockefeller Foundation, allowing Baylor to attract distinguished faculty and strengthen its programs. As enrollment increased, pressure to construct new buildings grew. During Brooks' tenure four major projects were finished, adding significant study and dormitory space in the growing university. These included a men's dormitory, named for Brooks (completed in 1921), the rebuilding of Carroll Library and Chapel after a disastrous fire in 1922, and Waco Hall, built by the citizens of Waco in 1930.[10] The fourth building, a new women's dormitory, was primarily financed by Baptist women and their organization, the Women's Missionary Union (WMU). The dormitory campaign was led by Mrs. J. M. (Willie) Dawson, who traveled tirelessly throughout the state to raise funds. Dedication services for the new building were held October 15, 1930.[11] With these projects completed and enrollment continuing to grow, President Brooks could look back with pride on having bolstered Baylor's reputation as a leading Baptist university in the country. He had worked with board president Pat Neff to keep Baylor in Waco and was beloved by Baptists throughout the state.

Apparently indefatigable in devotion to his work, Brooks had to be encouraged to take vacations. Thus, it was unusual that he asked for a leave of absence in October 1929 and toured abroad with his wife for three months. He returned to resume speaking statewide on behalf of the "Greater Baylor" fund-raising campaign. Although he did not feel well, he continued working until the drive was completed in January 1931.[12] The effort paid Baylor's debts and increased endowment funds. However, after the campaign, Baylor Board member Dr. J. M. Dawson, observing Brooks' shrunken frame and lines of pain in his face, exclaimed: "But at what cost?" After spending time at several hospitals in Texas and in Michigan, Brooks came home to enter a Waco hospital on May 2, 1931, for exploratory surgery. Neff returned from his Railroad Commission duties several times to visit him in the hospital, and Neff and Dr. Dawson were with him and his family in his final days.[13] Brooks died May 14, 1931, of abdominal cancer, at the age of sixty-seven.

The Baylor Board immediately appointed William Sims Allen, dean of the College of Arts and Sciences, as acting president. Brooks' two children later said their father had expected Allen would succeed him as president.[14] But Neff's name came up immediately. The *Dallas Morning News* story from the Austin bureau, datelined the day of Brooks' death, mentioned Neff as a successor and analyzed the appointment in terms of its effect on Texas politics if Neff left the Railroad Commission.[15] The Brooks' children said they thought their father "would have been utterly amazed to think that Neff would succeed him."[16] Their opinion was shared by several of the faculty but not by others knowledgeable about Baylor and Baptist activities. Neff had been a Baylor trustee since 1904, president of the board since 1907, president of the Baptist General Convention of Texas from 1926 to 1929, as well as prominent in state and national politics. The *Dallas Morning News* story stated that he was unhappy in his minority position on the Railroad Commission and that going to Baylor would be going to his "old love."

Because of both the presidential vacancy and a looming financial crisis, the Baylor Board and its executive committee met frequently over the summer and fall of 1931. An all-day board meeting on June 26 voted down a motion to proceed with electing a president. In July, influential board member D. K. Martin wrote fellow board member Carr P. Collins, soliciting his vote for Dr. George W. Truett, pastor of Dallas' First Baptist Church.[17] Nothing came of this initiative. Newspaper reports indicated that several others were discussed, including Dean Allen.[18]

The board (and the Waco Executive Committee in between board meetings) continued to meet during the fall of 1931 and into the winter—unable to focus on selecting a president because of the worsening financial crisis. Without President Brooks, endowment income was next to nothing and with the Depression, student enrollment was dropping, thus reducing current income from tuition and fees drastically. In the meantime, overhead expenses continued—obviously, something had to be done. By February 1932, the situation was critical. An audit covering the fall quarter of 1931 showed just how critical. The audit, covering from September 1 to November 30, 1931, showed a fall quarter operating loss of $4,180.65, compared with a profit in the same quarter in 1930 of $24,095.51, a decrease of $28,276.14.[19] In that era, such a deficit was huge, and a further downhill slide seemed inevitable. A committee of the board recommended extreme actions. Salaries were cut and a portion of them were issued in scrip, the *Baylor Monthly* magazine was discontinued, and the acting president was directed to eliminate as many employees as possible.[20] At that same meeting, the board again voted down a plan to select a president, but it decided that permanent leadership was essential and agreed to address the issue at a February 23 session.[21]

On February 23, with twenty-one of the twenty-six board members present, the board went into executive session as a committee of the whole, with the vice-president, Dr. J. T. Harrington, presiding. There was no discussion and no verbal nominations were made. Written ballots were distributed and Neff received a majority of the votes. Board member Martin later wrote that Neff received every vote except Neff's own, which went to Mrs. Willie Dawson, who had done Herculean work for Baylor.[22] Neff's annual salary was set at $8,400. He delayed accepting the offer for more than a month, not at all sure that he was the right man. Neff's secretary at the Railroad Commission, Emma Shirley, remembered his agonizing over the decision. She related later that Dr. George W. Truett had come to Austin to address a joint session of the legislature and Dr. Truett and Neff had walked back to Neff's office, where the minister had told Neff that "the Lord has put His hand on your shoulder to tell you that you must come to Baylor. It is His will." Mrs. Shirley remembered that Neff had replied: "If you say it is the Lord's will, I believe you. I'll come." Then the two men knelt in prayer.[23]

Portrait of the New President

Time magazine recognized that a unique figure was entering the education field and devoted ten inches in its Education section of April 18 to a flamboyant description of the former governor. The executive board of the Baptist General Convention of Texas adopted a resolution on March 8, 1932 endorsing Neff's selection and pledging united support.

Why did Neff accept the challenge? Was it his love for Baylor? Was it his lifelong relationship to the Baptist faith instilled by his mother? Or was it something equally important that pulled him back like a magnet in his subconscious mind—his love of the land? His family's history was rooted in the land they had risked their lives to gain in Texas. Land, by heritage and experience from boyhood, became his source of strength, his teacher of skills to survive nature's capricious punishment inflicted through erratic droughts and floods. He had learned survival techniques of spirit, body, and mind, studying his pocket dictionary as he plowed; sharpening his mind in the penny-pinching horse-trading tactics of buying and selling livestock and cotton to sustain a widowed mother with nine children; and strengthening his body while slopping hogs, baling hay, clearing brush, sawing wood, and carrying water from the spring—in summer's heat and winter's freezing northers. He had driven a wagon with a bale of cotton twenty miles from his farm home to Waco and sold it to pay tuition as a Baylor freshman. He had earned expense money selling eggs to Wacoans. Years of public service in the capital of the state and of the nation strengthened rather than diminished his ties to his roots: the Coryell County Leon River bottom land, the Baptist Church, and his law practice. As his mother's legal advisor and confidant, he had managed and expanded the family's land holdings.

As he had done throughout his adult life, Neff would continue as president of Baylor to follow his own advice and return periodically to this land when problems weighed heavily on him. His ties to his farm roots were reflected in his thousands of speeches in small towns and in big cities all over the nation with references to personal lessons learned from the land and the animals. To identify this complex man primarily as a lover of land or any other single thing, however, is a mistake. As a piece of sculpture must be observed from all sides in order to be evaluated, the people who came in contact with Neff had to study all sides to find the whole man. Pat Neff as land lover and gentleman farmer was not the image Wacoans had of him. He was a celebrity in quiet and conservative Waco, where many residents still had not traveled outside the county. Neff had been a national official in Washington, D.C., and the highest state official in Austin. He had traveled to South America and to many of the states in the U.S. He had had his photo taken with U.S. presidents and close friends like Senator Tom Connally. Candidates for elected offices at all levels sought his endorsement.

He had spoken all over the nation and he had delivered many funeral orations with such melodious and moving sentimental praise that the funeral was a special event. His commanding voice could set fire to words in a thunderous tone or descend to soothing ones that delivered sweet bouquets. Gubernatorial biographer Frederick L. Collins described his voice as "soft-flowing with a sigh in it."[24] It was slightly nasal and there were occasions when his words took on an East Texas drawl— he would occasionally pronounce his university "Bayla."[25] He wrote his own speeches and then spoke without notes.

The celebrity image was enhanced by Neff's personal appearance. He towered at six feet tall, weighing 200 pounds. He had a head of wavy, thick black hair, with just a few streaks of white at sixty years of age. (It later turned totally, dramatically white.) His high forehead descended to thick black eyebrows over steel-gray eyes whose piercing gaze withered one miscreant freshman who had reported to his office to discuss a breach of discipline. He said: "Neff knew what I did. But he did not act or look angry or threaten me, but he suggested that I had betrayed Baylor. Then he gave me that IMPOSING LOOK. He didn't HAVE to say anything. I went back to the dorm and packed my bags."[26] He was not expelled.

Neff's large ears framed an oval face and a thin-lipped mouth which were dominated by his nose—the "Neff nose," as it was called by the family. One of his faculty members would later recall: "[H]e was a magnificent individual to look at. He had a prominent, hawk-type nose. He looked very much like an Indian . . . because he had very sharp features and a sharp nose and a great mane of white hair."[27] When he was born, the nose was so big in proportion to his small body that a neighbor who visited the new addition said the cradle was behind a door. She thought Mrs. Neff put it there because the nose covered his face and thus made him an ugly baby.[28]

His confident stride—with his back ramrod straight, his head held high above his broad shoulders—was so impressive that one family friend who became a drama faculty member described him as "the only man I ever saw who could strut standing still."[29] He said he thought Neff had a detachment about what he was doing as if he were off looking at himself, including when he made a talk. "He had this marvelous kind of belief in his own power. And I think that was the center core of him."[30]

His unique clothing, worn since he was a freshman college student, emphasized this persona. He wore a black suit with a single-breasted longer jacket, black shoes with rounded toes, either high-tops or semi-high-tops, a white starched wing-tip collar (a style derived from colonial days, with the tip of each side turned down in front to form the wing), a white shirt, and a black string tie. Because starched collars and string ties were no longer worn and hard to find, he kept a large supply on hand, taking extras with him in a small milk canister when he traveled. When he appeared at four a.m. at a campus fire, formally dressed as always, including his big hat and black suit with the addition of a red rose in his lapel, the students were convinced he slept in his clothes. "When we saw him, we knew things were under control," student Jerry Ratliff remembered.[31]

A standard Stetson hat, in the western cowboy style with a rather large brim, added to his already imposing height. He wore Stetsons year-round in black felt and white felt, wearing a natural straw hat only in the hottest summer months. His size and carriage were such that the hat fit his total image, never appearing that he added it to look like a cowboy. His comfortable ease with wearing a hat may have come from having worn one in the sun as a youth rounding up cattle on the farm. When the hat came off, his hair was noticed. His hair, too, was part of his image. His haircut style never changed. Patsy Neff, a sister-in-law, operated a beauty salon in Suite 1312 of the Amicable Building, and it was well known in Waco that she styled Neff's hair. A former student and fellow Mason remembered a Neff mannerism sixty years later: "When Neff would stand to speak, he would take the palm of his right hand and thumb and place them on his forehead and go right over that beautiful white hair, moving above his ear and down the back of his neck, stroke it in place as he would arise from his chair in his stately manner. . . ."[32]

Neff enjoyed prestige and financial success, but he did not flaunt it in his lifestyle. He and his family lived modestly, except in 1932 when they drove a seven-passenger sleek, black Lincoln limousine, which was luxurious in Waco and Austin terms. The car itself became famous when it sold in December 1933 for $157 and began a new life with a Texas western swing band called the Texas Playboys. The band had come to Waco from Fort Worth, where it had gained some degree of fame as the Light Crust Doughboys on a radio show emceed by W. Lee "Pappy" O'Daniel, a flour salesman who would later become Governor of Texas. In January 1934 the band changed its name to Bob Wills and His Texas Playboys and headed to Oklahoma. The seven musicians "rode part of the way and pushed [the Lincoln] too much of the way."[33] Meanwhile, Neff bought a little Chevrolet coupe to drive to and from Baylor.

As president of Baylor, Neff expected respect and made that clear to a freshman who greeted him with an exuberant "Hello, Prexy" in the hall outside the new president's office. Neff "drew himself up to his full height, glared angrily and shook his finger" at the student: "Young man, I want you to know that I am President Pat M. Neff." The student never again addressed him informally, even in later years as a Baylor staff member.[34] The Waco newspaper later reported that Neff told students and faculty members they could call him anything they wanted, but not "Prexy" or "Doctor." A Baylor ex-student who referred to him in correspondence as the "Ex-Governor of Texas" was corrected: "Young man, there are ex-convicts but *former* governors."[35] He received, without demanding it, similar respect even from family and friends, who prefaced his name with "Brother," "Uncle," and the like, or as "Governor," "Mr. Neff," "Friend Pat," but never "Pat."

Newspapermen frequently failed to share the public's awe-inspired admiration of Neff. A respected journalist, later Baylor administrator, and historian Thomas E.

Turner Sr., who wrote about Neff while serving as Waco bureau chief for the *Dallas Morning News*, described Neff as "hard to know, distrustful of people, had to be in charge of every situation, unable to compromise, quietly loved the limelight, self-confident to the point of arrogance, not as close as normal to his own family and friends."[36] A *Houston Post* newsman, George Robinson, agreed with Turner's assessment of Neff's aloofness: "Pat Neff has few intimacies, not that he is too proud to have friends, but. . . he is so taken up with fine phrases that he has no time for mingling with his fellows on terms of intimacy." He maintained that Neff's fine phrases demonstrated he was a poet, one who should never have been in political strife "but in the pulpit, preaching salvation to lost sinners."[37]

Turner refuted accusations of Neff's duplicity regarding his moral principles. He said he received many anonymous calls accusing Neff of hypocrisy about his no-smoking and no-drinking stand and his strict moral principles generally, but he "never unearthed one whit of confirmation."[38] Detractors sporadically accused Neff of womanizing. Neff's answer one day to a Baylor staffer was succinct: "I thought that rumor was quite a compliment to a seventy-two-year-old man."[39] W. R. "Bob" Poage, who served for forty-two years as U.S. Congressman from the Eleventh District, which included Waco, described Neff as actually timid:

> He was reluctant to hurt anyone's feelings but he was more reluctant to allow what he considered to be a wrong to pass unpunished. . . . He had a great vision for Texas, for Baylor University, but he was not a visionary. He was a practical man who faced realities. He stood his ground against student criticism.[40]

Neff Takes Charge—June 1932

With the unrelenting Great Depression as a formidable foe, Neff had reason to be discouraged when he sat at his desk that first day. Baylor was back in debt—Brooks' absence from the field meant endowment income was virtually zero and enrollment was dropping. Neff later said that the debt reached a peak of more than $375,000 in September of his first year.[41] At that same time, he stated that none of the faculty or employees had been paid for the three previous summer months. In another report to the Baptist General Convention of Texas, he pegged the debt when he took office as $202,000.[42] Neff is not to be faulted for the disparity in these figures. Business managers and auditors changed several times in those early years, and the form of financial reporting used by both internal and external financial officials changed as a result. In one report, Neff even told of going downtown one day that first summer to the First National Bank of Waco to borrow $100 for some "small current needs," only to be told that the bank would not lend Baylor even one dollar. He reported that, in the academic world, Baylor had a star beside its name indicating that it was a probational member of the Southern Association of Colleges and Secondary Schools, primarily because of its financial condition.[43]

The Depression meant less income for Baylor's prime supporters—churches and individuals. Some of these individuals even left Texas. As Harry Leon McBeth wrote: "Many hopeless families, including Baptists, joined the migrant trail westward toward California."[44] The economic disaster struck another group of strong Baylor supporters—Wacoans. In Waco and the surrounding area, the price of cotton fell precipitously, causing twenty-one cotton gins and numerous banks to close. Jobless people moved out of town to live along creek banks in makeshift shelters. Those who had some money bought small tracts of land south of Waco and east of the river to grow food they could not afford to buy. Waco Congressman Poage remembered fewer law clients, less construction, more hot checks, and more unpaid and uncollectible bills.[45]

On March 4, 1933, the U.S. banking system collapsed. More than 12 million individuals were unemployed by that time. Franklin Delano Roosevelt was sworn in later that same day and uttered his well-known line: "The only thing we have to fear is fear itself." FDR began his whirlwind 100 days and the nation was soon deluged with an alphabet soup of federal programs to fight the economic disaster—AAA, CCC, FERA, NRA, WPA, and others.[46] The Depression was so severe that Baylor rationed pencils, pens, paper clips, and other office supplies to staff and faculty to save money. Daily stacks of mail on Neff's desk came from desperate men and women seeking teaching or staff positions. When a Baylor faculty member died, telegraphed applications for his job were in Neff's office before the man was buried. Neff answered every inquiry with sympathy, compassion, and sometimes suggestions for avenues of help.[47]

Neff took hold immediately. He had buildings, and he had faculty. He needed to maintain a level of students, but to do that, he had to be able to pay the faculty, maintain the buildings, and help students financially; otherwise, many would not be able to attend the university. He decided that the principal place he could free up money was in staff costs—personnel for building and grounds maintenance, the university press, secretarial help, and similar areas. He figured that he could save money by eliminating a few faculty positions and replacing many nonfaculty staffers with student help and crediting student salaries to their tuition and fees rather than paying them in cash. He immediately began laying off electricians, plumbers, press employees, and others. For all, it meant hardship, but for two individuals, it meant their lives: the reaction to being laid off and unable to find another job resulted in the premature death of one faculty member and the suicide of a staff member. In the latter case, a man tried to take care of his family by opening a small business, only to be unable to collect on credit that he extended; the strain was too much for him.[48] Unfortunately, such casualties were common during the Depression as the fight for economic survival forced leaders to make difficult—even cruel—decisions.

Moving steadily forward with his cost-cutting campaign, Neff wiped out cash costs to Baylor at the campus hospital by eliminating a salaried doctor and replacing him with three Waco physicians who agreed to rotate their services without charge. He also found graduate nurses who wanted to finish their college work and gave them their college expenses in lieu of salary.[49] If a husband and wife were both employed, the wife was forced to quit even though she had a doctoral degree, as Dr. Cornelia Smith recalled from her personal experience.[50] And there was no recourse on these decisions, for there were no contracts, no pensions, no sick benefits. Understanding the sacrifices staff were making, Neff told teachers and employees "to see him privately if they needed money for shoes or other essentials."[51] He strongly encouraged faculty and staff to stay in a dormitory, and he then subtracted the room and board from their salaries, thus reducing Baylor's cash outlay.[52] During the summer, dormitory rooms were rented to out-of-town visitors coming to Baylor. Neff, with board approval, had virtually dictatorial powers. When Dean Allen, who had been acting president and was a strong stickler for accreditation, approached him about Baylor's possible loss of accreditation because of salary and other cuts, Neff replied: "Well, Mr. Allen, would you rather have a live unaccredited university or a dead accredited university?"[53]

History Professor Guy B. Harrison remembered Neff's first faculty meeting. Neff took over and said bluntly: "Now I want to explain to you what the situation is. We have no money. We cannot borrow a penny. . . . We don't have money for books. . . . [We must] use a book and repair it until it can't be repaired any more, and then take a brick and lay it on top of it to keep the pages from blowing away."[54]

In a worsening salary crunch, faculty members who taught during the 1932 summer term were paid entirely in scrip. In September, full payment in cash was resumed, only to be reduced to half pay shortly thereafter. The other half was credited to their accounts, to be liquidated at an unspecified date when funds were available.[55] One faculty member described "scrip" as looking something like a stock certificate. Waco merchants, who took the scrip beginning February 9, 1932, were gambling that Baylor would make it through the Depression. A variety of prominent stores—clothing, furniture, and jewelry—accepted the scrip. One local bank redeemed the scrip for cash, but with a 50 percent discount. Instead of keeping the scrip and hoping for a chance to redeem it later, some faculty members used it for such things as household furnishings and clothing that they ordinarily would not have bought.[56]

Naturally, faculty reaction was very negative. Most of them had expected—and wanted—Allen, not Neff, to succeed Brooks. Dean E. N. Jones called Neff's election a bombshell.[57] Dr. Cornelia Smith, who lost her position because her husband was also a faculty member, was convinced Neff had solicited the presidency, but she later admitted that Allen probably could not have saved Baylor in those dark days.[58] Several other faculty members shared this view. Chemistry Professor William R. Stephens, for example, while agreeing that most of the faculty would have been happier with Allen, called Neff a born leader who, in his view, was not dictatorial.[59]

The earlier 15 percent cut in salaries meant some faculty were making less than $100 per month. Free or inexpensive events and evening visits with friends provided a social life. Professor Harrison described one scenario: "We just scratched by. We played bridge and always pulled the shades down when we did, because that was, among our Baptist brethren, verboten; . . . sometimes it was hot . . . just smothering . . . but the shades stayed down so that people couldn't see us and report us to the president."[60] Another group of faculty members was bolder. They gathered after football games to play penny ante bingo. On one occasion, football coach Ralph Wolf and publications director Cal Newton played a joke on the crowd. Wolf came to the front door, and Newton opened it and said in a loud voice, "Well, President Neff, how do you do? Won't you come in?" Behind him, the faculty group scattered in all directions, "like a bunch of chickens frightened by an animal."[61] Faculty caution about following rules was prompted by Neff's threat: "If you smoke on Pike's Peak, I'll know it." Both faculty and students were convinced he had a "BBI" (Baylor Bureau of Investigation) because he seemed to know everything anyone did.[62]

One student remembered that social life for students was also affected by the Depression. Most of the boys had no suit and no coat. Professor Will Rogers had one suit and generously loaned the coat to boys for special occasions. On some, the hands stuck far out of the sleeves and on others, the hands were hidden entirely. A date could cost a boy ten cents if it included a visit to the campus drugstore, where a Coke cost five cents.[63]

Neff knew that cutting expenses was not the total answer; he had to get out in the field and persuade students to come to Baylor who might otherwise stay at home. He reasoned that high school graduates in the Waco area were the best potential source of enrollment. Just nineteen days after he assumed office, he and other Baylor officials and faculty fanned out over Waco and spoke in seventeen Waco churches on a Sunday that was proclaimed Baylor Day. At each church, the spokesperson extolled the quality of Baylor's teaching and facilities and then appealed to the parents: "Your sons and daughters can go to Baylor and remain at home for much less than it would cost you to send them elsewhere."[64]

Neff also knew he needed more than students from Waco. As soon as he accepted the position in the spring, the board authorized him, Dean Allen, and Mrs. Willie Dawson to undertake a month-long trip through Texas with boxes of brochures about Baylor. Allen answered specific questions about Baylor's costs and courses, and Mrs. Dawson inspired students with powerful testimony about Baylor. The trip included many small towns of 5,000 or fewer where meeting Neff, a former governor and Washington official, was an experience to be treasured by young people. Years later, the lure of Neff's "Governor" mystique would be recalled by former Congressman and Texas Supreme Court Justice Jack Hightower, originally from the tiny town of Memphis in Northwest Texas, who said in his memoirs that he was influenced to go to Baylor by the fact that Neff was its president.[65]

Neff's first commencement was August 17, 1932, the end of the summer session. He presented diplomas to eighty-one graduates. Price Daniel Sr., whose father, M. P., had been an early contributor to Baylor and a friend of Neff's, prized a note on his diploma stating that his was the first diploma signed by Neff as president of the university. Daniel framed the diploma and cherished it throughout his distinguished career as a Texas Attorney General, Governor, Supreme Court Justice, and U.S. Senator.[66]

Enrollment was down in the fall of 1932 by almost 100 students from the autumn of 1931 (1,125 compared with 1,214 the previous year); yet an air of excitement filled the campus. Neff proclaimed that the quality of incoming freshmen had never been higher, with the new students racking up the highest average on the Brown Psychological Examination (the SAT of its time) of any previous Baylor class. While the Brown exam was designed to predict college scores, Neff, reporting to the Baptist General Convention in 1932, said many other factors were involved in a student's success. He castigated "wasting time on the corner or in the drug store" as a negative pastime. (The intersection at Fifth and Speight Streets and the drug store were favorite gathering places for students before, during, and after Neff's time.) However, Neff himself, in an undated manuscript among his papers, wrote: "I have long since forgotten at least four-fifths of the things I learned out of books as a student in Baylor, but I breathed lessons of life that would not be forgotten. . . . The student who does not get anything out of his college career but the information he gets out of books, studied in vain."[67]

Recruiting Students

Neff's personality showed an unfamiliar softness during the summer and fall of 1932 as he responded to desperate letters arriving in his office. To a father who said he couldn't cover costs for the last two terms of the current school year and requested a note for a year, Neff suggested making a note for a term at a time, thus saving interest costs. In an effort to help a girl who wanted to sell her piano to Baylor as payment for her tuition. Neff turned her note over to the head of the Music Department, who wrote her that Baylor did not need a piano, but gave her a list of instruments that the school would buy if she could trade the piano for a needed instrument. From five different individuals who desperately wanted to enroll in Baylor, Neff accepted four acres of land, two milk cows, a truck, and bushels of grapefruit for tuition.[68]

Neff did not live to see what may have been the greatest payback to Baylor. Monroe Ferrell, the youngest of four children, was orphaned as an infant. At the urging of his high school coach, a Baylor graduate, Ferrell entered Baylor in 1930, only to have to withdraw after three terms because of the Depression. During the next four years, he drifted from job to job barely eking out an existence. Seeking admission again, he told Neff that he was pretty good with a hammer and saw, and Neff gave him a job in the carpenter's shop. Ferrell graduated in 1938 and went on to become a successful businessman. After Ferrell's death in 1981, his family decided to honor him and a son who died in 1967 while a sophomore at Baylor by providing the major construction costs of the $12.5 million Ferrell Center on the Baylor campus, completed in 1988. The facility seats 12,000 for graduation ceremonies. The 10,184-seat arena is the home of Baylor men's and women's basketball and was the home court of the 2005 NCAA women's basketball champions.[69]

Neff, recognizing the hardships that families were enduring, set an example of frugality and selflessness. He asked the board to defer his salary initially and accepted a reduced salary later.[70] He traveled at night to save hotel fees. One time, when he missed train connections forty miles from Baylor, he stood beside the Waco highway until a farmer gave him a ride.[71] On trips to recruit students and by invitation to special events, he stayed overnight in the homes of hosts whenever possible. If he had to stay in a hotel room, he requested the cheapest rate.[72] He saved Baylor a substantial amount of money because he had passes on the Interurban rail line, which ran from Waco to Dallas, on the Greyhound Bus Lines, and on several railways. During these journeys, he spoke as many as five times a day to high school students "in an effort to draw students from as many high schools as possible."[73]

Knowing that her husband would be busy that first summer, Myrtie went to California for the entire summer.[74] Hallie Maude and Pat Jr. continued to live at home on Austin Avenue, and while Pat Jr. stayed busy with his law practice, Hallie Maude conducted her annual trip to Europe after training as a tour guide with Baylor Professor A. J. Armstrong.[75] Neff and his wife were not known for their social events, but the two children forged their own lives. Both Hallie Maude and Pat Jr. were popular in Waco. Hallie Maude had made her debut in Austin. Pat Jr. was a good dancer, and Hallie Maude enjoyed dancing with him. "Both had inherited the Neff nose which kept them from seeming handsome to me," close friend Bobbie Barnes said. Barnes described Myrtie as a "sweet little Victorian wife."[76] To the parents' dismay, Hallie Maude took up drinking and smoking as a young adult, but Neff apparently did not upbraid her for either. She didn't smoke or drink in his presence, according to Barnes.[77]

In the fall, Neff issued an executive order that weekday chapel attendance would be compulsory not only for students but for all instructors and employees. (The only exception was Wednesdays were for freshmen only to receive orientation and other special information.) Neff's goal was to weld the campus into a genuine community and to provide for fast delivery of essential announcements to the entire university. Neff did not invent the chapel session, but he adopted it with great pleasure, calling it "his class" throughout his tenure.[78]

Neff Presides at Chapel

It was an impressive and colorful sight on the morning of September 20, 1932, as more than 1,000 students, faculty, and staff streamed forth from buildings all over the campus and funneled down to the bottom of the steps leading up to Waco Hall for chapel. As Neff stepped to the podium—claiming it with the confidence of a man coming home and fully in command—the auditorium became quiet. At that first session, Neff both praised the faculty and challenged the students: "I can claim no credit for the faculty since it was chosen by another, but I gladly testify to the fact that it is the equal of any teaching force in this country." To the students he urged: "Make the best of your opportunities. . . .The start you make today . . . will in a large measure determine the destiny to which you will have attained forty years from now. Many of you students will get homesick, but remember that you never die from homesickness, and, like seasickness, homesickness does not last long."[79] Neff paid tribute to Brooks and expressed the hope that the faculty would be more than teachers: they would be friends who would be ready to help students in every way. A masterful planner and director of programs, Neff concluded the full program in its scheduled forty minutes.

Compulsory attendance could not be enforced the first session because seat assignments had not been made, but by the second session chapel seats had been assigned, men and women were separated, and grumbling ensued. Students signed up as chapel checkers to help earn their way through school, and a sliding scale of demerits was established for miscreants. Chapel checkers reported student names and descriptions of unacceptable conduct: "read the *Lariat* during Neff's speech," "carried on a conversation with the girl across the aisle in pantomime," "spit on the floor and studied."[80] Some of Baylor's most prominent graduates wound up with a number of demerits but not enough for suspension. Many students would later write that they were grateful for the chapel experience.[81] Neff did not share the stage gladly, but eventually he began to bring in outstanding religious, political, and business figures. One student said, "These were not inconsequential speeches; you wouldn't dare give an inconsequential speech in front of Pat Neff."[82]

During chapel, Neff introduced the students to his colorful oratorical style, declaring, for example:

> The boy who mows the lawns or sweeps the floor and comes to chapel wearing overalls, wears a badge of distinction and an emblem of honor, while the beads of sweat they wear upon their foreheads form a nobler crown than ever pressed the brow of royalty in any age, anywhere in the world.[83]

However, Neff's flights of oratory, which had captivated audiences in decades past, did not generally go over with the students. Neff asked Sara Lowrey, speech instructor, to critique him. She cautioned him to change his delivery and techniques in response to the audience—and he did. Drama instructor Paul Baker, whom Neff brought to the university, described Neff's style: "dynamic stage presence, gestures alive and vital, strong and melodic voice, clear diction, a wonderful sense of humor, gave audience time to hear and digest his ideas. . . I think he loved to see himself making a speech and enjoyed every minute of it."[84] A former student remembered how Neff demonstrated his unquestioned command in a chapel session. A ministerial student rose up from his seat one day when the audience had become quiet, awaiting the opening prayer. "President Neff," he said, "the Lord asked me to lead the prayer today." Without the slightest hesitation, Neff replied, "Young man, if the Lord wants you to lead the prayer, He will tell me!"[85]

If all students did not appreciate the value of the chapel sessions, ambitious outsiders did. Within three months, Neff began receiving requests from individuals who wanted to appear onstage and make a presentation, including a telegram from a father wanting to bring his five-year-old son to recite the history of Texas, using Neff's book, *Making Texans*, as his source. Neff was hesitant but finally agreed to twenty minutes only. But when the man responded with a request to take up a collection, Neff cancelled the invitation.[86]

Neff commanded the students' full attention in the December 9 chapel session when he announced that the U.S. flag, flying at half mast on the campus, was evidence of Baylor's sorrow that two of the upperclassmen and star athletes had been caught hazing weaker men and had been sent home. Neff called their names—students from Dallas and Fort Worth, both two-sport athletes. He said they had beaten their victims until they were unable to sit down. Neff announced that hazing would not be tolerated, regardless of a student's athletic abilities, social or financial influence, or scholastic rating. The Associated Press distributed the story statewide, with its clear message of the new president's intention to rigidly enforce traditional Baptist standards at Baylor. Letters, telegrams, and postcards arrived almost immediately in the president's office, overwhelmingly supporting his action.[87] The American Legion protested the lowering of the flag on grounds that this was an unauthorized display of the flag.[88]

Neff's style of expelling students in a chapel session brought mixed reactions through the years. One faculty member thought that his method was an outgrowth of his district attorney days, that he believed strongly that making a public example of culprits had a positive example on others.[89] It contrasted sharply with Brooks' method of calling students into his office for dismissal. In the chapel session, the rules against missing chapel, hazing, smoking (although boys were allowed to smoke in Brooks Hall, their dormitory), dancing, and drinking would be spelled out in detail in warning speeches and in public punishment of offenders. Neff knew that, off campus, some students violated one or more of these rules, but he was determined that it would not happen on the Baylor campus. In addition, female students were reminded about strict rules: no more than two dates a week for freshmen; no evening parked car dates; no student marriages; reduced date privileges until a failing grade was passing.[90] These rules were not new—in fact, in earlier years, students were expected to attend church on Sundays, and young ladies residing in Burleson Hall were to attend First Baptist Church if no other church was designated by her parents.

Promoting Baylor

Throughout his adult life, Neff had demonstrated unerring promotional abilities—from the "cannon episode" at the University of Texas Law School; to his days as prosecuting attorney when he convicted a McGregor liquor dealer by paraphrasing the Old Testament, the Twenty-third Psalm, and the patriotic song "America"; to boldly campaigning in a single-engine flying machine to become the first airborne Texas candidate; to issuing a gubernatorial pardon for famed blues singer Leadbelly—Pat Neff knew how to become newsworthy.

His greatest promotion occurred in 1933 when he hatched the idea that would bring Baylor not just national but international acclaim. He remembered that during the fall of 1932 he had been on a program in Oklahoma with a set of quadruplets, the Keys sisters—Leota, Mary, Mona, and Roberta. He discovered they were church-going Baptists and that they would finish high school in the spring of 1933. Indeed they were the first quadruplets in the United States to live to maturity. Neff immediately persuaded the executive committee of the board to approve his request to offer the "quads" four-year scholarships.[91] He then went to work, persuading A. M. Goldstein, secretary-treasurer of one of Waco's major department stores, Goldstein-Migel, to "present each, at the beginning of the season, with a nice dress, hat, pair of shoes, and a pair of silk hose."[92] A first cousin of the quads, Louise Shepperd, who was a sophomore at Baylor at the time, agreed to help persuade the quads that Baylor was the college they should attend.[93] With the girls nearing graduation in their hometown of Hollis, Oklahoma (population 964), Neff set out on an important journey. The authors interviewed the last surviving quad, Roberta Keys Torn in 2000, then nearing ninety years of age in Houston, and she related the story of their first meeting:

> It was a big thing then for Governor Neff to come to Hollis. He spoke to the high school assembly and all the people came. I was valedictorian. We played our saxophones. He was very impressive. He looked like a governor, a senator, or something. He stayed in our one hotel. I think he stayed another day. By the time he left, he had absolutely promised us the school. He saw the value of publicity. He was a publicity fiend, and thank goodness for his being that. He was trying to get more kids to come

to Baylor. He offered us free tuition, no book fees, no fees of any kind; we paid nothing: no room, no board, and a laundry furnished our laundry at no charge the whole time we were in Baylor. The Waco and Rivoli Theaters gave us free picture show passes. Goldstein-Migel gave us clothes. A store in Hollis gave us some clothes, too. There was no contract. . . I think Mr. Neff and my daddy shook hands.[94]

Neff had indeed scored a coup for Baylor. The Keys quads were born June 4, 1915, in the little town of Hollis in southwestern Oklahoma. (Later, the town would be the home of Darrell Royal, famed University of Texas football coach in the 1960s.) The Keys family already had two boys and two girls, and as Mrs. Keys' pregnancy had progressed with the quads, no one could figure out her huge weight gain. The girls arrived with no real problems at birth, weighing approximately four pounds each. Roberta Keys related that she and her sisters were put out on the big enclosed porch of the house, all on one bed. Mrs. Keys nursed the babies for nine months, relying on the same liquid stimulant that Myrtie had used in 1903—beer. Because Mrs. Keys needed so much, the beer came in a tanker, but the staunch Baptist Keys insisted that the label be removed from the truck to conceal the contents. The girls began to sing at three years of age. At eleven, they were invited to Hollywood and posed with Gary Cooper; they had offers from some of the studios, but their father wouldn't hear of show business careers—he wanted them to grow up to be normal, Roberta remembered. Neff made a favorable impression on the parents, and the girls enrolled at Baylor in September 1933. As will be revealed later, their arrival on campus would be a win-win situation for the entire Baylor community.

In January 1933, seven months after he had actually taken the reins, inaugural plans for the Neff presidency were unveiled. The ceremonies were planned for April 19-21 with an impressive array of speakers, including poet Robert Frost, a 200-voice choir, and invited representatives from more than 200 colleges and universities from around the country. Six thousand invitations were mailed nationwide in February, but the inauguration was cancelled in March because of the economic crisis. The decision to cancel was Neff's, undoubtedly a very difficult one for a man who loved pomp and ceremony and respected its power to add significance and draw attention and publicity to such an event.[95]

Neff concluded his first year as president by presiding over the university's spring commencement, May 27-31. A play in Waco Hall Saturday night launched the festivities. A baccalaureate sermon Sunday morning and an organ recital that afternoon were followed by two days honoring parents and alumni. Commencement day on Wednesday climaxed the celebrations. Honorary degrees were awarded to eight distinguished individuals, including two women and the commencement speaker, Southern Methodist University President C. C. Selecman. Neff's first two honor guests were David E. Colp, chairman of the Texas Parks Board for the past ten years, and Louis W. Kemp of Houston, noted member of the State Historical

Board. Neff added a personal touch that was appreciated—asking the parents of each graduate to stand as the student shook hands with Neff and received his or her degree.

As Neff completed his first twelve months as Baylor's president, the nation's hungry still stood in bread lines. Baylor's faculty were still eating beans and holding warrants and vouchers for unpaid salaries—their investment in Baylor's future, which was their future also. They had been invaluable partners in Neff's assaults on indebtedness and shared credit for the budget cuts that the times demanded.

When Neff had lifted his head from his desk after a moment of despair on his first day as president back in June 1932, he had fixed his eye on his goal of saving Baylor with the support of the Baylor Board, the Baptist governing bodies, and the faculty. He had proceeded to unleash his formidable personal energy and ingenuity in a life-or-death battle for Baylor, leaving in his wake scars on staff job security and family budgets and on countless academic egos. His strategies were working and he was determined to maintain the momentum, knowing full well, after being given unlimited freedom by the governing board, it was *his* personal life-and-death battle, too. Criticism of his methods would continue to parallel praise as he plunged forward with the zeal of a Bible hero who had heard God's voice, embraced His personal call, and accepted His divinely designated authority.

CHAPTER 10

The Promoter: Baylor from 1933 to 1939

Pat Neff: the greatest showman on earth.
—*Daily Lariat*, February 2, 1938

P at Neff's second summer as Baylor's chief executive started with a loss, but one that he and friends grudgingly expected. On February 20, 1933, the U.S. Congress proposed the Twenty-first Amendment to the U.S. Constitution, repealing the Eighteenth Amendment, which had outlawed the manufacture and sale of liquor. Neff made several speeches against the amendment during the spring and summer, but in letters to two friends, he expressed pessimism.[1] On August 26, Texas became the twenty-third state to vote for national repeal. At the same time, Texas voters authorized the manufacture and sale of 3.2 percent beer. In Texas, repeal won a whopping majority of more than 100,000 in a turnout of some 450,000.[2] National Prohibition ended four months later when the thirty-sixth state of the forty-eight approved the amendment. However, Neff continued his anti-liquor battle on the home front, fighting the return of saloons, especially those planned near the Baylor campus.[3]

In September 1932, faculty members had begun getting paychecks again, thanks to Neff's playing a shell game of shuffling from one local bank to another, paying off loans and taking out new ones.[4] The General Education Board of the Rockefeller Foundation came through with another $142,000 in 1933, primarily because the board visitor to Waco was impressed by the absence of smoking on campus and the genuine "spiritual atmosphere" that he sensed in the faculty and students.[5]

Two Indispensable Men

Baylor's Depression days were made more bearable by the work of Neill Morris Sr. and Morris Goebel, the nearest thing to indispensable men at Baylor in the early to mid-1900s. Neill Morris graduated from Baylor in 1927 and had already accumulated five years of work on the university's grounds and maintenance by graduation time. From 1927 to 1935, he was assistant superintendent of the Buildings and Grounds Department, and then he served in the top spot for thirty-eight

185

years until 1973. Although Morris did not have to contend with the complications of air conditioning and the like until later years, he cobbled together students and materials during the 1930s to keep the university plant operating without shut-downs. In a series of oral interviews in 1975, Morris recalled improvising a lot and building from scratch. "We infringed on several patents, I'm sure, but we didn't have the money to buy anything."[6] In 1934, Morris' "boys" were aided by federal education relief funds coming to Baylor from the State of Texas for stu-dent assistance. And in 1935, the National Youth Administration (NYA), one of FDR's counter-Depression programs, opened for business. Morris remembered being sent 150 students every quarter, many of them through the NYA program. Judge Abner McCall, Baylor president from 1961 to 1981, worked for Morris for a short time, as did Judge Charles Barrow and thousands of other Baylor graduates, now scattered over the country. McCall and Barrow shared two other distinctions: both served on the Texas Supreme Court and as dean of the Baylor Law School over the course of their careers. In his oral memoirs, Barrow recalled meeting Neff, "the most distinguished man I ever knew," when as a recent high school graduate, he and his family were looking at colleges. Neff happened to spot them, introduced himself, and offered Barrow a job mowing grass so that he could go to school. As Barrow noted in his memoirs, "Nobody was giving you jobs in 1938." He started work immediately that summer and entered school in the fall, giving Pat Neff all the credit.[7]

Neff was continuing to display his uncanny knack for spotting future talent. Morris Goebel was manager of the Baylor University Press from 1920 to 1952. His son, Marvin, succeeded him and served another thirty-six years, until he retired in 1988. The elder Goebel is credited for the growth and maturity of the Press. Dur-ing the administrations of Brooks and Neff, the Press consistently employed a dozen or more students at one time, in the office, the bindery, and the pressroom. It printed the *Daily Lariat*, the four annual bulletins published during those years, *The Baylor Monthly* magazine (later *The Baylor Line*), and football and drama pro-grams, as well as catalogs and hardcover books.

Neff applied for and began receiving NYA funds for impoverished youth shortly after he took over at Baylor. Nationally in 1936, the NYA claimed to reach 10 percent of all college enrollment.[8] In the period 1935-1937, Baylor might have received more than its regular allotment as the state director of the NYA was Lyndon Johnson. He and Neff exchanged several letters during that period, with Neff writ-ing on one occasion: "I count you as one of my boys."[9] The program continued until 1943. At its peak, Baylor had students on the payroll who were doing clerical, library, and promotional work, as well as buildings and grounds maintenance, gen-erally at the rate of thirty-five cents per hour.[10]

Climbing Out of the Depression

By November 1934, Neff was able to report to the Baptist General Convention of Texas that the school had paid every monthly salary and had not added any debt.[11] In the 1935 report, he proudly announced that the General Education Board had made another grant to Baylor, this time to purchase 2,500 new books for the library.[12] In 1936, Neff told the convention that the school did not borrow any new money and was paying down debt of previous years, but the campus was in dire need of additional buildings.[13] In 1937, he was able to report that the university at Waco was out of debt and had actually paid off $453,837 in debt and interest since 1932.[14]

Thanks to Neff's aggressive student aid programs and his promotional activities around the state, the fall enrollment, which had dipped in 1932, began rising one year later. The 1933 fall figures showed 1,532 in Waco, an increase of nearly 400 from the previous year, with another 625 in Dallas.[15] The number included the quadruplets from Oklahoma. Roberta remembered: "We saw students peeking around the corner at us. They didn't seem to know what they were supposed to do." But curiosity soon turned to "wonderful friendships that week."[16] Neff gave each of the quads a card—all they had to do was flash that card and books and other necessities were theirs. They were immediately placed in the band at its next concert and, with lessons from the Music Department to improve their singing and saxophone skills, they soon joined Neff on his tours of the state, recruiting other students and gathering money from the Baptist brethren for Baylor.[17]

By 1935, Neff was able to report the largest enrollment in Baylor history—1,894 students from twenty-two states and six foreign countries.[18] Enrollment continued to rise through the 1939-1940 school year.[19] The figures for the latter part of the 1930s showed a dramatic increase over the 1932 enrollment and naturally created a great strain on both faculty and facilities. The increase in student aid opportunities played a part in the growth, but the major reason for the jump in enrollment was undoubtedly the promotional abilities of the man many still called Governor Neff. Of his five governmental posts, only his four years as governor had required him to be a booster of his state. He had used his bully pulpit then to rally Texans around better roads and parks, but he had frequently been thwarted by a legislature that was more interested in the status quo. Now, at Baylor, he had an opportunity—in fact, the situation demanded it—to sell Baylor up and down the state and beyond. He let few opportunities escape him. Neff quickly recognized the power of the new medium of radio. In the fall of 1933, he began a thirty-minute weekly program over Waco station WACO. Neff frequently took part of the program, but he wanted his audience to see the depth and breadth of faculty and student musical talent, so for most shows, he featured vocalists and instrumentalists from the Music School. Realizing that WACO reached only the Central Texas area, he began wooing Fort Worth radio station

WBAP and was soon presenting an hour-long program over that station to a much bigger audience. In the late 1930s, the Baylor Variety Hour began broadcasting over the twenty-three stations of the Texas State Network on Wednesday afternoons.[20] In 1935, the faculty approved a new course in radio broadcasting to be housed in the Department of Speech.

The president was needed on campus every hour of every day. Neff's papers contain several letters offering to meet individuals on Saturday afternoon or Sunday morning—he did not go to Sunday School, which caused some discussion in his church, but he pled Baylor business and the congregation left him alone. To Neff, Baylor was his "ox in the ditch." Although he was faithful in attending the morning worship service and knew he was needed at home, he felt he had to go out and bring in students and money, and he spent many hours on the road. In the 1930s, he spoke to crowds at ceremonies marking historic events at Crockett, Independence, San Jacinto, and Fort Parker.[21] On a three-day North Texas trip, he spoke to the Plainview Chamber of Commerce, filled the pulpit of an Amarillo Baptist Church on a Sunday morning, and visited with Baylor alumni in both cities.[22] In those years, he also spoke to statewide associations of nurses, attorneys, teachers, and newspaper editors.[23] Neff was ecumenical in many ways: once when the regular pastor of Texas' largest Methodist church—First Methodist in Houston—was absent, Neff was asked to deliver the morning sermon.[24] He also accepted out-of-state invitations to help spread Baylor's name. In 1938, Neff delivered the principal address on the 129th anniversary of the birth of Abraham Lincoln in Springfield, Illinois. Previous lectures had been given by ambassadors, cabinet secretaries, and governors.[25] That same year, he represented Texas Governor James V. Allred in Valley Forge ceremonies in Pennsylvania.[26] He combined that trip with visits in New York City; Columbus, Ohio; Memphis, Tennessee; and St. Louis, Missouri, interviewing prospective faculty members for Baylor.[27]

Of course, radio was fine, but nothing took the place of face-to-face convocations, particularly in Baptist churches. Baptist churchgoers—in and out of Texas—loved to hear that "old-fashioned religion" brought to them by one of the most skilled orators in the country. And as he occupied pulpits on Sunday mornings and evenings, and many times during the week, he told his audience they had to send their children to Baylor. On many of his trips, he took the Keys sisters, a surefire way to attract even those who did not care for his elocution. By their junior year in 1935-1936, the quads were polished vocalists and saxophonists, bringing the house down wherever they appeared. They sang to the Texas Legislature in 1935[28] and, in their trips to all parts of Texas, it was not unusual for them to appear as many as three times in one day.[29] A lenient faculty let them take their assignments with them when they were gone during weekdays, and the conscientious foursome diligently kept up with their studies.[30] On one occasion, the largest congregation ever assembled in Second Baptist Church, Houston, turned out to hear Neff and the quads; the crowd overflowed the sanctuary and "many people sat in cars to listen over the radio."[31]

The Keys Quads and the Dionne Quints

Neff's great coup with the quads came in 1936. In 1924 as governor, Neff had officially launched the movement to celebrate the one hundredth anniversary of Texas independence.[32] In 1932, despite the Depression, voters endorsed a constitutional amendment authorizing an official Texas Centennial celebration and instructed the legislature to make necessary financial arrangements.[33] In June 1934, the Texas Centennial Commission of Control, with Neff as one of nine members, was established to supervise the celebrations statewide.[34] Soon after, an idea was born to have the Keys quads visit the Dionne quintuplets of Canada as part of the Centennial promotion. The Dionnes, born in May 1934, were the world's first surviving quintuplets. The initiative took hold immediately and plans were laid for a ten-day visit to the quintuplets that would include stops in St. Louis, Chicago, Toronto, New York and Washington.[35] Neff was to be their chaperone and, feeling an awesome responsibility to the parents, he would rarely leave their side. Newspapers carried the day-to-day stories of this unusual visit, but the quads told even better tales in their letters to their parents in Hollis. In the first letter, covering their first two days, Roberta wrote that they were having the time of their lives. She recounted leaving Waco (Friday, May 8) in their new blue outfits with photographers everywhere they went, making stops in Dallas and Denison as they rode in a "swanky train," and playing bridge in the lounge car as they traveled to St. Louis. They toured St. Louis, went to an American League baseball game, and ended with a fancy dinner, dance, and floor show until late that night. Traveling through the night, they arrived in Chicago the next morning. After a quick tour of Chicago and still more picture-taking, they left for Toronto.[36]

Several photographers met the girls outside Toronto and rode with the entourage all night to North Bay, some thirteen miles from Calendar, the site of the hospital housing the quints. The quads were met in North Bay by more reporters and photographers. At the hospital, Dr. Allan Roy Dafoe, who had delivered the quintuplets, allowed only Neff and the four girls through two gates and to a glass separating the quints from the outside world.[37] "We knocked on the glass. . . . They immediately began squealing and laughing and moving about," wrote Roberta. The quads gave their gifts to Dr. Dafoe for the quints, including college scholarships to Baylor. That night, at the doctor's invitation, Neff and the Baylor girls saw his movie of the quints, a treat not open to the public. Traveling again all night back to Toronto, the quads spent the day in that city, welcomed by everyone from the mayor to the speaker of the Parliament. They left that afternoon for Niagara Falls. After a few hours there, they boarded the train again for New York City.[38]

The group arrived in New York City early Wednesday morning, May 13, with Dodie (Leota) almost cursing (in a letter to her family) because she had not been able to take a bath since they left Waco.[39] They immediately spent two and a half hours with "four movie cameras grinding at once." Taken on another tour in the afternoon, they appeared on the Fred Allen show twice (the second at midnight for the West Coast audience), and then at a Manhattan night club. According to Dodie's letter, they finally climbed on a train for Washington at 3:30 in the morning, then wearily got out of bed four hours later to be ready for another day dealing with curious media. They breakfasted with Senator Tom Connally, posed for photographs with Vice President John Nance Garner, and went to the gallery of the House of Representatives, where the Oklahoma and Texas delegations vied for pictures with the girls. Originally scheduled to leave that night, Neff and the quads decided to stay over another day to tour Washington and Mount Vernon. Dodie closed her letter with the vow that she was "going to get that bath if I have to keep the whole Congress waiting."[40] The quads' last letter, written on the train on the way home, recounted their Washington tour, including a visit with U.S. Supreme Court Chief Justice Charles Evans Hughes and his wife in their home.[41]

The Keys quads arrived home in Waco to a heroines' welcome on Sunday, May 17, and reported on their trip at chapel the following week, a trip that Neff calculated at 5,000 railroad miles.[42] In a later letter to the girls, Neff wrote that the publicity department of the Texas Centennial believed the free publicity received during the trip would have ordinarily cost some $250,000.[43]

Kenneth B. Ragsdale, in his book on the Centennial, labeled the trip a "stunt" that "while being newsworthy in 1936, appears ludicrous or downright bizarre a half-century later."[44] He admitted that the Keys trip generated more than 4,000 newspaper clippings from forty-five states, plus Cuba and six provinces in Canada, and he reported that Neff and the girls received mixed reviews from the eastern press.[45] Ragsdale's preference for publicity was the Texas Centennial Press Train. The latter was impressive: Governor James V. Allred and 125 prominent Texans, along with the University of Texas Longhorn Band, made a ten-day trip to seventeen cities across the nation to promote the Centennial.[46] But many would say that the sets of quints and quads trumped the governor.

The quads never wore religion on their sleeves, but they also didn't shy from expressing their faith. Just two weeks before graduation in 1937, their church in Waco—the First Baptist—honored them before more than 2,000 worshippers who had turned out to hear Neff present the girls. Leota, speaking on behalf of the sisters, declared: "We are glad we chose the campus where Christ walks side by side with each student."[47]

On May 31, 1937, the quads graduated with their original class. As President Neff handed the quads their diplomas, he turned to Mr. and Mrs. Keys and said:

Four years ago, you sent to this institution and entrusted to our keeping for the time being, these laughing, singing, playing, and working daughters of yours. They were bright silver Keys when they came to us, and as a result of their four years of training and service in this institution, we return them to you, no longer just silver Keys but highly polished and burnished golden Keys—Keys that will unlock the door of opportunity for them wherever they go. And in turning them back to you, I wish to thank you for the compliment you paid Baylor in entrusting to this institution for polishing for a time these rich jewels of yours.[48]

Neff received permission from the Baylor Board of Trustees to place a plaque on the door of the suite the quads had occupied in Memorial Dormitory. He determined to make it an honor suite by selecting outstanding Baylor students to occupy it each year.[49]

After graduation, the quads returned to Oklahoma, moving to Oklahoma City, and all four took up teaching careers. Several individuals tried to take advantage of their fame to entice them into all sorts of commercial ventures, but Roberta said her "common-sense father" kept them out of trouble.[50] All four married, and each couple had children, a total of fifteen children altogether. They returned to Baylor periodically, and Neff also visited them several times in Oklahoma.[51] By 1999, three of the four had died, leaving Roberta Keys Torn as the only surviving quad. In 1998, the Baylor Alumni Association presented Roberta with its first annual Abner V. McCall Award, honoring individuals "who support the causes of religious liberty and humanitarianism." Roberta was honored for initiating several volunteer programs at M.D. Anderson Cancer Center in Houston and for creating the Sojourn House, which supplied low-cost housing to hundreds of outpatients each year. The official record of her service, as of January 1998, totaled 11,270 hours.[52]

The Faculty Shines

By 1936, Neff the promoter had almost outstripped the ability of faculty and buildings to accommodate the increase in students. The president was able to begin adding faculty in 1935, and finally in that year the university required that all professors have some sort of college degree.[53] By the next year, Neff boasted that the school had twenty-seven faculty with doctoral degrees, and that sixty universities were represented by the faculty as a whole, including Ivy League schools and numerous others around the country.[54] By 1939, Neff could write an aspiring faculty member that the university did not employ anyone who did not have a doctoral degree.[55]

Neff held on to the responsibility for selecting and firing faculty and setting their salaries. Not until 1947, his last year in office, did he turn the real decisions over to the respective department.[56] He did not apologize for his method of setting salaries. He wrote one neighboring college president: "I just sit down on my side of the desk and 'horse trade' with prospective teachers on the other side of the desk."[57] Oral memoirs of former faculty members reveal that only the hardiest and skilled of individuals were likely to obtain what they felt was a reasonable salary. His method of selecting individuals for salary increases or promotions in rank was equally subjective: "I have no formula of any kind by which I go."[58] Contracts were unheard of: "We write him a letter and if he accepts, we count that as a contract."[59] Neff initiated several forced resignations; he took the name to the board, and they ratified his actions without questions. Neff justified his dictatorial stance: he had his eye on a single goal—keeping Baylor afloat until economic times got better.

Neff had been blessed with many dedicated teachers when he assumed the presidency, several already celebrating their silver anniversary with the institution before he arrived. Giants such as Browning scholar Dr. A. J. Armstrong and Bible expert Dr. J. B. Tidwell were honored later as buildings were erected and named for them. Other stalwarts already on the faculty in 1932 included History Professors Guy B. Harrison, Jefferson Davis Bragg, and Francis Guittard; administrator and Chemistry Professor W. T. Gooch; Chemistry Professor W. R. Stephens; Journalism Professor Frank Burkhalter; Speech Department director Sara T. Lowrey; Spanish Professor Andres Sendon; and two individuals who would be better known for their administrative abilities, E. N. Jones and William Sims Allen, interim president. All but Sendon and Harrison had doctoral degrees.

If Neill Morris and Morris Goebel were the indispensable men spanning the Brooks and Neff eras and beyond, Lily Russell was the essential woman. A graduate of Baylor, Russell taught five years at Baylor before moving to Oregon and then returning to Waco to become assistant dean of women and, in 1931, dean of women. She served in that capacity until 1940 when Neff asked her to become director of education extension and public relations. A letter from Neff was effusive in its praise of her initiative in seeing something that needed to be done, even outside her scope of responsibility, and getting it done.[60]

Neff's uncanny knack for selecting individuals of outstanding potential for key positions, honed in his gubernatorial days, continued at Baylor. Given Neff's flair for the dramatic and his love of oratory, it is not surprising that two early hires would be future stars in theater and debate. Both Paul Baker, head of the Drama Department, and Glenn Capp, who chaired the debate section of the Speech Department, began their careers with Neff in 1934. Baker's father and grandfather were both Presbyterian preachers from the Comanche Springs area, a stone's throw from Neff's home base of Eagle Springs. Baker graduated from Trinity University in San Antonio, attended Yale Drama School, at that time considered the greatest theater school in the country, and went on to the Central School of Speech in London. In the job interview, President Neff asked him: "Was your grandfather Parson Baker?" When Baker said he was, Neff replied:

"Well, then, you must be all right, because that was one of the most marvelous old men I have ever known."

Neff still negotiated with Baker on his initial salary, but from that first day on, Neff and Baker had a "honeymoon" that lasted through Neff's entire tenure. Neff believed Baker to be an honorable individual who, while reaching into uncharted theatrical waters, would honor his forebears' Christian heritage. Hence, Neff never questioned his work and Baker never disappointed him. Baker married Sallie Kathryn (Kitty) Cardwell in 1936; she became a math professor at Baylor and later would complement her husband's work by establishing a Children's Theater in Waco.[61] Baker completed a master's degree in fine arts at Yale in 1939 and in the succeeding years fashioned an international reputation.[62]

Neff's debating and oratorical skills were well known. He had been an active member of the early literary societies at Baylor and loved the contests sponsored by student groups. When he became president, Neff also claimed the title of chairman of the Speech Department and taught a course called Platform Speaking. In 1933, Baylor's debate teams lost to a twosome from Oklahoma Baptist University (OBU) that included a young man named Glenn Capp. Neff was not used to losing—he had won twenty political elections without a loss. He started inquiring and found that Capp was graduating from OBU and looking for a law school. Neff made a deal with him: while teaching speech and debate at Baylor, he could also take one law school class each semester.[63] Capp graduated from Baylor Law School in 1938 but never practiced law—his love was debate, and he had quickly shown he knew how to transfer his considerable skills to his students. From a foundation laid by Dr. Luther Courtney and Dr. Sara Lowrey, Capp quickly elevated Baylor to one of the nation's foremost schools for debate and extemporaneous speech. In 1935, the school began the first Baylor speech tournament. By 1939, it had become the largest such tournament in the Southwest, attracting more than 500 competitors from several states.[64] Under Capp's tutelage, Baylor brought home a national debate title in 1936 when its three-man, three-woman team scored highest among the 120 college teams and won the championship sweepstakes in the prestigious Pi Kappa Delta Tournament.[65] By the end of the decade, debate and extemporaneous speaking trophies were overflowing trophy cases; some at Baylor even considered melting them down to raise funds for the school, but Neff vetoed the idea.[66] In 1939, the debate fraternity announced that Baylor was again first in the country, this time based on its six-year record in debate, oratory, and extemporaneous speaking.[67] Capp taught at Baylor until 1981; he had been honored by his own Oklahoma Baptist University with an honorary Doctor of Philosophy degree in 1965. The list of Baylor graduates, men and women, who owe their initial training in the art of speaking to Capp is a Who's Who of outstanding Texans. These include, among others, former Texas Governor Ann Richards, former Stetson University president and Baylor executive vice-president Paul Geren, media giant and philanthropist

Joe Allbritton, and minister Dr. Ralph Phelps.[68] Waco Congressman O. H. Cross was so proud of the program that he established a cash prize to be awarded to the top speaker in the school.[69]

In his oral memoirs, Capp credited Neff with having more influence on the major decisions in his life than any other person.[70] Neff also had some effect on Capp's chapel attendance. Picking up the telephone one day, Capp heard the president at the other end, saying, "I haven't seen you in chapel in three days." Capp's quick reply was, "No you haven't, but I'll bet you one thing; I'll bet you see me there tomorrow." Neff couldn't help but laugh, agreeing that Capp had understood the message.[71] Neff thought so highly of Capp that he offered him three different jobs when Capp finished law school. Over time, Capp would be offered the chairmanship of speech departments in three other universities, but he turned them all down to remain at Baylor.

A third star employed by Neff was Abner V. McCall. A graduate of the Masonic Home in Fort Worth, McCall heard Baylor had a good law school and he wanted to be a lawyer, so he entered Baylor in 1933. He worked off his tuition like most students in those days, primarily working in the Business Office and then supervising a little candy and soda pop store in Brooks Hall. The store had been started by two other students on a private basis, but Neff moved in and took it over and added the profits to help Baylor's strapped situation.[72] McCall graduated from law school in 1938, went to Longview intending to practice law, only to return immediately to start teaching in the Baylor Law School in the fall of 1938. The Baylor Law School closed during World War II, and McCall was an FBI agent for three years. He returned to the Law School after the war as acting dean in October 1948 and assumed the deanship permanently in April 1949. In 1956, he was appointed by Governor Price Daniel to fill a seat on the Texas Supreme Court, which he held until the next election. In the summer of 1959, he became executive vice-president of Baylor with full administrative authority under President William R. White and on April 18, 1961, was named president, a position he held for twenty years.[73]

In addition to these stars, there were many other outstanding additions. Neff lured Dr. Charles D. Johnson back to Baylor in 1938 from Mississippi; Johnson had left Baylor in 1917 to become president of Ouachita College in Arkansas. He returned to the university as director of publicity and chairman of the publications board. In that position, he established *The Baylor Monthly* for alumni and friends of Baylor. Neff made him chairman of the Sociology Department in 1939, a post he held until his retirement in 1960. Neff did not forget old friends, either. Emma Shirley, his efficient secretary at the Texas Railroad Commission, went to the University of Texas to work when Neff left the commission, but shortly thereafter, Neff invited her to Baylor to teach shorthand and typing.[74] In 1938, Shirley wrote her master's thesis for the University of Texas on Neff's gubernatorial years. Baylor reprinted it as a *Baylor Bulletin* later the same year.[75]

During the 1930s, Neff also had administrative and faculty resignations. The major loss was Dean William Sims Allen. Allen was of course disappointed that he was not named president in 1932, and in 1934 he went to Florida to be president of Stetson University, a position he held until 1947, when he resigned because of illness.[76]

By his third year in the saddle, Neff was strengthening and broadening curriculum offerings to make Baylor a true university. In 1936, he appointed a faculty committee to study Baylor's curriculum compared with that of leading universities in the country, and two years later he set up a committee to study Baylor's degree requirements. In his annual reports to the Baptist General Convention each fall, he did not forget the faculty—initially praising their staying through difficult times, then in 1936 listing and bragging on individual faculty accomplishments, and in 1938 and other years, listing the universities represented by the faculty and calling attention to the wide range of learning available to Baylor students.

In 1933, he proclaimed that Dr. J. B. Tidwell was celebrating twenty-five years of service and deserved a building for his Bible collection. Neff further argued that Dr. A. J. Armstrong deserved his own building for his burgeoning Browning collection.[77] Neff knew that new buildings just then were out of the question, but he laid the groundwork that would remain until those buildings were actually constructed. For the time being, the two collections were forced to share space with the Texas History Collection begun by Dr. K. H. Aynesworth.

The year 1936 was an academic highlight for lawyer Neff. He announced that the Baylor Law School had been granted full membership in the American Association of Law Schools. This was a great achievement for the school, which had been reestablished in 1920 after having been closed when the University of Texas established its Law School in 1883.

Building a Greater Baylor

As Neff recruited more faculty to handle the increasing enrollment, the president and board struggled to build, buy, and rent temporary quarters until finances allowed the university to construct permanent buildings.[78] Neff wrote board member D. K. "Dock" Martin that Baylor had spent $117,000 to provide land "that Waco is under obligation to purchase."[79] He turned to the Waco citizenry and Chamber of Commerce to complete their 1928 commitment to raise $1 million, and they came through with several hundred thousand dollars to acquire nearby property. Wacoans also agreed to obtain the property on Dutton Avenue, one mile south of the campus, for an athletic facility, thereby freeing up the property in the middle of the campus for other buildings.

With enrollment, faculty, and course offerings expanding, Neff also announced in 1936 that Baylor could accommodate no more students until more buildings were added. "Our libraries will not hold our books; our dormitories will not accommodate our students; our classrooms are heavily loaded," he told the Baptist messengers (delegates) gathered in Mineral Wells at the annual meeting of the Baptist General Convention that fall.[80] He laid the problem squarely before the delegates: either share the responsibility of meeting the dilemma or prepare for a policy of restricted enrollment. Neff knew how to get Baptists' attention, for many of the persons present at the Baptist Convention had sons and daughters expecting to enroll in Baylor. Neff said the university had to have a new administration building, a fine arts building, another to house domestic science classes, and more room for physical education.[81]

Neff had thought about constructing a temporary frame structure to be used as a gymnasium. In February 1937, board trustee Earl Hankamer wrote Neff, asking him to hold off on his plans. Hankamer stated that several of the trustees thought they could raise money to build a permanent building.[82] In an exchange of letters, trustees Carr P. Collins and D. K. Martin joined the long-distance discussion, and Hankamer and Martin were instrumental in eventually persuading San Antonio rancher and oilman Marrs McLean to contribute $60,000 toward a brick and steel gymnasium and indoor swimming pool in memory of his mother. McLean later added to his gifts and eventually contributed almost one-half of the cost of the $180,000 building.[83] The Rena Marrs McLean Physical Education Building was built on South Fifth Street across from the athletic field on land obtained earlier by friends of Waco and Baylor and held in trust by the city until transferred to Baylor in August 1937. The cornerstone was laid on February 1, 1938, in elaborate ceremonies, a *Daily Lariat* column describing Neff's production as coming from "the greatest showman on earth."[84] The gymnasium featured 2,700 seats for basketball surrounding a regulation basketball court, an auxiliary playing floor, a swimming pool, handball courts, dressing rooms and lounges, and office space for coaches and physical education staff.[85] The building was the first permanent building Baylor itself had built since Brooks Hall in 1921. (Funds to build Waco Hall were contributed by the citizens of Waco and construction of Memorial Dormitory was funded by the statewide drive of Baptists led by Mrs. Willie Dawson.)

Despite soaring enrollment, a new administration building became the only other permanent building Baylor constructed during the 1930s. Until the new building was completed in 1939, Carroll Science Hall's first floor housed not only the president's office but also the business offices, the dean of women, and the college dean, reducing the space available for classes. Carroll Library's overcrowded book stacks and reading rooms shared the building with classes. The administrative offices, academic classrooms and offices, and library all desperately needed more room. Again the General Education Board came to the rescue, declaring that "if Baylor would construct a new building to house administrative functions and the overflow of classes, and also would undertake the necessary remodeling of the space thus freed for library use and scientific laboratories, the Board would make the University a gift of $50,000."[86] In May 1938, Neff presented plans for a $150,000 building, stating that outside contributions could cover half the cost and the school would fund the rest. Four years later, in a letter to a university colleague in another state, he wrote that the university actually paid all of the cost of the building—which finally ran to $275,000—from current university funds.[87] Groundbreaking took place in August 1938, and a little more than a year later, portions of the unfinished building were placed into service to accommodate the heavy 1939 fall enrollment.[88]

The administration building went without a name until November 1939, when board president Dr. J. T. Harrington stated that he had received many suggestions that the structure be named for Neff. The board agreed unanimously and the name was settled: Pat Neff Hall.[89] Neff had recommended the name Historic Hall but did not object when the trustees overruled him.[90] He also added his own touch by adding inscriptions around the building. On the Speight Street side Neff's own words can still be seen: "The preservers of history are as heroic as its makers." On the Seventh Street side is found the Bible verse that Neff left Ma Ferguson when he retired as governor: "Thy word is a lamp unto my feet." The dome of the building is believed to be the first stainless steel dome in the state.

Although Cullen Thomas had favored moving Baylor to Dallas ten years earlier, he and Neff had been through too many political battles as friends and colleagues to let any differences separate them in the long term. Thus, early on, Thomas offered to give $15,000 for a set of chimes if the architect would design a fitting home atop Pat Neff Hall. A tower was added to Pat Neff Hall and the Cullen F. Thomas Carillon lifted into place during the Christmas season of 1939.[91] Faculty and students were grateful—the chimes replaced a bell system for beginning and ending classes that could not be heard throughout the campus and also took the place of the bugler at Brooks Hall and the flashing of lights at 10:10 each night to signal "lights out" in the dormitories.[92] Pat Neff Hall, the office of the president and key officials, remains in place at the heart and center of Baylor's campus and is one of the university's icons.

The first floor of the structure, housing the administrative and financial functions of the school, was equipped with air-conditioning—the first in any Baylor building. Neff's own office was completely furnished by friend Harvey Couch, Arkansas utility and railroad magnate. The upper floors became classrooms and, in addition, the home of the Texas History Collection and the Baylor Museum. The classrooms were named for notable Baylorites, including Henry F. Gillette, who organized the first classes at Independence, and John S. Tanner, one of the foremost intellectuals in Texas at the turn of the twentieth century.[93]

The only other noteworthy permanent addition to the campus in this decade was the statue of Judge R. E. B. Baylor. Neff commissioned his favorite sculptor, Pompeo Coppini, for this recognition of the man for whom the institution was named. Coppini, born in Italy, came to the United States in 1896 and moved to San Antonio in 1901 to answer a need for sculptors for government grounds. He completed the statue of Jefferson Davis on the Texas Capitol grounds in 1903, the full-length likeness of Rufus Burleson on the Baylor campus in 1903, and the Littlefield Fountain Memorial at the entrance of the University of Texas campus in 1928. Neff decided to put the Baylor statue on Founders Mall between Waco Hall and Pat Neff Hall. On its completion in 1939, the president wrote the sculptor that one of the Baylor coeds had remarked, "Every time I come out here and look at this statue, I feel like climbing up there and sitting in the old Judge's lap." Neff commented, "If that's not a fine compliment, I don't know what is."[94]

Although the gymnasium and administration building were the only two permanent buildings constructed during this decade, serious planning took place for three other additions—a Bible building to honor Dr. J. B. Tidwell, a building for student activities, and a structure to house the Browning Library. The Tidwell Library Collection, located in the Carroll Library Building, was dedicated in 1934, and two years later, Tidwell's students and alumni had formulated a plan to raise $100,000 for construction of a building to house the library and classrooms for Bible classes.[95] At about the same time, Waco physician and Baylor benefactor Dr. Kenneth H. Aynesworth and prominent local businessman George Belew led a fundraising effort to build a student union. Such a building would not only meet the entertainment needs of students but provide rooms for meetings of all types— trustee, alumni, faculty, and others. The statewide campaign for funds yielded many pledges but little cash. The Baylor Centennial Foundation, the vehicle for raising funds, decided to take the plunge with only a fraction of the funds on hand and broke ground in the summer of 1940. The Union Building remained a skeleton until 1946, when funds finally became available to complete it.[96] Meanwhile, the indefatigable Dr. A. J. Armstrong was raising funds for a building to house his constantly growing collection honoring Robert and Elizabeth Barrett Browning. Armstrong would eventually get his building, which would attract worldwide attention, but it would take almost twenty years.[97]

Students—The Pulse of the University

President Neff loved the sound of hammer and saw for new buildings going up, and he enjoyed hiring new faculty, but he knew that physical facilities and even the faculty were only the superstructure of a university. The student was the pulse, and the success of such an institution was determined by the kind of experience a student encountered during those four years away from home. Neff was determined that at Baylor that experience would continue the tradition of "Christian Education." After being president a little over a year, he told the delegates to the 1933 Baptist General Convention that he would "keep Baylor loyal to all its fine ideals and principles, and continue to build upon the solid foundations so ably laid by those who have gone on before. Baylor will continue as heretofore to stress scholarship, but scholarship that is genuinely Christian. Baylor must continue to be the Baptist bulwark for the faith of our fathers."[98] Of course, Neff was not taking a new stance. Baylor had been the Texas Baptists' flagship university for a long time. Previous Baylor presidents had established a strong tradition of student churchgoing, compulsory chapel, and emphasis on education for the ministry. Faculty members were always expected to set the example by active church membership and exemplary lives.

Neff's annual reports to the Baptist General Convention delegates in the 1930s frequently led off with a section on the religious life at Baylor. This would include not just statistics on the work of the ministerial students but the religious activities of the student body generally. One Baylor staff member later recalled that he did not remember Neff's being directly involved in religious affairs at Baylor. However, Neff did not feel that he had to prove his spirituality to anyone. He had worked in the "vineyard of the Lord" all his life, not only serving as officer of and speaking to numerous Baptist organizations, but also serving on many executive boards and committees of both the state and southern conventions, attending meetings that sometimes must have bored the action-oriented Neff.

Besides, the acknowledged spiritual leader of Baylor was Dr. Josiah Blake (J. B.) Tidwell, who fulfilled that title admirably. Tidwell had joined Baylor in 1908; he became head of the Bible Department, as an academic department, in 1910. In 1933, Neff asked Tidwell to also assume responsibility for leadership in the religious life of the school. In that year, Neff reported a large and active voluntary mission band and a Young Woman's Auxiliary of about 150 members. He told the delegates at the 1933 convention that "regular preaching services were held in the jails, at the poor farm, and on the streets where many were served."[99] Neff noted that Dr. Tidwell had preached at the annual Revival Week at Baylor in lieu of bringing in an outside speaker and "every teacher made a talk on religion to each of his classes." The first weekly prayer meeting in the fall of 1933 drew more than 600 students; 85 percent of all students were enrolled in some religious activity, and 113 ministerial students were pastoring at sixty-five churches.[100]

Later in the decade Neff began inviting outstanding Baptist ministers, primarily from Texas, to lead the weeklong event, recognizing that "practically all our students are members of some church."[101] Dr. George W. Truett spoke at the special week in 1938. In a lengthy letter setting up his visit, Neff told the eminent Dallas preacher that he would speak at chapel Monday morning through Friday morning, "taking what time you want." Neff stated that his morning audience would consist of 2,244 students and about 150 teachers and employees. Truett would also speak in the evening the first four days of the week, again with no time limit. To further prepare him, the president sent Dr. Truett a sheet showing the church membership of the students and indicating that the "twenty-eight non Christians on the list would be the subject of solicitude by the students generally and will not be overlooked."[102] The services evidently served their purpose. Afterward, Neff reported to an interested observer in Oklahoma that "there were now only about ten students who do not confess any faith or conviction. . . . Hundreds of students rededicated their lives [during the week]."[103] During this period, the *Daily Lariat* reported that six Baylor athletes presented the program for the Baylor Religious Hour. Billy Patterson, football passing ace, and Sam Boyd, one of his principal receivers, were two of the stars praising the university for its emphasis on religion. Boyd, choking with emotion, closed his remarks by thanking the faculty and students for "bringing us into closer contact with God" and asking them to "keep trying to make Christ preeminent on the campus."[104]

That same year, Neff, who was responsible for keeping the ship afloat financially, pointed out at the General Convention that the university was providing free tuition not only to ministerial students but also to ministers' wives, children, and missionary students. He reported that in the previous five years, Baylor had contributed more than $140,000 in tuition to those individuals. He also informed the messengers that a like amount had been granted to high school honor graduates, making a total of more than $280,000 in the five-year period.[105] One justification for calling the amount to the attention of the convention was that the free tuition made it much more difficult for Baylor to fulfill the minimum student expenditure per capita to meet accreditation standards of the Southern Association of Colleges and Secondary Schools. It was gratifying then to all concerned to receive a letter in early 1940 pointing to a statement in the Southern Baptist *Commission* publication that in the preceding seven years, Baylor had contributed one-fourth of all missionaries from twenty-two Southern Baptist colleges to foreign fields.[106] Addressed to Neff, the letter writer's comments on those statistics were particularly pleasing to Neff: "In spiritual as in material affairs, you have served our denomination worthily."[107]

Neff's Class—The Chapel Hour

President Neff took a personal interest in the half-hour chapel session, planning every agenda. So memorable were some of the activities that many a Baylor memoir contains chapel tales. Mary Sendon, wife of Spanish Professor Andres Sendon, remembered Neff's asking her husband to give the invocation in Spanish, then in English. For the English version, Neff asked him to read Scripture from Mother Neff's Bible.[108] Neff himself often read his favorite Bible passage, Psalms 1, the first verse of which reads: "Blessed is the man that walketh not in the counsel of the ungodly, nor standeth in the way of sinners, nor sitteth in the seat of the scornful." The verse would generally be followed by the Doxology. Until 1939, at some point during the thirty minutes, one might hear "The Eyes of Texas" before closing with

"The Good Old Baylor Line." As athletic rivalry became more fierce and the "Eyes" became better known as the official song of the University of Texas, Neff switched to "Texas, Our Texas," the winning song in the competition Neff had initiated as governor in search of an official state song.[109]

Chapel musical programs varied widely and included the Baylor Band, the choir of the Texas Penitentiary, and a performance by opera singer Helen Jepson. On one occasion, Neff had Baylor foreign students dress in their native costume and sing or perform. Paul Baker's Theater Department also staged several short plays to provide more variety to the class.

Neff spoke occasionally, repeating some of his declamations from previous years. He received wide acclaim whenever he orated "The Flag." Attorney Matt Dawson, son of Neff's minister and Baylor Board colleague Dr. J. M. Dawson, admitted in his memoir that he had memorized that particular speech in high school. When Neff gave it one day in chapel, Dawson mimicked it, staying just a step ahead of Neff. He was careful that only those in the few rows around him could hear him and thus he escaped Neff's wrath.[110]

The chapel audience was surprised October 23, 1933, when Neff escorted an equally surprised black Baylor employee to the stage. Pulled from his job by the president, he was in shirt sleeves and wearing his work boots. Neff introduced Arch Long, a faithful Negro laborer who had worked forty-one years under four Baylor presidents, a record unsurpassed at that time. He had been born thirty miles from Waco to slave parents. "Today is Arch Long Day," Neff informed the smiling black man and praised him effusively. He complimented Long for never missing a day of work and never smoking, drinking, cursing, or setting a bad example for a Baylor boy. Neff told the audience that Long had saved his money and paid for a home, raised a creditable family, and given his children better opportunities than he had had. Long was very humbled by the recognition, saying only: "I have tried through all the years to be a good servant and to never do a disorderly thing."[111]

Neff's overall philosophy on and relations with the Negro race are not well documented in his papers. Negroes were not appointed to state boards or executive positions in the 1920s when he was governor, and although he did not sign the bill establishing all-white primaries, he also did not veto it and allowed it to become law without his signature. As discussed in chapter 7, Neff maintained a political middle ground on the Ku Klux Klan as governor—while he clearly did not condone the group's use of violence, he never directly mentioned the Klan's name in his public statements about crime and law enforcement. In an interesting contrast, his pardoning of Leadbelly, the black blues singer, was certainly positive, especially in light of his otherwise tough stance on crime. As Baylor president, Neff again gave off mixed signals. On several occasions of social intercourse with the black Paul Quinn College in Waco, there were both positive and negative outcomes. On the one hand, he allowed their basketball team the use of

Baylor's gymnasium facilities when the Paul Quinn court was damaged by fire.[112] He also received the grateful thanks of Paul Quinn College President A. S. Jackson for helping the college become certified as a four-year college by the Texas State Department of Education.[113]

On the other hand, in his oral memoirs, Dr. J. M. Dawson remembered that Neff had reacted very negatively to hearing that a "joint discussional meeting" was to take place between Baylor and Paul Quinn students. Dawson recalled that although the rumor that he was trying to arrange such a meeting was false, Neff told him on the phone that he would "positively forbid any Baylor student from attending."[114] Racial integration of Baylor, in athletics and in the classroom, would not occur for some fifteen years after Neff's retirement.[115]

Overall, then, Neff's record on race relations was not a particularly strong one, despite the occasional positive actions. His stance was in line with the majority of Texans in those times, but in retrospect it is regrettable that he didn't choose to use his power and influence more often on behalf of the black minority.

The lessons imparted during Neff's chapel sessions were often of a practical nature. He received several critical letters in 1939 when Frank Baldwin, editor of the *Waco News-Tribune*, spoke in chapel, advocating the country's entry into the war. Neff defended the speech, saying that while he also disagreed with Baldwin, university students were old enough to hear differing views and sort out the "wheat from the chaff."[116] Former students recall other instances of Neff's practical outlook. Former State Senator George Nokes remembers Neff telling the students on more than one occasion: "Life is a constant readjustment."[117] Nokes now repeats this advice to his grandchildren, saying he has found it to be true in his own life. In a classic example of Neff's ability to adjust to the circumstances, former cheerleader Lester Harrell remembered a cloudy, dark day when the lights in Waco Hall went out during chapel; Neff didn't miss a beat as he continued a monologue until the lights came back on.[118] Not all students appreciated Neff's efforts to plan interesting programs, however: some were known to pay other students a nickel or a dime to sit in their seats so they wouldn't be marked absent. And not infrequently, names of students would be called out in chapel for missing chapel.[119]

"Thou Shalt Not"

Neff also used chapel as the place for serious discussion of disciplinary matters. The 1932 dismissal of two athletes was but a prelude to the November 16, 1933, chapel hour, which would send shock waves statewide. Later, many alumni would consider that hour the most traumatic event in Neff's fifteen-year tenure as president. As the students began to take their assigned seats in Waco Hall that day, many felt a foreboding in the air. Campus rumors were floating around about possible expulsions. The students were quiet, noticing not only faculty on the stage but a number of strangers. Only a few recognized several of them as members of the board of trustees. When Neff moved to the podium, he scanned the audience with a piercing gaze, his mouth pursed tightly and his body rigid. He looked a foot taller than his six-foot frame. He began ominously: "As this is an historic and epoch-making chapel service, I have asked that it be stenographically reported from the opening ode to the closing prayer." The students stood and sang the opening song, "He Leadeth Me." Neff followed with a scripture reading from Solomon: "Fear God and keep His commandments." Neff said that that meant to revere God, and "thus it is with an institution of learning." The tension was electric as Neff announced he was placing in the hands of the trustees present his resignation as president, effective at the end of the chapel service. He said none of the trustees or faculty knew why they had been asked to be present, and that he assumed full responsibility for his actions. He went on for several minutes praising the history of Baylor and what it had stood for. He told the trustees that the campus had a "wonderful student body" overall. He declared, however, that all students must conform to a set of principles and rules that was not negotiable. First, he said, "there will be no hazing at Baylor; secondly, there shall be no getting drunk on the Baylor campus or in the dormitories; thirdly, . . . students will not only attend chapel, but be quiet, attentive and respectful during any chapel services." Finally, his climatic statement came: "the constituted authorities, and not the students, are going to run Baylor University." He again lauded the student body as a whole, but said: "This morning, we are taking the first step to rid Baylor of those students who reflect discredit and dishonor on our student body. . . . Contrary to the practice of preceding years, these students shall be publicly expelled."

He then called the names of seven students, giving a short sketch of their misdeeds, and declared them to be indefinitely suspended and ordered them to leave the hall. The transgressions ranged from hazing, to drinking, to the general statement "for the good of the University." The transcript of the chapel service did not record that Newell Davis of Fort Worth offered the only response to Neff. He paused long enough as he left to say, "Looks to me like a melodrama—with the president taking the part of a clown." An angry Neff again ordered him from the hall. "That is typical of the attitude of the handful of students who are not in sympathy with Baylor's ideals," he added.[120] A freshman student remembered the incident: "You could have heard a pin drop. I was literally scared to death. I thought lightening would strike that boy before the sun went down. Everybody was intimidated. I expect the faculty as well."[121] But Neff was not through. He said he had the names of thirty other students "who ought to leave this institution" and he was writing them that day to put them on notice that if they violated any rule in the future, they would be expelled, too.

Then, group by group, he asked for confirmation of his action and his policies. He first asked the faculty to stand if they supported him—all stood and the students applauded. He next asked the trustees to stand if they agreed with him—all stood and were applauded by the faculty and students. Finally, he asked the student body. The transcript of the chapel session stated that every student stood. This, however, was not the case. In an interview in September 2000, Matt Dawson, a prominent attorney and Baylor booster (and son of Dr. and Mrs. J. M. Dawson), told an interviewer that he and Abner McCall, future Baylor president, did not stand. When Neff instructed the chapel checkers to record the names of those who did not stand, Abner and Matt began to worry about their punishment. They were relieved that the dreaded summons to Neff's office never came.[122] Neff then turned to the trustees and stated that his resignation was in their hands. Chairman Harrington immediately called the trustees into session on the stage, and they unanimously endorsed "everything the President has done and refused to accept his resignation."[123]

Outside, Elizabeth Hightower wiped tears from her eyes, not from disagreement with Neff, but for his "public humiliation of the students in front of their friends."[124] Newspapers in the state headlined the story, and several wrote supporting editorials. Heavy mail response to the epochal chapel session was predominantly supportive. The Reverend W. R. White, who later succeeded Neff as president, wrote his support.[125] One board member took issue with Neff as to public discipline, writing that he had heard a great deal of criticism over this method of expulsion.[126] Neff replied that he firmly believed that making the suspension at a public meeting was the surest way to stop the violations of Baylor policy. Several faculty believed he was harking back to his district attorney days when his reputation as a hard-nosed prosecutor was widely known.[127] The University of Texas student newspaper, the *Daily Texan*, condemned the action as having the makings of a "reform school."[128]

Several of the expelled students later asked for reinstatement. One notable student given another chance was Truett Smith of McGregor. He was readmitted, finished Baylor, including law school, became an attorney in Waco, and served on the Waco City Council from 1954 to 1958. In his last year of service, 1957-1958, he was elected mayor by his colleagues.[129]

More than twenty individuals were expelled in the 1930s. At least two sons of preachers were among those expelled in those years, as well as several outstanding athletes. Although mostly male, Neff did not hesitate to suspend female students—most frequently for smoking or drinking. One woman, who was expelled for drinking while a student, threatened to sue the authors of this book if her name were revealed—some seventy years after the incident occurred. Responding to criticism for expelling three young women for smoking, Neff's response was, "I am not saying they can't smoke. I simply am saying they can't be a Baylor student if they smoke."[130]

One young man was suspended for marrying in secret—another forbidden activity. Later he became another mayor—Pete McNee, twenty-three-year-old mayor of Henderson. McNee returned to the campus three years after his expulsion to address the student Esquire Club and Neff introduced him. Neff did not readmit him to school, but President Abner McCall later withdrew McNee's suspension.

Eugene Wisdom, a business student suspended in 1939, was readmitted in 1940 and went on to become an outstanding actuary in Texas. Most of the students were readmitted after sitting out one quarter and writing abject letters of apology.

Students who checked attendance at chapel—"chapel checkers"—were also occasionally disciplined. Alumnus Bob Middleton remembered an artificial coughing incident that took place during these years. The students were not always impressed with the quality of speakers Neff brought in and began to protest more and more with artificial coughing. At one program when there was a speaker who had not only poor delivery but a message of little relevance to the students, the coughing became louder. Neff ordered the chapel checkers to take names of the coughers. Middleton intentionally did not report those in his section and, as a result, lost his $19 per week job. "That was a lot of money in those depression days," Middleton recalled.[131]

The second most publicized suspension by Neff in his presidency was the expulsion of three students in 1938 for printing and distributing a "yellow sheet" comparing Neff to Adolf Hitler. In a memoir handwritten in 1987, Elton Miles, one of the three students, gave a day-by-day account of the thoughts of the three as they chafed against the tight restrictions that they felt Neff had imposed on all students.[132] Miles was the cartoonist for the paper, and Carey Williams and Norman Smith contributed prose. Miles suggested the banner design of *Il Popolo*, the state-controlled newspaper of Fascist Italy. Swastikas decorated the cover sheet on both sides of the title. Printed on a mimeograph machine one night, the papers were available at various places on the campus in the morning. The administration quickly confiscated the copies, learned where the paper was bought, and called Miles into Neff's office. At chapel the next day, Neff called the three up, then publicly expelled them from the campus. At this point, the students in the audience began coughing and Neff yelled, "Chapel checkers, get those names." In his memoir, Miles wrote that he regretted comparing Neff to Hitler—"it was disgraceful of me." Miles was readmitted the next year and went on to a long and distinguished teaching career at Sul Ross State University in Alpine. Williams finished his law degree away from Baylor and practiced law in Houston. Before the end of the year, Norman Smith committed suicide. Some believed that the expulsion was the cause. Miles, however, wrote: "I have never believed it. He was a brilliant, lonely, moody young man with few friends and no girl friend."[133]

The New Testament Paul

President Pat Morris Neff was the ultimate in contradictions. It was difficult to imagine, but this same Old Testament Moses was also a New Testament Paul who cared deeply about his people. He defended the maturity of students, honoring their conflicting views on possible war and challenging their maturity when he publicly punished them for disobeying the rules. Contrariwise, he was also known to extend a helping hand to both faculty and students on numerous occasions, particularly in the Depression when so many Texans were having such hard financial times.

When Music Professor Robert Hopkins, a Welshman, wanted to take his family to his ancestral home in Wales the summer of 1938 to visit his and his wife's elderly parents, Neff secured $400 in advance salary from the board for Hopkins, making the trip possible.[134] Glenn Capp recalled that one summer, he expressed a desire to Neff to attend graduate school at the University of Southern California but didn't have the $350 tuition. Neff disappeared and, in five minutes, came back with the money.[135]

His generosity to students went unnoticed in many instances. One year, he answered a letter from the student loan committee of the San Antonio Rotary Club by highly recommending a "young Mexican of highest ideals," Enrique Ramirez. In his letter, Neff said he had found the boy in a Civilian Conservation Corps (CCC) camp in the Big Bend, thought he was a "budding artist," and invited him to enter Baylor knowing that the boy had no money.[136] Neff gave him work, and personal check records reflect that Neff wrote him small checks for at least three years to help with his expenses. Neff's papers contain multiple letters telling of his advancing money (not necessarily with his own funds) for a student's tuition. Other letters reflect a 100 percent repayment by the families involved. In one instance, the family overpaid, and Neff sent a refund by personal check. In still another letter, he told an employer that a particular young man would get his degree in August, rather than June, but said this was not the fault of the student and urged that company to go ahead and employ him. Several letters in his papers are also directed to the Business Office, asking staff to be patient with one student or another in payment of their bills.[137] He also advised the Business Office, in some cases, to honor a student's version of the amount owed Baylor rather than insist on the sum originally sought by the university.[138]

Several faculty members later recalled in their memoirs the informal Neff who could relax and banter with them. Historian Guy B. Harrison actually remembered Neff as being "hilarious at times, . . . he knew more jokes, . . . he'd just keep you in stitches!"[139] The informal Neff was also seen frequently at student events. One of the most notable school holidays in those days was All University Day, held in the spring each year. The highlight of that day was the donkey race, with Neff and Dean of Education Lorena Stretch vying to outrace the other. On more than one occasion, female students in Burleson or Memorial kitchens would look up to see the president in their midst. In one incident, a student threw a dish towel at him and said, "Get to work," and he willingly obliged. Neff circulated enough among the students to be named "the alumnus who best represents the spirit of Baylor" in a *Daily Lariat* poll in 1935.[140]

National fraternities and sororities did not come to Baylor until much later, but a wide variety of clubs offered friendship and fellowship for most students. These included several organizations whose name made their membership self-evident—the Red Head Club, the International Club, the Twins Club, the Little Theater, and the Classical Club.

One of the most unusual and visible groups was the Nose Brotherhood. In a book of remembrances published in 1997, Brother Short Nose Long (otherwise known as Dr. Willie C. Long, Temple physician and one-time member of the Baylor Board of Regents), wrote that the exact date of the founding and the founder of the organization varies according to which individuals were questioned.[141] Long has written that the most likely date is 1926, and the Nose, which claims to be the oldest social unit on the campus, was apparently formed to rival the presumed "student leadership" group, the Baylor Chamber of Commerce, organized in 1919.[142] The Nose humor in the *Lariat* and occasionally the university annual, *The Round-up*, their appearance at homecoming parades, and their antics on the campus were usually designed to view and conduct events in reverse. Their language used reverse syntax, their "Holy Temple" was built from the top thirty-eighth floor down, and their "Holy Law" was a very thick industrial supply book with inserts of toilet paper for additions. Their annual event was the Pink Tea and their dates were called their "Fortunates." In 1938, the men and their "fortunates" were transported to the Roosevelt Hotel for their Pink Tea on a hook and ladder truck from the Waco Fire Department. The girls emerged from Memorial Dormitory in long dresses and carrot corsages.[143] As with President Brooks before him, Neff paid little attention to the group, but it is still alive and well along with Baylor's other historic traditions.

Neff was never one for informal partying, but he did see to it that the minimum amenities with the faculty were observed. While Myrtie rarely entertained the wives' Baylor Round Table or the faculty in their home on Austin Avenue, Neff and Myrtie did host the annual President's Reception on the lawn of Memorial Dorm or the Quadrangle between the two Carroll halls. In the spring of most years, Neff would play host to a faculty barbecue at either the old "home place" or Mother Neff Park.[144]

While the Nose Brotherhood tweaked the establishment, Neff paid it tribute by awarding a number of honorary degrees to distinguished businessmen, academic officials, and religious leaders in the early years of his presidency. One of the first was to Mrs. Willie Dawson, tireless wife of Dr. J. M. Dawson, for her fundraising and other efforts. FDR's independent-thinking wife—Eleanor Roosevelt—was a campus visitor in the 1930s, but Neff, reading his board's political disposition, did not award her a degree, although he welcomed her to speak.[145] One former faculty member who did not want to be identified told one of the authors that "if you were rich, you were going to get a degree. He built Baylor that way." Whatever he did, his board of trustees was behind him—they knew that Baylor was coming out of the woods and it was due almost entirely to the administrative and promotional abilities of the former governor.

Hail to the Vice-President

In 1936, the Keys quads' trip to visit the Dionne quintuplets was followed by another major publicity event—the awarding of an honorary degree to Vice-President John Nance Garner in Waco on November 21. Neff broke all precedent by writing his old friend that he wanted to honor Mrs. Garner as well. For the occasion, Neff assembled an all-star cast of political figures from U.S. Senator Tom Connally to Governor James V. Allred and former Governor Miriam Ferguson. The black-robed dignitaries marched to Waco Hall under the lens of the national news organizations, including Paramount and Fox Movietone News.[146] On stage, both Garners were awarded honorary Doctor of Laws degrees, with Neff having warm words to say about Mrs. Garner's contribution to the vice-president's successful political career.[147]

Garner had gone from the Texas House of Representatives to Congress in 1903, serving in the House for thirty years, until March 4, 1933. He worked to gain friends on both sides of the aisle and in 1931 was elected Speaker of the U.S. House of Representatives. He had some backing for the presidential nomination in 1932 and secured the ninety votes of California and Texas, which a candidate had to have to be nominated. As historian Lionel Patinaude noted: "When he gave his votes to Franklin D. Roosevelt on the fourth ballot, Roosevelt became indebted to Garner and to the State of Texas. As a result, Garner was offered the vice-presidential nomination, which he reluctantly accepted."[148] Garner came close to becoming president before Inauguration Day. A would-be assassin had missed Roosevelt by inches seventeen days earlier.[149]

A Waco columnist properly described the Waco event honoring Garner, although Neff, publicly at least, would have argued with his statement:

> On the basis of 100 percent, the affair may be divided 10 percent to honor the vice-president and his wife and 90 percent to put Baylor in the national limelight. It is one of those several master strokes which Pat Neff has engineered for the University since he became president and of all the people who will enjoy the program, there will be no one whose enjoyment exceeds the former governor's.[150]

That same columnist predicted an additional enrollment in Baylor of "five hundred in two years" and, as Neff had planned, the prediction came true. Neff was criticized by several Baptist officials for honoring the "whiskey-drinking, poker-playing" Garner, but he sloughed it off.[151]

Saving the Medical School

Perhaps the best-kept secret of Neff's fifteen years at Baylor was that if he had not moved decisively in 1938, Baylor at Dallas might have gone into receivership for lack of honoring its bonded indebtedness. As president of Baylor's Board of Trustees before he became university president, Neff had dealt with the College of Medicine in Dallas, so the experience was not entirely new to him, but in 1932, he became the school's chief executive. In November 1937, when he was able to announce that Baylor at Waco was out of debt, he could turn his attention to Baylor at Dallas. Dallas had always been treated like a stepchild—the same board of trustees governed Waco and Dallas, but the main attention had always been on the Waco campus. Immediately that fall, the Dallas operation could no longer be ignored.

Baylor at Dallas consisted of the College of Medicine, the School of Nursing, the College of Dentistry, and a hospital, a total of some twelve buildings valued at more than $2 million. In 1929, Dr. Justin F. Kimball, former Dallas school superintendent, had become vice-president of the Dallas operations.[152] As early as April 1933, Dr. Kimball had reported to the board of trustees that of $1.1 million first mortgage bonds issued against the Dallas school dated January 1, 1925, $893,000 was still outstanding. Also, an additional $325,000 was owed to the First National Bank of Dallas, amounting to an aggregate interest charge of $75,000 per year.[153] Neff received several letters from individuals in 1934 complaining that Baylor at Dallas had refused to pay principal or interest on outstanding bonds.[154] The university was forced to issue refunding bonds in 1934 to postpone the financial impact of maturing bonds. Over the next three years, as the Depression deepened, Baylor Hospital incurred more bad debts, and gifts to the Dallas school dropped precipitously, the university was forced to take more drastic action. Neff and Earl B. Smyth, president of the Fidelity Union Life Insurance Company in Dallas and vice-president for Dallas affairs of the Baylor Board, went to St. Louis on October 15, 1937, to visit the investment securities firm of Bitting and Company.[155] Neff had met William Bitting three years before at a church meeting in North Carolina and they had stayed in touch occasionally since that time. Smyth was Neff's strong liaison to the Dallas school, and the insurance executive spent many hours in the 1930s trying to help salvage the Dallas operations.[156]

Bitting suggested another refunding with bonds to become due October 10, 1949, and pledged his best efforts to get the present bondholders to refrain from taking Baylor to court on the default. Neff was adamant about keeping Baylor out of court, writing to Bitting: "I would take the last shirt off my back and then go afield to actually hold up a wealthy friend of the Institution and demand money from him before I could agree to throw Baylor into a receivership."[157] Bitting, Neff, and Smyth worked out the finances, but not before all three agreed that immediate steps had to be taken to economize on day-to-day operations in Dallas. In addition to the bondholders, the school had many unhappy vendors who had not been paid, some threatening to turn the delinquent accounts over to a bill collector.[158] In the same letter to Bitting, Neff revealed that he had already started his second "bloodletting" in his six-year tenure at Baylor. Neff spent several days during the last week of November 1938 in Dallas. In his letter, he told Bitting that he had only worked on the hospital payroll and hadn't touched the medical or dentistry schools yet. In Baylor Hospital alone, he had eliminated forty-nine employees, reduced the salaries of twenty-four of the "higher-ups," and taken away the "free meal" privilege that seventy-four employees had enjoyed. He promised Bitting that more layoffs and reduced salaries would follow within the next month.[159] To his credit, Dr. Kimball had been taking some steps before Neff stepped in, but after eight years at the helm, he was too close to many of the officials and employees to make the hard decisions that were necessary. Kimball had been forced to resign his superintendency of the Dallas School District in 1924 because of poor health, and now, he told the board that again, he was "worn out." The board reluctantly accepted his resignation shortly after 1939 began.[160] At that same meeting, Smyth reported on Neff's efforts, saying that the president had cut more than $35,000 in operating expenses in just three months, a 20 percent reduction.[161] The work of the three men—Neff, Bitting, and Smyth—kept the medical school going until another crisis came a few years later.

On a positive note in 1939, a group of Dallas businessmen had organized a foundation to raise $5 million for support of medical research at Baylor. Unfortunately, the endowment did not materialize, partially as a result of the threat of war.[162] When the decade ended, Baylor at Dallas continued to harbor dreams and suffer disappointments.

Athletics and the Board of Trustees

Earl Smyth was one of the five or six most active board members in Neff's early years. Another was Carr P. Collins, who had been the one who made the motion in the spring of 1933 for Neff to be given full authority to make any changes or additions that he felt necessary to carry out his plans without referring matters to the board. Other members were Houston businessman Earl Hankamer Sr., San Antonio insurance executive D. K. "Dock" Martin, and Waco attorney Alva Bryan. Dr. J. T. Harrington, president of the board, and Dr. J. M. Dawson were also Waco members and presumably talked face to face with Neff frequently about school issues, as little is found in the Neff papers in writing. Dr. George W. Truett, the Dallas pastor, confined his advice primarily to religious matters and interfered very little in the Waco operation. The virtually "dictatorial authority" given to Neff extended to academic and finance matters, but several letters to and from Smyth, Collins, Hankamer, and Martin raised questions about faculty performance as well as about speakers invited to the campus.[163] The four were all conservative businessmen and had no use for FDR and his New Deal nor for Texas Governor James V. Allred.[164] They had not objected to the honorary degree for Vice-President Garner because he was "one of them," but when Dr. A. J. Armstrong invited Frances Perkins, U.S. Secretary of Labor, to the campus in 1939, Martin wrote a strong letter to Neff, deploring the idea. Martin told Neff that the president had made a real hit with the trustees present at a recent chapel when he had said he did not countenance any "isms" except "Americanism." He reminded Neff that outside gifts were necessary to build buildings on the campus and "we are not going to get any of these gifts from disciples of Frances Perkins."[165] Armstrong himself wired Martin back the same day Neff received the letter, stating he had cancelled the invitation and asking whether U.S. Senator Champ Clark would be satisfactory to Martin.[166] In regard to Governor Allred, Neff and Martin simply "agreed to disagree."

The board's interference in administrative matters was most notable in athletic activities. The board was well aware that Neff had no fondness for or interest in competitive sports. Some may believe that the obsession of some university alumni and friends with success in collegiate athletics is a recent phenomenon, but almost eighty years ago, Neff learned that such was not the case. Baylor championships in football, basketball, and other sports sanctioned by the Southwest Conference were as rare in the twentieth century as they continue to be into the twenty-first. Just before Neff took office in 1932, students and alumni celebrated a basketball championship, but this would be the only one in the 1930s. Football teams came close—in 1937 and 1938—but could not quite complete the final victories.[167]

All of these near championships were frustrating to alumni and also to several of the board members. The board had formally established a position of athletic business manager just after Neff took over in the fall of 1932. It was to be filled by the board on recommendation of the president, so it should have been apparent to Neff from the beginning that the board was going to get heavily involved in athletic matters.[168] Just two years later, the board approved Neff's annual recommendations for faculty salaries, but appointed a committee to work with Neff to work out athletic salaries.[169] In 1936, trustee Hankamer told the board that Baylor needed to do better in the athletic arena, and he received approval for a board committee to aid Baylor athletic teams in whatever way necessary to keep Baylor a leader in the Southwest Conference.[170] Neff and the committee sparred repeatedly on salaries of athletic director Ralph Wolf and head football coach Morley Jennings.[171] Neff felt the athletic committee of the board was moving salaries of the athletic staff out of line with academic salaries, and he resisted it. He attended many football games but continually exasperated the board members whom he hosted. On one occasion, Martin, an avid fan, complained that Neff paid no attention to the game and just wanted to talk about Baylor problems.

If Baylor was less than successful on the football field in those years, it could not be blamed on its yell leaders. One of the most enthusiastic was Bill Daniel, known on campus as "Hoot." Neff's longtime friend M. P. Daniel, of Liberty, wrote him in 1933, pleading for a job for Bill so that he could come to Baylor. Neff came through, and Daniel later reciprocated with substantial gifts to the university.[172] Bill Daniel received his law degree in 1938 but not before capping his yell-leading career. He got so overwrought at the 1937 Baylor-TCU game that he fainted and had to be hospitalized overnight.[173] His zeal for Baylor never abated, and the Bill Daniel Student Center and the endowed Bill and Vara Faye Daniel Professorship in Law are part of his legacy.

Off to the Country

The pigskin Neff was interested in had yet to be taken to the slaughterhouse. Raised on the acreage he called the "home place," Neff never really left it in many ways. Sometimes it appeared he could hardly wait to free up a weekend, put on his old clothes, and take on the chores of a farmer. Although he had hired help, Neff actively participated in the operation of the farm and often gave specific and detailed instructions on farm operations to his relatives (who sometimes lived on the place) and farm employees. Neff raised a variety of animals on his farm, and the copies of bank checks in his papers reveal that in the decade of the 1930s he spent thousands of dollars on farm equipment, supplies, and salaries to men employed by him. In 1936, in a letter to Coryell County agent Guy Power, Neff sought help in determining how the federal government's cotton rules applied to his farm. Neff related that he owned 1,700 acres of land in the county, 850 acres being cultivated and the remaining 850 consisting of wooded pasture land.[174] His letter revealed that he had several tenant farmers on the land as well as a hired hand tending some of his acreage. He then set forth eleven specific questions regarding his cotton allotment, along with questions on oats, corn, and maize. Neff's papers also contain three letters from the Internal Revenue Service, questioning his farm operations and seeking small additional tax payments from Neff.[175]

Neff knew that Mother Neff Park was inadequate as it was originally donated by his mother. Thus on May 13, 1934, he announced that he was giving another 250 acres to the park area.[176] In giving the additional land to the State of Texas, Neff was going to be sure it was properly cared for and thus let it be known that he was going to follow very closely how the area was maintained and improved.[177]

Neff took early advantage of FDR's Depression-fighting new programs. When the Civilian Conservation Corps (CCC) was established in 1933, he quickly got in line to have a camp stationed at Mother Neff Park to construct needed buildings and make general improvements.[178] A CCC company for Mother Neff Park arrived on December 28, 1934, to set up camp and begin work. Neff persuaded his friend Governor Allred to make two trips to the park within a week's time in May 1935: Allred shoveled the first dirt for a new clubhouse at the park and then returned four days later to deliver the Mother's Day address at the park.[179] Work proceeded during the summer, but on October 12, 1935, Neff fired off four identical letters to federal and state officials in charge of the CCC work, including Conrad Wirth, director of the National Park Service in Washington. The letter was critical to the point of being highly sarcastic:

> For nearly a year the clubhouse at Mother Neff Park has been discussed, planned, considered, and proposed from Washington to Austin. . . . After the passing of these many months, the laboring mountain has brought forth a wonderful clubhouse. It actually consists of two water toilets and a cold drink stand, separated by a large, open hallway marked "pavilion."[180]

Neff did not let up for three and a half single-spaced pages, castigating the design and work on everything from the park entrance to a water tank and observation tower. He wrote that he could not believe that any of the four to whom the letter was addressed were responsible for the "measly plans" and poor execution. Finally, to try to make some amends, he stated that "it is going to be a real park," and that he and the local people would make the best of what was offered.[181] Eight days later, however, he wired Wirth that the men in charge on the ground, named Nason and Maier, "were temperamentally unfit to direct the work of the park." He declared that he would take necessary steps in the courts or with members of Congress to prevent a situation allowing "two small men to make either a joke or a farce of this particular park."[182]

In 1936, new faces appeared all around and work proceeded smoothly on the clubhouse, as well as other major improvements to the park. By the spring of 1937, the clubhouse was ready, and Neff made big plans for a dedication ceremony on Mother's Day, May 7. He decided that the occasion would be a great time to get all six former living Texas governors together for a reunion. Letters went out in April to all five former governors: the two Fergusons, Hobby, Moody, Sterling, and the current governor, Allred. [183] Neff would make the count seven. He stated that he was not going to have the reunion unless all seven governors agreed to come. He soon learned that he was the only one who could get along with all of the other six. Governors Moody and Sterling wrote that if certain former governors were to be present, they would not be coming.[184] The reference was, in all probability, to the two Fergusons, with whom Moody and Sterling had never been on good terms. The Fergusons, perhaps sensing hostility, wrote Neff that they did not think "such a meeting would promote harmony, and very likely it would result in a lack of congeniality."[185] Thus, on April 20, Neff was forced to write former Governor Hobby that he was calling the whole thing off.[186] On May 7, 1937, a subdued biennial Mother's Day program was held, featuring one of the Keys' sisters last performances.[187]

Neff's next park crisis was not long in coming. In early 1938, federal officials announced that the CCC had completed its job at Mother Neff Park and the company of men would be moving on to other parks. Neff knew that more needed to be done and began contacting Waco's state representative, Earl Huddleston, as well as Congressman Bob Poage.[188] With pressure from all, the National Park Service announced that the company would not leave until June 30 and beyond that a contingent of fifty men would remain behind to finish up the work.[189] The park improvements were completed to Neff's satisfaction, and Neff dedicated the park on Mother's Day, May 14, 1938. He arranged for several highway patrolmen to handle the crowd, estimated at several thousand, and also wrote radio stations and newspapers prior to the event. The program went off without a hitch.

In 1933, Governor Ma Ferguson had asked Neff to be a member of the Texas State Parks Board. Because of his love of parks and his long affiliation with the movement in the state, Neff accepted, despite his Herculean work load at Baylor.[190] Two years later, on the death of David E. Colp, the board elected him chairman.[191] Over his six-year term, he attended most board meetings, perhaps a little partial to his own park. When Governor O'Daniel failed to reappoint him in 1939, Neff wrote a five-page letter to the Parks Board, explaining his role over the past years to Mother Neff Park and the personal monies he had put into the park. During his time on the board, Neff had a "gentlemen's agreement" to develop the park as he "thought wise to do so" as long as it did not place any financial obligations on the state. In the letter, Neff related that he had bought several items of equipment for the caretaker at the park, given him $300 to initially stock the little store for supplies to be sold to campers and visitors in the park, and paid for an ice box for cold drinks for the store. Perhaps his major contribution was to secure National Youth Administration youth to take the old lumber left by the CCC and build five one-room camp buildings, augmented by community toilet and bathing facilities, kitchen, and barbecue pit. Finally, he reported that he had arranged for an additional entrance road to the park to spare some visitors a longer route. He reported over $1,400 in expenditures but stated he was not asking for any reimbursement.[192] Neff subsequently reported to the board that he had leased the little store to Claude Jones and his sisters, V. Marie and Tullie, and set them up in business. The board named Neff superintendent of the park, and the new chairman wrote Neff in October that he was doing such a good job "could we not persuade you to take over the duties at these [other] parks, at the same salary, of course?"[193]

The Family—Celebration and Sadness

The 1930s held both highs and lows for the Neff family. Neff and Myrtie were pleased in 1933 when Hallie Maude concluded a long courtship with Frank L. Wilcox, prominent Waco accountant. The wedding took place December 5 at the

Neff home with only a few family members in attendance. Several years later, in July 1938, the Neff household was saddened when Hallie Maude's twins (a boy and a girl) died the day they were born.[194] The couple did not have other children. Just before Hallie Maude's marriage, Pat Jr. had moved to Austin, having been appointed an assistant attorney general by Governor Allred. Pat Jr. would serve successive attorneys general, including William McCraw and Gerald Mann, ending his state service in 1941.

The Neffs lived simply. It helped that railroads and buses continued to honor free passes not only for Neff's Baylor travel but for personal travel for the family as well. In addition to his Baylor income, Neff had some income from a limited law practice and from his land holdings in several Texas counties earned from previous law work. He was supportive of his church; check records reflect numerous contributions to the First Baptist Church in the 1930s, ranging from as little as $2.50 to as much as $100.[195] As the decade closed, Neff received board fees of $140 for the year 1938 from Texas Power and Light Company in Dallas, the only commercial firm in which he had agreed to participate. His one share of stock also brought in a $7 dividend that year.[196]

The End of the Decade

As Neff stood before the messengers to the annual meeting of the Baptist General Convention of Texas in November 1939 in San Antonio, he could look back with a great deal of pride on a highly successful seven and one-half years at the helm of the world's largest Baptist university. He had saved both the Waco and Dallas campuses from extinction, and he reported a current endowment of $1,638,197 at Baylor in Waco. In addition, Baylor at Dallas was in a markedly better financial situation when compared to previous years. In summary, Neff foresaw a future in which Baylor would be a "University which in Christian influence, stands without a peer."[197]

Neff celebrated success in San Antonio, and a month later the decade would come to a resounding close with the stately, dignified president being hoisted onto the shoulders of six exuberant Baylor students for a wild campus ride from Pat Neff Hall to Waco Hall, as hundreds of students belted out "For He's a Jolly Good Fellow." The occasion: Neff had just agreed to let the students out one day early for Christmas! George Bevil, a student, was there when Neff was lowered to the sidewalk of Waco Hall. "How did it feel?" George asked. Neff's answer: "Like Jesus riding into Jerusalem on the backs of asses."[198]

Christmas came and went, but Neff was not about to let the six students have the final word. At the first chapel after the holidays, Neff ordered the six to report to his office that afternoon. Six timid souls showed up, not knowing what the president had in mind but fearing the worst. Neff thundered that the boys had committed a grave and unpardonable offense against the dignity of his presidential office. Just at the tensest moment, Neff suddenly smiled, pulled from his desk six photographs of himself, and presented one to each of the boys.

Autographed across the bottom of each were the words: "In memory of a triumphant ride. Pat M. Neff."[199]

CHAPTER 11

Baylor at War, 1940-1945

The present war is a total war, and we are involved in it.

—Pat Neff

Americans' attention was diverted from domestic problems to the international scene in the late 1930s and early 1940s as madman Adolf Hitler took control of Germany and began to invade other European countries and bomb England. Headlines on January 1, 1940, told of fierce fighting between German and French troops and of the Finnish army trying to hold off the Russians' invasion. Americans were deeply divided. Many thought the war could be confined to Europe and the U.S. should keep its distance, while others passionately believed that the country needed to take action to keep the war away from our shores. A policy of "lend-lease" of military equipment to Great Britain and France demonstrated friendliness of the United States toward those countries, but U.S. citizens remained unwilling to declare war until the sneak attack on Pearl Harbor, Hawaii, by the Japanese on December 7, 1941.[1]

Preparing for War

Indeed, in 1940 the war was thousands of miles away, but President Neff was already anticipating the effects of the defense effort on Baylor University. In August 1939, Neff took a proposal to the board's Waco Executive Committee (WEC) for Baylor to train pilots for the Civil Aeronautics Authority.[2] The U.S. government's goal was to have a large number of trained pilots in case of a national emergency. It took the WEC a year to decide that such an operation would not conflict with Baylor's tradition as a Christian school.[3] By the summer of 1941, sixty-five students had earned their pilot's licenses.[4] The beginning of the pilot training program at Baylor had coincided with the first peacetime draft signed into law by President Roosevelt in September 1940. The draft required all males between eighteen and thirty-five years of age to register for military service—a move that cast a pall over college students everywhere.

By contrast, Baylor's financial picture brightened considerably in 1940. First, Herbert L. Kokernot, Alpine and San Antonio rancher and businessman, gave Baylor

$600,000, the largest single donation the university had ever received. The gift pushed Baylor's total endowment to more than $2 million.[5] The annual meeting of the Baptist General Convention of Texas in Houston in November 1940 heralded more good news. After pleas from Neff for several years for direct financial support, the convention agreed to give Baylor $30,000 per year for five years.[6] Two months later, Baylor's accreditation agency, the Southern Association of Colleges and Secondary Schools (SACS), notified Neff that Baylor had been taken off its probationary list and restored to full membership.[7] SACS had been advising Neff for several years that the university needed to strengthen its financial base. Baylor would remain in good standing with SACS for the remainder of Neff's presidency.

At commencement in 1940, Neff dispelled the notion that Baylor would award honorary degrees only to those from whom it hoped to profit. The two honorees in 1940 were Grace Noll Crowell and Pompeo Coppini, both favorites of the Baylor president. Crowell, named Poet Laureate of Texas in 1935, had also been named as one of ten Outstanding American Women in 1938 by the biographical publication *American Women*. In the early 1940s, she was called "the most popular writer of verse in America."[8] Neff and sculptor Pompeo Coppini had been friends for nearly forty years. As noted earlier, Coppini was internationally acclaimed for his commemorative statues, which included works at the Texas State Capitol as well as the bronze statue of former Baylor President Rufus Burleson on the Baylor campus.

Another event brought joy to Baylor in the fall of 1940. In a football game played in San Antonio, Baylor beat Villanova University. Prior to the game, the president of the Baylor Club in San Antonio had sent out a letter announcing that, following the game, there would be a dance that night at the Gunter Hotel. Some Baptist preachers objected, and the dance was cancelled. Baylor Board member D.K ."Dock" Martin wrote Neff that he wished he could get the pastors to be as anxious to help Baylor as they were to criticize it. All in all, Martin called the matter a "tempest-in-a-teapot."[9]

Neff's efforts over seven and one-half years were rewarded in January 1941, when the WEC, acting for the Baylor Board of Trustees, raised his annual salary from $8,400 to $10,000.[10] That vote came the month before the beloved longtime football coach Morley Jennings announced he was tired of coaching and resigned. He was succeeded by Hardin Simmons University coach Frank Kimbrough, who signed a three-year contract for $5,000 per year.[11] Neff bit his tongue but did not appreciate that Kimbrough's salary was well above that of the heads of the Baylor's academic departments. In fact, the coach's salary in 1941 would not be reached by Dr. A. J. Armstrong, Paul Baker, and other key academics until near the end of Neff's presidency in 1947.[12]

Meanwhile, enrollment continued to climb. The fall enrollment of 1941 was the largest in Baylor's history.[13] As a result of enrollment increases in the late 1930s, the spring graduating class of 1941 was also the largest in the institution's history: 439 in Waco and another 135 in Dallas.[14]

Buildings for the Future

Neff was nevertheless concerned; he had been forced to turn away almost 100 young women from Baylor in the fall of 1938 because housing was simply not available.[15] He soon contacted Catherine Alexander, a woman of means, and persuaded her to make the lead gift on a women's dormitory.[16] The citizens of Waco came through with money for the land adjacent to Memorial Dormitory. On January 22, 1940, construction began on a facility for 165 young women. As plans progressed, the cost escalated—instead of $150,000, the bill finally became $325,000. Baylor went back into debt for $200,000 to pay for the building, but the bonds issued would be paid off by the rents paid by the girls.[17] The building construction was put on a "fast track," and the dormitory, appropriately named Catherine Alexander Hall, was occupied just nine months later.

Because of the shortage of materials during the war and the necessary attention to war-related matters by Neff and others, Alexander Hall was the only permanent building erected on campus until after the war. Hopes were high for the Student Union Building, with Carroll Field as the proposed site. Football had been moved from Carroll in 1936. In 1940, the university moved the remainder of athletic activities from Carroll Field to a new off-campus location considerably south on Dutton Street. The donation of a 600-by-600-foot plot of land by the City of Waco and the appropriation by the Baylor Board of $15,000 made possible the erection of a stadium for baseball and track as well as two practice fields for football.[18] The Student Union Building had a colorful ground-breaking on the site of the old field, and concrete pillars were erected, only to stand stark against the sky until 1946—no money and no materials.[19]

In 1941, in recognition of the innovative and imaginative work of Drama Professor Paul Baker, the General Education Board granted $15,000 to the university for a building to house the Baylor Theater.[20] Baylor matched that amount, and a simple "semi-permanent" building for the theater was erected that year. Baker then moved his operations from an upper floor of Old Main to the new building. Although a modest building, Baker put his creative talents to work. His design of that small theater at Fifth and Speight marked the beginning of Baker's theater design work. Arthur J. Rogers, designer of more than twenty theaters and auditoriums, would later write: "No single person has contributed more to its [theater architecture's] development than Paul Baker."[21] Studio One of the theater featured "stages surrounded by the audience seated in swivel chairs. Chairs could be placed on the stages to convert the total space into an arena theater. In the rear, sliding doors could transform the front lobby into a proscenium stage or a sixth stage with a balcony."²² The *Fort Worth Star-Telegram* gave the theater rave reviews in an extensive story on September 29, 1941. Shakespeare's *Macbeth* opened the season. That fall Baker attracted the first guest appearances of numerous theatrical and Hollywood celebrities. An early visitor was playwright Lynn Riggs, author of *Green Grow the Lilacs*, the play that later became the long-running Broadway musical hit *Oklahoma*.²³

During the war years, Neff continued his efforts to finance and build appropriate buildings for both the Tidwell Bible Collection and Dr. A. J. Armstrong's Browning Collection. At a board meeting April 27, 1944, Neff recommended that the university push ahead on both buildings "as soon as war conditions permit."²⁴ In 1945, Tidwell and his son-in-law, architect Guy A. Carlander of Amarillo, presented an ambitious plan for a ten-story tower and a biblical garden, with shrubs and trees from the Holy Land.²⁵ In early January 1945, Neff wrote what might be interpreted as a sheepish letter—half apologetic—to the WEC, asking that a major commitment he had made to Dr. Armstrong be ratified.²⁶ According to Dr. J. M. Dawson's book, *A Thousand Months to Remember*, "Dr. A," as he was affectionately known by his students, had been furious that Neff had found money to build the administration building (Pat Neff Hall), and had not put that money into the proposed Browning building. At the January meeting, Neff told the WEC that he had saved $100,000 from operating expenses—in 1943—and had invested it. At the same time, "without authority of the Board of Trustees," he had told Dr. Armstrong that Baylor would give him this money for the Browning building if Armstrong himself would raise a matching amount. Neff reported that Armstrong had actually raised $150,000, and Neff was then asking the WEC in 1945 for approval to place the total $250,000 with the Baptist Foundation in Dallas to be invested until such time as the university could erect the Browning building. Neff told the WEC that he thought Armstrong had "added more to the culture and scholarship . . . of Baylor than any other faculty member at any time connected with the institution, that the Browning Collection is more widely known in some places than Baylor itself."²⁷ The WEC was not exactly pleased—the minutes record only that "after much discussion," a motion was approved to accept Neff's recommendation. Dr. Dawson requested that the minutes show that he did not vote. When Neff told Armstrong of the WEC action, the two embraced and Armstrong was overcome with emotion.²⁸ Neff and Armstrong had an "off and on" relationship. Faculty member Lois Douglas Murray Strain, who knew them both intimately, wrote that they clashed on numerous occasions but would always come back together again for the greater good of Baylor. She noted that they were both very strong personalities, but she thought Armstrong was actually the more formidable.²⁹ The estimated cost of both the Tidwell and the Browning buildings far surpassed any monies on hand, so the proposals remained in the "hoped for" stage for several years. In place of brick and stone, wooden buildings on the campus were erected and renovated.

In 1940, Brooks Hall was the only men's dormitory. Until 1941, private off-campus housing for men had not been regulated. In 1941, W. W. Wendt, director of Brooks Hall, wrote almost 100 families that the university would require that owners of private homes renting to male students register with Baylor before students could reside in them. All freshmen would continue to be housed in Brooks. The homeowners had to sign an agreement not to permit drinking, hazing, or gambling on their premises and to report any violation to Wendt.[30]

With the enrollment increase in 1941, Neff asked the board for several additions to the faculty. His letter of September 11 recommended fourteen new individuals, including Robert S. Denny as director of religious activities, Dr. Loyd W. Rowland as head of the Psychology Department, and Gideon Waldrop as band director.[31] The additions also included his "Mexican lad" friend, Enrique Ramirez, whom Neff had personally helped with his finances. Ramirez was recommended as a teacher in Spanish. Neff said Ramirez had never taught, but the students in class with him thought he could handle the work.[32] In addition, Neff recommended two women who would play important roles in coming years with the university: Billie Murray in political science and Merle McClellan in history. Murray, a Baylor law graduate, would become a confidante to Neff during his tenure and fill a variety of unrelated positions. Neff named McClellan as Baylor's armed services representative during the war, and she took the time to stay in touch with a number of Baylor students after they went into the service.[33]

Baylor faculty members were sources of enrichment not always strictly academic. Students of those years who took Dr. Charles D. Johnson's sociology class became familiar with the Chicago White Sox baseball team and Baylor's and Johnson's personal hero, pitcher Ted Lyons.[34] Others who sat through Alta Jack's French class usually left the room in a cloud of chalk dust as Jack scribbled so furiously on the blackboard that she left her dress a white and black creation.[35] But many students, before and after Neff's days, would strongly argue that the most entertaining professor was undoubtedly Guy B. Harrison. In his memoir, Harrison admitted he cultivated the image of a "friendly, vigorous, eccentric, and colorful member" of the faculty.[36] A student in his class did not fall asleep lest he miss the opportunity to sit on the lectern on top of Harrison's desk with a crown on his head and a scepter in his hand to see how a king felt high above his subjects or have the professor imitate the flirting of a king's mistress. He would sometimes enter the classroom by the fire escape—the signal for a "pop test."

One of Neff's proudest moments in 1941 was awarding an honorary Doctor of Laws to his close friend from Magnolia, Arkansas, days—Harvey Couch. Couch was the near dropout whom Neff had persuaded to stay in school when Neff was teaching at Magnolia. The two had stayed in touch since then and by 1941, Couch was an internationally known businessman and political power. At the degree ceremony, Neff gave a long and glowing tribute to Couch.[37]

Students Seeking Recognition

Fall 1941 was a memorable season for Baylor students. November 8 marked the first of two unforgettable events. On that day, the University of Texas football team, featured on the cover of *Life* magazine the week of the game as the nation's premier team, came to town to play the lowly Baylor Bears. The Bears had already lost three of their first six games and would go on after the Texas game to lose their last three games. Thomas E. Turner, noted *Dallas Morning News* scribe and later executive assistant to Baylor President Abner McCall, would later explain: "Baylor is so superior in every other way that the Lord uses football to keep us humble."[38] Jinx Tucker, famed sports editor of the *Waco News-Tribune*, predicted that Texas would win by a score of 50-0 and said he was leaving town because he did not want to see the slaughter. Baylor men had other ideas. Holding Texas to a 7-0 lead through most of the game, the Bears scored in the last four minutes and kicked the extra point; the game ended in a 7-7 tie. Jubilant students, including one of this book's coauthors, poured out of the stands and launched a parade to downtown Waco, chanting "Lynch Jinx Tucker." The throng gathered at the entrance of the newspaper office on Sixth Street, but Tucker was nowhere to be found. Thwarted by Tucker's absence, the students began shouting "Holiday on Monday." Neff got word of the demand while attending the annual meeting of Texas Baptists in Abilene and promptly wired back to the campus that any student not in class on Monday would be suspended.[39] Brother Worm (Master) Nose John L. Bates remembered that most "good" teachers failed to check roll on Monday.[40]

Bates, a noted Waco attorney who died in 2005, was also the primary source for the fall 1941 "alarm clock" incident, possibly the wildest prank during Neff's tenure. Others, including H. C. Pittman, Jr., later a respected Texas state official and trade association executive, hinted at possible involvement but, even decades after the prank, were reluctant to admit participation. In Willie Long's history of the Nose Brotherhood, Bates remembered that the president had invited world-famous preacher Dr. George Truett to inspire the Baylor student body to greater spiritual awareness. Bates and some of the other Nosemen decided to "liven" Dr. Truett's sermon. The night before the event they gathered about ten wind-up alarm clocks, climbed into the attic of Waco Hall above the stage, and set the alarm clocks to go off at three-minute intervals beginning after Neff's introduction of Truett the next morning. Bates gives this account of the incident:

> Dr. Truett commenced his sermon and on schedule the first clock went off. Dr. Truett
> looked up to see if God had sounded the alarm, but the first alarm created little

interest. However, beginning with the third alarm, pandemonium reigned. Dr. Truett took the incident very well, but I thought President Neff might have a stroke. To this day when I attend functions in Waco Hall, I wonder if my alarm clock is still up there. Needless to say, none of us claimed our alarm clocks.[41]

Neff angrily dismissed chapel early; the perpetrators were never found.

Neff was the target of several other pranks before the war sobered faculty and students alike. A rare snowfall in Waco provided the setting for two pranks that, to Neff's credit, he took with good humor. Bob Nelson, outstanding center on the Bears football team, accepted a dare one day in 1940 and ran across the snow to tackle Neff and sprawl him in the snow. Nelson offered his hand to help the president up but then quickly ran off, though not before being recognized. Later in the day a frightened Nelson was summoned to Neff's office where, instead of receiving a suspension from the university, he received an autographed picture of the president.[42] C. E. Bryant, Baylor publicist during Neff's tenure, remembered another snow day when class was dismissed and a gang of celebrating students jubilantly rolled Neff in the snow when he stepped out of his car. When Bryant asked him for a statement, Neff quickly replied, "They are all professionals; not an amateur in the bunch."[43] Again, no disciplinary action resulted. Neff had made his point on discipline in the early years of his presidency, and the 1940s saw fewer students dismissed for unacceptable conduct.

Neff's 1941 and 1942 fall reports to the Baptist General Convention of Texas (BGCT) stressed three different areas almost equally—faculty and curriculum accomplishments, accommodation to the war effort, and student religious activity. He proudly pointed out advances in the Law School under the leadership of Neff-recruited, Harvard-educated Dean Leslie Jackson. Neff ticked off three specific accomplishments: a full-time law librarian, an outstanding practice court class initiated by Judge James P. Alexander, who went on to become Chief Justice of the Texas Supreme Court, and a record enrollment of eighty-two men and one woman.[44] In a *Daily Lariat* story November 12, 1942, Dean Jackson said he wanted to recruit more female students, citing a recent letter from Todd Shipyards Corporation seeking female lawyers. Unfortunately, the absence of the great majority of male students due to war service forced the closing of the Law School in May 1943 for duration of the war. Neff assured everyone that the American Bar Association had stated that the temporary closure would not affect Baylor's accreditation. Baylor had assured the Bar Association that the university would continue to buy $1,000 worth of law books each year to keep the Law Library current.[45] One of the Law School graduates in 1942, Peeler Williams of Waco, made the highest grade in Texas on the state bar examination in 1943.[46]

Debate teams continued their strong record in the early 1940s. The women's team entered five tournaments during the 1941-1942 school year and won all of them as well as the coveted top spot in the national Pi Kappa Delta Tournament in Minneapolis. The speakers brought home more than fifty individual trophies and medals during that season.[47]

One major administrative change in 1942 was the resignation of popular and effective Dean E. N. Jones. Jones was headed upward. Texas Arts and Industries College at Kingsville named him president in 1942, and six years later he went to Texas Technological College in Lubbock as vice-president with the expectation that he would succeed to the presidency. He did so in 1952 and served in that capacity for seven years before retiring under pressure from arch conservative J. Evetts Haley (who had been appointed to the Texas Tech Board in 1955) and like-minded colleagues.[48]

The War Intrudes

Following the declaration of war in December 1941, Neff believed strongly that a church school had as much responsibility as a state-supported university to support the war effort. He organized a defense council, composed of both faculty and students, to study ways to make Baylor's war service an all-out effort.[49] The civil pilot training course continued; the Business School and the Law School, with support from the federal government, began offering evening courses for both Waco adults and Baylor students to better prepare them for war service; and radio courses adapted to the national emergency were added. Faculty, with students serving under them, joined local defense units and received training as air raid wardens, along with attending first aid courses. The university began requiring compulsory physical education courses for all male students. The school set up a special booth at the Baylor Book Store for the sale of war stamps and bonds; campus clubs in 1942 sold more than $15,000 worth.[50] Neff himself participated fully in the effort. In 1941 and 1942 alone, he wrote eight personal checks for more than $2,200 for war bonds.[51]

Neff pointed out early in the war that Rear Admiral William Robert Munroe, a Baylor man, was commander of Battleship Division Three of the United States Fleet.[52] Some students, eager for war action, had signed up for the Royal Canadian Air Force (RCAF) or the British Royal Air Force (RAF) well before Pearl Harbor and, after that tragedy, numerous male and some female students volunteered for one of the armed services. Neff himself felt the shock of the war when he was notified that a young person named for him had been killed in action while flying for the RCAF. Pat Neff Templeton was the son of District Judge R. H. Templeton of Wellington, whom Neff had appointed to the bench when he was governor.

Also in 1942, the university received word that Lieutenant William Silver Edgar, one of the early student volunteers deciding to fly for the British Royal Air Force, along with three Baylor classmates had been killed in action. Edgar's parents donated

$250 to erect a memorial lamp in his honor, stimulating the formation of the Wings Club, organized to place lamps at various points on the campus to memorialize former students killed in the war. By the 1946 homecoming, 125 lamp posts had been erected.[53] The gravity of the war began to sink in on Baylor faculty, staff, and students in early 1942 with the deaths of volunteers in the RCAF and RAF, the presence of military uniforms on campus, and, of course, the headlines day after day announcing that the United States military was taking a pounding from the Japanese forces in the South Pacific. Neff felt the time was appropriate for an intense week of spirituality.

In February, the university held its first Religious Focus Week, designed to saturate the school with the Word of God. An impressive roster of fourteen speakers took turns speaking in Waco Hall and then fanning out over the campus to every class, lecturing and conducting discussions on vital issues and student concerns. Most the speakers were officials in the Southern Baptist Convention, headquartered in Atlanta, but the list also included several Texas preachers and Dr. Homer Price Rainey, president of the University of Texas. Few knew that Dr. Rainey was an ordained Baptist minister and fewer still that he had been a professional baseball player for a short time and was a veteran of World War I. Neff knew Rainey from educational circles and had a great deal of respect for him.[54] Robert Denny, director of the Baptist Student Union at Baylor, coordinated the week.

The Focus Week was repeated in 1943 and 1944. In the latter year, a missionary component was added at the end of the week. On Friday and Saturday afternoons, students conducted a religious census, attempting to visit every home in Waco "to find and win the unsaved." On Friday night, in the words of the *Baylor Lariat*, "the students took religious services to colored, Spanish, and underprivileged white sections of town." On Saturday afternoon, "street meetings were held on the public square."[55]

The enlistees for U.S. Army service in early 1942 included a nonstudent, Assistant Attorney General Pat Neff Jr. Neff's only son had begun working for Attorney General James V. Allred in 1933 and was reappointed twice, by succeeding Attorneys General William McCraw in 1935 and Gerald C. Mann in 1939. Pat Jr. entered active duty on August 1, 1942. As a lawyer, he came on duty as a captain assigned to the Judge Advocate General's Office (the army's legal arm). On March 11, 1943, he was promoted to major. In late 1942 and again in 1943, Pat Jr. sought overseas combat duty, only to fail a required physical examination.[56] He underwent surgery for a possible hernia in June 1943 and for an undisclosed leg condition in October of the same year. Complications resulted from the leg operation, and he was given an honorable discharge for service-connected disability on April 5, 1944.[57] Later, Baylor graduate and famed war crimes trial attorney Leon Jaworski of Houston hailed young Neff's persistence in pursuing the overseas assignment: "I saw this soldier voluntarily enter a government hospital and undergo a serious and painful operation to enable him to go overseas."[58]

The nature of the operation was never revealed. Less than three months after his discharge, Pat Jr. joined the Vinson and Elkins law firm in Houston. Neff wrote his son frequently in the days after his army service. In January 1945, Neff wrote Judge James A. Elkins, thanking him for letting Pat Jr. take some time off to rest. Neff wrote that Pat Jr. had unwillingly "submitted to the operation [in the Army] with bad results that will probably go with him through the years."[59] Pat Jr. rested at the family farm for an undisclosed period of time.

In early 1942, the U.S. government approved Baylor as a training institution for the Deferred Service Plan, permitting high school graduates to enlist in one of the armed forces reserve units, but remain in college for two years or, in some cases, until graduation. Nearly 500 Baylor students signed up for the plan.[60] The Air Corps Reserve was called up in February 1943, followed in the next five months by the Army, Navy, and Marine reserves. Other men who had not enlisted in one of the reserves enlisted or were drafted during the year. As a result, Baylor's male enrollment plummeted sharply in the fall of 1943.[61]

The program of informing existing male students of their options did not involve "strangers" coming on the Baylor campus. However, in 1942, Baylor University received several requests from the U.S. government to participate in training of soldiers, sailors, and airmen. In order that there be no questions raised later, Neff took the requests to the WEC in July 1942 with the following statement:

> It is my thought that Baylor should cooperate as far as our abilities and equipments will permit with the Federal government in this education and training of our men for military services. In doing this, we may be violating some of the fundamental principles of our denominational teachings, but the present war is a total war, and we are involved in it.[62]

Neff reminded the WEC that they had previously approved the pilot training program. He now told them that the government wanted to send men to Baylor to be trained for general military service. The first quota was a class of thirty. The men would be at the university for eight weeks, and the school would be allowed $100 per man for room and board and transportation plus $185 per man for tuition costs. The WEC approved the general arrangements with the understanding that the soldiers would be required to conform with all the rules and regulations of Baylor.[63]

In June 1942, the Civil Aeronautics Authority contracted with the U.S. War Department to train naval aviation cadets at Baylor. During the training, the 100 young men lived in Brooks Hall with the civilian students. In May 1943, the Army added a new unit at Baylor, called the Army Specialized Training Program (ASTP).

When that occurred, the pilot trainees moved to Burleson Hall, and the spring quarter was shortened to free up Brooks Hall for the 400 trainees in the ASTP program. Housing continued to be a problem. In the summer of 1943, an unprecedented number of women applied for admission. The administration's choice was to either turn away many daughters of Baptist church members, or ask the girls to accept more crowded conditions, which was finally done. Bunk beds appeared in all the dormitories and adjacent residences, and Memorial Dormitory dining room became a cafeteria.[64]

Housing was not the only problem caused by the increase in military students. To fill the need for more classes, Neff quickly added another thirty faculty members. This situation was not viewed as a negative one by Neff, however. In his 1943 report to the BGCT, he was effusive in his praise of the military students, stating that they had fit into the campus extremely well. He cited as example of the generosity and patriotism of the military men that they had donated 151 pints of blood to the blood bank in Waco. Neff proudly told the convention that the young men had been accepted into the social program of the university and the "seriousness and earnestness of the soldiers' bearing . . . have tended to raise the tone of the whole campus."[65]

Baylor's war fortunes changed for the worse in 1944. Washington sensed victory in Europe and began to plan for the final push. As part of that plan, the defense establishment needed all available manpower and began eliminating university training programs for Army and Navy personnel. In November, Baylor's ASTP, which had utilized Brooks Hall as its barracks since April 1943, was eliminated and the men dispersed to Army units around the globe. Before it closed, 351 ASTP members had received diplomas from Baylor.[66] ASTP was disbanded nationwide. One of those affected was a young man named Sam Johnson—no relation to LBJ—who had entered Baylor in 1938, took some time off, returned, and was called into army service in 1943. He was assigned to an ASTP unit but, like many others, never made it to a college for training. Instead, he went into combat and was wounded in the Battle of Metz in 1944. After the war, Johnson returned to Baylor and then to the University of Texas Law School. A distinguished judicial career, including a stint on the Texas Supreme Court, was climaxed in 1979 when President Jimmy Carter named him to the U.S. Fifth Circuit Court of Appeals, the highest judicial honor ever held by a Baylor graduate. Baylor named him a distinguished alumnus in 1978. He died in 2002 with Metz battle shrapnel still in his body.[67]

The training for Navy combat pilots, which came to Baylor in 1942, was inactivated in July 1944. The withdrawal of the two units freed up Brooks and Burleson dormitories. The latter was showing its age and, to entice the Centennial women's class to move there, Neff told the WEC that the university needed to spend several thousand dollars to rewire, build closets, polish floors, paint rooms, and generally give it a fresh look.[68]

The Medical School Moves to Houston

Neff had saved Baylor's medical complex at Dallas from foreclosure in 1939, but in 1942 the situation again demanded his attention. It became fairly obvious that neither the Baptist denomination nor the citizens of Dallas appreciated the tremendous asset represented by the medical, dental, and nursing schools (the pharmacy school had closed in 1934) and the Baylor University Hospital. The denomination seemed to be interested only in the spiritual condition of the units, and the Dallas business community was parsimonious in its financial support of the schools and hospital.[69] In 1939, the Dallas business community formed a Southwestern Medical Foundation, but it was 1942 before the group finally announced plans for a large medical center to be built on Hines Boulevard in Dallas.[70]

The buildings would belong solely to the foundation, and the medical complex would be governed by a committee of three members appointed by the foundation and two by Baylor.[71] Baylor University Hospital was not a part of the proposal. Although the foundation had not provided any endowment or financial assistance to Baylor-Dallas in its three years of operation, the sixteen-point agreement set forth was quickly endorsed by the Dallas medical community and the "uncritical popular support of the citizens."[72] Baylor was put in the position of being an ungrateful recipient unless it acquiesced to the plan.

In his comprehensive book on the history of Baylor College of Medicine, Dr. Walter H. Moursund Sr., dean of the college from 1923 to 1953, wrote that the Medical Foundation stressed that it was nonsectarian in nature and that foundation officials felt Baylor was handicapped in soliciting endowment and operating funds because it was controlled by the Baptists. Moursund rejected that argument, pointing out that he was Presbyterian and that neither applicants for faculty positions nor students had ever been screened for their religious beliefs. He observed that the faculty and student body represented many faiths and that there were many denominationally controlled medical schools in the country. Moursund and others were also disturbed by the stated intent of the foundation to control the major decisions of the schools.[73] Neff was put into a very difficult position. The Dallas members of his board of trustees were strongly in support of the foundation initiative while board members from San Antonio, Waco, and Houston were generally opposed. Despite misgivings, the agreement was approved by the Baylor Board on June 23, 1942, and by the executive board of the Baptist Convention on July 7.[74]

But opposition continued. Influential board member Dock Martin of San Antonio wrote Neff stinging letters in July and again in August that he would resign from the board before he would turn over control of the school to the foundation.[75] He was joined in his concerns by Earl Hankamer and Marrs McLean, both longtime major supporters of the university.

Meanwhile, Martin's August 25 letter then disclosed for the first time the possibility of moving the medical school to Houston: "There is a great benevolent foundation in Houston of some $20,000,000. It is my judgment that this Foundation would be glad to get behind Baylor with all their funds, buy us a site, erect such buildings as we need, and pledge future support to the operation of a great medical center."[76] Martin wrote that officials of the Houston foundation had told him that they "would trust Baylor with control" of the institution. Despite misgivings, the messengers to the annual BGCT meeting in Fort Worth approved the Dallas contract in November.[77] In March 1943, the contract was approved by the Dallas City Council and that same month the Dallas Medical Alumni Association wrote an open letter to the Baylor and the foundation boards strongly defending the agreement.[78] However, it became increasingly clear that the foundation read the contract as giving it exclusive control of the medical complex; for that reason, the Baylor Board of Trustees cancelled the contract on April 27, 1943.[79]

The Houston foundation referred to in Martin's letters in mid-1942 was the M. D. Anderson Foundation, created by one of the founders of Anderson, Clayton and Company, one of the world's largest cotton merchandising firms. That foundation, established in 1936, decided in 1941 to sponsor a comprehensive medical center in Houston. Sensing the growing displeasure of the Baylor Board with the Dallas contract, officials of the Anderson Foundation wasted no time making their bid for Baylor. On May 5, only eight days after the Dallas contract was abrogated, the Houston foundation submitted its proposal, and three days later the Baylor Board enthusiastically approved the agreement.[80]

The M. D. Anderson Foundation offered a twenty-acre site for the exclusive use of the medical and dental schools (Baylor later decided to leave the dental school in Dallas), $1 million for construction of permanent buildings for the schools, and $100,000 per year for ten years for research purposes. Management and control would remain with Baylor, and the university would agree to continue to admit students of all faiths and select its faculty and administrative officials on the basis of scholarship and qualifications without regard to a religious faith.[81] Neff and the Baylor Board's jubilation was multiplied when, a week later, the Houston Chamber of Commerce agreed to raise $50,000 annually for ten years for operating expenses of the college. The total of $500,000 was subscribed in a relatively short time.[82]

With the Houston announcement, all hell broke loose in Dallas. The Southwestern Medical Foundation, stung by the planned move to Houston, immediately organized an independent Southwestern Medical College and put tremendous pressure on Baylor faculty, doctors, students, and staff to remain in Dallas with the new medical school.[83] Dallas reaction was so strong that Marrs McLean wrote a draft of a Letter to the Editor to be printed in the *Dallas Morning News*.[84]

Things moved quickly that summer. Baylor officials met with Houston doctors and officials of Jefferson Davis Hospital, a key Houston hospital, in mid-May and secured their wholehearted support for the move. On May 31, 1943, Baylor held its last medical school commencement in Dallas. The Baylor College of Medicine opened in temporary quarters (an old Sears, Roebuck building) in Houston on July 12 with 131 students. One day later, the Baylor Board met for the first time in its ninety-eight-year history in Houston. Neff's exuberant recounting of the Houston move in his annual report to the BGCT meeting in San Antonio in November 1944 stressed that for the first time in its history, the medical school was "unhampered with financial worries . . . [and the staff was] happy beyond words."[85] Moursund's book recounts the successful first years in Houston and the construction of permanent buildings beginning in 1945. In his book, the modest Moursund makes no reference to his own dedication and commitment to Baylor over a thirty-year period. After overseeing the move to Houston, he was rewarded by the trustees with an honorary Doctor of Laws degree at the commencement of the first graduating class in Houston on March 13, 1944.[86] Neff spent several days in May and June in Dallas, trying to placate his Dallas board members—Dr. George W. Truett, Carr P. Collins, and Charles R. Moore. He was successful in getting Army officials to say that all of their Army medical students would stay with Baylor, wherever Baylor went.[87]

The Baptists Honor Neff

In the middle of all the turmoil, Neff was elected president of the Southern Baptist Convention (SBC) and spent a week in Nashville organizing his presidency. In the mid-1940s, Southern Baptists claimed more than 25,000 churches with 5.5 million members. Church properties were valued at a quarter of a billion dollars, and Southern Baptists gave some $50 million for local work and another $13 million for missions.[88]

Neff had been active for many years on various committees and the executive board of the SBC. The promotion was a natural recognition of his Christian stewardship and his leadership of the largest Baptist university in the world. He had been nominated for president in 1935 but had refused to be considered because of his pressing duties at Baylor.[89] In May 1942, at its annual meeting in San Antonio, the messengers would not be denied. Neff was elected unanimously to a rising ovation, the first lay person to head the SBC in thirty-two years.[90] According to tradition, he should have held a single one-year term, but the 1943 meeting was cancelled because of the war and he retained the presidency for a second term. Neff and the SBC officers urged Baptist churches and members to use the money they would have spent on the 1943 convention to retire the SBC debt of more than $6 million. The suggestion was accepted, and in January 1944 the debt was retired.[91]

In 1944, despite his advance statement asking to be relieved, Neff was reelected for a third term at the meeting in Atlanta in May.[92] His popularity as a leader was due not only to his remarkable administrative abilities but also to the palette of skills and attributes that allowed him to rise to every occasion. His 1944 presidential address—"Manhood on the March"—received widespread approval both for its content and its style. Neff preached that "No narrow, parochial, intellectual horizon should be ours," but rather that out of the war "must come a brotherhood of comity, collaboration, and cooperation."[93] This lofty reference to the fruits of war struck a chord with his war-weary audience. Chase S. Winfrey, in his dissertation for the University of Denver in 1951, noted that Neff frequently used alliteration to emphasize his points, and "comity, collaboration, and cooperation" was a good example. Winfrey also quoted several passages of this same speech to illustrate how Neff was flexible in his oratorical style—ranging from highly ornate language to practical words and phrases. As part of his study of Neff's oratory and leadership style, Winfrey interviewed contemporaries of Neff to get first-hand appraisals of his attributes. In discussing Neff as a churchman, noted preacher Dr. Robert G. Lee, at that time president of the Southern Baptist Convention, said Neff's effectiveness as a church leader could be attributed to his "unquestioned character as a Christian, his faith in God, and his stand for the right always."[94]

Neff saw his role as chief executive officer of an organization to be different from that of chairing an assembly meeting. In the former, he could be and often was autocratic. As a presider at the SBC sessions, he reverted to the role he had played when Speaker of the Texas House. As in 1903 with state representatives in Austin, his openness and fairness as a presiding officer at the SBC meetings brought letters of praise at the end of his tenure. Baptist columnist Henry W. Tiffany called the 1944 convention "the most democratic meeting we have ever attended." The columnist went on: "The messengers on the floor were frequently given preference over the members and women on the stage; those who had not spoken were given preference over those who had spoken on any given issue, and the presiding officer directed the business of the convention in a way that delighted the heart of everyone present."[95] Finally, at the 1946 convention in Miami, Neff passed the torch. During his four-year tenure, the financial status of the SBC had improved dramatically.

Neff's Christian character was displayed through financial commitment as well as words. In the period 1940-1945, his papers contain numerous cancelled checks to the First Baptist Church for amounts ranging from $5 to $250. In 1941, he paid $215 for a loudspeaker for the church. He also wrote a $250 check to the Baylor Centennial Foundation in 1941. In addition, in 1942 alone, he supported the Waco Community Chest (an amalgamation of several social service organizations) with gifts of at least $215 while keeping up his membership in the Karem Temple, Waco Rotary Club, and Waco Chamber of Commerce.[96] As related earlier in this book and elaborated above, Neff was a joiner, choosing to participate in a wide variety of organizations. It must have come as a particular pleasure, therefore, when he was selected in 1940 as a member of the prestigious Philosophical Society of Texas, one of the very few organizations in Texas that could trace its lineage beyond that of Baylor.[97]

The SBC presidency added another layer of responsibility to Neff's exhausting workload but did not seem to affect him physically. Neff did no physical exercise except his occasional work on the farm and some horseback riding. He usually had family as well as hired help on the farm, but he loved to don his old clothes and help out. He tried to have regular physical examinations, but they were generally confined to urine specimens.[98] Despite the lack of strenuous and regular exercise and only a one-week vacation in August each year at the Baker Hotel and Crazy Hotel in Mineral Wells,[99] he was seldom sick. There were two major exceptions: he was out of the office for health reasons in December 1944 when he was hospitalized with pneumonia for some four weeks,[100] and he was confined to the hospital for five weeks in December and January of 1941-1942 because of an automobile accident, which he admitted to friends was his fault.[101] His careless driving was apparently part of the Neff "package." He had several other minor wrecks over the years and was lectured one time on his way to the farm by a motorist who claimed that Neff "cut him off." Neff apologized and continued his journey.[102]

Neff's hectic work schedule and seemingly stern demeanor belied his sense of humor. He was especially fond of humanizing the complimentary closing to letters he wrote. When he left a shirt at the Baker Hotel in 1941, he wrote and asked the manager to mail it to him at his expense, signing the letter, "Your shirtless friend." On writing a long letter to an old friend who was joining the faculty, he listed "orders" she was to follow (mainly about resting from her academic stress) until she reported for duty—then signed it, "Yours for regulations." A favorite closing used numerous times was, "Yours until the last roundup."

Radio at Baylor Broadens Its Horizons

Radio, through the campus station and its programs, remained a strong attribute of Baylor in the early 1940s, in its community service activities as well as its classroom teaching. The Texas State Network was delighted with the Baylor programs, and its educational director wrote Neff that "we have found these weekly features to be high caliber."[103] In his 1942 report to the BGCT, Neff bragged that Baylor had produced more radio broadcasts and had more time on the air than any other educational institution in Texas.[104] Radio at Baylor, then in its seventh year, produced seventy-eight broadcasts, with the participation of 136 individuals, including faculty, students, and guests. Neff himself was the star on the Baptist Hour, sponsored by the radio committee of the Southern Baptist Convention.[105]

In 1943, radio at Baylor took a giant leap. On January 14, Neff presented a generous proposal to the board of trustees. Carr P. Collins, insurance tycoon and member of the Baylor Board since 1924, offered to give Baylor a 50,000-watt radio station located in Reynosa, just across the Texas-Mexico border from McAllen. He would move the station equipment from Reynosa to Corpus Christi and pay Baylor an annual rental of $25,000. All expenses would be Collins' responsibility, and Baylor could have whatever time it wanted for broadcasting at no cost. Any time not used by Baylor would be available to Collins, who agreed that any of his programs would meet Baylor's high standards and that the station would carry no alcohol advertising.[106] The board approved the package, and Collins resigned from the board at that same meeting to avoid a conflict of interest. Neff also reported to the board that a campus radio station, KOED, had opened and ninety members of the Baylor Radio Workshop were preparing to air programs over the entire Gulf Coast area when the new station, KWBU, "hit the air." Collins secured a permit for the station from the Federal Communications Commission and Baylor began operating the station later that year. In his thesis on the history of radio broadcasting at Baylor, M. John Kulesz wrote that "although KWBU was a commercial station, it quickly became an outlet for an assortment of religious, educational, and variety productions by Baylor radio," including chapel services, daily newscasts, and some fifteen programs produced by the Baylor Radio Workshop.[107] In the spring of 1944, a weekly variety show was added as well as a daily news commentary, "Women and the News," by Speech Department chair Sara Lowrey. By then, Baylor was reaching a potential audience of 3.5 million from Brownsville to Gulfport, Mississippi. In 1944, the *Baylor Lariat* claimed that Baylor was the second university in the country to own a commercial radio station, Loyola University in New Orleans being the first. In September 1944, radio had become such an important part of the curriculum at Baylor that it was separated from the Speech Department.[108]

Baylor's Diverse Board of Trustees

Collins was arguably the most colorful of the trustees Neff worked for in his fifteen years as president. With only one year of college, Collins built an insurance empire, beginning with the Fidelity Union Life Insurance Company. Over his business life, he was engaged in numerous unrelated business companies and activities and was active in Texas politics. His most famous business venture was selling his Crazy Water Crystals to consumers all over the country. He probably sold more than $3 million of the "laxative" before federal regulators declared them to be worthless.[109] His major political activity was working as an early and strong backer of W. Lee O'Daniel in his successful race in 1941 against Congressman Lyndon B. Johnson for a Texas Senate seat. In that race, a Texas Senate investigating committee accused Collins of giving a large block of radio time to O'Daniel. Collins told the committee that the time was paid for but he could not remember the names of the donors. The committee did not pursue the matter further.[110]

Collins served on the Baylor Board for twenty-one years, and continued to contribute to Baylor after Neff retired. He provided the key gift for a girls' dormitory named for his wife and for a chair in the Business School. Although known as a conservative in politics, he worked for better conditions for African-Americans and helped bring Bishop College to Dallas in 1961.[111]

Collins' conservative views were shared by several others on the board—Earl Hankamer, Dock Martin, and Alva Bryan, among others. Neff walked a tightrope on some issues, since he also had his socially conscious pastor, Dr. J. M. Dawson, and a number of other Baptist ministers on the board. Neff adroitly managed the board through the Depression; he was essentially given a free hand to keep Baylor open. Until about 1942, he usually gave the board *fait accompli* decisions. Board agendas, committee reports, minutes of past meetings, and similar information would be given to the board as they gathered for a meeting. Dr. Dawson spoke up in 1942 and requested that the board be given materials in advance of board meetings.[112] Neff complied. Neff's public dismissal of students also caught the board's attention about the same time. A policy was enacted that the Waco Executive Committee would approve any such dismissals before action was taken.[113] With the exigencies of the war, some of Neff's autocratic methods resurfaced, bothering some board members, but his masterful administration of the university's affairs usually kept them from taking issue with him, at least until after the war. Only in athletics did the board exercise week-to-week administrative authority in matters relating to coaches, their salaries, and their working conditions.

An Old War Horse Can't Stay Out of the Fray

Neff was a political animal, so at Baylor he was reluctant to give up his interest in politics. However, because saving Baylor was almost an around-the-clock job for several years, he virtually disappeared from the political scene during his first six or seven years there. Reappearance on the political scene came in 1939 in Neff's support of his old Texas House of Representatives friend, then Vice-President John Nance Garner. The Roosevelt-Garner ticket had overwhelmed the Republican opposition in 1936 as it had in 1932, and FDR's New Deal was sweeping the country. By then, Garner was growing increasingly critical of several of Roosevelt's policies. The president's backing of sit-down strikers that year and his plan to overhaul the U.S. Supreme Court and "pack" it with new Rooseveltian judges in 1937 signaled the beginning of the end of FDR and Garner's friendship. As vice-president presiding over the Senate, and as a former thirty-year member of the U.S. House, Garner had been Roosevelt's strong ally in shepherding his policies through the Congress.[114] But Garner disapproved of many of FDR's programs. In late 1938, the two met and attempted reconciliation but failed. During the last two years of FDR's second term, Garner actually became the leader and brains of the opposition to the president.[115] As talk began to emerge that Roosevelt was needed for a third term to finish his Depression-fighting programs and to give continuity to the nation's increasing concern with Germany's and Japan's military ambitions, those opposed to Roosevelt's "liberal" programs began to look for an alternative. In Texas, that meant Garner, and in June 1939 a Garner-for-President committee was formed. Cochairs E. B. Germany, Dallas oilman, and Clara Driscoll, Corpus Christi businesswoman, wrote Neff asking him to be a member of the executive committee of the movement, and Neff readily accepted.[116] In a later letter, Neff stated that he did not think Garner had "any chance whatever for the presidency," but he was for him because he was a native son of Texas and Neff did think he would make a good president.[117]

In late May 1940, the State Democratic Convention met in Waco Hall on the Baylor campus with FDR and Garner backers geared for a fight. Historian Seth Shepard McKay paints a vivid picture of the "riot which lasted practically all morning," causing Waco Police Chief C. C. Maxey to remark, "You'd never know they're supposed to be the smartest men in Texas."[118] Neff was asked to take the chair by common consent and he managed to calm the delegates. McKay pointed out that the convention was a scene unlike anything Neff had ever allowed before. After the Garner delegates won and some semblance of order was restored, the crowd lustily sang "Beer Barrel Polka" and other songs not often sung on the campus. The Associated Press stories out of Waco related how Neff sat on the platform and "watched smoke from hundreds of Democratic cigars curl toward the vaulted ceiling of Waco Hall."[119] Neff's tolerance for the delegates' behavior, which was in marked contrast with his intolerance of such behavior by Baylor students, was curious but not entirely out of character. Although he could not have approved of the rowdiness, his role was political, not administrative, and he was among his peers. In the fall, Roosevelt supporters nationwide were much too strong for any Garner movement; the president was nominated handily and indicated preference for Henry Wallace as his vice-president.

Several businessmen organized a Democrats-for-Willkie group, and in October, Neff received a telegram from Mike Hogg (son of Neff's idol, former Governor James Stephen Hogg), pleading with him to join Hogg and others in protesting a third term for FDR.[120] Neff's reply to Hogg made it clear that even if Garner could not be nominated, Neff would stick with the party and support the president.[121] Both Dock Martin and Marrs McLean also wrote Neff lengthy letters in 1940 urging him to come out against Roosevelt. McLean raved that if Roosevelt were successful in seeking a third term, "we will have National Socialism fastened on us so hard that America will never break its shackles."[122] Neff's reply to Martin was clear: while he thought the party made a mistake in nominating FDR for a third term, he "believed in party organizations . . . [and] the party has been kind, generous, and indulgent with me, as I sought public honors at its hands."[123]

Political matters had really begun to unravel with the election in 1938 of W. Lee O'Daniel as governor. On April 9, 1941, U.S. Senator Morris Sheppard died after suffering a brain hemorrhage. O'Daniel clearly indicated that he would run for Sheppard's unexpired term when he named eighty-six-year-old Andrew Jackson Houston, the only surviving son of Sam Houston, as the temporary replacement for Sheppard. Houston became the oldest man ever to enter the Senate and then one of the shortest-serving officeholders in history when he died less than a month after taking the oath of office.[124] O'Daniel called the special election for June 28. When O'Daniel, Congressman Lyndon B. Johnson, Texas Attorney General Gerald Mann, Congressman Martin Dies, and a host of minor candidates announced for Sheppard's seat, Dock Martin quickly let Neff know that he thought Johnson would be a huge mistake. Johnson was the Texas Congressman with the strongest ties to FDR and his policies."[125] Martin was almost livid when he wrote Neff, castigating board president J. T. Harrington for speaking on behalf of Johnson on the Baylor campus.[126] Martin claimed that Harrington was sullying Baylor's name and had no right to get into politics. Neff defended his board president, reminding Martin that Baylor men had always been involved in politics. This included Dr. Burleson's run for governor while he was president of Baylor and Brooks' run for the U.S. Senate later while he was president. Neff did say that he had tried to avoid getting involved in any campaigns and that personally, he "rather shared your view on matters of this kind." But he strongly defended Harrington's right to air his views.[127] O'Daniel vanquished Congressman Lyndon B. Johnson in the hotly contested Senate race, and Lieutenant Governor Coke Stevenson succeeded to the governor's chair.

At the State Democratic Convention in Austin in September 1942, Neff gave the keynote address. Summoning his most flowery oratorical style, Neff gave a speech that was interrupted several times with applause as he stirred the crowd to an almost fever pitch of patriotism. Leaving Gregory Gym on the campus of the University of Texas after the speech, Neff nearly took a tumble on the slick steps outside the gymnasium. Ever the master of the quick comeback, the stately Neff picked out a nearby female delegate and said, "I was watching you and nearly fell!"[128] That November, O'Daniel bested Allred, Moody, and Floyd Ryan in the primary and then barely eked out Allred in the runoff for the U.S. Senate, 451,000 to 433,000. Stevenson had no trouble winning his first full term as governor.[129]

By 1944, America was winning battles in both Europe and the South Pacific, but the war was far from over. Although everyone agreed that pursuing ultimate victory was the nation's number one goal, the Roosevelt administration continued to face criticism from Texas and elsewhere for its domestic policies. Democratic precinct and county conventions passed a multitude of resolutions, ranging from complete support of the administration to one urging Texas not to participate at all in the national convention. As the state convention got underway in Austin in late May, it was obvious that the state was badly split. Again Neff was called on to mediate the differing views, and he "restored a measure of order and good humor as he declared that he had never bolted the Democratic Party or the Baptist Church."[130] Most of the delegates were anti-New Deal and became known as the Texas Regulars. The Roosevelt supporters had left the Senate Chamber and were meeting in the House of Representatives Chamber. Although Neff had confessed earlier to having doubts about the wisdom of nominating Roosevelt for a fourth term, he again remained loyal to the party. In a telegram just before the election in November 1944, State Democratic Executive Chairman Harry L. Seay of Dallas wired Neff and the other former governors seeking their position; Neff immediately wired back, "I shall vote for our nominees—the Roosevelt-Truman ticket."[131] Dock Martin, Marrs McLean, and the other Regulars could claim only that they had succeeded in getting rid of "liberal" Henry Wallace as vice-president and securing Senator Harry Truman to succeed him.

Baylor's Centennial

Baylor University would be 100 years old in 1945, and Neff had begun planning an elaborate celebration nine years earlier in 1936. In that year, Waco physician Dr. K. H. Aynesworth had founded the Baylor Centennial Foundation, with collaboration from Wacoans Wilford W. Naman, George H. Belew, and Grady Yates. Aynesworth had been a student at Baylor with Neff before the turn of the century, had become a noted physician (including serving as president of the American Medical Association), and had the energy to be not only a strong supporter of Baylor but also a regent of the University of Texas. He and Neff persuaded Nell Whitman Gurley to become field secretary of the organization founded to weld Baylor alumni together and raise money for a student union building.[132] She began fundraising and promotional work in 1936, and the effort never let up until the celebration in 1945. Neff went to the board of trustees in December 1939 to get official sanction for the Centennial, and the board approved Lily Russell as "Promoter of Projects and Chairman" of the coming event.[133] The country's entry into the war in 1941 did not slow preparations; Neff and Russell were determined to have a celebration of some kind, even if it was curtailed by travel restrictions and other limitations.

As the end of 1944 brought the war closer to a successful conclusion, Neff and Russell knew that their plans to kick off the year-long celebration on February 1, 1945, could be definitely scheduled. Neff had one distraction in the fall of 1944. His friend, Dr. Homer Price Rainey, president of the University of Texas, was fired on November 1.[134] Less than two weeks later, in a Baylor Board meeting in Houston, trustee Dock Martin reported that he had been called to Austin to meet Governor Stevenson, who told him that the seventy-two-year-old Neff was being considered to take Rainey's place.[135] Two separate newspaper stories reported that Neff was under consideration, but the only two University of Texas regents interviewed both stated that Neff had not been discussed.[136] The regents appointed zoologist Dr. Theophilus S. Painter as acting president.

While Baylor was holding ceremonies between February and May commencement, momentous events were unfolding worldwide. In early February at the Yalta Conference, Roosevelt, British Prime Minister Winston Churchill, and Soviet leader Joseph Stalin agreed that their three countries plus France would occupy Germany and that Russia would enter the war against Japan. On February 19, U.S. Marine forces landed on Iwo Jima, a key Japanese island. On April 12, FDR died, and hours later Harry S. Truman was sworn in as president. On May 7, Germany surrendered and May 8 was declared V-E (Victory in Europe) Day. None of these events changed the Baylor Centennial schedule.

The first official event of the Centennial was Founders' Day on February 1. The date commemorated the 100th anniversary of the chartering of Baylor by the Republic of Texas on that day in 1845. The church-like service featured several outstanding Baptist preachers, the Baylor choirs, and an address by Dr. Kenneth Scott Latourette, professor of missions and chairman of the Department of Religion in the Graduate School of Yale University. After his address, Baylor conferred honorary doctorate degrees on Latourette, Dr. Frederick Eby, and Dr. Dixon Wecter. Eby and Neff were old friends. He had taught at Baylor in the Brooks days and then gone to the University of Texas, where he had an outstanding record of accomplishments; he was often referred to as the father of the junior college movement in Texas.[137] Wecter graduated from Baylor in 1925, received a doctorate from Yale in 1936, and was a widely known and respected academic and social historian. On the afternoon of Founder's Day, the Baylor University Historical Society met, and both Eby and Wecter made major addresses. The day closed with dedication that evening of memorial pillars dedicated to Baylor founders Reverend James Huckins and Reverend William James Tryon. The pillars, erected on the Pleasance (Founders Mall), were a gift of the Baylor class of 1945, and the program climaxed with the lighting of the pillar lamps, a carillon concert, and finally a concert by the Baylor University Symphony.[138]

Once again, Neff heard from two of his board members, this time with criticism of Wecter's afternoon speech, in which Wecter had chastised the University of Texas regents for firing President Rainey. Ray Dudley, Gulf Oil executive from Houston and board member since 1937, wrote Neff the day after he saw the newspaper story on the celebration and objected to what he termed Wecter's "lack of taste" in attacking a sister school, particularly his comment that he "would accept the judgment of the average student body of a university rather than that of a board of regents."[139] Neff's diplomatic reply a week later both agreed and disagreed with Dudley. He first said that he was in accord with several of Dudley's conclusions in his letter, but then quickly added that Wecter's speech "as a whole was scholarly, effectively delivered, and had many splendid thoughts in it."[140] The other letter from board member and San Antonio oilman Marrs McLean had much the same tone as Dudley's. McLean wrote that he was glad that Wecter was *"from* Baylor instead of *in* Baylor, for if he was *in,* one of us would have to get out."[141] Neff's tactful reply again started with saying that he agreed with some of McLean's thoughts but noted: "I really appreciate a person who says some things that I do not believe to be true. It engenders thought."[142] Governor Coke Stevenson was present at the event, but there is no record of the taciturn Stevenson's commenting on Wecter's criticism of his (Stevenson's) board of regents members.

The next event was a Centennial meeting of the board of trustees, held May 15, 100 years to the day after their predecessors first met at Brenham, Texas.[143] Planned as a largely ceremonial meeting by Neff, the session drew twenty-three of the twenty-seven trustees, the largest attendance in at least eleven years. Neff made a report of his thirteen-year tenure as president and presented faculty salary recommendations for the forthcoming academic year.[144]

Commencement weekend, a three-day celebration, began on Saturday, May 26, with traditional student ceremonies and activities. Sunday events included the baccalaureate sermon, a visit to Oakwood Cemetery to decorate the graves of past Baylor presidents Burleson and Brooks, and an evening memorial to students and alumni who "had died in service to Church and State."[145] As the Centennial theme, Neff chose the phrase "Christian Education: Safeguard of Democracy."

On commencement day, Monday, May 28, an impressive procession of trustees, guests, administrators, faculty, and graduates marched down the walks to Waco Hall. After the opening choir numbers, Neff introduced the commencement speaker he had chosen, Dr. Francis Pendleton Gaines, president of Washington and Lee University in Lexington, Virginia. Neff had admired Gaines as a fellow Baptist and president of Baylor's sister Baptist university, Wake Forest College (1927-1930). Neff also respected Gaines' record since 1930 at Washington and Lee, where he raised academic standards while improving the university's financial standing. After the address, it was time for the awarding of honorary degrees.

Neff had carefully assembled an outstanding cast of honorary degree recipients. Now seventy-three, he had grown even more autocratic with age. He had taken the names of the fourteen men and two women whom he had chosen to receive Baylor's highest honors to the Waco Executive Committee only four days before commencement.[146] It was fortunate that none of these honorees was controversial, but it must have bothered the WEC and the board as a whole that he took them for granted in such important matters. The two women were Dallas concert pianist Isabel Scionti and Washington, D.C., attorney and longtime Neff friend Marguerite Rawalt. Rawalt was unable to be present and would receive her honor in 1947. A total of fifteen individuals actually walked across the stage that day.

The fourteen men honored included two ministers: Dr. Ellis A. Fuller, president of the Southwestern Baptist Seminary in Louisville, Kentucky, and Dr. Perry

Webb, pastor of the First Baptist Church in San Antonio. Three philanthropists were honored: Houston oilman Hugh Roy Cullen, cheese manufacturer and Baptist layman James L. Kraft of Chicago, and San Antonio rancher and businessman Herbert L. Kokernot. Although Neff had, in previous years, written other university presidents that Baylor did not award honorary degrees to its alumni, he made an exception in 1945, honoring Dr. Joseph M. Jones, former U.S. State Department official and then associate editor of *Fortune* magazine. The event concluded with the awarding of diplomas to 240 candidates for bachelor's and master's degrees.

The graduates included future Hollywood actress Carole Cook (listed in the program as Mildred Frances Cook, but known at Baylor from President Neff on down as "Cookie"). Trained under Paul Baker, to whom she freely gave credit, she was "discovered" by comedian Lucille Ball and brought to Hollywood to star on the screen, although her first love had always been the stage. In 1995, Baylor honored her as a distinguished alumna. Returning that year to speak to Baylor's Heritage Club meeting, she delighted the returning alumni by relating how she had once sat on Pat Neff's lap "and a big smile came on his face."[147] Spring 1945 graduates also included future distinguished alumnus Bettye Ruth Caldwell (then McDonald), who became an internationally known child care advocate.[148]

Students Launch Youth for Christ

Notable evidence of Baylor students' commitment to spiritual growth was manifested in the Centennial spring of 1945 when a small group of dedicated students organized the first Waco Youth for Christ revival. Administrative leadership was provided by Robert Denny, director of the Baptist Student Union on campus. Well-liked by students, Denny's method of leadership was more that of a coach; when a group came to him to ask advice about the 1945 revival, he encouraged them not to look to the Youth for Christ movement in Chicago for guidance but to organize, finance, and carry out the revival themselves.[149] The inspiring story of that 1945 revival and others to follow was written by one of the principals, Bruce McIver, in a book published shortly after his death in 2001.[150] McIver, who in 1972 was awarded an honorary Doctor of Laws from Baylor and in 1997 the George W. Truett Distinguished Church Service Award, served as pastor of the Wilshire Baptist Church in Dallas for thirty years and was a Baylor trustee from 1963 to 1972. As a student at Baylor, McIver was one of three key leaders in the Youth for Christ movement. M. D. Oates and Reiji Hoshizaki were the other two.[151] Oates, from San Diego, California, was known mostly for his outstanding tennis talents. Hoshizaki was one of eight children of a Buddhist Japanese family who had migrated from Japan to California and worked as tenant farmers. Hoshizaki's family was part of a group of 120,000 individuals of Japanese descent ordered to be interned for the balance of the war by President Roosevelt. Reiji Hoshizaki was born in this country, graduated from high school, and went to Dallas to work in 1939. Influenced by Baylor-educated preachers Ellred Thomas and John Havalick, Hoshizaki became a Christian and decided to go to Baylor and become a minister. In Waco, Hoshizaki was continually harassed; one time, a student stepped in between him and a tire-tool-toting service station operator. Despite these incidents, Hoshizaki stayed at Baylor, and in 1945, he teamed up with McIver and Oates. McIver relates the gripping story of how the three were joined by others whose names would be synonymous with the Baptist ministry—Ralph Langley, B. O. Baker, LeRay Fowler, and Angel Martinez—to plan and execute the revival. McIver reported in his book that the revival services "soared nightly above the 3,000 mark and . . . there were 281 public commitments made to Christ and to Christian ministries."[152]

The War Draws to a Close

The Centennial year marked the formal chartering of the Waco Baylor Foundation. The Waco community, after originally pledging the $1 million in 1928 to retain Baylor, continued to pay off that pledge year by year through the 1930s and 1940s. The purpose of the foundation was to fund land acquisition in preparation for further expansion of the university's facilities. President Neff promised the businessmen of the city that if they would "acquire and deliver certain described pieces of property to Baylor University," the institution would pledge "to construct on the property and on the present campus one million dollars worth of new buildings immediately upon materials being made available after cessation of hostilities."[153]

As the war drew to a close, Baylor Board members and sports enthusiasts Martin, McLean, Bryan, and Hankamer were happy to announce that the Baylor Bears, out of Southwest Conference action in 1943 and 1944, would resume conference football competition in the fall of 1945. R. E. "Bill" Henderson would be football coach until Frank Kimbrough could be released from the Navy. All other teams in the conference had continued the sport during the war.[154] The 1945 Baylor football team ended the season with a 5-5-1 record. Baylor also began to plan for the resumption of spring sports in 1946.

That fall, students were greeted by Josephine, the newest of bear mascots for the university. Josephine had originally been called Joe College III until it was discovered that "he" was a female.[155] The Baylor Chamber of Commerce also purchased a new trailer for the bear, one of the first vehicles of its type for a university mascot in the country. The "bear pit," home of the mascots for many years, was located on the south bank of Waco Creek next to the site of the Student Union Building. In the early 1940s, a bear escaped, causing a group of coeds, sunbathing on a warm spring day across the street at the gymnasium, to scatter in all directions as the mascot roamed around briefly before being recaptured.[156]

The greatest news of the fall was the end of the war. Baylorites and all the United States had been shocked by the news that on August 6, the U.S. Air Corps had dropped the world's first atomic bomb on Hiroshima, Japan, killing an estimated 75,000 persons and injuring thousands more. Three days later, a second bomb had hit Nagasaki, killing some 40,000. The bombs took all of the fight out of the fanatical Japanese armed forces and their government, and Japan agreed to surrender five days later. V-J (Victory over Japan) Day, Japan's formal surrender, was September 2.

Neff reported to the BGCT in November 1945 that approximately 3,000 Baylor men, including 110 chaplains, had entered the military service over the course of the war and that 116 were on Baylor's list of war dead, with 12 still missing and 7 reported as prisoners of war.[157] He went on to say that several Baylor men were known to have worked on the atom bomb. Baylor's contribution included two Congressional Medal of Honor recipients, John "Killer" Kane and Jack Lummus. The Congressional Medal of Honor is the highest award that can be given to a member of the military. Kane was a survivor of the tragic 1927 bus-train wreck in Round Rock that took the lives of ten of his Baylor basketball teammates. He joined the Army Air Corps in 1932 and became a legendary bomber commander. According to a Baylor press release, "On August 1, 1943, he led what at the time was called the deadliest air battle in history—a low-level, long-range bombing raid on Hitler's oil-refining complex at Ploesti, Romania."[158] Lummus starred in Baylor baseball for four years (1938-1941) and in football for three of those years. He played professional football for the New York Giants for one season before joining the Marines. He received the Medal of Honor posthumously after performing heroically during the Iwo Jima invasion. Lummus' story was published in a book by veteran newspaper and radio journalist Mary Hartman in 1997.[159] Lummus' family also developed a web site highlighting his Marine service.[160]

Several years after the war, Baylor established a Granite Ring of Honor, immediately in front of Pat Neff Hall, to honor Baylor's most notable war heroes. In 2004, the late Chaplain Robert P. Taylor joined Kane and Lummus as one of three Baylor heroes thus honored. Taylor graduated from Baylor in 1933 and began his chaplaincy with U.S. infantry forces in the Philippines in 1941. He was awarded the Silver Star for gallantry in action for his services in the Battle of Bataan, became a member of the Bataan Death March of U.S. prisoners, and then ministered to 10,000 patients at the prison camp hospital at Cabanatuan. He later underwent torture at the hands of the Japanese, testifying on his release, "I'm going to live and you are too, because God is going to give us strength." Upon his return to the United States, he became the third chief of chaplains for the U.S. Air Force.[161]

Baylor closed the war years with a record enrollment in the fall of 1945, leaping almost 400 above the 1944 figure.[162] The enrollment of 1,816 was two-thirds women—1,203 compared with 613 men, including 161 veterans. But Neff and the campus braced for 1946, for this is when the great majority of individuals would be discharged from the military. The G. I. Bill of Rights, with veterans' education paid for by the federal government, would reinvigorate Baylor and every other university in the country and educate a new generation of political, business, and religious leaders.

CHAPTER 12

Neff Signs Off

I am bound to Baylor by tender ties and mellow memories.

—Pat Neff

B y the spring of 1946, Neff and Baylor were inundated by hundreds of veterans returning from World War II ready for a college education. Neff and his staff were almost overwhelmed by the task of providing housing, faculty, and classroom space for the growing student body. In the fall of 1945, the Baylor Board had set an enrollment cap of 2,300 students on the Waco campus. Neff thought total enrollment should be that which could be accommodated by Baylor's present facilities. Less than six months later, he went back to the board to expand that recommendation. In a board meeting on April 30, 1946, the board clarified the number by exempting three classes of students: returning servicemen, other previous students who wanted to return, and those whose parents or grandparents had attended Baylor.[1]

The policy was established but board member Alva Bryan did not think it was working. In July 1946, he wrote an impassioned letter to Neff charging that Dean James P. Cornette was turning down numerous applications from veterans despite the explicit directions from the board. His letter went into detail, stating that housing and classroom space were available and if they did not "seize the opportunity to make Baylor a great university and go all out in helping the Government take care of the G.I.'s, as well as to be compensated handsomely therefore, it is a matter that cannot be explained to the general board, or to the convention."[2] Neff's defense of Dean Cornette in this matter and later of Dean of Women Sadie Crawley, who displeased the board for some unknown reason, did not enhance his relationship with the board members, who were increasingly questioning his judgment and decisions.

In September 1946, 3,712 individuals enrolled: 2,432 men, of whom 1,825 were veterans, and 1,280 women. The number included 375 ministerial students.[3] Even then, hundreds of students, primarily out-of-state applicants, were turned away. Men's housing included prefabricated houses from the Bluebonnet Ordinance Plan in McGregor, which were set up just east of Brooks Hall and reserved for married veterans. Another 100 trailers were secured from the government and placed on ground owned by Baylor. Five dormitories, a cafeteria, and a study hall at the old National Youth Administration center at the Circle in Waco accommodated 304 men. The surge of students swallowed up all this space plus barracks at the old Blackland Army Airfield, which housed another 1,000 veterans.[4] Finally, at Neff's urging, Wacoans opened their homes to rent bedrooms. H. L. Kokernot, San Antonio rancher and businessman, helped matters by giving $1 million to the university; groundbreaking for a new men's dormitory, named in his honor, was held in May 1946.[5]

Obviously, more faculty and classroom space had to be provided. Twenty-five teachers were added and class time was extended to five in the afternoon, with some night classes also added. Neff was forced to give up his compulsory chapel service, as Waco Hall could seat only 2,412 students. Upperclassmen and married students were excused, and other students who seemed to have any kind of excuse were exempted from the chapel service.[6] Another Baylor custom severely tested after the war was Neff's "no smoking" policy. He continued to enforce it to the end of his presidency in 1947 for female students, but it was unpopular with many of the returning veterans. Roger Edens, who operated the drug store at Fifth and Speight for many years, remembered that students who had been soldiers frequently sat on the store's window sills outside the drug store and smoked. "Pat Neff stood on the Baylor side [where Carroll Library is located] one day and shook his finger at the soldiers/students and one of them retorted, 'Aw, why don't you go on back to your office?'"[7] Obviously, times had changed, but President Neff wasn't ready to accept that fact.

An Athlete and Student Preacher Comes to Baylor

Although three-fourths of the entering men students in the fall of 1946 were veterans, the board's policy also called for admission of children of Baylor graduates. One person who fit the latter description was Robert Jackson "Jackie" Robinson, both of whose parents graduated from Baylor. Robinson graduated from Paschal High School in Fort Worth and brought two of his teammates from the state high school champion basketball team to Baylor with him. He led the Baylor basketball team to a heart-throbbing win over Texas A&M on February 22, 1946, and the team thereby claimed the first Southwest Conference title in any sport for Baylor in fourteen years. In 1948, Robinson would lead the Bears to a second place standing in the country and then he would go on to help the United States win a gold medal in the 1948 Olympics in London. He played before 90,000 spectators, including the King and Queen of England.[8]

Jackie Robinson came to Baylor to study for the ministry. He was not there when the 1945 "Waco Youth for Christ" revival galvanized the community, but he was quickly drawn into the 1946 experiences. The second revival introduced Robinson and another student who would be heard from for many years—Howard

E. Butt Jr., son of multimillionaire Howard E. Butt Sr., whose Texas grocery chain profits were generously shared with communities and organizations in their service area. In his memoir, Robinson remembered going out with Howard Jr. to preach to both "blacks and whites" at the then segregated venereal disease clinics on Friday nights. Robinson related that Howard Jr. could reach "the back row of a crowd of twenty thousand people" and could "outpreach Billy Graham."[9] Robinson would go on to pastor several major churches, and Butt would become chief executive of the Butt Foundation and a leading Protestant layman in the country into the twenty-first century.[10] Those revival days are captured in even more detail by one of the participants—Bruce McIver—who went on to have an outstanding pastoral and administrative career in the Baptist denomination.[11] McIver wrote about another student who became an international figure in Baptist circles, Charles Wellborn. Wellborn returned to Baylor in 1946 after serving three years in Italy as a member of an Army ski patrol. Embittered by the war and not a Christian, Wellborn only wanted to earn a few more credits before entering Harvard Law School in September 1947. Robinson's testimony in chapel for a Christian life changed Wellborn's direction. Beginning in the summer of 1947, he became one of the key preachers in the Youth Revival Movement. Following seminary training, Wellborn pastored the campus-located Seventh and James Baptist Church for ten years and later went to Florida State University, becoming director of its overseas studies in London. The Waco revival in April 1946 drew more than 4,000 attendees and exactly 500 conversions.[12] It was followed by summer revivals in Dallas, Fort Worth, and Houston and then began to spread across the South.[13] One of the key vocalists and song leaders was Bob Feathers, who would later become a vice-president for development for Baylor for several years.[14]

And Still They Came

The students kept pouring in. September 1947 saw another 21 percent increase in enrollment to 4,506, the largest in Baylor's history. Almost 600 came from out of state, according to Neff's report to the Baptist General Convention that fall. The flood of students meant more faculty, more classes, and more space problems. Frances Landreth was just twenty years old when President Neff hired her in 1947 to teach math—but she already had a master's degree and two years' experience at the University of Southern California. She still vividly remembers those years right after the war:

> There were so many students and so little classroom space that one year, I had an 8 a.m. class and a session that began at 8 p.m the same day. We found that we had more students than chairs in several classes and were told: "Weed out the less capable students in the early weeks until the chairs and the students even out."[15]

Overcrowding was not the only issue Landreth faced. She recalled that in her first faculty meeting in the fall of 1947, President Neff laid out the rules for the newcomers. He told them that women faculty members would wear hose anytime they were on campus. To young, financially struggling single women, this was quite a sacrifice because nylon hose were still in short supply after the war and the women wanted to save those expensive wardrobe additions for church and dates with young men.

The university kept scrambling for housing, although business manager Roy McKnight thought the school could accommodate 5,000 students.[16] To Neff's dismay, Kokernot Hall and the Student Union were the only two buildings the university was able to erect in the postwar years before his departure in December 1947. Neff had taken the matter of the Student Union Building to the board in November 1945, stating that construction had started in 1940 but was discontinued in June 1942 for lack of funds. He told the board that the construction company had estimated it would take $400,000 to complete the building and the alumni association apparently had abandoned the project. The board persuaded Neff to continue to work with the alumni to complete the building.[17]

The idea of alumni being primarily responsible for funding a Student Union Building appears to have originated with the Centennial Foundation in 1936. Several references appear in the alumni edition of *The Baylor Bulletin* of clubs pledging money for the building.[18] The Depression economy and then World War II had prevented the building's completion. In January 1946, Neff gave the ex-students an office in Pat Neff Hall, and former football star Lieutenant Billy Patterson, fresh out of the Naval Air Force, was hired by Baylor to go into the field and raise money for the building.[19] Neff gave Patterson a letter addressed to "Friends of Baylor," seeking contributions and saying the Union Building was sorely needed by September 1 so that it could accommodate the influx of students expected.[20] Patterson had planned to open a law practice in McAllen on March 1, 1946, but he agreed to spend January and February "working for Baylor, crisscrossing the state to raise money to finish the building." In his memoir, he estimated that he raised some "$75,000 -$100,000" with "some to come later."[21] When Jack Dillard was employed by Baylor to succeed Patterson, Neff gave him the same "Dear Friends" letter. Several rooms on the third floor of the new Student Union were pressed into service as classrooms in September 1947, but the formal dedication of the building would not take place until September 1948, after Dr. W. R. White became president.

Despite Neff's and Dr. Armstrong's best efforts, groundbreaking for the Browning Building would also be delayed until 1948. The delay was almost as much a disappointment to Neff as it was to the world-renowned Browning scholar. Neff had praised the professor extravagantly when he told the board that he had promised him $100,000 in 1943. Despite strong financial support from board members, especially Earl Hankamer and Marrs McLean, the university was not successful in broadening the fundraising sufficiently to begin construction. The frustrated Armstrong would not give up. He cajoled, challenged, and besieged every student and ex-student of his. Former student and Baylor faculty member Lois Smith Douglas painted a tender portrait of Armstrong in her biography of him published by Baylor in 1951. In the book, she also describes his colorful classroom demeanor that both outraged and endeared him to thousands of Baylor students over a teaching career of more than forty years.[22]

Notwithstanding Baylor's Baptist heritage and ownership by the churches of Texas, money for the Tidwell Bible Building was even more difficult to raise. It would be 1953, almost two decades after talk began of the necessity for such a structure, before the building could be started.[23]

In the meantime, in December 1945, the relocated Baylor College of Medicine, warmly welcomed by Houston, celebrated the groundbreaking for a new building there, to be located near Hermann Hospital as part of a 134-acre Texas Medical Center, purchased from the City of Houston by the M. D. Anderson Foundation. As construction proceeded on the new building, it was realized that the total cost would be considerably higher than expected. Baylor trustees had no ready solution for sourcing the expected shortfall. On March 1, 1947, Houston oilman Hugh Roy Cullen, already a multimillion-dollar philanthropist, came to the rescue. He and Mrs. Cullen agreed to give Baylor $800,000—half to pay the remainder of the construction cost and half to be used for equipment for the new building. Neff saw the actual check drawn in October 1947 and was also proud to see the announcement by the Cullens that their foundation would donate the balance of $2.25 million to cover the entire cost of the new building.[24]

In the post-war 1940s, Professor Glenn Capp and his students continued to accumulate first-place trophies from debate tournaments, and Dr. Daniel Sternberg and his Music Department enriched Waco's cultural life by producing operas entirely with campus talent. Other departments and faculty shone as well. Because of increased enrollment and interest, the Bible Department expanded from three teachers in 1932 to twelve in 1947. The Education Department developed a visual education component that served schools and communities from El Paso to Texarkana. In the sciences, Baylor boasted one of the highest rates of students accepted for medical school.[25]

Next to Dr. Armstrong's international reputation for his Browning Collection, Paul Baker and his Drama Department were probably better known than any other Baylor academic area. In the postwar years, Neff proudly pointed out that the department had undertaken a strong religious drama movement in the Waco churches. Baker had continued leadership of the Baylor Civic Theater, enlisting Waco citizens as well as students, and also of the Children's Theater and the Southwest Summer Theater.[26]

The issue of Baylor's accreditation with the country's standard-setting bodies for higher education came to the forefront in 1947. Baylor received full recognition from the Southern Association of Colleges and Secondary Schools in 1940 but had never been accredited by the Association of American Universities (AAU). In 1945, Baylor submitted an application to that body. After a field review by Dean A. O. Brogan of the University of Texas, Baylor was turned down and told that eleven fields needed improvement before the AAU would approve Baylor.[27] Neff immediately set the faculty to work to correct the shortcomings. The president told the faculty that accreditation itself was not the goal, that the goal was for Baylor to be "what our founding fathers dreamed of."[28] AAU accreditation became a moot point in 1949 when the AAU ceased its accreditation function in order to concentrate on its original mission—serving as an organization of selected universities and colleges with strong graduate programs.[29]

Personal Matters Intervene

At the fall 1945 meeting of the Baylor Board, Neff announced that if the Masonic Grand Lodge followed its usual course, he would be elected Grand Master (the top position in the state) when the Grand Lodge convened in Waco in December. Although Neff told them the position would require some work and travel, the board told him to go ahead and accept it if offered. Neff's election on December 6, 1945, gave him the unique honor of holding, at the same time, the highest office in two institutions that were organized when Texas was a Republic—Baylor University and the Masonic Grand Lodge. He also became the only man in Texas history to have held the top positions in two of the state's major fraternal organizations during his lifetime—the Knights of Pythias in 1918 and then the Masons in 1946.

Neff's 1946 was enough to exhaust a man half his age. In addition to the challenges of steering a record enrollment and captaining the Masonic Grand Lodge, his son decided to run for Texas Attorney General, and for at least three months in the spring and summer of 1946, Pat Sr. was deeply involved in that campaign.

Pat Jr. had been thinking of running for the state's chief legal officer position since he worked in that office as an assistant attorney general before going into the Army. He felt his eight years in the office under three separate attorneys general gave him a depth and breadth of experience that would serve the citizens of Texas well. In 1946, Grover Sellers, the incumbent attorney general, had announced for governor, and that meant the office was wide open. Several men toyed with the idea of running, but in the end, it was two Baylorites—Pat Jr. and Price Daniel—who decided to run. Daniel was a 1932 graduate of Baylor Law School and a three-term member of the Texas House of Representatives, serving as speaker in 1943. He left the House to enroll in the Army and served until 1946, with a short stint overseas after fighting stopped. The two were friends and hated to run against each other, but each had arrived at his decision independently and neither wanted to back down.

Newspaperman Weldon Hart, later to be a key staff member for both Governor Beauford Jester and then Governor Allan Shivers, ran Pat Jr.'s campaign. He wrote Neff several times asking for advice and imploring him to get more deeply involved. Neff wrote his hundreds of friends across the state asking them to support his son. Former Governor James V. Allred wrote Neff that the Baylor president needed to place some personal telephone calls to several influential newspaper publishers, and Neff responded by calling publishers Amon Carter (the *Fort Worth Star-Telegram*), former Governor William P. Hobby Sr. (*Houston Post*), and one of his friends at the *Dallas Morning News*.[30]

Both candidates campaigned vigorously throughout the state, but Daniel covered more ground and campaigned harder than Pat Jr. On election night, July 27, the lead surged back and forth, but at the end of the night, Daniel had edged out Pat Jr. by 13,580 votes out of 1,129,128 cast. Pat Jr.'s political life was over. Daniel, on the other hand, went on to hold more high state and national offices than any other Texan had ever achieved, spoiled only by a defeat by John Connally when Daniel attempted to win an unprecedented fourth term for governor in 1962.[31]

By 1946, the Baylor Board of Trustees and its sub-unit, the Waco Executive Committee, were beginning to chafe under Neff's continuing mode of independent action. Board member Alva Bryan had reacted strongly to Dean Cornette's ignoring board policy by refusing to admit a number of veterans. Neff bristled at what he felt was board interference, and the board backed off slightly but reiterated that it wanted as many G.I. students as possible to be welcomed to the campus. In March 1947, Neff's antipathy toward athletics resulted in another rebuke to the president. The board's athletic committee reported to the Waco Executive Committee (WEC) that Neff had ignored decisions made by the athletic group and refused to pay the coaching staff it had selected. The WEC had written the full board in March, reminding that body and Neff that, under board policy, the WEC had been acting as the final authority in recruiting and setting the pay scale for the Athletic Department. The WEC had employed Bob Woodruff as football coach to succeed Frank Kimbrough, set his salary, and approved assistant coaches for his staff. Neff's refusal to pay the staff placed the WEC "in a most embarrassing position." The WEC supported the athletic committee and authorized it to continue to act for the WEC and the full board in the future.[32] The above incidents would not be sufficient in isolation to cause serious rift in the relations between Neff and the board, but there were more.

Truman's Honorary Degree

Neff's usual practice in awarding honorary degrees was to take the names before the board or the WEC (there seemed to be no pattern) just days away from commencement after the invitations had been extended to the recipients. On

November 16, 1945, in a regular meeting of the WEC, Neff informed them that some months previously, he had extended an invitation to President Harry Truman to accept an honorary degree from Baylor on December 5, 1945.[33] Truman had replied that he would be present "unless something unforeseen prevented" his trip. A few days after that, Truman canceled all his engagements outside Washington. On November 2, Neff wrote the president that he understood and the degree would be waiting for him whenever he could make the trip to Waco.[34]

Neff informed the WEC, in case they had not already heard the news, that just the day before the WEC meeting, the Baptist General Convention of Texas had passed, by unanimous vote, the following resolution: "Because of the attitude of the President of the United States as a Baptist toward gambling and drinking, and because of the invitation of Baylor University to confer upon him the high recognition of an honorary degree, I move that we instruct trustees of our colleges and universities not to confer any honorary degree on those holding to such positions." Neff asked for guidance from the WEC on the matter. Dr. J. M. Dawson spoke first, emphasizing that Baylor was owned and controlled by the Baptist Convention, and urged that the university "adhere to the wishes of the Convention." Trustees Alva Bryan, J. W. Hale, J. T. Harrington, and E. R. Nash Jr. all expressed support for the degree and authorized Neff to proceed. Dr. Dawson did not vote.[35]

In January 1947, President Truman decided to combine a trip to talk with Mexican President Miguel Aleman with a trip to Waco to receive the degree. Both were set for early March. When one of Truman's Arkansas lawyer friends wrote him about the forthcoming Baylor honor, the president replied in one of his typical salty exchanges:

> The President of Baylor University is a former Governor of Texas and he is all wool and a yard wide. He didn't pay any attention to the demagogue preachers, who were trying to get a little publicity by attacking their member who happens to be in the White House. It is a wonderful thing we don't have a Baptist Pope."[36]

The expression "all wool and a yard wide" was a fairly common one in that era. It is generally considered to have come from the clothing industry and meant wool of high quality and cut extra wide. Applied to individuals, it meant they were "genuine, sincere, honorable and of excellent quality."[37]

Except for a driving rain, the Truman visit measured up to all that Baylor could have wished for. Truman delivered a major policy address that appealed to all nations to lower trade barriers and follow a course of free commerce. Truman and his party stayed for a brief luncheon —supervised by Neff's daughter, Hallie Maude— and departed soon after to return to Washington, D.C. On his return, the president wrote a cordial letter to Neff, stating that he thought Baylor was a good place to deliver his major address and that he prized his honorary degree.[38]

Although Senator Tom Connally and Congressman Bob Poage had reinforced Neff's invitation, it may well have been Truman's old schoolteacher at Independence, Missouri, Ardelia Palmer, who actually clinched the deal for the Waco visit. Palmer prided herself on being a Browning scholar, and she wrote Truman that she had been a guest lecturer at one of Dr. A. J. Armstrong's classes. Dr. Armstrong had taken her to meet Neff and she was enchanted by the visit; she heaped praise on Armstrong, Neff, and the university and urged President Truman to accept the proffered invitation from Neff.[39]

But Neff had put the board in an embarrassing position. He had issued the invitation to Truman in 1945 before the annual meeting of the BGCT. When the convention blasted the move, board members felt they could do nothing but back up their president even though it went against the wishes of the convention. It did not help that six weeks after the Truman visit, Neff addressed the April 29 board meeting, stating that he wanted "to have it recorded here as a part of the permanent file that on October 6, 1945, by authority of the Board and the entire faculty," he had extended the original invitation.[40] The minutes of the board, the WEC, and the faculty do not show any such approval in 1945. Neff had cut corners and put the board in an awkward position, but once again he had gotten Baylor University significant national coverage.

The Beginning of the End

Events were closing in on Neff. His longtime friend and supporter, board president Dr. J. T. Harrington, died the same day as the spring 1947 board meeting on April 29. The board became aware of his death before adjournment and elected Alva Bryan of Waco as the new chair. Although Bryan and Neff had been at loggerheads on athletic matters, Bryan was generally a Neff supporter. This friendship did not help Neff, however, as Bryan presided at only two meetings and was not reappointed to the board by the BGCT in November. Bryan blamed Neff, but the president told him in a letter that the preachers "got him" because he was not a church-going Baptist.[41]

At the April 29 meeting, Neff asked for the annual approval of administrative officers, including business manager Roy McKnight, public relations director Lily Russell, and registrar Truett K. Grant. All three were approved unanimously. The fourth appointment, Dean Cornette, was discussed at length by the board and Neff was forced, once more, to defend Cornette when several board members again accused Cornette of refusing veterans enrollment.[42] The appointment was approved only after an impassioned promise by Neff that Cornette would carry out the policies of the board. Neff was also forced to withdraw the nomination of Sadie Crawley for dean of women when eleven out of seventeen members voted against her retention. Board minutes do not carry the reasons for her adverse vote.[43]

After the meeting, Dock Martin sought to bolster Neff's feelings by saying that after having some original concerns, he thought the board meeting had been very positive and "you are in better favor . . . than you have been in five years."[44] Neff's antennae told him something different. In a reply to Martin a week later, he wrote: "I felt that there were some undercurrents and countercurrents that were brewing but did not culminate. I felt apprehensive with each passing moment of the meeting, fearful of what might be suggested."[45]

The spring semester and summer seemed to be quiet. Neff brought Harvard President James E. Conant to campus for an address and an honorary degree on February 13, 1947. In May, he was able to grant the delayed honorary degree to his longtime friend Marguerite Rawalt. Rawalt had been a secretary to Neff when he was governor. He saw her potential and pushed her to further her education. She went on to college, then to law school, and became the first female president of the Federal Bar Association in Washington and also served as president of the National Association of Women Lawyers. Rawalt was a fitting capstone to Neff's commitment to recognizing the possibilities of women in filling challenging positions. He saw his mother's steely courage in the way she faced the premature death of her husband and two of her children, and in her proven ability to manage the family farm. He decided early on that women had been wrongly denied the opportunity to take their rightful place in the business and professional world. He blazed a new trail when he was governor by appointing the first women to several key positions. He followed this path at Baylor by bringing in more women professors and by honoring other distinguished women with honorary degrees from the university.

September came and Neff remained apprehensive. He sensed that business manager Roy McKnight and alumni secretary Jack Dillard were conspiring to remove him as president. McKnight wrote Neff an impassioned letter on October 5 that he had heard some things that "surprised and disturbed me greatly." He went on to pledge his unqualified support for Neff, stating: "I am not involved in any plot against you and do not know of any such."[46] Dillard, however, made no such protestation. Dillard and his alumni group had grown increasingly unhappy at Neff's coolness, even outright opposition at times, to Baylor's athletic programs. Several alumni were well aware of Neff's refusal to honor the athletic committee's actions in regard to Coach Woodruff and his staff. Thus, although most observers thought the "conspiracy" theory Neff held in regard to McKnight and Dillard was a figment of Neff's imagination, there were several close to the situation who later stated there could have been some truth to the matter, especially regarding Dillard.

Neff Resigns

It seems, however, that Neff felt he had taken enough grief from the board and others. The *Dallas Morning News* ran a story on October 11, 1947, that Neff had intended to resign at the October 10 meeting of the board, but this was heatedly denied by Neff. McKnight took the opportunity to write Neff from his sickbed that he was "100 percent loyal to Neff" and reiterated his complete support.[47] On November 7, Neff announced that he was indeed resigning effective December 31, 1947, after fifteen years of service as the chief executive. His official letter was positive and pleasant: "Since my early youth, I have had some connection with Baylor University. I am bound to her by tender ties and mellow memories. Should I live a thousand years . . . , I could not to her pay the debt of gratitude I owe."[48] With his resignation letter, Neff filed his final report, the same that he would present later that month to the annual meeting of the BGCT in Amarillo. The fifty-six pages contrasted Baylor as Neff found it in 1932 with the status in 1947 of finances, faculty, enrollment, buildings, religious life, and many other areas for which Neff was responsible, at both Waco and Dallas. It was an impressive accounting of fifteen years of dedicated, laborious effort.[49]

Two days after Neff's resignation announcement, the faculty, by unanimous vote, called on him to withdraw his resignation. The Baylor Student Council passed a similar resolution, and in chapel student leaders urged their fellow students to sign petitions asking Neff to stay and the trustees to reject his resignation. When Neff went to Amarillo to the annual meeting of the BGCT, he confused matters by telling a group at a dinner honoring him that he would "serve as long as the school trustees think I should." In Amarillo, Neff was not helped by his longtime friend and fellow Baylor graduate Caso March, who lobbied the convention to pass a resolution asking the trustees to keep Neff. Despite his good intentions, March, an eccentric law professor at Baylor, had run for Texas Governor as a "liberal" Democrat in 1946, which meant he was not in favor with a majority of the Baylor Board of Trustees.[50] Editorials praising Neff's presidency came quickly. The *Dallas Morning News* (November 10, 1947), the *Waco News-Tribune* (November 8, 1947), and the *Daily Lariat* (November 11 and December 19, 1947) all paid tribute to his accomplishments. Numerous individuals wrote Neff asking that he withdraw his resignation.[51]

On November 24, Neff wrote business manager Roy McKnight and alumni secretary Jack Dillard that they were "released from any further business connection or association with Baylor University." Neff stated he was taking the action so that his successor would have "an open field and a free hand in organizing his working staff."[52] Neff still felt the two were somehow conspiring against him and ordered Dillard from the office he was occupying in Pat Neff Hall. When the letter was written, McKnight was at home recuperating from illness; he was bewildered and heartbroken. Dillard did not reply to his letter, but instead mobilized the alumni across the state to call the board members and urge them to follow through and accept Neff's resignation. Headlines in the November 25 *Waco Times-Herald* screamed BAYLOR EXES ASK BOARD TO LET NEFF OUT. Telegrams and telephone calls came to Dillard and the board from all over Texas. The outcry reflected the effective work of Dillard, Patterson, and a number of other outraged alumni. Letters of support for Dillard and McKnight came from many individuals, including noted attorney Leon Jaworski and Texas Attorney General Price Daniel.[53] Dillard later claimed that Neff's resignation was a ploy to obtain a show of support for his continued service from the board of trustees.

Within the next two days, Neff's original "voluntary" resignation became what could only be characterized as an involuntary one. The board was now determined to accept Neff's resignation even if he tried to renege on it.[54] They met in a special called meeting in Houston November 28, and Neff's resignation was read. Neff was outside the room but was invited in to make a statement. He stated that his association with Baylor had been pleasant and happy and asked the board to accept his resignation. The board expressed its appreciation for his service in a formal resolution and named him to a new position of president emeritus, effective January 1, 1948, with a salary of $3,000 per year but with no duties or authority. *Dallas Morning News* Waco correspondent Thomas Turner, along with other reporters, was just outside the door as Neff came out of the meeting room. Turner remembered Neff's quipping: "I came, I saw, I was conquered."[55]

However, Neff had to have the last word, at least with the reporters. He proudly told them that he had, on three occasions, been offered the presidency of two of Texas' state schools, the University of Texas and Texas Technological College.[56] There is no official record of the latter, but Neff's signing the legislation creating the school could possibly have given him that position. As described earlier in this book, Neff had been offered the presidency of the University of Texas in 1924, but wisely turned it down. He was well aware that his good friend and influential alumnus, Will C. Hogg, was dead set against any "politician" and Neff did not want that fight. In 1944, there had been talk of his succeeding Homer Price Rainey, but several regents were quoted as saying that his name had not been discussed.

After the Baylor Board accepted Neff's resignation, it then took up the matter of the firing of McKnight. It was ruled that Neff did not have the authority to discharge any person elected or approved by the board. A motion passed reversing the dismissal and giving McKnight a leave of absence with pay until January 1 to give him time to recuperate from his illness. In the case of Dillard, the board found that neither Neff nor the board had any authority over him since Baylor was not paying his salary or supervising his work. Dr. W. T. Gooch was named acting president, Dean Carroll was named acting dean, and, finally, a committee of five was named to make recommendations for a new president.[57]

Neff gave his farewell speech in chapel on December 18. He told the students that he had "recognized the need for a new voice" and he asked the students to "remember me at my best."[58] There was no trace of bitterness in his remarks. He received a standing ovation, and then Pat Luckett, chairman of the Student Council, presented him with a gavel and a bouquet of forty-five roses, representing the forty-five years of Neff's association with Baylor. (Neff came back to the 1948 commencement and, on request, signed a number of diplomas. Luckett was delighted that on his diploma, Neff added the words "Thanks to you" above his signature.) Neff's last "class" closed with "The Good Old Baylor Line" and "The Eyes of Texas."

What prompted Neff's resignation? Two individuals uniquely qualified to comment do not vary greatly in their assessment. Baylor historian Eugene Baker wrote:

> After the war, there were probably several things that led to Neff's gradual loss in effectively administering the University—his age, his inability to alter his course, his jealousy of others in the limelight, and his failure to recognize the changing times. Regardless of these shortcomings, Neff always had the good of the University at heart.[59]

Thomas E. Turner, who covered Waco and Baylor for the *Dallas Morning News* for several years before and after Neff's resignation, wrote similar comments in his book of narrative portraits of the presidents of Baylor:

> To the returning G.I.s and Rosie the Riveters of '45 and after, many of the rules of Baylor were out of tune with the times. The "football crowd" thought Neff was not supportive enough of that ancient pastime, and the alumni and faculty wanted a bigger say in the running of their school.[60]

Several Baylor observers had thought Neff was going to retire in 1945—"graduate with the Centennial class." Neff hinted at such, but then could not bring himself to turn loose of the reins. In his oral memoir, Dr. W. J. Wimpee stated that he had come to Neff during his last months in office in 1947 and told him that he would support him all the way, but added: "Honestly, sir, I thought you made a mistake in not retiring in 1945, because in that Centennial year, you would have been remembered with great appreciation by everyone." Neff's reply was: "I really didn't relish not having a job and not having a load to carry that I've carried all these years."[61]

In a conversation recorded for the Baylor Alumni Association, Jack Dillard stated that he thought Neff wanted to eliminate football and limit the size of the school to the number that could be accommodated in Waco Hall—"his class"—both concepts opposed by many alumni and board members.[62] Dillard was not only reinstated by his alumni board, but went on to breathe new life into the alumni group and into *The Baylor Line* magazine and was later named a distinguished alumnus of the university. Dillard remained angry at Neff, disparaging his contributions to Baylor and making several misstatements about the former president. Billy Patterson, president of the exes in 1947, differed from Dillard in his estimation of Neff. He felt Neff was "respected, even liked" by the student body, and that they were "glad to have him as president." Although one of Dillard's charges was that Neff did not want to finish the Student Union Building, Patterson did not recall any opposition on Neff's part to the building.[63]

Neff proffered various reasons for his resignation as he answered letters of inquiry. He wrote about spending more time at Mother Neff Park, tending his sheep at the farm, doing some writing, or exploring some vague new pursuits. Although he saw his opposition coming for several months, he could not bring himself to think seriously about any future beyond Baylor. He had spent his entire professional life assuming and wielding power, and retirement to a life without power or prestige was a foreign concept.

Baylor Retrospective

The greatest achievement of Neff's fifteen-year tenure as president was undoubtedly the astounding feat of keeping the doors of Baylor, both at Waco and at Dallas, open during the Great Depression. His statewide and national reputation brought faculty and students to Baylor who would otherwise have gone to other colleges or passed up college entirely. His flair for promotion (through, for example, the Keys quads and the Garner and Truman honorary degrees) gave Baylor international publicity that money could not buy. His autocratic methods became outdated perhaps even before he retired, but during his tenure he used those powers—at that critical time in the Baylor's history—to keep the largest Baptist college in the world afloat and solvent.

Neff found Baylor a small Central Texas college; he left it a nationally known university, respected across the country in a wide variety of disciplines—law, speech, theater, and music, among others, as well as a college highly prized by most Baptist congregations in Texas and the South. As is the case with many leaders whose tenures span more than a decade, changing conditions and expectations eventually eroded Neff's ability to lead effectively. His inability to change with the times was somewhat ironic in light of his earlier advice to students that "life is a constant readjustment." But that short period of decline did not in any way diminish Neff's accomplishments, and Baylor University remains a testament to his enduring legacy.

The Last Curtain

At its meeting on January 3, 1948, the board of trustees elected Dr. William Richardson (W. R.) White as president of Baylor at a salary of $12,000 annually plus a home. At the same meeting, board member Dr. Wallace Bassett, minister of the Oak Cliff Baptist Church in Dallas, "made some remarks concerning the inadvisability of President Emeritus Neff having an office on the Baylor campus." A motion was approved appointing a committee to confer with Neff and ask him to vacate his office in Pat Neff Hall by February 1. The board also adopted a policy that the $250 per month compensation to Neff was supposed to pay for any expenses he incurred after January 1 and that Baylor would not be responsible for any such expenditures.[64] Both actions hurt Neff terribly, but he duly vacated his office and rented space at the Amicable Building, where he had officed for many years. When Neff vacated his office in Pat Neff Hall on February 1, he left papers, trophies, and other personal possessions in several rooms. In July, board member George M. Irving wrote Neff that the university needed those rooms and asked him to move his collection "at the earliest possible moment."[65]

Professor Guy B. Harrison remembered Neff as being "very bitter." Harrison said he tried to "mellow" Neff after his resignation and finally went to President White, telling him that Neff was so bitter that he was going to leave all his papers to the University of Texas. President White had been cordial to Neff, inviting him to share the 1948 commencement platform and including him in many functions. However, he failed to realize the severity of Neff's bruised feelings. Harrison told White, "Neff's papers must come here," and Dr. White asked him, "What will it take?" Harrison told him Neff wanted space for all his accumulated records and files.[66] White wrote Neff a friendly letter, asking that his collection be left to Baylor and stating that he was making Room 410 in Pat Neff Hall available for this purpose.[67] Harrison worked with Neff five days a week until Neff's death, helping him arrange his papers.[68] After Neff's death, the family officially tendered all his records to Baylor.[69]

One of the most regrettable results of Neff's resignation was the loss of his friendship with Alva Bryan and his longtime close friend Dock Martin. In 1950, Martin wrote Neff that Bryan "went to his grave with a conviction that you had broken friendship with him." The Neff-Martin relationship would be strained even longer. In the same letter, Martin pleaded with Neff for reconciliation. Martin was hurt that Neff had not even spoken to him at a Rotary Club meeting in Waco when Dr. White was introduced to the club. Further, Martin said that Neff had not answered his last three letters. Martin closed saying, "I would indeed like to be your friend."[70] There is no record of a reply to this letter from Neff. At some point, Neff had gotten the idea that Martin had turned on him, and nothing Martin said could change his mind.

For the four years after leaving Baylor until his death in January 1952, Neff was alternately bitter and forgiving. He was still in demand as a speaker, but not at the pace he had been accustomed to. Shortly after his retirement, he went to Detroit to make one of his then famous Lincoln Day addresses. He also attended the long-awaited ground-breaking for the Armstrong Browning Library at Baylor in 1948 and was heartened later by an effusive letter from Dr. "A" that "the glory of the Browning Library belongs to you."[71] In 1950, he was bolstered by a short visit from his protégé, Senator Lyndon B. Johnson, who was in town for a short stay.[72] He also was cheered by Baylor news—Carr Collins wrote him that the radio station

Collins and Neff had pushed the board to approve was earning $8,000 a month for the university.[73]

Three years after his last day at Baylor and less than a year before his death, he was finally able to stand back and view his years in perspective. He told dissertation writer Chase Winfrey in an interview: "I found Baylor poor and struggling. It is strong enough now to withstand the strains of time. It will weather the storm. I can watch it in peace, with others at the helm."[74]

About this same time, he was being pushed by his longtime friend, secretary, and professor Emma Shirley to write his autobiography, which she offered to put in final form.[75] There is no record of a response from Neff. He continued to live his life rather than write about it. The campaigner who never lost an election bragged that he had not missed a gubernatorial inauguration in fifty years. In an *Austin American* story in 1951, reporter Wick Fowler wrote that Neff was the only former governor spotted in the crowd for Governor Allan Shivers' swearing in on January 16, 1951.[76]

The wife he had left alone so many nights was his final companion. After a night out with Myrtie, Neff died of a heart attack on the morning of January 20, 1952. The following day, more than 2,000 mourners filled the First Baptist Church of Waco, including Senator Tom Connally, Governor Allan Shivers, and former Governor Dan Moody, who was a pallbearer. Dr. Forrest C. Feezor, pastor of the church and president of the Baptist General Convention, and W. R. White, president of Baylor, officiated.[77] Dr. J. M. Dawson—Neff's pastor, friend, and Baylor Board member for many years—had taken a position in Washington, D.C. as executive director of the Baptist Joint Committee on Public Affairs for the United States, and did not attend the funeral. However, his telegram was shared during the service.[78]

Neff was buried in Oakwood Cemetery where Hallie Maude's twins were interred. Not far from his grave are the tombs of two other Texas governors from Waco, Richard Coke and Lawrence S. Ross; the grave of his friend and fellow former Baylor President Samuel Palmer Brooks; and the grave of Rufus C. Burleson, first president of Baylor at Waco.[79]

Describing the funeral the following day in the *Waco News-Tribune*, newspaper correspondent Thomas Turner aptly wrote:

> Pat Neff returned to his beloved earth Monday. It was a perfect union—the two had never been far apart. No matter how far Pat Neff went in public life—and his career as a statesman and educator stands unchallenged—he always came back home to the soil.[80]

Neff would be joined eighteen months later by his wife Myrtie, who died on July 19, 1953, just weeks before her eightieth birthday. Neff's sister, Sallie Calvert, died in 1954. Her son and Neff's nephew, Robert S. Calvert, had been elected Texas Comptroller of Public Accounts in 1948 and went on to serve in that position for twenty-six years, the longest-serving comptroller in Texas history. Hallie Maude continued to be an active citizen of Waco until she died at the age of seventy-six on November 21, 1977, four months after the death of her husband, Frank Wilcox. In her final years she bequeathed numerous Neff memorabilia to historic houses in Waco, to the Governor's Mansion, and to the Texas Collection at Baylor. Pat Neff Jr. died on January 8, 1986, at the age of eighty-two.

Pat Neff III and his wife had a son, whom they named Pat Neff IV, and later a daughter, Gretchen Nan Neff. She married Robert Daniel Watson on September 1, 1990, in Houston. During the 1990s, the couple had two sons and a daughter, giving Pat Sr. (some forty years after his death) two great-great-grandsons and one great-great-granddaughter.

Pat Neff's name also lives on through several individuals who are named for him, including a girl, Pat Neff Pratt of Commerce, Texas, as well as through Pat Neff Hall at Baylor, the Pat Neff Society for major givers to Baylor, Pat Neff Middle School in San Antonio, and Pat Neff Elementary School in Houston.

A Final Portrait

After all is said and done, who was Pat Morris Neff?

He was, first and foremost, the man his mother wanted him to be—well-educated, faithful to the teachings and mandates of the Baptist Church, highly successful in all of his professional undertakings, and deeply committed to public service. Beyond those qualities, Pat Neff was also a man of many talents, most notably in the art of oratory. He learned early that there was power in words if they were carefully crafted and delivered well, and he used that power extremely effectively in the courtroom, on the campaign trail, in the House Chamber, at the pulpit, in the Baptist Convention boardroom, in the Masonic Lodge, and in his chapel "class" at Baylor. For reasons that remain a mystery, he failed to make use of his oratory powers in his dealings with the legislature as governor, which undermined his success in that arena. This instance was an exception, however, and his reputation as one of the best orators in Texas remained intact throughout his life.

Neff's accomplishments as governor, which were numerous despite his problems with the legislature, were tied to his personal priorities—his love of the land, his fondness for highway travel, his respect for the rights and abilities of women, and his commitment to higher education. A farm boy by birth and a lifelong weekend farmer by choice, he believed strongly in the importance of land ownership, and by extension, of public ownership and protection of open spaces. As governor, he led the drive to create a state parks system in Texas and then contributed to its development by donating part of the Neff family farm to form one of the state's first state parks—Mother Neff Park. Soon after his death, the Texas State Parks

Board issued a memorial resolution recognizing Neff as "the Father of the Texas Parks System."[81]

The passage in 1923, on Neff's recommendation, of $600,000 for topographic and hydrographic surveys of the upper reaches of the state's major rivers must also be ranked as one of Neff's major achievements. In fact, in 1938, as he reviewed his governorship, he considered his park work and the attention to conservation of floodwaters as the most far-reaching of any of his accomplishments.

The launching of a "true" state highway system was an accomplishment that lives on as one of Neff's greatest legacies. In his second term as governor, he led the way to give the Highway Department its first substantial source of income—the state gasoline tax. He also secured six-year terms for highway commissioners to at least partially insulate them from politics, and he engineered legislation that would allow the state to move from a patchwork of county-controlled roads to a coordinated system of state highways.

Neff's respect for women, no doubt stemming from his admiration for his mother, led him to appoint an unprecedented number of women to important posts in government. Following on the heels of woman suffrage, this was more than a symbolic gesture, reflecting a genuine desire to open up new opportunities for talented women and to set a precedent for future governors.

Neff's strong support of an adequate public educational system was demonstrated throughout his life. From defending appropriations for the University of Texas on the floor of the Texas House in 1899 to serving as president of the Conference on Education in Texas in 1913, he had earned his credentials in educational circles long before he became governor. He accelerated that advocacy in his first gubernatorial campaign, constantly pushing the state's citizens and lawmakers to increase their support for both public and higher education. In the field of education, Neff's two terms were marked by the establishment of Texas Technological College in West Texas and South Texas State Teachers College at Kingsville, specific appropriations for rural education in both terms, acceptance of federal aid for vocational training in the public schools, and a law permitting former armed service personnel to attend state colleges tuition free. Neff's call for an educational survey commission to review the whole field of education was also approved.

As noted earlier in this chapter, Neff's accomplishments as Baylor president were also substantial and of enduring importance. His labors on behalf of his alma mater began with the Herculean task of saving the institution from financial ruin during the Depression—a task he undertook with extraordinary administrative skill—and continued over the next fifteen years as he made full use of his charismatic powers and promotional instincts on its behalf. During his tenure as president, enrollment at Baylor jumped from 1,200 to more than 4,000, the area of the campus doubled in size, and the university's academic programs and special collections (including the world-renowned Browning Collection) prospered.

Neff's career trajectory, which moved from law to government to higher education administration, was complemented by the spiritual dimension of his life. Born of parents who rested the seventh day each week on their hazardous weeks-long wagon trip from Virginia to Texas, who became pillars of their little church in Eagle Springs, and who lived their religion in their everyday life, Neff came by his deep spiritual principles naturally. His love of the Bible led him to weave favorite verses into his court appearances as an attorney, to leave a marked verse for his successor in the governor's office, and to select the same verse—"Thy word is a lamp unto my feet"—to be inscribed on the side of the building named for him at Baylor University. The same leadership skills that took him to the highest levels of his profession also propelled him to the upper echelons of the Baptist Church organization, where he served as president of the Waco Baptist Association, then the Baptist General Convention of Texas, and finally, the Southern Baptist Convention. He was a popular and effective lay minister, invited often to take the pulpit at churches around the state, and he also provided religious leadership through his daily chapel sessions at Baylor, campus revivals, and his beloved Chautauquas.

Any portrait of Pat Neff must include some mention of his shortcomings and failures, particularly as they relate to his leadership style and performance. As noted elsewhere in this book, he was in many ways a man of contradictions. There was a dramatic contrast between the democratic, consensus-building approach that he used so effectively as Texas Speaker of the House and as head of the State Democratic Convention, and the autocratic approach that he used as governor and as Baylor president. As noted earlier, he chose to work in isolation from rather than in partnership with the legislature when he was governor, with mixed results. As president of Baylor, he was given absolute power by the board of trustees to handle the financial crises of the 1930s—a power he wielded effectively and with relish—but then he found it difficult to relinquish any part of that power, even though he must have known that the autocracy could not and should not be sustained. He was a firm believer in the sanctity of the balance of powers in government, but he failed to maintain that balance as a chief executive, particularly at Baylor. In choosing to serve as the rule-making and rule-enforcing agents as well as the top executive, he eventually fell victim to his own unchecked powers.

A related problem was his failure to delegate. An early version of what we now call a "workaholic," Neff insisted on handling most of his own affairs, including running his own election campaigns, working (in his words) eighteen-hour days in the governor's office, and micromanaging the Baylor faculty and administration. Although this quality in itself is not necessarily a bad thing, in Neff's case it seemed to be tied to his inability to delegate responsibility—and power—to others. This approach took its toll on his relationships with the legislature and the Baylor Board of Trustees.

There was one area in which Neff was absolutely consistent—his lifelong abhorrence of alcohol. He once said, "I was taught at my mother's knee to hate the saloon with the intensity that Hannibal was taught to hate Rome,"[82] and this hatred was manifested through his work on the Anti-Saloon League and other Texas extensions of the Prohibition movement. His intolerance extended almost equally to smoking, dancing, card playing, and other "sinful vices" prohibited by the Baptist religion, and his opposition persisted even as public (and Baptist) standards relaxed a bit after World War II.

In the end, then, Pat Neff was a man a bit out of step with the times, but more than fifty years after his death, he remains a larger-than-life figure in Texas history. Despite his flaws, he provided leadership and direction at a difficult time and under difficult circumstances. As respected historian and educator Rupert N. Richardson observed, "Pat M. Neff earned a place in even a short list of great Texans of all time."[83]

Pat Morris Neff: Condensed Timeline

Noah Neff and Isabella Shepherd marry	10-26-1854
Pat Morris Neff born (last of 9 children)	11-26-1871
Neff arrives at Baylor	12-31-1888
Neff graduates from Baylor with B.A. degree	6-06-1894
Neff begins teaching at Southwestern Academy (Magnolia, Arkansas)	12-03-1894
Neff completes two academic years of teaching at Southwestern	5-1896
Neff enters University of Texas Law School	9-1896
Neff graduates from University of Texas Law School with LL.B. degree	6-1897
Neff begins practice of law in Waco	8-1897
Neff elected to 26th Legislature, Texas House of Representatives	11-08-1898
Neff sworn into office as member of Texas House of Representatives	1-10-1899
Neff marries Myrtle Mainer	5-31-1899
Neff receives master's degree from Baylor	6-1899
Neff elected to 27th Legislature	11-06-1900
Neff sworn into office in 27th Legislature	1-08-1901
Hallie Maude Neff born	4-13-1901
Neff elected to 28th Legislature	11-04-1902
Neff sworn into office and elected Speaker, Texas House	1-13-1903
Pat Neff Jr. born	12-19-1903
Neff's third term in Texas House of Representatives officially ends	1-09-1905
Time in Legislature: 6 years	
Neff elected County Attorney (Prosecuting Attorney), McLennan County	11-06-1906
Neff assumes office as County Attorney	12-12-1906
Neff elected to second term as County Attorney	11-03-1908
Neff elected to third term as County Attorney	11-08-1910
Neff's final term as County Attorney officially ends	12-12-1912
Time as County Attorney: 6 years	
Neff serves as president of Conference on Education in Texas	1913-1915
Neff serves as Grand Chancellor of Knights of Pythias of Texas	1918-1919
Neff announces for Governor	7-27-1919
Neff finishes second to Joseph W. Bailey in primary election	7-24-1920

Neff beats Bailey in runoff election   8-28-1920

Neff wins general election and is elected Governor   11-02-1920

Neff sworn in as 14th Governor since Reconstruction   1-18-1921

Neff wins Democratic Party nomination for second term as Governor   7-22-1922

Neff sworn in as Governor for second term   1-16-1923

Neff's last day as Governor   1-20-1925

Time as Governor: 4 years

Neff serves as president, Baptist General Convention of Texas   1926-1929

Neff confirmed by U.S. Senate as member of U.S. Board of Mediation   2-14-1927

Neff not confirmed by U.S. Senate for reappointment; last day in office   3-04-1929

Time on Board of Mediation: 2 years

Neff sworn in as Chairman, Texas Railroad Commission   10-16-1929

Neff's last day as Chairman, Texas Railroad Commission   1-28-1931

Time as Chairman of Railroad Commission: 1 year, 2 months

Neff continues as elected member, Texas Railroad Commission   1-29-1931

Neff resigns; last day as member, Texas Railroad Commission   6-04-1932

Total time on Railroad Commission: 2 years, 7 months

Neff appointed President, Baylor University   2-23-1932

Neff assumes office as President, Baylor University   6-08-1932

Baylor University Board of Trustees names new administration
building Pat Neff Hall   11-07-1939

Neff serves as president, Southern Baptist Convention   1942-1946

Neff serves as grand master, Masonic Grand Lodge of Texas   1946

Neff resigns as President, Baylor University   11-08-1947

Neff's last day as President, Baylor University   12-31-1947

Total time as President, Baylor University: 15 years, 6 months

Neff's date of death   1-20-1952

Myrtie Neff's date of death   7-19-1953

Hallie Maude Neff Wilcox's date of death   11-21-1977

Pat Neff Jr.'s date of death   1-08-1986

APPENDIX B

Brief History of the
Baylor Alumni Association

The first association for former Baylor students was created by Baylor President Rufus C. Burleson in 1859, fourteen years after Baylor University in Independence was chartered by the Republic of Texas. By June of that year, forty-two former students qualified for membership.[1]

In 1881, the first semblance of an alumni publication appeared. Called the *Baylor Aegis,* the magazine was published only two years. The next alumni-sponsored magazine, called the *Baylor Literary*, was published from 1893 to 1915. In 1909, in conjunction with the first Baylor homecoming, a preliminary directory of alumni was produced.

In 1921, Baylor President Samuel Palmer Brooks recruited Mayes Berhman, a 1916 graduate, to come to the university as Baylor's first full-time alumni secretary at a salary of $3,600 annually.[2] Brooks would give credit to Behrman for the founding in April 1925 of the first publication devoted exclusively to alumni concerns, the *Baylor Monthly.*[3] Dr. J. M. Dawson served as editor of the magazine until the Depression forced the university to suspend publication in 1932 and close the alumni office.

In 1936, President Pat M. Neff pushed for creation of a Baylor Centennial Foundation to plan for the university's Centennial in 1945. As foundation officials began to solicit funding, they discovered that they lacked any comprehensive listing of potential donors.[4] Despite Baylor's being out of official touch with its former students, hundreds of dedicated Baylorites had been meeting in clubs as far away as Los Angeles for many years. As early as the 1930s, Baylor clubs were active in Dallas, Houston, Henderson, Wichita Falls, Gregg County, and other locations in Texas. Many were reactivated with the aid of Nell Whitman Gurley, field secretary for the foundation.[5] To keep in touch with alumni, the university developed a new magazine in 1938, the *Baylor Century*, with Dr. C. D. Johnson serving as editor.

In 1941, the State of Texas granted the Baylor Ex-Students Association a charter. The purpose clause stated that the group sought to "promote all educational and other activities of Baylor."[6]

In the last issue of the *Baylor Century* in August 1946, editor C. D. Johnson introduced Jack Dillard as the head of the Ex-Students Association and declared that the October issue of the magazine (renamed the *Baylor Line*) would be under Dillard's editorship. Dillard had resigned his service with the Federal Bureau of Investigation in the spring of 1946 to become the Ex-Students Association's first full-time executive secretary. Dillard served until 1954 when he moved to Austin to become administrative assistant to Texas Governor Allan Shivers.

In April 1976, the organization changed its name to the Baylor Alumni Association. In 1978, the Alumni Association was legally incorporated as a nonprofit organization and was relocated from the Student Union Building to the new Hughes-Dillard Alumni Center.[7] The organization continued with full-time executive directors, with varying levels of financial help from the university over the years. In 2007, the association launched the Sesquicentennial Campaign in anticipation of its 150th anniversary in 2009. The campaign is designed to raise the organization's endowment to the extent that it could become financially self-sufficient. The association continues to publish the *Baylor Line*, as well as a monthly e-mail newsletter, *Between the Lines.*[8]

Notes—Appendix B

1. Baylor Alumni Association, "History of BAA: Key Dates in the History of the Baylor Alumni Association," online: http://www.bayloralumni.com/index.php?id=25453.

2. Minutes, Baylor University Board of Trustees, March 25, 1921, p. 88; April 20, 1921, p. 93; March 14, 1922, p. 112.

3. President S. P. Brooks, "Alumni Secretary Resigns," *Baylor Monthly*, June 1926.

4. Kent Keeth, "Looking Back," *Baylor Line*, September 1987.

5. Nell Whitman Gurley, ed., *Baylor Bulletin* 40, no. 3 (August 1937).

6. *Baylor Century* 4, no. 6 (May 1942).

7. Baylor Alumni Association, "History of BAA."

8. Online: http://www.baylor.edu/buaa/baylorline/splash.php and http://www.bayloralumni.com/index.php?id=25400 .

The Texas State Song: "Texas, Our Texas"

In 1924 Governor Pat Neff, lamenting the fact that his native state had no state song, initiated a contest with a $1,000 prize for music and lyrics that might be adopted as an official state song. By the contest deadline of December 1, 1924, 286 songs had been submitted. Neff formed a committee of sixteen individuals from all over the state to evaluate the entries. The committee met for two days in Austin and chose "Texas, Our Texas," written by W. J. Marsh and Gladys Yoakum Wright of Fort Worth.* Legislatures in 1925 and 1927 could not agree on the adoption of any song. Finally, the 41st Legislature in 1929 adopted the song originally recommended by Neff's committee. Only one revision has been made since its adoption. In 1959, when Alaska statehood meant Texas was no longer the largest state, the word "Largest" in the third line was changed to "Boldest."

Lyrics

Texas, our Texas! All hail the mighty State!
Texas, our Texas! So wonderful, so great!
Boldest and grandest, Withstanding ev'ry test;
O Empire wide and glorious. You stand supremely blest.

(Refrain) God bless you Texas! And keep you brave and strong,
That you may grow in power and worth, Thro'out the ages long.

Texas, O Texas! Your freeborn single star,
Sends out its radiance to nations near and far;
Emblem of freedom! It sets our hearts aglow,
With thoughts of San Jacinto and glorious Alamo.

(Refrain)

Texas, dear Texas! From tyrant grip now free,
Shines forth in splendor your star of destiny!
Mother of heroes! We come your children true,
Proclaiming our allegiance, our faith, our love for you.†

---

* Pat M. Neff, *Battles of Peace* (Fort Worth: Pioneer Publishing Co., 1925), pp. 195-205.
† Reprinted with permission of Southern Music Company.

APPENDIX D
"That Good Old Baylor Line"

In 1906, a student penned humorous words to the tune of "In the Good Old Summer Time" and they became generally accepted among the student body as the school song. However, in 1931, Mrs. Enid Eastland Markham, wife of music professor Robert Markham, feeling the words were neither dignified enough nor representative of the total university, wrote new lyrics which were presented in chapel in November and soon sanctioned as the official school song. The "Good Old Summer Time" tune was later arranged to fit Mrs. Markham's "Baylor Line" through the work of Jack Goode, Donald I. Moore, and Charles F. Brown. Several other arrangements have been produced as well. *

Lyrics

That good old Baylor line!
That good old Baylor line!
We'll march forever down the years,
As long as stars shall shine.
We'll fling our green and gold afar
To light the ways of time,
And guide us as we onward go;
That good old Baylor line!

Copyright ® 1952, Baylor University.
All rights reserved.

*Reprinted from the Baylor University web site, "Traditions Q & A," http://www.baylor.edu/about/index.php?id=5560.

270

Notes on Endnotes

Pat M. Neff Papers: The authors' research in the Neff Papers in the Texas Collection at Baylor University Library began in the 1990s. At that time, the papers were arranged in the order they had been received from the Neff family in the 1950s. In 2006 the archivists of the Texas Collection began consolidating files with similar contents, arranging series of letters in chronological order, and refiling misfiled items in preparation for microfilming the contents. Because of these imminent changes within the papers, archivist Ellen Brown advised the authors to use only the "Neff Papers" citation without further elaboration. Major subdivisions—e.g., gubernatorial correspondence, Baylor correspondence, job applications, etc.—have been retained in the archive collection. Readers/researchers seeking further information beyond notes included in this book should be able to find that information in the Neff Papers using these major headings.

Location of Other Named Collections/Papers: Collections and papers cited in the endnotes are housed in the following locations (selected list):

> Blodgett Collection (private collection)
> Austin, Texas

> David L. Scott Collection (private collection)
> Gatesville, Texas

> Hallie Maude Neff Wilcox Papers, Texas Collection
> Baylor University, Waco, Texas

> Roberta Keys Torn Collection (private collection)
> Houston, Texas

> National Archives
> Washington, D.C.

Baylor Oral History Program: Dr. Thomas L. Charlton arrived on the Baylor University campus in 1970 and soon found himself serving as chairman of an ad hoc committee on oral history. The committee submitted an ambitious proposal for a Baylor University Program for Oral History (BUPOH), which was approved by Dr. Herbert H. Reynolds, then executive vice-president of Baylor. The name of the program was changed to the Baylor University Institute for Oral History (BUIOH) in August 1982 to reflect its larger role in the state of Texas. The notes in this book have distinguished between oral history memoirs completed under the original program (BUPOH) and those completed under its successor (BUIOH).

Minutes, Baylor University Board of Trustees and Waco Executive Committee: Until March of 1921, actions requiring approval of the policy body of Baylor University were taken by the Baylor Board of Trustees. The board generally met twice each year, one time in Waco and one time in Dallas. On March 25, 1921, in recognition of the increasing growth and complexity of the university's operations, the Baylor Board adopted bylaws that established two executive committees—the Waco Executive Committee (WEC) and the Dallas Executive Committee. The board thus gave cognizance to the two campuses comprising Baylor—the main campus in Waco and the components making up the medical complex in Dallas. The pertinent section of the newly adopted bylaws read: "Such matters as do not require the action of the whole Board may be referred by the Board to the Executive Committee more nearly concerned in the subject matter to be considered." Originally, the minutes of the two executive committees were a part of the minute books of the total board. Beginning with a meeting of the WEC on November 28, 1933, that body initiated its own minute book. However, in many instances, minutes of the WEC were still entered in the minute books of the board. Because of the critical financial problems during the Great Depression and then World War II, the WEC met much more often than the board as a whole and took many actions that one might think should be taken only by the board. Throughout the book, the authors have attributed actions exactly as recorded in the minutes, either by the WEC or by the Baylor Board in its entirety. The minutes are no longer in book form; they are referenced in these notes by date only.

Newspaper Citations: Major Texas newspapers after about 1920 are generally available in multiple locations, including libraries, so the endnotes do not provide source locations for news articles from 1920 forward. Earlier newspapers may be less accessible, and therefore locations are provided; a large number of early news clippings are archived in the Neff Papers.

The Baylor Student Newspaper: Over the years, the student newspaper at Baylor was alternately named the *Daily Lariat,* the *Lariat,* and the *Baylor Lariat.* The endnotes use the name associated with the particular article cited.

Endnotes

Chapter 1. Gone to Texas

1. This scene is a composite description of the sequence of events leading up to Neff's encounter with Melvin Maxwell.

2. Melvin Maxwell, interview by David L. Scott, Dorothy Blodgett, and Terrell Blodgett, September 26, 1998, Blodgett Collection.

3. Neff to Pat Jr., February 23, 1945, Neff Papers.

4. Theme, Pat Neff, Baylor University, February 1890, Neff Papers.

5. Joel Blair to Noah Neff, January 16, 1852, Neff Papers.

6. Notebook of Pat Neff, Neff Papers, as quoted in Macklyn Ward Hubbell, "The Life of Pat Neff," master's thesis, University of Houston, Houston, Texas, 1953, p. 5.

7. Pat Neff, interview by R. Bryan Nichols, n.d., as quoted in R. Bryan Nichols, "Pat M. Neff: His Boyhood and Early Political Career," master's thesis, Baylor University, Waco, Texas, 1951, p. 8.

8. Isabella Neff to David Deyerle, February 26, 1855, Neff Papers.

9. Noah Neff to David Deyerle, February 26, 1855, Neff Papers.

10. Hubbell, "The Life of Pat Neff," pp. 6-7.

11. Theme, Pat Neff, Baylor University, February 1890, Neff Papers.

12. Noah Neff to David Deyerle, September 3, 1856, Neff Papers.

13. Ibid.

14. Patsy Neff to Neff, April 17, 1944, Patsy Britton Collection.

15. David L. Scott, *On the Banks of Onion Creek, The Eagle Springs Baptist Church, 140th Anniversary* (Gatesville, Tex., 1998), p. 1.

16. Neff Family Bible, Neff Papers.

17. Notes on brochure from an interview with Pat Neff, undated, Neff Papers.

18. John Holt, "This is Pat Neff," *Bulletin of the Southern Baptist Convention*, January 1943, p. 4, as quoted in Chase Sherwin Winfrey, "Pat Morris Neff: A Personality-Oratorical Study," Ph.D. diss., University of Denver, Denver, Colorado, 1951, p. 7.

19. Isabella Neff to David Deyerle, February 21, 1861, Neff Papers.

20. Ibid.

21. 1850 Census, Roanoke County, Virginia, pp. 310, 317.

22. Tax receipts, Neff Papers.

23. Mildred Watkins Mears, "Coryell County Scrapbook, 1863," Statement by Noah Neff, p. 188.

24. Government document, 1867, Neff Papers.

25. 1870 Census, Coryell County, Texas, p. 290.

26. Coryell County Deeds, Coryell County Clerk's Office, Gatesville, Texas, Book F, pp. 404-405.

27. Mrs. Patsy Neff, interview by Macklyn Ward Hubbell, April 23, 1953, as quoted in Hubbell, "The Life of Pat Neff," p. 9.

28. Neff to Crawford, September 2, 1920; Neff to Curry, September 11, 1951; both in Neff Papers.

29. Isabella to Cefe Shepherd, January 22, 1872, Neff Papers.

30. Betty Seawright and Edgar Perryman, interview by David L. Scott, September 13, 2004, David L. Scott Collection.

31. Pat Neff Jr., interview by Macklyn Ward Hubbell, April 6, 1953, as quoted in Hubbell, "The Life of Pat Neff," p. 10.

32. Ibid., April 7, 1953, p. 12.

33. Neff to Mother Neff, March 22, 1918, Charlotte Calvert Papers, David L. Scott Collection.

34. Clay Patterson, interview by Dorothy Blodgett, January 10, 1992, Blodgett Collection.

35. J. M. Price, ed., *Ten Men from Baylor* (Kansas City, Kan.: Central Seminary Press, 1945), p. 29.

36. Pat Neff, interview by Chase Sherwin Winfrey, April 16, 1951, as quoted in Winfrey, "Pat Morris Neff," p. 12.

37. Hubbell, "The Life of Pat Neff," pp. 12-13.

38. Theme, Pat Neff, Baylor University, February 1890, Neff Papers.

39. Ibid.

40. David B. Parker, "Bill Arp (Charles Henry Smith, 1826-1903)," *New Georgia Encyclopedia*, online: www.georgiaencyclopedia.org/nge/Article.jsp?id=h-757&hl=y .

41. Winfrey, "Pat Morris Neff," p. 13.

42. Neff Family Bible, Neff Papers.

43. R. G. Lee, "Interview of Pat M. Neff," n.d., as quoted in Nichols, "Pat M. Neff," p. 24.

44. Neff to Mother Neff, March 22, 1918, Charlotte Calvert Papers, David L. Scott Collection.

45. Theme, Pat Neff, Baylor University, February 1890, Neff Papers.

46. Ibid.

47. District Court Records, McLennan County District Clerk's Office, Waco, Texas; *Waco Daily News*, December 10, 1890.

48. Records of the U.S. District Court for the Western District, San Antonio Division, RG21.46.48, National Archives, Southwest Region, Federal Records Center, Fort Worth, Texas; see also Jeff Burton, "No Train Robbers Ever Worked Harder at Their Trade Than the Cornett-Whitley Gang," *True West*, February-March 1973, pp. 18-53.

49. Sallie Calvert to Neff, January 27, 1889, Neff Papers.

50. Mother Neff to Neff, November 13, 1889, Neff Papers.

51. Mother Neff to Neff, March 9, 1890, Neff Papers.

Chapter 2. Riding to Baylor

1. *Waco News-Tribune*, July 31, 1917. Neff made this statement more than eighteen years after his arrival at Baylor.

2. Edward Neff, "Pat Neff," 1935, Marie Taylor Neff Papers, David L. Scott Collection.

3. Ledger, Neff Papers.

4. Theme, Pat Neff, Baylor University, "How I Spent the Holidays," undated, Neff Papers.

5. Neff to Myrtie Mainer, July 1892, Neff Papers.

6. Mother Neff to Neff, May 29, 1891, Neff Papers.

7. Neff to Myrtie Mainer, July 1892, Neff Papers.

8. Neff to Mother Neff, February 7, 1892, Neff Papers.

9. Neff to Myrtie Mainer, July 1892, Neff Papers.

10. Myrtie Mainer to Neff, September 25, 1892, Neff Papers.

11. Neff to Myrtie Mainer, February 26, 1893, Neff Papers.

12. Neff to Mother Neff, October 4, 1892, Neff Papers.

13. Myrtie Mainer to Neff, October 4, 1892, Neff Papers.

14. Myrtie Mainer to Neff, October 29, 1892, Neff Papers.

15. Neff to Myrtie Mainer, December 4, 1892, Neff Papers.

16. Neff to Mother Neff, April 2, 1893, Neff Papers.

17. Academic records, Pat Neff, Baylor University, 1892-1893, Texas Collection.

18. Neff to Myrtie Mainer, May 7, 1893, Neff Papers.

19. Neff to Myrtie Mainer, July 29, 1893, Neff Papers.

20. "Voices from the 1893 World's Columbian Exposition," http://japan.park.org/Guests/WWWvoice/1893chi.html.

21. Neff to Mother Neff, August 14, 1893, Neff Papers.

22. Neff to Mother Neff, August 21, 1893, Neff Papers.

23. "Voices from the 1893 World's Columbian Exposition."

24. Neff to Sallie Neff Calvert, August 1893, Charlotte Calvert Papers, David L. Scott Collection.

25. Neff to Myrtie Mainer, August 23, 1893, Neff Papers.

26. Academic records, Pat Neff, Baylor University, 1893-1894, Texas Collection.

27. Neff to Mother Neff, October 6, 1893, Neff Papers.

28. Neff to Sallie Neff Calvert, September 6, 1893, Charlotte Calvert Papers, David L. Scott Collection.

29. Neff to Mother Neff, November 14, 1893, Neff Papers.

30. Neff to Mother Neff, January 14, 1894, Neff Papers.

31. Neff to Myrtie Mainer, September 8, 1894, Neff Papers.

32. Neff to Myrtie Mainer, August 4, 1894, Neff Papers.

33. Neff to Myrtie Mainer, August 13, 1894, Neff Papers.

34. Neff to Myrtie Mainer, August 4, 1894, Neff Papers.

35. Neff to Mother Neff, November 10, 1894, Neff Papers.

36 Ibid.

37. Neff to Myrtie Mainer, November 29, 1894, Neff Papers.

38. Neff to Mother Neff, January 27, 1895, Neff Papers.

39. Neff to Myrtie Mainer, January 27, 1895, Neff Papers.

40. Neff to Mother Neff, March 24, 1895, Neff Papers.

41. Neff to Mother Neff, October 27, 1895, Charlotte Calvert Papers, David L. Scott Collection.

42. Winston P. Wilson, *Harvey Couch: The Master Builder* (Nashville, Tenn.: Broadman Press, 1947), pp. 18-22, 84, 200-205.

43. "Harvey Crowley Couch, 1877-1941," *Encyclopedia of Arkansas History and Culture* (Little Rock, Ark.: Butler Center for Arkansas Studies, 2006).

44. The Baylor University Law School, organized in 1857, closed in 1883 and did not reopen until 1920.

45. Guittard to Neff, January 17, 1897, Neff Papers.

46. Neff to Myrtie Mainer, September 2, 1896, Neff Papers.

47. Jim Nicar, "A Holiday with a Spiked Cannon," Texas Exes UT Heritage Society, Texas Exes-University of Texas Alumni Association, Austin, Texas, n.d.

48. Neff to Ben Neff, January 24, 1897, Neff Papers.

49. Neff to Myrtie Mainer, January 3, 1897, Neff Papers.

50. Neff to Ben Neff, January 24, 1897, Neff Papers.

51. Ibid.

52. Tom Connally, with Alfred Steinberg, *My Name is Tom Connally* (New York: Thomas Y. Crowell Company, 1954), pp. 30-32; *The Cactus* (Austin: University of Texas, 1897), pp. 52-58; Neff to Mother Neff, March 14, 1897, Neff Papers. See also *Waco News-Tribune*, March 1, 1941; *Austin Daily Statesman*, March 3-4, 1897; *Daily Texan*, March 1, 1959; Margaret Catherine Berry, *UT Austin: Traditions and Nostalgia* (Austin: Shoal Creek Publishers, Inc., 1975), pp. 81-82; *The Alcalde* (weekly journal), University of Texas, March 3, 1897; George H. Carter, "Who Spiked the Cannon?" *The Alcalde* (magazine)1, no. 1 (April 1913); Nicar, "A Holiday with a Spiked Cannon."

53. Nicar, "A Holiday with a Spiked Cannon."

54. Neff to Mother Neff, March 14, 1897, Neff Papers.

55. Ibid.

56. See chapters 9 and 10 in this book for descriptions of Neff's often draconian approach to disciplining students in his early years as president of Baylor.

57. Neff to Mother Neff, May 14, 1897, Neff Papers.

58. Neff to Sallie Neff Calvert, September 9, 1897, Charlotte Calvert Papers, David L. Scott Collection.

59. Neff would finish his coursework a year later. Neff to Mother Neff, January 4, 1899, Neff Papers.

Chapter 3. Mr. Speaker

1. Kansas State Historical Society, "Carry Nation: The Famous and Original Bar Room Smasher," online exhibit: http://www.kshs.org/exhibits/carry/carry1.htm.

2. Samuel Eliot Morison, *The Oxford History of the American People,* vol. 3 (New York: Meridian, 1994), pp. 117-129.

3. Tom Connally, with Alfred Steinberg, *My Name is Tom Connally* (New York: Thomas Y. Crowell Company, 1954), p. 38.

4. Joe B. Frantz, *Texas: A Bicentennial History* (New York: W. W. Norton, 1976), p. 148.

5. Robert C. Cotner, et al., *James Stephen Hogg, A Biography* (Austin and London: University of Texas Press, 1959), p. vii.

6. *Handbook of Texas Online,* s.v. "Waco, Texas," http://www.tsha.utexas.edu/handbook/online/articles/WW/hdw1.html .

7. Ibid.

8. Tony Duty, "Waco at the Turn of the Century," *Waco Heritage and History* 3, no. 2 (summer 1972): 14.

9. Ibid.

10. *Handbook of Texas Online,* s.v. "Cooper, Madison Alexander Jr.," http://www.tsha.utexas.edu/handbook/online/articles/CC/fco59.html .

11. Ibid.

12. Handwritten notes, Madison Cooper Papers, Texas Collection, Baylor University, Waco, Texas.

13. *Waco Times-Herald,* April 26, 1898, Neff Papers.

14. Neff to Myrtie, April 8, 1898, Neff Papers.

15. Myrtie to Neff, April 14, 1898, Neff Papers.

16. Neff to Myrtie, May 24, 1898, Neff Papers.

17. Myrtie to Neff, August 28, 1898, Neff Papers.

18. See letters between Neff and Myrtie, August to October 1898, Neff Papers.

19. Minutes, Commissioners Court, McLennan County, Texas, January 5, 1899.

20. Neff to Mother Neff, November 12, 1898, Neff Papers.

21. *Austin Daily Statesman,* December 21, 1898, Neff Papers.

22. Rupert Norval Richardson, *Colonel Edward M. House: The Texas Years, 1858-1912* (Abilene, Tex.: Hardin-Simmons University, 1964).

23. *House Journal,* 26th Leg., Reg. Sess., 1899, January 10, 1899, p. 2.

24. Neff to Mother Neff, January 27, 1899, Neff Papers.

25. Neff to Myrtie, August 2, 1898, Neff Papers.

26. Neff to Myrtie, January 24, 1899, Neff Papers.

27. Neff to Mother Neff, April 4, 1899, Neff Papers.

28. "The Freeze of 1899 and Other Phenomena of Waco Weather," *Waco Heritage and History* 15, no. 2 (Winter 1986): 1-2.

29. Ibid., p. 4.

30. Robert M. Utley, *Lone Star Lawmen: The Second Century of the Texas Rangers* (New York: Oxford University Press, 2007), pp. 217-220; A. R. "Babe" Schwartz, telephone interview

by Terrell Blodgett, April 27, 2007, Blodgett Collection. Schwartz, a veteran legislator, said he hosted two trips to Galveston in the 1980s, but the experience wasn't the same as in the past and he didn't make a further attempt to revive the tradition.

31. *House Journal*, 26th Leg., Reg. Sess., 1899, May 4, 1899, p. 1199.

32. *Waco Times-Herald*, May 1, 1899, Neff Papers.

33. Ibid.

34. Some agencies received increases of 5-10 percent, but none rivaled the 23 percent increase for the University of Texas. *General and Special Laws of the State of Texas*, 25th Leg., 1st Called Sess., 1897, pp. 17-38; 26th Leg., Reg. Sess., 1899, pp. 267-297.

35. Normal colleges later became "teachers' colleges." The word "normal" in this context came from the Latin word *norma*, originally a carpenter's square, a device used to create right angles. W. H. Bruce, president of North Texas State Normal College, offered this description to the Legislative Committee to Make a Survey of Higher Education in Texas in 1923: "In an abstract sense, a carpenter's square is a pattern for perpendicularity, so a norm came to refer to a pattern of behavior or a standard of measurement. 'Normal' took on the meaning of 'standard-ized' or 'uniform,' and normal schools aimed to turn out standardized teachers." *Senate Journal*, 38th Leg., Reg. Sess., 1923, January 22, 1923, pp. 220-221. The names of the various state colleges were not changed from "normal" colleges to "state teachers" colleges until 1923.

36. See letters between Neff and his mother and between Neff and Myrtie, January to March 1899, Neff Papers.

37. Neff to Myrtie, August 2, 1896, Neff Papers.

38. Myrtie to Neff, January 17, 1899, Neff Papers.

39. *Crockett Courier*, June 16, 1899, Neff Papers.

40. Neff to Mother Neff, June 16, 1899, Neff Papers.

41. Neff to Mother Neff, November 25, 1899, Neff Papers.

42. *Waco Times-Herald*, May 8, 1899, Neff Papers.

43. See discussion in chapter 5. See also letters from Hoge to Neff, June 16, 1920; Sandefer to Neff, June 21, 1920; and Scott to Neff, June 22, 1920; all in Neff Papers.

44. Neff to Mother Neff, January 26, 1900, Neff Papers.

45. *Who's Who in America*, vol. 11, 1920-1921 (Chicago: A. N. Marquis and Co., 1920), p. 2081.

46. *Waco Times-Herald*, May 7, 1899, Neff Papers.

47. *Houston Post*, April 30,1900, Neff Papers.

48. Minutes, McLennan County Commissioners Court, vol. F, p. 305.

49. David G. McComb, *Galveston: A History* (Austin: University of Texas Press, 1986), p. 122.

50. James A. Clark and Michel T. Halbouty, *Spindletop* (New York: Random House, 1952), p. 79.

51. Connally, *My Name is Tom Connally*.

52. *House Journal*, 27th Leg., Reg. Sess., 1901, February 14, 1901, p. 383.

53. *Senate Journal*, 27th Leg., Reg. Sess., 1901, January 23, 1901, pp. 95-97.

54. *Waco Times-Herald*, February 11, 1901, Neff Papers.

55. Neff to Mother Neff, February 26, 1901, Neff Papers.

56. Her first name came from Myrtie's friend Hallie Crook of Crockett, her middle name from Maud (without the *e*) Davenport Neff, the wife of Neff's brother, David Leslie Neff. Throughout her life, her middle name would be spelled both "Maude" and "Maud." Since her birth certificate and marriage certificate both give the former spelling, it will be used throughout the book.

57. Neff to Mother Neff, April 15, 1901, Neff Papers.

58. Frederic D. Ogden, *The Poll Tax in the South* (University, Ala.: University of Alabama Press, 1958), p. 11.

59. *San Antonio Express,* October 25, 1902, as quoted in Laura Snow, "The Poll Tax in Texas: Its Historical, Legal, and Fiscal Aspects," master's thesis, University of Texas, Austin, Texas, 1936, pp. 47-48.

60. Alwyn Barr, *Black Texans* (Austin: Jenkins, 1973), pp. 79-80.

61. Abner McCall, Oral Memoirs, interview by Thomas Lee Charlton and Thomas E. Turner Sr., September 14, 1981, p. 245, Baylor University Institute for Oral History, Waco, Texas, hereafter cited as BUIOH.

62. Walter L. Buenger, *The Path to a Modern South: Northeast Texas between Reconstruction and the Great Depression* (Austin: University of Texas Press, 2001), p. 88.

63. See discussion in chapter 7. See also *San Antonio Express,* March 16, 1923. The bill passed was Senate Bill 44, and is on page 74 in the *General Laws of the State of Texas,* passed by the 38th Legislature, lst, 2nd, and 3rd Called Sessions.

64. *Waco Times-Herald,* May 9, 1902, Neff Papers.

65. Office of Elections Administrator, McLennan County, Texas, *Record of Election Returns,* vol. 1, p. 3, 1902.

66. John Nance Garner to Neff, November 4, 1901, Neff Papers.

67. Hogg to Neff, December 4, 1902, Neff Papers.

68. J. W. Baines to Buck Gray, October 21, 1902, Neff Papers.

69. *House Journal,* 28th Leg., Reg. Sess., 1903, January 13, 1903, pp. 1-6.

70. Ibid., p. 8.

71. Connally, *My Name is Tom Connally,* p. 52.

72. *House Journal,* 28th Leg., Reg. Sess., 1903, January 13, 1903, pp. 8-9.

73. *Presiding Officers of the Texas Legislature, 1846-2002* (Austin: Texas House of Representatives, 2002).

74. *House Journal,* 28th Leg., Reg. Sess., 1903, January 16, 1903, pp. 75-82.

75. Neff made this claim numerous times. He also did not correct others who made it on his behalf. See S. P. Brooks, "Biographical Sketch," in Pat M. Neff, *A Collection of Twenty-three Addresses* (Waco: Philomathesian Literary Society, Baylor University, c. 1914.), Neff Papers. Also see Emma Morrill Shirley, "The Administration of Pat M. Neff, Governor of Texas, 1921-1925," *Baylor Bulletin* 41 (December 1938): 5.

76. *House Journal,* 28th Leg., Reg. Sess., 1903, January 21 1903, p. 118 (appeal withdrawn); *House Journal,* 28th Leg., Reg. Sess., 1903, February 19, 1903, p. 444 (ruling of speaker sustained); *House Journal,* 28th Leg., 1st Called Sess., 1903, April 7, 1903, p. 11

(ruling of speaker sustained).

77. *House Journal*, 28th Leg., Reg. and Called Sess., 1903.

78. Original Myers Capitol Drawings, Drawing No. 004—Mylar, Archives and Information Services Division, Texas State Library and Archives Commission, Austin, Texas.

79. Bonnie Ann Campbell, "Furnishing the Texas State Capitol," *Southwestern Historical Quarterly* 92, no. 2 (October 1988): 334.

80. *Austin Daily Statesman*, January 29, 1891, and March 4, 1895, Austin History Center.

81. Ibid., February 24, 1897.

82. Neff to Jung, November 14, 1938, Neff Papers.

83. Theodosia Bell, as quoted in *Today in Texas* 4, no. 5 (May 1945), Neff Papers.

84. Pat Stoffregen, "Our Great White Father," paper, History 204, Baylor University, Winter Quarter 1947, p. 12; R. Bryan Nichols, "Pat M. Neff: His Boyhood and Early Political Career," master's thesis, Baylor University, Waco, Texas, 1951, Neff Papers. Both papers were written during Neff's lifetime and contain information from interviews with Neff, although the occupancy of the apartment is not cited specifically as coming from an interview. See also the speech by Emma Shirley to Daughters of the American Revolution, undated, Neff Papers.

85. Judy Zelio, Program Director, Fiscal Affairs, National Conference of State Legislatures, telephone interview by Terrell Blodgett, November 8, 2006, Blodgett Collection.

86. The boy's full name was Pat Mainer Neff Jr. (Mainer was Myrtie's maiden name). Strictly speaking, he was not a "junior," as his father was named Pat Morris Neff. The Mainer middle name was later carried on with the son and grandson of Pat Jr.— Pat M. Neff III and Pat M. Neff IV.

87. *Austin Statesman*, April 2, 1903, Neff Papers.

88. Neff to Myrtie, October 3, 1901, Neff Papers.

89. Myrtie to Mother Neff, August 15, 1904, Neff Papers.

90. A review of a dozen medical books in the Texas Medical Association library, all written between 1880 and 1930 but most around the turn of the century, revealed a wide discrepancy in medical opinion regarding the use of beer to aid nursing mothers in lactation. See, for example, Alfred Cleveland Cotton, M.D., *The Medical Diseases of Infancy and Childhood* (Philadelphia: J. P. Lippincott, 1906), pp. 96-98.

91. *Texas State Journal of Medicine*, December 11, 1911.

92. Anthony Whitmars, "The Disappearance of Neurasthenia," *Emerge* (summer 1998). Online: http://home.vicnet.net.au/~mecfs/general/neurasthenia.html. See also David G. Schuster, "Neurasthenia and a Modernizing America," *Journal of the American Medical Association* 290, no. 17 (November 5, 2003): 2327-2328.

93. Leland E. Hinsie, M.D., and Robert Jean Campbell, M.D., *Psychiatric Dictionary* (London: Oxford University Press, 1970).

94. *Austin Statesman*, March 18, 1903, Neff Papers.

95. *Austin Statesman*, May 4, 1903.

Chapter 4. Prosecuting and Defending: Prelude to Higher Office

1. *West News*, July 31, 1905, Neff Papers.

2. *Houston Post*, October 8, 1905, Neff Papers.

3. *Texas Baptist Annual* (Waco: Baptist General Convention of Texas, 1904), p. 89.

4. Minutes, Baylor University Board of Trustees, June 5, 1905, Texas Collection, Baylor University, Waco, Texas.

5. *Texas Baptist Annual* (Dallas: Baptist General Convention of Texas, 1905), p. 13.

6. Campaign booklet, undated, Neff Papers.

7. Campaign flyer, undated, Neff Papers.

8. *Waco Times-Herald*, August 2, 1906, Neff Papers; Office of McLennan County Elections Administrator, *Record of Election Returns*, vol. 1, p. 26.

9. *McLennan County Deed Records*, vol. 189, p. 37, release recorded October 23, 1907.

10. Myrtie to Mother Neff, January 6, 1907, Neff Papers.

11. Neff to Mother Neff, July 22, 1907, Neff Papers.

12. Announcement flyer, undated, Neff Papers.

13. Minutes, Baylor University Board of Trustees, November 19, 1907, p. 49.

14. Various city directories and Baylor publications.

15. *Waco Semi-Weekly Tribune*, October 2, 1909, Neff Papers.

16. *Peoria Star*, June 19, 1908, Neff Papers.

17. Postcard, Neff to Mother Neff, June 18, 1908, Neff Papers.

18. Rosa McClintock to Mother Neff, October 1, 1908, Neff Papers.

19. *Waco Semi-Weekly Tribune,* August 5, 1908, Neff Papers.

20. Office of McLennan County Elections Administrator, *Record of Election Returns*, vol. 1, p. 43.

21. *Waco Semi-Weekly Tribune*, November 6, 1909, Neff Papers.

22. Ibid.

23. Ibid.

24. Pat M. Neff, *A Collection of Twenty-three Addresses* (Waco: Philomathesian Literary Society, Baylor University, c. 1914), pp. 80-104.

25. *Waco Semi-Weekly Tribune*, April 3, 1910, Waco-McLennan County Library, Waco, Texas.

26. Burns to Neff, August 17, 1909, Neff Papers; *Waco Semi-Weekly Tribune*, January 2, 1909, Neff Papers.

27. Endowment Bond marked "paid" by E. H. Sparkman, May 5, 1915, Neff Papers.

28. *Austin Tribune*, March 12, 1909, Neff Papers.

29. *Waco Tribune-Herald*, October 15, 1961, Neff Papers. See also Lavonia Jenkins Barnes, *The Texas Cotton Palace* (Waco: Heritage Society of Waco, 1964).

30. Pat M. Neff, *Making Texans: Five Minute Declamations* (Austin: Gammel's Bookstore, n.d.).

31. As quoted in *Waco Semi-Weekly Tribune*, May 14, 1910, Neff Papers.

32. *Waco Times-Herald*, July 26, 1910, Neff Papers.

33. Office of McLennan County Elections Administrator, *Record of Election Returns*, vol. 1, p. 53.

34. *Waco Semi-Weekly Tribune*, October 25, 1911, Neff Papers.

35. Ibid.

36. Alvin V. Sellers, *Classics of the Bar: Stories of the World's Great Legal Trials and a Compilation of Forensic Masterpieces*, vol. 5 (Baxley, Ga.: Classic Publishing Co., 1919), pp. 143-180.

37. Neff, *Collection of Twenty-three Addresses*, pp. 138-174.

38. *Waco Times-Herald*, October 20, 1912, Neff Papers.

39. *Waco Daily Times-Herald*, October 11, 1912, Neff Papers.

40. Neff to Mother Neff, October 12, 1912, Neff Papers.

41. 167 S.W. 733, *Southwestern Reports, Annotated (Texas Cases)*, vols. 167 and 168, June–August 1914 (St. Paul, Minn.: West Publishing Co., 1914).

42. Neff to Sharp, October 13, 1933, Neff Papers.

43. *Waco Semi-Weekly Tribune*, November 2, 1912, Neff Papers.

44. Neff, *Collection of Twenty-three Addresses*, pp. 214-220.

45. Interview with Bob McClain, McLennan County District Clerk, by Chase Winfrey, June 5, 1951, as quoted in Chase Sherwin Winfrey, "Pat Morris Neff: A Personality-Oratorical Study," Ph.D. diss., University of Denver, Denver, Colorado, 1951, p. 50.

46. Interview with Neff, May 6, 1951, as quoted in ibid., p. 42.

47. "Final Report of County Attorney Pat M. Neff for the Two Years Ending December 12, 1912," Neff Papers. During Neff's tenure as prosecuting attorney, he was assisted by an able group of assistants who became well known in their own careers. These included John B. McNamara, who succeeded Neff; Harvey Richey, who later became a judge; and Alva Bryan, who had been with Neff since his first election in 1906. Bryan later became a member of the Baylor Board of Trustees and was active in Masonic Lodge, holding its highest position in the state at one time.

48. Abner Vernon McCall, Oral Memoirs, interview by Thomas Lee Charlton, W. Frank Newton, and R. Matthew Dawson, June 2, 1975, pp. 123-125, Baylor University Institute for Oral History, Waco, Texas, hereafter cited as BUIOH.

49. Myrtie to Mother Neff, September 1911, Neff Papers.

50. Mrs. L. V. Johnson to Mother Neff, May 8, 1912, Neff Papers.

51. Myrtie to Mother Neff, October 11, 1912, Neff Papers.

52. Sallie Neff Calvert to Mother Neff, October 25, 1912, Neff Papers.

53. Tabulation from numerous court cases, Blodgett Collection.

54. *Terrell v. Middleton*, Supreme Court of Texas, motion for rehearing denied, March 28, 1917; 108 Tex. 14 at 39.

55. Lemly became one of the celebrated heroes of the chiropractic profession, serving as president of the Texas Chiropractic Association in 1920-1921 and pursuing the establishment of the Texas Chiropractic Examiners Board.

56. Pat Ireland Nixon, M.D., *A History of the Texas Medical Association, 1853-1953* (Austin: University of Texas Press, 1953), p. 312.

57. *Waco Times-Herald*, December 1, 1916, Neff Papers.

58. *Waco Morning News*, December 1, 1916, Neff Papers.

59. Texas Court of Criminal Appeals, decision affirmed, June 19, 1918; 84 Tex. Crim. 115; 205 S.W. 662.

60. Neff argument to jury, Frank Finks trial, Neff Papers.

61. Conduct Register, 43058-44968, State Penitentiaries, Huntsville, Texas, Texas State Archives, Texas State Library and Archives Commission, p. 248.

62. Cicely S. Goff, "The Conference for Education in Texas," class paper, Education 384s, 1929, Frederick Eby Papers, Texas Collection, Baylor University.

63. C. E. Evans, *The Story of Texas Schools* (Austin: Steck Company, 1955), p. 115.

64. Frederick Eby, *The Development of Education in Texas* (New York: Macmillan Company, 1925), p. 221.

65. Arthur Gray Jones, *Thornton Rogers Sampson, 1852-1915* (Richmond, Va.: Richmond Press, 1917), pp. 117-118.

66. Oran Lonnie Sinclair, "Samuel Palmer Brooks, President of Baylor University, 1902-1920," master's thesis, Baylor University, Waco, Texas, 1961, p. 268. See also Lewis L. Gould, *Progressives and Prohibitionists: Texas Democrats in the Wilson Era* (Austin: University of Texas Press, 1973). The details of the Senate race are covered in depth by Gould in his coverage of politics during that era. Gould researched the papers of Bailey, Colquitt, and Campbell as well as numerous other sources to present a comprehensive account of the campaign.

67. Tom Connally, with Alfred Steinberg, *My Name is Tom Connally* (New York: Thomas Y. Crowell Company, 1954), p. 66.

68. *Waco Morning News*, May 16, 1916, Neff Papers.

69. National Association for the Advancement of Colored People (NAACP), "The Waco Horror," supplement to *Crisis*, July 1916.

70. *Waco Morning News*, May 16, 1916; *Waco Semi-Weekly Tribune*, May 17, 1916; both in Neff Papers.

71. James M. SoRelle, "The Waco Horror: The Lynching of Jesse Washington," paper presented to annual meeting of the Texas State Historical Association, reprinted in *Southwestern Historical Quarterly* 86, no. 4 (April 1983): 532.

72. The terrible event was revisited in a recent book by Patricia Bernstein, *The First Waco Horror: The Lynching of Jesse Washington and the Rise of the NAACP*, published by Texas A&M University Press in 2005. Reviews of this book publicized the story again, and an editorial in the May 3, 2005, issue of the *Houston Chronicle* called for Waco to acknowledge the atrocity as a cleansing mechanism to "boldly expose a past it rejects." In 2006, the Waco City Council approved a resolution "condemning lynchings that occurred in the past" without specifically mentioning the Jesse Washington lynching. A month earlier, the McLennan County Commissioners Court had refused to adopt a similar resolution. See *Austin American-Statesman*, June 21, 2006, and *Austin American-Statesman*, May 17, 2006. For more treatment of lynching in Central Texas generally, including that of Jesse Washington, see also William D. Carrigan, *The Making of a Lynching Culture: Violence and Vigilantism in Central Texas, 1836-1916* (Urbana and Chicago: University of Illinois Press, 2004).

73. *Waco Semi-Weekly Tribune*, October 13, 1917, Waco-McLennan County Public Library, Waco, Texas.

74. Ibid.

75. *Waco Morning News*, October 21, 1917, and October 24, 1917, Neff Papers.

76. *Dallas Morning News*, October 20, 1918 (recounting one year after Prohibition election in Dallas); *Waco Semi-Weekly Tribune,* August 25, 1917, Neff Papers.

77. *Fort Worth Record*, May 16, 1918, Neff Papers.

78. *Texas Pythian News-Nuggets*, August-September 1919, Neff Papers.

79. *Handbook of Texas Online*, s.v. "Knights of Pythias," http://www.tsha.utexas.edu/handbook/online/articles/KK/vnk1.html .

80. Only a few of the Children's Home's graduates had been able to go on to college. These included Blair Cherry, who later became head football coach at the University of Texas. On one of Neff's trips, he discovered that three of the girls who would be graduating from high school in 1919 desired to enter Baylor University in the fall. He took personal responsibility for their education but gave other Pythians the opportunity to contribute $5 to assist; Neff's papers record $5 donations for the girls from a number of friends, including Congressman Tom Connally.

81. Neff to Mother Neff, October 8, 1918, Charlotte Calvert Papers, David L. Scott Collection.

82. See discussion in chapter 5 of the alleged discrepancy in records of Neff's birthdate and the accusation that he avoided the draft.

83. Minutes, First Baptist Church, Waco, Texas, February 16, 1918, Texas Collection, Baylor University.

84. Emma Shirley, "Mrs. Pat M. Neff," as quoted in Ray Earl Bennett, "Pat M. Neff: His Denominational Leadership," master's thesis, Baylor University, Waco, Texas, 1959, p. 10.

85. Joseph Martin Dawson, *A Thousand Months to Remember: An Autobiography* (Waco: Baylor University Press, 1964).

86. See minutes, Baylor University Board of Trustees, 1913-1919.

87. Neff to Mother Neff, September 1, 1915, Charlotte Calvert Papers, David L. Scott Collection.

88. Hallie Maude to Neff, unknown date, 1917, Neff Papers.

89. *Baptist Standard*, March 6, 1919, Texas Baptist Historical Collection.

90. Mineral Wells is a small town about forty miles west of Fort Worth. Not long after the discovery of its "magic" water in 1877, the destination was drawing visitors from all thirty-eight states. According to J. W. Register: "In the early 1900s, visitors to Mineral Wells, a town of 8,000 inhabitants, numbered 150,000 annually; in one twelve-month period (from 1902 to 1903), the railroad sold 45,000 tickets to Mineral Wells." Register, "Mineral Wells, Famous Resort," *Texas Magazine* 2, no. 3 (July 1910): 63-64, as quoted in Janet Mace Valenza, *Taking the Waters in Texas: Springs, Spas, and Fountains of Youth* (Austin: University of Texas Press, 2000), p. 40. Valenza's book contains an excellent summary of the history of baths and springs worldwide before discussing in great detail their development in Texas. Her book, extensively researched and documented, lists over 200 "medicinal wells and springs" in Texas that were in operation at one time or another.

Chapter 5. From a Mule to an Airplane: Campaigning for Governor

1. Ledger titled "Fees and Expenses, Year 1917, Pat M. Neff"; "Fees for Year 1918"; both in Hallie Maude Neff Wilcox Papers, Texas Collection, Baylor University.

2. *General Laws of the State of Texas,* 35th Leg., 1st Called Sess., 1917, pp. 117, 198.

3. O'Bryan to Neff, February 17, 1916; Matthews to Neff, November 1, 1917; *Kosse Cyclone,* n.d., 1915; all in Neff Papers.

4. James A. Clark, with Weldon Hart, *The Tactful Texan: A Biography of Governor Will Hobby* (New York: Random House, 1958), p. 143; Jean Houston Daniel, Price Daniel, and Dorothy Blodgett, *The Texas Governor's Mansion: A History of the House and Its Occupants* (Austin: Texas State Library and Archives Commission; Liberty: Sam Houston Regional Library and Research Center, 1984), p. 150.

5. Clark, *The Tactful Texan,* pp. 45-47.

6. Ibid., p. 55.

7. *House Journal,* 35th Leg., Reg. Sess., 1917, January 15, 1917, pp. 120-125.

8. Ibid., 3rd Called Sess., September 26, 1917, p. 211.

9. Clark, *The Tactful Texan,* p. 95.

10. *General and Special Laws of the State of Texas,* 35th Leg., 4th Called Sess., 1918: statewide Prohibition, pp. 37-40; woman suffrage, pp. 61-64; majority vote in elections, pp. 191-193; prostitution law, pp. 27-29.

11. Clark, *The Tactful Texan,* p. 126.

12. Ledger titled "Fees, 1919," Hallie Maude Neff Wilcox Papers.

13. Sim Palmer Brooks and Aurelia Brooks Harlan, Oral Memoirs, interview by Kent Keeth, January 19, 1982, pp. 147-149, Baylor University Institute for Oral History, Waco, Texas, hereafter referred to as BUIOH.

14. Brooks to Gambrell, July 7, 1913, Brooks Papers, as quoted in Oran Lonnie Sinclair, "Samuel Palmer Brooks: President of Baylor University, 1902-1920," master's thesis, Baylor University, Waco, Texas, 1961; and Brooks to H. L. Darwin, April 8, 1913, Brooks Papers, Texas Collection, Baylor University.

15. Brooks to Dr. Wallace Buttrick, January 5, 1921, Brooks Papers, as quoted in Sinclair, "Samuel Palmer Brooks."

16. Sam Hanna Acheson, *Joe Bailey: The Last Democrat* (New York: MacMillan Co., 1932), pp. 384-385.

17. T. C. Richardson, *East Texas: Its History and Its Makers,* ed. Dabney White (New York: Lewis Historical Publishing Co., 1940), vol. 4, p. 33.

18. Election to Texas House of Representatives, *House Journal,* 35th Leg., Reg. Sess., 1917, January 9, 1917, pp. 1-3; election as speaker, *House Journal,* 36th Leg., Reg. Sess., 1919, January 14, 1919, pp. 5-6.

19. Norman D. Brown, *Hood, Bonnet, and Little Brown Jug: Texas Politics, 1921-1928* (College Station: Texas A&M University Press, 1984), p. 4.

20. *House Journal,* 36th Leg., 2nd Called Sess., 1919, July 15, 1919, pp. 442-445.

21. Neff to Mother Neff, July 25, 1919, Charlotte Calvert Papers, David L. Scott Collection.

22. Mother Neff to Neff, July 28, 1919, Neff Papers.

23. *Waco News-Tribune*, November 19, 1919, Neff Papers.

24. Neff to Nichols, August 6, 1919, Neff Papers.

25. Neff to Stewart, August 23, 1919, Neff Papers.

26. Notes, political campaign folders, Neff Papers.

27. Neff to McDonald, September 10, 1919, Neff Papers.

28. Neff to J. W. McDaniel, September 20, 1919, Neff Papers.

29. Neff to Pickett, October 4, 1919, Neff Papers.

30. The "Smiths" and thousands of other Texas voters responded: Preston Smith was elected and served as governor of the state from 1969 to 1973. Jimmy Banks, *Money, Marbles, and Chalk: The Wondrous World of Texas Politics* (Austin: Texas Publishing Company, Inc., 1971), p. 45.

31. Neff to McIntyre, October 17, 1919, Neff Papers.

32. Neff to F. G. Fitzgerald, November 20, 1919, Neff Papers.

33. Brooks to Davis, November 5, 1919, Neff Papers.

34. Robert Ewing Thomason, *The Autobiography of a Federal Judge*, ed. and ann. by Joseph M. Ray (El Paso: Texas Western Press, University of Texas at El Paso, 1971), p. 13.

35. Ibid., p. 22.

36. Richardson, *East Texas*, vol. 4, p. 33.

37. Ibid.

38. *Brownwood Semi-Weekly*, December 30, 1919; *Beaumont Enterprise,* December 7, 1919; both in Neff Papers.

39. *Brownwood Semi-Weekly*, December 30, 1919, Neff Papers.

40. *Beaumont Enterprise,* December 7, 1919, Neff Papers.

41. Opening address, gubernatorial campaign, 1919, Neff Papers.

42. Ibid.

43. Neff to "Dear Mr. Editor," December 9, 1919, Neff Papers. As an example, a copy of the postcard returned from Collier Smith of the *Wise County Messenger* had the figure "1,200" in the blank for number of copies of the speech, the figure $50 in the blank indicating the amount of payment due, and written on the postcard by Smith was, "Put the word 'advertisement' at bottom of page."

44. Lewis L. Gould, *Progressives and Prohibitionists: Texas Democrats in the Wilson Era* (Austin and London: University of Texas Press, 1973), pp. 249-277.

45. Ibid., pp. 259-260.

46. This section highlights Neff's major speeches and utilizes other Neff papers and official documents to complement theses on his first gubernatorial campaign. Comprehensive coverage of Neff's travels in his 1920 campaign is found in Eugene Baker's Baylor University master's thesis of 1961 entitled "The First Gubernatorial Campaign of Pat. M. Neff." In his thesis, Baker traces the race week by week, making extensive use of documents in the Neff Papers and newspaper stories of his campaign speeches. Emma Shirley's monograph based on her master's thesis—"The Administration of Pat M. Neff, Governor of Texas, 1921-1925," *Baylor Bulletin* 41, no. 4 (December 1938)—also has excellent coverage of the campaign.

47. *Brownsville Herald*, January 12, 1920, Neff Papers.

48. Neff to Ramsey, February 9, 1920, Neff Papers.

49. Ibid.

50. *Amarillo News,* February 2, 1920, Neff Papers.

51. Neff to Pat Jr., December 19, 1924, Neff Papers.

52. Pat M. Neff, *The Battles of Peace* (Fort Worth: Pioneer Publishing Co., 1925), p. 8.

53. *Oil City Visitor,* Sour Lake, Texas, January 28, 1920, Neff Papers.

54. *Orange Leader*, January 29, 1920, as quoted in Baker, "The First Gubernatorial Campaign," pp. 11-12.

55. Gould, *Progressives and Prohibitionists*, p. 262.

56. *Hillsboro Mirror*, February 25, 1920, Neff Papers.

57. *Cleburne Review*, April 14, 1920; *Waco Daily Times-Herald*, April 2, 1920, Neff Papers.

58. *Waco Daily Times-Herald*, April 15, 1920, Neff Papers.

59. Notes, political campaign folder, Neff Papers.

60. *Pharr Clarion*, undated, Neff Papers.

61. *Houston Post*, May 13, 1920, Neff Papers.

62. *Houston Chronicle*, May 30, 1920, Neff Papers.

63. *Waco News-Tribune*, May 26, 1920, Neff Papers.

64. Neff to Mother Neff, May 20, 1920, Hallie Maude Neff Wilcox Papers, Texas Collection.

65. Lary to Harrington, June 11, 1920, Neff Papers, as quoted in Baker, "The First Gubernatorial Campaign," pp. 40-41.

66. Neff to Morris, June 14, 1920, Neff Papers.

67. *Farm and Labor Journal*, June 17, 1920, Neff Papers.

68. *Abilene Reporter*, June 6, 1920, Neff Papers.

69. *Temple Telegram*, July 8, 1920, Neff Papers.

70. S. G. Reed, *A History of the Texas Railroads and of Transportation Conditions under Spain and Mexico and the Republic and the State* (Houston: St. Clair Publishing Co., 1941), p. 728.

71. Scott to Brooks, June 22, 1920, Neff Papers.

72. Sandefer to Neff, June 21, 1920, and Hoge to Neff, June 16, 1920, Neff Papers.

73. Notes, political campaign folder, Neff Papers.

74. Ibid.

75. *Brownsville Herald,* June 29, 1920, Neff Papers.

76. Barcus to O'Brien and Springer, June 16, 1920, Neff Papers.

77. *Abilene Reporter*, June 6, 1920, Neff Papers.

78. For example, see J. W. Hale to Benton McMillin, July 5, 1920, Neff Papers.

79. Betty Ann McCartney McSwain, ed. *The Bench and Bar of Waco and McLennan County, 1849-1976.* (Waco: Texian Press, 1976), p. 335.

80. Neff, *The Battles of Peace,* p. 8.

81. Ibid., p. 9.

82. *Quanah Observer*, July 1, 1920, Neff Papers. The newspaper drew the quote from

Brooks' introductory biographical statement in a collection of Neff's addresses: "He is a na-tive-born Texan and a rustic who has never shot a gun, baited a hook, used tobacco in any form, or drunk anything stronger than Brazos water" (Neff, *A Collection of Twenty-three Addresses* [Waco: Philomathesian Literary Society, Baylor University, c.1914]). Obviously Brooks' statement was intended as a compliment, not a criticism.

83. Ibid.

84. Frederick L. Collins, *Our American Kings* (New York and London: Century Co., 1924), p. 163. Collins describes the reaction to Neff's hunting and fishing in colorful terms: "In the popular imagination, Pat Neff became the Wild Man from Waco. He jumped clean out of his ruffles into his corduroys." See also, "At Home with the Governors—Pat and His Hat," *Woman's Home Companion*, August 1924, p. 24, as quoted in Baker, "The First Gubernatorial Campaign," p. 48.

85. Notes, campaign folder, Neff Papers.

86. Judith N. McArthur and Harold L. Smith, *Minnie Fisher Cunningham: A Suffragist's Life in Politics* (New York: Oxford University Press, 2003), p. 93.

87. Campaign flyer, Neff Papers.

88. Neff to Mrs. Lovejoy, November 13, 1919, and Neff to Mrs. Gerhardt, November 14, 1919, Neff Papers.

89. *Dallas Morning News*, July 24, 1920, Neff Papers.

90. Clark, *The Tactful Texan*, p. 95.

91. Thomason, *Autobiography*, p. 24.

92. *Austin American*, August 3, 1954.

93. *Whitney Messenger*, July 30, 1920, Neff Papers.

94. *Waco News-Tribune*, August 5, 1920, as quoted in Baker, "The First Gubernatorial Campaign," p. 63.

95. Baker, "The First Gubernatorial Campaign," p. 64.

96. Patsy Neff to Isabella Neff, August 6, 1920, Hallie Maude Neff Wilcox Papers, Texas Collection.

97. Among these were the *Martindale American Law Directory* and the *Legislative Year Book, 1905*.

98. *Cleburne Morning Review*, August 28, 1920, Neff Papers.

99. Interview with Neff, April 15, 1951, as quoted in Chase Sherwin Winfrey, "Pat Morris Neff: A Personality-Oratorical Study," Ph.D. diss., University of Denver, Denver, Colorado, 1951, p. 64. Some stories of Neff's campaign state that he traveled in a Ford. The reference to a Buick car in this interview corroborates the information contained in a letter written by Neff to W. T. Herrick on June 6, 1921, and a *Farm and Labor Journal* article on May 27, 1920, both of which state that he traveled Texas in a Buick.

100. James V. Allred to Chase Winfrey, April 18, 1951, as quoted in Winfrey, "Pat Morris Neff," pp. 65-66.

101. Neff, *The Battles of Peace*, p. 8.

102. *Dallas Morning News*, August 28, 1920, Neff Papers.

103. Official returns, *Dallas Morning News,* September 7, 1920, as quoted in Alexander

Heard and Donald S. Strong, *Southern Primaries and Elections: 1920-1949* (University, Ala.: University of Alabama Press, 1950), pp. 134-136.

104. Acheson, *Joe Bailey;* pp. 388-389.

105. Walter L. Buenger, *The Path to a Modern South: Northeast Texas between Reconstruction and the Great Depression* (Austin: University of Texas Press, 2001), p. 200.

106. *Dallas Morning News,* August 24, 1920; *Houston Post,* August 11, 1920; *Amarillo Tribune,* August 22, 1920; all in Neff Papers.

107. *Timpson Times,* August 15, 1920, Neff Papers.

108. *General Laws of the State of Texas,* 36th Leg., Reg. Sess., 1919, ch. 88, p. 139.

109 Campaign contribution and expenses statements of candidates, Texas Secretary of State: Neff (June 26, 1920; July 13, 1920; August 28, 1920); Looney (June 28, 1920; July 14, 1920; August 2, 1920); Thomason (May 27, 1920; July 14, 1920; July 30, 1920); Bailey (June 28, 1920; July 14, 1920; July 28, 1920; August 18, 1920). Texas State Library and Archives Commission, Archives and Information Services Division, Austin, Texas.

110. *Austin Statesman,* November 12, 1918.

111. Neff to "Dear Mr. Editor." See endnote 43. Dozens of these returned postcards were found in the Neff Papers.

112. Neff to Tyssowski, July 9, 1920, Neff Papers.

113. Barcus to Guinn, August 15, 1920, Neff Papers.

114. *Farm and Labor Journal,* September 16, 1920, Neff Papers.

115. *Sherman Democrat,* September 10, 1920, Neff Papers.

116. Neff to Mother Neff, September 12, 1920, Charlotte Calvert Papers, David L. Scott Collection.

117. Neff to Morris Neff, September 29, 1920, Neff Papers.

118. Neff to Mother Neff, October 2, 1920, Charlotte Calvert Papers, David L. Scott Collection.

119. *Senate Journal,* 37th Leg., Reg. Sess., 1921, January 17, 1921, pp. 91-95.

120. Neff to Mother Neff, November 26, 1920, Neff Papers.

121. Peeler to Neff, November 15, 1920, Neff Papers.

122. *Baptist Standard,* December 2, 1920.

123. Neff to Mother Neff, December 29, 1920, Charlotte Calvert Papers, David L. Scott Collection.

124. Mother Neff to Neff, December 29, 1920, Neff Papers.

125. Mother Neff to Neff, January 5, 1921, Neff Papers.

Chapter 6. Fussin' and Feudin'

1. *Austin American*, January 19, 1921.

2. Ibid.

3. *Austin Statesman*, January 18, 1921.

4. *Austin American*, January 19, 1921.

5. Fred Gantt Jr., *The Chief Executive in Texas: A Study in Gubernatorial Leadership* (Austin: University of Texas Press, 1964), pp. 336-337, 341.

6. *General and Special Laws of the State of Texas*, 66th Leg., Reg. Sess., 1979, table 2, "Votes on Amendments to Constitution," p. 3252.

7. Robert Caro, *Means of Ascent* (New York: Alfred A. Knopf, 1990), p. 158.

8. Census, 1920, U.S. Bureau of the Census.

9. *Austin Statesman*, January 3, 1921.

10. During the Capitol renovation in the late 1900s, the building became the Capitol Visitors' Center.

11. It was Governor John Connally who, coming in the mid-1960s from luxurious offices in his two previous positions—as attorney for oilman Sid Richardson in Fort Worth and then U.S. Secretary of the Navy in Washington—found the governor's quarters "dismal and very inadequate," in the words of Larry Temple, a former aide. Connally immediately set out to improve and expand the chief executive's offices. In the original drawings of the Capitol, a large room on the second floor immediately above the Governor's Business Office was assigned to the Capitol Post Office and was later taken over by the Senate. Longtime Senate Secretary Betty King remembered that when Governor Connally took office in 1963, Senator Ottis Lock of Lufkin and other senators were occupying that large space. Connally negotiated with Lock and Lieutenant Governor Preston Smith to vacate the space and then set about renovating that area as well as the remainder of the governor's space on the second floor. He also secured the construction of a private elevator where the back stairs had been from the first to second floor. According to Curator of the Capitol Ali James, the expanded governor's space remains the same into the twenty-first century, with the governor occupying the large office just to the east of the public reception room and members of the governor's staff normally occupying all four of the rooms (first and second floors) with the south exposure. The only exception is that Governor Ann Richards forsook the large office and operated from the second floor "consultation" office nearest the front entrance.

12. *San Antonio Express*, May 2, 1925.

13. *House Journal*, 42nd Leg., Reg. Sess., 1931, January 15, 1931, vol. 1, pp. 29-36; *House Journal*, 43rd Leg., Reg. Sess., 1933, January 13, 1933, vol. 1, pp. 63-72. In 1935, James V. Allred beat Witt and four other candidates in the Democratic primary on July 28 (see *San Antonio Express*, July 29, 1935) and then went on to defeat Tom Hunter in the Democratic runoff in August. He was elected in the general election in November.

14. *Handbook of Texas Online*, s.v. "Parr, Archer," http://www.tsha.utexas.edu/handbook/online/articles/PP/fpa35.html .

15. *Senate Journal*, 37th Leg., Reg. Sess., 1921, January 30, 1921, p. 125; January 27, 1921, p. 161; February 3, 1921, p. 230; February 17, 1921, pp. 463-465; February 21, 1921, pp. 502-503.

16. *General Laws of Texas,* 36th Leg., 2nd Called Sess., 1919, p. 399.

17. J. A. Bullock to Neff, October 21, 1921; J. B. Bennett to Neff, December 9, 1920; both in Neff Papers.

18. Neff to Board of Pardon Advisors, January 22, 1921, Neff Papers.

19. *Senate Journal,* 37th Leg., Reg. Sess., 1921, January 28, 1921, pp. 171-175.

20. Ibid.

21. *Houston Chronicle,* January 29, 1921.

22. *Dallas Morning News,* February 1, 1921.

23. *General Laws of the State of Texas,* 37th Leg., Reg. Sess., 1921, pp. 14-15, 225.

24. Holman to Neff, October 25, 1920, Neff Papers.

25. *Senate Journal,* 37th Leg., Reg. Sess., 1921, February 1, 1921, pp. 201-202.

26. *Austin American,* March 6, 1921.

27. *Austin American,* April 3, 1921.

28. *House Journal,* 37th Leg., Reg. Sess., 1921, February 3, 1921, pp. 373-374.

29. *Senate Journal,* 37th Leg., Reg. Sess., 1921, March 12, 1921, p. 1182.

30. *Dallas Morning News,* February 14, 1921.

31. *San Antonio Express,* February 14, 1921.

32. *San Antonio Express,* March 13, 1921.

33. Governor Thomas Campbell to Neff, January 31, 1921; *Dallas Journal,* January 31, 1921; Hugh Nugent Fitzgerald to Neff, January 31, 1921; George M. Bailey to Neff, January 31, 1921; all in Neff Papers.

34. *Austin American,* February 1, 1921.

35. *General Laws of the State of Texas,* 37th Reg. Sess., 1921, pp. 45-54.

36. The activation of these two counties left only three to fill out the full complement of 254 counties. Cochran County was organized in 1924, Crane in 1927, and Loving in 1931.

37. Veto proclamation, *Senate Journal,* 37th Leg., Reg. Sess., 1921, February 21, 1921, p. 513.

38. *House Journal,* 37th Reg. Sess., 1921, February 18, 1921, p. 589.

39. Legislative Reference Library, State of Texas, "Vetoed Bills 1860-2005: Vetoed Bills—Governor Pat N. (sic) Neff, 37th Regular Session (1921)," online: http://www.lrl.state.tx.us/legis/vetoes/vetoesbySession.cfm?legSession=37-0.

40. Proclamation, Governor of Texas, April 1, 1921, Texas Office of the Governor, located in Archives and Information Services Division, Texas State Library and Archives Commission, Austin, Texas.

41. Homer Dale Wade, *Establishment of Texas Technological College, 1916-1923* (Lubbock, Tex.: Texas Tech Press, 1956), pp. 56-63. See also Jane Gilmore Rushing and Kline A. Nall, *Evolution of a University: Texas Tech's First Fifty Years* (Austin: Madrona Press, 1975), pp. 11-14.

42. *Houston Post,* April 3, 1921.

43. Legislative Reference Library, "Vetoed Bills," online. The proclamation vetoing House Bill 161, known as the Minimum Wage Bill, may be found under that heading.

44. Neff to Unknown, March 3, 1921, Neff Papers.

45. Neff to Cordelia Shepherd, April 22, 1921, Neff Papers.

46. News clipping, unidentified newspaper, undated, Neff Papers.

47. Telegram, Neff to Pat Jr., February 11, 1921, Neff Papers.

48. The Governor's Mansion, its history and its changes, has been extensively described in *The Texas Governor's Mansion*, by Jean Houston Daniel, Price Daniel, and Dorothy Blodgett, published in 1984 by the Texas State Library and Archives Commission. Through the years, there had been talk of demolishing the mansion, particularly during Governor Hogg's administration, but no governor felt the state had the money or seemingly wanted to take on the potentially controversial challenge. Similarly, in the late twentieth century, there would be consideration of converting the mansion to a museum and buying the old Pease mansion in west Austin, which would be more "child friendly" in its location. Again, such conversation went nowhere. The Pease mansion was finally sold to an individual for use as a private residence in 2003.

49. Mary D. Farrell and Elizabeth Silverthorne, *First Ladies of Texas: The First Hundred Years, 1836-1936* (Belton, Tex.: Stillhouse Hollow Publishers, 1976), pp. 299-300.

50. Daniel, Daniel, and Blodgett, *Texas Governor's Mansion*, p. 160.

51. A detailed description of the mansion and its furniture and decorations as of 1921 is reported in an October 23, 1921, *Austin Statesman* story, "Where the Governors of Texas Live and Transact Their Business," by Mary Jimperieff.

52. Myrtie to Pat Jr., June 11, 1921, Neff Papers.

53. Farrell and Silverthorne, *First Ladies of Texas*, p. 312.

54. Isabella to Patsy Neff, February 11, 1921, Marie Taylor Neff Collection.

55. *Dallas Morning News*, May 20, 1921.

56. Neff to Mother Neff, May 11, 1919, Neff Papers.

57. Neff to Marsh, May 28, 1921, Neff Papers.

58. Farrell and Silverthorne, *First Ladies of Texas*, p. 312.

59. Bobbie Barnes, interview by Dorothy Blodgett, May 30, 1992, Blodgett Collection.

60. Myrtie to Hallie Maude, August 26, 1922, and September 11, 1923, Neff Papers. Myrtie had started changing her name when she went to Mineral Wells as early as 1903, when Neff was speaker of the House of Representatives. See Neff to Myrtie, April 23, 1903, in reply to a postcard from Myrtie; Neff Papers.

61. Pat Jr. to Myrtie, April 5, 1921, Charlotte Calvert Papers, David L. Scott Collection; Pat Jr. to Hallie Maude, April 19, 1921, Hallie Maude Neff Wilcox Papers, Texas Collection.

62. Neff to Patterson, March 17, 1921, Neff Papers.

63. *Senate Journal*, 37th Leg., Reg. Sess., 1921; *Senate Journal*, 38th Leg., Reg. Sess., 1923, January 30, 1923, pp. 352-355. (Neff's fall 1922 appointments had to be ratified by the Senate when it met in 1923.)

64. Nancy Baker Jones and Ruthe Winegarten, *Capitol Women: Texas Female Legislators, 1923-1999* (Austin: University of Texas Press, 2000), p. 82.

65. Ibid., p. 84.

66. Neff to Adams, January 12, 1922, Neff Papers.

67. Neff to Lewis, August 20, 1921, Neff Papers.

68. *Austin Statesman*, January 1, 1921.

69. *San Antonio Express*, May 13, 1921.

70. Vaughn to Neff, May 22, 1921, Neff Papers.

71. Bryan to Neff, July 7, 1921, Neff Papers.

72. *Amarillo Daily News*, July 16, 1921.

73. *San Antonio Express*, July 18, 1921.

74. *Senate Journal*, 37th Leg, 1st Called Sess., 1921, July 18, 1921, pp. 7-17.

75. Ibid., pp. 8-10.

76. *General and Special Laws of the State of Texas*, 66th Leg., Reg. Sess., 1979, table 2, p. 3252.

77. Herring to Senator Gwinn Williams, Chairman, Penitentiary Committee, February 25, 1921, Neff Papers. This five-and-a-half-page single-spaced letter gives an excellent status report of the Texas prison system from Herring's viewpoint. It includes comments on prisoner health, location of prisons, use of the strap for punishment, and prisoner discipline, among other subjects.

78. Neff to Mrs. Ruth Walker, November 7, 1921; Neff to Gus Taylor, November 7, 1921; both in Neff Papers.

79. *General Laws of the State of Texas*, 37th Leg., 1st and 2nd Called Sess., 1921, pp. 42-52, approved by the governor, August 10, 1921.

80. *House Journal*, 37th Leg. 2nd Called Sess., 1921, August 17, 1921, p. 2.

81. Ibid., August 19, 1921, pp. 15-16.

82. *General Laws of the State of Texas*, 37th Leg., 1st and 2nd Called Sess., 1921, signed August 31, 1921: eleemosynary institutions, pp. 68-107; American Legion Memorial Sanitorium, pp. 110-111; Orphan's Home, Corsicana, pp. 120-121; rural aid for schools, pp. 141-146.

83. Neff actually cut only fourteen positions from the 772. The 758 positions remaining included fifty Texas Rangers but did not include the employees of the penitentiaries or eleemosynary and higher education institutions.

84. *General Laws of the State of Texas*, 37th Leg., 1st and 2nd Called Sess., 1921, pp. 172-215.

85. Hogg to Ousley, October 24, 1921, William Clifford Hogg Papers, Center for American History, University of Texas at Austin.

86. Hogg to Neff, February 1, 1921, William Clifford Hogg Papers.

87. Legislative Reference Library, "Vetoed Bills," online.

88. *Dallas Morning News*, September 7, 1921.

89. Charles Comer Alexander, "Crusade for Conformity: The Ku Klux Klan in Texas, 1920-1927," master's thesis, University of Texas, Austin, Texas, 1959, pp. 3-5.

90. Norman D. Brown, *Hood, Bonnet, and Little Brown Jug: Texas Politics, 1921-1928* (College Station: Texas A&M University Press, 1984), pp. 49-87.

91. Ibid., pp. 49-52.

92. Charles C. Alexander, *The Ku Klux Klan in the Southwest* (Lexington: University of Kentucky Press, 1965), pp. 33-34. See also Robert A. Calvert, Arnoldo De Leon, and Gregg

Cantrell, *The History of Texas,* 3rd ed. (Wheeling, Ill.: Harlan Davidson, Inc., 2002).

93. Neff, Press Release, February 1, 1921, Neff Papers.

94. Alexander, "Crusade for Conformity," p. 35.

95. Linda Elaine Kilgore, "The Ku Klux Klan and the Press in Texas, 1920-1927," master's thesis, University of Texas, Austin, Texas, 1964, pp. 22-38.

96. Ibid., pp. 35-38.

97. *Dallas Morning News,* June 18, 1921.

98. Nancy Beck Young, *Wright Patman: Populism, Liberalism, and the American Dream* (Dallas: Southern Methodist University Press, 2000). See also Janet Louise Schmelzer, "The Early Life and Early Congressional Career of Wright Patman: 1894-1941," Ph.D. diss., Texas Christian University, Fort Worth, Texas, 1978.

99. *House Journal,* 37th Leg., 1st and 2nd Called Sess., 1921, July 27, 1921, p. 74.

100. *Austin American,* September 3, 1921.

101. Shawn Lay, *War, Revolution, and the Ku Klux Klan* (El Paso: Texas Western Press, 1985), p. 74.

102. Alexander, "Crusade for Conformity," pp. 48, 56, 58, 73.

103. Foster to Neff, November 10, 1921, Neff Papers.

104. Neff to Foster, November 12, 1921, Neff Papers.

105. John B. Thomas to Neff, January 28, 1921, Neff Papers.

106. Robert Denny, Oral Memoirs, interview by William L. Pitts, September 22, 1983, pp. 62-63, BUIOH.

107. *Centennial History of the Texas Bar: 1882-1982* (Austin: Eakin Press, 1981), p. 109.

108. Diana Davids Olien and Roger M. Olien, *Oil in Texas: The Gusher Age, 1895-1945* (Austin: University of Texas Press, 2002), pp. 120-121.

109. Ibid., p. 121.

110. Neff, *Battles of Peace,* p. 72.

111. Ibid., p. 73.

112. *Report of State Ranger and Martial Law Activities of the National Guard of Texas, 1921 and 1922, to Honorable Pat M. Neff, Governor,* Legislative Reference Library, Austin, Texas, and Neff Papers.

113. Ken Anderson, *You Can't Do That, Dan Moody: The Klan Fighting Governor of Texas* (Austin: Eakin Press, 1998).

114. Frank M. Stewart, *Highway Administration in Texas: A Study of Administrative Methods and Financial Policies,* University of Texas Bulletin no. 3423, June 15, 1934 (Austin: University of Texas, 1934), pp. 40-43.

115. *Dallas Morning News,* April 9, 1922.

116. *Dallas Morning News,* April 29, 1922; *Fort Worth Star-Telegram,* April 28, 1922. The newspaper speculation appears to be just that. Neff was not concerned with the issue as a social problem; at that time he saw it entirely as a budgetary challenge.

117. *Dallas Morning News,* May 7, 1922.

118. "Extracts from an Address delivered by Governor Pat M. Neff to the Texas Bankers' Association at Fort Worth, Texas, May 17, 1922," Neff Papers.

119. *Dallas Morning News,* April 18, 1922.

120. *Texas Highway Bulletin* 4, no. 8 (August 1924).

121. *Handbook of Texas Online,* s.v. "Daniels, Bebe Virginia," http://www.tsha.utexas.edu/handbook/online/articles/DD/fda10_print.html .

122. *Dallas Morning News,* January 22, 1922.

123. Ibid.

124. Ibid.

125. Ibid.

126. Wasson to Neff, February 7, 1922, Neff Papers.

127. Kilgore, "Ku Klux Klan," pp. 38-43.

128. Ibid., p.123.

129. Ibid.

130. Ibid., p. 4.

131. Ibid., pp. 54-58, 122.

132. Ibid., pp. 43, 123, 125-163.

133. Joseph Martin Dawson, *A Thousand Months to Remember: An Autobiography* (Waco: Baylor University Press, 1964), p. 165.

134. Monte Akers, *Flames after Midnight: Murder, Vengeance, and the Desolation of a Texas Community* (Austin: University of Texas Press, 1999), p. 77.

135. According to author Robert M. Utley, Neff did send National Guardsmen and Texas Rangers to Lufkin in 1924 to quell a possible lynching, but the Klan was by that time in decline. Utley, *Lone Star Lawmen: The Second Century of the Texas Rangers* (Oxford and New York: Oxford University Press, 2007), pp. 103-104.

Chapter 7. Reelection

1. *San Antonio Express*, October 21, 1921.

2. *Dallas Morning News*, April 28, 1922.

3. *Waco Daily Times-Herald*, June 4, 1922.

4. *Dallas Morning News*, June 5, 1922.

5. *Houston Chronicle*, July 4, 1922.

6. A review of the major state newspapers during the campaign reveal that King's name is hardly mentioned. He did not conduct a campaign of any sort.

7. Original manuscript, "Address of Governor Pat M. Neff, Candidate for Reelection," June 24, 1922, Neff Papers.

8. Neff to Watkins, June 23, 1922, Neff Papers.

9. *Dallas Morning News,* July 9 and July 12, 1922.

10. *Dallas Morning News*, July 13, 1922.

11. Ibid.

12. *Dallas Morning News*, July 14, 1922.

13. James A. Clark, *The Tactful Texan: A Biography of Governor Will Hobby* (New York: Random House, 1958), p. 133.

14. *General Laws of the State of Texas*, 36th Leg., 4th Called Sess., 1920, p. 7.

15. *Austin Statesman*, July 22, 1922.

16. *Tyler Courier Times*, July 14, 1922, as quoted in Lola Matthews Laughlin, "The Speaking Career of Pat Morris Neff," master's thesis, Baylor University, Waco, Texas, 1951, p. 185.

17. Pat M. Neff, *The Battles of Peace* (Fort Worth, Tex.: Pioneer Publishing Company, 1925), p. 74.

18. Mark Stanley argues in his 2005 thesis that the Denison strike and the Mexia oil field problem were the two most important events of Neff's governorship. He also comments, as does Lewis Gould in his 1973 book, that Neff was a "shrewd, practical politician." See Mark Stanley, "Booze, Boomtowns, and Burning Crosses: The Turbulent Governorship of Pat M. Neff of Texas, 1921-1925," master's thesis, University of North Texas, Denton, Texas, 2005, summary (unnumbered page) and p. l. Also see Lewis L. Gould, *Progressives and Prohibitionists: Texas Democrats in the Wilson Era* (Austin and London: University of Texas Press, 1973), p. 272. Both writers place Neff in the forefront of the "progressive" movement in the 1920s, but also agree that Neff was a complex individual who defied easy classification.

19. Norman D. Brown, *Hood, Bonnet, and Little Brown Jug: Texas Politics, 1921-1928* (College Station: Texas A&M University Press, 1984), pp. 49-87; Walter L. Buenger, *Northeast Texas between Reconstruction and the Great Depression* (Austin: University of Texas Press, 2001), pp. 203-214; Arnold S. Rice, *The Ku Klux Klan in American Politics* (Washington, D.C.: Public Affairs Press, 1962), pp. 13-17; Robert M. Utley, *Lone Star Lawmen: The Second Century of the Texas Rangers* (New York: Oxford University Press, 2007), pp. 87-88.

20. Charles Comer Alexander, "Crusade for Conformity: The Ku Klux Klan in Texas, 1920-1927," master's thesis, University of Texas, Austin, Texas, 1959, pp. 150-194; Alexander, *The Ku Klux Klan in the Southwest* (Norman: University of Oklahoma Press, 1965), pp. 77-82.

21. *Dallas Morning News*, July 19, 1922.

22. *Dallas Morning News*, July 23, 1922.

23. *Dallas Morning News*, July 23 and 24, 1922.

24. *Senate Journal*, 38th Leg., Reg. Sess., 1923, January 9, 1923, pp. 1-21.

25. Brown, *Hood, Bonnet, and Little Brown Jug*, p. 95.

26. Ibid., p. 99.

27. *Dallas Morning News*, August 6, 1922.

28. Undated Ma Ferguson campaign poster, "Boys, We Are Winning," signed by James E. Ferguson, Neff Papers.

29. *Corpus Christi Caller*, July 17, 1922; *Houston Post*, July 21, 1922.

30. Gross to Neff, June 24, 1922, Neff Papers.

31. Walthall to Cooper, July 14, 1922, Neff Papers.

32. Quinn to Neff, July 24, 1922; Wolters to Neff, July 24, 1922; Powers to Neff, June 16, 1922; Green to Neff, July 22, 1922; Bigham to Neff, July 19, 1922; Kelly to Walthall, July 16, 1922; all in Neff Papers. See also marked ballot in envelope postmarked Houston, Texas, July 20, 1922, Neff Papers.

33. *Dallas Morning News*, August 6, 1922.

34. Neff, *Battles of Peace*, pp. 73-76.

35. *Report of State Ranger and Martial Law Activities of the National Guard of Texas, 1921 and 1922, to the Honorable Pat M. Neff, Governor of Texas, from Thomas D. Barton, Adjutant General of Texas* (Austin: Von Boeckmann-Jones Co., 1923), p. 23.

36. *Texas Conservation News*, August 12, 1922, Neff Papers.

37. Hallie Maude to Myrtie, August 10, 1922, Hallie Maude Neff Wilcox Papers; Myrtie to Hallie Maude, August 26, 1922, Neff Papers.

38. Neff to Hallie Maude, August 25, 1922, Neff Papers. September 1 was the beginning of the fiscal year for the state.

39. The deed was not recorded until May 16, 1927. Coryell County Deed Records, Coryell County Clerk's Office, Book 108, p. 56l.

40. For Neff, see *Senate Journal*, 38th Leg., Reg. Sess., 1923, January 15, 1923, pp. 61-67; for Mayfield, see *Dallas Morning News*, November 8, 1922, and *Texas Almanac* (Dallas: Dallas Morning News, 2006), p. 401.

41. Neff, *Battles of Peace*, p. 28.

42. *Dallas Morning News,* December 6, 1922.

43. *San Antonio Express*, December 18, 1922.

44. *San Antonio Express*, December 23, 1922.

45. *San Antonio Express*, January 1, 1923.

46. *San Antonio Express*, January 4, 1923.

47. *San Antonio Express*, January 10, 1923.

48. *Senate Journal*, 38th Leg., Reg. Sess., 1923, January 16, 1923, p. 88.

49. *Austin Statesman*, April 8, 1923.

50. *San Antonio Express*, April 27, 1923.

51. *San Antonio Express*, April 28, 1923.

52. Barcus to Neff, January 2, 1923, Neff Papers.

53. *San Antonio Express*, January 10, 1923.

54. *San Antonio Express*, December 27, 1922.

55. *House Journal*, 38th Leg., Reg. Sess., 1923, January 12, 1923, pp. 56-57.

56. Barcus to Neff, January 2, 1923, Neff Papers.

57. *Austin Statesman*, January 14, 1923.

58. *San Antonio Express,* January 16, 1923.

59. *Austin Statesman*, December 8, 1922.

60. *Dallas Morning News*, December 19, 1922.

61. *General Laws of the State of Texas*, 38th Leg., Reg. Sess., 1923, pp. 235-237.

62. *General Laws of the State of Texas,* 38th Leg., 1st, 2nd, and 3rd Called Sess., 1923, Prohibition law, pp. 53-55; driving while intoxicated, p. 56; injunctions against hotels, pp. 57-58.

63. *Austin Statesman*, January 13, 1923.

64. *Senate Journal*, 38th Leg., Reg. Sess., 1923, education, January 18, 1923, pp. 106-109; taxation, January 19, 1923, pp. 128-135; prison system, January 22, 1923, pp. 154-157; highways, January 25, 1923, pp. 196-300; manufacturing, January 30, 1923, pp. 345-347.

65. Fred Gantt Jr., *The Chief Executive in Texas: A Study in Gubernatorial Leadership* (Austin: University of Texas Press, 1964), p. 203.

66. *Senate Journal*, 38th Leg., Reg. Sess., 1923, January 18, 1923, pp. 106-109.

67. *General Laws of the State of Texas*, 38th Leg., Reg. Sess., 1923, pp. 258-260.

68. Ibid., p. 341.

69. Education bill in third session, *General Laws of the State of Texas*, 38th Leg., 1st, 2nd and 3rd Called Sess., 1923, p. 292.

70. Rural school bill in third session, *General Laws of the State of Texas*, 38th Leg., 1st, 2nd, and 3rd Called Sess., 1923, pp. 302-306.

71. *Senate Journal*, 38th Leg., Reg. Sess., 1923, January 19, 1923, pp. 128-135.

72. Ibid.

73. *San Antonio Express*, February 7, 1923.

74. *General Laws of the State of Texas,* 38th Leg., Reg. Sess., 1923, gasoline dealers, pp. 275-277; sulphur, pp. 337-338; textbook publishers, pp. 352-353.

75. *San Antonio Express*, May 16, 1923.

76. Ibid.

77. *Senate Journal*, 38th Leg., Reg. Sess., 1923, January 22, 1923, pp. 238-240.

78. *General Laws of the State of Texas*, 38th Leg., Reg. Sess., 1923, pp. 178-179.

79. *Senate Journal*, 38th Leg., Reg. Sess., 1923, January 23, 1923, pp. 175-184.

80. Ibid.

81. *San Antonio Express*, February 17, 1923.

82. *Senate Journal*, 38th Leg., Reg. Sess., 1923, January 25, 1923, pp. 296-300.

83. *Galveston Daily News*, October 27, 1911, as quoted in John David Huddleston, "Good Roads for Texas: A History of the Texas Highway Department," Ph.D. diss., Texas A&M University, College Station, Texas, 1981, p. 27.

84. The Texas Highway Association later again became the Texas Good Roads Association and under that name was regarded as one of the most potent lobbying groups in the latter

part of the twentieth century. For a history of the State Highway Department, see Huddleston, "Good Roads for Texas." See also *Facing the Texas Highway Crisis* (Austin: Texas Highway Association, 1923), as quoted in Frank M. Stewart, *Highway Administration in Texas*, University of Texas Bulletin 3423, Austin, Texas, June 15, 1934.

85. For example, the *Dallas Morning News* and the *San Antonio Express* both had extensive automobile sections in their Sunday newspapers in 1923.

86. *General Laws of the State of Texas,* 38th Leg., Reg. Sess., 1923, state control, pp. 155-162; pay raise and six-year term for highway commissioners, pp. 325-326. 1st, 2nd, and 3rd Called Sess., gasoline tax, pp. 158-164.

87. Veto Proclamation, House Bill 35, June 23, 1923.

88. Homer Dale Wade, *Establishment of Texas Tech College, 1916-1923* (Lubbock: Texas Tech Press, 1956), p. 2.

89. Ibid., pp. 52-55.

90. Ibid., pp. 60-63.

91. Ibid.

92. Ibid., p. 91.

93. Ibid., pp. 104-105.

94. Ibid., p. 109. See also Jerry Flemmons, *Amon: The Texan Who Played Cowboy for America* (Lubbock: Texas Tech Press, 1998).

95. McLennan County Clerk's Office, Wills, File E/5641.

96. Ibid.

97. Jeffrey Fritz Crunk, "Breathing Spots for the People: Pat M. Neff, David E. Colp, and the Emerging Idea of State Parks in Texas," master's thesis, Baylor University, Waco, Texas, 1994, p. 75.

98. Original manuscript, "Address of Governor Pat M. Neff, Candidate for Reelection," Neff Papers.

99. *Senate Journal,* 38th Leg, 1st, 2nd, and 3rd Called Sess., 1923, May 1, 1923, pp. 117-118.

100. *General Laws of the State of Texas,* 38th Leg., 1st, 2nd, and 3rd Called Sess., 1923, pp. 58-60.

101. Crunk, "Breathing Spots," pp. 75-82.

102. *San Antonio Express,* March 16, 1923; *General Laws of the State of Texas,* 38th Leg., 1st, 2nd, and 3rd Called Sess., 1923, p. 74. In July 1924, Dr. Lawrence Nixon, a black El Paso physician, attempted to vote in the Democratic primary in that city and was turned away. He began what became a series of lawsuits, with the U.S. Supreme Court upholding the challenger in case after case, and the State Democratic Party fighting year after year to keep the status quo. Finally, over a quarter of a century and two more lawsuits later, the white party officials gave up, and Negroes turned their attention in the 1950s to educational opportunities that were being denied them. See Charles L. Zelden, *The Battle for the Black Ballot: Smith v. Allwright and the Defeat of the Texas All-White Primary* (Lawrence: University Press of Kansas, 2004). Zelden's book traces the Nixon case and other lawsuits. See also Conrey Bryson, *Dr. Lawrence Nixon and the White Primary,* rev. ed. (El Paso: Texas Western Press, 1992); and Clinton Cross, "Law Day, 2004," *El Paso Bar Bulletin* (January-April 2004).

103. *Senate Journal*, 38th Leg., Reg. Sess., 1923, March 10, 1923, p. 1075.

104. Legislative Reference Library, State of Texas, "Vetoed Bills 1860-2005: Vetoed Bills—Governor Pat N. (sic) Neff, 38th Regular Session (1923)," online: http://www.lrl.state.tx.us/legis/vetoes/vetoesbySession.cfm?legSession=38-0 .

105. Ibid.

106. Ibid.

107. As cited in Betty Ann McCartney McSwain, ed., *The Bench and Bar of Waco and McLennan County* (Waco: Texian Press, 1976), pp. 278-279.

108. David M. Horton and Ryan Kellus Turner, *Lone Star Justice* (Austin: Eakin Press, 1999), p. 267.

109. Lloyd E. Price, *Backwoods to Border*, ed. Mody C. Boatright and Donald Day, Publications of the Texas Folklore Society, no. 18 (Austin: Texas Folklore Society; Dallas: University Press, Southern Methodist University, 1943), pp. 214, 216-217.

110. *San Antonio Express,* February 27, 1923.

111. In 1927, Splawn went to Washington and served in a variety of positions until he was appointed to the Interstate Commerce Commission (ICC) in 1934. His nineteen-year tenure on the ICC was made all the more remarkable by the fact that he served much of time while completely blind. When he took the ICC office, he did not forget Neff, writing to him that when Neff appointed him to the Railroad Commission, "you started something" (Splawn to Neff, February 15, 1934, Neff Papers). He retired to Austin to write a voluminous history of the University of Texas, dictating the manuscript to a corps of students and graduate assistants.

112. "Chatterbox," unidentified columnist, unidentified newspaper, 1924, Neff Papers.

113. Neff to "My Dear Friends," August 1, 1923, Neff Papers.

114. Myrtie to Pat Jr., August 3, 1923, Neff Papers.

115. Myrtie to Hallie Maude, September 11, 1923, Neff Papers.

116. Sturdivant to Hallie Maude, August 2, 1923, Neff Papers.

117. Bryan to Neff, August 14, 1923, Neff Papers.

118. Neff to Smith, September 7, 1923, Neff Papers.

119. *Fort Worth Record*, August 25, 1923.

120. Petition, Burleson County Neff for President Club, June 27, 1923, Neff Papers.

121. Neff to Curtis, June 22, 1923, Neff Papers. Thesis author Mark Stanley contends that Neff had an intense interest in the presidency but "pursued a back door strategy that alienated his political base among Texas Democrats." See Stanley, "Booze, Boomtowns, and Burning Crosses," summary page (unnumbered).

122. *Austin American*, February 27, 1923.

123. Ibid.

124. *Dallas Morning News*, June 6, 1923.

125. *The Alcalde* (August 1924): 197-205, Center for American History, University of Texas at Austin. If the University of Texas ex-students did not appreciate Neff, the Baylor University Board of Trustees certainly did. In the middle of all of the events going on at the University of Texas, the Baylor Board voted to award Neff an honorary Doctor of Laws. See Minutes, Baylor University Board of Trustees, Book E, May 28, 1924, pp. 6-7.

126. Neff to Stark, telegram, May 16, 1924, Neff Papers.

127. *Daily Texan,* May 18, 1924.

128. *Alcalde* (August 1924).

129. Ibid.

130. Unidentified newspaper and date, Neff Papers.

131. Lou Maysel, *Here Come the Texas Longhorns* (Fort Worth: Stadium Publishing Co., 1970), p. 88.

132. Harry Marsh, "A Day the Longhorns Would Like to Forget," in Kent Keeth, *Looking Back at Baylor* (Waco: Baylor University, 1985), p. 68.

133. Kenneth B. Ragsdale, *Centennial '36: The Year America Discovered Texas* (College Station: Texas A&M University Press, 1987), p. 5.

134. *Dallas Morning News,* November 7, 1923.

135. *Fort Worth Star-Telegram,* November 13, 1923.

136. *Austin American,* January 19, 1925.

137. In 1935, Neff was appointed by Governor James V. Allred to the Commission of Control for the Texas Centennial Celebrations. See *Senate Journal,* 44th Leg., Reg. Sess., 1935, May 10, 1935, pp. 1817 and 1865. Neff was appointed by Allred and confirmed by the Senate on the same day. The Commission of Control was charged with the broad authority to supervise disbursement of the $3 million appropriation for the Centennial approved by the 44th Legislature. *General and Special Laws of the State of Texas,* 44th Leg., Reg. Sess., 1935, pp. 417-437.

138. William Neff Patman, interview by Terrell Blodgett, Austin, Texas, October 20, 2006, Blodgett Collection.

139. The case was styled *Johnson v. Darr* (114 Tex 516).

140. Cureton to Neff, March 8, 1924, Neff Papers.

141. *Dallas Morning News,* January 2 and 3, 1925.

142. Watkins to Neff, January 3, 1925, Neff Papers; *Dallas Morning News,* January 8, 1925. The story of Neff's appointment of three female attorneys to serve as special justices to hear this one case has been the subject of several scholarly papers by lawyers and law students. The most recent of these at the time of publication of this book was a comprehensive paper presented to the annual meeting of the Texas State Historical Association in 2004 by Dallas attorney Jeffrey D. Dunn. He reviews the theories as to Neff's thinking set out by Sue Hall and other writers and then proceeds to set forth his own. He states that the evidence does not suggest that Neff appointed a total female court for any political advantage, arguing, with good reason, that Neff already was known as a strong supporter of women's causes. Dunn's conclusion: Neff was genuinely interested in advancing the status of women. See Jeffrey D. Dunn, "The Legacy of *Johnson v. Darr*: The 1925 Decision of the All-Woman Supreme Court," paper presented at the annual meeting of the Texas State Historical Association, Austin, Texas, March 6, 2004. Other works on the subject are cited in his paper. An interesting side note: Neff attempted to blaze the way for additional women appointments to Texas courts, but his effort went for naught until 1935. In that year, Governor James V. Allred appointed Sarah T. Hughes to a state district court position.

143. Charles Wolfe and Kip Lornell, *The Life and Legend of Leadbelly* (New York: Harper Collins, 1992), front jacket flap.

144. John Lightfoot, "Early Texas Bluesmen," in *The Roots of Texas Music*, ed. Lawrence Clayton and Joe W. Specht (College Station: Texas A&M University Press, 2003).

145. Wolfe and Lornell, *Leadbelly,* p. 134.

146. Subsequent years brought both heartache and fame to the blues singer. Five years after his pardon by Neff, Leadbelly was back in prison in Louisiana on assault charges. This time, famed folklorist John Lomax came to his rescue, succeeded in getting him released early from the Louisiana prison, and, in 1935, took him to New York City to perform. *Time* and *Life* magazines both featured articles on the convict. See also jazz historian Dave Oliphant's history of Texas jazz music, *Texan Jazz* (Austin: University of Texas Press, 1996).

147. *Senate Journal*, 39th Leg., Reg. Sess., 1925, January 14, 1925, p. 23.

148. Ibid., January 19, 1925, p. 80.

149. Ibid., January 20, 1925, p. 82.

150. Ibid., January 29, 1925, pp. 179-180.

151. Ibid., February 9, 1925, pp. 321-322.

152. Neff to Colp, September 21, 1923, Neff Papers.

153. Colp's extensive work, beginning in 1924 and terminated by his premature death in 1935, is detailed in Jeffrey Fritz Crunk's excellent thesis, "Breathing Spots for the People," cited earlier. Utilizing the David E. Colp Papers at the University of Texas, Crunk paints a vivid picture of Colp's cross-country travels around the state of Texas as he persuaded, cajoled, and virtually bribed property owners to donate land to the state.

154. *San Antonio Express*, March 20, 1924.

155. *San Antonio Express*, July 20, 1924.

156. *San Antonio Express*, July 16, 1924.

157. Unattributed newspaper clipping, November 1924, Neff Papers.

158. *House Journal*, 39th Leg., Reg. Sess., 1925, February 4, 1925, pp. 362-363.

159. James Wright Steely, *Parks for Texas: Enduring Landscapes of the New Deal* (Austin: University of Texas Press, 1999), p. 8.

160. Governor Ma Ferguson appointed Neff to the State Parks Board in 1933. See *Senate Journal*, 43rd Leg., Reg. Sess., 1933, May 11, 1933, p. 1712. He was confirmed by the Senate on May 15, 1933. See *Senate Journal*, 43rd Leg., Reg. Sess., 1933, May 15, 1933, p. 1777.

161. Shortly after the unveiling on January 19—Neff's next-to-last day in office—Neff was delighted to receive a letter from Philip Ashton Rollins, noted author of *The Cowboy: An Unconventional History of Civilization on the Old-Time Cattle Range* (a 1936 report published by the Oklahoma University Press in 1997), one of the early definitive studies of the cowboy species. Rollins stated in his letter that he had "ridden the Northern range for years" and the Warren statue was the single piece "in bronze or stone" that successfully represented the Texas cowboy. Rollins to Neff, January 13, 1925, Neff Papers.

162. Neff, *Battles of Peace,* pp. 267-270.

163. Jacque Barcus, interview by Dorothy Blodgett and David L. Scott, Austin, Texas, April 21, 1998, Blodgett Collection.

164. Ouida Wallace Ferguson Nalle, *Two Fergusons of Texas, or "Two Governors for the Price of One"* (San Antonio: Naylor, 1946).

165. May Nelson Paulissen and Carl McQueary, *Miriam: Miriam Amanda Ferguson of Bell County, The Southern Belle Who Became the First Woman Governor of Texas* (Austin: Eakin Press, 1995), p. 184.

166. *Austin American*, January 17, 1925.

167. See Robert C. Cotner, *James Stephen Hogg: A Biography* (Austin and London: University of Texas Press, 1959). Two notable biographies of John B. Connally are Ann Fears Crawford and Jack Keever, *John B. Connally: Portrait in Power* (Austin: Jenkins Publishing Company, 1973), and James Reston Jr., *The Lone Star: The Life of John Connally* (New York: Harper and Row, 1989).

168. The gubernatorial years of the Fergusons have been decried by historians from earlier days, including Norman D. Brown (*Hood, Bonnet, and Little Brown Jug*, see pp. 253-296) and Lewis Gould (*Progressives and Prohibitionists*, see pp. 185-221), as well as by more recent writers such as James L. Haley (*Passionate Nation*, see pp. 464-484) and Robert Utley (*Lone Star Lawmen*, see p. 118). In what was proclaimed in 1995 as the first definitive biography of Ma Ferguson, authors May Nelson Paulissen and Carl McQueary, on pp.117-160, paint an unflattering picture of the Fergusons, both in regard to various types of governmental contracts they awarded as well as their dealings with the state's pardon and parole function. James E. Ferguson remains into the twenty-first century the only Texas governor to be impeached by the Texas House of Representatives and subsequently convicted by the Texas Senate and barred from future office.

169. A. Garland Adair and Ellen Bohlender Coats, *Texas: Its History* (Philadelphia: John C. Winston Co., 1954), p. 220; and June Rayfield Welch, *The Texas Governor* (Dallas: G. L. A. Press, 1977), p. 136.

170. Steely, *Parks for Texas*, front jacket flap.

171. Martin to Shirley, January 13, 1937, as quoted in Emma Shirley, "The Administration of Pat M. Neff: Governor of Texas, 1921-1925," *Baylor Bulletin* 41, no. 4 (December 1938): 110. Although Martin was a good friend of Neff's and might be expected to speak favorably of his contributions, his credibility in making this assessment is evident in the fact that two governors after Neff valued his advice sufficiently to reappoint him to the commission.

172. *General Laws of the State of Texas*, 38th Leg., Reg. Sess., 1923, pp. 258-260.

173. Shirley, "Administration of Pat Neff," p. 109.

174. Ibid., pp. 112-113.

175. *Austin American*, January 21, 1925.

176. *Dallas Morning News*, January 21, 1925.

177. Gantt, *Chief Executive in Texas*, p. 303.

178. Lee Simmons, *Assignment Huntsville: Memoirs of a Texas Prison Official* (Austin: University of Texas Press, 1957), p. 192.

179. *Dallas Morning News*, January 19, 1925; *Austin American*, January 19, 1925.

180. *Dallas Morning News*, January 26, 1952.

181. Neff, *Battles of Peace*, pp. 261-265.

182. Minutes, Baylor University Board of Trustees, January 30, 1925, pp. 22, 27.

183. Connally to Neff, telegram, January 9, 1925, Neff Papers.

Chapter 8. Two Appointments, Two Headaches

1. Pat M. Neff, *The Battles of Peace* (Fort Worth: Pioneer Publishing Co., 1925), p. 261.

2. Myrtie to Hallie Maude, April 6, 1925, Hallie Maude Neff Wilcox Papers, Texas Collection, Baylor University.

3. Diary of Pat Neff, Neff Papers.

4. Myrtie to Hallie Maude, April 28, 1925, Hallie Maude Neff Wilcox Papers.

5. Neff to Hallie Maude, May 25, 1925, Neff Papers.

6. Neff to Ione Neff, June 17, 1925, Neff Papers.

7. The Chautauqua movement began in 1874 to provide training for Sunday School teachers in Protestant churches. Named for Lake Chautauqua located in southwestern New York State, the experience, over the next fifty years, became highly popular as it broadened from a religious experience to include educational and musical components. The early Chautauqua programs in New York featured speeches by U.S. presidents and other notables (including Pat Neff in 1922) and continue to attract individuals each summer from around the country to participate in its unique combination of music, art, drama, religion, stimulating discussion, history, and recreation. See Joseph E. Gould, *The Chautauqua Movement* (New York: State University of New York), 1961. See also Jeffrey Simpson, *Chautauqua: An American Utopia* (New York: Henry N. Abrams, Inc., in association with the Chautauqua Institution, 1999).

8. *Waco Times-Herald,* July 3 and 10, 1925.

9. Neff to Sallie Calvert, December 24, 1925, Neff Papers.

10. Bell to Hallie Maude, February 13, 1923, Hallie Maude Neff Wilcox Papers.

11. Bobbie Barnes, interview by Dorothy Blodgett, April 30, 1992, Blodgett Collection.

12. Cause 7098, Mandate, Court of Civil Appeals, Third Supreme Judicial District at Austin, February 14, 1928.

13. Mary C. Byers, interview by Dorothy Blodgett, September 8, 1997, Blodgett Collection; Myrtie to Neff, April 5, 1926, Neff Papers; Jacque Barcus, interview by Dorothy Blodgett and David L. Scott, April 21, 1998, Blodgett Collection.

14. Direct Index to Minutes, District Court, Travis County, vol. 2, 1914-1933, A-Z, Case 42,218, pp. 305, 399.

15. Index, Criminal Minutes, No. 1, Travis County District Court, 1878-1936, Cause 19142, pp. C 256, 276, 394, D 115.

16. Bell had gone to college in New York and worked briefly there after the World War. In New York, he married the widow of a wealthy investment banker and returned with her to Austin about 1943. She died a few years later, and he met and married a nurse. Bell became general counsel for the State Health Department, a position he held until his retirement in 1970 (Mary C. Byers, interview, 1997; *Austin American-Statesman,* December 6, 1975). He became a prominent member of the Presbyterian Church in Austin and in 1967 founded Westminster Manor, which continues to be one of Austin's premier retirement homes into the twenty-first century. To honor him, the home gave Bell and his wife a penthouse apartment for life and named the home's community gathering room Harris Bell Hall for him. (Margaret C. Berry, *Westminster Manor: The First Thirty-Five Years* [Austin: Nortex Press, 2003], pp. 23, 55.)

17. *San Antonio Express*, November 21, 1924.

18. Norris to Neff, December 12, 1925, Neff Papers.

19. Norris to Neff, August 9, 1926, Neff Papers.

20. Harry Leon McBeth, *Texas Baptists: A Sesquicentennial History* (Dallas: Baptistway Press, 1998), p. 225.

21. *Texas Baptist Annual* (San Antonio: Baptist General Convention of Texas, 1926), p. 179. For discussion of Neff's denominational leadership generally, see Ray Earl Bennett, "Pat M. Neff: His Denominational Leadership," master's thesis, Baylor University, Waco, Texas, 1960.

22. *Waco Times-Herald*, August 6, 15, 16, 1926.

23. U.S. Board of Mediation, *Annual Report of the United States Board of Mediation, 1927* (Washington, D.C.: Government Printing Office, 1927), pp. 1-9.

24. Mayfield to Neff, telegram, February 9, 1927, Neff Papers.

25. *San Antonio Express*, February 15, 1927.

26. Neff to Groner, March 7, 1927, Neff Papers.

27. Marrinan to Neff, May 5, 1927, National Archives and Records Administration.

28. Winslow to Neff, telegram, September 1, 1927, National Archives and Records Administration.

29. Neff to Winslow, telegram, October 4, 1927, National Archives and Records Administration.

30. Winslow to Neff, telegram, October 6, 1927, National Archives and Records Administration.

31. Marrinan to Neff, March 6, 1928, National Archives and Records Administration.

32. Charles Comer Alexander, "Crusade for Conformity: The Ku Klux Klan in Texas, 1920-1927," master's thesis, University of Texas, Austin, Texas, 1959. Mayfield was still identified with the Klan, and Alexander writes: "By the end of 1927, the Invisible Empire was no more. The Klan was finished—dethroned, debased, discredited" (p. 277). See also Seth Shepard McKay, *Texas Politics, 1906-1944; with Special Reference to the German Counties* (Lubbock: Texas Tech Press, 1952), pp. 164-174.

33. Kelly to Neff, January 14, 1928, Neff Papers.

34. Neff to Hallie Maude, July 5, 1928, Neff Papers.

35. Raskob to Neff, telegram, August 10, 1928, Neff Papers.

36. *Waco News-Tribune*, September 7, 1928.

37. *Texas Almanac 2006-2007* (Dallas: Dallas Morning News, 2006), p. 399.

38. Mayfield to Coolidge, December 4, 1928; Sanders, Secretary to the President, to Mayfield, December 7, 1928, National Archives and Records Administration.

39. Connally to Neff, telegram, December 17, 1928, Neff Papers.

40. Mayfield to Neff, telegram, December 26, 1928, Neff Papers.

41. Gallagher, Kinsley, Goodridge, and Steadhouse to Sheppard, December 12, 1928, Neff Papers.

42. *Nomination of Hon. Pat M. Neff, Hearings before the Committee on Interstate Commerce Commission, United States Senate, Seventieth Congress, Second Session* (Washington, D.C.,

Government Printing Office, 1929). For fuller coverage of Neff's service on the Mediation Board, see Stephen Edward Gooch, "Pat Neff and the National Mediation Board," master's thesis, Baylor University, Waco, Texas, 1968.

43. Neff to President Hoover, March 15, 1929, Neff Papers.

44. Couch to President Hoover, March 4, 1929, Neff Papers.

45. Neff to President Hoover, March 15, 1929, Neff Papers.

46. Colquitt was confirmed by the U.S. Senate on May 10, 1929. See George Portal Huckaby, "Oscar Branch Colquitt: A Political Biography," Ph.D. diss., University of Texas, Austin, Texas, 1946, p. 468.

47. *Fort Worth Star-Telegram,* June 17, 1928; Neff calendar book, 1929, Neff Papers.

48. Neff to Hallie Maude, June 7, 1928; Neff to Hallie Maude, July 30, 1929; both in Hallie Maude Neff Wilcox Papers.

49. *Baptist Standard,* November 24, 1927.

50. *Dallas Morning News,* April 28, 1928.

51. Roger N. Conger, ed., *The Best of Brann: The Iconoclast* (Waco: Texian Press, 1967), p. 109. Brann actually wrote: "As a small Waco property owner, I will give it [Baylor] $1,000 any time to move to Dallas, and double that amount if it will go to Honolulu or hell. . . . Baylor is a disgrace to the community."

52. Kent Keeth, "Looking Back at Baylor 1928," pts. I and II, reprinted in *Baylor Line* (November 1988 and January 1989).

53. Ibid., pts. II and III, January 1989, and March 1989.

54. Ibid., pt. III, March 1989.

55. Ibid., pt. IV, May 1989.

56. Ibid.

57. Daniel to Neff, July 19, 1929, Neff Papers.

58. Cranfill to Neff, October 7, 1929, Neff Papers.

59. *Austin Statesman,* September 27, 1929.

60. *Austin American,* October 17, 1929.

61. The story of the East Texas oil fields has been captured in a number of books, several of them on the oil industry as a whole, but featuring individual chapters on that particular event. Among the books are Diana Davids Olien and Roger M. Olien, *Oil in Texas: The Gusher Age, 1895-1945* (Austin: University of Texas Press, 2002); Carl Coke Rister, *Oil! Titan of the Southwest* (Norman: University of Oklahoma Press, 1949); William R. Childs, *The Texas Railroad Commission: Understanding Regulation in America to the Mid Twentieth Century* (College Station: Texas A&M University Press, 2005); Nicholas George Malavis, *Bless the Pure and Humble: Texas Lawyers and Oil Regulation, 1919-1936* (College Station: Texas A&M University Press, 1996).

62. Childs, *Texas Railroad Commission.*

63. J.W.H. to Carlisle, June 22, 1929; *Dallas Morning News,* July 19, 1930.

64. *Handbook of Texas Online,* s.v. "Johnson, Rebekah Baines," http://www.tsha.utexas.edu/handbook/online/articles/JJ/fjo22.html.

65. May Nelson Paulissen and Carl McQueary, *Miriam: Miriam Amanda Ferguson of Bell*

County: The Southern Belle Who Became the First Woman Governor of Texas (Austin: Eakin Press, 1995), p. 125.

66. Gene Barnwell Waugh, interview by Dorothy Blodgett, September 20, 2000, Blodgett Collection.

67. Sam Houston Johnson, *My Brother, Lyndon*, ed. Enrique Hank Lopez (Cowles Book Co., 1970), pp. 31-34.

68. Neff to Lyndon B. Johnson, May 17, 1924, Neff Papers.

69. "Notes of the President's Meeting with Ronnie Dugger, March 23, 1968," Appointment File Diary Backup, Lyndon Baines Johnson Presidential Library, Austin, Texas.

70. Ava Johnson Cox, interview by Dorothy Blodgett and David L. Scott, October 29, 1992, Blodgett Collection.

71. Alfred Steinberg, *Sam Johnson's Boy: A Close-up of the President from Texas* (New York: Macmillan Co., 1968), pp. 50-53.

72. Neff to Sam Johnson, June 7, 1930; Sam Johnson to Neff, June 8, 1930; both in Neff Papers.

73. Neff to Sam Johnson, June 21, 1930, Neff Papers.

74. Welly K. Hopkins, interview by Eric F. Goldman, May 11, 1965, Lyndon Baines Johnson Presidential Library.

75. Wilton Woods, interview by Michael L. Gillette, December 6, 1979, Lyndon Baines Johnson Presidential Library.

76. Neff to Johnson, August 8, 1930. Seven years later, Johnson's mother wrote Baylor President Neff asking him to help her son in his first congressional race. In her letter of March 2, 1937, found in the Neff Papers, she wrote that Johnson's ambition was "to be like Pat Neff" and that Neff had been "his political hero." The mother closed stating: "I have great hopes for my son." Neff promptly replied, saying he had talked with Lyndon by telephone and that "he knows just where I can be of assistance to him." Neff to Mrs. Sam Johnson, March 9, 1937, Neff Papers.

77. Burkett to Neff, June 24, 1930; Lomax to Neff, June 24, 1930; Burkett to Neff, June 25, 1930; Coplin to Neff, June 26, 1930; Cain to Neff, June 27, 1930; Elliott to Neff, June 27, 1930; Pierson to Neff, July 11, 1930; all in Neff Papers. Neff's use of state employees in his campaign was in line with the prevailing practices, including those of his colleagues on the Railroad Commission. It would be more than a half century later (1983) before the legislature enacted laws prohibiting the use of state employees and other state resources for campaign purposes.

78. *Dallas Morning News,* August 21, 1930.

79. *Dallas Morning News* and *San Antonio Express*, November 5, 1930.

80. *Austin American,* January 29, 1931.

81. Childs, *Texas Railroad Commission*, p. 173.

82. Hallie Maude to Myrtie, September 29, 1929, Hallie Maude Neff Wilcox Papers.

83. Myrtie to Hallie Maude, September 24, 1931, Hallie Maude Neff Wilcox Papers.

84. For an excellent overall description of the Depression in Texas, see *Handbook of Texas Online*, s.v. "Great Depression," http://www.tsha.utexas.edu/handbook/online/articles/GG/npg1.html.

85. Neff to Garner, telegram, undated, Neff Papers.

86. Childs, *Texas Railroad Commission*, p. 148.

87. Ibid., p. 206.

88. *Handbook of Texas Online*, s.v. "East Texas Oilfield," http://www.tsha.utexas.edu/handbook/online/articles/EE/doe1.html .

89. David F. Prindle, *Petroleum Politics and the Texas Railroad Commission* (Austin: University of Texas Press, 1981), p. 25.

90. Olien and Olien, *Oil in Texas,* p. 183.

91. Neff to Smith, July 28, 1931; Neff to Terrell, October 1, 1931; Neff to Petet, July 37, 1931; Neff to Guy, March 22, 1931; all in Neff Papers.

92. *House Journal*, 42nd Leg., 1st Called Sess., 1931, July 14, 1931, pp. 1-526.

93. "Testimony of Texas Railroad Commissioner Pat M. Neff," *House Journal,* 42nd Leg., 1st Called Sess., 1931, appendix A, "Proceedings of Investigating Committee of the Whole House of Representatives Relating to the Oil and Gas Industry, July 24, 1931," pp. 239, 241.

94. Ibid., "Testimony of Texas Railroad Commissioner C. V. Terrell," July 29, 1931, p. 491.

95. *Austin American*, July 28, 1931.

96. *MacMillan v. Railroad Commission*, 51 F 2d 400 (W.D. Tex, 1931).

97. Childs, *Texas Railroad Commission*, p. 210; Olien and Olien, *Oil in Texas*, p. 185.

98. Olien and Olien, *Oil in Texas*, p.185.

99. Ibid., p. 186; Childs, *Texas Railroad Commission*, p. 205.

100. Childs, *Texas Railroad Commission*, p. 214.

101. Ibid., pp. 195, 206.

102. Minutes, Texas Railroad Commission, June 4, 1932, p. 24, Texas State Library and Archives.

Chapter 9. Miracle on the Brazos

1. Neff, "Remarks to the Faculty," January 30, 1947, unpublished manuscript, Neff Papers.

2. The information about Baylor's early days is drawn from three sources: Eugene W. Baker, *To Light the Ways of Time: An Illustrated History of Baylor University, 1845-1986* (Waco: Baylor University Press, 1987); Thomas E. Turner, *Instruments of Providence: Biographical Vignettes of the Charter Trustees of Baylor University* (Waco: Baylor University Press, 1989); Lois Smith Murray, *Baylor at Independence* (Waco: Baylor University Press, 1972).

3. Marquis James, *The Raven: A Biography of Sam Houston* (Indianapolis: Bobbs-Merrill, 1976), p. 385. Sam Houston later became a donor to Baylor at Independence.

4. Baker, *To Light the Ways of Time,* pp. 46-56.

5. Ibid., p. 66.

6. Harry Leon McBeth, *Texas Baptists: A Sesquicentennial History* (Dallas: Broadway Press, 1998), pp. 96-98. McBeth wrote that Truett criss-crossed the state, traveling by "train, horse-back, buggy, wagons, and on foot."

7. Ibid., p. 126.

8. *Baylor Monthly,* May 1927, p. 4; *Texas Baptist Annual* (Fort Worth: Baptist General Convention of Texas, 1901), pp. 40-44; Baker, *To Light the Ways of Time,* pp. 108-109.

9. Brooks to Dr. E. C. Sage, General Education Board, New York, N.Y., undated, Brooks Papers, Texas Collection, Baylor University.

10. In 2006, the Baylor Board of Trustees voted to raze the original Brooks Hall and replace it with another, retaining the name and the landmark Brooks arch through which thousands of students had passed over its eighty-five-year life. See Kent Keeth, *Looking Back at Baylor: A Collection of Historical Vignettes* (Waco: Baylor University, 1985), p. 21; *Baylor Flash,* online newsletter, Baylor University, February 3, 2006, http://www.baylor.edu/pr/news.php?action=story&story=38780 .

11. Baker, *To Light the Ways,* p. 147.

12. Ibid.

13. Joseph Martin Dawson, *Brooks Takes the Long Look* (Waco: Baylor University Press, 1931), pp. 26-45.

14. Sims Palmer Brooks and Aurelia Brooks Harlan, Oral Memoirs, interview by Kent Keeth, October 4, 1984, p. 240, Baylor University Institute for Oral History (hereafter referred to as BUIOH).

15. *Dallas Morning News,* May 15, 1931.

16. Brooks and Harlan, Oral Memoirs, pp. 240-241.

17. Martin to Collins, July 27, 1931, Neff Papers.

18. Allen had two factors working against him. He did not have the state and national persona, both in the Baptist brotherhood and in politics, which Neff had; secondly, he had already invited a "liberal" to give the 1932 spring commencement address. The "liberal" was Dr. Kirby Page, editor of the *World Tomorrow* (a publication not favorably viewed in conservative political circles). Board members, most of them of a conservative bent, undoubtedly felt even further vindicated in passing on Allen when, during his commencement address,

Page "openly declared capitalism dead and himself a socialist." See *Waco Tribune Herald*, June 2, 1932.

19. Minutes, Baylor University Board of Trustees, February 9, 1932, pp. 99-104.

20. Ibid.

21. Jenkins (Secretary of Baylor Board of Trustees) to Neff, February 10, 1932, Neff Papers.

22. Martin to Reverend Loyd Lester, March 12, 1947, Neff Papers; Joseph Martin Dawson, *A Thousand Months to Remember: An Autobiography* (Waco: Baylor University Press, 1964), p. 137.

23. Emma Shirley, "A Baylor Memory," *Waco Citizen*, August 7, 1975, reprinted in Keeth, *Looking Back*, p. 47.

24. Frederick L. Collins, *Our American Kings* (New York and London: Century Co., 1924), p. 165.

25. Audiotape of Neff's final chapel address, December 18, 1947, Texas Collection, Baylor University, Waco, Texas.

26. Brian DeGraffenreid, telephone interview by Dorothy Blodgett, June 16, 1998, Blodgett Collection.

27. Guy B. Harrison Jr., Oral Memoirs, interview by Thomas L. Charlton, June 20, 1974, p. 223, Baylor University Program for Oral History (hereafter referred to as BUPOH).

28. Cathryn Chapin, telephone interview by Dorothy Blodgett, February 28, 1992, Blodgett Collection.

29. Paul Baker, interview by Dorothy Blodgett, December 12, 1996, Blodgett Collection. Robert Caro, in his first book on Lyndon B. Johnson, wrote that a Johnson City resident remembered Lyndon's father and one of his brothers "strutting." The resident stated that "the Johnsons could strut sitting down." See Robert A. Caro, *The Years of Lyndon Johnson: The Path to Power* (New York: Alfred A. Knopf, 1982), p. 42. The Johnson City resident quoted was apparently Ohlen Cox or Stella Gliddon; it is not possible from the book's notes to determine exactly which person was quoted. See Caro, p. 794. The origin of the saying "strutting standing still" or "strutting sitting down" is not known.

30. Paul Baker, interview by Dorothy Blodgett, December 12, 1996, Blodgett Collection.

31. Jerry Ratliff, interview by Dorothy Blodgett, November 20, 1997, Blodgett Collection; *Lariat*, March 24, 1938.

32. Sam H. Shurtleff Jr., interview by Dorothy Blodgett, December 16, 1997, Blodgett Collection.

33. See Charles R. Townsend, *San Antonio Rose: The Life and Music of Bob Wills* (Urbana and Chicago: University of Illinois Press, 1976), pp. 88-89.

34. Cal Newton, interview by Dorothy Blodgett and Terrell Blodgett, September 22, 1998, Blodgett Collection.

35. Jim Bowmer to Dorothy Blodgett, October 31, 2003, Blodgett Collection.

36. Thomas E. Turner to Dorothy Blodgett, February 24, 1998, Blodgett Collection.

37. George Robinson, "Pat M. Neff, Baylor Chief," editorial, *Houston Post*, March 22, 1932.

38. Turner to Blodgett, February 24, 1998, Blodgett Collection.

39. C. E. Bryant to Dorothy Blodgett, April 9, 1996, Blodgett Collection.

40. W. R. Poage, *Politics, Texas Style* (Waco: Texian Press, 1974), pp. 93, 96.

41. *Texas Baptist Annual* (El Paso: Baptist General Convention of Texas, 1937), p. 33.

42. *Texas Baptist Annual* (Amarillo: Baptist General Convention of Texas, 1947), p. 28.

43. Ibid.

44. McBeth, *Texas Baptists*, pp. 187-188.

45. William Robert "Bob" Poage, Oral Memoirs, interview by Thomas L. Charlton, March 19, 1979, pp. 228-230, BUIOH.

46. Rexford G. Tugwell, *The Democratic Roosevelt: A Biography of Franklin D. Roosevelt* (Garden City, N.Y.: Doubleday, 1957).

47. Neff, Letters, 1932-1937, Depression Job Applications, Neff Papers.

48. Guy B. Harrison, Jr., Oral Memoirs, interview by Thomas L. Charlton, June 20, 1974, pp. 228-229, BUPOH; Marvin Goebel, interview by Terrell Blodgett, July 12, 2000, Blodgett Collection.

49. Neff to Groner, October 8, 1934, Neff Papers.

50. Cornelia Marshall Smith, Oral Memoirs, interview by Kay Clifton, March 22, 1978, p. 90, BUPOH; Dixon Wecter, *The Age of the Great Depression, 1929-1941* (New York: Macmillan, 1948), pp. 25-26.

51. Hallie Maude (Neff) Wilcox, April 24, 1953, as quoted in Macklyn Ward Hubbell, "The Life of Pat Neff," master's thesis, University of Houston, Houston, Texas, 1953.

52. Paul Baker, interview by Dorothy Blodgett, December 12, 1996, Blodgett Collection.

53. Neill Coker Morris, Oral Memoirs, interview by Rufus B. Spain, June 18, 1975, p. 135, BUPOH.

54. Harrison, Oral Memoirs, pp. 226-229.

55. Keeth, *Looking Back*, p. 16.

56. Morris, Oral Memoirs, pp. 132-133.

57. E. N. Jones, Oral Memoirs, interview by Thomas L. Charlton, May 10, 1972, pp. 89-91, BUPOH.

58. Smith, Oral Memoirs, pp. 104-105.

59. William Richmond Stephens, Oral Memoirs, interview by Thomas L. Charlton, October 2, 1975, pp. 121, 124-125, BUPOH.

60. Harrison, Oral Memoirs, p. 236.

61. Newton, interview by Dorothy Blodgett and Terrell Blodgett, September 22,1998, Blodgett Collection.

62. Harrison, Oral Memoirs, p. 229.

63. Louise Durham Denham, Oral Memoirs, interview by Lois Myers, December 3, 1998, pp. 108, 124, BUIOH.

64. *Waco Tribune Herald*, June 26, 1932.

65. Jack Hightower, interview by Terrell Blodgett, April 5, 2002, Blodgett Collection.

66. David Rupert Murph, "Price Daniel: The Life of a Public Man, 1910-1956," Ph.D. diss., Texas Christian University, Fort Worth, Texas, 1975, p. 49.

67. Neff, "The Invisible in a University," manuscript, undated, Neff Papers.

68. Neff to Dr. T. C. Hairston; unidentified newspaper clipping, undated; Neff to Weldon Alexander, August 22, 1933; all in Neff Papers; as quoted in James Franklin Palmer, "Pat Morris Neff, President of Baylor University, 1932-1939," master's thesis, Baylor University, Waco, Texas, 1960, pp. 112-113.

69. "Convocation/Dedication Commemorating the 144th Year of Baylor University and the Dedication of the Ferrell Center and the Paul J. Meyer Arena" (program), November 18, 1988, online: http://baylorbears.collegesports.com/school-bio/bay-theferrellcenter.html .

70. Baker, *To Light the Ways of Time*, p.157.

71. *Dallas Morning News*, April 4, 1943.

72. Neff to Driskill Hotel, Austin, October 13, 1933, Neff Papers.

73. Neff to Barlow, May 15, 1934, Neff Papers.

74. Myrtie to Neff, July 3, 1932, Neff Papers.

75. Since 1925, Hallie Maude had taken her summer trip to Europe six of the past eight years.

76. Bobbie Barnes, interview by Dorothy Blodgett, April 30, 1992, Blodgett Collection.

77. Ibid.

78. Michael Beaty, Todd Buras, and Larry Lyon, "Baptist Higher Education: A Conflict of Terms?" *Baylor Line* (winter 1997): 47.

79. *Waco Times-Herald*, September 22, 1932.

80. Special reports made by chapel checkers for the fall quarter, October 11, 1935, as quoted in Palmer, "Pat Morris Neff," pp. 142-143.

81. Harry M. Provence, "The Chapel Hour—What It Meant to Me," *Baylor Bulletin* 40, no. 3 (August 1937): 64-65; Lady Ray Eastland, "In Favor of Chapel," *Baylor Bulletin* 40, no. 3 (August 1937): pp. 65-68.

82. Louise Yelvington Denham, interview by Dorothy Blodgett, November 30, 1998, Blodgett Collection.

83. *Waco News-Tribune*, October 4, 1932.

84. Paul Baker, interview by Blodgett, December 12, 1996.

85. Bowmer to Dorothy Blodgett, October 31, 2003, Blodgett Collection.

86. Telegram, November 9, 1932, Neff Papers.

87. Among the supporting letters Neff received was one from his old friend at the University of Texas, Dr. Frederick Eby, December 13, 1932, Neff Papers.

88. Unidentified newspaper clipping, December 14, 1932, Neff Papers.

89. Harrison, Oral Memoirs, p. 229.

90. Keeth, *Looking Back*, p. 61.

91. Minutes, Executive Committee, Baylor University Board of Trustees, February 14, 1933, p. 219.

92. Goldstein to Neff, May 27, 1933, Neff Papers.

93. Mrs. George B. Graves to Mary D. Farrell, January 17, 1975, Neff Papers.

94. Roberta Keys Torn, interview by Dorothy Blodgett and Terrell Blodgett, September 22, 2000, Blodgett Collection.

95. Smyth to Neff, March 9, 1933; *Lariat,* March 14, 1933.

Chapter 10. The Promoter

1. Neff to Norris, July 14, 1933; Neff to Thomas, August 4, 1933; both in Neff Papers.

2. *Dallas Morning News,* August 27, 1933.

3. Eugene W. Baker, *To Light the Ways of Time: An Illustrated History of Baylor University, 1845-1986* (Waco: Baylor University Press, 1987), pp. 158, 160.

4. Kent Keeth, *Looking Back at Baylor: A Collection of Historical Vignettes* (Waco: Baylor University, 1985), p. 16.

5. *Texas Baptist Annual* (Fort Worth: Baptist General Convention of Texas, 1933), pp. 45-46.

6. Neill Coker Morris, Oral Memoirs, interview by Rufus B. Spain, June 18, 1975, p. 139, Baylor University Program for Oral History, hereafter cited as BUPOH.

7. Charles Wallace Barrow, Oral Memoirs, interview by Rebecca Sharpless, December 3, 1993, p. 9, Baylor University Institute for Oral History, hereafter cited as BUIOH.

8. Press release, National Youth Administration, no month or day, 1936, Neff Papers.

9. Neff to Johnson, June 9, 1936, Neff Papers.

10. Proposed Work Plan, National Youth Administration, no month or day, 1942, Neff Papers.

11. *Texas Baptist Annual* (San Antonio: Baptist General Convention of Texas, 1934), p. 53.

12. *Texas Baptist Annual* (Houston: Baptist General Convention of Texas, 1935), p. 38.

13. *Texas Baptist Annual* (Mineral Wells: Baptist General Convention of Texas, 1936), p. 41.

14. *Texas Baptist Annual* (El Paso: Baptist General Convention of Texas, 1937), p. 33.

15. *Texas Baptist Annual* (Fort Worth: Baptist General Convention of Texas, 1933), p. 47.

16. Roberta Keys Torn, interview by Dorothy Blodgett and Terrell Blodgett, September 22, 2000, Blodgett Collection.

17. Ibid.

18. *Texas Baptist Annual* (Houston: Baptist General Convention of Texas, 1935), p. 37.

19. Enrollment climbed slowly but steadily through the 1939-1940 school year. See *Texas Baptist Annual* (San Antonio: Baptist General Convention of Texas, 1939), p. 32.

20. M. John Kulesz Jr., "A History and Analysis of Radio Broadcasting at Baylor University, 1935-1968," master's thesis, Baylor University, Waco, Texas, 1968.

21. *Houston Chronicle,* September 16, 1934.

22. *Daily Lariat,* February 24, 1938.

23. *Daily Lariat,* April 27, 1938.

24. *Daily Lariat,* November 2, 1935.

25. *Daily Lariat,* February 11, 1938.

26. Speech File, Invitations Accepted and Declined, Baylor Years, Neff Papers. The folder containing a listing of speech invitations accepted and declined is especially interesting for the declinations. In the 1930s, the listing by year of invitations declined includes literally dozens of invitations from churches, universities, high schools, and civic and fraternal organizations.

27. *Waco Times-Herald,* August 8, 1938.

28. *Daily Lariat,* February 13, 1935.

29. *Daily Lariat,* April 8, 1937.

30. Torn, interview by Blodgett and Blodgett, September 22, 2000.

31. *Waco News-Tribune,* March 8, 1937.

32. *Fort Worth Star-Telegram,* November 13, 1923.

33. Kenneth B. Ragsdale, *The Year America Discovered Texas: Centennial '36* (College Station: Texas A&M University Press, 1987), p. 29.

34. Ibid., p. 33.

35. Ibid., pp. 147-148.

36. Roberta Keys to "Dearest Folks," May 10, 1936, Roberta Keys Torn Papers.

37. As of 2004, only two of the Dionne quintuplets remained. The three deceased sisters lived to the ages of twenty, thirty-six, and sixty-seven. Their story is a tragic contrast to the Keys story. The quints were taken from their parents at birth, placed in a theme-park type environment for eight years, and finally returned to their parents in 1943. Later, the sisters filed suit against the Ontario government, claiming they were commercially exploited and wrongly deprived of a share of the earnings from tourists. In 1998, the three surviving sisters were awarded $4 million in compensation from the Ontario government. The scholarship offers from Baylor were never pursued.

The Dionne sisters told their story through two autobiographies: *We Were Five: The Dionne Quintuplets' Story,* by James Brough, with Annette, Cecile, Marie, and Yvonne Dionne (New York: Simon and Schuster, 1965); and *Family Secrets: The Dionne Quintuplets' Own Story,* by Jean-Yves Soucy, with Annette, Cecile, and Yvonne Dionne (Toronto: Stoddart Publishing Co., 1996).

38. Roberta to "Dearest Folks," May 11, 1936, Roberta Keys Torn Papers.

39. Dodie to "Dearest Family," May 14, 1936, Roberta Keys Torn Papers.

40. Ibid.

41. Roberta to "Dearest Folks," May 16, 1936, Roberta Keys Torn Papers.

42. Schaefer to Neff, May 17, 1936, Neff Papers.

43. Neff to Quadruplets, June 22, 1936, Neff Papers.

44. Ragsdale, *The Year America Discovered Texas,* p. 147.

45. Ibid., p. 148.

46. Ibid., p. 150.

47. *Daily Lariat,* May 11, 1937.

48. *Waco News-Tribune,* June 1, 1937.

49. Neff to Baylor University Board of Trustees, July 29, 1937; *Daily Lariat,* November 4, 1937; both in Neff Papers.

50. Torn, interview by Blodgett and Blodgett, September 22, 2000.

51. Neff to Leota Keys, November 6, 1942; Neff to Keys sisters, May 9, 1939; *Daily Lariat,* October 20, 1938, and October 25, 1940.

52. *Baylor Lariat,* March 19, 1998. In 2005, Roberta celebrated her ninetieth birthday with a party for more than 300 friends and family. Her decreased mobility has forced her to give up her volunteering, but a telephone conversation with her in mid-2006 revealed a still

vibrant, inquisitive personality. On a National Public Radio broadcast in early 2007, her daughter described her as "a real character who has character."

53. *Waco Times-Herald*, April 5, 1935.

54. *Texas Baptist Annual* (Mineral Wells, Tex.: Baptist General Convention of Texas, 1936), p. 37.

55. Neff to Lowe, July 20, 1939, Neff Papers.

56. Neff to Johnson, January 8, 1947, Neff Papers.

57. Neff to Taylor, July 1, 1947, Neff Papers.

58. Neff to Gersbacher, August 13, 1943, Neff Papers.

59. Neff to Kraushaar, January 16, 1939. Neff Papers.

60. Neff to Russell, June 28, 1940, Neff Papers.

61. Robert Flynn and Eugene McKinney, ed., *Paul Baker and the Integration of Abilities* (Fort Worth: TCU Press, 2003), pp. 1-4.

62. Flynn and McKinney's book on Baker gives a detailed account of his achievements.

63. Capp to Neff, July 7, 1934; Neff to Capp, August 2, 1934; both in Neff Papers.

64. *Waco News-Tribune*, January 14, 1939.

65. Baker, *To Light the Ways of Time*, p. 164.

66. James Franklin Palmer, "Pat Morris Neff, President of Baylor University, 1932-1939," master's thesis, Baylor University, Waco, Texas, 1960, p. 96.

67. *Baylor Century*, October 1940, p. 10.

68. The late Governor Ann Richards credited Professor Capp with teaching her "how to say" things.

69. Glenn R. Capp Sr., *"Prof" and Speech Communication at Baylor* (Waco: Baylor University, 1981), pp. 1:109-1:113.

70. Ibid., 1:83.

71. Ibid., 1:87.

72. Matt Dawson, "The Early Years," in *Abner McCall: One Man's Journey*, ed. Sherry Boyd Costello, Gary Cook, and Thomas Turner (Waco: Baylor University, 1981), p. 60.

73. Baker, *To Light the Ways of Time*, p. 294-297.

74. Emma Shirley, Oral Memoirs, interview by Ann Armistead, October 18, 1976, pp. 27-28, BUPOH.

75. Emma Morrill Shirley, "The Administration of Pat M. Neff, Governor of Texas, 1921-1925," *Baylor Bulletin* 41, no. 4 (December 1938).

76. "Historical Timeline," Stetson University, online: http://www.stetson.edu/iro/HistoricalTimeline.htm .

77. *Texas Baptist Annual* (Fort Worth: Baptist General Convention of Texas, 1933), p. 41.

78. Minutes, Waco Executive Committee, Baylor University, December 28, 1937, p. 156.

79. Neff to Martin, September 13, 1939, Neff Papers.

80. *Texas Baptist Annual* (Mineral Wells. Tex.: Baptist General Convention of Texas, 1936), p. 41.

81. Ibid.

82. Hankamer to Neff, February 27, 1937, Neff Papers.

83. Business Office to Neff, October 27, 1947, Neff Papers.

84. *Daily Lariat,* February 2, 1938.

85. Ibid.

86. Keeth, *Looking Back,* p. 28.

87. Neff to Holmes, February 20, 1942, Neff Papers.

88. *Waco Times-Herald,* August 10, 1938.

89. Minutes, Baylor University Board of Trustees, November 7, 1939, p. 42.

90. Neff to Holmes, February 20, 1942, Neff Papers.

91. *Baylor Century,* February 1940.

92. *Daily Lariat,* May 30, 1938. When the chimes quit working in the 1970s, the administration decided to raise funds to install a true carillon with bronze bells. In 1988, the McLane Carillon was dedicated, a gift of the Drayton McLane family and the McLane Company, Inc., of Temple.

93. *Daily Lariat,* February 1, 1940.

94. Neff to Coppini, October 18, 1938, Neff Papers.

95. Baker, *To Light the Ways of Time,* p. 171.

96. Kent Keeth, "Building the Living Room," *Baylor Line* (September 1986, November 1986, February 1987).

97. The Armstrong-Browning building was not dedicated until December 2, 1951. White to Neff, November 13, 1951.

98. *Texas Baptist Annual* (Fort Worth: Baptist General Convention of Texas, 1933), p. 49.

99. Ibid., p. 37.

100. Ibid., p. 38.

101. Neff to Head, October 5, 1939, Neff Papers.

102. Neff to Truett, October 4, 1938, Neff Papers.

103. Neff to Heard, November 18, 1938, Neff Papers.

104. *Daily Lariat,* December 1, 1938.

105. *Texas Baptist Annual* (Dallas: Baptist General Convention of Texas, 1938), p. 41.

106. *The Commission* (Richmond, Va.: Foreign Mission Board, March 1940), p. 79.

107. Clay to Neff, March 20, 1940, Neff Papers.

108. Mary Kemendo Sendon, Oral Memoirs, interview by Lois E. Myers, February 22, 1994, p. 623, BUIOH.

109. Pat M. Neff, *The Battles of Peace* (Fort Worth: Pioneer Publishing Co., 1925), pp. 195-205. In response to Neff's call for a state song in 1924, 286 entries were submitted. A sixteen-member committee appointed by Neff recommended "Texas, Our Texas," but the legislatures in 1925 and 1927 reopened the competition. In 1929, the legislature finally adopted the song that was first recommended, and it remains the official state song of Texas today. See appendix C for the song's lyrics.

110. Matt Dawson, telephone interview by Dorothy Blodgett, September 14, 2000, Blodgett Collection.

111. *Waco News-Tribune,* October 24, 1933.

112. Garrett to Neff, October 4, 1939; Neff to Garrett, October 6, 1939; both in Neff Papers.

113. Neff to Hereford, January 7, 1938; Jackson to Neff, February 8, 1938; Jackson to Neff, April 19, 1938; Neff to Jackson, April 20, 1938; all in Neff Papers.

114. Joseph Martin Dawson, Oral Memoirs, interview by Thomas L. Charlton, April 2, 1971, p. 65, BUOPH.

115. The Baylor University Board of Trustees voted in November 1963 to integrate academic classes. The *Waco Times-Herald* reported in its January 28, 1964, issue that the university had accepted its first five Negro students for enrollment in the evening division. On November 23, 1963, the athletic council announced integration of all athletic teams, effective with the opening of the spring semester, January 30, 1964. See *Waco Times-Herald*, November 24, 1963. Baylor was the first Southwest Conference team to use a black player in a football game. This occurred on September 10, 1966, when John Westbrook played for Baylor in its game with Syracuse University. See Richard Pennington, *Breaking the Ice: The Racial Integration of Southwest Conference Football* (Jefferson, N.C.: McFarland and Co., Inc., 1987), ch. 3. A review of the process of campus integration that took place at Baylor at the time can be found in an article by Vince Clark called "Integrating Baylor," *Baylor Line* (spring 2004): 33-39.

116. Garrett to Neff, October 4, 1939; Neff to Garrett, October 6, 1939; both in Neff Papers.

117. George Nokes, Jr., interview by Terrell Blodgett, November 2, 2006, Blodgett Collection.

118. Lester Harrell, interview by Terrell Blodgett, October 22, 2003, Blodgett Collection.

119. Lucille Carson Harrell and June Page Johnson, interview by Terrell Blodgett, October 22, 2003, Blodgett Collection.

120. *Waco Times-Herald*, November 16, 1933.

121. Louise Yelvington Denham, interview by Dorothy Blodgett, November 30, 1998, Blodgett Collection.

122. Matt Dawson, telephone interview by Dorothy Blodgett, September 14, 2000, Blodgett Collection.

123. Neff, "An Epoch-Making Chapel Service of Baylor University," November 16, 1933, Neff Papers.

124. Elizabeth (Logue) Hightower, telephone interview by Dorothy Blodgett, November 12, 2003, Blodgett Collection.

125. White to Neff, December 6, 1936, Neff Papers, as quoted in Palmer, "Pat Morris Neff," p. 170.

126. Dudley to Neff, April 22, 1938; Neff to Dudley, June 8, 1938; both in Neff Papers.

127. Guy B. Harrison Jr., Oral Memoirs, interview by Thomas L. Charlton, June 20, 1974, p. 229, BUPOH.

128. Palmer, "Pat Morris Neff," p. 172.

129. Ervin to Blodgett, April 18, 2007, Blodgett Collection.

130. Bryant to Dorothy Blodgett, April 9, 1996, Blodgett Collection.

131. Bob Middleton, telephone interview by Dorothy Blodgett, November 17, 2003, Blodgett Collection.

132. Elton Miles, Oral Memoirs, 1987, Texas Collection, Baylor University.

133. Ibid., p. 8.

134. Neff to Board of Trustees, June 22, 1938, Neff Papers.

135. Glenn R. Capp Sr., Oral Memoirs, interview by Gary Wayne Hull, August 31, 1976, p. 29, BUPOH.

136. Neff to Student Loan Committee, September 10, 1938, Neff Papers.

137. Mixson to Grant, September 20, 1940, Neff Papers.

138. The Neff Papers contain two full folders of letters from Neff to the Baylor Business Office, instructing staff to make financial arrangements for hundreds of students on an individual basis.

139. Guy B. Harrison Jr., Oral Memoirs, interview by Thomas L. Charlton, June 20, 1974, p. 233, BUPOH.

140. *Daily Lariat,* January 8, 1935.

141. Brother Short Nose (William B.) Long and Most Fortunate Mary Cole Farrow Long, eds., *The Nose Brotherhood Knows: A Collection of Nothings and Non-Happenings: 1926-1965* (Belton, Tex.: Bear Hollow Publishers, 1997) p. 3.

142. Ibid., p. 4.

143. Ibid., p. 15.

144. *Daily Lariat,* April 19, 1934.

145. *Waco Sunday Tribune-Herald,* March 12, 1939.

146. *Waco Sunday Tribune-Herald,* November 22, 1936.

147. Ibid.

148. *Handbook of Texas Online,* s.v. "Garner, John Nance," http://www.tsha.utexas.edu/handbook/online/articles/GG/fga24.html.

149. Blaise Pecchi, *The Five Weeks of Giuseppe Zangara: The Man Who Would Assassinate FDR* (Chicago: Academy Chicago Publishers, 1998).

150. Unidentified newspaper clipping, Scrapbook 8, as quoted in Palmer, "Pat Morris Neff," p. 111.

151. Neff to Talbott, January 7, 1937, Neff Papers.

152. Walter H. Moursund Sr., "A History of Baylor University College of Medicine, 1900-1953," Faculty Publication, Baylor University College of Medicine, Houston, Texas, 1956, p. 83.

153. Minutes, Baylor University Board of Trustees, April 25, 1933, p. 117.

154. Gribbs to Neff, May 31, 1934; Cohn to Neff, January 18, 1934; both in Neff Papers.

155. Bitting to Neff, October 15, 1937, Neff Papers.

156. Neff to Smyth, numerous letters, 1938 and 1939, medical school folders, Neff Papers.

157. Neff to Bitting, December 5, 1938, Neff Papers.

158. Smyth to Neff, January 6, 1939, January 19, 1939, and January 23, 1939, all in Neff Papers.

159. Neff to Bitting, December 5, 1938, Neff Papers.

160. Minutes, Baylor University Board of Trustees, April 28, 1939, p. 1.

161. Ibid.

162. Moursund, "History of Baylor College of Medicine," pp. 93-94.

163. Hankamer to Neff, December 10, 1938; Martin to Neff, April 2, 1937; Neff to Martin, June 27, 1947; all in Neff Papers.

164. Neff to Martin, August 14, 1940, Martin to Neff, June 18, 1941, both in Neff Papers.

165. Martin to Neff, May 8, 1939, Neff Papers.

166. Armstrong to Martin, May 12, 1939, Neff Papers.

167. "SWC Football, 80 Years, 1915-1995, Roster and Records," photocopy, 1994.

168. Minutes, Waco Executive Committee, November 23, 1932, p. 169.

169. Minutes, Baylor University Board of Trustees, April 19, 1934, p. 1.

170. Ibid., March 26, 1936, p. 36.

171. Minutes, Athletic Committee, Baylor University Board of Trustees, April 29, 1937, p. 84; April 19, 1938, p. 139.

172. M. P. Daniel to Neff, June 12, 1937; M. P. Daniel to Neff, December 15, 1937; both in Neff Papers; *Waco News-Tribune,* May 20, 1938.

173. *Daily Lariat,* November 5, 1937.

174. Neff to Power, April 19, 1936, Neff Papers.

175. Internal Revenue Service to Neff, May 18, 1942; May 28, 1942; June 29, 1942; all in Neff Papers.

176. *Waco Times-Herald,* May 14, 1934.

177. Coryell County Deed Records, Coryell County Clerk's Office, vol. 115, pp. 634-635.

178. "The CCC was designed to give unemployed young men useful work, preventing them from drifting into subversive organizations, and to help conserve natural resources." Samuel Eliot Morrison, *The Oxford History of the American People,* vol. 3 (New York: Penguin, 1994), p. 3:303.

179. *Daily Lariat,* May 9, 1935.

180. Neff to Conrad Wirth, George Nason, Herbert Maier, and D. E. Colp, October 12, 1935, Neff Papers.

181. Ibid.

182. Neff to Wirth, telegram, October 20, 1935, Neff Papers.

183. Neff to James E. Ferguson and other former governors, April 6, 1937, Neff Papers.

184. Moody to Neff, April 18, 1937; Sterling to Neff, April 23, 1937; Neff Papers.

185. James E. Ferguson to Neff, April 9, 1937, Neff Papers.

186. Neff to Hobby, April 20, 1937, Neff Papers. Neff had written Hobby calling off the gathering three days before Sterling's letter was written, but Sterling expressed the same negative sentiments as Moody.

187. *Daily Lariat,* May 7, 1937.

188. Neff to Huddleston, April 7, 1938; Huddleston to State Parks Board, March 24, 1938; Huddleston to Poage, March 24, 1938; Huddleston to Neff, March 24, 1938; all in Neff Papers.

189. Demaray to Neff, May 12, 1938, Neff Papers.

190. Neff was appointed on May 11, 1933. See *Senate Journal,* 43rd Leg., Reg. Sess., 1933, May 11, 1933, p. 1712. He was confirmed by the Senate on May 15, 1933. See *Senate Journal,* 43rd Leg., Reg. Sess., 1933, May 15, 1933, p. 1777.

191. *Daily Lariat,* January 28, 1936.

192. Neff to State Parks Board, August 26, 1939, Neff Papers.

193. Mayes to Neff, October 3, 1939, Neff Papers. Marie Jones soon married Monroe Jones (no relation to Marie's family), and the four Joneses (Marie, Monroe, Tullie, and Claude) took care of the park for several years. Claude Jones was the brother of Marie and Tullie and no relation to Monroe Jones.

194. Records, Compton's Funeral Home, Waco, Texas.

195. Cancelled checks, First National Bank, Waco, Texas, 1925-1948, Neff Papers.

196. Van Horn to Neff, January 28, 1939, Neff Papers.

197. *Texas Baptist Annual* (San Antonio: Baptist General Convention of Texas, 1939), pp. 32-35.

198. C. E. Bryant to Dorothy Blodgett, April 9, 1996, Blodgett Collection.

199. *Daily Lariat,* January 5, 1940.

Chapter 11. Baylor at War, 1940-1945

1. John Keegan provides an interesting account of the war in *The Second World War* (New York: Viking Penguin, 1990).

2. Minutes, Waco Executive Committee, August 17, 1939, p. 202.

3. Ibid., September 7, 1940, p. 233.

4. *Texas Baptist Annual* (Abilene: Baptist General Convention of Texas, 1941), p. 38.

5. Eugene W. Baker, *To Light the Ways of Time: An Illustrated History of Baylor University: 1845-1986* (Waco: Baylor University Press, 1987), p. 185.

6. Ibid., p. 189.

7. Norton to Neff, January 8, 1941, Neff Papers.

8. *Handbook of Texas Online*, s.v. "Crowell, Grace Noll," http://www.tsha.utexas.edu/handbook/online/articles/CC/fcr57.html .

9. Martin to Neff, September 21, 1940, Neff Papers.

10. Minutes, Waco Executive Committee, January 3, 1941, p. 236.

11. Ibid., February 24, 1941, p. 238.

12. Chart, Baylor University Faculty, 1947-1948, Neff Papers.

13. *Texas Baptist Annual* (Abilene: Baptist General Convention of Texas, 1941), p. 37.

14. Ibid.

15. *Texas Baptist Annual* (Dallas: Baptist General Convention of Texas, 1938), p. 40.

16. Minutes, Waco Executive Committee, November 29, 1939, p. 217.

17. *Texas Baptist Annual* (Houston: Baptist General Convention of Texas, 1940), p. 41.

18. Minutes, Baylor University Board of Trustees, April 16, 1940, p. 57.

19. Ibid., November 8, 1945, p. 57.

20. Minutes, Waco Executive Committee, June 27, 1941, p. 245.

21. Arthur J. Rogers, "Paul Baker and Theater Architecture," in *Paul Baker and the Integration of Abilities*, ed. Robert Flynn and Eugene McKinney (Fort Worth: TCU Press, 2003), p. 29.

22. Ibid., p. 251.

23. Flynn and McKinney, *Paul Baker and the Integration of Abilities*; Meg Cullar, "Stage Presence," *Baylor Line* (fall 2001); *Austin American-Statesman*, November 9, 2003; *Paul Baker Theater: A Photo History* (Waco: Central Texas Printing, n.d).

24. Minutes, Baylor University Board of Trustees, April 27, 1944, p. 271.

25. Carol Whitcraft, interview by Dorothy Blodgett, March 30, 1998, Blodgett Collection.

26. Minutes, Waco Executive Committee, January 11, 1945, p. 62.

27. Ibid., pp. 62-64.

28. Joseph Martin Dawson, Oral Memoirs, interview by Kay Nowlin, November 25, 1971, p. 251, Baylor University Program for Oral History (hereafter referred to as BUPOH).

29. Lois Smith Douglas Murray Strain, interview by Dorothy Blodgett, April 30, 1992, Blodgett Collection.

30. Wendt to Neff, April 17, 1941, "General Housing Rules for Men" (enclosure), Neff Papers.

31. Neff to Board of Trustees, September 11, 1941, Neff Papers.

32. Ibid.

33. Merle Mears McClellan Duncan, Oral Memoirs, interview by Janelle Easley, January 12, 1977, p. 48, BUPOH; personal recollection, Terrell Blodgett.

34. Personal recollection, Terrell Blodgett.

35. Ibid.

36. *Waco Times-Herald*, August 29, 1969.

37. Winston P. Wilson, *Harvey Couch: The Master Builder* (Nashville, Tenn.: Broadman Press, 1947), pp. 201-203.

38. Thomas E. Turner, "The Triumphs and Tribulations of Baylor Football," *Retired Professors Newsletter* 12 (December 1, 1996): 12.

39. Brother Short Nose (William B.) Long and Most Fortunate Mary Cole Farrow Long, eds., *The Nose Brotherhood Knows: A Collection of Nothings and Non-Happenings, 1926-1945* (Belton, Tex.: Bear Hollow Publishers, 1997), p. 142.

40. Ibid.

41. Ibid.

42. *Baylor Line*, September 1984.

43. Bryant to Dorothy Blodgett, May 27, 1996, Blodgett Collection.

44. *Texas Baptist Annual* (Abilene: Baptist General Convention of Texas, 1941), p. 36.

45. *Texas Baptist Annual* (Dallas: Baptist General Convention of Texas, 1943), p. 31.

46. Ibid.

47. *Texas Baptist Annual* (Fort Worth: Baptist General Convention of Texas, 1942), p. 34.

48. Jane Gilmore Rushing and Kline A. Nall, *Evolution of a University: Texas Tech's First Fifty Years* (Austin: Madrona Press, 1975).

49. *Texas Baptist Annual* (Fort Worth: Baptist General Convention of Texas, 1942), pp. 32-33.

50. Ibid.

51. Cancelled checks, First National Bank, Waco, Texas, 1925-1948, Neff Papers. A more complete history of Baylor's wartime activities is provided in Kevin Michael Brady's "Baylor at War," master's thesis, Baylor University, Waco, Texas, 2002.

52. *Texas Baptist Annual* (Fort Worth: Baptist General Convention of Texas, 1942), p. 33.

53. Baker, *To Light the Ways of Time*, p. 192.

54. The ties between Homer Price Rainey and Neff went back to early days. Rainey was from Lovelady, Myrtie's home town, became an ordained Baptist minister, and then became president of Franklin College (1927-1931) and Bucknell University (1931-1935). He was appointed president of the University of Texas in 1939. Neff admired Rainey and would support him in Rainey's losing race for governor in 1946.

55. *Baylor Lariat*, February 10, 1944.

56. Taylor to Neff, September 24, 1942; Hyer to Neff, August 21, 1943; both in Neff Papers.

57. "Pat M. Neff Jr.," biographical sketch by Pat Neff Jr., undated, Neff Papers.

58. Quoted in ibid.

59. Neff to Elkins, January 10, 1945, Neff Papers.

60. *Texas Baptist Annual* (Fort Worth: Baptist General Convention of Texas, 1942), p. 27.

61. *Texas Baptist Annual* (Dallas: Baptist General Convention of Texas, 1943), p. 27.

62. Minutes, Waco Executive Committee, July 2, 1942, p. 11.

63. Ibid., pp. 10, 11.

64. *Texas Baptist Annual* (Dallas: Baptist General Convention of Texas, 1943), p. 29.

65. Ibid., pp. 27-29.

66. *Texas Baptist Annual* (San Antonio: Baptist General Convention of Texas, 1944), p. 30.

67. June Johnson, interview by Terrell Blodgett, December 2, 2003, Blodgett Collection.

68. Minutes, Waco Executive Committee, June 6, 1944, p. 53.

69. Henry Franklin Carman, Oral Memoirs, interview by Daniel B. McGee, March 30, 1972, p. 19, BUPOH; Neff to Moore, January 24, 1944; Walter H. Moursund Sr., "A History of Baylor University College of Medicine, 1900–1953," Baylor University College of Medicine, Houston, Texas, 1956, p. 116.

70. Moursund, "History of the Baylor University College of Medicine," pp. 93, 100-102. Extensive discussion of the Dallas proposal and agreement and the subsequent proposal and agreement from Houston may also be found in the official minutes of the Baylor University Board of Trustees, May 5, 1942, pp. 175-180; April 27, 1943, pp. 217-218; May 3 and July 13, 1943, pp. 220-246.

71. Moursund, "History of the Baylor College of Medicine," pp. 102-109.

72. Ibid., p. 110.

73. Ibid., p. 111.

74. Minutes, Baylor University Board of Trustees, June 23, 1944, pp. 185-192; Moursund, "History of the Baylor College of Medicine," p. 111.

75. Martin to Neff, July 1942, Neff Papers.

76. Martin to Neff, August 25, 1942, Neff Papers.

77. *Texas Baptist Annual* (Fort Worth: Baptist General Convention of Texas, 1942), pp. 70-75.

78. Public Relations Committee of the Dallas Baylor Medical Alumni to the Trustees of Baylor University and the Trustees of Southwestern Medical Foundation, March 23, 1943, Neff Papers.

79. Minutes, Baylor University Board of Trustees, April 27, 1943, pp. 217-218.

80. Ibid., May 8, 1943, p. 220. In a note appended to the minutes of May 8, the following statement appeared: "5-31-43, Exec Bd of BGCT approved both termination of contract with SW Med Foundation and acceptance of Anderson Foundation."

81. Moursund, "History of the Baylor College of Medicine," pp. 114-116.

82. Ibid., p. 118.

83. Ibid., p. 116.

84. McLean to Neff, May 27, 1943, Neff Papers.

85. *Texas Baptist Annual* (San Antonio: Baptist General Convention of Texas, 1944), p. 36.

86. Minutes, Waco Executive Committee, March 10, 1944, p. 44.

87. Neff to Crawley, May 20, 1943, Neff Papers; Moursund, "History of the Baylor College of Medicine," pp. 125, 134, 136.

88. Henry W. Tiffany, "The Southern Baptist Convention," *Watchman-Examiner* 32, no. 22 (June 1, 1944): 532.

89. *Daily Lariat,* May 17, 1935.

90. *Baptist Standard,* May 28, 1942.

91. Gilmore to Neff, January 4, 1944, Neff Papers.

92. *Daily Lariat,* May 19, 1944.

93. Neff, "Manhood on the March," original manuscript, 1944, Neff Papers.

94. Lee to Winfrey, April 12, 1951, as quoted in Chase Sherwin Winfrey, "Pat Morris Neff: A Personality-Oratorical Study," Ph.D. diss., University of Denver, Denver, Colorado, 1951, p. 94.

95. Tiffany, "Southern Baptist Convention," pp. 532-533.

96. Cancelled checks, First National Bank, Waco, Texas, 1925-1948, Neff Papers.

97. Briggs to Neff, October 25, 1940; Neff to Briggs, November 18, 1940; both in Neff Papers. The Philosophical Society of Texas was founded in 1937, but after a series of occasional meetings, became inactive before the annexation of Texas (1845). The organization was reestablished in 1935, four years after Baylor President Samuel Palmer Brooks' death. Neff was the first president of Baylor to be admitted to the society, and three others followed—W. R. White, Abner McCall, and Herbert H. Reynolds. The society remains into the twenty-first century a virtual Who's Who in Texas of academics, business people, and individuals in the arts.

98. Fiedler to Neff, December 11, 1946, Neff Papers.

99. Neff to Crazy Hotel, Mineral Wells, Texas, August 17, 1940, Neff Papers.

100. Neff to Smith, December 21, 1944, Neff Papers.

101. Neff to Couch, January 23, 1942, Neff Papers.

102. Newspaper clipping, no attribution, undated, Neff Papers.

103. Clough to Neff, June 27, 1940, Neff Papers.

104. *Texas Baptist Annual* (Fort Worth: Baptist General Convention of Texas, 1942), p. 34.

105. Lowe to Johnson, March 24, 1942, Neff Papers.

106. Collins had recently bought the station from Dr. John R. Brinkley, known then as the "purveyor of health and youth through goat glands." Brinkley's station, XEAW, had an official rating of 180,000 watts and could be heard clearly over a wide area of Texas and beyond. Collins had intended to operate the station in Reynosa and use it to advertise his Crazy Water Crystals (dehydrated minerals), a product Collins and his brother Hal had concocted to package the "crazy water" discovered in Mineral Wells. With a single box of crystals (which cost $1.50) and tap water, a sufferer could whip up a full five gallons of the solution. Shortly after Collins bought the station, the Mexican government moved in with troops, closed the station, and gave the frequency to a station in Monterrey, Mexico. Collins finally got permission from the Mexican government to move the disassembled station equipment to Corpus Christi, and with a bribe to the Reynosa police chief, a caravan of sixty-five trucks

hastily crossed the border. See Dorothy Neville, *Carr P. Collins: Man on the Move* (Dallas: Park Press, 1963), p. 87; Richard Schroeder, *Texas Signs On: The Early Days of Radio and Television* (College Station: Texas A&M University Press, 1998); and Gene Fowler and Bill Crawford, *Border Radio* (Austin: Texas Monthly Press, 1987).

107. M. John Kulesz, Jr., "A History and Analysis of Radio Broadcasting at Baylor University, 1935-1968," master's thesis, Baylor University, Waco, Texas, 1968, p. 41.

108. *Texas Baptist Annual* (San Antonio: Baptist General Convention of Texas, 1944), p. 33.

109. Tom Peeler, "Nostalgia: Healing Waters," *D Magazine* (November 1983): 65-73.

110. George Norris Green, *The Establishment in Texas Politics: The Primitive Years, 1938-1957* (Westport, Conn.: Greenwood Press, 1979), pp. 37-38.

111. *Handbook of Texas Online*, s.v. "Collins, Carr P.," http://www.tsha.utexas.edu/handbook/online/articles/CC/fco90_print.html .

112. Minutes, Baylor University Board of Trustees, May 5, 1942, p. 150.

113. Ibid., May 1, 1941, p. 96.

114. Lionel V. Patenaude, *Texans, Politics, and the New Deal* (New York: Garland, 1983). See chapter 2 particularly.

115. Ibid. See chapter 4 particularly.

116. Neff to Germany, May 22, 1939, Neff Papers.

117. Neff to Granbery (clerk), April 24, 1940, Neff Papers.

118. Seth Shepard McKay, *Texas Politics, 1906-1944, with Special Reference to the German Counties* (Lubbock: Texas Tech Press, 1952), pp. 420, 422.

119. Newspaper clipping, no attribution, undated, Neff Papers.

120. Hogg to Neff, telegram, October 25, 1940, Neff Papers.

121. Neff to Hogg, October 29, 1940, Neff Papers.

122. McLean to Neff, August 16, 1940, Neff Papers.

123. Neff to Martin, August 14, 1940, Neff Papers.

124. Green, *Establishment in Texas Politics*, p. 34.

125. McKay, *Texas Politics*, p. 353.

126. Martin to Neff, June 28, 1941, Neff Papers.

127. Neff to Martin, July 3, 1941, Neff Papers.

128. *Plainview Herald*, September 9, 1942, Neff Papers.

129. *Texas Almanac, 2006-2007* (Dallas: Dallas Morning News, 2006), pp. 401, 407.

130. McKay, *Texas Politics*, p. 436.

131. Neff to Seay, telegram, November 2, 1944, Neff Papers.

132. Aynesworth to Directors, January 12, 1937, Neff Papers; *Baylor Bulletin* 40, no. 3 (August 1937): 213-221.

133. Neff to Board of Trustees, December 18, 1939, Neff Papers.

134. Homer P. Rainey, *The Tower and the Dome: A Free University versus Political Control* (Boulder, Colo.: Pruett Publishing Co., 1971).

135. Minutes, Baylor University Board of Trustees, November 13, 1944, p. 9.

136. *Austin American*, November 12 and 22, 1944.

137. *Handbook of Texas Online*, s.v. "Eby, Frederick," http://www.tsha.utexas.edu/handbook/online/articles/EE/feb3_print.html .

138. *Waco Times-Herald*, February 2, 1945.

139. *Dallas Morning News*, February 2, 1945; Dudley to Neff, February 3, 1945; both in Neff Papers.

140. Neff to Dudley, February 10, 1945, Neff Papers.

141. McLean to Neff, February 3, 1945, Neff Papers.

142. Neff to McLean, February 9, 1945, Neff Papers.

143. Minutes of the Baylor University Board of Trustees, Independence, Texas, May 15, 1845, p. 7, as quoted in Thomas E. Turner, *Instruments of Providence: Biographical Vignettes of the Charter Trustees of Baylor University* (Waco: Baylor University Press, 1989), p. 18.

144. Minutes, Baylor University Board of Trustees, May 15, 1945, pp. 31-56.

145. Kent Keeth, "Marking the Milestones: Part 3, Celebrating the 1945 Centennial," *Baylor Line* (spring 1995).

146. Minutes, Waco Executive Committee, May 24, 1945, pp. 75-78.

147. Cook, telephone conversation with Dorothy Blodgett, July 11, 1995, Blodgett Collection.

148. In 2006, Caldwell was the second person selected to the Alumni 150, a program begun by the Baylor Alumni Association in 2006 to honor 150 Baylor alumni (out of some 130,000 Baylor ex-students) for exceptional achievement.

149. Robert S. Denny, Oral Memoirs, interview by William L. Pitts, September 22, 1983, p. 70, Baylor University Institute for Oral History, hereafter referred to as BUIOH.

150. Bruce McIver, *Riding the Wind of God: A Personal History of the Youth Revival Movement* (Macon, Ga.: Smyth and Helwys Pub., 2002).

151. Howard E. Butt Jr. and Katy Jennings Stokes, Oral Memoirs, interview by Thomas L. Charlton, L. Katherine Cook, and Katy Jennings Stokes, May 13, 1982, p. 23, BUIOH.

152. McIver, *Riding the Wind*, p. 33.

153. Eugene Baker, "Enhancing the Foundation," draft manuscript, May 9, 2003, p. 333.

154. Harold V. Ratliff, *The Power and the Glory: The Story of Southwest Conference Football* (Lubbock: Texas Tech Press, 1957), p. 68.

155. Baker, "Enhancing the Foundation," p. 335.

156. Newspaper clipping, no attribution, undated, Neff Papers.

157. In 2002, the Office of Public Relations of Baylor stated that the total service figure was more than 4,000 and the number killed or who died as a result of the war was 125.

158. Baylor University, Office of Public Relations, "ROTC Pays Tribute to Medal of Honor Alumni," December 6, 2002, online: http://www.baylor.edu/pr/news.php?action=story& story=4362 .

159. Mary Hartman, *Texas Granite* (Dallas: Hendrick-Long, 1997).

160. http://www.jacklummus.com .

161. Baylor University, Office of Public Relations, "Former Air Force Chaplain Presented War Heroes Award," January 9, 2004. Online: http://www.baylor.edu/pr/news.php?action=story&story=6325 .

162. Baker, *To Light the Ways of Time*, p. 206.

Chapter 12. Neff Signs Off

1. Minutes, Baylor University Board of Trustees, April 30, 1946, p. 85.
2. Minutes, Waco Executive Committee, July 28, 1946, pp. 125-128.
3. *Texas Baptist Annual* (Mineral Wells: Baptist General Convention of Texas, 1946), p. 30.
4. Ibid.
5. Eugene Baker, *To Light the Ways of Time: An Illustrated History of Baylor University, 1845-1986* (Waco: Baylor University Press, 1987), p. 208.
6. *Texas Baptist Annual* (Mineral Wells: Baptist General Convention of Texas, 1946), p. 31.
7. Roger Edens, interview by Dorothy Blodgett, April 11, 2002, Blodgett Collection.
8. Robert Jackson Robinson, Oral Memoirs, interview by Thomas L. Charlton, May 21, 1982, pp. 102-105, Baylor University Institute for Oral History (hereafter cited as BUIOH). In 1948, Robinson would become the first athlete in Baylor's history to be named a first team all Southwest Conference player for three straight years. In sports history books, Robinson's exploits would occur about the same time that an African-American with the same name would capture most of the national headlines by breaking the color barrier in major league baseball. On April 15, 1947, Californian Jackie Robinson, a four-sport athlete at the University of California at Los Angeles, took the field for the Brooklyn Dodgers.
9. Ibid., interview by L. Katherine Cook, May 20, 1982, p. 21, BUIOH.
10. According to information provided by the H. E. Butt Foundation, Howard E. Butt Jr. teamed with Billy Graham in the 1950s to create Layman's Leadership Institutes, which generated a host of spiritual programs for business professionals. He has written several books about Christian leadership and sponsors a web site, TheHighCalling.org, which offers an extensive library of articles, interviews, and radio messages to guide Christians in their daily work.
11. Bruce McIver, *Riding the Wind of God: A Personal History of the Youth Revival Movement* (Macon, Ga.: Smyth and Helwys Pub., 2002).
12. Ibid., p. 53.
13. Ibid., chapters 8 and 9 particularly.
14. In addition, McIver is lavish in his praise of the guiding force of Robert Denny and later Dr. W. J. Wimpee, who succeeded Denny as director of the Baylor Baptist Student Union in 1945. McIver dedicated his book to Dr. W. F. Howard, director of Student Work for Baptists in Texas, whom he called the "Gentle Giant" of the Youth Revival Movement. McIver also expresses gratitude to Howard E. Butt Sr., who underwrote some of the early revivals. In preparation for the Houston series, Butt called a friendly Jewish competitor, Joseph Weingarten, and persuaded him to donate fourteen billboards to advertise the forthcoming revival.
15. Frances Landreth Etheridge, telephone interview by Terrell Blodgett, May 16, 2007.
16. Minutes, Waco Executive Committee, January 16, 1947, p. 145.
17. Minutes, Baylor University Board of Trustees, November 8, 1945, p. 57.
18. *Baylor Bulletin* 40, no. 3 (August 1937), p. 109.
19. *Century* 8, no. 2 (January 1946). Patterson played quarterback in the famed 1939 New Year's Shrine East-West game, later played professional football for Chicago and Pittsburgh while at Baylor Law School, and then went into the Navy in World War II.

20. Neff to Friends of Baylor, January 9, 1946, Neff Papers.

21. Joseph William "Bill" Patterson, Oral Memoirs, interview by Thomas E. Turner, September 17, 1981, p. 32, BUIOH.

22. Lois Smith Douglas, *Through Heaven's Back Door: A Biography of A. Joseph Armstrong* (Waco: Baylor University Press, 1951).

23. Baker, *To Light the Ways of Time*, p. 235.

24. The Baylor University College of Medicine continued to grow and in 1969, the relationship with Baylor University and the Baptist General Convention of Texas was terminated by mutual agreement. The school dropped "University" from its name, and it became a free-standing corporation, governed by a self-perpetuating board of trustees. Similarly, over the years, Baylor University Hospital in Dallas broadened its name to become Baylor Health Care System and on March 31, 1997, established autonomy from Baylor University. The Health Care System signified that it would continue to work closely with the Baylor School of Nursing. On August 1, 1971, Baylor Dental College in Dallas became Baylor College of Dentistry, ended its association with Baylor University, and became a nonprofit, nonsectarian educational corporation. In 1996, the college became a part of the Texas A&M University System. This left only the School of Nursing in Dallas as one of nine schools and colleges operated by Waco-based Baylor University, the only one not in Waco in the early twenty-first century. In 1999, that school became the Louise Herrington School of Nursing, named after Louise Herrington Ornelas, who made a $13 million endowment gift to the school, the third-largest gift from an individual in Baylor's history.

25. *Texas Baptist Annual* (Amarillo: Baptist General Convention of Texas, 1947), p. 40.

26. Unfortunately, in 1963, President Abner McCall took exception to the language in the presentation of Eugene O'Neill's *Long Day's Journey into Night*. McCall and Baker could not reconcile their differences, and Baker and eleven of his faculty and staff resigned. Immediately, Trinity University (San Antonio) President James W. Lairie announced the appointment of Baker as head of the Speech and Drama Department at that university, and Trinity agreed to hire five of Baker's key staff. The resulting furor on the Baylor campus included strong backing of McCall by Baptist preachers statewide and condemnation of McCall's actions by *The Baylor Lariat*. In addition, *Baylor Line* editor Frances Provence, wife of the *Waco News-Tribune* editor, Harry Provence, resigned when she was not allowed to write the story as she saw it.

27. Brogan to Neff, January 22, 1947, Neff Papers.

28. Neff, "Remarks of President Pat M. Neff in Presenting the Eleven-Point Improvement Program to the Faculty on January 30, 1947," Neff Papers.

29. Ann Speicher, Assistant Director of Communications and Public Affairs, Association of American Universities, telephone interview by Terrell Blodgett, November 27, 2006, Blodgett Collection.

30. Allred to Neff, June 20, 1946; Neff to Allred, July 10, 1946; both in Neff Papers.

31. David Rupert Murph, "Price Daniel: The Life of a Public Man, 1910-1956," Ph.D. diss., Texas Christian University, Fort Worth, Texas, 1975.

32. Minutes, Waco Executive Committee, March 20, 1947, p. 150.

33. Ibid., November 16, 1945, p. 90.

34. Neff to Truman, November 2, 1945, Truman Papers, President's Secretary's File, Chronological Name File, Box 245, Harry S. Truman Presidential Library, Independence, Missouri; hereafter cited as Truman Papers.

35. Minutes, Waco Executive Committee, November 16, 1945, p. 90.

36. Truman to Quillin, February 4, 1947, Truman Papers.

37. Truman co-owned and operated a clothing store in Kansas City from 1919 to 1922. It was his first job after his service in the First World War. When the store failed in 1922, the Pendergast machine helped him begin his upward career in government. See David McCullough, *Truman* (New York: Simon and Schuster, 1992), pp. 143-166.

38. Truman to Neff, March 10, 1947, Truman Papers.

39. Palmer to "Harry," October 3, 1945, Truman Papers.

40. Minutes, Baylor University Board of Trustees, April 29, 1947, p. 101.

41. Neff to Bryan, November 19, 1947, Neff Papers.

42. Dean Cornette saw the "handwriting on the wall" and resigned at the end of 1947 to become executive vice-president of West Texas State College at Canyon. In less than a year, he became president and the college later became known as West Texas State University. In his twenty-five years there, he brought the college and himself numerous honors, and when he stepped down in 1973, the new university library was named for him.

43. Minutes, Baylor University Board of Trustees, April 29, 1947, p. 101.

44. Martin to Neff, April 30, 1947, Neff Papers.

45. Neff to Martin, May 5, 1947, Neff Papers.

46. McKnight to Neff, October 5, 1947, Neff Papers.

47. McKnight to Neff, October 20, 1947, Neff Papers.

48. Neff to Belew, Secretary, Board of Trustees, November 8, 1947, Neff Papers.

49. *Texas Baptist Annual* (Amarillo: Baptist General Convention of Texas, 1947), pp. 28-55.

50. David Keith Chrisman, "The Public Life of Caso March: Anti-Establishment Campaigns in the Democratic Party, 1946-1950," master's thesis, Baylor University, Waco, Texas, 1990.

51. Included in the numerous letters Neff received when he announced his resignation were letters from U.S. Senator Tom Connally (December 26, 1947), Matt Dawson (October 23, 1947), Gladys Allen (November 7, 1947), Judge Whitfield Davidson (November 8, 1947), Carr P. Collins (November 10, 1947), and many others, all in Neff Papers.

52. Neff to Dillard and McKnight, November 24, 1947, Neff Papers.

53. Jaworski to Dillard, November 25, 1947; Daniel to Dillard, December 13, 1947, Baylor University Alumni Association Archives. Daniel's letter indicated he had earlier voiced his support for Dillard.

54. Neff became the third Baylor president to submit an involuntary resignation. The others were Dr. Rufus C. Burleson in 1897 and Oscar Henry Cooper in 1902.

55. Turner to Dorothy Blodgett, February 24, 1998, Blodgett Collection.

56. *Daily Lariat*, November 29, 1947.

57. Minutes, Baylor University Board of Trustees, November 28, 1947, pp. 127-134.

58. *Daily Lariat*, December 19, 1947.

59. Baker, *To Light the Ways of Time*, p. 217.

60. Thomas E. Turner, *The Presidents of Baylor University* (Waco: Baylor University Press, 1981), p. 48.

61. W. J. Wimpee, Oral Memoirs, interview by Thomas L. Charlton, May 1, 1980, pp. 37-38, BUIOH.

62. "Those Who Were There," *Baylor Line* (fall 1998). Transcript of a taped conversation between Jack H. Dillard, Roger Edens, and George Stokes, Hughes-Dillard Alumni Center, Baylor University, Waco, Texas, November 1, 1985.

63. Patterson, Oral Memoirs, September 17, 1981, pp. 18, 32.

64. Minutes, Baylor University Board of Trustees, January 3, 1948, p. 135.

65. Irving to Neff, July 15, 1948, Neff Papers.

66. Guy B. Harrison Jr., Oral Memoirs, interview by Thomas L. Charlton, June 20, 1974, p. 243, Baylor University Program for Oral History.

67. White to Neff, April 30, 1951, Neff Papers.

68. Harrison, Oral Memoirs, June 20, 1974, pp. 242-243.

69. *Dallas Morning News*, July 27, 1952.

70. Martin to Neff, October 31, 1950, Neff Papers.

71. Armstrong to Neff, March 4, 1950, Neff Papers.

72. Johnson to Neff, February 14, 1950, Neff Papers.

73. Collins to Neff, May 19, 1950, Neff Papers.

74. Chase Sherwin Winfrey, "Pat Morris Neff: A Personality-Oratorical Study," Ph.D. diss., University of Denver, Denver, Colorado, 1951, p. 3.

75. Shirley to Neff, July 26, 1951, Neff Papers.

76. *Austin American*, January 17, 1951.

77. " 'Noble Warrior' Pat Neff Buried," *Waco News-Tribune*, January 22, 1952.

78. Dawson to W. R. White, telegram, January 21, 1952, Neff Papers. The telegram read: "Pat Neff stood foremost among the greatest laymen produced by the Baptists. Into political life from county attorney to governor, he carried the lofty ideals learned in his Christian home, in the First Baptist Church, and in Baylor University. As distinguished president he bought [sic] Baylor to unprecidented [sic] heights. Through thirty-one years of my pastorate at First Baptist Church he was a steadfast friend and loyal member and I loved him devotedly. I would offer the highest tribute to be paid by Baptists north and south to his noble example of enduring contribution and unsurpassed service."

79. *Daily Lariat*, January 23, 1952.

80. "Last Tribute Paid Ex-Governor Neff," *Waco News-Tribune*, January 22, 1952.

81. Resolution, Texas State Parks Board, February 29, 1952, Neff Papers.

82. "Iron Will, Silver Tongue Made Pat Neff an Unforgettable Part of Baylor History," *Baylor Lariat*, June 24, 1959.

83. Rupert N. Richardson to W. R. White, telegram, January 21, 1952, Neff Papers.

Bibliography

Books

Abernethy, Francis Edward, ed. *Legendary Ladies of Texas*. Dallas: E-Heart Press, 1981.

Acheson, Sam Hanna. *Joe Bailey: The Last Democrat*. New York: Macmillan Co., 1932.

Adair, A. Garland, and Ellen Bohlender Coats. *Texas: Its History*. Philadelphia: John C. Winston Co., 1954.

Ainslie, Ricardo C. *No Dancin' in Anson: An American Story of Race and Social Change*. Northvale, N.J.: Jason Aronson, Inc., 1995.

Akers, Monte. *Flames after Midnight: Murder, Vengeance, and the Desolation of a Texas Community*. Austin: University of Texas Press, 1999.

Alexander, Charles C. *The Ku Klux Klan in the Southwest*. Norman, Okla.: University of Oklahoma Press, 1995.

Allen, Frederick Lewis. *The Big Change: America Transforms Itself, 1900-1950*. New York: Harper Bros., 1952.

———. *Only Yesterday (the 20s)*. New York: Harper Bros., 1939.

———. *Since Yesterday (the 30s)*. New York: Harper Bros., 1986.

Allen, James, Hilton Als, Congressman John Lewis, and Leon F. Litwack. *Without Sanctuary: Lynching Photography in America*. Santa Fe: Twin Palms, 2000.

Anderson, Ken. *You Can't Do That, Dan Moody: The Klan Fighting Governor of Texas*. Austin: Eakin Press, 1998.

Annuals, Baylor University, 1941 thru 1945.

Bailey, Beth L. *From Front Porch to Back Seat: Courtship in Twentieth Century America*. Baltimore, Md.: Johns Hopkins University Press, 1988.

Bainbridge, John. *The Super-Americans: A Picture of Life in the United States, as Brought into Focus, Bigger than Life, in the Land of the Millionaires—Texas*. Garden City, N.Y.: Doubleday and Co., 1961.

Baker, Eugene. *To Light the Ways of Time: An Illustrated History of Baylor University 1845-1986*. Waco: Baylor University Press, 1987.

Balmer, Randall. *Grant Us Courage: Travels along the Mainline of American Protestantism*. New York: Oxford University Press, 1996.

Banks, Jimmy. *Money, Marbles, and Chalk: The Wondrous World of Texas Politics*. Austin: Texas Publishing Co., Inc., 1971.

Barnes, Lavonia Jenkins. *The Texas Cotton Palace*. Waco: Heritage Society of Waco, 1964.

Barnes, William W. *Southern Baptist Convention, 1845-1953*. Nashville, Tenn.: Broadman Press, 1954.

Barr, Alwyn. *Black Texans: A History of the Negroes in Texas, 1528-1971.* Austin: Jenkins Publishing Co., 1973.

———. *Reconstruction to Reform: Texas Politics, 1876-1906.* Austin: University of Texas Press, 1971.

Barr, Alwyn, and Robert A. Calvert, eds. *Black Leaders: Texans for Their Times.* Austin: Texas State Historical Association, 1981.

Bellesiles, Michael A. *Arming America: The Origins of a National Gun Culture.* New York: Alfred A. Knopf, 2000.

Bernstein, Patricia. *The First Waco Horror: The Lynching of Jesse Washington and the Rise of the NAACP.* College Station: Texas A&M University Press, 2005.

Berry, Margaret Catherine. *UT Austin: Traditions and Nostalgia.* Austin: Shoal Creek Publishers, Inc., 1975.

———. *Westminster Manor: The First Thirty-Five Years.* Austin: Nortex Press, 2003.

Blackwelder, Julia Kirk. *Now Hiring: The Feminization of Work in the United States, 1900-1995.* College Station: Texas A&M University Press, 1997.

Bolton, Paul. *Governors of Texas.* Corpus Christi: Corpus Christi Caller-Times, 1947.

Brinkley, Alan. *Culture and Politics in the Great Depression.* Charles Edmondson Historical Lecture, Baylor University. Waco: Baylor University Press, 1999.

Brough, James, with Annette, Cecile, Marie, and Yvonne Dionne. *We Were Five: The Dionne Quintuplets' Story.* New York: Simon and Schuster, 1965.

Brown, Norman D. *Hood, Bonnet, and Little Brown Jug: Texas Politics, 1921-1928.* College Station: Texas A&M University Press, 1984.

Bryson, Conrey. *Dr. Lawrence Nixon and the White Primary.* Rev. ed. El Paso: Texas Western Press, 1992.

Buenger, Walter L. *The Path to a Modern South: Northeast Texas between Reconstruction and the Great Depression.* Austin: University of Texas Press, 2001.

Cable, Mary, and the editors of American Heritage. *American Manners and Morals.* New York: American Heritage Publishing Co., 1969.

Calvert, Robert A., Arnoldo De Leon, and Gregg Cantrell. *The History of Texas,* 3rd ed. Wheeling, Ill.: Harlan Davidson, Inc., 2002.

Capp, Glenn R., Sr. *"Prof" and Speech Communication at Baylor.* Waco: Baylor University, 1981.

Caro, Robert. *Means of Ascent.* New York: Alfred A. Knopf, 1990.

Carr, Waggoner, and Byron Varner. *Texas Politics in My Rearview Mirror.* Plano, Tex.: Wordware Publishing, 1993.

Carrigan, William D. *The Making of a Lynching Culture: Violence and Vigilantism in Central Texas, 1836-1916.* Urbana and Chicago: University of Illinois Press, 2004.

Carter, Paul A.. *The Twenties in America.* 2d ed. American History Series. Wheeling, Ill.: Harlan Davidson, Inc., 1975.

Carver, Charles. *Brann and the Iconoclast.* Austin: University of Texas Press, 1957.

The Catalogue of Baylor University, 1902-1903. Waco: Baylor University Bulletin, 1902.

Centennial History of the Texas Bar: 1882-1982 (Austin: Eakin Press, 1981).

Childs, William R. *The Texas Railroad Commission: Understanding Regulation in America to the Mid Twentieth Century.* College Station: Texas A&M University Press, 2005.

Clark, James. *Three Stars for the Colonel.* New York: Random House, 1954.

———. *Spindletop.* New York: Random House, 1952.

Clark, James, and Michel T. Halbouty. *The Last Boom.* New York: Random House, 1972.

Clark, James, with Weldon Hart. *The Tactful Texan: A Biography of Governor Will Hobby.* New York: Random House, 1958.

Cocke, William. *The Bailey Controversy in Texas, with Lessons from the Political, Life Story of a Fallen Idol.* Vol. 1. San Antonio: Cocke Co., 1908.

Collins, Frederick L., *Our American Kings.* New York and London: Century Co., 1924.

Conaway, James. *The Texans.* New York: Alfred A. Knopf, 1976.

Conger, Roger N., ed. *The Best of Brann: The Iconoclast.* Waco: Texian Press, 1967.

Conger, Roger Norman. *Highlights of Waco History.* Waco: Hill Printing and Stationery Co., 1945.

Connally, Tom, with Alfred Steinberg. *My Name is Tom Connally.* New York: Thomas Y. Crowell Co., 1954.

Cooper, Madison. *Sironia, Texas.* 2 vols. Boston: Houghton Mifflin Co., 1952.

Copp, Tara, and Robert L. Rogers. *The Daily Texan: The First 100 Years.* Austin, Eakin Press, 1999.

Costello, Sherry Boyd, Gary Cook, and Thomas Turner, ed. *Abner McCall: One Man's Journey.* Waco: Baylor University, 1981.

Cotner, Robert C. *Texas Cities and the Great Depression.* Texas Memorial Museum Miscellaneous Papers No. 3. Austin: Texas Memorial Museum, 1973.

Cotner, Robert C., et al. *James Stephen Hogg, A Biography.* Austin and London: University of Texas Press, 1959.

Cotton, Alfred Cleveland, M.D. *The Medical Diseases of Infancy and Childhood.* Philadelphia: J. P. Lippincott, 1906.

Crawford, Ann Fears, and Jack Keever. *John B. Connally: Portrait in Power.* Austin: Jenkins Publishing Co., 1973.

Crawford, Ann Fears, and Crystal Sasse Ragsdale. *Women in Texas: Their Lives, Their Experiences, Their Accomplishments.* Burnet, Tex.: Eakin Press, 1982.

Danbom, David B. *Born in the Country: A History of Rural America.* Baltimore: Johns Hopkins University Press, 1995.

Daniel, Jean Houston, Price Daniel, and Dorothy Blodgett. *The Texas Governor's Mansion: A History of the House and Its Occupants.* Austin: Texas State Library and Archives Commission; Liberty, Tex.: Sam Houston Regional Library and Research Center, 1984.

Dawson, Joseph Martin. *Brooks Takes the Long Look.* Waco: Baylor University Press, 1931.

———. *A Thousand Months to Remember: An Autobiography.* Waco: Baylor University Press, 1964.

Downs, Fane, and Nancy Baker Jones. *Women and Texas History: Selected Essays.* Austin: Texas State Historical Association, 1939.

Drepperd, Carl W. *Pioneer America: Its First Three Centuries.* Garden City, N.Y.: Doubleday and Co., 1949.

Eby, Frederick. *The Development of Education in Texas*. New York: Macmillan Co., 1925.

Ellis, Joseph Henry Harrison. *Sam Houston and Related Spiritual Forces*. Houston: Concord Press, 1945.

Executive Board of the Baptist General Convention of Texas. *Centennial Story of Texas Baptists*. Chicago: Hammond Press, W. B. Conkey Co., 1936.

Farrell, Mary D., and Elizabeth Silverthorne. *First Ladies of Texas: The First One Hundred Years, 1836-1936*. Belton, Tex.: Stillhouse Hollow Publishers, Inc., 1976.

Fiedler, Leslie A. *The Return of the Vanishing American*. New York: Stein and Day, 1971.

Flemmons, Jerry. *Amon: The Texan Who Played Cowboy for America*. Lubbock: Texas Tech Press, 1998.

Flynn. Robert, and Eugene McKinney, ed. *Paul Baker and the Integration of Abilities*. Fort Worth: TCU Press, 2003.

Foley, Neil. *The White Scourge: Mexicans, Blacks, and Poor Whites in the Cotton Culture*. Berkeley: University of California Press, 1997.

Fowler, Gene. *Crazy Water: The Story of Mineral Wells and Other Texas Health Resorts*. Fort Worth: Texas Christian University Press, 1991.

Fowler, Gene, and Bill Crawford. *Border Radio*. Austin: Texas Monthly Press, 1987.

Frantz, Joe. *Texas: A Bicentennial History*. New York: W.W. Norton and Co.; Nashville: American Association for State and Local History, 1976.

———. *The Forty-Acre Follies: An Opinionated History of the University of Texas*. Austin: Texas Monthly Press, 1983.

Gabriel, Ralph H. *The Course of America Democratic Thought: An Intellectual History since 1815*. New York: Ronald Press Co., 1940.

Gantt, Fred Jr. *The Chief Executive in Texas: A Study in Gubernatorial Leadership*. Austin: University of Texas Press, 1964.

Gantt, Fred Jr., Irving O. Dawson, and Luther G. Hagard Jr., eds. *Governing Texas: Documents and Readings*. 3d ed. New York: Thomas Y. Crowell, 1974.

Gould, Joseph E. *The Chautauqua Movement*. New York: State University of New York, 1961.

Gould, Lewis L. *Progressives and Prohibitionists: Texas Democrats in the Wilson Era*. Austin: University of Texas Press, 1973.

Graber, Doris A. *Verbal Behavior and Politics*. Chicago: University of Illinois Press, 1976.

Green, George Norris. *The Establishment in Texas Politics: The Primitive Years, 1938-1957*. Westport, Conn.: Greenwood Press, 1979.

Greenawalt, Kent. *Religious Convictions and Political Choice*. New York: Oxford University Press, 1988.

Greene, A. C. *A Personal Country*. New York: Alfred A. Knopf, 1969.

Griggs, William Clark. *Parson Henry Renfro: Free Thinking on the Texas Frontier*. Austin: University of Texas Press, 1994.

Hadas, Moses. *The Basic Works of Cicero*. New York: Random House, 1951.

Haley, James L. *From Spindletop through World War II*. New York: St. Martin's Press, 1993.

Harrison, Guy Bryan. *The Texas Collection of Baylor University*. Waco: Baylor University Press, 1940.

Hartman, Mary. *Texas Granite: Story of a World War II Hero.* Dallas: Hendrick-Long Pub. Co., 1996.

Heard, Alexander, and Donald S. Strong. *Southern Primaries and Elections, 1920-1949.* University, Ala.: University of Alabama Press, 1950.

Henderson, Lana. *Baylor University Medical Center.* Waco: Baylor University Press, 1978.

Henderson, Richard B. *Maury Maverick: A Political Biography.* Austin: University of Texas Press, 1970.

Hendrickson, Kenneth E., Jr. *Chief Executives of Texas: From Stephen F. Austin to John B. Connally, Jr.* College Station: Texas A&M University Press, 1995.

Hendrickson, Kenneth E., Jr., and Michael L. Collins, eds. *Profiles in Power: Twentieth-Century Texans in Washington.* Arlington Heights, Ill.: Harland Davidson, Inc., 1991.

Henson, Margaret Swett, and Deolece Parmelee. *The Cartwrights of San Augustine: Three Generations of Agricultural Entrepreneurs in Nineteenth-Century Texas.* Austin: Texas State Historical Association, 1993.

Herring, Charles, Jr., and Walter Richter. *Don't Throw Feathers at Chickens: A Collection of Texas Political Humor.* Plano, Tex.: Wordware Publishing, 1992.

Horton, David M., and Ryan Kellus Turner. *Lone Star Justice: A Comprehensive Overview of the Texas Criminal Justice System.* Austin: Eakin Press, 1999.

Hyer, Julien. *The Land of Beginning Again: The Romance of the Brazos.* Atlanta: Tupper and Love, 1952.

Jackson, Pearl Cashell. *Texas Governors' Wives.* Austin: E. L. Steck, 1915.

Jakle, John A., and Keith A. Sculle. *The Gas Station in America.* Baltimore: Johns Hopkins University Press, 1994.

James, Marquis. *The Raven: A Biography of Sam Houston.* Indianapolis, Ind.: Bobbs-Merrill, 1976.

Johnson, Charles A. *The Frontier Camp Meeting: Religion's Harvest Time.* Dallas: Southern Methodist University, 1955, 1985.

Johnson, Sam Houston. *My Brother, Lyndon.* Ed. Enrique Hank Lopez. New York: Cowles Book Co., 1970.

Jones, Arthur Gray. *Thornton R. Sampson: A Life Sketch.* Richmond, Va.: Richmond Press, 1917.

Jones, Nancy Baker, and Ruthe Winegarten. *Capitol Women: Texas Female Legislators, 1923-1999.* Austin: University of Texas Press, 2000.

Journey in Faith. The Story of the Baylor Presidents, 1845-1995. Waco: Baylor University, n.d.

Keegan, John. *The Second World War.* New York: Viking Penguin, 1990.

Keeth, Kent. *Looking Back at Baylor: A Collection of Historical Vignettes.* Reprinted from the series in the *Baylor Line*, 1975-1985. Waco: Baylor University, 1985.

Kelley, Dayton, ed. *Handbook of Waco and McLennan County.* Waco: Texian Press, 1972.

Kesselus, Ken. *Alvin Wirtz: The Senator, LBJ, and LCRA.* Austin: Eakin Press, 2002.

Kightlinger, Flora N. *The Star Speaker.* Jersey City, N.J: Star Publishing Co., 1892.

King, Rufus. *Gambling and Organized Crime.* Washington, D.C.: Public Affairs Press, 1969.

Larson, Erik. *Isaac's Storm.* New York: Crown Publishers, 1999.

Lay, Shawn. *War, Revolution, and the Ku Klux Klan*. El Paso: Texas Western Press, 1985.

Lefever, Alan J. *Fighting the Good Fight: The Life and Work of Benajah Harvey Carroll*. Austin: Eakin Press, 1994.

Link, Arthur S. *Woodrow Wilson: Revolution, War, and Peace*. Wheeling, Ill.: Harlan Davidson, Inc., 1979.

Link, Richard McKeon, ed. *Introduction to Aristotle*. New York: Random House, Inc., 1992 ed.

Lloyd, Grann. *White Supremacy in the United States. An Analysis of Its Background with Especial Reference to the Poll Tax*. Washington, D.C.: Public Affairs Press, 1952.

Long, William B., and Mary Cole Farrow Long, eds. *The Nose Brotherhood Knows: A Collection of Nothings and Non-Happenings, 1926-1965*. Belton, Tex.: Bear Hollow Publishers, 1997.

Lynch, Dudley. *The President from Texas: Lyndon Baines Johnson*. New York: Thomas Y. Crowell Co., 1975.

Malavis, Nicholas George. *Bless the Pure and Humble: Texas Lawyers and Oil Regulation, 1919-1936*. College Station: Texas A&M University Press, 1996.

Malone, Ann Patton. *Women on the Texas Frontier: A Cross-Cultural Perspective*. El Paso: Texas Western Press, University of Texas at El Paso, 1983.

Malone, Bill C. *Country Music, U.S.A.: A Fifty Year History*. Austin: University of Texas Press, for the American Folklore Society, 1974.

Marsden, George M. *The Outrageous Idea of Christian Scholarship*. New York: Oxford University Press, 1997.

Maysel, Lou. *Here Come the Texas Longhorns, 1893-1970*. Fort Worth: Stadium Publishing Co., 1970.

McBeth, Harry Leon. *Texas Baptists: A Sesquicentennial History*. Dallas: Baptistway Press, 1998.

McComb, David G. *Galveston: A History*. Austin: University of Texas Press, 1986.

McCullough, David. *John Adams*. New York: Simon and Schuster, 2001.

———. *Truman*. New York: Simon and Schuster, 1992.

McIver, Bruce. *Riding the Wind of God: A Personal History of the Youth Revival Movement*. Macon, Ga.: Smyth and Helwys Pub., 2002.

McKay, Seth Shepard. *Texas Politics, 1906-1944, with Special Reference to German Counties*. Lubbock: Texas Tech Press, 1952.

McPherson, Harry. *A Political Education: A Washington Memoir*. Austin: University of Texas Press, 1995.

McSwain, Betty Ann McCartney, ed. *The Bench and Bar of Waco and McLennan County*. Waco: Texian Press, 1976.

Merk, Frederick. *History of the Westward Movement*. New York: Alfred A. Knopf, 1978.

Miller, Ray. *Texas Parks: A History and Guide*. Austin: Cordovan Press,1984.

Mills, Betty J. Savage. *Calico Chronicle: Texas Women and Their Fashions 1830-1910*. Lubbock: Texas Tech Press, 1985.

Moore, Walter B. *Governors of Texas*. 2d ed. Dallas: Dallas Morning News, 1969.

Morrison, Samuel Eliot. *The Oxford History of the American People*. Vol. 3. New York: Meridian, 1994.

Murray, Lois Smith. *Baylor at Independence.* Waco: Baylor University Press, 1972.

Myres, Sandra L. *Westering Women and the Frontier Experience, 1800-1915.* Albuquerque: University of New Mexico Press, 1982.

Nalle, Ouida Wallace Ferguson. *The Fergusons of Texas; or, "Two Governors for the Price of One." A Biography of James Edward Ferguson and His Wife, Miriam Amanda Ferguson, Ex-Governors of the State of Texas, by Their Daughter Ouida Ferguson Nalle.* San Antonio, Tex.: Naylor Co., 1946.

Neff, Pat M. *The Battles of Peace.* Fort Worth: Pioneer Pub. Co., 1925.

———. *A Collection of Twenty-three Addresses.* Waco: Philomathesian Literary Society, Baylor University, c. 1914.

———. *Making Texans: Five Minute Declamations.* Austin: Gammel's Bookstore, n.d.

Neuhaus, Richard John. *The Naked Public Square: Religion and Democracy in America.* Grand Rapids, Mich.: William B. Eerdmans Publishing Co., 1984.

Neville, Dorothy. *Carr P. Collins: Man on the Move.* Dallas: Park Press, 1963.

Newcomer, Velda Wilbern. *Texas First Ladies Historic Costume Collection: Texas Woman's University.* Denton: University Press, Texas Woman's University, 1978.

Nixon, Pat Ireland, M.D. *A History of the Texas Medical Association, 1853-1953.* Austin: University of Texas Press, 1953.

O'Brien, Esse Forrester. *The Baylor Bear Mascots.* Waco: Baylor Chamber of Commerce, 1950.

Ogden, Frederic D. *The Poll Tax in the South.* University, Ala.: University of Alabama Press, 1958.

Olien, Diana Davids, and Roger M. Olien. *Oil in Texas: The Gusher Age, 1895-1945.* Austin: University of Texas Press, 2002.

Oliphant, Dave. *Texan Jazz.* Austin: University of Texas Press, 1996.

Patenaude, Lionel V. *Texans, Politics, and the New Deal.* New York: Garland, 1983.

Paul Baker Theater: A Photo History. Waco: Central Texas Printing, n.d.

Paulissen, May Nelson, and Carl McQueary. *Miriam: Miriam Amanda Ferguson of Bell County—The Southern Belle Who Became the First Woman Governor of Texas.* Austin: Eakin Press, 1995.

Pecchi, Blaise. *The Five Weeks of Giuseppe Zangara: The Man Who Would Assassinate FDR.* Chicago: Academy Chicago Publishers, 1998.

Pennington, Richard. *Breaking the Ice: The Racial Integration of Southwest Conference Football.* Jefferson, N.C.: McFarland and Co., Inc., 1987.

Perry, George Sessions. *The Story of Texas A and M.* New York: McGraw-Hill Book Co., 1951.

Phares, Ross. *The Governors of Texas.* Gretna, La.: Pelican Publishing Co., 1976.

———. *Texas Tradition.* Gretna, La.: Pelican Publishing Co., 1975.

Pittman, H. C. *Inside the Third House: A Veteran Lobbyist Takes a 50-Year Frolic through Texas Politics.* Austin: Eakin Press,1992.

Poage, W. R. *McLennan County—Before 1980.* Waco: Texian Press, 1981.

———. *Politics, Texas Style.* Waco: Texian Press, 1974.

Pool, William C., Emmie Craddock, and David E. Conrad. *Lyndon Baines Johnson: The Formative Years.* San Marcos, Tex.: Southwest Texas State College Press, 1965.

Porterfield, Nolan. *Last Cavalier: The Life and Times of John A. Lomax, 1867-1948.* Chicago: University of Illinois Press, 1996.

Presiding Officers of the Texas Legislature, 1846-2002. Austin: Texas House of Representatives, 2002.

Price, John Milburn. *Ten Men from Baylor.* Kansas City, Kan.: Central Seminary Press, 1945.

Price, Lloyd E. *Backwoods to Border.* Ed. Mody C. Boatright and Donald Day. Publications of the Texas Folklore Society, no. 18. Austin: Texas Folklore Society; Dallas: University Press, Southern Methodist University, 1943.

Prindle, David F. *Petroleum Politics and the Texas Railroad Commission.* Austin: University of Texas Press, 1981.

Provence, Harry. *The Citizen's National Bank of Waco, 1884-1982.* Waco: Waco Republic Bank, 1982.

Ragsdale, Kenneth B. *The Year America Discovered Texas: Centennial '36.* College Station: Texas A&M University Press, 1987.

Rainey, Homer P. *The Tower and the Dome: A Free University versus Political Control.* Boulder, Colo.: Pruett Publishing Co., 1971.

Rankin, Rev. George C. *Rum on the Run in Texas: A Brief History of Prohibition in the Lone Star State.* Dallas: Johnston Printing Co., 1910.

Ratliff, Harold V. *The Power and the Glory: The Story of Southwest Conference Football.* Lubbock: Texas Tech Press, 1957.

Reed, S. G. *A History of the Texas Railroads and of Transportation Conditions under Spain and Mexico and the Republic and the State.* Houston: St. Clair Publishing Co., 1941.

Reston Jr., James. *The Lone Star: The Life of John Connally.* New York: Harper and Row, 1989.

Rice, Arnold S. *The Ku Klux Klan in American Politics.* Washington, D.C.: Public Affairs Press, 1962.

Richardson, Rupert Norval. *Colonel Edward M. House: The Texas Years, 1858-1912.* Abilene: Hardin Simmons University, 1964.

Richardson, T. C. *East Texas: Its History and Its Makers.* Ed. Dabney White. New York: Lewis Historical Publishing Co., 1940.

Rioux, Terry Lee, and G. W. Carroll. *Southern Capitalist and Dedicated Beaumont Baptist.* Austin: Eakin Press, 2001.

Rushing, Jane Gilmore, and Kline A. Nall. *Evolution of a University: Texas Tech's First Fifty Years.* Austin: Madrona Press, 1975.

Schroeder, Richard. *Texas Signs On: The Early Days of Radio and Television.* College Station: Texas A&M University Press, 1998.

Scott, Anne Firor. *Making the Invisible Woman Visible.* Chicago: University of Illinois Press, 1984.

Scott, Bess Whitehead. *You Meet Such Interesting People.* College Station: Texas A&M University Press, 1989.

Scott, David L. *On the Banks of Onion Creek—Eagle Springs Baptist Church, 1858-1998, 140th Anniversary.* Gatesville, Tex., 1998.

Scott, Zelma. *A History of Coryell County, Texas.* Austin: Texas State Historical Association, 1965.

Sellers, Alvin V. *Classics of the Bar: Stories of the World's Great Legal Trials and a Compilation of Forensic Masterpieces.* 8 vols. Baxley, Ga.: Classic Publishing Co., 1909-1921.

Sibley, Marilyn McAdams. *Lone Stars and State Gazettes: Texas Newspapers before the Civil War.* College Station: Texas A&M University Press, 1983.

Silverthorne, Elizabeth. *Christmas in Texas.* College Station: Texas A&M University Press, 1990.

Simmons, Frank. *History of Mother Neff Memorial State Park.* Gatesville, Tex.: Freeman Printing Plant, 1949.

Simpson, Jeffrey. *Chautauqua: An American Utopia.* New York: Henry N. Abrams, Inc., in association with the Chautauqua Institution, 1999.

Sitton, Sarah C. *Life at the Texas State Lunatic Asylum, 1857-1997.* College Station: Texas A&M University Press, 1999.

Slate, Audrey N. J., and the Association of Graduate Schools in the Association of American Universities. *AGS: A History.* Austin: University of Texas Press, 1994.

Soucy, Jean-Yves, with Annette, Cecile, and Yvonne Dionne. *Family Secrets: The Dionne Quintuplets' Own Story.* Toronto: Stoddart Publishing Co., 1996.

Steely, James Wright. *Parks for Texas: Enduring Landscapes of the New Deal.* Austin: University of Texas Press, 1999.

Steen, Ralph W., ed. *The Texas News: A Miscellany of Texas History in Newspaper Style.* Austin: Steck Co., 1955.

———. *The Texas Story.* Rev. ed. Austin: Steck Co., 1960.

Steinberg, Alfred. *Sam Johnson's Boy: A Close-up of the President from Texas.* New York: Macmillan Co., 1968.

———. *Sam Rayburn: A Biography.* New York: Hawthorn Books, 1975.

Stewart, Frank M. *Highway Administration in Texas: A Study of Administrative Methods and Financial Policies.* University of Texas Bulletin no. 3423, June 15, 1934. Austin: University of Texas, 1934.

Stone, Ron. *The Book of Texas Days.* Austin: Eakin Press, 1984.

Tarpley, Fred. *1001 Texas Place Names.* Austin: University of Texas Press, 1980.

Tatum, Ray E. *Conquest or Failure? A Biography of J. Frank Norris.* Fort Worth: Manney Co., 1976.

Texas Almanac 2006-2007. Dallas: Dallas Morning News, 2006.

Texas Baptist Annual. Baptist General Convention of Texas, various locations, various dates.

Texas Education Agency. *Texas Public Schools, 1854-1954: A Centennial Handbook.* Austin: Texas Education Agency, 1954.

Texas Society, Daughters of the American Revolution. *Historic Costumes and Furnishings.* Temple, Tex.: American Printing Co., 1940.

Thomason, Robert Ewing. *Thomason: The Autobiography of a Federal Judge.* Ed. and ann. by Joseph M. Ray. El Paso: Texas Western Press, University of Texas at El Paso, 1971.

Timmons, Bascom N. *Garner of Texas: A Personal History.* New York: Harper, 1948.

Townsend, Charles R. *San Antonio Rose: The Life and Music of Bob Wills.* Urbana and Chicago: University of Illinois Press, 1976.

Toynbee, Arnold. *An Historian's Approach to Religion.* New York: Oxford University Press, 1956.

Travis, Marion. *Waco's Champion: Selections from the Papers of Roger Norman Conger*. Waco: Historic Waco Foundation, 1990.

Tugwell, Rexford G. *The Democratic Roosevelt: A Biography of Franklin D. Roosevelt*. Garden City, N.Y.: Doubleday, 1957.

Turner, Thomas E. *Instruments of Providence: Biographical Vignettes of the Charter Trustees of Baylor University*. Waco: Baylor University Press, 1989.

———. *The Presidents of Baylor University*. Waco: Baylor University Press, 1981.

Turner, Thomas, Sherry Boyd Casello, and Gary Cook, eds. *One Man's Journey*. Waco: Baylor University, 1981.

Utley, Dan K., and James W. Steely. *Guided with a Steady Hand: The Cultural Landscape of a Rural Texas Park*. Waco: Baylor University Press, 1998.

Utley, Robert Marshall. *Lone Star Lawmen: The Second Century of the Texas Rangers*. New York: Oxford University Press, 2007.

Valenza, Janet Mace. *Taking the Waters in Texas: Springs, Spas and Fountains of Youth*. Austin: University of Texas Press, 2000.

Wade, Homer Dale. *Establishment of Texas Technological College, 1916-1923*. Lubbock: Texas Tech Press, 1956.

Walker, Donald R. *Penology for Profit: A History of the Texas Prison System, 1867-1912*. College Station: Texas A&M University Press, 1988.

Wallace, Patricia Ward. *Waco: A Sesquicentennial History*. Virginia Beach, Va.: Donning Company, 1999.

Webb, Walter Prescott. *The Great Frontier*. Austin: University of Texas Press edition, 4th printing, 1975.

———. *The Texas Rangers: A Century of Frontier Defense*. 2d ed. Austin: University of Texas Press, 1995.

Wecter, Dixon. *The Age of the Great Depression, 1929-1941*. New York: Macmillan, 1959.

Welch, June Rayfield. *The Texas Governor*. Dallas: G.L.A. Press, 1977.

Wilson, Winston P. *Harvey Couch: The Master Builder*. Nashville, Tenn.: Broadman Press, 1947.

Wolfe, Charles K., and Kip Lornell. *The Life and Legend of Leadbelly*. New York: Harper Collins, 1992.

Wolfe, J. A. L. *A Consideration of the Legal Status of Chiropractors: More Particularly of the Question Whether or Not Chiropractors Are Included within the Terms of the Texas Medical Practice Act of 1907*. Austin: Council of Medical Defense, 1918.

Yergin, Daniel. *The Prize: The Epic Quest for Oil, Money and Power*. New York: Simon and Schuster, 1991; Fort Worth: Miramar Publishers, 1983.

Zelden, Charles L. *The Battle for the Black Ballot: Smith v. Allwright and the Defeat of the Texas All-White Primary*. Lawrence: University Press of Kansas, 2004.

Articles and Chapters

Allen, W. S. "Historical High Points of Baylor University." *Baylor Monthly* 1 (November 1927).

"A Look Back: Class Rings." *Baylor Line* (summer 2002).

Armstrong, A. J. "Baylor University's Browning Collection." *Baylor Bulletin* 30 (December 1927).

Asher, Lisa. "Turn the Radio On." *Baylor Line* (winter 2003).

Banta, John. "Old Corn Road Reaches Back into History." *Waco Tribune-Herald,* July 29, 1962.

"The Baptist General Convention of Texas." *Baptist Standard,* December 10, 1925.

"Baptist in the Middle of the Road." *Literary Digest* (June 1926).

"Baptist $75 Million Campaign." *Baptist Standard* 33, no. 32 (July 24, 1919).

Baylor University, Office of Public Relations. "Former Air Force Chaplain Presented War Heroes Award." January 9, 2004. Online: http://www.baylor.edu/pr/news.php?action=story& story=6325 .

———. "ROTC Pays Tribute to Medal of Honor Alumni." December 6, 2002. Online: http://www.baylor.edu/pr/news.php?action=story&story=4362.

Beaty, Michael, Todd Buras, and Larry Lyon. "Baptist Higher Education: A Conflict of Terms?" *Baylor Line* (winter 1997).

Bodine, Max N. "Letter to Editor." *Baylor Line* (fall 1992).

Bragg, J. D. "Waco University." *Southwestern Historical Quarterly* 51, no. 3 (January 1948).

Brooks, S. P. "About Baylor University." *Baptist Standard* 24, no. 1 (January 4, 1912).

———. "Concerning Removal of Baylor University." *Baylor Monthly* 4, no. 1 (April 1928).

———. "The Inaugural Address." *Baylor Bulletin* 6 (November 1902).

———. "The President's Page." *Baylor Monthly* 6, no. 7 (January 1931).

———. "Some Things Educational." *Baptist Standard* 24, no. 32 (8 August 1912).

———. "The Thatness of the Somewhat." *Baylor Literary* 5, no. 5 (January 1897).

Brown, Ellen Kuniyuki. "Samuel Palmer Brooks and the Evolution Controversy at Baylor University, 1921-1923." *Texas Baptist History, Journal of the Texas Baptist Historical Society* 1 (1981).

Brown, Ellen Kuniyuki, and Paula Price Tanner. "Building Baylor." *Baylor Line (*fall 1994).

Brown, Margaret Cannon. "The Cotton Palace Pageant: The Beginning." *Waco Heritage and History* 11, no. 1 (spring   1980): 11-18.

Burton, Jeff. "No Train Robbers Ever Worked Harder at Their Trade Than the Cornett-Whitley Gang." *True West*, February-March 1973, pp. 18-53.

Campbell, Bonnie Ann. "Furnishing the Texas State Capitol." *Southwestern Historical Quarterly* 92, no. 2 (October 1988): 334.

Carter, George H. "Who Spiked the Cannon?" *Alcalde* 1, no. 1 (April 1913).

Clark, Vince. "Integrating Baylor," *Baylor Line* (spring 2004): 33-39.

———."Why 'The Ten' Remain Immortal." *Baylor Line* (winter 1997).

Claypool, Mrs. T. H. "Religious Educational Activities in Baylor University." *Baptist Standard* (April 1, 1920).

"Commencement 1924—Before and After." *Alcalde* 12, no. 87 (August 1924).

"Convocation/Dedication Commemorating the 144th Year of Baylor University and the Dedication of the Ferrell Center and the Paul J. Meyer Arena." Program. November 18, 1988. Online: http://baylorbears.collegesports.com/school-bio/bay-theferrellcenter.html .

Copeland, Todd. "An Academic Restructuring." *Baylor Line* (winter 1995).

———. "The Immortal Ten." *Baylor Line* (winter 2002).

Cullar, Meg. "Stage Presence." *Baylor Line* (fall 2001).

Curry, William H. "The Auditorium." *Waco Heritage and History* 3, no. 4 (winter 1972).

———. "The Big Crush" "*Waco Heritage and History* 8, no. 3 (fall 1977): 1-5.

Cross, Clinton. "Law Day, 2004." *El Paso Bar Bulletin* (January-April 2004).

Dawson, Joseph M. "W. C. Brann, 1855-1898." *Waco Heritage and History* 23, no. 1 (June 1993).

Dawson, Matt. "The Early Years." In *Abner McCall: One Man's Journey.* Ed. Sherry Boyd Costello, Gary Cook, and Thomas Turner. Waco: Baylor University, 1981.

Duty, Tony E. "Waco at the Turn of the Century." *Waco Heritage and History* 3, no. 2 (summer 1972).

Eastland, Lady Ray. "In Favor of Chapel." *Baylor Bulletin* 40, no. 3 (August 1937): 65-68.

Finney, L. E. "The Convention." *Baylor Monthly* 4 (June 1928).

"The Freeze of 1899 and Other Phenomena of Waco Weather." *Waco Heritage and History* 15, no. 2 (Winter 1986).

Hall, Ida Legett. "The Blacks in Waco, 1800-1950." *Waco Heritage and History* 14, no. 3 (spring 1984).

Handbook of Texas Online, s.v. "Collins, Carr P." http://www.tsha.utexas.edu/handbook/online/articles/CC/fco90_print.html.

Handbook of Texas Online, s.v. "Cooper, Madison Alexander Jr.," http://www.tsha.utexas.edu/handbook/online/articles/CC/fco59.html.

Handbook of Texas Online, s.v. "Crowell, Grace Noll." http://www.tsha.utexas.edu/handbook/online/articles/CC/fcr57.html.

Handbook of Texas Online, s.v. "Daniels, Bebe Virginia." http://www.tsha.utexas.edu/handbook/online/articles/DD/fda10_print.html.

Handbook of Texas Online, s.v. "East Texas Oilfield." http://www.tsha.utexas.edu/handbook/online/articles/EE/doe1.html.

Handbook of Texas Online, s.v. "Eby, Frederick." http://www.tsha.utexas.edu/handbook/online/articles/EE/feb3_print.html.

Handbook of Texas Online, s.v. "Garner, John Nance." http://www.tsha.utexas.edu/handbook/online/articles/GG/fga24.html.

Handbook of Texas Online, s.v. "Great Depression." http://www.tsha.utexas.edu/handbook/online/articles/GG/npg1.html.

Handbook of Texas Online, s.v. "Johnson, Rebekah Baines." http://www.tsha.utexas.edu/handbook/online/articles/JJ/fjo22.html.

Handbook of Texas Online, s.v. "Knights of Pythias." http://www.tsha.utexas.edu/handbook/online/articles/KK/vnk1.html.

Handbook of Texas Online, s.v. "Parr, Archer." http://www.tsha.utexas.edu/handbook/online/articles/PP/fpa35.html.

Handbook of Texas Online, s.v. "Waco, Texas." http://www.tsha.utexas.edu/handbook/online/articles/WW/hdw1.html.

Harrison, Guy B., Jr. "The Texas Collection of Baylor University." *Baylor Bulletin* 44 (December 1940).

Hartman, Fred. "Burleson Hall Traditions Linger." *Baylor Monthly* 4, no. 9 (December 1928).

"Harvard vs. Yale." *Sports Illustrated on Campus* (November 18, 2003).

"Harvey Crowley Couch, 1877-1941." *Encyclopedia of Arkansas History and Culture.* Little Rock, Ark.: Butler Center for Arkansas Studies, 2006.

Herring, B. O. "The Bible Department Building." *Baylor Bulletin* 40, no. 3, pt. 1 (August 1937): 235.

Hinsie, Leland E., M.D., and Robert Jean Campbell, M.D. *Psychiatric Dictionary.* London: Oxford University Press, 1970.

Hunt, Eleanor L. "Towers Going Back atop Baylor's Old Main, Burleson Hall." *Waco Heritage and History* 6, no. 2 (summer 1975).

"Iron Will, Silver Tongue Made Pat Neff an Unforgettable Part of Baylor History." *Baylor Lariat,* June 24, 1959.

Jennings, Morley. "Baylor's Department of Physical Education." *Baylor Bulletin* 40, no. 3, pt. 4 (August 1937): 228-229.

Kansas State Historical Society. "Carry Nation: The Famous and Original Bar Room Smasher." Online exhibit: http://www.kshs.org/exhibits/carry/carry1.htm.

Keeth, Kent. "Building the Living Room," *Baylor Line* (September 1986, November 1986, February 1987).

———."The Businessmen's March." *Baylor Line* (May 1990).

———. "The Campus as Playground." *Baylor Line* (summer 1994).

———. "A Cheer for the Carrolls." *Baylor Line* (April 1979).

———. "The Day the Carroll Library Burned." *Baylor Line* (winter 1993).

———. "The Death of Burleson." *Baylor Line* (summer 1995).

———. "From the Literary to the Monthly." *Baylor Line* (June 1987).

———. "Keeping in Touch." *Baylor Line* (April 1987).

———. "The Lariat's Debut." *Baylor Line* (November 1985).

———. "Looking Back at Baylor 1928." Four parts. Reprinted in *Baylor Line* (November 1988—May 1989).

———. "Marking the Milestones: Part 3, Celebrating the 1945 Centennial," *Baylor Line* (spring 1995).

———. "A Roundabout Road to Baylor, Part 1 ." *Baylor Line* (winter 1994).

"Last Tribute Paid Ex-Governor Neff." *Waco News-Tribune,* January 22, 1952.

McSwain, Betty Ann. "Take the Interurban." *Waco Heritage and History* 6, no. 3 (summer 1975).

———. "Texas Christian University in Waco, 1902-1910." *Waco Heritage and History* 6, no. 2 (summer 1975).

Measures, Royce. "Fundamentalism Texas Style." *Texas Baptist History: The Journal of the Texas Baptist Historical Society* 1 (1981).

Miller, Neil Colgin. "Make Do and Do Without: Wartime Reminiscences." *Waco Heritage and History* 21, no. 2 (December 1991): 105-107.

Ming, Virginia. "Letters to Hallie Maude Neff." *Waco Heritage and History* 9, no. 2 (summer 1978): 39-48.

Morehouse, Henry L. "An Educational Revival." *Baylor Bulletin* 6, no. 1 (November 1902).

Morris, C. Gwin. "J. Frank Norris and the Baptist General Convention of Texas." *Texas Baptist History: The Journal of the Texas Baptist Historical Society* 1 (1981).

Nash, J. M. "Baylor's Endowment." *Baylor Bulletin,* 40, no. 3, pt. 3 (August 1937): 84-86.

National Association for the Advancement of Colored People (NAACP), "The Waco Horror," supplement to *Crisis,* July 1916.

Neff, Pat M. "Baylor University." *Baylor Bulletin* 40, no. 3, pt. 1 (August 1937): 33-34.

———. "Ex-Governor Pat M. Neff Paints Word Pictures." *Baylor Monthly* 3, no. 5 (August 1927).

———. "Our Alma Mater." *Southland* 11, no. 4 (April 1902): 83-86.

" 'Noble Warrior' Pat Neff Buried." *Waco News-Tribune,* January 22, 1952.

Padgitt, Clint. "Brooks Hall, Site of an Historic Waco Event." *Baylor Bulletin* 40, no. 3, pt. 1 (August 1937): 20-22.

Parker, David B. "Bill Arp (Charles Henry Smith, 1826-1903)" *New Georgia Encyclopedia.* Online: www.georgiaencyclopedia.org/nge/Article.jsp?id=h-757&hl=y .

Peeler, Tom. "Nostalgia: Healing Waters." *D Magazine* (November 1983).

Provence, Harry. "The Chapel Hour—What It Meant to Me." *Baylor Bulletin* 40, no. 3, pt. 3 (August 1937): 64-65.

Radford, Garry Hamilton. "The History of the Black Man in Waco, Texas, from June 10, 1866 to January 1, 1984." *Waco Heritage and History* 14, no. 3 (spring 1984).

Riddle, D. Q. "Baylor University Celebrates Her Seventy-fifth." *Baptist Standard* (June 24, 1920).

———. "The Texas Baptist Encampments." *Baptist Standard* (June 17, 1920).

Robinson, George. "Pat M. Neff, Baylor Chief." Editorial. *Houston Post,* March 22, 1932.

Rogers, Arthur J. "Paul Baker and Theater Architecture." In *Paul Baker and the Integration of Abilities,* ed. Robert Flynn and Eugene McKinney. Fort Worth: TCU Press, 2003.

Routh, E. C. "Samuel Palmer Brooks—An Appreciation." *Baptist Standard* 27, no. 46 (November 18, 1915).

Schuster, David G. "Neurasthenia and a Modernizing America." *Journal of the American Medical Association* 290, no. 17 (November 5, 2003).

"She Who Nurses One Must Nourish Two." *Texas State Journal of Medicine* (December 1911): 9.

Shirley, Emma Morrill. "The Administration of Pat M. Neff, Governor of Texas, 1921-1925." *Baylor Bulletin* 41, no. 4 (December 1938).

Shirley, Mrs. Newton A. "Mrs. Pat Neff." *Henry Downs Chapter, Daughters of the American Revolution* (n.d., circa 1930): 1-6.

SoRelle, James M. "The Waco Horror: The Lynching of Jesse Washington." Paper presented to annual meeting of the Texas State Historical Association, reprinted in *Southwestern Historical Quarterly* 86, no. 4 (April 1983).

Strecker, John K. "Baylor's Museum in New Quarters." *Baylor Monthly 3* (October 1927).

"Testament." *Sampson-Vinson Heritage Society Newsletter of the Austin Presbyterian Theological Seminary* (spring 2001).

"Texas Baptists and Our Negro Brethren." *Baptist Standard,* April 22, 1920.

"Those Who Were There." *Baylor Line* (fall 1998).

"Through the Century to the Line." *Baylor Line* (September 1987).

Turner, Thomas E. "The Triumphs and Tribulations of Baylor Football." *Retired Professors Newsletter* 12 (December 1, 1996).

———. "U.S. Presidents at Baylor: Not All Fun and Fanfare." *Waco Heritage and History* 1, no. 2 (December 1989).

Veazey, D. Raymond. "Neff in Effigy." *Baylor Line* (fall 1992): 75.

Veit, Richard J. "All I Want for Christmas is a Blackout Curtain." *Waco Heritage and History* 21, no. 2 (December 1991): 108-112.

———. "The Waco Jailbreak of Bonnie and Clyde." *Waco Heritage and History* 20, no. 2 (December 1990): 3-20.

"Voices from the 1893 World's Columbian Exposition." *Internet 1996 World Exposition.* Online: http://japan.park.org/Guests/WWWvoice/1893chi.html.

Whitmars, Anthony. "The Disappearance of Neurasthenia." *Emerge* (summer 1998). Online: http://home.vicnet.net.au/~mecfs/general/neurasthenia.html.

"Women at Baylor, 1845-1980: She Was a Phantom of Delight." *Waco Heritage and History* 25, no. 1 (summer 1995): 38-50.

Theses, Dissertations, and Unpublished Papers and Manuscripts

Adams, Charles Scott. "Twentieth Century Baylor University Presidents and Christian Education: The Educational Philosophies of Samuel Palmer Brooks, Pat Morris Neff, and William Richardson White." Master's thesis, Baylor University, Waco, Tex., 1964.

Alexander, Charles Comer. "Crusade for Conformity: The Ku Klux Klan in Texas, 1920-1927." Master's thesis, University of Texas, Austin, Tex., 1959.

Baker, Eugene. "As We Onward Go: Baylor University in the Twentieth Century." Unpublished manuscript, Baylor University, Waco, Tex., May 2003. Texas Collection.

———. "Enhancing the Foundation." Draft manuscript, May 9, 2003.

———. "The First Gubernatorial Campaign of Pat M. Neff." Master's thesis, Baylor University, Waco, Tex., 1961.

———. "History of the Baylor Law School." Unpublished manuscript, Baylor University, Waco, Tex., 2001. Texas Collection.

Bean, Robyn Carlyle. "The Role of the Commercial-Civic Elite in the Desegregation of Public Facilities in Waco, Texas." Master's thesis, Baylor University, Waco, Tex., 1990.

Bennett, Ray Earl. "Pat M. Neff: His Denominational Leadership." Master's thesis, Baylor University, Waco, Tex., 1960.

Bettis, Nat C. "History of Baylor University 1845-1942." Term paper, Baylor University, Waco, Tex., 1942.

Brady, Kevin Michael. "Baylor at War." Master's thesis, Baylor University, Waco, Tex., 2002.

Bryant, C. E. "A Review of the Neff Administration." Unpublished manuscript, Baylor University, Waco, Tex., 1941.

Cagle, Louise Moore. "The Life of Francis Gevrier Guittard." Master's thesis, Baylor University, Waco, Tex., 1951.

Chrisman, David Keith. "The Public Life of Caso March: Anti-Establishment Campaigns in the Democratic Party, 1946-1950." Master's thesis, Baylor University, Waco, Tex., 1990.

Crow, Herman Lee. "A Political History of the Texas Penal System, 1829-1951." Ph.D. dissertation, University of Texas, Austin, Tex., 1962.

Crunk, Jeffrey Fritz. "Breathing Spots for the People: Pat M. Neff, David E. Colp, and the Emerging Idea of State Parks in Texas, 1900-1925." Master's thesis, Baylor University, Waco, Tex., 1994.

Davis, James Michael. "Horace Sherman Miller and the U.S. Klans." Master's thesis, Baylor University, Waco, Tex., 1989.

Dickinson, William Colvin. "Baylor University: A Century of Discipline, 1845-1947." Master's thesis, Baylor University, Waco, Tex., 1962.

Dunn, Jeffrey D. "The Legacy of *Johnson v. Dare*: The 1925 Decision of the All-Woman Supreme Court." Paper presented at the annual meeting of the Texas State Historical Association, Austin, Tex., March 6, 2004.

Goff, Cicely S. "The Conference for Education in Texas." Term paper, Baylor University, 1929. Frederick Eby Papers, Texas Collection, Baylor University, Waco, Tex.

Gooch, Stephen Edward. "Pat M. Neff and the National Mediation Board." Master's thesis, Baylor University, Waco, Tex., 1968.

Healey, Jane Frances, "An Annotated Bibliography of Privately Published Autobiographies." Master's thesis, Baylor University, Waco, Tex.,1986.

Henderson, Robert L. "The Baylor Administration of Pat M. Neff, 1939-1947." Master's thesis, Baylor University, Waco, Tex., 1960.

Hubbell, Macklyn Ward. "The Life of Pat Neff." Master's thesis, University of Houston, Houston, Tex., 1953.

Huckaby, George Portal. "Oscar Branch Colquitt: A Political Biography." Ph.D. dissertation, University of Texas, Austin, Tex., 1946.

Huddleston, John David. "Good Roads for Texas: A History of the Texas Highway Department." Ph.D. dissertation, Texas A&M University, College Station, Tex., 1981.

Johnson, Aimee Harris. "Prostitution in Waco, 1889-1917." Master's thesis, Baylor University, Waco, Tex., 1990.

Kilgore, Linda Elaine. "The Ku Klux Klan and the Press in Texas, 1920-1927." Master's thesis, University of Texas, Austin, Tex., 1964.

Kulesz, M. John, Jr. "A History and Analysis of Radio Broadcasting at Baylor University, 1935-1968." Master's thesis, Baylor University, Waco, Tex., 1968.

Laughlin, Lola Matthews. "The Speaking Career of Pat Morris Neff." Master's thesis, Baylor University, Waco, Tex., 1951.

Mackenzie, Charles Alfred. "A History of the Baylor University School of Law: From the

Lectures of Abner S. Lipscomb through the Deanship of Abner V. McCall." Master's thesis, Baylor University, Waco, Tex., 1988.

Moore, Loise M. "Pat M. Neff and His Achievements." Master's thesis, Texas College of Arts and Industries, Kingsville, Tex., 1941.

Moursund, Walter H., Sr. "A History of Baylor University College of Medicine, 1900-1953." Faculty publication, Baylor University College of Medicine, Houston, Tex., 1956.

Murph, David Rupert. "Price Daniel: The Life of a Public Man, 1910-1956." Ph.D. dissertation, Texas Christian University, Fort Worth, Tex., 1975.

Neff, Pat M. "The Life of Pat M. Neff, An Autobiography." Class paper, Baylor University, 1890. Pat Neff Papers, Texas Collection, Baylor University, Waco, Tex.

Nicar, Jim ."A Holiday with a Spiked Cannon." Texas Exes UT Heritage Society, Texas Exes-University of Texas Alumni Association, Austin, Tex., n.d.

Nichols, R. Bryan. "Pat M. Neff, His Boyhood and Early Political Career." Master's thesis, Baylor University, Waco, Tex., 1951.

Owens, Estelle. "An Analysis of the Rationale of Representative Southern Baptist Intellectuals, 1835-1900." Master's thesis, Baylor University, Waco, Tex., 1975.

Palmer, James Franklin. "Pat Morris Neff, President of Baylor University, 1932-1939." Master's thesis, Baylor University, Waco, Tex., 1960.

Parr, Ottis. "The Public Services of Pat M. Neff." Master's thesis, Texas Technological College, Lubbock, Tex., 1951.

Parrish, Thomas Michael. "'This Species of Slave Labor': The Convict Lease System in Texas, 1871-1914." Master's thesis, Baylor University, Waco, Tex., 1976.

Renberg, James Bernard. "Samuel Palmer Brooks, President of Baylor University, 1920-1931." Master's thesis, Baylor University, Waco, Tex., 1963.

Schmelzer, Janet Louise. "The Early Life and Early Congressional Career of Wright Patman: 1894-1941." Ph.D. dissertation, Texas Christian University, Fort Worth, Tex., 1978.

Shirley, Emma Morrill. "Mother Neff State Park: The Mother of the Entire Texas Park System." Unpublished manuscript, Baylor University, n.d. Pat Neff Papers, Texas Collection, Baylor University, Waco, Tex.

Sinclair, Oran Lonnie. "Samuel Palmer Brooks: President of Baylor University, 1902-1920." Master's thesis, Baylor University, Waco, Tex., 1961.

Snow, Laura. "The Poll Tax in Texas: Its Historical, Legal, and Fiscal Aspects." Master's thesis, University of Texas, Austin, Tex., 1936.

Stanley, Mark. "Booze, Boomtowns, and Burning Crosses: The Turbulent Governorship of Pat M. Neff of Texas, 1921-1925." Master's thesis, University of North Texas, Denton, Tex., 2005.

Stoffregen, Pat. "Our Great White Father." Term theme, Baylor University, 1947. Texas Collection.

Stricklin, David B. "The Development of the Musical Career of Bob Wills, 1929-1938: Folk Forces and Commercialization." Master's thesis, Baylor University, Waco, Tex., 1978.

Stroud, Roy Wallace. "The Run-off Primary." Master's thesis, University of Texas, Austin, Tex., 1941.

"SWC Football, 80 Years, 1915-1995, Roster and Records." Photocopy, 1994.

Williams, Earl Francis. "History of Baylor University." Ph.D. dissertation, Baylor University, Waco, Tex., 1941.

Winfrey, Chase Sherwin. "Pat Morris Neff: A Personality-Oratorical Study." Ph.D. dissertation, University of Denver, Denver, Col., 1951.

Ying, Wang. "Samuel Palmer Brooks, Pat Morris Neff, and William Richardson White: Their Different Methods in Administration." Master's thesis, Baylor University, Waco, Tex., 1988.

Interviews

Adkins-Grantham, Donna. Interview by Dorothy Blodgett. Tape recording. Waco, Tex., May 16, 1992. Blodgett Collection, Austin, Tex.

Baker, Eugene. Interview by Dorothy Blodgett. Waco, Tex., September 26, 1985. Blodgett Collection, Austin, Tex.

Baker, Paul, and Kitty Baker. Interview by Dorothy Blodgett. Tape recording. Waelder, Tex., December 12, 1996. Blodgett Collection, Austin, Tex.

Barcus, Jacque. Interview by Dorothy Blodgett and David L Scott. Tape recording (2 tapes). Austin, Tex., April 21, 1998. Blodgett Collection, Austin, Tex.

Barnes, Bobbie. Interview by Dorothy Blodgett. Tape recording. Waco, Tex., April 30, 1992. Blodgett Collection, Austin, Tex.

Bowmer, Jim D. Interview by Dorothy Blodgett. Correspondence. Killeen, Tex., October 21, 2003. Blodgett Collection, Austin, Tex.

Boyles-Brooks, Judy. Interview by Dorothy Blodgett. Correspondence. Mendocina, Calif., August 23, 1995. Blodgett Collection, Austin, Tex.

Bratcher, Ed. Telephone interview by Dorothy Blodgett. Durham, N.C., January 22, 2003. Blodgett Collection, Austin, Tex.

Brewer-Miles, Gladys. Telephone interview by Dorothy Blodgett. Austin, Tex., May 28, 1996. Blodgett Collection, Austin, Tex.

Bryant, C. E. Interview by Dorothy Blodgett. Correspondence. Spartanburg, S.C., April 4 and July 7, 1996; Fairview Heights, Ill., August 10, 1997. Blodgett Collection, Austin, Tex.

Byers, Mary C. Interview by Dorothy Blodgett. Austin, Tex., September 8, 1997. Blodgett Collection, Austin, Tex.

Chapin, Cathryn. Telephone interview by Dorothy Blodgett, Austin, Tex., February 28, 1992. Blodgett Collection, Austin, Tex.

Combs, Juanita. Interview by David Scott. Corpus Christi, Tex., March 24, 2002. David L. Scott Collection, Gatesville, Tex.

Cox, Ava Johnson. Interview by Dorothy Blodgett and David L. Scott. Tape recording. Johnson City, Tex., October 29, 1992. Blodgett Collection, Austin, Tex.

Culpepper, E. A. "Vena". Interview by David Scott. Moody, Tex., September 28, 1991. David L. Scott Collection, Gatesville, Tex.

Davis, Clay, and Joan Davis. Interview by Dorothy Blodgett and Terrell Blodgett. Coryell County Farm near Mother Neff Park, Tex., October 26, 1998. Blodgett Collection, Austin, Tex.

Dawson, Matt. Telephone interview by Dorothy Blodgett. Tape recording. Waco, Tex., September 14, 2000. Blodgett Collection, Austin, Tex.

DeGraffenreid, Brian. Telephone interview by Dorothy Blodgett. Austin, Tex., June 16,1998. Blodgett Collection, Austin, Tex.

Denham, Louise Yelvington. Interview by Dorothy Blodgett. Tape recording. Austin, Tex., November 30, 1998. Blodgett Collection, Austin, Tex.

Dillard, Dorothy. Telephone interview by Dorothy Blodgett. Austin, Tex., October 17, 1997. Blodgett Collection, Austin, Tex.

Dillard, Jack, and Roger Edens. Interview by George Stokes. Tape recording. Waco, Tex., November 1, 1985. Blodgett Collection, Austin, Tex.

Dismukes, Diane. Interview by Dorothy Blodgett. Austin, Tex., October 29, 2003. Blodgett Collection, Austin, Tex.

Dodd, Ella. Interview by David Scott. Tape recording. Lovelady, Tex., May 14, 1992. Blodgett Collection, Austin, Tex.

Edens, Roger. Interview by Dorothy Blodgett. Waco, Tex., April 11, 2002. Blodgett Collection, Austin, Tex.

Goebel, Marvin. Interview by Terrell Blodgett. Tape recording. Waco, Tex, July 12, 2000. Blodgett Collection, Austin, Tex.

Hamilton, Oleta Maxwell. Interview by David Scott, Dorothy Blodgett, and Terrell Blodgett, September 26, 1998. Arrowhead Ranch, Coryell County, Tex. (home of Barbara Hamilton Wright). Blodgett Collection, Austin, Tex.

Harrell, Lucille, and Lester Harrell. Interview by Dorothy Blodgett. Correspondence. October 22, 2003. Blodgett Collection, Austin, Tex.

Harrell, Lucille Carson, and June Page Johnson. Interview by Terrell Blodgett, Austin, Tex., October 22, 2003, Blodgett Collection.

Hightower, Elizabeth (Logue). Telephone interview by Dorothy Blodgett. November 12, 2003. Blodgett Collection, Austin, Tex.

Hightower, Judge Jack. Interview by Terrell Blodgett. Tape recording. Austin, Tex., April 5, 2002. Blodgett Collection, Austin, Tex.

Hopkins, Welly K. Interview by Eric F. Goldman, May 11, 1965. Lyndon Baines Johnson Presidential Library, Austin, Tex.

Jenkins, Warwick. Interview by Terrell Blodgett. Tape recording. Waxahachie, Tex., July 13, 2000. Blodgett Collection, Austin, Tex.

Johnson, June. Interview by Terrell Blodgett. Austin, Tex., December 2, 2003. Blodgett Collection, Austin, Tex.

Jones, Bess. Interview by Dorothy Blodgett. Austin, Tex., September 10, 1998. Blodgett Collection, Austin, Tex.

Jones, Carol, and George Jones. Interview by Dorothy Blodgett. Tape recording. Austin, Tex., March 30, 1998. Blodgett Collection, Austin, Tex.

Jones, Johnny, and Wilma Jones. Interview by Dorothy Blodgett and Terrell Blodgett. Austin, Tex., October 1, 2000. Blodgett Collection, Austin, Tex.

Jones, Monroe, V. Marie Jones, Tullie Jones, and Clyde Jones. Interview by Dorothy Blodgett. Tape recording. Moody, Tex., October 27, 1985. Blodgett Collection, Austin, Tex.

Jones, V. Marie. "The Day I Met Bonnie Parker and Clyde Barrow." Interview by David Scott. McGregor, Tex., 1985. Blodgett Collection, Austin, Tex.

Keeth, Kent. Telephone interview by Dorothy Blodgett. Waco, Tex., November 3, 1995. Blodgett Collection, Austin, Tex.

Logue, Bill. Telephone interview by Dorothy Blodgett. Waco, Tex., April 2, 1998. Blodgett Collection, Austin, Tex.

Long, Willie. Interview by Dorothy Blodgett. Correspondence. Belton, Tex., April 18, 2001. Blodgett Collection, Austin, Tex.

Maxwell, Melvin. Interview by David Scott, Dorothy Blodgett, and Terrell Blodgett. Arrowhead Ranch, Coryell County, Tex. (home of Barbara Hamilton Wright), September 26, 1998. Blodgett Collection, Austin, Tex.

Middleton, Bob. Telephone interview by Dorothy Blodgett, November 17, 2003. Blodgett Collection, Austin, Tex.

Murphy, Pat. Telephone interview by Dorothy Blodgett and Terrell Blodgett. Little Rock, Ark., June 30, 2000. Blodgett Collection, Austin, Tex.

Napier, Mary Isabella. Interview by David L. Scott. Fort Worth, Tex., May 14, 1997. David L. Scott Collection, Gatesville, Tex.

Neff-Price, Sara. Interview by Dorothy Blodgett and Terrell Blodgett. Tape recording. Niceville, Fla., January 25, 1999. Blodgett Collection, Austin, Tex.

Newton, Cal, and India Newton. Interview by Dorothy Blodgett and Terrell Blodgett. Tape recording. Uvalde, Tex., September 22, 1998. Blodgett Collection, Austin, Tex.

Nokes, George, Jr. Interview by Terrell Blodgett. Austin, Tex., November 2, 2006, Blodgett Collection.

Patman, William Neff. Interview by Terrell Blodgett. Austin, Tex., October 20, 2006. Blodgett Collection, Austin, Tex.

Patterson, Clay. Interview by Dorothy Blodgett. McGregor, Tex., January 10, 1992. Blodgett Collection, Austin, Tex.

Pickle, Joe. Interview by Terrell Blodgett. Tape recording. Austin, Tex., February 27, 2001. Blodgett Collection, Austin, Tex.

Pittman, H. C. Telephone interview by Dorothy Blodgett. Tape recording. Austin, Tex., June 9, 1999. Blodgett Collection, Austin, Tex.

Ratliff, Jerry. Interview by Dorothy Blodgett. Correspondence. Austin, Tex., Island at Lake Travis, November 20, 1997. Blodgett Collection, Austin, Tex.

Schwartz, A. R. "Babe." Telephone interview by Terrell Blodgett. Austin, Tex., April 27, 2007. Blodgett Collection, Austin, Tex.

Seawright, Betty, and Edgar Perryman. Interview by David L. Scott. McGregor, Tex., September 13, 2004. David L. Scott Collection, Gatesville, Tex..

Shelburne, Estelle. Interview by Dorothy Blodgett and David Scott. Tape recording. Crockett, Tex., May 1, 1992. Blodgett Collection, Austin, Tex.

Shurtleff, Sam, Jr. Interview by Dorothy Blodgett. Tape recording. Waco, Tex., December 16, 1997. Blodgett Collection, Austin, Tex.

Smith Douglas Murray Strain, Lois. Interview by Dorothy Blodgett. Tape recording. Waco, Tex., April 30, 1992. Blodgett Collection, Austin, Tex.

Smith, Laura Dossett. Telephone interview by Dorothy Blodgett. Waco, Tex., October 22, 2003. Blodgett Collection, Austin, Tex.

Speicher, Ann. Telephone interview by Terrell Blodgett. Austin, Tex., November 27, 2006. Blodgett Collection, Austin, Tex.

Stovall-Killion, Velma. Interview by Dorothy Blodgett. Correspondence. Paradise Valley, Ariz., March 18, 1996. Blodgett Collection, Austin, Tex.

Torn, Roberta Keys. Interview by Dorothy Blodgett and Terrell Blodgett. Houston, Tex., September 22, 2000. Blodgett Collection, Austin, Tex.

Townsend, Charles R. Interview by Dorothy Blodgett. Canyon, Tex., April 17, 2002. Blodgett Collection, Austin, Tex.

Turner, Thomas E. Interviews by Dorothy Blodgett. Correspondence. 1998-2001. Blodgett Collection, Austin, Tex.

Waugh, Gene Barnwell. Interviews by Dorothy Blodgett. Telephone and correspondence. Austin, Tex., September 20, 2000. Blodgett Collection, Austin, Tex.

Whitcraft, Carol. Interview by Dorothy Blodgett. Austin, Tex., March 30, 1998. Blodgett Collection, Austin, Tex.

Wilcox, Hallie Maude (Neff). Interview by Macklyn Ward Hubbell. Waco, Tex., April 17, 2002. (Cited by Hubbell in his master's thesis, "The Life of Pat Neff," University of Houston, Houston, Tex., 1953.) Neff Papers, Texas Collection, Baylor University, Waco, Tex.

Willis, Jimmy. Telephone interview by David L. Scott. June 9, 1998. Blodgett Collection, Austin, Tex.

Willis, Juanita. Interview by Dorothy Blodgett. Waco, Tex., October 18, 1986. Blodgett Collection, Austin, Tex.

Oral Memoirs

The oral memoirs listed here were produced by the Baylor University Institute for Oral History, previously called the Baylor University Program in Oral History, and deposited in the Texas Collection, Baylor University, Waco, Texas.

Barrow, Charles Wallace. Oral Memoirs. Interview by Rebecca Sharpless, December 3, 1993.

Brooks, Sims Palmer, and Aurelia Brooks Harlan. Oral Memoirs. Interviews by Kent Keeth, January 19, 1982; October 4, 1984.

Butt, Howard E., Jr., and Katy Jennings Stokes. Oral Memoirs. Interview by Thomas L. Charlton, L. Katherine Cook, and Katy Jennings Stokes, May 13, 1982.

Capp, Glenn R., Sr. Oral Memoirs. Interview by Gary Wayne Hull, August 31, 1976.

Carman, Henry Franklin. Oral Memoirs. Interview by Daniel B. McGee, March 30, 1972.

Dawson, Joseph Martin. Oral Memoirs. Interview by Thomas L. Charlton, April 2, 1971.
———. Oral Memoirs. Interview by Kay Nowlin, November 25, 1971.
Denham, Louise Durham. Oral Memoirs. Interview by Lois Myers, December 3, 1998.
Denny, Robert S. Oral Memoirs. Interview by William L. Pitts, September 22, 1983.
Duncan, Merle Mears McClellan. Oral Memoirs. Interview by Janelle Easley, January 12, 1977.
Harrison, Guy B., Jr. Oral Memoirs. Interview by Thomas L. Charlton, June 20, 1974.
Jones, E. N. Oral Memoirs. Interview by Thomas L. Charlton, May 10, 1972.
McCall, Abner Vernon. Oral Memoirs. Interview by Thomas Lee Charlton and Thomas E. Turner Sr., September 14, 1981.
Miles, Elton. Oral Memoirs. Various dates in 1987.
Morris, Neill Coker. Oral Memoirs. Interview by Rufus B. Spain, June 18, 1975.
Patterson, Joseph William "Bill." Oral Memoirs. Interview by Thomas E. Turner, September 17, 1981.
Poage, William Robert "Bob". Oral Memoirs. Interview by Thomas L. Charlton, March 19, 1979.
Robinson, Robert Jackson. Oral Memoirs. Interview by L. Katherine Cook, May 20, 1982; interview by Thomas L. Charlton, May 21, 1982.
Sendon, Mary Kemendo. Oral Memoirs. Interview by Lois E. Myers, February 22, 1994.
Shirley, Emma. Oral Memoirs. Interview by Ann Armistead, October 18, 1976.
Smith, Cornelia Marshall. Oral Memoirs. Interview by Kay Clifton, March 22, 1978.
Stephens, William Richmond. Oral Memoirs. Interview by Thomas L. Charlton, October 2, 1975.
Wimpee, W. J. Oral Memoirs. Interview by Susie Valentine, May 1, 1980.

Government Documents

General and Special Laws of the State of Texas, various legislative sessions. Legislative Reference Library, State of Texas, Austin, Texas.
Journal of the Texas House of Representatives (cited as *House Journal*), various legislative sessions. Legislative Reference Library, State of Texas, Austin, Texas.
Journal of the Texas Senate (cited as *Senate Journal*), various legislative sessions. Legislative Reference Library, State of Texas, Austin, Texas.
Nomination of Hon. Pat M. Neff, Hearings before the Committee on Interstate Commerce Commission, United States Senate, Seventieth Congress, Second Session. Washington, D.C.: Government Printing Office, 1929.
Report of State Ranger and Martial Law Activities of the National Guard of Texas, 1921 and 1922, to Honorable Pat M. Neff, Governor. Legislative Reference Library, State of Texas, Austin, Texas, and Neff Papers.
U.S. Board of Mediation. *Annual Report of the United States Board of Mediation, 1927*. Washington, D.C.: Government Printing Office, 1927.
"Vetoed Bills 1860-2005: Vetoed Bills—Governor Pat N. (sic) Neff, 37th Regular Session (1921)." Legislative Reference Library, State of Texas, Austin, Texas. Online: http://www.lrl.state.tx.us/legis/vetoes/vetoesbySession.cfm?legSession=37-0 .

"Vetoed Bills 1860-2005: Vetoed Bills—Governor Pat N. (sic) Neff, 38th Regular Session (1923)." Legislative Reference Library, State of Texas, Austin, Texas. Online: http://www.lrl.state.tx.us/legis/vetoes/vetoesbySession.cfm?legSession=38-0 .

Index

governors who attended, iv, ix
graduates of, 43, 139, 141
hazing at, 203
honorary degrees, 183, 207-08, 218, 230,
    238–40, 250–53
Institute for Oral History, 271-72
Johnson family affiliation with, 161. *See
    also* Johnson, Lyndon B.
Law School
    accreditation for, 195
    closing of during war, 194
    dean, 186, 223
    faculty, 34
    funding for, 151
    Neff, Pat Jr. at, 158
literary societies, 14–15, 193
location of, 158–59, 167–68
Medical School, 209–10, 228–30, 248,
    328 note 24
Moody and Jesse Jones Library, xiv
move from Waco to Dallas, 158–59
Music Department, 178, 187, 206, 248
Myrtie Neff as student, 11, photo section
Neff as student, 10–20, 29, photo section
Neff Club, 81
Neff for Governor Club, 71
Nursing School, 209, 328 note 24
oral history project, 271–72
presidents of
    Andrews, Reddin, 168
    Brooks, Samuel Palmer, 11, 43–44,
        46, 56–57, 61, 65, 67, 72, 124,
        154, 159, 163, 168–69, 174, 176,
        181, 186, 267
    Burleson, Rufus, 11, 167–68, 218,
        267, 329 note 54
    McCall, Abner, 34, 50, 186, 191, 194,
        204–05, 222
    Neff, Pat. *See* Neff as Baylor president
    White, William R., 194, 204, 257–59
promoting, 182–84
Psychology Department, 221
racial integration at, 201–02, 317 note
    115
real estate acquisition for, 61, 195–96,
    219, 229, 248
recruitment, 178–79, 186–87
religious life at, 199, 225, 245-46
Revival Week, 199

school song, 270
social activities at, 10-12
Sociology Department, 194
Speech Department, 188, 192–93
Student Council, 254
student financial aid, 178–79, 186–87
Texas Collection at, xi, xiii, xiv
and Waco's support, 47, 56, 158–59
yearbook, 48
Baylor University Board of Trustees. *See also*
    Waco Executive Committee
    agendas, 61
    and athletics, 210–12, 218, 250
    Dawson on, 60, 220, 234, 251
    Martin (Dock) on, 96, 149, 170, 195–96,
        210-11, 228–29, 234-37, 253, 258
    members of, 1, 42–43, 60–61, 64, 141,
        159, 163, 166, 169–70, 182, 184,
        191, 196–97, 203, 207, 209–11, 218,
        220, 228–29, 233–34, 236–41, 244,
        247, 249–59, 262, 272
    president of, 43–44, 60, 64, 96, 154, 209
    vice-president of, 42
Baylor University Press, 186
Baylor Variety Hour, 188
Beaumont Enterprise, 65, 106
beer, 39, 183, 185, 280 note 90
Belew, George H., 237
Bell, Harris, 153–54, 304 note 16
Bell, Theodosia, 37
Benedict, H. Y. (Dr.), 141
Berhman, Mayes, 237, 267
Bevil, George, 215
BGCT. *See* Baptist General Convention of
    Texas
Bible, 62, 86, 127, 144, 147, 182, 199, 262
Bill and Vara Faye Daniel Professorship, 212
Bill Daniel Student Center, 212
Bitting, William, 209–10
Blackland Army Airfield, 245
blacks. *See* African-Americans
Blair, Joel, 2
Blue Back Speller, 6
Board of Prison Commissioners, 105
Bob Wills and His Texas Playboys, 173
Bolton, Herbert Eugene, 142
Boyd, C. D., 76
Boyd, Sam, 200
Boyd, Walter, 144. *See also* Leadbelly

Neff, Marie Taylor, xiii
Neff, Martha Frances, xiii
Neff, Myrtle (Myrtie) Mainer
 and Sunday School class, 60
 assistants to, 103
 Barnes on, 179
 as Baylor student, 11, photo section
 children born, 32–33, 38
 correspondence from Mother Neff, 39,
  43, 50, 51
 correspondence from Pat, 11, 12, 13, 14,
  15, 16, 17, 18, 19, 20, 24, 25, 26, 27,
  28, 33, 39
 courtship with Pat, 12, 15, 17, 19, 24,
  25, 28, 33, 38
 death of, 259–60
 description of, 89
 family of, xiii
 first home of, 29
 as first lady, 91
 in Governor's Mansion, 101–03, photo
  section
 and Hallie Maude, 33, 127, 153, 214–15
 health problems of, 33, 38–40, 41, 44–
  45, 50–51, 62
 and Isabella (mother-in-law), 28–29, 43,
  50–51, 102
 marriage, 28–30, 37, photo section
 nursing children, 39, 280 note 90
 at Mineral Wells, 33, 38, 51, 62, 90, 103,
  127, 140, 158
Neff, Noah, 2–8, 102, 265–66, photo section
Neff, Pat III, 127, 260
Neff, Pat IV, 260
Neff, Pat Jr.
 attorney general race, 249-50
 in army, 225–26
 in Austin, 92, 215
 at Baylor Law School, 158
 birth of, 38–39, 280 note 86
 career of, 225–26, 249–50
 childhood of, 50, photo section
 death, 260
 and family homestead, 127
 high school graduation of, 101, 103
 law practice, 179
 at Mineral Wells, 62
 timeline, 165-66
 at Neff victory, 89

 on twenty-first birthday, 77
 at University of Texas, 140
Neff, Pat Morris
 at Baylor (student, board president,
  university president)
 accepting presidency, 166
 and athletics, 210–12, 222, 241, 245–
  46
 and Baptist church and organizations,
  230–31
 and Baptist General Convention of
  Texas, 42–43, 58–59, 60–61, 155,
  169–71, 171, 174, 178, 187, 195,
  196, 199–200, 215, 223, 228, 230,
  242, 251–52, 254, 262
 and Baylor Centennial, 237–40
 and buildings, 195–98, 219–21, 247–
  48
 on Board of Trustees, 42, 43–44, 48,
  60, 64, 141, 154, 158–59, 163,
  233–34, 250, 252–57
 relationship to Dr. Brooks, 11, 56, 61,
  72, 82–83, 163, 169
 chapel attendance, 180, 194
 chapel generally, 179–82, 200–02
 commencements, 183–84, 190–91,
  218, 221–22, 239-40, 253
 Dallas Morning News, 169–70, 174,
  253–54
 death of, 259–60
 description of Neff by newspapermen,
  173–74
 and discipline, 181–82, 202–05, 215–
  16, 222
 and enrollment, 218–19, 244–45,
  246–47
 and faculty, 191–95, 223–24, 248–49
 and family, 179, 214–15
 final portrait, 260–63
 and financial problems, ix, 167, 174–
  79, 184–87
 first day as president, 167
 and his farm, 1, 171, 212, photo
  section
 and generosity, 205-06
 graduation from Baylor, 15, 20
 awarding honorary degrees, 183, 207–
  08, 218, 23–40, 250–53, photo
  section

war bonds, 59
Ward, Hortense, 144
Warehouse and Marketing Department, 97
Warner, Harry T., 120, 121, 126
Warner, Phebe Kerrick, 145
Warren, Constance Whitney, 146
Washington, D.C., 78, 79, 87, 93, 122, 131,
    146, 148, 155–58, 160, 171, 189, 190,
    251, 259
Washington, Jesse, 56–57, 283 note 72
Wasson, Alonzo, 118
water conservation, 74, 115, 116, 149, 261.
    See also flood control
Waters-Pierce Oil Company, 25, 68
Watson, T. R., 53
Weeks, John W., 122
Wellborn, Charles, 246
Welder, Katie Owens, 145
Wendt, W. W., 221
West News, 48
West Texas
    associates in, 71, 80
    colleges in, 136, 149
    drought in, 59
    Looney in, 85
    park land in, 146
    Pat Jr. in, 103
    property purchased in, 46–47
    Sam Neff in, 12, 103,163
    speaking in (Neff), 41, 115–16
West Texas Chamber of Commerce, 100,
    136, 140
West Texas State Teachers College, 132
White, William Richardson (W. R.), 194,
    204, 247, 257, 259, 324 note 97
"white primary" bill, 138, 150, 201
white supremacy, 33, 110
Whitley, William, 9
Whittier, John Greenleaf, 45
Who's Who in America, 30
Wichita Falls, 43, 86, 94, 115, 267
Wilcox, Frank L., 214–15, 260, photo
    section
William Jewell College, 7
Williams, Carey, 205
Williams, Carl, 155
Williams, Peeler, 223
Williamson County Sun, 83

Wilmans, Edith E., 129, 144
Wilson, Will, 27
Wilson, Woodrow, 26, 56, 58, 59, 68, 75,
    79, 87, 88, 147
Wimpee, W. J. (Dr.), 256
Winfrey, Chase, 86, 259
Wings Club, 225
Winslow, Samuel E., 156
Winston, George T., 19
Witt, Edgar E., 95
WMU. *See* Women's Missionary Union
Wolf, Ralph, 177, 211
Wolfe, Charles, 144
Wolters, Jacob F. (Brig. Gen.), 114
Woman Suffrage Association, Texas, 83
women. *See also* suffrage
    advocates, 125
    all-woman Texas Supreme Court, 143,
        144, 148, 301 note 142
    at Baylor, 182, 219, 227, 253
    clubs and organizations, 71, 83, 116, 145,
        253
    dean of, Baylor, 192
    in Democratic Party, 104
    Ku Klux Klan on, 118
    Neff's support of, 83, 104, 140, 144, 148,
        159, 260, 261
    Outstanding American, 218
    in state legislature, 104, 129
    and voting rights, 66, 69, 72, 73, 78, 83,
        87, 104, 107
Women's Clubs, Texas Federation of. *See*
    Texas Federation of Women's Clubs
Women's Missionary Union, 169
Women's Press Association, Texas, 104
Wood, Wilton, 162
Woodmen of America. *See* Modern
    Woodmen of America
Woodmen of the World, 41, 144
Woodruff, Bob, 250, 253
World War I, 49, 59, 68–69, 72, 75, 86, 93,
    104, 142, 225
World War II, 194, 217, 219, 224–27, 244,
    247, 263, 272
World's Fair (Chicago), 13
WOW. *See* Woodmen of the World
Wright, Gladys Yoakum, 269